PREFACE

According to the Oxford English dictionary, a tertiary definition of the word "trot," when used as a noun, is "a literal translation of a text used by students; a crib." As one who, back in the mists of time, passed through a Jesuit prep school allegedly reading classics, a trot was an indispensable little friend secreted in the back of our Greek and Latin texts that helped us survive the oral recitation of Xenophon, Homer and Cicero without incurring imprecation or penal servitude at the hands of our instructors.

Fortunately, the mnemonic rigor of the classicist is not indispensable to the practice of law for as the English Court said in Montriou and Jeffreys, 2 C&P 113 (1825): "No attorney is bound to know all the law; God forbid that it should be imagined that an attorney or a counsel, or even a judge is bound to know all the law."

Thus, the modest ambition of this book is simply to be a "trot", a quick reference to the various ways in which the courts have translated the text of the Federal Rules of Evidence, hopefully with sufficient case authority to survive or overcome a particular objection and with reference to the treatises for deeper study, when necessary. Its loftier ambition, however, is to be as useful to those who have practiced for thirty or forty years as it might be for those who are trying their first case.

I extend my sincere thanks to my colleague Attorney Chris Amar for his help with this edition.

CHARLES B. GIBBONS

Pittsburgh
December 2011

ABOUT THE AUTHOR

Charles B. Gibbons is a litigation partner at Buchanan Ingersoll & Rooney, Pittsburgh, Pennsylvania. A graduate of the Scranton Preparatory School, the University of Scranton and Boston College Law School, he is a Fellow of the American College of Trial Lawyers and a member of the American Law Institute.

Attorney Mike Manzo

1948-2011
B.S.E. Princeton University
M.B.A. University of Scranton
J.D. University of Virginia

Fellow, American College of Trial Lawyers
Past President, Academy of Trial Lawyers of Allegheny County, Pennsylvania
Partner, Buchanan Ingersoll & Rooney, Pittsburgh

A Prayer for Princeton

O eternal God, the Creator and Preserver of all, we beseech Thee to bestow upon this University Thy manifold gifts of grace; Thy truth to those who teach, Thy laws to those who learn, Thy wisdom to those who administer, and Thy steadfastness to all who bear her name. Bind us together by these gracious influences of Thy Spirit into the fellowship which can never fail, throughout all ages, world without end. Amen.

Donald B. Aldrich,
Dean, Princeton University Chapel, 1928

Table of Contents

APPENDIX

ARGUMENTATIVE

See:

Fed.R.Evid. 611(a)
Mil.R.Evid. 611(a)

Objection

- Objection. The question is argumentative.
- Objection. Counsel is arguing with the witness.

Response

- I have properly phrased my question to elicit evidence from this witness.

Commentary

Fed.R.Evid. 611(a) provides that the court shall exercise reasonable control over the mode of interrogating witnesses. Any question which is actually an argument is improper. *Cf. Mendez v. County of San Bernardino*, 540 F.3d 1109 (9th Cir. 2008). Argumentative questions are those questions which are not intended to elicit new information but which are intended to argue to the jury through the witness, or which call for an argument in answer to an argument contained in the question. Typically, such a question states a conclusion and asks the witness to agree with it, or is asked in a sarcastic tenor:

> "Do you mean to tell me . . . " or "Doesn't it seem strange that . . . "

The impropriety of such questions is illustrated in: *Smith v. Estelle*, 602 F.2d 694, 700 n.7 (5th Cir. 1979) ("[Y]ou're kind of the hatchet man down here for the District Attorney's Office, aren't you?"); *U.S. v. Micklus*, 581 F.2d 612, 617 n.3 (7th Cir. 1978) ("It wouldn't bother you any, to come in here and lie from the time you started to the time you stopped, would it?"); *U.S. v. Briscoe*, 839 F. Supp. 36, 39 (D.D.C. 1992) ("Isn't what you told this jury on its face ridiculous?").

Additional References

Graham, Handbook of Federal Evidence § 611:20 (7th ed. 2012)

Treatises and Practice Aids

Goode and Wellborn, Courtroom Handbook on Federal Evidence Chapter 5, Rule 611 and Obj. 2 (annual ed.)

Wright & Graham, Federal Practice and Procedure: Evidence 2d §§ 5036, 5042
McCormick, Evidence, Chapter 2 (6th ed. 2006)
Park, Trial Objections Handbook § 6:8 (2nd ed. 2001)

ASKED AND ANSWERED

See:

Fed.R.Evid. 611(a)
Mil.R.Evid. 611(a)

Objection

- Objection. The question has been asked and answered.
- Objection. The question is repetitive.

Response

- The witness has not answered this question.
- I have not asked this question previously.

Commentary

If a question has been asked and answered, the trial court has broad discretion to limit or exclude repetitive questions. Fed.R.Evid. 611(a); *Gray v. Hoffman-La Roche, Inc.*, 82 Fed. Appx. 639 (10th Cir. 2003); *U.S. v. Perez-Montanez*, 202 F.3d 434 (1st Cir. 2000); *Price v. Kramer*, 200 F.3d 1237 (9th Cir. 2000); *U.S. v. Laboy-Delgado*, 84 F.3d 22 (1st Cir. 1996). Repetition wastes time and places undue emphasis on certain evidence through cumulative testimony. The form of the question does not have to be absolutely identical in order to raise this objection. If a new question calls for an answer which has essentially already been given, the question is objectionable as repetitious. The objection applies not only when an answer already has been given but also when a witness previously has testified that he does not know about or remember a matter.

Additional References

Graham, Handbook of Federal Evidence § 611.17 (7th ed. 2012)

Treatises and Practice Aids

Goode and Wellborn, Courtroom Handbook on Federal Evidence Chapter 5, Rule 611 and Obj. 3 (annual ed.)
McCormick, Evidence Chapter 2 (6th ed. 2006)
Park, Trial Objections Handbook § 6:21 (2nd ed. 2001)

ASSUMING FACTS NOT IN EVIDENCE

See:

Fed.R.Evid. 611(a)
Mil.R.Evid. 611(a)

Objection

- Objection. The question assumes facts that have not been introduced into evidence.

Response

- The question is proper cross-examination; I am entitled to test the credibility or memory of the witness. The witness can deny the asserted facts if he disagrees with the assertion.
- Your Honor, I will establish the fact [and its relevancy] in subsequent testimony. I request that the witness assume the fact for purposes of this question.

Commentary

A question which assumes the existence of a fact not established by the evidence is improper. *U.S. v. Adames*, 56 F.3d 737 (7th Cir. 1995) (questions about alleged involvement in murder properly excluded when counsel failed to provide good faith basis for them); *U.S. v. Davenport*, 753 F.2d 1460 (9th Cir. 1985) (new trial ordered where government failed to establish factual predicate for question about planning other bank robberies); *U.S. v. Harris*, 542 F.2d 1283 (7th Cir. 1976) (improper for government to ask question that implies factual predicate which examiner knows he cannot support by evidence or which he has no reason to believe is true); *Braun v. Powell*, 77 F. Supp. 2d 973, 1005 (E.D. Wis. 1999), rev'd on other grounds, 227 F.3d 908 (7th Cir. 2000) (improper to ask witnesses questions of the "when did you stop beating your wife?" variety). In certain situations, counsel may ask the court to permit the question to stand as asked, upon representation that the assumed fact will be proven later. Such a representation, however, should not be made if it cannot be fulfilled.

With respect to examination of witnesses, A.B.A. Standards for Criminal Justice (3d ed. 1992), The

Prosecution Function, § 3-5.7(d), provides:

> A prosecutor should not ask a question which implies the existence of a factual predicate for which a good faith belief is lacking.

The Defense Function, § 4-7.6(d), is identically worded. *See* 6 J. Wigmore, Evidence § 1808, at 371 (J. Chadbourn rev. ed. 1976) ("When a counsel puts such a question, believing that it will be excluded for illegality or will be negatived, and also having no reason to believe that there is a foundation of truth for it, he violates professional honor.")

Similarly, Professor Alan M. Dershowitz has written:

> The law requires an attorney to have a 'good-faith basis' before asking any question on cross-examination. This important rule is designed to prevent the irresponsible prosecutor or defense attorney from planting a fictitious accusation in the minds of the jurors by the framing of questions. Without this salutary rule, a lawyer could ask all kinds of variations on the "When did you stop beating your wife?" theme . . .. The rule does not require that the cross-examining lawyer must have proof of the assertion underlying the question, but simply that there must be a good-faith basis—a concept difficult to define.

Dershowitz, Reversal of Fortune, pp. 220–221 (Pocket Books, 1990).

The principle is also illustrated in the following cases: *U.S. v. Taylor*, 522 F.3d 731 (7th Cir. 2008) (when sidebar revealed proposed questions were just shots in the dark without good faith basis, court properly barred them); *U.S. v. Elizondo*, 920 F.2d 1308 (7th Cir. 1990) (when prosecution asks damning questions that go to central issue in case, those questions must be supported by evidence, available or inferable); *U.S. v. Jungles*, 903 F.2d 468 (7th Cir. 1990) (government does not have duty in every case to introduce factual predicate for a potentially prejudicial question, particularly where there is a reasonable suspicion that circumstances underlying question might be true); *U.S. v. Wolf*, 787 F.2d 1094 (7th Cir. 1986) (line of questioning improper; prosecution was insinuating defendant's guilt of other crimes which government was not prepared to prove); *U.S. v. Silverstein*, 737 F.2d 864 (10th Cir. 1984) (reversible error where prosecutor could not prove substance of his questions about alleged conversations between defendant and another inmate because latter inmate escaped prison before trial and was not recaptured until after trial).

Courts require a "good faith" basis before permitting a party to cross-examine regarding prior bad acts. *U.S. v. Foley*, 508 F.3d 627 (11th Cir. 2007) (character witness could be cross-examined about defendant's prior misconduct as long as it is relevant and government has good faith basis for incidents inquired about); *U.S. v. Ovalle-Marquez*, 36 F.3d 212, 219 (1st Cir. 1994). "While the purpose of cross-examination is to impeach the credibility of a witness, the basis for the impeachment cannot be speculation and innuendo with no evidentiary foundation." *Id.* "The general rule in such situations is that the questioner must be in possession of some facts which support a genuine belief that the witness committed the offense or the degrading act to which the questioning relates." *U.S. v. Sampol*, 636 F.2d 621, 658 (D.C. Cir. 1980).

Treatises and Practice Aids

Goode and Wellborn, Courtroom Handbook on Federal Evidence Chapter 5, Rule 611 and Obj. 4 (annual ed.)

Wright & Graham, Federal Practice and Procedure: Evidence 2d § 5036

Park, Trial Objections Handbook § 6:7 (2nd ed. 2001)

AUTHENTICATION OF PHYSICAL EVIDENCE

See:

Fed.R.Evid. 901, 902, 903
Mil.R.Evid. 901, 902, 903

Objection

- Objection. The exhibit has not been properly authenticated.

Response

- The exhibit was authenticated by the testimony of the witness that:
  - he was present at the scene at the time in question and that the [*photograph*] [*videotape*] fairly and accurately represents the particular condition at the time in question;
  - he saw the author [*compose*] [*sign*] the document;
  - he recognizes and is familiar with this handwriting;
  - he knows that this letter came in reply to his own earlier letter.

Commentary

The proponent of physical evidence is generally required to prove its authenticity as a condition precedent to admissibility. *Peals v. Terre Haute Police Dept.*, 535 F.3d 621 (7th Cir. 2008). Rule 901 states that the foundational requirement of authentication or identification is satisfied by evidence sufficient to support a finding that the matter in question is what its proponent claims. *See U.S. v. Iribe*, 564 F.3d 1155 (9th Cir. 2009); *U.S. v. Hampton*, 464 F.3d 687 (7th Cir. 2006); *U.S. v. Perez-Gonzalez*, 445 F.3d 39 (1st Cir. 2006) (Rule 901 requires *prima facie* showing of genuineness, leaving it to jury to decide true authenticity and probative value of evidence); *U.S. v. Ruggiero*, 928 F.2d 1289 (2d Cir. 1991) (burden of authentication does not require proponent of evidence to rule out all possibilities inconsistent with authenticity, or to prove beyond any doubt that evidence is what it purports to be; standard for authentication is one of reasonable likelihood); *Link v. Mercedes-Benz of North America, Inc.*, 788 F.2d 918 (3d Cir. 1986) (burden of proof for authentication is slight; all that is required is foundation from which fact-finder could legitimately infer that evidence is what proponent claims it to be); *Langbord v. U.S. Dept. of Treasury*, 2011 WL 2623315 (E.D. Pa. 2011) (same); *Zielinski v. Pabst Brewing Co., Inc.*, 360 F. Supp. 2d 908 (E.D. Wis. 2005) (when a witness with personal knowledge swears that the document is what she says it is, the authenticity requirement is met). The court need not find that the evidence is necessarily what the proponent claims, but only that there is sufficient evidence that the jury ultimately might do so. *U.S. v. Safavian*, 435 F. Supp. 2d 36 (D.D.C. 2006).

One variation of this principle-the chain of custody rule-requires a showing that the evidence is in substantially the same condition as it was during the relevant period of time. *U.S. v. Moore*, 425 F.3d 1061 (7th Cir. 2005); *see* Chain of Custody, *infra*.

In matters of authentication, the trial court serves a gatekeeping function. *See generally* Fed.R.Evid. 104(a); *Lowe v. Experian*, 340 F. Supp. 2d 1170 (D. Kan. 2004) (authentication is condition precedent to admissibility and court will not consider evidence not properly admitted in compliance with requirements of the evidentiary rules). If the court discerns enough support in the record to cause a reasonable person to determine that the evidence is what it purports to be, then Rule 901(a) is satisfied, and the weight to be given to the evidence is left to the jury. *U.S. v. Paulino*, 13 F.3d 20 (1st Cir. 1994).

Depending upon the particular evidence involved, the proof can be as simple as testimony by a person with knowledge that he recognizes a writing, document or photograph as genuine or that it accurately represents a particular condition; or proof may be so complex as to require expert testimony to substantiate authenticity. *American Wrecking Corp. v. Secretary of Labor*, 351 F.3d 1254 (D.C. Cir. 2003) (photo may be authenticated if witness with knowledge of scene testifies it accurately depicts scene it purports to represent); *U.S. v. Tank*,

200 F.3d 627 (9th Cir. 2000) (child pornography prosecution where government made *prima facie* showing of authenticity of Internet chat room logs through testimony of person who had created logs); *U.S. v. Mills*, 194 F.3d. 1108 (10th Cir. 1999) (videotape of inmate transfer authenticated by corrections officer who took it); *U.S. v. Oriakhi*, 57 F.3d 1290 (4th Cir. 1995) (defendant's voice on audio tape identified by co-conspirator who had known him for almost one year and by DEA agent who heard defendant speak on three occasions); *U.S. v. McGlory*, 968 F.2d 309 (3d Cir. 1992) (handwriting expert testified to numerous similarities between signature on documents and defendant's handwriting exemplar); *Lucero v. Stewart*, 892 F.2d 52 (9th Cir. 1989) (approximate date of photograph adequate for authentication).

A document may be authenticated by direct proof, such as the testimony of a witness who saw the author sign the document; acknowledgment of execution by the signer; admission of authenticity by an adverse party; or proof that the document or its signature is in the purported author's handwriting. *U.S. v. Samet*, 466 F.3d 251 (2d Cir. 2006) (witness gained familiarity with defendant's handwriting by examining numerous documents during lengthy investigation); *U.S. v. Apperson*, 441 F.3d 1162 (10th Cir. 2006) and *Estate of Genecin ex rel. Genecin v. Genecin*, 363 F. Supp. 2d 306 (D. Conn. 2005) (similar); *Pahl v. C.I.R.*, 150 F.3d 1124 (9th Cir. 1998) (witness saw taxpayer/petitioner sign document); *U.S. v. Dozie*, 27 F.3d 95 (4th Cir. 1994) (jury could compare signature on tax return admittedly signed by defendant with other documents to draw legitimate inference that defendant prepared false claim documents); *U.S. v. Bello-Perez*, 977 F.2d 664 (1st Cir. 1992) (circumstantial evidence showed that anonymous correspondence was sufficiently distinctive in appearance, contents, substance, internal patterns or other distinctive characteristics within meaning of Rule 901(b)(4) to meet authentication requirement); *U.S. v. Tipton*, 964 F.2d 650 (7th Cir. 1992) (co-worker familiar with defendant's handwriting qualified to give lay witness opinion testimony per Rule 701 identifying signature and handwriting); *U.S. v. Dreitzler*, 577 F.2d 539 (9th Cir. 1978) (based on her familiarity with defendant's handwriting, former secretary could testify he had forged names on loan documents).

A document may also be authenticated by circumstantial evidence. In determining authenticity based on circumstantial evidence, a court can consider whether the appearance, contents, substance, internal patterns, or other distinctive characteristics, taken in conjunction with circumstances, indicate that the evidence is what the party purports it to be. *U.S. v. Smith*, 223 F.3d 554, 570 (7th Cir. 2000). Certain recurrent patterns of circumstantial evidence have come to be recognized as distinct rules. These include the "ancient documents" rule (Rule 901(b)(8)) and the "reply letter" rule. The ancient document rule provides that authentication may be supplied by a demonstration that a document is in such condition as to create no suspicion concerning its authenticity; was in a place where, if authentic, it likely would be, and has been in existence twenty years or more at the time it is offered. *U.S. v. Stelmokas*, 100 F.3d 302 (3d Cir. 1996) (World War II German Army records of voluntary police units found in government archives in Vilnius, Lithuania and certified by archival personnel deemed to be authentic). A letter can be authenticated by testimony or other proof that it was sent in reply to a duly authenticated writing. *U.S. v. Henry*, 164 F.3d 1304 (10th Cir. 1999) (false workers compensation forms sufficiently authenticated where forms replied to mailings to defendant and contained information personal to him); *U.S. v. Reilly*, 33 F.3d 1396 (3d Cir. 1994) (in illegal dumping case where vessel's captain authenticated his own radiotelegrams asking for instructions, reply messages could reasonably be attributed to defendant who was shown to be in charge of operation).

The following cases illustrate authentication by circumstantial evidence: *U.S. v. Lauder*, 409 F.3d 1254 (10th Cir. 2005) (fingerprint cards can be authenticated under Rule 901(b)(4)'s distinctive characteristics language); *U.S. v. Thornton*, 197 F.3d 241 (7th Cir. 1999) (documents such as utility bills, merchandise receipts and business cards seized from co-conspirator sufficiently distinctive to qualify as self-authenticating without testimony by actual authors); *U.S. v. Trujillo*, 146 F.3d 838 (11th Cir. 1998) (notes taken from defendant's mouth and toilet, each with number "591" authenticated by tapes indicating 591 kilos of air-dropped cocaine belonged to Columbians); *U.S. v. Jones*, 107 F.3d 1147 (6th Cir. 1997) (postcard contained personal information from which it could be inferred defendant authored document); *U.S. v. Luisi*, 9 F. Supp. 2d 422 (S.D. N.Y. 1998) (ring reported as stolen but seized at time of arrest authenticated by, *inter alia*, identifiable markings and inventory control number); *Gonzalez v. Digital Equipment Corp.*, 8 F. Supp. 2d 194 (E.D. N.Y. 1998) (documents and videos produced in discovery by nonparty keyboard manufacturers sufficiently authenticated because materials were clearly labeled as to source and contained information indicating they were internal materials of producing companies).

Computer Records

It is not necessary that the computer programmer testify in order to authenticate computer-generated records. *U-Haul Intern., Inc. v. Lumbermens Mut. Cas. Co.*, 576 F.3d 1040 (9th Cir. 2009). A computer printout may be authenticated by one who has knowledge of the particular record system. *U.S. v. Miller*, 771 F.2d 1219, 1237 (9th Cir. 1985). Similarly, a party need not produce expert testimony as to the mechanical accuracy of a computer where it presented evidence that the computer was sufficiently accurate so that the company relied on it in conducting its business. *Id., citing U.S. v. De Georgia*, 420 F.2d 889, 893 n.11 (9th Cir. 1969).

Self-Authentication: Amendments of December 1, 2000

The business records of American companies are now admissible in civil and criminal cases without the need to call a witness if: (1) accompanied by a written declaration by the custodian or other qualified person that the records (a) were made at or near the time of the occurrence at issue or from information transmitted by a person with knowledge, (b) were kept in the ordinary course of business, (c) were created by the business as a regular practice; and (2) the offering party gives notice of intended use to all adverse parties and opportunity to inspect the records and the declaration so as to provide a fair opportunity to challenge them. Rule 902(11). Under Rule 902(11), the custodian of the records need not have personal knowledge of the actual creation of the document. The custodian's written declaration does not violate *Crawford v. Washington*, 541 U.S. 36, 56, 124 S. Ct. 1354, 158, 158 L. Ed. 2d 177 (2004) which said that business records by their nature are not testimonial. *U.S. v. Adefehinti*, 510 F.3d 319 (D.C. Cir. 2007).

The same procedure applies to foreign business records to be used in civil cases. Rule 902(12). A statute, 18 U.S.C.A. § 3505, already provides a similar route to admissibility in criminal cases and has withstood Confrontation Clause challenges. *U.S. v. Garcia Abrego*, 141 F.3d 142, 178–79 (5th Cir. 1998) (collecting cases).

The following decisions illustrate evidence rejected for lack of proper authentication: *U.S. v. Lawson*, 494 F.3d 1046 (D.C. Cir. 2007) (photos properly excluded because they could not be authenticated); *Sherman v. Sunsong America, Inc.*, 485 F. Supp. 2d 1070 (D. Neb. 2007) (uncertified court records); *Figueroa v. U.S. Postal Service*, 422 F. Supp. 2d 866 (N.D. Ohio 2006) (incomplete document without signature); *S.E.C. v. Franklin*, 348 F. Supp. 2d 1159 (S.D.Cal. 2004) (rejecting documents offered by S.E.C. without the written declaration required by Rule 902(11)); *Medite of New Mexico, Inc. v. N.L.R.B.*, 72 F.3d 780 (10th Cir. 1995) (witness who made tape of picketing activities unable to testify how tape had been edited prior to trial); *John Paul Mitchell Systems v. Quality King Distributors, Inc.*, 106 F. Supp. 2d 462 (S.D. N.Y. 2000) (although circumstantial evidence such as appearance and content may serve to authenticate documents, paid informant's records rejected where he never testified to authenticity or provided other genuine documents to use as basis for comparison); *Haiman v. Village of Fox Lake*, 79 F. Supp. 2d 949 (N.D. Ill. 2000) (employment discrimination case where log book allegedly kept by village treasurer not properly authenticated; book not titled, signed or dated; no witness had firsthand knowledge of it nor could anyone identify it); *Lamberti v. U.S.*, 22

F. Supp. 2d 60 (S.D. N.Y. 1998) ("exploding" letter bore no indicia of authenticity and was palpably incredible); *Teton West Const. Inc. v. Two Rivers Const. Inc.*, 961 F. Supp. 1422 (D. Idaho 1997) (in patent infringement suit, blueprint of potato storage building would be disregarded where nothing in record authenticated it); *U.S. v. Yousef*, 175 F.R.D. 192 (S.D. N.Y. 1997) (foreign public records not admissible where government failed to provide either final certification required by Rule 902(3) or explanation to support finding of good cause for failure to obtain certification); *Bullock v. Widnall*, 953 F. Supp. 1461 (M.D. Ala. 1996) (unauthenticated letters).

Additional References

Graham, Handbook of Federal Evidence §§ 901 *et seq.* (7th ed. 2012)

Treatises and Practice Aids

Goode and Wellborn, Courtroom Handbook on Federal Evidence Chapter 5 and Obj. 13 (annual ed.)

Mueller & Kirkpatrick, Federal Evidence, §§ 9:6, 9:8, 9:11 (3d ed., 2007)

Wright & Gold, Federal Practice and Procedure: Evidence §§ 7101 *et seq.*

McCormick, Evidence Chapter 22 (6th ed. 2006)

Park, Trial Objections Handbook Chapter 9 (2nd ed. 2001)

AUTHENTICATION: VOICE-TELEPHONE CONVERSATIONS, TAPE RECORDINGS

See:

Fed.R.Evid. 901(b)(5),(6)
Mil.R.Evid. 901(b)(5),(6)

Objection

- Objection. The alleged phone conversation/ tape recording is inadmissible. There is [*no*] [*insufficient*] foundation establishing the identity of the speaker.

Response

- A proper foundation for the testimony has been established. Identity has been established by [*voice recognition*] [*sufficient circumstantial evidence [specify]*].

Commentary

Telephone Conversations

A telephone conversation between a witness and another person is admissible only when the identity of the person with whom the witness was speaking is satisfactorily established. Rule 901(b)(5),(6); *see U.S. v. Miller*, 771 F.2d 1219 (9th Cir. 1985).

Proving identity is no different than proving any other fact and may be accomplished by direct or circumstantial evidence. *U.S. v. Gilbert*, 181 F.3d 152 (1st Cir. 1999); *U.S. v. Garrison*, 168 F.3d 1089 (8th Cir. 1999); *U.S. v. Espinoza*, 641 F.2d 153 (4th Cir. 1981).

The speaker's identity can be authenticated by testimony from a witness that he recognizes the speaker's voice. Rule 901(b)(5); *see U.S. v. Recendiz*, 557 F.3d 511 (7th Cir. 2009) (D.E.A. agent familiar with defendant's voice because of prior personal contact); *U.S. v. Brown*, 510 F.3d 57 (1st Cir. 2007) (same); *U.S. v. Zepeda-Lopez*, 478 F.3d 1213 (10th Cir. 2007) (accepting voice identification of tapes spoken in Spanish which FBI agent did not speak); *U.S. v. Bush*, 405 F.3d 909 (10th Cir. 2005) (Rule 901(b)(5) sets low threshhold for voice identification and only requires witness be minimally familiar with voice to identify it; jury will assess issues re extent of familiarity); *U.S. v. Magana*, 118 F.3d 1173 (7th Cir. 1997) (accepting voice identification of tapes spoken in English even though officer's prior conversation with defendants had been in Spanish). *But see Yeatman v. Inland Property Management, Inc.*, 845 F. Supp. 625 (N.D. Ill. 1994) (purported identification of phone caller's voice rejected as tainted and unreliable because only one tape recording of one voice was played; witness knew of critical need for evidence of recognition; and there had been three-year time lapse and only one brief prior exposure to voice in question).

When the witness is unable to identify the speaker's voice, identity may be established by circumstantial evidence. Rule 901(b)(6); *see U.S. v. Khan*, 53 F.3d 507 (2d Cir. 1995) (Medicaid fraud case where witness left message for defendant and received return call that day to discuss matters familiar to both; caller gave defendant's father's address as place where payments to be sent); *U.S. v. Espinoza*, 641 F.2d 153 (4th Cir. 1981) (circumstantial evidence of phone records, shipment, invoice, all tending to identify defendant as person with whom witness spoke in ordering kiddie porn; establishing identity of person by evidence that he replied or responded in manner that was expected to be evoked by communication made to him by another is well-recognized and time-honored). The illustrations in Rule 901(b)(6) are examples only and not limitations on methods of identification that may be used. *U.S. v. Alessi*, 638 F.2d 466 (2d Cir. 1980).

While mere assertion of identity by a person talking on the telephone is not in itself sufficient to authenticate that person's identity, some additional evidence, which "need not fall in[to] any set pattern," may provide the necessary foundation. Rule 901(b)(6) Advisory Committee's Note, example 6; *U.S. v. Garcia*, 447 F.3d 1327 (11th Cir. 2006) (self-identification together with contents of conversations). Self-identification of a person who is called at a place where his presence reasonably could be expected has long been regarded as sufficient. *O'Neal v. Esty*, 637 F.2d 846 (2d Cir. 1980). On the other hand, self-identification by the speaker alone is insufficient to authenticate the source of a telephone call. *Khan*, 53 F.3d at 516; *U.S. v. Roberts*, 22 F.3d 744 (7th Cir. 1994).

Audio Tape Recordings

The party introducing a sound recording must show that the tape as played is an accurate representation of the conversation or other sounds at issue. *U.S. v. Eberhart*, 467 F.3d 659 (7th Cir. 2006) (Rule 901 requires government to offer evidence sufficient to support finding that tape is what its proponent claims, i.e. showing by clear and convincing evidence that tape is a true, accurate and authentic recording of conversation between the parties). In some courts, this requires a demonstration of such factors as: (i) the operator's competency, (2) the fidelity of the recording equipment, (3) the absence of material alterations, and (4) the identification of material sounds or voices. *U.S. v. Wells*, 347 F.3d 280 (8th Cir. 2003); *U.S. v. Buchanan*, 70 F.3d 818 (5th Cir. 1995). A recording may be admitted without strict adherence to all foundational requirements, if after independent examination, the court is convinced that the tape is an accurate reproduction. *U.S. v. Doyon*, 194 F.3d 207 (1st Cir. 1999) (while some courts have strict recipe for evidentiary foundation, First Circuit simply requires facts necessary under circumstances to prove tape accurately reflects conversation); *U.S. v. Stone*, 960 F.2d 426 (5th Cir. 1992) (similar); *U.S. v. Byrne*, 83 F.3d 984 (8th Cir. 1996) (existence of audiotapes establishes equipment was properly functioning and operator was sufficiently skilled); *U.S. v. Cisneros*, 59 F. Supp. 2d 58 (D.D.C. 1999) (most important criterion for admission is that tapes accurately reflect conversations they purport to record).

Poor quality and partial unintelligibility do not render tapes inadmissible unless the unintelligible portions are so substantial as to render the recording as a whole untrustworthy. *U.S. v. Wesley*, 417 F.3d 612 (6th Cir. 2005); *U.S. v. Dukes*, 139 F.3d 469 (5th Cir. 1998); *U.S. v. Larkins*, 83 F.3d 162 (7th Cir. 1996); *U.S. v. Crouse*, 227 F.R.D. 36 (N.D. N.Y. 2005). Inaudibility of a portion of a tape, which is otherwise generally audible, is relevant to its weight, not its admissibility. *U.S. v. Robinson*, 956

F.2d 1388 (7th Cir. 1992).

Questions concerning the credibility of the identifying witness also go to the weight that the jury accords the recording, not its admissibility. *U.S. v. Capers*, 61 F.3d 1100 (4th Cir. 1995).

The court has broad discretion in deciding whether to permit the use of written transcripts as an aid to the jury in listening to recorded conversations. *U.S. v. Howard*, 80 F.3d 1194 (7th Cir. 1996); *Capers*, 61 F.3d at 1107; *U.S. v. Posada Carriles*, 486 F. Supp. 2d 599 (W.D. Tex. 2007) (transcript too inaccurate and unreliable to be given to jury); *U.S. v. Broadnax*, 475 F. Supp. 2d 783 (N.D. Ind. 2007) (court provided jury with written instruction as to limited use to be made of transcripts).

Additional References

Graham, Handbook of Federal Evidence § 901.5 to 901.6 (7th ed. 2012)

Treatises and Practice Aids

Goode and Wellborn, Courtroom Handbook on Federal Evidence Chapter 5 and Obj. 39 (annual ed.)

Mueller & Kirkpatrick, Federal Evidence, §§ 9:3, 9:13, 9:17 (3d ed. 2007)

Wright & Gold, Federal Practice and Procedure: Evidence §§ 7110, 7111

McCormick, Evidence Chapter 22 (6th ed. 2006)

Park, Trial Objections Handbook § 9:27 (2d ed. 2001)

BEST EVIDENCE RULE

See:

Fed.R.Evid. 1002
Mil.R.Evid. 1002

Objection

- Objection. This exhibit is not the best evidence of the written contract between the parties.
- I object to this exhibit on grounds of the best evidence rule. The original writing has not been accounted for.
- Objection. There is no competent excuse for nonproduction of the original.

Response

- Your Honor, we have established a legally sufficient reason for nonproduction.
- The contents of the document are not in issue.
- The contents are merely collateral, and, therefore, the best evidence rule does not apply.

Commentary

When the *contents* of a writing, recording or photograph are directly in issue, the original writing must be produced unless the original is unavailable through no fault of the proponent. Fed.R.Evid. 1002; *Ridgway v. Ford Dealer Computer Services, Inc.*, 114 F.3d 94 (6th Cir. 1997); *U.S. v. Ross*, 33 F.3d 1507 (11th Cir. 1994).

Rule 1002 applies in cases where the pertinent substantive law treats the *contents* of a writing, recording or photograph as indispensable to prove a case or establish a defense or accords such contents a primary significance. Wright and Gold, Federal Practice and Procedure, Evidence § 7184. *See, e.g., U.S. v. Humphrey*, 104 F.3d 65 (5th Cir. 1997) (testimony of former lawyer not best evidence of civil judgment); *Amin v. Loyola University Chicago*, 423 F. Supp. 2d 914 (W.D. Wis. 2006) (in ERISA case where university claimed plaintiff was not a plan member, defense witness' testimony regarding content of retirement plan was inadmissible where no copy of plan was submitted and there was no claim the document was lost, destroyed or unobtainable); *Marshak v. Treadwell*, 58 F. Supp. 2d 551 (D.N.J. 1999) (written contract lost or destroyed in fire; photocopy admissible as duplicate under Rule 1003 or as "other evidence" under Rule 1004).

The factors a court considers when deciding whether proposed testimony seeks to establish content of document or merely its existence, for purpose of applying best evidence rule, are: (1) relative importance of content in case, (2) simplicity or complexity of content and consequent risk of error in admitting testimonial account, (3) strength of proffered evidence of content, taking into account corroborative witnesses or evidence and presence or absence of bias or self-interest on part of witnesses, (4) breadth of margin for error within which mistake in testimonial account would not undermine point to be proved, (5) presence or absence of actual dispute as to content, (6) ease or difficulty of producing writing, and (7) reasons why proponent of other proof of its content does not have or offer writing itself. *Railroad Management Co., L.L.C. v. CFS Louisiana Midstream Co.*, 428 F.3d 214, 218–219 (5th Cir. 2005).

The rationale for the best evidence rule is described as follows in *Seiler v. Lucasfilm, Ltd.*, 808 F.2d 1316, 1319 (9th Cir. 1986):

> The modern justification for the rule has expanded from prevention of fraud to a recognition that writings occupy a central position in the law. When the contents of a writing are at issue, oral testimony as to the terms of the writing is subject to a greater risk of error than oral testimony as to events or other situations. The human memory is not often capable of reciting the precise terms of a writing, and when the terms are in dispute only the writing itself, or a true copy, provides reliable evidence.

Rule 1003 creates an exception to the best evidence rule in that a duplicate is admissible to the same extent as an original except where there is a genuine question as to the authenticity of the original or where it would be unfair to admit the duplicate in lieu of the original. *U.S. v. Hampton*, 464 F.3d 687 (7th Cir. 2006) (photocopies of certificates of insurance admissible duplicates; bank tellers testified that they recognized copies as copies of the certificates possessed by or posted in their banks, all copies bore dates of issuance before the robberies, and bank tellers stated banks were currently insured); *U.S. v. Haddock*, 956 F.2d 1534 (10th Cir. 1992) (court should be wary of admitting duplicates where circumstances surrounding execution of writing present substantial possibility of fraud); *Boswell v. Jasperson*, 266 F. Supp. 2d 1314 (D. Utah 2003) (where original deed was never produced and authenticity was in issue; altered deed did not pass muster under Best Evidence Rule); *U.S. v. Szehinskyj*, 104 F. Supp. 2d 480 (E.D. Pa. 2000) (no unfairness in admitting copies of Nazi concentration camp documents; originals were old, in delicate condition and held in various nations' archives).

Rule 1004 also creates an exception to the best evidence rule. Where the document cannot be produced because, for example, it is lost, destroyed or cannot be obtained by legal process, production of the original is excused unless the proponent lost or destroyed the original in bad faith. Rule 1004(1); *Beeler v. U.S.*, 894 F. Supp. 761 (S.D. N.Y. 1995) (original returns filed with IRS not destroyed in bad faith but pursuant to normal IRS document retention procedures). Once the terms of Rule 1004 are satisfied, the party seeking to prove the contents of a writing, recording or photograph may do so by any kind of secondary or substitute evidence. Fed.R.Evid. 1004; *U.S. v. Gerhart*, 538 F.2d 807 (8th Cir. 1976). The trial judge determines whether there is sufficient proof to establish that the original document is unavailable. *Id.* There are no degrees of secondary evidence and thus there is no requirement that a document be introduced in preference to oral testimony in order to prove the contents of the unavailable original document. *U.S. v. Billingsley*, 160 F.3d 502 (8th Cir. 1998).

The best evidence rule does not prohibit a witness from testifying about a fact or conversation simply because that fact or conversation can also be found in or supported by a written document or tape recording. *U.S. v. Blaylock*, 535 F.3d 922 (8th Cir. 2008) (nothing in Rules of Evidence prohibits government from relying on testimony of officers who seized items during a search instead of introducing the items themselves); *U.S. v. Donato-Morales*, 382 F.3d 42 (1st Cir. 2004) (in larceny case, prosecution not required to offer scanner display reflecting price of videocassette recorder rather than security officer's testimony regarding price); *U.S. v. Branham*, 97 F.3d 835 (6th Cir. 1996) (tape recordings were admissible but testimony by participant was equally admissible and sufficient to establish what was said); *Allstate Ins. Co. v. Swann*, 27 F.3d 1539 (11th Cir. 1994) (error to exclude testimony that homeowner did not qualify for insurance; no need to produce underwriting guidelines); *R & R Associates, Inc. v. Visual Scene, Inc.*, 726 F.2d 36 (1st Cir. 1984) (permissible for witness to testify to damage amount without introducing written documentation); *McKeown v. Woods Hole*, 9 F. Supp. 2d 32 (D. Mass. 1998) (vessel's chief engineer could testify about work assignment even though there existed document listing tasks); *Strahan v. Coxe*, 939 F. Supp. 963 (D. Mass. 1996) (testimony about giving notice of suit was sufficient; precise contents of letter need not be established).

Where an object has been inscribed, the trial court has discretion to treat the evidence as a chattel or as a writing. McCormick, Evidence § 232; *U.S. v. Duffy*, 454 F.2d 809 (5th Cir. 1972) (allowing testimony about laundry markings on shirt seized from stolen car without requiring production of shirt). *See also Segrets, Inc. v. Gillman Knitwear Co., Inc.*, 42 F. Supp. 2d 58 (D. Mass. 1998) (copyright infringement claim where court overruled objection that photographs of uniquely designed sweater violated "best evidence rule"; court expressed doubt that sweater came within meaning of best evidence rule since it was not a writing, recording or photograph).

Occasionally, the best evidence rule is cited for propositions which find no support in case law. For example, in a situation where several people know something, there is no requirement that the party call the person who knows it "best". There is no rule that proof of a fact will be excluded unless its proponent furnishes the best evidence in his power. *Simas v. First Citizens' Federal Credit Union*, 170 F.3d 37 (1st Cir. 1999) (plaintiff could prove he filed car loan application through his own trial testimony without introducing documents). Also there is no rule that oral testimony is inadmissible because the same facts could be proven by better evidence, *i.e.*, documents or recordings. *U.S. v. Martin*, 920

F.2d 393 (6th Cir. 1990) (Rule 1002 does not apply and witness was free to testify to conversation which had also been tape recorded; government's intention in playing tape was not to prove content of recording but to corroborate conversation).

Additional References

Graham, Handbook of Federal Evidence §§ 1002.1 to 1002.5 (7th ed. 2012)

Treatises and Practice Aids

Goode and Wellborn, Courtroom Handbook on Federal Evidence Chapter 5, Rule 1002 and Obj. 14 (annual ed.)

Mueller & Kirkpatrick, Federal Evidence, §§ 10:1 *et seq.* (3d ed., 2007)

Wright & Gold, Federal Practice and Procedure: Evidence §§ 7161 *et seq.*

McCormick, Evidence Chapter 23 (6th ed. 2006)

Park, Trial Objections Handbook §§ 9:1 to 9:8 (2nd ed. 2001)

BEYOND THE SCOPE

See:

Fed.R.Evid. 611(b)
Mil.R.Evid. 611(b)

Objection

- Objection. This is beyond the scope of direct examination. This matter was not mentioned in direct testimony; counsel must call this witness in his own case if he wishes to go into this evidence.
- This is not within the scope of proper redirect examination. It is not responsive to anything covered in the cross-examination.

Response

- The question is proper:
  - it is addressed to the [*inference*] [*deduction*] [*conclusion*] which the witness sought to create in his direct testimony;
  - credibility is always in issue;
  - I am entitled to show the [*bias*] [*interest*] of the witness;
  - I am entitled to test [*memory*] [*perception*].

Commentary

Rule 611(b) limits the scope of cross-examination "to the subject matter of the direct examination and matters affecting the credibility of the witness." *U.S. v. Ellis*, 156 F.3d 493 (3d Cir. 1998) (where agent's testimony was limited to authenticity of tape recordings which defendant did not challenge, he could not be examined on other topics because his credibility was not in issue); *U.S. v. Route*, 104 F.3d 59 (5th Cir. 1997) (no error in terminating cross-examination where defendant would not restrict questioning to scope of direct testimony). This scope is broadly defined as the right to elicit testimony which explains or destroys the effect of the direct testimony, including inferences, deductions or conclusions which may be drawn from the challenged testimony. *See, e.g., Macaulay v. Anas*, 321 F.3d 45, 54 (1st Cir. 2003) (it is unrealistic to expect that direct examination and cross-examination will be perfectly congruent; cross-examiners must be given reasonable latitude to delve into areas related to witness's direction examination); *U.S. v. Jones*, 913 F.2d 1552 (11th Cir. 1990) (in cocaine case where defendant attempted to create impression he was changed man leading responsible life, it was proper impeachment to show that impression was false); *U.S. v. Carter*, 910 F.2d 1524 (7th Cir. 1990) (in cross-examination of girlfriend, prosecution allowed to exceed scope of direct testimony to challenge some of defendant's alibis; Rule 611(b) grants court discretion to "permit inquiry into additional matters as if on direct examination").

Questions which test perception or memory or which show bias, prejudice or motivation are also proper. *Davis v. Alaska*, 415 U.S. 308, 316–17, 94 S. Ct. 1105, 1110, 39 L. Ed. 2d 347 (1974) ("The exposure of a witness' motivation in testifying is a proper and important function of the constitutionally protected right of cross-examination."); *U.S. v. Harris*, 185 F.3d 999, 1008 (9th Cir. 1999) ("Cross examination for bias is often on topics outside the scope of the direct examination, but that is not a reason to exclude inquiry into the potential bias."); *U.S. v. Alexius*, 76 F.3d 642 (5th Cir. 1996) (reversible error to refuse to allow defendant to cross-examine government witness about pending drug charges because charges were relevant to motive or bias); *Harbor Ins. Co. v. Schnabel Foundation Co., Inc.*, 946 F.2d 930, 935 (D.C. Cir. 1991) (abuse of discretion to restrict cross-examination where purpose was to show that construction expert witness lacked personal knowledge of other construction sites he referenced in giving his opinion; "where a party is seeking to impeach a witness whose credibility could have an important influence on the outcome of the trial, the district court should be cautious in limiting cross-examination.")

The court has judicial discretion to enlarge cross-examination into areas not explored on direct examination. Rule 611(b); *see U.S. v. Lara*, 181 F.3d 183 (1st Cir. 1999); *Losacco v. F.D. Rich Const. Co., Inc.*, 992 F.2d 382 (1st Cir. 1993); *U.S. v. Arnott*, 704 F.2d 322 (6th Cir. 1983); *U.S. v. Raper*, 676 F.2d 841 (D.C. Cir. 1982). *But cf. Lis v. Robert Packer Hospital*, 579 F.2d 819, 823 (3d Cir. 1978) (confining exercise of discretion under Rule 611(b) to "special circumstances" because "to allow the practice in every case is not to exercise discretion; it is to use no discretion whatever.") But when a party is permitted to go beyond the scope of direct examination, counsel cannot ask leading questions but must proceed as if on direct examination. Rule 611(b).

In civil cases, cross-examination is a due process right. *Demenech v. Secretary of the Dept. of Health and Human Services*, 913 F.2d 882 (11th Cir. 1990). Refusal to permit cross-examination of a witness concerning matters testified to on direct examination constitutes prejudicial error. *Francis v. Clark Equipment Co.*, 993 F.2d 545 (6th Cir. 1993) (in product liability case against forklift manufacturer, new trial awarded where jury heard plaintiff's expert testify about feasibility of operator restraint technology but defendant was precluded from cross-examining on that subject because plaintiff abandoned theory).

In criminal cases, the Sixth Amendment guarantees the accused the right to cross-examine prosecution witnesses fully and fairly. *Delaware v. Fensterer*, 474 U.S. 15, 106 S. Ct. 292, 88 L. Ed. 2d 15 (1985); *Pointer v. Texas*, 380 U.S. 400, 405, 85 S. Ct. 1065, 1068, 13 L. Ed. 2d 923 (1965) (right of cross-examination is "an essential and fundamental requirement for the kind of fair trial which is this country's constitutional goal."); *U.S. v. Skelton*, 514 F.3d 433 (5th Cir. 2008).

The right to confront witnesses, however, is not unlimited. *Danner v. Motley*, 448 F.3d 372, 377 (6th Cir. 2006); *U.S. v. Ortega*, 150 F.3d 937 (8th Cir. 1998); *Miranda v. Cooper*, 967 F.2d 392 (10th Cir. 1992). The trial court retains broad discretion to limit cross-examination that is marginally relevant or to prevent harassment, prejudice, repetition or confusion of the issues. *See Delaware v. Van Arsdall*, 475 U.S. 673, 106 S. Ct. 1431, 89 L. Ed. 2d 674 (1986); *U.S. v. Papajohn*, 212 F.3d 1112 (8th Cir. 2000) (where witness had refused to answer prosecutor's questions, no error to bar cross-examination because there was no direct testimony to confront). The trial court's discretionary authority arises *only after* sufficient cross-examination has been granted to satisfy the Sixth Amendment.

U.S. v. Landerman, 109 F.3d 1053 (5th Cir. 1997); *U.S. v. Restivo*, 8 F.3d 274, 278 (5th Cir. 1993) ("The Confrontation Clause of the Sixth Amendment is satisfied where defense counsel has been permitted to expose to the jury the facts from which jurors, as the sole triers of fact and credibility, could appropriately draw inferences relating to the reliability of the witness.").

A defendant may not introduce his defense by way of cross-examination of witnesses. *U.S. v. Smith*, 44 F.3d 1259 (4th Cir. 1995) (court properly disallowed certain cross-examination beyond scope of IRS agent's direct testimony but invited defendant to recall agent in her own case to pursue inquiry); *U.S. v. Sampol*, 636 F.2d 621 (D.C. Cir. 1980) (no error to prohibit cross-examination about possible CIA complicity in assassination of former Chilean official where it was beyond scope of government witnesses' direct testimony; defendants were free to recall witnesses in their own case and government agreed to make them available); *U.S. v. Stamp*, 458 F.2d 759 (D.C. Cir. 1971) (trial judge correct in not allowing defense to cross-examine prosecution witness with respect to matters only relevant to affirmative defense not yet brought into case); *Baker v. U.S.*, 401 F.2d 958 (D.C. Cir. 1968) (same).

Redirect examination may be used to rebut false impressions arising from cross-examination, *U.S. v. Burns*, 432 F.3d 856, 860 (8th Cir. 2005); *U.S. v. Naiman*, 211 F.3d 40 (2d Cir. 2000), and its scope is a matter of judicial discretion, *U.S. v. Diaz*, 176 F.3d 52 (2d Cir. 1999). Absent the introduction of any new matter on redirect examination, the rule is that recross-examination is not permitted. *U.S. v. Fleschner*, 98 F.3d 155, 157 (4th Cir. 1996) ("Without something new, a party has the last word with his own witness") (quoting Wharton's Criminal Evidence, 14th ed., 1986, Vol. 2, p. 698). If a new subject is raised in redirect examination, the trial court must allow recross-examination concerning the new matter. *U.S. v. Riggi*, 951 F.2d 1368 (3d Cir. 1991). "To deny recross examination on matter first drawn out on redirect is to deny the defendant the right of any cross-examination as to that new matter." *U.S. v. Caudle*, 606 F.2d 451, 458 (4th Cir. 1979).

BEYOND THE SCOPE

Additional References

Graham, Handbook of Federal Evidence §§ 611.11 to 611.13 (7th ed. 2012)

Treatises and Practice Aids

Goode and Wellborn, Courtroom Handbook on Federal Evidence Chapter 5, Rule 611 and Obj. 26 (annual ed.)

Mueller & Kirkpatrick, Federal Evidence, § 6:60 (3d ed. 2007)

Wright & Gold, Federal Practice and Procedure: Evidence § 6165

McCormick, Evidence Chapter 4 (6th ed. 2006)

Park, Trial Objections Handbook §§ 6:14 to 6:15 (2nd ed. 2001)

CHAIN OF CUSTODY

See:

Fed.R.Evid. 901
Mil.R.Evid. 901

Objection

- Objection. The exhibit has not been properly authenticated. There is insufficient evidence to demonstrate that the identity of this object [*and/or its condition*] is unimpaired.

Response

- A proper foundation for admission has been established. We have met our burden of demonstrating that there has been no [*alteration/substitution/change of condition*]. Any alleged gap in the chain of custody since the time of the incident goes to the weight of the evidence, not its admissibility.

Commentary

Real evidence (i.e. material objects) consists of the actual objects involved in a particular event (e.g. the murder weapon, the seized drugs, the defective product). The "chain of custody" rule derives from the principle that real evidence must be authenticated prior to its admission into evidence. Fed.R.Evid. 901. The purpose of requiring proof of a chain of custody of physical evidence is to ensure that evidence is not lost, adulterated, or changed pending trial on the merits of a case. *U.S. v. Ellis*, 15 F. Supp. 2d 1025 (D. Colo. 1998). Evaluating the admissibility of real evidence is within the sound discretion of the trial judge. *U.S. v. Dixon*, 132 F.3d 192 (5th Cir. 1997).

When physical evidence has distinctive characteristics which make it unique, readily identifiable and relatively resistant to change, its foundation for admission may be established simply by testimony that the evidence is what its proponent claims it to be. *U.S. v. Mills*, 194 F.3d 1108 (10th Cir. 1999); *U.S. v. Cardenas*, 864 F.2d 1528 (10th Cir. 1989). But when the evidence is not readily identifiable and is susceptible to alteration by tampering or contamination, the trial court requires proof of a chain of custody of the item with sufficient completeness to make it improbable that the original item has been exchanged with another, tampered with, or contaminated. *U.S. v. Wilson*, 565 F.3d 1059 (8th Cir. 2009); *U.S. v. Lothridge*, 332 F.3d 502 (8th Cir. 2003).

Proof of the chain of custody need not be perfect for the evidence to be admissible. *U.S. v. Lee*, 502 F.3d 691 (7th Cir. 2007); *U.S. v. Guidry*, 406 F.3d 314 (5th Cir. 2005); *U.S. v. Humphrey*, 208 F.3d 1190 (10th Cir. 2000). The offering party is not always required to produce every individual who came into contact with an item of evidence, *U.S. v. Rose*, 587 F.3d 695 (5th Cir. 2009); *U.S. v. Howard-Arias*, 679 F.2d 363 (4th Cir. 1982), nor must it rule out every conceivable chance that somehow the identity or character of the evidence underwent change. *Ballou v. Henri Studios, Inc.*, 656 F.2d 1147 (5th Cir. 1981); *U.S. v. Lane*, 591 F.2d 961 (D.C. Cir. 1979); *U.S. v. Haldeman*, 559 F.2d 31 (D.C. Cir. 1976). Proof of a perfect chain of custody is not required so long as the evidence, direct and circumstantial, establishes a reasonable inference that the identity and condition of the item has remained the same from the time it was first obtained until the time of trial. *Reed v. U.S.*, 377 F.2d 891 (10th Cir. 1967). A break in the chain of custody usually goes to the weight of the evidence and not its admissibility. *Melendez-Diaz v. Massachusetts*, 552 U.S. 1256 (2008); *U.S. v. Moreland*, 437 F.3d 424 (4th Cir. 2006); *U.S. v. Cartagena-Carrasquillo*, 70 F.3d 706 (1st Cir. 1995); *U.S. v. Sparks*, 2 F.3d 574 (5th Cir. 1993); *Tirado v. Senkowski*, 367 F. Supp. 2d 477 (W.D. N.Y. 2005). Once admitted, the jury evaluates the defects and, based on its evaluation, may accept or disregard the evidence. *U.S. v. Huggins*, 191 F.3d 532 (4th Cir. 1999) (break in chain caused by theft of marijuana from state office adequately addressed by testimony of perpetrator and agent who later found marijuana in original container); *U.S. v. Rodriguez*, 162 F.3d 135 (1st Cir. 1998) (agent who did not witness controlled drug buy could testify about narcotics despite five-minute time gap in transfer from buyer to undercover agent and then to the witness); *Huenefeld v. Maloney*, 62 F. Supp. 2d 211 (D. Mass. 1999) (aware that bloodstained car used in murder thereafter was loaned to another person for short period and later turned over to prosecutor, jury could assign whatever weight it thought appropriate to chemical analysis); *Lentz v. Mason*, 32 F. Supp. 2d 733 (D.N.J. 1999) (common sense suggests that average person does not have access to torpedo tubes; pieces sent to expert for analysis came from hazardous material for which plaintiff landowner sought clean-up costs); *U.S. v. Ellis,* 15 F.Supp.2d at 1032 (confusion and contradiction resolved against prosecution where suspected drugs were improperly handled and combined; military policewoman who searched defendant's purse had never seen methamphetamine and could not identify it; court could not tell which, if any, investigator had field tested substance).

Merely raising the possibility of tampering is insufficient to render evidence inadmissible. *U.S. v. Allen*, 106 F.3d 695 (6th Cir. 1997).

Where items have been in official custody and there is no affirmative evidence of tampering, there is a presumption that public officers have discharged their duties properly to preserve the items' original condition. *U.S. v. Prieto*, 549 F.3d 513 (7th Cir. 2008); *U.S. v. Broadnax*, 475 F. Supp. 2d 783 (N.D. Ind. 2007).

In *Melendez-Diaz v. Massachusetts*, supra, the trial court had admitted into evidence state laboratory affidavits with forensic analysis results showing material seized from defendant was cocaine. The United States Supreme Court said that the laboratory reports fell within the core class of testimonial statements since they has been created for the sole purpose of providing evidence against a defendant. Acknowledging that the Confrontation Clause may make prosecution of criminals more burdensome, the Court held that crime laboratory reports may not testimony and subject themselves to cross-examination. Accord *Bullcoming v. New Mexico*, ____ U.S. ____ (2001).

Additional References

Graham, Handbook of Federal Evidence § 901.1 (7th ed. 2012)

Treatises and Practice Aids

Goode and Wellborn, Courtroom Handbook on Federal Evidence Chapter 5, Rule 901 and Obj. 16 (annual ed.)

Chain of Custody

Mueller & Kirkpatrick, Federal Evidence, § 9:10 (3d ed. 2007)
Wright & Gold, Federal Practice and Procedure: Evidence § 7106
McCormick, Evidence Chapter 22 (6th ed. 2006)
Park Trial Objections Handbook § 9:28 (2nd ed. 2001)

CHARACTER WITNESS: HYPOTHETICAL QUESTION ASSUMING GUILT

See:

Fed.R.Evid. 405
Mil.R.Evid. 405

Objection

- Objection. Any question assuming guilt of the charges in question here is improper.

Response

- Withdraw the question.*
- The question asks no more than what the defendant has already admitted in his own testimony. It does not assume guilt and, therefore, is proper.

Commentary

When a defendant calls a character witness, Rule 405(a) allows the government to cross-examine that witness regarding his/her knowledge of specific instances of the defendant's misconduct in order to help the jury evaluate the quality of the character testimony.

However, a majority of circuits which have addressed the issue hold that the prosecution may not cross-examine a defendant's character witness by asking whether his or her opinion of the defendant would change if the defendant were guilty of the charges against him. The prosecution also may not ask whether the witness is aware that the defendant is guilty. The Fifth Circuit has said that guilt-assuming hypotheticals have no probative value, assume facts which are the subject of the litigation, strike at the very heart of the presumption of innocence and have no place in a criminal trial. *U.S. v. Candelaria-Gonzalez*, 547 F.2d 291, 294 (5th Cir. 1977). Although the questions at issue in *Candelaria-Gonzalez* were posed to character witnesses who were testifying about the accused's reputation in the community, these questions are

---

[Character etc.]

*See discussion re District of Columbia Circuit.

equally inappropriate when asked of witnesses who are testifying about their personal knowledge of the defendant's character. *U.S. v. Guzman*, 167 F.3d 1350 (11th Cir. 1999); *U.S. v. Mason*, 993 F.2d 406 (4th Cir. 1993); *U.S. v. Oshatz*, 912 F.2d 534 (2d Cir. 1990); *U.S. v. Barta*, 888 F.2d 1220 (8th Cir. 1989); *U.S. v. McGuire*, 744 F.2d 1197 (6th Cir. 1984); *U.S. v. Williams*, 738 F.2d 172 (7th Cir. 1984); *U.S. v. Polsinelli*, 649 F.2d 793 (10th Cir. 1981). *But see U.S. v. Kellogg*, 510 F.3d 188 (3d Cir. 2007) (collecting cases and examining the distinction between reputation character evidence (where hypothetical questions are improper) and opinion character evidence (where, in some cases, such hypotheticals usefully test the character witness' own standards and bias)); *U.S. v. White*, 887 F.2d 267, 274–75 (D.C. Cir. 1989) (court saw nothing wrong with guilt-assuming questions posed to witnesses who had given their personal opinions of defendant's character but acknowledged such questioning of reputation witnesses "may be inappropriate.")

See also U.S. v. Russo, 110 F.3d 948 (2d Cir. 1997) (because defense counsel "opened the door" by asking character witness whether, in his opinion, defendant's character was consistent with charges against him, government allowed to determine how familiar witness was with those charges); *U.S. v. Wilson*, 983 F.2d 221 (11th Cir. 1993) (questions did not assume guilt because character witnesses were asked nothing more than defendant had already admitted on stand); *U.S. v. Velasquez*, 980 F.2d 1275 (9th Cir. 1992) (no error where prosecutor asked character witnesses how they would interpret acts-walking into bank with hand grenade and asking manager to open vault-that defense counsel admitted in his opening statement had occurred).

Additional References

Graham, Handbook of Federal Evidence § 405.1 (7th ed. 2012)

Treatises and Practice Aids

Goode and Wellborn, Courtroom Handbook on Federal Evidence Chapter 5, Rule 610 and Obj. 83 (annual ed.)

Mueller & Kirkpatrick, Federal Evidence, § 4:41 (3d ed. 2007)

Wright & Graham, Federal Practice and Procedure: Evidence §§ 5261 *et seq.*
McCormick, Evidence § 48 (6th ed. 2006)

CLOSING ARGUMENT

See:

Fed.R.Crim.P. 29.1

Objection

- Your Honor, I must object. Counsel is: [*stating her own personal belief about a witness's credibility*] [*misstating the law*] [*stating the law in a manner calculated to confuse the jury*] [*mischaracterizing the evidence*] [*engaging in comment which is inappropriate, inflammatory and prejudicial*]. I request an immediate cautionary instruction. [*I hereby move for a mistrial*].

Response

- Your Honor, my comments are fair deductions and legitimate inferences from the evidence presented and are well within the boundaries of proper advocacy. [*I have stated the law correctly*] [*I have stated the facts accurately and the record will reflect that*].

Commentary

The function of a closing argument is to provide counsel the opportunity to marshal the evidence and to present it, along with permissible inferences, to the jury in the best possible light on behalf of the client and to attempt to explain away the evidence which is unfavorable. *U.S. v. Taylor*, 54 F.3d 967 (1st Cir. 1995).

The right to present a summation is a component of the Sixth Amendment right to representation by counsel. *Herring v. New York*, 422 U.S. 853, 95 S. Ct. 2550, 45 L. Ed. 2d 593 (1975). Counsel must be afforded reasonable latitude in presenting a case to a jury, and must be allowed to present his or her arguments with logical force and vigor. *U.S. v. Wilner*, 523 F.2d 68, 74 (2d Cir. 1975) ("[A] prosecuting attorney is not an automaton whose role in summation is limited to parroting facts . . .. He is an advocate who is expected to prosecute diligently and vigorously, albeit without appeal to prejudice or passion.")

The length of closing argument is within the discretion of the trial court. *U.S. v. Apperson*, 441 F.3d 1162 (10th Cir. 2006) (ninety minutes allotted by court for each defendant was entirely reasonable); *Conde v. Henry*, 198 F.3d 734 (9th Cir. 1999); *U.S. v. Gray*, 105 F.3d 956 (5th Cir. 1997) (in reviewing time limitations the crucial question is whether counsel were permitted to advocate effectively for their clients); *U.S. v. Donato*, 99 F.3d 426 (D.C. Cir. 1996) (prosecutor's error in mischaracterizing evidence compounded by trial judge who improperly shortened time defense counsel could use for closing argument).

During final argument, counsel may describe and discuss: all facts and opinions which are part of the record; reasonable inferences from the evidence that the jury has seen and heard, *see U.S. v. Lopez-Medina*, 596 F.3d 716 (10th Cir. 2010) (the cardinal rule of closing argument is that counsel must confine comments to evidence in the record and to reasonable inferences from that evidence); *U.S. v. Hernandez*, 218 F.3d 58 (1st Cir. 2000); *U.S. v. Ward*, 211 F.3d 356 (7th Cir. 2000); *U.S. v. Reeder*, 170 F.3d 93 (1st Cir. 1999); how the law applies to the facts to support the verdict sought and how the evidence supports the legal theories; and anecdotes, analogies and metaphors involving common life experiences. The closing argument is the last opportunity the attorney has to explain the specific result the attorney wants and to convince the jury that the facts and the law support a verdict in favor of the client. *See* Haydock and Sonsteng's Trial: Advocacy Before Judges, Jurors and Arbitrators Chapter 11 (2nd ed.1999).

Visual aids that summarize other evidence are generally permissible devices, especially when used to organize complex testimony or transactions for the jury. Such aids need not be admitted into evidence. *U.S. v. Reyes*, 157 F.3d 949 (2d Cir. 1998) (blown up map of New York to show distance traveled by gang members to visit defendant in prison); *U.S. v. Crockett*, 49 F.3d 1357 (8th Cir. 1995) (transparencies summarizing testimony).

Trial counsel, however, is not permitted to:

1. misstate admitted evidence or misquote a witness' testimony, *U.S. v. Watson*, 171 F.3d 695 (D.C. Cir. 1999); *Donato*, 99 F.3d at 426;

2. misstate the law or state it in a manner calculated to confuse the jury, *U.S. v. Gonzalez-Montoya*, 161 F.3d 643 (10th Cir. 1998);
3. comment on the credibility of witnesses by stating a personal opinion (vouching) about whether a witness has testified truthfully, *U.S. v. Jones*, 468 F.3d 704 (10th Cir. 2006); *Byrd v. Collins*, 209 F.3d 486 (6th Cir. 2000); *U.S. v. Thornton*, 197 F.3d 241 (7th Cir. 1999); *Rodriguez v. Scillia*, 193 F.3d 913 (7th Cir. 1999); *U.S. v. Dispoz-O-Plastics, Inc.*, 172 F.3d 275 (3d Cir. 1999); *U.S. v. Loayza*, 107 F.3d 257 (4th Cir. 1997). *See U.S. v. Adams*, 799 F.2d 665, 670 (11th Cir. 1986) (distinguishing between "I believe that the defendant is guilty," which is impermissible vouching, and "I believe the evidence has shown the defendant's guilt," which is permitted argument);
4. refer to facts which are not in evidence, *Slagle v. Bagley*, 457 F.3d 501 (6th Cir. 2006); *U.S. v. Beckman*, 222 F.3d 512 (8th Cir. 2000) (closing argument asserted facts not in evidence and attempted to argue and imply inferences therefrom); *U.S. v. Brisk*, 171 F.3d 514 (7th Cir. 1999) (argument that children were present while cocaine was being packaged was improper attempt to argue facts not in evidence); *U.S. v. Maddox*, 156 F.3d 1280 (D.C. Cir. 1998) (attorney makes himself unsworn witness offering blatant hearsay when referring to matters not in evidence);
5. make remarks that are not justified by the testimony and which are unfairly prejudicial to the accused, *U.S. v. Richardson*, 161 F.3d 728 (D.C. Cir. 1998) (improper argument that defense was based on racial stereotyping and defense attorney was out of touch with inner-city world of prosecution witnesses and jury). Comments will be deemed unfairly prejudicial where their unavoidable effect is to create in the jurors such bias and hostility toward a party that they could not weigh the evidence objectively and render a true verdict. *Hodge v. Hurley*, 426 F.3d 368 (6th Cir. 2005) (defense counsel provided ineffective assistance when he failed to object to closing loaded with error and unfairly prejudicial comment); *Moore v.*

Gibson, 195 F.3d 1152 (10th Cir. 1999) (court does not condone prosecutorial remarks encouraging jury to allow sympathy to influence its decision); *Whitehead v. Food Max of Mississippi, Inc.*, 163 F.3d 265 (5th Cir. 1998) (tort action remanded for new trial on damages because counsel persisted in contrasting Mississippi plaintiffs with large Michigan corporation in an appeal to local bias); *Guaranty Service Corp. v. American Employers' Ins. Co.*, 893 F.2d 725 (5th Cir. 1990) (arguments which invite jury to act on behalf of a litigant become improper "conscience of the community" arguments when parties' relative popularity, identities, or geographical locations are invoked to prejudice jurors); *U.S. v. Hernandez*, 865 F.2d 925 (7th Cir. 1989) (prosecutor prohibited from making race-conscious arguments because it draws jury's attention to a characteristic the Constitution generally demands that jury ignore).

A "Golden Rule" argument in which the jurors are asked to put themselves in the shoes of the plaintiff or defendant has been deemed improper because it encourages the jurors to depart from neutrality and to decide the case on the basis of personal interest and bias rather than on the evidence. *Lovett ex rel. Lovett v. Union Pacific R. Co.*, 201 F.3d 1074 (8th Cir. 2000); *Whitehead*, 163 F.3d at 265; *Edwards v. City of Philadelphia*, 860 F.2d 568 (3d Cir. 1988); *Spray-Rite Service Corp. v. Monsanto Co.*, 684 F.2d 1226 (7th Cir. 1982); *Arnold v. Eastern Air Lines, Inc.*, 681 F.2d 186 (4th Cir. 1982); *Loose v. Offshore Nav., Inc.*, 670 F.2d 493 (5th Cir. 1982); *cf. Shultz v. Rice*, 809 F.2d 643 (10th Cir. 1986); *Burrage v. Harrell*, 537 F.2d 837 (5th Cir. 1976) ("Golden Rule" argument improper only when used with respect to issue of damages and not when issue is liability); *Heimlicher v. Steele*, 615 F. Supp. 2d 884 (N.D.Iowa 2009) (Golden Rule universally condemned).

It is also improper to ask a jury to "send a message" to other potential tortfeasors when asking for compensatory damages. Like any other defendant, a tortfeasor is entitled to be judged solely on its own wrongdoing and not used as an example to others. *Third Wave Technologies, Inc. v. Stratagene*

Corp., 405 F. Supp. 2d 991 (W.D. Wis. 2005).

Criminal Proceedings

While a prosecutor " 'may strike hard blows, he is not at liberty to strike foul ones.' " *United States v. Young*, 470 U.S. 1, 7, 105 S. Ct. 1038, 1042, 84 L. Ed. 2d 1 (1985) (quoting *Berger v. United States*, 295 U.S. 78, 88, 55 S. Ct. 629, 79 L. Ed. 1314 (1935)). The prosecutor is free to comment on what the evidence shows concerning the credibility of a witness, including the defendant. *U.S. v. Moreland*, 509 F.3d 1201 (9th Cir. 2007) (it is neither unusual nor improper for prosecutor to voice doubt about veracity of defendant who has taken the stand); *U.S. v. Isler*, 429 F.3d 19 (1st Cir. 2005) (when defendant puts his credibility at issue by testifying, prosecutor can comment on implausibility of testimony or its lack of evidentiary foundation). He can speak fully, although harshly, concerning the conduct and actions of the accused if the evidence supports the comments. Defense counsel has the same license to comment on evidence and witnesses. *U.S. v. Durham*, 211 F.3d 437 (7th Cir. 2000); *U.S. v. Russell*, 109 F.3d 1503 (10th Cir. 1997).

It is improper for a prosecutor to suggest that a jury has a civic duty to convict. *Thornburg v. Mullin*, 422 F.3d 1113 (10th Cir. 2005).

To obtain a reversal based on prosecutorial misconduct to which there was a proper objection, a defendant must show that: (1) the prosecutor's remarks or conduct were improper, and (2) the remarks or conduct so infected the trial with unfairness as to make the resulting conviction a denial of due process. *Donnelly v. DeChristoforo*, 416 U.S. 637, 94 S. Ct. 1868, 40 L. Ed. 2d 431 (1974).

Fifth Amendment Violation

In criminal cases, a prosecutor violates the Fifth Amendment by commenting, directly or indirectly, on a defendant's decision not to testify. *Griffin v. California*, 380 U.S. 609, 85 S. Ct. 1229, 14 L. Ed. 2d 106 (1965); *U.S. v. Brown*, 508 F.3d 1066 (D.C. Cir. 2007); *U.S. v. Wesley*, 422 F.3d 509 (7th Cir. 2005). A prosecutor's comment that the government's evidence on an issue is 'uncontradicted,' 'undenied,' 'unrebutted,' 'undisputed,' etc., will be a violation of the defendant's Fifth Amendment rights if the only person who could have contradicted, denied, rebutted or disputed the government's evidence was the defendant himself. *U.S. v. Balsam*, 203 F.3d 72 (1st Cir. 2000) (government may focus on absence of impeachment of its witnesses during cross-examination so long as comments are sufficiently circumscribed and do not necessarily implicate defendant's assertion of Fifth Amendment right not to testify); *U.S. v. Bey*, 188 F.3d 1 (1st Cir. 1999) (no error because defense had an available witness capable of rebutting government's evidence); *U.S. v. McClellan*, 165 F.3d 535 (7th Cir. 1999) (same); *U.S. v. Roberts*, 119 F.3d 1006 (1st Cir. 1997) (when defendant advances "theory of the case," door is opened to appropriate response by prosecution; comment on quality of witnesses or weak foundation of theory is permitted; however, suggesting defendant has responsibility to present compelling case is reversible error); *U.S. v. Lewis*, 40 F.3d 1325 (1st Cir. 1994) (government entitled, to some extent, to comment on defendant's failure to produce evidence supporting defense theory); *U.S. v. Parker*, 903 F.2d 91 (2d Cir. 1990) (prosecutor who wishes to argue government's evidence is largely uncontradicted must walk fine line; she is entitled to comment on defendant's failure to call witnesses to contradict government's case or to support theory of defense but must avoid commenting in a way that trenches on defendant's constitutional rights and privileges). *Cf. U.S. v. Golding*, 168 F.3d 700 (4th Cir. 1999) (misconduct warranting reversal where prosecutor commented on wife's failure to testify which invaded her marital privilege).

Silence

Generally, a prosecutor may not comment on a defendant's post-arrest, post-*Miranda* silence to create an inference of guilt without violating the guarantee of fundamental fairness embodied in the Due Process Clause. *See Doyle v. Ohio*, 426 U.S. 610, 96 S. Ct. 2240, 49 L. Ed. 2d 91 (1976); *U.S. v. Rosenthal*, 793 F.2d 1214 (11th Cir. 1986) (virtually any description of a defendant's silence following arrest and a *Mirana* warning will constitute a

Doyle violation). However, the Supreme Court has articulated an exception to the *Doyle* rule whereby a prosecutor may comment on defendant's silence as a "fair response" to an argument by defense counsel based on defendant's silence. *U.S. v. Robinson*, 485 U.S. 25, 108 S. Ct. 864, 99 L. Ed. 2d 23 (1988).

Vouching

A prosecutor vouches for the credibility of a witness when she states or implies that the government can guarantee the witness' veracity in either of two ways: by (1) placing the prestige of the government behind a witness through personal assurances of the witness' veracity, or (2) suggesting that information not presented to the jury supports the witness' testimony. *U.S. v. Johnson*, 587 F.3d 625 (4th Cir. 2009); *U.S. v. Martinez-Larraga*, 517 F.3d 258 (5th Cir. 2008); *U.S. v. Weatherspoon*, 406 F.3d 636 (9th Cir. 2005) (no lawyer, either public or private, should lay his or her own credibility on the line by expressing his or her own opinion about a witness' believability); *U.S. v. Francis*, 170 F.3d 546 (6th Cir. 1999) (bolstering and vouching are alike and go to heart of fair trial; bolstering occurs when prosecutor implies witness' testimony is corroborated by evidence known to government but not known to jury); *Buehl v. Vaughn*, 166 F.3d 163 (3d Cir. 1999) (prosecutor's expression of personal opinion about credibility of witnesses or guilt of defendant creates risk that jury will trust government's judgment rather than its own view of evidence); *U.S. v. Renteria*, 106 F.3d 765 (7th Cir. 1997) (same); *U.S. v. Baptista-Rodriguez*, 17 F.3d 1354 (11th Cir. 1994) (referring to fact that witness took polygraph test may amount to implicit vouching for credibility of witness); *cf. U.S. v. Auch*, 187 F.3d 125 (1st Cir. 1999) (confronted with prosecutorial misconduct, court's recourse not limited to public hand-wringing in pages of federal reporters; in appropriate case offending prosecutor will be referred to Department of Justice for investigation and discipline). The rule applies both ways; defense counsel also must refrain from injecting personal beliefs into the presentation of his case. *U.S. v. Grabiec*, 96 F.3d 549 (1st Cir. 1996). *See also* Model Rules of Prof'l Conduct R. 3.4(e) (2002) (prohibiting a lawyer from stating a personal opinion as to the justness of a cause, the credibility of a witness, the culpability of a civil litigant or the guilt or innocence of an accused).

Although the government may present evidence about its witnesses' plea agreements and their concomitant obligations to be truthful, the court should not permit unnecessarily repetitive references to truthfulness. *See U.S. v. Collins*, 223 F.3d 502 (7th Cir. 2000) (no vouching occurred when prosecutor argued that government witnesses had entered plea agreements requiring truthfulness and jury ought to consider that fact when evaluating their testimony).

Oratorical Flair

While traditionally tolerant of oratorical flair during argument, courts have universally condemned religiously charged arguments as confusing, unnecessary and inflammatory. *U.S. v. Roach*, 502 F.3d 425 (6th Cir. 2007); *Sandoval v. Calderon*, 231 F.3d 1140, 1151 (9th Cir. 2000) (religious arguments have been condemned by virtually every federal and state court to consider their challenge); *Bennett v. Angelone*, 92 F.3d 1336 (4th Cir. 1996) (prosecution's religiously loaded sentencing arguments with references to Noah and the flood, Jesus and the crucifixion, were highly improper); *Cunningham v. Zant*, 928 F.2d 1006 (11th Cir. 1991) (improper to compare defendant's statement to Peter's denial of Christ); *cf. Bussard v. Lockhart*, 32 F.3d 322 (8th Cir. 1994) (quoting Bible acceptable merely for poetic but accurate explanation of law; as distinguished from misusing Bible to invoke wrath of God or to suggest that jury apply divine law).

Use of insults, slurs and other intemperate language is inappropriate, *Darden v. Wainwright*, 477 U.S. 168, 180–181, 106 S. Ct. 2464, 2471, 91 L. Ed. 2d 144 (1986) (where defendant was referred to as animal who should not be out of prison without a leash, Court declined relief but cautioned that closing arguments could become so infected with unfairness that conviction would be denial of due process); *Wilson v. Sirmons*, 536 F.3d 1064 (10th Cir. 2008) (describing defendant as an "animal" and "unadulterated evil" unprofessional, inappropriate and unworthy of an officer of the court); *Shurn v. Delo*, 177 F.3d 662 (8th Cir. 1999) (death sentence vacated; closing linked defendant with notorious mass-murderer Charles Manson); *Martin v. Parker*, 11 F.3d 613 (6th Cir. 1993) (granting writ of habeas corpus; defendant compared to Hitler); *U.S. v. Steinkoetter*, 633 F.2d 719 (6th Cir. 1980) (judgment vacated; defendant compared to Pontius Pilate and Judas Iscariot). *Cf. U.S. v. Gartmon*, 146 F.3d 1015 (D.C. Cir. 1998); *U.S. v. Rude*, 88 F.3d 1538 (9th Cir. 1996); *U.S. v. Catalfo*, 64 F.3d 1070 (7th Cir. 1995); *Moore v. U.S.*, 934 F. Supp. 724 (E.D. Va. 1996) (collecting cases suggesting there is no reason why the words "lie" and "lying" should be banned from the vocabulary of summation).

Other Misconduct

Attacks on defense counsel can constitute prosecutorial misconduct. *See, e.g. U.S. v. Young*, 470 U.S. 1, 9, 105 S. Ct. 1038, 84 L. Ed. 2d 1 (1985) (counsel "must not be permitted to make unfounded and inflammatory attacks on the opposing advocate."). Courts have held that the prosecutor commits misconduct by: denigrating the defense as a sham, *Dubria v. Smith*, 197 F.3d 390 (9th Cir. 1999); attacking the integrity of defense counsel, *U.S. v. Eagle*, 515 F.3d 794 (8th Cir. 2008); *U.S. v. Childress*, 58 F.3d 693 (D.C. Cir. 1995); *U.S. v. Smith*, 962 F.2d 923 (9th Cir. 1992); and applauding at end of defense summation as a sarcastic commentary on the closing argument, *U.S. v. Burns*, 104 F.3d 529 (2d Cir. 1997).

Ordinarily, prejudicial statements can be remedied by striking them with a curative instruction. *U.S. v. Gainey*, 111 F.3d 834 (11th Cir. 1997); *Murray v. Groose*, 106 F.3d 812 (8th Cir. 1997). Mistrial is generally a matter for the trial court's discretion. *U.S. v. King*, 150 F.3d 644 (7th Cir. 1998). An abuse of discretion depends upon whether: (1) the conduct was isolated or deliberate and repeated; (2) the trial court gave a strong and explicit cautionary instruction; and (3) the likelihood that any prejudice surviving the judge's instruction could have affected the outcome of the case. *U.S. v. Joyner*, 191 F.3d 47 (1st Cir. 1999). *See* Curative Instruction.

Treatises and Practice Aids

Wright, Federal Practice and Procedure: Criminal 4th § 471

Park, Trial Objections Handbook Chapter 10 (2nd ed. 2001)

COMPOUND QUESTION

See:

Fed.R.Evid. 611(a)
Mil.R.Evid. 611(a)

Objection

- Objection. Compound question.
- Objection. Counsel is asking two questions at the same time.

Response

- I withdraw the question and will ask separate questions.

Commentary

Fed.R.Evid. 611(a) provides that the court shall exercise reasonable control over the mode of interrogating witnesses so as to make the interrogation effective for the ascertainment of truth. A multiple or compound question presents two or more questions within a single question. It is objectionable because the answer usually will be ambiguous. An example of a compound question is, "On that date, did you go to the Red Sox game that afternoon and the Boston College-Notre Dame game that evening?" If only one of the two facts in the compound question is true, neither a "yes" nor a "no" answer will be accurate. Answers to multiple or compound questions, which sometimes seem straightforward and understandable in the courtroom, can become extremely confusing when reviewing the record. For example, in *U.S. v. Watson*, 171 F.3d 695, 699 (D.C. Cir. 1999), on a critical point of proof the prosecutor asked what was in essence a compound question: "Mr. Thomas, you believe that you know Watson's girlfriend, Tyra Jackson, right?" In so doing, he effectively asked both whether the witness knew Ms. Jackson and whether the witness knew her to be the defendant's girlfriend. This compound question yielded an ambiguous response ("I never testified I knew her or not.") and led to reversible error when the testimony was misstated and misquoted in the prosecution's closing. *See U.S. v. Smith*, 354 F.3d 390, 396 (5th Cir. 2003) (on cross-examination, government's attorney asked: "Are you aware that two weeks ago, your wife called Keisha and Meredith [and] asked if they would testify today that Josh Booty was at Kristenwood on January 23rd, as late as 8:00 o'clock?" witness responded: "Yes"; court held that this was an objectionable compound question as it was impossible for the jury to determine whether witness was testifying solely that the phone call occurred, or whether he also was confirming the government's allegation that the purpose of the call was to affect testimony.); *U.S. v. Matthews*, 222 F.3d 305 (7th Cir. 2000) (upward adjustment of sentence could not be predicated on testimony which was unclear due to compound nature of questions).

Additional References

Graham, Handbook of Federal Evidence § 611.16 (7th ed. 2012)

Treatises and Practice Aids

Goode and Wellborn, Courtroom Handbook on Federal Evidence Chapter 5 Rule 611 and Obj. 5 (annual ed.)

Wright & Gold, Federal Practice and Procedure: Evidence § 6164

Park, Trial Objections Handbook § 6:12 (2nd ed. 2001)

CONTINUING OBJECTION

See:

Fed.R.Evid. 103(a)(1)
Mil.R.Evid. 103(a)(1)

Form

- I object to all testimony concerning this witness's identification of Exhibit 5 on grounds that [*here state specific grounds*].
- Your Honor, may the record show my continuing objection to all testimony concerning this witness's identification of Exhibit 5 on grounds that [*here state specific grounds*].

Commentary

Where an objection has been overruled and the trial court clearly indicates that its ruling will apply to all questions on the same matter, the objecting attorney should consider making a "continuing" objection to every subsequent question and answer on the same subject. *See U.S. v. Carpenter*, 494 F.3d 13 (1st Cir. 2007) (where during course of trial, court granted continuing objection to testimony comparing defendant's conduct to gambling, that objection was sufficient to cover prosecution's closing argument based on same testimony); *Clay v. Ford Motor Co.*, 215 F.3d 663 (6th Cir. 2000) (continuing objection to all aspects of expert's testimony). A continuing objection eliminates the need for the attorney to object repeatedly after each question or answer, which may annoy the judge and/or jury. On this latter point, *see, e.g., U.S. v. DeSantis*, 134 F.3d 760, 766 (6th Cir. 1998) (where trial court granted continuing objection and instructed counsel "you don't have to get up every time.")

Because the federal rules require a timely and specific objection at the proper stage in the questioning of a witness, Fed.R.Evid. 103(a)(1); *U.S. v. Polasek*, 162 F.3d 878 (5th Cir. 1998), reliance on only a general request "for a continuing objection" or a general objection "to this entire line of questioning" may be insufficient to preserve all grounds of objection for appeal. *See also U.S. v. Sumlin*, 489

F.3d 683, 688 (5th Cir. 2007) (where counsel first objected without specifying that objection was continuing, testimony between that initial objection and a later continuing objection was not preserved).

The lawyer must initially define the scope of the continuing objection as precisely as possible, and must be alert to any additional grounds for objection that arise during subsequent testimony. If another ground becomes apparent during the line of questioning, that ground must also be stated to create an adequate record for appeal.

A continuing objection serves to obviate repeated objections only to evidence admitted within the scope of the court's specific evidentiary ruling. *See, e.g., U.S. v. Gomez-Norena*, 908 F.2d 497 (9th Cir. 1990) (specific objection protects record to extent of grounds specified and no further); *U.S. v. Ladd*, 885 F.2d 954 (1st Cir. 1989) (party may argue violation of Rule 403 on appeal because it posited continuing objection on basis of that particular rule); *U.S. v. Verrusio*, 803 F.2d 885 (7th Cir. 1986) (continuing objection on hearsay grounds would preserve appeal of admission of subsequent hearsay statements); *U.S. v. Marshall*, 762 F.2d 419, 425 (5th Cir. 1985) (overruling of timely specific objection amounted to continuing objection, thereby preserving right of appeal for "subsequent evidence admitted within the scope of the ruling") (citing 21 Wright & Graham, Federal Practice and Procedure § 5037 at 191 to 92 (1977); *United States v. Gillette*, 189 F.2d 449 (2d Cir. 1951) (party may not rely on continuing objection lodged on one evidentiary ground to argue different ground on appeal)).

Note: In *U.S. v. McVeigh*, 153 F.3d 1166, 1199 (10th Cir. 1998), the court reiterated its view that "the considerations bearing upon a decision whether to admit or exclude evidence under Rules 404(b) and 403 are sufficiently complex that ordinarily neither counsel nor the trial court should rely on a standing objection with respect to evidence coming within the purview of these rules."

Additional References

Graham, Handbook of Federal Evidence § 103.2 (7th ed. 2012)

Treatises and Practice Aids

Goode and Wellborn, Courtroom Handbook on Federal Evidence Chapter 5, Rule 103 (annual ed.)

Mueller & Kirkpatrick, Federal Evidence, § 1:10 (3d ed. 2007)

Wright & Graham, Federal Practice and Procedure: Evidence 2d § 5037

McCormick, Evidence § 52 (6th ed. 2006)

Park, Trial Objections Handbook § 1:8 (2nd ed. 2001)

CUMULATIVE

See:

Fed.R.Evid. 403, 611(a)
Mil.R.Evid. 403, 611(a)

Objection

- Objection. This testimony/evidence is cumulative. The matter has been covered by [*e.g. three other witnesses / six other exhibits*].

Response

- This testimony/evidence will add important details to the evidence already admitted.
- It is not improperly cumulative because corroborative evidence from additional sources is needed to support the facts being proved.

Commentary

Evidence is cumulative when it adds very little to the probative force of the other evidence in the case and thus does not warrant the time spent in introducing it. Fed.R.Evid. 403; *Carrasquillo v. City of Troy*, 251 Fed. Appx. 688 (2d Cir. 2007) (judge has discretion to exclude evidence if it is cumulative of evidence already in the record); *Goodwin v. MTD Products, Inc.*, 232 F.3d 600 (7th Cir. 2000); *U.S. v. Williams*, 81 F.3d 1434 (7th Cir. 1996); *U.S. v. Davis*, 40 F.3d 1069 (10th Cir. 1994). Absent a clear abuse of discretion, a trial judge retains a wide latitude to exclude repetitive or cumulative evidence. Fed.R.Evid. 611(a); *U.S. v. Kizeart*, 102 F.3d 320 (7th Cir. 1996); *International Minerals and Resources, S.A. v. Pappas*, 96 F.3d 586 (2d Cir. 1996); *U.S. v. Holmes*, 44 F.3d 1150 (2d Cir. 1995). If the evidence is important, however, more witnesses or exhibits may relate to some facts without being cumulative. But when many witnesses testify to the same event or when many nearly identical exhibits are offered, they serve no useful purpose and are cumulative. *See, e.g., U.S. v. Zimmermann*, 509 F.3d 920 (8th Cir. 2007) (court has broad discretion as to number of witnesses a party may call on a point at issue); *In re Air Crash Disaster*, 86 F.3d 498, 527 (6th Cir. 1996) (no error in excluding testimony by additional experts where there was no suggestion of new information "as opposed to the refrain 'me too' "); *Finke v. Hunter's View, Ltd.*, 596 F. Supp. 2d 1254 (D. Minn. 2009) (where expert reports overlapped, only one expert was permitted to testify re adequacy of product warnings while the other expert could address other matters).

Additional References

Graham, Handbook of Federal Evidence § 403.1 (7th ed. 2012)

Treatises and Practice Aids

Goode and Wellborn, Courtroom Handbook on Federal Evidence Chapter 5, Rule 103 (annual ed.)
Mueller & Kirkpatrick, Federal Evidence, §§ 4:11, 4:12, 4:15 (3d ed. 2007)
Wright & Graham, Federal Practice and Procedure: Evidence §§ 5220, 6164
McCormick, Evidence, § 185 (6th ed. 2006)

CURATIVE INSTRUCTIONS

See:

Fed.R.Evid. 611(a)
Mil.R.Evid. 611(a)

Form

- I object and move to strike the [*statement*] [*answer*] of this witness on grounds [*state specific reason*]. Further, I ask the Court to instruct the jury to disregard this testimony and to direct them not to consider it for any purpose in this case.

Commentary

During the trial, the judge will give curative instructions to the jury after an inappropriate event has occurred, after some inadmissible evidence has been improperly referred to, or after trial misconduct. *Greer v. Miller*, 483 U.S. 756, 107 S. Ct. 3102, 97 L. Ed. 2d 618 (1987) (prejudicial effects of improper question generally cured by objection and issuance of curative instruction); *Hall v. Arthur*, 141 F.3d 844 (8th Cir. 1998) (inadvertent difficulties frequently arise at trial and cautionary instructions are generally sufficient to alleviate mistakes occurring during trial). Such instructions can be given on the judge's own initiative. *See Igo v. Coachmen Industries, Inc. (Sportscoach Corp. of America Div.)*, 938 F.2d 650 (6th Cir. 1991) (trial court cannot sit quietly while counsel inflames passions of jury with improper conduct, even if opposing counsel does not object). Counsel, however, bears the primary responsibility for making a timely specific objection and for insuring that any error is cured in the manner most advantageous to his client. *U.S. v. Conley*, 186 F.3d 7 (1st Cir. 1999). A request for a curative instruction to the jury, explaining that inadmissible evidence cannot be considered in reaching its verdict, always should be accompanied by a motion to strike the inadmissible evidence.

A mistrial is not necessary where cautionary instructions are adequate to overcome prejudice. *U.S. v. Glenn*, 389 F.3d 283 (1st Cir. 2004); *U.S. v. Pospisil*, 186 F.3d 1023 (8th Cir. 1999); *U.S. v.*

Randall, 162 F.3d 557 (9th Cir. 1998); *U.S. v. Awon*, 135 F.3d 96 (1st Cir. 1998).

Prompt curative instructions have been found effective in numerous situations, including: where inadmissible evidence is offered, *U.S. v. Cortez*, 252 Fed. Appx. 887 (10th Cir. 2007); *U.S. v. Talley*, 194 F.3d 758 (6th Cir. 1999); *Warren v. Miller*, 78 F. Supp. 2d 120 (E.D. N.Y. 2000); reference to unrelated prior criminal activity, *U.S. v. Layne*, 192 F.3d 556 (6th Cir. 1999); violation of defendant's Fifth Amendment rights by commenting on his failure to testify, *U.S. v. Griffith*, 118 F.3d 318 (5th Cir. 1997); prosecutorial misconduct during cross-examination, *U.S. v. Gordon*, 173 F.3d 761 (10th Cir. 1999); and counsel's expression of personal opinion about defendant's guilt, *U.S. v. Nelson*, 137 F.3d 1094 (9th Cir. 1998).

Where evidence is so improper and unduly prejudicial that it cannot be cured by a cautionary instruction, the court should grant a mistrial if there is a timely request. *U.S. v. Garcia*, 405 F.3d 1260 (11th Cir. 2005). *See, e.g., Holbrook v. Flynn*, 475 U.S. 560, 106 S. Ct. 1340, 89 L. Ed. 2d 525 (1986) (customary courtroom security force supplemented by uniformed state troopers sitting in gallery); *Bruton v. United States*, 391 U.S. 123, 88 S. Ct. 1620, 20 L. Ed. 2d 476 (1968) (admission of co-defendant's confession implicating defendant); *Sheppard v. Maxwell*, 384 U.S. 333, 86 S. Ct. 1507, 16 L. Ed. 2d 600 (1966) (pretrial publicity combined with disruptive influences in courtroom); *Remmer v. United States*, 350 U.S. 377, 76 S. Ct. 425, 100 L. Ed. 435 (1956) (associate of defendant attempted to bribe juror); *U.S. v. Mannie*, 509 F.3d 851 (7th Cir. 2007) (jury witnessed courtroom intimidation, outbursts and violence); *U.S. v. Ham*, 998 F.2d 1247 (4th Cir. 1993) (in mail fraud case, effect of prejudicial evidence concerning child molestation, homosexuality and abuse of women could not be cured with cautionary instruction); *Government of Virgin Islands v. Pinney*, 967 F.2d 912 (3d Cir. 1992) (cautionary instruction on testimony of child molestation could not reduce risk of jury considering such evidence for improper purpose); *U.S. v. Bland*, 908 F.2d 471 (9th Cir. 1990) (curative instruction could not obviate prejudice from evidence that defendant had outstanding warrant for molestation, torture and murder of young girl).

Additional References

Graham, Handbook of Federal Evidence § 103.3 (7th ed. 2012)

Treatises and Practice Aids

Wright & Graham, Federal Practice and Procedure: Evidence §§ 5756, 5757

McCormick, Evidence § 4 (6th ed. 2006)

DISCOVERY RULES: FAILURE TO COMPLY (CIVIL CASES)

See:

Fed.R.Civ.P. 37

Objection

- Objection. [*Plaintiff*] [*Defendant*] failed to disclose the existence of this [*evidence*] [*witness*] during pretrial discovery despite our formal requests for disclosure. I respectfully request the [*evidence be excluded*] [*witness be precluded from testifying*].

Response

- There is no prejudice, surprise or bad faith [*citing specifics*]. If the court is persuaded [*plaintiff*] [*defendant*] is entitled to some additional time to meet this evidence, then I would respectfully request that a continuance be granted with trial to resume in two days.

Commentary

The trial court possesses the inherent power to sanction attorney or party misconduct with respect to pretrial discovery, case management and to ensure obedience to its orders. *Chambers v. NASCO, Inc.*, 501 U.S. 32, 111 S. Ct. 2123, 115 L. Ed. 2d 27 (1991); *Aloe Vera of America, Inc. v. U.S.*, 376 F.3d 960 (9th Cir. 2004). Inherent power sanctions include preclusion of evidence, adverse evidentiary inferences, default judgment, fines, awards of fees and expenses and contempt citations. *Shepherd v. American Broadcasting Companies, Inc.*, 62 F.3d 1469 (D.C. Cir. 1995).

Fed.R.Civ.P. 37 also permits the court to impose sanctions for failure to comply with pretrial discovery rules. *Zenith Electronics Corp. v. WH-TV Broadcasting Corp.*, 395 F.3d 416 (7th Cir. 2005) (damages evidence precluded for failure to answer contention interrogatories). Rule 37(c)(1) states that "a party that without substantial justification fails to disclose information required by Rule 26(a) or 26(e)(1), or to amend a prior response to discovery as required by Rule 26(e)(2), is not, unless such failure is harmless, permitted to use as evidence at a trial . . . any witness or information not so disclosed. In addition to or in lieu of this sanction, the court . . . may impose other appropriate sanctions." *Yeti by Molly, Ltd. v. Deckers Outdoor Corp.*, 259 F.3d 1101 (9th Cir. 2001) (where defendants produced expert report two years after close of discovery and just 28 days prior to trial, exclusion was appropriate remedy for failing to fulfill disclosure requirements of Rule 26(a) even though there was no explicit court order to produce report and even absent a showing of bad faith or wilfulness); *Wilson v. Bradlees of New England, Inc.*, 250 F.3d 10 (1st Cir. 2001) (expert videotape properly excluded because not disclosed pursuant to court's discovery deadlines); *Sheek v. Asia Badger, Inc.*, 235 F.3d 687 (1st Cir. 2000) (no error to exclude portions of expert testimony; defendant failed to file supplementary discovery responses indicating change in expert's medical opinion). The sanction of exclusion is automatic and mandatory unless the party to be sanctioned can show that its violation of Rule 26 was either justified or harmless and therefore deserving of some lesser sanction. *Finley v. Marathon Oil Co.*, 75 F.3d 1225, 1230 (7th Cir. 1996); *Montes v. Phelps Dodge Industries, Inc.*, 481 F. Supp. 2d 700 (W.D. Tex. 2006) (evidence excluded; plaintiff failed to show how violation was harmless).

Rule 37 envisions a procedure by which the court, when confronted with a failure or refusal to provide discovery, will exercise judicial discretion to formulate an appropriate sanction order. This requires the court to select a punishment which "fits the crime." *Crown Life Ins. Co. v. Craig*, 995 F.2d 1376 (7th Cir. 1993) (choice of sanction should be guided by concept of proportionality between offense and sanction); *Aoude v. Mobil Oil Corp.*, 892 F.2d 1115 (1st Cir. 1989) (court must properly calibrate the scales to ensure that gravity of sanction corresponds to misconduct). *See Taylor v. TECO Barge Line, Inc.*, 517 F.3d 372 (6th Cir. 2008) (mere fact that party has not fully complied with pretrial orders does not mandate exclusion of evidence; inadvertent and small mistakes are excused).

The choice of an appropriate sanction is necessarily a highly fact-based determination based on the course of the discovery process leading up to the sanction. Cases upholding particular sanctions at trial suggest the importance of prejudice or surprise and bad faith. *See Santiago-Diaz v. Laboratorio Clinico Y De Referencia Del Este And Sara Lopez, M.D.*, 456 F.3d 272 (1st Cir. 2006) (expert testimony precluded; a party's violation of a time-specific order is not cured by subsequent compliance at his leisure); *R.M.R. ex rel. P.A.L. v. Muscogee County School Dist.*, 165 F.3d 812 (11th Cir. 1999) (affirming exclusion of plaintiff's witness not listed in pretrial order nor identified until third day of trial; plaintiff could have minimized prejudice by seeking continuance or requesting mistrial); *Salgado by Salgado v. General Motors Corp.*, 150 F.3d 735 (7th Cir. 1998) (excluding expert witness where, even after extensions, reports were late and incomplete); *Harre v. Muegler*, 113 F.3d 909 (8th Cir. 1997) (imposition of sanctions preventing defendant from introducing undisclosed evidence not abuse of discretion where there was almost a complete failure to provide discovery); *Konstantopoulos v. Westvaco Corp.*, 112 F.3d 710 (3d Cir. 1997) (exclusion of expert witness where report was never filed and witness not disclosed until three weeks before trial; opponent not required to attempt to cure prejudice by last-minute scrambling to meet new evidence); *Langley by Langley v. Union Elec. Co.*, 107 F.3d 510 (7th Cir. 1997) (court properly disallowed all evidence re existence or use of allegedly faulty furnace in wrongful death action, resulting in summary judgment where plaintiff failed to produce furnace and then "lost" it); *Barrett v. Atlantic Richfield Co.*, 95 F.3d 375 (5th Cir. 1996) (striking of expert witness as sanction for failure to comply with discovery order setting dates for identification and deposition of experts not abuse of discretion where there was no explanation for failure to meet deadline or seek timely continuance; importance of expert testimony underscored need for compliance); *Finley.*, 75 F.3d at 1225 (no error in excluding exhibits disclosed shortly before trial where discovery violation neither justified nor harmless); *Labadie Coal Co. v. Black*, 672 F.2d 92 (D.C. Cir. 1982) (trial court erred in admitting documents first produced by defendant on final day of trial where records were requested during discovery); *Texas Instruments, Inc. v. Hyundai Electronics Industries, Co. Ltd.*, 50 F. Supp. 2d 619 (E.D. Tex. 1999) (defendant's failure to timely disclose prior art information warranted exclusion of evidence in patent infringement action; last-minute ambush deprived plaintiff of critical discovery and valuable trial preparation time).

Sanctions may be imposed even if failure to comply was not willful, but instead the result of gross or even simple negligence. *Argo Marine Systems, Inc. v. Camar Corp.*, 755 F.2d 1006 (2d Cir. 1985); *Cine Forty-Second St. Theatre Corp. v. Allied Artists Pictures Corp.*, 602 F.2d 1062 (2d Cir. 1979) (negligent wrongs are appropriate for general deterrence though courts should avoid the harshest of sanctions where failure to comply due to mere oversight); *U.S. v. Veal*, 365 F. Supp. 2d 1034 (W.D. Mo. 2004) (default judgment, as a discovery sanction for counsel's misconduct, may be appropriate even without a finding of bad faith or willful misconduct on the part of the party).

Where a sanction is disproportionate in terms of the offense and its impact, it will not be upheld. *See, e.g., Sherrod v. Lingle*, 223 F.3d 605 (7th Cir. 2000) (excluding experts unjustified considering harmless nature of failure to comply with discovery order); *Gonzalez v. Trinity Marine Group, Inc.*, 117 F.3d 894 (5th Cir. 1997) (dismissal of case reversed because not least onerous sanction that would address plaintiff's conduct in fabricating evidence during discovery); *Bonds v. District of Columbia*, 93 F.3d 801 (D.C. Cir. 1996) (setting aside order barring defendant from calling any fact witnesses at trial in favor of lesser sanction precluding only witnesses who had not been deposed; when discovery sanction denies party right to trial on the merits, court must make finding supported by record that more severe sanction is necessary to avoid prejudice to opposing party or to court's calendar or to prevent a benefit to non-disclosing party, or-if sanction is based only on deterring future discovery misconduct-more severe sanction must be supported by finding of flagrant or egregious misconduct); *Banghart v. Origoverken, A.B.*, 49 F.3d 1302 (8th Cir. 1995) (reversing sanction because no prejudice where photographs were inadvertently omitted from exhibit list); *Price v. Seydel*, 961 F.2d 1470 (9th Cir. 1992) (refusing to allow plaintiff to call defendant for failure to list as witness was abuse of discretion; defendant, as a party, could have expected to be cross-examined and there was no attempted surprise or bad faith); *Southwest Whey, Inc. v. Nutrition 101, Inc.*, 126 F. Supp. 2d 1143 (C.D. Ill. 2001) (excluding plaintiff's untimely expert report inappropriate where no indication of harm and impact could be $1 million counterclaim award to defendant via summary judgment).

Because dismissal is the most severe sanction, it should be imposed only in extreme circumstances, and a trial court is required to balance the equities carefully and dismiss only where the violation of the discovery rules is willful and the opposing party has been prejudiced. *ClearValue, Inc. v. Pearl River Polymers, Inc.*, 560 F.3d 1291 (Fed. Cir. 2009); *In re Golant*, 239 F.3d 931 (7th Cir. 2001); *Comiskey v. JFTJ Corp.*, 989 F.2d 1007 (8th Cir. 1993).*

A party is prejudiced if the failure to make discovery impairs the party's ability to determine the factual merits of the opponent's claim or defense. *Avionic Co. v. General Dynamics Corp.*, 957 F.2d 555 (8th Cir. 1992). Before imposing the harsh sanction of dismissal, the trial court must weigh several factors: (1) the public's interest in expeditious resolution of litigation; (2) the court's need to manage its docket; (3) the risk of prejudice to the party seeking sanctions; (4) the public policy favoring disposition of cases on their merits; and (5) the availability of less drastic sanctions. *Keefer v. Provident Life and Acc. Ins. Co.*, 238 F.3d 937 (8th Cir. 2000); *see Greviskes v. Universities Research Ass'n, Inc.*, 417 F.3d 752 (7th Cir. 2005) (suit dismissed for fraudulent conduct in discovery and attempts to hide conduct by further fraud and deceit); *Harmon v. CSX Transp., Inc.*, 110 F.3d 364

[Discovery etc.]

*Fed.R.Civ.P. 37(b)(2)(C) authorizes the court to impose sanctions upon parties who fail to comply with discovery orders, but dismissal may be imposed as a sanction only if there is: (1) an order compelling discovery, (2) a willful violation of that order, and (3) prejudice to the other party. *See Schoffstall v. Henderson*, 223 F.3d 818 (8th Cir. 2000).

(6th Cir. 1997) (persistent failure to provide discovery sufficiently egregious to justify dismissal as first and only sanction); *In re Exxon Valdez*, 102 F.3d 429 (9th Cir. 1996) (total refusal to provide discovery obstructed resolution of claims and merited dismissal); *Anheuser-Busch, Inc. v. Natural Beverage Distributors*, 69 F.3d 337 (9th Cir. 1995) (affirming dismissal of counterclaim where defendant concealed documents and repeatedly lied about their destruction; courts have inherent power to dismiss action when party has willfully deceived court and engaged in conduct utterly inconsistent with orderly administration of justice); *Shepherd*, 62 F.3d at 1467 (reversing default judgment as sanction for discovery misconduct because district court failed to find by clear and convincing evidence that lesser sanction would not sufficiently punish and deter the abusive conduct while allowing full and fair trial on the merits); *Tyler v. Iowa State Trooper Badge No. 297*, 158 F.R.D. 632 (N.D. Iowa 1994) (pro se litigant's failure to comply with court order to prepare for trial warranted dismissal).

NOTE: Rule 26 disclosure requirements do not apply to materials to be presented **solely** for impeachment. Fed.R.Civ.P. 26(a)(3). However, the distinction between substantive evidence and impeachment evidence can be difficult to discern, especially because some evidence serves both functions. Substantive evidence is that which is offered to establish the truth of the matter to be determined by the trier of fact. Impeachment evidence is that which is offered to discredit a witness or otherwise to reduce the effectiveness of testimony by bringing forth evidence which explains why the jury should not believe the testimony. The circuits divide on their interpretation of the word "solely" in Rule 26(a)(3). Some read "solely" to mean that the evidence could be used for nothing other than impeachment, i.e., the evidence has no substantive value. Other circuits construe "solely" to mean that the evidence was offered only as impeachment and not in the offeror's case-in-chief. *Hayes v. Cha*, 338 F. Supp. 2d 470 (D.N.J. 2004). *Compare Klonoski v. Mahlab*, 156 F.3d 255 (1st Cir. 1998) (remanding for new trial because late wife's letters contradicting husband's testimony about state of marriage were not revealed until cross-examination and constituted trial by ambush; evidence had substantive and impeachment value and was covered by disclosure requirements of Rule 26, including duty to supplement responses) *and Chiasson v. Zapata Gulf Marine Corp.*, 988 F.2d 513 (5th Cir. 1993) (video surveillance tape not solely impeachment evidence and should have been disclosed prior to trial) *with Halbasch v. Med-Data, Inc.*, 192 F.R.D. 641 (D. Or. 2000) (admitting evidence offered through cross-examination as impeachment that had not been disclosed in pretrial discovery).

Treatises and Practice Aids

Wright, Miller & Marcus, Federal Practice and Procedure: Civil 3d §§ 2281 *et seq.*

Park, Trial Objections Handbook §§ 11:1, 11:10, 11:12 (2nd ed. 2001)

DISCOVERY RULES: FAILURE TO COMPLY (CRIMINAL CASES)

See:

Fed.R.Crim.P. 16
R.C.M. 701

Objection

- Objection. The [*government / defendant*] failed to disclose the existence of this evidence during pretrial discovery despite our request for any such evidence. We ask that it be excluded.

Response

- There is no prejudice, surprise or bad faith [*citing specifics*]. If the court is persuaded that [*government / defendant*] is entitled to some additional time to meet this evidence, then I would respectfully request that a continuance be granted, with trial to resume in [*specify*] days.

Commentary

Fed.R.Crim.P. 16 gives a defendant the right to request discovery of his own statements, prior criminal record, documents and tangible items material to the defense, results of tests and experiments, and disclosure of testifying experts.

Discovery under the criminal rules is reciprocal: if defendant requests discovery, then upon compliance by the government, the prosecutor may request discovery of similar items under defendant's control. Rule 16(b).

"One of the objectives of Rule 16 is to eliminate the idea that a criminal trial is a sporting contest in which the game of cat and mouse is acceptable." *U.S. v. Howell*, 231 F.3d 615, 626 (9th Cir. 2000).

A party failing to comply with the requirements of Rule 16 is subject to sanctions by the trial court which "may order such party to permit the discovery or inspection, grant a continuance, or prohibit the party from introducing evidence not disclosed, or it may enter such other order as it deems just under the circumstances." Fed.R.Crim.P. 16(d)(2).

The factors to be considered in determining

whether a sanction is appropriate are: (1) the reasons for the delay in producing the requested materials, including whether or not the party acted in bad faith; (2) the extent of prejudice to the other party; and (3) the feasibility of curing the prejudice with a continuance. *U.S. v. Davis*, 514 F.3d 596 (6th Cir. 2008); *U.S. v. Garrett*, 238 F.3d 293 (5th Cir. 2000); *U.S. v. Nichols*, 169 F.3d 1255 (10th Cir. 1999). These factors are not exhaustive, nor is each necessarily required to support a sanction. *U.S. v. Russell*, 109 F.3d 1503 (10th Cir. 1997).

Appellate courts generally have indicated that the trial court should impose the least severe sanction that will accomplish prompt and full compliance with the court's discovery orders. *See, e.g., U.S. v. Marshall*, 132 F.3d 63 (D.C. Cir. 1998) (a severe sanction such as suppression of evidence will rarely be appropriate if trial court finds violation was not in bad faith and where less dramatic remedy, such as a continuance, would mitigate any prejudice); *U.S. v. Wicker*, 848 F.2d 1059 (10th Cir. 1988); *U.S. v. Sarcinelli*, 667 F.2d 5 (5th Cir. 1982). Additionally, if the court intends to impose the ultimate sanction of dismissal, circuit courts have instructed that not only should the above factors be considered, but the discovery violation must actually meet the two requirements of prejudice and willful misconduct, the same standard applicable to dismissal for a *Brady* violation. *Government of Virgin Islands v. Fahie*, 419 F.3d 249, 259 (3d Cir. 2005).

The following cases illustrate the operation of the Rule: *U.S. v. Young*, 248 F.3d 260, 270 (4th Cir. 2001) (excluding audiotape of conversation between defendant and prosecution witness which had not been provided to prosecution in violation of court's discovery order; "Exclusion of undisclosed evidence is a permissible sanction for a violation of Rule 16."); *U.S. v. Garrett*, 238 F.3d at 293 (trial court abused its discretion in excluding 25 government witnesses from testifying as sanction for tardy discovery compliance; there was no bad faith, any prejudice could be cured by continuance and sanction would obliterate government's case); *U.S. v. Vega-Figueroa*, 234 F.3d 744 (1st Cir. 2000) (where government's disclosure was delayed but defendant did not move for a continuance and could not show real prejudice, no error in permitting introduction of evidence; when the issue is one of delayed disclosure rather than total nondisclosure, the applicable test is whether defense counsel was prevented by the delay from using the disclosed material effectively in preparing and presenting the defendant's case; generally courts view the failure to ask for a continuance as an indication that defense counsel was satisfied he had sufficient opportunity to use the evidence advantageously); *U.S. v. Johnson*, 219 F.3d 349 (4th Cir. 2000) (prohibiting defense expert from testifying; although defense claimed it turned over expert's resume, Rule 16(b)(1)(C) obligated disclosure of a written summary of expert's expected testimony, including opinions, the bases and reasons therefor, all of which was not done); *U.S. v. DeCoteau*, 186 F.3d 1008 (8th Cir. 1999) (sanctioning the government by striking all of its witnesses and dismissing the indictment without first making any findings as to prejudice constitutes a clear abuse of discretion); *U.S. v. Nichols*, 169 F.3d at 1268 (where defense violated Rule 16(b)(1)(C) by failing to identify expert and provide written summary of his testimony, no error for trial court to exclude evidence, in major part, out of concern that three-month trial would extend into holidays; sometimes, even in absence of prejudice, integrity and scheduling considerations alone may justify suppression of otherwise admissible evidence offered by delinquent party); *U.S. v. Gonzales*, 164 F.3d 1285 (10th Cir. 1999) (where government intentionally violated discovery orders and misrepresented whereabouts of witness, sanctions were merited but complete suppression of testimony was inappropriate when lesser sanctions could have cured any prejudice); *U.S. v. Russell*, 109 F.3d at 1509 ("Excluding witnesses for failure to comply with discovery orders, if not an abuse of discretion, does not violate a defendant's Sixth Amendment right to compulsory process."); *U.S. v. Jackson*, 51 F.3d 646, 651 (7th Cir. 1995) (noting the extent of detail required by Rule 16(a)(1)(E) depends on the nature of the expert testimony and holding disclosure re drug courier profile testimony "barely" sufficient; "Other contexts, such as cases involving technical or scientific evidence, may require greater disclosure, including written and oral reports, tests, investigations, and any other information that may be recognized as a legitimate basis for an opinion under Fed.R.Evid. 703."); *U.S. v. Saa*, 859 F.2d 1067 (2d Cir. 1988) (disclosure of identity or address of confidential informant is not required unless informant's testimony is shown to be material to the defense); *see also*, Privilege, Confidential Informer, *infra*; *U.S. v. Diabate*, 90 F. Supp. 2d 140 (D. Mass. 2000) (dismissal without prejudice was appropriate sanction for government's numerous violations of discovery obligations which had substantially prejudiced defendant).

Brady v. Maryland

In *Brady v. Maryland*, 373 U.S. 83, 83 S. Ct. 1194, 10 L. Ed. 2d 215 (1963), the Supreme Court held that due process requires disclosure by the prosecution of evidence favorable to the accused that is material to guilt or punishment. However, this duty is a constitutional requirement and does not constitute a form of pretrial discovery subject to Rule 16. *U.S. v. Maniktala*, 934 F.2d 25, 28 (2d Cir. 1991) (*citing U.S. v. Starusko*, 729 F.2d 256, 262 (3d Cir. 1984)); *U.S. v. Beasley*, 576 F.2d 626, 630 (5th Cir. 1978) ("*Brady* is not a discovery rule but a rule of fairness and minimum prosecutorial obligation.").

The basic *Brady* rules are outlined here for the convenience of bench and bar.

Under *Brady*, the prosecution has a constitutional obligation to disclose exculpatory evidence to a criminal defendant if it is "material" either to guilt or to punishment. *Brady*, 373 U.S. at 87; *Towery v. Schriro*, 641 F.3d 300 (9th Cir. 2010); *U.S. v. Risha*, 445 F.3d 298 (3d Cir. 2006) (all evidence that is favorable to the defense must be disclosed); *see also White v. McKinley*, 514 F.3d 807 (8th Cir. 2008) (*Brady's* protections also extend to actions of other law enforcement officers such as investigating officers). This obligation extends to evidence that could be used to impeach a government witness, *United States v. Bagley*, 473 U.S. 667, 676, 105 S. Ct. 3375, 3380, 87 L. Ed. 2d 481 (1985), and to evidence that was not requested by the defense. *Id.* at 682; *Dickson v. Quarterman*, 453 F.3d 643

(5th Cir. 2006). Evidence is material if "there is a reasonable probability that, had the evidence been disclosed to the defense, the result of the proceeding would have been different. A 'reasonable probability' is a probability sufficient to undermine confidence in the outcome." *Bagley*, 473 U.S. at 682; *see also Kyles v. Whitley*, 514 U.S. 419, 434, 115 S. Ct. 1555, 1565, 131 L. Ed. 2d 490 (1995); *U.S. v. Skilling*, 554 F.3d 529 (5th Cir. 2009) (defendant need not prove his trial would have had different outcome; a lack of faith in the result is sufficient); *Beuke v. Houk*, 537 F.3d 618 (6th Cir. 2008). The final determination of materiality is based on the "suppressed evidence considered collectively, not item by item." *Kyles*, 514 U.S. at 436–37; *Cooper v. Brown*, 510 F.3d 870 (9th Cir. 2007) (mere possibility that undisclosed information might have helped defense or might have affected outcome of trial is insufficient to establish materiality in the constitutional sense). Additionally, in order to be material information within the meaning of *Brady*, the undisclosed information or evidence acquired through that information must be admissible. *U.S. v. Kennedy*, 890 F.2d 1056 (9th Cir. 1989).

The existence of a duty to disclose witness statements at trial pursuant to the Jencks Act, 18 U.S.C.A. § 3500,* does not eviscerate the government's *Brady* obligation to disclose witness statements well in advance of trial if those statements also fall under *Brady*. *See U.S. v. Tarantino*, 846 F.2d 1384 (D.C. Cir. 1988).

It is the government's responsibility in the first instance to determine whether information in its possession is *Brady* material. While it generally is not the court's role to "referee . . . disagreements about materiality and supervise the exchange of information," the government acts at its own risk when it withholds even arguably favorable evidence. *U.S. v. McVeigh*, 954 F. Supp. 1441, 1451 (D. Colo. 1997).

[Discovery etc.]

*The Jencks Act provides that in criminal prosecutions brought by the United States, no statement made by a government witness may be the subject of discovery until after that witness has testified at trial. *U.S. v. Jordan*, 316 F.3d 1215 (11th Cir. 2003).

The Supreme Court has never expressly held that evidence that is turned over to the defense during trial has been suppressed within the meaning of *Brady*. The Fifth Circuit holds that a defendant is not prejudiced if the evidence is received in time for its effective use at trial. Other courts have reached a similar conclusion. *U.S. v. Lee*, 573 F.3d 155 (3d Cir. 2009) (undisclosed evidence that upsets a defendant's trial strategy may be admissible if defendant has opportunity to adjust trial strategy and respond to new evidence; here, however, conviction vacated because of prejudice); *Powell v. Quarterman*, 536 F.3d 325 (5th Cir. 2008) (collecting cases).

Rules For Courts-Martial

Article 46 of the Uniform Code of Military Justice establishes that both the prosecutor and defense counsel "shall have equal opportunity to obtain witnesses and other evidence . . .." 10 U.S.C.A. § 846 (1995). *See U.S. v. Williams*, 50 M.J. 436, 439 (C.A.A.F. 1999) (the military justice system has been a leader with respect to open discovery); *U.S. v. Enloe*, 35 C.M.R. 228, 230 (C.M.A. 1965) (congressional intent to provide a military accused with a broader right of discovery than civilian defendants). The "equal access" rule is reflected in the Rules for Courts-Martial and to a lesser extent in the Military Rules of Evidence. R.C.M. 701 "Discovery" sets out the basic disclosure requirements governing both the prosecution and defense.

If at any time during the court martial it is brought to the attention of the military judge that a party has failed to comply with discovery, the military judge may: (i) order the party to disclose the material; (ii) grant a continuance; (iii) dismiss charges; (iv) prohibit the party from introducing evidence, calling a witness or raising a defense not disclosed; and (v) enter such other order as is just under the circumstances. R.C.M. 701(g)(3); *U.S. v. Pomarleau*, 57 M.J. 351 (C.A.A.F. 2002); *U.S. v. Dancy*, 38 M.J. 1 (C.M.A. 1993); *U.S. v. Preuss*, 34 M.J. 688 (N.M.C.M.R. 1991); *U.S. v. Trimper*, 28 M.J. 460 (C.M.A. 1989).

Additional References

Levenson, Federal Criminal Rules Handbook, Rule 16 (annual ed.)

Discovery Rules: Failure to Comply (Criminal Cases)

Treatises and Practice Aids

Wright, Federal Practice and Procedure: Criminal 4th §§ 251 *et seq.*

Park, Trial Objections Handbook §§ 11:1, 11:10 to 11:12 (2nd ed. 2001)

EVIDENCE EXCLUDED BY STATUTE: CLASSIFIED INFORMATION PROCEDURES ACT

See:

18 U.S.C.A. App. III §§ 1 et seq.

Objection

- Objection. The Government asserts surprise. Defendant's Section 5(a) notice contained no mention of this information. Since there was no prior disclosure, any questions or evidence concerning this matter are improper.

Response

- The question is proper. Defendant did state with particularity those items of classified information which he expected to be revealed by his defense and this matter was covered in the Section 6 hearing by [specify].

Commentary

The use of classified information in criminal trials is regulated by the Classified Information Procedures Act ("CIPA"), 18 U.S.C.App. III §§ 1 to 16 (1988). CIPA's purpose is to harmonize a criminal defendant's right to obtain and present exculpatory material with the government's need to withhold information from discovery when disclosure would be inimical to national security. *In re Terrorist Bombings of U.S. Embassies in East Africa*, 552 F.3d 93 (2d Cir. 2008); CIPA also addresses the practice of "graymail" by criminal defendants, i.e. threatening to disclose classified information with a Hobson's choice: either allow disclosure of the classified information or dismiss the indictment against the defendant. *U.S. v. Collins*, 720 F.2d 1195, 1196–97 (11th Cir. 1983); *See* Salgado, Note, Government Secrets, Fair Trials, and the Classified Information Procedures Act, 98 Yale L.J. 427, 427 (1988). CIPA mitigates this dilemma by prescribing pretrial procedures to help resolve issues of discovery and admissibility of classified information.

CIPA requires defendants who expect to disclose classified information to notify the court and the government of their intention to do so. 18 U.S.C.App. III § 5; *U.S. v. Giffen*, 473 F.3d 30, 33 (2d Cir. 2006); *U.S. v. Rosen*, 518 F. Supp. 2d 798 (E.D. Va. 2007). Upon the government's request, the court must then "conduct an in camera hearing to make all determinations concerning the use, relevance, or admissibility of classified information that would otherwise be made during the trial or pretrial proceeding." *Id.* § 6(a); *U.S. v. Salah*, 462 F. Supp. 2d 915 (N.D. Ill. 2006); *U.S. v. Cardoen*, 898 F. Supp. 1563 (S.D. Fla. 1995). If the court determines that the defendant's proffered evidence is irrelevant or otherwise inadmissible, it should issue a ruling *in limine* precluding the introduction of that evidence at trial. If the evidence would be admissible at trial, the burden shifts to the government to offer in lieu of the classified evidence either a statement admitting relevant facts that the classified information would tend to prove or a summary of the specific classified information. The court shall allow a substitution if it finds that the alternate submission will provide the defendant with substantially the same ability to present his or her defense as would disclosure of the specific classified information. § 6(c); *Al Odah v. U.S.*, 559 F.3d 539 (D.C. Cir. 2009); *U.S. v. Dumeisi*, 424 F.3d 566 (7th Cir. 2005) (upholding approval of substitution that provided defendant with substantially the same ability to make his defense as would disclosure of the specific classified information); *U.S. v. Moussaoui*, 365 F.3d 292 (4th Cir. 2004) (standard in CIPA adequately conveys fundamental purpose of a substitution; to place defendant as nearly as possible in the position he would be in if the classified information were available to him). Only when specific classified information is necessary to the full presentation of the defense does the government face the dilemma of permitting disclosure or dismissing the charges.

As the *Salah* court recognized, some tension exists between CIPA's procedures and a defendant's right to confront a witness. The court must strike a balance between the defendant's right to confrontation and CIPA's mandates to protect and restrict classified information "in a way that does not impair the defendant's right to a fair trial." *Dumeisi*, 424 F.3d at 578. If the substitutions would deprive defendant of his constitutional rights, the court can dismiss the indictment or take other appropriate actions.

If the defendant fails to comply with the notice requirement, the court may preclude disclosure of any classified information not made the subject of notification and may prohibit the examination by the defendant of any witness with respect to any such information. 18 U.S.C.App. III § 5(b).

CIPA does not create new law governing the admissibility of evidence. *U.S. v. Abu Ali*, 528 F.3d 210 (4th Cir. 2008); *U.S. v. Zazi*, 2011 WL 2532903 (E.D.N.Y. 2011). It simply ensures that questions of admissibility will be resolved under controlled circumstances calculated to protect against premature and unnecessary disclosure of classified information. Thus, the district court may not take into account the fact that evidence is classified when determining its "use, relevance, or admissibility." *U.S. v. Juan*, 776 F.2d 256, 258 (11th Cir. 1985); *accord Collins*, 720 F.2d at 1199. The relevance of classified information in a given case is governed solely by the standards set forth in the Federal Rules of Evidence. *U.S. v. Baptista-Rodriguez*, 17 F.3d 1354 (11th Cir. 1994); *U.S. v. Anderson*, 872 F.2d 1508 (11th Cir. 1989). If the classified information is admissible under ordinary evidentiary standards, then the burden falls upon the government to propose an alternative way of conveying the information to the jury that is less damaging to national security.

Treatises and Practice Aids

Goode and Wellborn, Courtroom Handbook on Federal Evidence Chapter 5, Prop. Rule 509 (annual ed.)

Wright & Graham, Federal Practice and Procedure: Evidence §§ 5662, 5672, 5683

Rothstein and Crump, Federal Testimonial Privileges Chapter 5 (annual ed.)

McCormick, Evidence § 107 (6th ed. 2006)

EVIDENCE EXCLUDED BY STATUTE: FEDERAL HIGHWAY SAFETY ACT

See:

3 U.S.C.A. § 409

Objection

- Objection. 23 U.S.C.A. § 409 excludes this evidence.

Response

- The question is proper. While this type of information may have been included in federal reports, this particular data was originally generated independent of the federal program and for other purposes.

Commentary

23 U.S.C.A. § 409 is a federal exclusionary statute that withdraws the broad latitude of discretion ordinarily allowed judges in evidentiary matters and bars the reception of evidence compiled for purposes of safety enhancement of highways, bridges and railroad crossings.

Section 409 states:

> Notwithstanding any other provision of law, reports, surveys, schedules, lists, or data compiled or collected for the purpose of identifying, evaluating, or planning the safety enhancement of potential accident sites, hazardous roadway conditions, or railway-highway crossings, pursuant to sections 130, 144, and 152 of this title or for the purpose of developing any highway safety construction improvement project which may be implemented utilizing Federal-aid highway funds shall not be subject to discovery or admitted into evidence in a Federal or State court proceeding or considered for other purposes in any action for damages arising from any occurrence at a location mentioned or addressed in such reports, surveys, schedules, lists, or data.

Section 130, dealing with payment of costs of railway-highway crossings, requires the state to conduct surveys, *see* 23 U.S.C.A. § 130(d); to establish and implement schedules, *see id.*; and to make annual reports which include lists and compilations and analyses of data, *see* 23 U.S.C.A. § 130(g). Section 144, dealing with highway bridge replacement programs, requires the Secretary of Transportation, in conjunction with the states, to inventory and classify bridges, *see* 23 U.S.C.A. § 144(b), and requires the Secretary to submit his report to Congress biannually, *see* 23 U.S.C.A. § 144(i). Section 152, dealing with elimination of highway hazards, requires each state to conduct engineering surveys of public roads, to establish and implement schedules of projects for their improvement, *see* 23 U.S.C.A. 152(a); and to submit an annual report to Congress on the progress being made to eliminate highway hazards, *see* U.S.C.A. § 152(g). This annual report is required to contain compilations and analyses of extensive data, and is the basis for the annual report that the Secretary of Transportation must file with Congress.

The purpose of Section 409 is to promote candor in administrative evaluations of highway, grade crossing and bridge safety hazards and to prohibit federally required record-keeping from being used as a tool in private litigation. *Harrison v. Burlington Northern R. Co.*, 965 F.2d 155 (7th Cir. 1992); *Robertson v. Union Pacific R. Co.*, 954 F.2d 1433 (8th Cir. 1992); *Rodenbeck v. Norfolk & Western Ry. Co.*, 982 F. Supp. 620 (N.D. Ind. 1997); *Taylor v. St. Louis Southwestern Ry. Co.*, 746 F. Supp. 50 (D. Kan. 1990).

Courts have tended to give § 409 a rather expansive scope. The Seventh Circuit has held § 409 extends to any project that conceivably could have been financed by federal funds. *Harrison v. Burlington Northern R. Co.*; *Shots v. CSX Transp., Inc.*, 887 F. Supp. 204 (S.D. Ind. 1995). State reports do not fall outside the scope of § 409 merely because they are not compiled solely for federal reporting purposes and are available for other uses. *Lusby v. Union Pacific R. Co.*, 4 F.3d 639 (8th Cir. 1993) (reversible error to admit safety expert's testimony; fact that Section 409 materials also may have been available to State of Arkansas for other purposes does not give plaintiff's expert the right to use them in his testimony). Section 409 encompasses not only safety documents, but also any testimony based on those documents. *Robertson v. Union Pacific R. Co., supra* (text of 23 U.S.C.A. § 703 making safety evidence inadmissible "[n]otwithstanding any other provision of laws" supersedes provisions of Fed.R.Evid. 703 which permit experts to utilize inadmissible evidence).

Additional References

Graham, Handbook of Federal Evidence § 502.1 (7th ed. 2012)

Treatises and Practice Aids

Goode and Wellborn, Courtroom Handbook on Federal Evidence Chapter 5; Rule 501 and Obj. 73 (annual ed.)

McCormick, Evidence § 112 (6th ed. 2006)

EVIDENCE EXCLUDED BY STATUTE: FEDERALLY AUTHORIZED TAX PRACTITIONERS

See:

26 U.S.C.A. § 7525

Objection

- Objection. The question calls for disclosure of a privileged communication.

Response

- The evidence is not privileged because [*the witness was acting solely as an accountant and the communication was only for that purpose*] [*the communication would not be protected in an attorney-client context*] [*it relates to a tax shelter and is excluded from the scope of the statute*].

Commentary

The IRS Restructuring and Reform Act of 1998 extends the protections of the attorney-client privilege to federally authorized tax practitioners "to the extent the communication would be considered a privileged communication if it were between a taxpayer and an attorney." 26 U.S.C.A. § 7525(a)(1). See Privilege: Attorney-Client, *infra*.

Because the scope of this privilege depends on the scope of the common law protections of confidential attorney-client communications, courts look to the body of law interpreting the attorney-client privilege to interpret the § 7525 privilege. *U.S. v. BDO Seidman*, 337 F.3d 802 (7th Cir. 2003); *Pasadena Refining System Inc. v. U.S.*, 2011 WL 1938133 (N.D. Tex. 2011) (court must look to law of attorney-client privilege to inform its interpretation of the taxpayer-federally authorized tax practitioner privilege). *See generally U.S. v. Textron Inc. and Subsidiaries*, 577 F.3d 21 (1st Cir. 2009).

This statutory privilege is limited to noncriminal tax matters before the Internal Revenue Service or in federal court, brought by or against the United States. *Grant v. U.S.*, 2011 WL 3583399 (N.D. Cal. 2011) (privilege does not apply to a criminal investigation); 26 U.S.C.A. § 7525(a)(2). It does not apply to communications regarding corporate tax shelters. 26 U.S.C.A. § 7525(b). Nothing in the statute suggests that federally authorized tax practitioners are entitled to privilege when they are doing other than lawyers' work. *U.S. v. Frederick*, 182 F.3d 496 (7th Cir. 1999).

In contrast with certain states, federal courts do not recognize any accountant-client privilege. *United States v. Arthur Young & Co.*, 465 U.S. 805, 104 S. Ct. 1495, 79 L. Ed. 2d 826 (1984); *Couch v. United States*, 409 U.S. 322, 93 S. Ct. 611, 34 L. Ed. 2d 548 (1973); *In re Grand Jury Proceedings*, 220 F.3d 568 (7th Cir. 2000); *Wm. T. Thompson Co. v. General Nutrition Corp., Inc.*, 671 F.2d 100 (3d Cir. 1982).

Treatises and Practice Aids

Goode and Wellborn, Courtroom Handbook on Federal Evidence Chapter 5, Rule 501 and Obj. 73 (annual ed.)

Wright & Graham, Federal Practice and Procedure: Evidence §§ 5427, 5431

EVIDENCE EXCLUDED BY STATUTE: NATIONAL TRANSPORTATION SAFETY BOARD ("NTSB") REPORTS

See:

49 U.S.C.A. § 1154(b); 49 C.F.R. § 835.2

Objection

- Objection. The NTSB Report is not admissible in evidence and there are no exceptions.

Response

- If the party is attempting to use a formal NTSB report (as opposed to an investigator's report) there is no response because NTSB reports are inadmissible in civil litigation.

Commentary

The NTSB is an independent federal agency responsible for investigating airplane, highway, railroad, pipeline and marine accidents, determining probable cause and making recommendations to help protect against future accidents. 49 U.S.C.A. §§ 1131, 1132, 1135. An NTSB investigation is a fact-finding proceeding with no adverse parties. It is not conducted for the purpose of determining the rights or liabilities of any person. 49 C.F.R. § 831.4. The "report of the Board" typically contains the NTSB's opinions and probable cause finding.

49 U.S.C.A. § 1154(b) provides:

> No part of a report of the Board, related to an accident or an investigation of an accident, may be admitted into evidence or used in a civil action for damages resulting from a matter mentioned in the report.

NTSB investigatory procedures are not designed to facilitate litigation, and Congress has made it clear that the report of the Board should not be used to the advantage or disadvantage of any party in a civil lawsuit. *Chiron Corp. and PerSeptive Biosystems, Inc. v. National Transp. Safety Bd.*, 198 F.3d 935 (D.C. Cir. 1999); *Campbell v. Keystone Aerial Surveys, Inc.*, 138 F.3d 996 (5th Cir.1998); *Thomas Brooks Chartered v. Burnett*, 920 F.2d 634 (10th Cir.1990); *In re Air Crash at Charlotte, N.C.*

on July 2, 1994, 982 F. Supp. 1071 (D.S.C. 1996).

Investigator's reports are not "reports of the Board" for purposes of 49 U.S.C.A. § 1154(b). 49 C.F.R. § 835.2 defines the Board's accident report as "the report containing the Board's determinations, including the probable cause of the accident." *Id.* No part of this report "may be admitted as evidence or used in any suit or action for damages growing out of any matter mentioned in such reports." *Id.* A "factual accident report," on the other hand, is "an investigator's report of his investigation of the accident." *Id.* Because this latter type of report is not a "report of the Board," it is not barred by 49 U.S.C.A. § 1154(b) and is admissible. *See Chiron Corp.*, 198 F.3d at 935 (collecting and distinguishing older cases which created "exception" for factual data in Board reports; exception was subsequently eliminated by amended NTSB regulations that distinguish between inadmissible "Board report" and admissible "investigator's reports"); *Lidle v. Cirrus Design Corp.*, 2010 WL 1644958 (S.D.N.Y. 2010) (similar; collecting cases).

Additional References

Graham, Handbook of Federal Evidence § 502.1 (7th ed. 2012)

Treatises and Practice Aids

Goode and Wellborn, Courtroom Handbook on Federal Evidence Chapter 5, Rule 501 and Obj. 73 (annual ed.)

Wright & Graham, Federal Practice and Procedure: Evidence §§ 5437, 6273

McCormick, Evidence § 112 (6th ed. 2006)

EXPERT WITNESS: ASSESSING CREDIBILITY PROHIBITED

See:

Fed.R.Evid. 702
Mil.R.Evid. 702

Objection

- Your Honor, this testimony is improper because the witness will intrude on the jury's function of deciding credibility.

Response

- [*There is no response if the expert's evidence goes directly to the issue of witness credibility.*]
- The expert is not making impermissible credibility determinations. He is simply offering his opinion based upon certain factual assumptions supported by testimony in [*plaintiff's/defendant's*] case.

Commentary

A fundamental premise of our system of trial in both civil and criminal cases is that determining the weight and credibility of witness testimony is the responsibility of the jury. *United States v. Scheffer*, 523 U.S. 303, 313, 118 S. Ct. 1261, 140 L. Ed. 2d 413 (1998); *Aetna Life Ins. Co. v. Ward*, 140 U.S. 76, 88, 11 S. Ct. 720, 35 L. Ed. 371 (1891). It is this premise that underlies the principle that a witness's credibility is "not an appropriate subject matter for expert testimony." *See, e.g. U.S. v. Lombardozzi*, 491 F.3d 61 (2d Cir. 2007) (expert testimony may not be used to bolster credibility of fact witnesses); *Nimely v. City of New York*, 414 F.3d 381 (2d Cir. 2005) (forensic pathologist not permitted to render expert opinion as to tendencies of police officers to lie or to tell the truth); *Goodwin v. MTD Products, Inc.*, 232 F.3d 600 (7th Cir. 2000) (defendant not entitled to have expert give opinion as to veracity of plaintiff's testimony about circumstances of his accident); *Richman v. Sheahan*, 415 F. Supp. 2d 929 (N.D. Ill. 2006) (in excessive force case, experts could not make credibility determinations but could base opinions on a version of events which they assumed to be true based upon the testimony); *In re Vioxx Products Liability Litigation*, 414 F. Supp. 2d 574 (E.D. La. 2006) (validating or adding credibility to another witness' testimony is not the proper realm for an expert).

In the context of sexual abuse cases, a qualified expert can inform the jury of characteristics in sexually abused persons and describe the characteristics the alleged victim exhibits. *U.S. v. Two Elk*, 536 F.3d 890 (8th Cir. 2008); *U.S. v. Eagle*, 515 F.3d 794 (8th Cir. 2008); *Isely v. Capuchin Province*, 877 F. Supp. 1055 (E.D. Mich. 1995). However, an expert will not be permitted to opine on the credibility of the alleged victim or offer any opinion that the alleged victim, in fact, suffered the sexual abuse he or she claims. *U.S. v. Charley*, 189 F.3d 1251 (10th Cir. 1999) (collecting cases); *Discepolo v. Gorgone*, 399 F. Supp. 2d 123 (D. Conn. 2005).

Exclusion of expert testimony on eyewitness identification traditionally has been based on the notion that the question of accuracy of perception and memory can be adequately addressed in cross-examination and that such testimony intrudes too deeply on the province of the jury to assess witness credibility. *U.S. v. Carter*, 410 F.3d 942 (7th Cir. 2005); *U.S. v. Martin*, 391 F.3d 949 (8th Cir. 2004) (no abuse of discretion in excluding expert testimony because general reliability of eyewitness identification is a matter of common understanding); *U.S. v. Hall*, 165 F.3d 1095 (7th Cir. 1999) (the hazards of eyewitness identification are well within the knowledge of most lay jurors); *U.S. v. Harris*, 995 F.2d 532 (4th Cir. 1993) (affirming exclusion because jurors using common sense and faculties of observation can judge the credibility of an eyewitness identification, especially since deficiencies or inconsistencies in such testimony can be brought out with skillful cross-examination).

However, a number of circuits have suggested that, under certain circumstances, such evidence warrants a more hospitable reception. *See, e.g. U.S. v. Brien*, 59 F.3d 274, 277 (1st Cir. 1995) ("We are unwilling to adopt a blanket rule that qualified expert testimony on eyewitness identification must routinely be admitted or excluded;" district courts should examine each case, taking into account such concerns as "the reliability and helpfulness of the proposed expert testimony, the importance and the quality of the eyewitness evidence it addresses, and any threat of confusion, misleading of the jury, or unnecessary delay.").

The circumstances held sufficient to support introduction of expert testimony have included such problems as cross-racial identification, identification after a long delay, identification after observation under stress and such psychological phenomena as feedback factor (witnesses unconsciously reinforcing mistaken identities) and unconscious transference (confusing a person seen in one situation with someone seen in a different situation). *See U.S. v. Stevens*, 935 F.2d 1380 (3d Cir. 1991) (in prosecution for robbery and sexual assault, admitting testimony on lack of correlation between confidence in identification and accuracy); *U.S. v. Sebetich*, 776 F.2d 412 (3d Cir. 1985) (robbery conviction vacated and case remanded for hearing to determine admissibility of expert testimony where identification was made nineteen months later by single eyewitness to highly stressful robbery); *U.S. v. Smith*, 736 F.2d 1103 (6th Cir. 1984) (error, albeit harmless, to exclude expert who would have testified about cross-racial misidentification and unconscious transference; photo spread was three weeks after robbery, line-up four months later); *U.S. v. Lester*, 254 F. Supp. 2d 602, 612 (E.D. Va. 2003) (exposure time and retention interval are within common knowledge of jury while "the problem of cross-race recognition, the phenomenon of weapon focus, the relationship of different levels of stress on eyewitness perception, and the correlation (or lack thereof) between confidence and accuracy-do seem to fall outside the common sense of the average juror. At a minimum, it cannot confidently be said that these factors obviously would be within the common knowledge of the average juror."); *U.S. v. Jordan*, 924 F. Supp. 443 (W.D. N.Y. 1996) (testimony of expert in human memory and perception would be helpful to jury in bank robbery case where there was only one eyewitness and no physical evidence such as fingerprints, guns or surveillance photos). *See also U.S. v. Rincon*, 28 F.3d 921 (9th Cir. 1994) (upholding exclusion of expert testimony but noting the result reached was based upon an individualized inquiry rather than strict application of a past rule).

If there is any common thread perhaps it is that in criminal cases, various appellate courts have found no abuse of discretion where trial courts exclude eyewitness identification expert testimony where the eyewitness identification is only a small part of the prosecution's case.

Additional References

Graham, Handbook of Federal Evidence, § 702.6 (7th ed. 2012)

Treatises and Practice Aids

Goode and Wellborn, Courtroom Handbook on Federal Evidence Chapter 5, Rule 702 (annual ed.)

EXPERT WITNESS: COMPETENCE TO TESTIFY

See:

Fed.R.Evid. 702
Mil.R.Evid. 702

Objection

- Your Honor, I request an offer of proof as to the witness' testimony as well as the right to conduct voir dire.
- In light of the offer and my voir dire, I object to any testimony by this witness since his opinion is beyond the area of expertise in which he is qualified.

Response

- As a foundation for this testimony, I have established that the witness has sufficient [*skill*] [*knowledge*] [*experience*] [*training*] in the field of [*specify*] to qualify as an expert witness. I, therefore, ask for the court's ruling that he is recognized as an expert and permitted to testify to his opinions.

Commentary

A preliminary question under Rule 702 is whether the proffered expert possesses sufficient qualifications through knowledge, skill, training or experience to assist the trier of fact to understand the evidence or to determine a fact in issue. *Kumho Tire Co., Ltd. v. Carmichael*, 526 U.S. 137, 119 S. Ct. 1167, 143 L. Ed. 2d 238 (1999); *U.S. v. Two Elk*, 536 F.3d 890 (8th Cir. 2008); *Santoro ex rel. Santoro v. Donnelly*, 340 F. Supp. 2d 464, 478 (S.D. N.Y. 2004) (engineering background and experience in analogous gas-fired consumer products qualified witness as expert on safety of fireplace heaters).

There is no mechanical formula for determining whether an expert is qualified to offer opinion evidence in a particular field. The test is whether, under the totality of the circumstances, the witness can be said to be qualified as an expert in a particular field, through any one or more of the five bases enumerated in Rule 702 — knowledge, skill, experience, training or education. *Santos v. Posadas De Puerto Rico Associates, Inc.*, 452 F.3d 59 (1st Cir. 2006). The proponent of expert testimony must demonstrate by a preponderance of the evidence that the witness is qualified to testify competently regarding the matters he intends to address. *Cook ex rel. Estate of Tessier v. Sheriff of Monroe County, Fla.*, 402 F.3d 1092 (11th Cir. 2005); *Rink v. Cheminova, Inc.*, 400 F.3d 1286 (11th Cir. 2005).

Where a witness does not possess experience or education in the subject matter under investigation, he is incompetent to testify as an expert. *Wheeling Pittsburgh Steel Corp. v. Beelman River Terminals, Inc.*, 254 F.3d 706 (8th Cir. 2001) (although eminently qualified as a hydrologist, witness lacked education or personal experience to testify as expert in safe warehousing practices); *Ramos v. Philip Morris, Inc.*, 414 F. Supp. 2d 115 (D.P.R. 2005) (pathologist not qualified as expert on design or addictiveness of cigarettes); *Kolesar v. United Agri Products, Inc.*, 412 F. Supp. 2d 686 (W.D. Mich. 2006) (industrial hygienist unqualified to opine on causation of respiratory disease); *D & D Associates, Inc. v. Board of Educ. of North Plainfield*, 411 F. Supp. 2d 483 (D.N.J. 2006) (attorney who lacked knowledge of construction and public bidding laws not qualified to give expert opinion re whether school board attorney was deficient in obtaining easements and advising board on public bidding of construction contract); *Derienzo v. Trek Bicycle Corp.*, 376 F. Supp. 2d 537 (S.D. N.Y. 2005) (in product failure case, avid cyclist with electrical engineering degree not qualified to testify to matters involving bicycle design or metallurgical engineering but was qualified on cycling trends, habits and safety). Whether a witness is competent to testify as an expert is within the discretion of the trial court. *St. Martin v. Mobil Exploration & Producing U.S. Inc.*, 224 F.3d 402, 412 (5th Cir. 2000); *Jones v. Lincoln Elec. Co.*, 188 F.3d 709, 723 (7th Cir. 1999) (whether witness is qualified as expert can only be determined by comparing area in which witness has superior knowledge, skill, experience or education with the subject matter of the witness' testimony); *Windham v. Circuit City Stores, Inc.*, 420 F. Supp. 2d 1206 (D. Kan. 2006)

(Rule 702 requires court as gatekeeper to assess whether proposed expert is qualified).

The standard of qualification for an expert witness is a liberal one. *U.S. v. Parra*, 402 F.3d 752 (7th Cir. 2005) (court should consider proposed expert's full range of practical experience as well as academic or technical training when determining whether expert is qualified to render opinion in given area); *In re Paoli R.R. Yard PCB Litigation ("Paoli II")*, 35 F.3d 717, 741 (3d Cir. 1994) ("We have held that a broad range of knowledge, skills and training qualify an expert as such," and have "eschewed imposing overly rigorous requirements of expertise"); *Loeffel Steel Products, Inc. v. Delta Brands, Inc.*, 387 F. Supp. 2d 794 (N.D. Ill. 2005); *Corrigan v. Methodist Hosp.*, 234 F. Supp. 2d 494 (E.D. Pa. 2002). If a witness has any reasonable pretension to specialized knowledge on the subject under investigation, he may testify, and the weight to be given to his testimony is for the jury. *McCullock v. H.B. Fuller Co.*, 61 F.3d 1038, 1043 (2d Cir. 1995); *Davis v. American Jet Leasing, Inc.*, 864 F.2d 612 (8th Cir. 1988) (any gaps in education or experience went to testimony's weight and credibility, not its admissibility). To meet the standard, it is not necessary for the witness to possess all the knowledge in his or her field of activity. Although the witness must demonstrate some special knowledge or skill, there is no requirement that a witness acquire expertise as a result of formal schooling; expertise acquired by practical experience is sufficient. Fed.R.Evid. 702, Advisory Committee's Note; *U.S. v. Walker*, 657 F.3d 160 (3d Cir. 2011) (specialized knowledge can be based upon practical experience as well as academic training and credentials); *U.S. v. Gill*, 513 F.3d 836 (8th Cir. 2008) (court has broad discretion to allow law enforcement officials to testify as experts concerning modus operandi of drug dealers); *U.S. v. Sanchez-Hernandez*, 507 F.3d 826 (5th Cir. 2007) (similar); *U.S. v. Allen*, 269 F.3d 842, 846 (7th Cir. 2001) (experience is, in certain fields, the predominant, if not sole basis for a great deal of reliable expert testimony); *Dresser v. Cradle of Hope Adoption Center, Inc.*, 421 F. Supp. 2d 1024 (E.D. Mich. 2006) (lack of academic training, a college degree, and previous expert witness experience does not render expert testimony inadmissible); *Wisdom v. TJX Companies, Inc.*, 410 F. Supp. 2d 336 (D. Vt. 2006) (40 years of retail marketing experience qualified consultant on premises and safety issues to opine on hazards of clothing display rack); *U.S. E.E.O.C. v. E.I. Du Pont de Nemours & Co.*, 406 F. Supp. 2d 645 (E.D. La. 2005) (experience qualified witness to testify as expert in emergency evacuation of disabled individuals); *Merrifield v. Lockyer*, 388 F. Supp. 2d 1051 (N.D. Cal. 2005) (Federal Rules of Evidence do not require formal education or board certification to qualify as expert); *Shepherd v. Unumprovident Corp.*, 381 F. Supp. 2d 608 (E.D. Ky. 2005) (witness' extensive background and experience in insurance industry qualified her as expert despite lack of formal education in insurance). But if an expert witness is relying solely or primarily on experience, he must explain how that experience leads to the conclusion reached, why that experience is a sufficient basis for the opinion, and how that experience is reliably applied to the facts. *Mikeron, Inc. v. Exxon Co., U.S.A.*, 264 F. Supp. 2d 268 (D. Md. 2003); *see also Pizal v. Monaco Coach Corp.*, 374 F. Supp. 2d 653 (N.D. Ind. 2005) (experts can be qualified to testify upon personal knowledge and experience so long as experience and knowledge is reliable).

Experts in one area of medicine have been ruled qualified to address other areas of specialization where the specialties overlap in practice, or where the physician has experience in another related medical field. *Compare Gaydar v. Sociedad Instituto Gineco-Quirurgico y Planificacion*, 345 F.3d 15 (1st Cir. 2003) (proffered expert physician need not be specialist in a particular medical discipline to render expert testimony relating to that discipline); *Mitchell v. U.S.*, 141 F.3d 8 (1st Cir. 1998) (internist who was not a specialist in gastroenterology but who had substantial experience in use of Coumadin was qualified to give expert testimony where issue was malpractice in adjusting patient's anticoagulant levels before and after colonoscopy); *Holbrook v. Lykes Bros. S.S. Co., Inc.*, 80 F.3d 777, 782 (3d Cir. 1996) (in death action stemming from alleged exposure to asbestos-containing products, reversible error to exclude testimony of doctors specializing in internal and pulmonary medicine; court erroneously required expert to have specialization in cancer and radiation) *with Hartke v. McKelway*, 526 F. Supp. 97, 100–101 (D.D.C. 1981) (family practitioner unqualified to establish standard of care for sterilization surgery, where practitioner had never performed operation, had no training in the procedure and "major reason for her conclusion that there was negligence was that the result was unfavorable").

However, in civil actions in which state law supplies the rule of decision with respect to an element of a claim or defense, a witness' competency must be determined in accordance with state law. Fed.R.Evid. 601; *Legg v. Chopra*, 286 F.3d 286 (6th Cir. 2002) (examining interplay of expert testimony with Tennessee's medical malpractice statute and Federal Rules of Evidence and holding Texas physician properly excluded pursuant to competency requirements of state's malpractice statute); *McDowell v. Brown*, 392 F.3d 1283, 1295 (11th Cir. 2004) (following *Legg v. Chopra*); *Barton v. American Red Cross*, 829 F. Supp. 1290 (M.D. Ala. 1993) (holding that, under Rule 601, competency requirements under Alabama Medical Liability Act applied in federal court).

Generally the factual basis of an expert opinion goes to the credibility of the testimony, not its admissibility. It is up to the opposing party to examine the factual basis for the opinion in cross-examination. *Larson v. Kempker*, 414 F.3d 936 (8th Cir. 2005). However, expert testimony will be deemed incompetent if it lacks an adequate basis in fact. *Nebraska Plastics, Inc. v. Holland Colors Americas, Inc.*, 408 F.3d 410 (8th Cir. 2005) (expert opinion that fails to consider relevant facts of case is fundamentally unsupported and properly excluded); *Brooks v. Outboard Marine Corp.*, 234 F.3d 89 (2d Cir. 2000); *Macaluso v. Herman Miller, Inc.*, 2005 WL 563169 at *8 (S.D. N.Y. 2005) (concluding expert's testimony must be excluded under Daubert "because it is based on incorrect factual assumptions that render all of his subsequent conclusions purely speculative"); *Wurtzel v. Starbucks Coffee Co.*, 257 F. Supp. 2d 520 (E.D. N.Y. 2003). The expert is allowed to assume the truth of testimony already in evidence. *U.S. v. Scop*, 846 F.2d 135 (2d Cir. 1988). While an expert's opinion need not be based on absolute certainty, an opinion based on mere possibilities is not competent evidence. *Goebel v. Denver and Rio Grande Western R. Co.*, 346 F.3d 987, 991 (10th Cir. 2003). This means that expert testimony cannot be based solely upon conjecture or surmise. An expert must do more than guess. *Bryte ex rel. Bryte v. American Household, Inc.*, 429 F.3d 469 (4th Cir. 2005) (*Daubert* aims to prevent expert speculation). His assumptions must be based upon such facts as the jury would be warranted in finding from the evidence. *Richman v. Sheahan*, 415 F. Supp. 2d 929 (N.D.Ill. 2006) (collecting cases).

Because admissibility of expert opinion is highly case-specific, the following decisions simply serve to illustrate application of the rule.

Admitted: Burke v. TransAm Trucking, Inc., Civil Action No. 03: 06-CV-2090 (M.D.Pa. 5-20-09) (biomechanical expert can testify to forces exerted in accident and whether those forces could cause the types of injuries suffered; cannot testify to extent of injuries suffered by plaintiff which would require diagnosis of medical condition); *Bado-Santana v. Ford Motor Co.*, 482 F. Supp. 2d 192 (D.P.R. 2007) (although not a physician, neuropsychologist qualified to testify as expert on mild traumatic brain injury); *Hadix v. Caruso*, 461 F. Supp. 2d 574 (W.D. Mich. 2006) (by nature of practice and experience, primary care physicians qualified to offer opinions on psychiatric and psychological care).

Excluded: *Smith v. Goodyear Tire & Rubber Co.*, 495 F.3d 224 (5th Cir. 2007) (polymer scientist with no expertise in tire design, manufacture or malfunction not permitted to testify on cause of tire failure); *Botnick v. Zimmer, Inc.*, 484 F. Supp. 2d 715 (N.D. Ohio 2007) (witness did not qualify as expert in defective medical device case; general mechanical engineering was not particular to the science bearing on design or causation issues of alleged product defects); *McMillan v. Weeks Marine, Inc.*, 478 F. Supp. 2d 651 (D. Del. 2007) (actuarial economist should not have testified about plaintiff's future employment prospects; subject was outside his discipline and prior experience); *Pfizer Inc. v. Teva Pharmaceuticals USA, Inc.*, 461 F. Supp. 2d 271 (D.N.J. 2006) (rheumatologist not qualified to testify in patent infringement case on subject of whether other doctors were influenced by advertising and promotion in deciding whether to prescribe drug).

Additional References

Graham, Handbook of Federal Evidence § 702.2 (7th ed. 2012)

Treatises and Practice Aids

Goode and Wellborn, Courtroom Handbook on Federal Evidence Chapter 5, Rule 702 and Obj. 32 (annual ed.)

McCormick, Evidence § 13 (6th ed. 2006)

EXPERT WITNESS: LEGAL OPINION

See:

Fed.R.Evid. 702
Mil.R.Evid. 702

Objection

- [*To a question*] Objection. The question calls for a legal conclusion.
- [*To an answer*] I object and move to strike. The witness' testimony provides a legal opinion.

Response

- The question seeks only a factual answer. [*Explain*]
- The testimony provides relevant facts and not legal conclusions. [*Explain*]

Commentary

Rule 702 provides for the liberal admission of expert testimony regarding factual matters. However, "resolving doubtful questions of law is the distinct and exclusive province of the trial judge." *Nationwide Transp. Fin. v. Cass Info. Sys., Inc.*, 523 F.3d 1050, 1051 (9th Cir. 2008). Accordingly, federal courts typically prohibit lawyers, professors, and other experts from interpreting the law for the court or from advising the court about how the law should apply to the facts of a particular case. Testimony "which articulates and applies the relevant law . . . circumvents the [fact finder's] decision-making function by telling it how to decide the case." *Specht v. Jensen*, 853 F.2d 805 (10th Cir. 1988).

The principle that legal opinion evidence concerning the law is inadmissible is "so well-established that it is often deemed a basic premise or assumption of evidence law-a kind of axiomatic principle." *Holman Enterprises v. Fidelity and Guar. Ins. Co.*, 563 F. Supp. 2d 467, 472 (D.N.J. 2008); *In re Initial Public Offering Securities Litigation*, 174 F. Supp. 2d 61, 64 (S.D. N.Y. 2001) (quoting Baker, *The Impropriety of Expert Witness Testimony on the Law*, 40 U. Kan. Law Rev. 325,

352 (1992)). The rule regarding legal testimony has been stated as follows:

> A witness cannot be allowed to give an opinion on a question of law . . .. In order to justify having courts resolve disputes between litigants, it must be posited as an a priori assumption that there is one, but only one, legal answer for every cognizable dispute. There being only one applicable legal rule for each dispute or issue, it requires only one spokesman of the law, who of course is the judge . . .. To allow anyone other than the judge to state the law would violate the basic concept.

Specht v. Jensen, 853 F.2d at 807 (citation omitted). Courts have held that expert testimony by lawyers, law professors, and others concerning legal issues is improper. *See*, *U.S. v. Crockett*, 435 F.3d 1305 (10th Cir. 2006) (witness cannot be permitted to define the law of the case); *U.S. v. Stewart*, 433 F.3d 273 (2d Cir. 2006) (court correctly prevented securities law expert from testifying about legality of stock trade); *In re Initial Public Offering Sec. Litigation*, 174 F.Supp.2d at 64 (stating that "every circuit has explicitly held that experts may not invade the court's province by testifying on issues of law."); *Hygh v. Jacobs*, 961 F.2d 359 (2d Cir. 1992) (same); *U.S. v. Zipkin*, 729 F.2d 384, 387 (6th Cir. 1984) (reversing trial court's decision to allow bankruptcy judge to testify regarding his interpretation of the Bankruptcy Act, stating that "[i]t is the function of the trial judge to determine the law of the case."); *Bethea v. Equinox Fitness Club*, 544 F. Supp. 2d 398 (S.D. N.Y. 2008) (in Title VII action, report of human resources expert containing his views on appropriate legal standards re remedies was inadmissible); *Brill v. Marandola*, 540 F. Supp. 2d 563 (E.D. Pa. 2008) (expert's interpretation of legal documents usurp fact-finding role of jury); *Ji v. Bose Corp.*, 538 F. Supp. 2d 354 (D. Mass. 2008) (entertainment law attorney's testimony re legal impact of releases signed by model prior to photo shoot constituted improper legal conclusions); *Cryovac Inc. v. Pechiney Plastic Packaging, Inc.*, 430 F. Supp. 2d 346 (D. Del. 2006) (expert testimony on substantive areas of patent law is impermissible); *Wollan v. U.S. Dept. of Interior, Bureau of Land Management*, 997 F. Supp. 1397, 1403 (D. Colo. 1998) (expert's "legal opinion as to what the homestead laws say or do not say . . . inapposite

. . . .. Where the ultimate issue is a question of law, the opinion of a legal expert, even a lawyer, interferes with the judge's role as 'sole arbiter of the law' and should not be allowed.").

In addition to prohibiting legal expert testimony which defines the governing law, courts have also prohibited legal expert opinion which applies the law to the facts. Many courts have held that the judge is the sole arbiter of the law and its application to the facts. *See, Marx & Co., Inc. v. Diners' Club Inc.*, 550 F.2d 505, 508–11 (2d Cir. 1977) (court erred in permitting a lawyer to offer his opinions concerning securities law and the application of that law to the contract in dispute.); *Peterson v. City of Plymouth*, 60 F.3d 469, 475 (8th Cir. 1995) (error to allow testimony that police officers' conduct satisfied Fourth Amendment requirements stating that "[the expert's] testimony was not a fact-based opinion, but a statement of legal conclusion. These legal conclusions were for the court to make. It was an abuse of discretion to allow the testimony."); *Montgomery v. Aetna Cas. & Sur. Co.*, 898 F.2d 1537, 1541 (11th Cir. 1990) (finding that court abused its discretion by allowing witness to testify that defendant had a duty to hire tax counsel, stating "[a] witness also may not testify to the legal implications of conduct . . .."); *Specht v. Jensen*, 853 F.2d at 809 (stating that "testimony on ultimate issues of law by the legal expert is inadmissible because it is detrimental to the trial process.").

Other illustrative cases include: *Mola Development Corp. v. U.S.*, 516 F.3d 1370 (Fed. Cir. 2008) (proper interpretation of agency regulations is an issue of law; expert testimony should not be received, much less considered); *RLJCS Enterprises, Inc. v. Professional Ben. Trust Multiple Employer Welfare Ben. Plan and Trust*, 487 F.3d 494 (7th Cir. 2007) (legal arguments are costly enough without being subjects of experts' depositions and extensive debates in discovery); *DiBella v. Hopkins*, 403 F.3d 102, 121 (2d Cir. 2005) (inadmissible testimony that defendant's actions constituted extortion); *Miller v. Clark County*, 340 F.3d 959, 963 n.7 (9th Cir. 2003) (excluding testimony that dog bite constituted "deadly force"); *Bammerlin v. Navistar Intern. Transp. Corp.*, 30 F.3d 898 (7th

Cir. 1994) (excluding expert testimony regarding compliance with Federal Motor Vehicle Safety Standards; the meaning of federal regulations is a question of law, not a question of fact); *Suter v. General Acc. Ins. Co. of America*, 424 F. Supp. 2d 781 (D.N.J. 2006) (in bench trial, ability of expert witness to stray into court's territory is significantly lessened); *Safeway, Inc. v. Sugarloaf Partnership, LLC.*, 423 F. Supp. 2d 531 (D. Md. 2006) (report as to custom and usage of "continuous operation clauses" in shopping center leases not admissible); *Gallatin Fuels, Inc. v. Westchester Fire Ins. Co.*, 410 F. Supp. 2d 417 (W.D. Pa. 2006) (expert testimony that insurer deviated from industry standards admissible; testimony that insurer actually acted in bad faith inadmissible); *Sanders v. Mount Sinai School of Medicine*, 418 F. Supp. 2d 339 (S.D. N.Y. 2005) (admitting expert report describing claims included in original patent and elements lost as a result of prior judgment of U.S. Patent Office as foundation for opinion that hospital failed to commercialize patent); *Casper v. SMG*, 389 F. Supp. 2d 618 (D.N.J. 2005) (professor of law and economics precluded from testifying that labor agreement constituted anti-trust violation); *U.S. v. Caputo*, 374 F. Supp. 2d 632 (N.D. Ill. 2005) (government's expert could give opinion about safety testing of medical device and that notice was inadequate to warn purchasers of risks but could not opine whether defendants complied with federal statute or were materially misleading within meaning of statute or regulation); *Highway Materials, Inc. v. Whitemarsh Tp., Montgomery County, Pa.*, 2004 WL 2220974 at *20 (E.D. Pa. 2004) (excluding expert's opinion that defendants' actions satisfied "shocked the conscience" standard); *Wechsler v. Hunt Health Systems, Ltd.*, 381 F. Supp. 2d 135 (S.D. N.Y. 2003) (expert opinion that part of corporation's receivables were either non-reimbursable accounts or were disputed, denied, appealed or paid were factual and not legal conclusions).

But cf. Flores v. Arizona, 516 F.3d 1140, 1166 (9th Cir. 2008) (expert testimony on federal educational funding law properly admitted in *bench trial*; expert legal opinions generally inadmissible "but there may be 'instances in rare, highly complex and technical matters where a trial judge, utilizing limited and controlled mechanisms, and as a matter of trial management, permits some testimony seemingly at variance with the general rule,'" *citing Nieves-Villanueva v. Soto-Rivera*, 133 F.3d 92, 101 (1st Cir. 1997)); *U.S. v. McIver*, 470 F.3d 550 (4th Cir. 2006) (expert's opinion that defendant's treatment of certain patients was either illegitimate or inappropriate fell within the limited vernacular available to express whether doctor acted outside bounds of his professional practice); *U.S. v. Jacques Dessange, Inc.*, 2000 WL 294849 at *2 (S.D. N.Y. 2000) (approving expert testimony on issues of law regarding sophisticated aspects of regulatory system and industry practices to help fact-finder understand unfamiliar terms, concepts or standards of accepted practice); In *In re Prempro Products Liability Litigation*, 474 F. Supp. 2d 1040 (E.D. Ark. 2007) (expert's testimony that drug company was negligent permissible in complex, highly technical case).

Additional References

Graham, Handbook of Federal Evidence § 704.1 (7th ed. 2012)

Treatises and Practice Aids

Goode and Wellborn, Courtroom Handbook on Federal Evidence Chapter 5, Rule 702 and Obj. 35 (annual ed.)
McCormick, Evidence § 12 (6th ed. 2006)

EXPERT WITNESS: REQUISITE DEGREE OF CERTAINTY

See:

Fed.R.Evid. 702
Mil.R.Evid. 702

Objection

- Your Honor, I object and move to strike the testimony of this witness because his opinion has not been rendered to a reasonable degree of professional certainty.

Response

- The witness is not required to use "magic words" in order for the opinion to be admissible. Taken as a whole, the testimony expresses a reasonable certainty and absolute certainty is not required.

Commentary

The United States Supreme Court has said that an expert's opinion must consist of more than "subjective belief or unsupported speculation." *Daubert v. Merrell Dow Pharmaceuticals, Inc.*, 509 U.S. 579, 589–90, 113 S. Ct. 2786, 125 L. Ed. 2d 469 (1993).

An expert is generally required to give an opinion to a reasonable degree of [professional] certainty. *See, e.g. Gomez v. Martin Marietta Corp.*, 50 F.3d 1511 (10th Cir. 1995) (expert was able to express a reasonably accurate conclusion); *Friend v. Time Mfg. Co.*, 422 F. Supp. 2d 1079 (D. Ariz. 2005) (expert reached his conclusions within a reasonable degree of engineering certainty). It is not required that these "magic words" be used. As one court said:

> [T]he phase 'with a reasonable degree of medical certainty' is a useful shorthand expression that is helpful in forestalling challenges to the admissibility of expert testimony. Care must be taken, however, to see that the incantation does not become a semantic trap and the failure to voice it is not used as a basis for exclusion without analysis of the testimony itself.

Schulz v. Celotex Corp., 942 F.2d 204, 208 (3d

Cir. 1991); *accord U.S. v. Mornan*, 413 F.3d 372 (3d Cir. 2005) (phase "to a reasonable degree of scientific certainty" is not derived from the language of Rule 702 and court finds no authority to support position that questions regarding expert's "degree of scientific certainty" categorically render expert testimony inadmissible); *Holbrook v. Lykes Bros. S.S. Co., Inc.*, 80 F.3d 777, 785 (3d Cir. 1996) (trial court erred in disallowing cross-examination of expert to determine whether opinion met reasonable degree of certainty; "The Federal Rules of Evidence . . . do not require a particular phrase regarding the degree of certainty with which experts must form their opinions, but they certainly allow questions concerning the degree to which the opinion is held."). The opinion will be held sufficiently certain if review of the testimony, in its entirety, reveals reasonable certainty. *U.S. v. Mornan*, 413 F.3d 372 (3d Cir. 2005) (handwriting experts often give their opinions in terms of probabilities rather than certainties); *U.S. v. Ford*, 481 F.3d 215 (3d Cir. 2007) and *U.S. v. Allen*, 390 F.3d 944 (7th Cir. 2004) (proper to admit testimony by shoe-print expert that defendant's shoes could have made impression found at robbery site); *Goebel v. Denver and Rio Grande Western R. Co.*, 346 F.3d 987 (10th Cir. 2003) (absolute certainty is not required); *Dodge v. Cotter Corp.*, 328 F.3d 1212 (10th Cir. 2003) (same); *U.S. v. Charley*, 189 F.3d 1251 (10th Cir. 1999) (sexual abuse "could" explain child's other symptoms); *U.S. v. Rosario*, 118 F.3d 160, 163 (3d Cir. 1997) (opinion that defendant "probably" authored forged check was admissible); *U.S. v. Rahm*, 993 F.2d 1405, 1412 (9th Cir. 1993) ("In any area of science or social science, but particularly in matters of the mind, expecting an expert to reach a conclusion without the slightest doubt as to its accuracy is exceedingly unrealistic. Experts ordinarily deal in probabilities, in 'coulds' and 'mights'."); *U.S. v. Monteiro*, 407 F. Supp. 2d 351 (D. Mass. 2006) (although firearms expert permitted to testify to reasonable degree of ballistic certainty that spent cartridge cases matched defendant's gun, he was not allowed to say match was to any exact statistical certainty because science has not advanced to that point). *See also Roche v. Lincoln Property Co.*, 278 F. Supp. 2d 744 (E.D.

Va. 2003) (despite the fact that expert opinion was made "within a reasonable degree of medical certainty," it was inadmissible because conclusion was vague and general and diagnosis of injury caused by mold unsupported and unreliable).

Other linguistic formulations open an opinion to attack that it lacks the requisite certainty. However, an opinion that the alleged cause was "the most probable cause" is sufficient to meet this standard of certainty. *See, e.g. Kennedy v. Collagen Corp.*, 161 F.3d 1226 (9th Cir. 1998) (medical expert's opinion that, based on "reasonable medical probability," collagen injections caused plaintiff's lupus would assist trier of fact).

Conversely, an opinion may be excluded as lacking requisite certainty if it is couched in terms such as "possibility," "suspicious that it could have been," "could only guess," *Schulz v. Celotex Corporation*, 942 F.2d at 208 (citations omitted); *Lexington Ins. Co. v. Rounds*, 349 F. Supp. 2d 861 (D. Vt. 2004) (engineer's report that it should have been foreseeable that landowners "might" have to remove excess surface water and would be "inclined" to divert water over berm inadmissible; report couched in very speculative language with no basis for conclusions).

In certain instances, the degree of certainty required will depend on which party has the burden of proof. For example, a plaintiff expert, who holds the burden of proof on causation, would be required to testify to a reasonable degree of scientific certainty that toxin X caused the harm, whereas the defense expert may be permitted to testify that it "was a distinct possibility" that the harm was caused by a different factor. *See Holbrook v. Lykes Bros. S.S. Co. Inc.*, 80 F.3d at 786 (reasonable medical certainty not required because defendant did not have burden of proof with respect to the cause of plaintiff's cancer).

In criminal cases, it is not necessary that a prosecution expert testify that his conclusions are stated beyond a reasonable doubt. Whether an expert's testimony is persuasive beyond a reasonable doubt is a matter for the jury's consideration.

Additional References

Graham, Handbook of Federal Evidence § 702.1 (7th ed. 2012)

EXPERT WITNESS: REQUISITE DEGREE OF CERTAINTY

Treatises and Practice Aids

Goode and Wellborn, Courtroom Handbook on Federal Evidence, Rule 702 and Objs. 30, 34 and 35 (annual ed.)

EXPERT WITNESS: TESTIMONY BASED IN PART ON HEARSAY—CONDUIT WITNESS

See:

Fed.R.Evid. 703
Mil.R.Evid. 703

Objection

- Objection, hearsay. I move to strike this testimony since the witness has merely summarized the findings and conclusions of others.

Response

- The objection is not well-founded. The witness has used a variety of sources, along with her own professional experience, to arrive at her own opinion. We have established as foundation for this opinion that the data was of the type reasonably relied on by experts in the particular field. Her testimony is admissible expert testimony under Fed.R.Evid. 703 and not hearsay evidence.

Commentary

Although the common law restricted the expert to testimony based on personal observation or examination, the federal rules permit experts to give their opinions based, in part, upon reports, facts and data of others, which are not in evidence but upon which experts customarily rely in the practice of their profession. Fed.R.Evid. 703; *Monsanto Co. v. David*, 516 F.3d 1009 (Fed. Cir. 2008) (testimony in patent infringement case properly admitted from expert who did not conduct his own seed report tests); *Larson v. Kempker*, 414 F.3d 936 (8th Cir. 2005); *U.S. v. LeClair*, 338 F.3d 882 (8th Cir. 2003) (facts or data that form the basis for expert opinion need not be admissible in evidence in order for opinion to be admitted as long as evidence is a type reasonably relied on by experts in the field); *U.S. v. Dukagjini*, 326 F.3d 45 (2d Cir. 2003); *Terrell v. City of El Paso*, 481 F. Supp. 2d 757 (W.D. Tex. 2007) (same); *Ohio Environmental Development Ltd. Partnership v. Envirotest Systems Corp.*, 478 F. Supp. 2d 963 (N.D. Ohio 2007); *O2 Micro Intern.*

Ltd. v. Monolithic Power Systems, Inc., 420 F. Supp. 2d 1070 (N.D. Cal. 2006); *Olson v. Ford Motor Co.*, 410 F. Supp. 2d 855 (D.N.D. 2006).

The rationale for the exception is practical necessity and common sense. An expert's opinion may be based on years of professional experience, schooling and knowledge, not all of which can be presented on a first-hand basis in court. Moreover, the expert is assumed to have the ability to evaluate the trustworthiness of the data upon which he or she relies, both because the expert has demonstrated expert qualifications and because the expert regularly relies on and uses similar data in the practice of his or her profession. *See, e.g., U.S. v. Locascio*, 6 F.3d 924 (2d Cir. 1993) (an expert who meets the test of Rule 702 is assumed to have the skill to properly evaluate the hearsay, giving it probative force appropriate to the circumstances). Thus, when the expert witness has consulted numerous sources and uses that information, together with his or her own professional knowledge and experience to arrive at an opinion, that opinion is regarded as evidence in its own right and not as hearsay in disguise.

While often applied to the testimony of medical experts (*see, e.g., Ramirez v. Debs-Elias*, 407 F.3d 444 (1st Cir. 2005); *Adel v. Greensprings of Vermont, Inc.*, 363 F. Supp. 2d 683 (D. Vt. 2005) (to require scientists to develop all of their knowledge through their own clinical work or experiments is an unrealistic expectation which ignores the reality of science as a collaberative process)), the exception is not limited to the medical profession. *See Simpson v. Socialist People's Libyan Arab Jamahiriya*, 362 F. Supp. 2d 168 (D.D.C. 2005) (expert on terrorism and hostage taking could rely in part on newspaper articles); *Hambrick ex rel. Hambrick v. Ken-Bar Mfg. Co.*, 422 F. Supp. 2d 627 (W.D. Va. 2002) (expert could rely on survey performed by others).

However, an expert will not be permitted simply to repeat another's opinion or data without employing his own expertise and judgment. *Dura Automotive Systems of Indiana, Inc. v. CTS Corp.*, 285 F.3d 609 (7th Cir. 2002) (a scientist, however well credentialed, is not permitted to be the mouth piece of a scientist in a different specialty). This type of expert has been referred to as the "summary" or "conduit" expert, who serves to introduce the contents of extrajudicial statements or writings. *McCormick, Evidence,* §§ 15 and 324.3. *See, e.g., Matter of James Wilson Associates*, 965 F.2d 160 (7th Cir. 1992) (expert cannot be used as vehicle for circumventing the rule against hearsay); *Bouygues Telecom, S.A. v. Tekelec*, 472 F. Supp. 2d 722 (E.D. N.C. 2007) (wholesale adoption of another expert's opinion not within intent of Rule 702); *Loeffel Steel Products, Inc. v. Delta Brands, Inc.*, 387 F. Supp. 2d 794 (N.D.Ill. 2005) (if allowed to testify, expert would be hiding behind three other experts and acting as their mouthpiece when he had absolutely no knowledge of whether their theory was valid and reliable). In such a situation, the non-testifying expert is not on the witness stand and truly is unavailable for cross-examination. *See, e.g., TK-7 Corp. v. Estate of Barbouti*, 993 F.2d 722 (10th Cir. 1993). However, an expert witness is permitted to use assistants in formulating his expert opinion. *McReynolds v. Sodexho Marriott Services, Inc.*, 349 F. Supp. 2d 30 (D.D.C. 2004) (collecting cases).

Rule 703, as amended in 2000, clarifies that the expert generally may not disclose otherwise inadmissible evidence unless the trial court determines its probative value outweighs its prejudicial effect. If otherwise inadmissible information is admitted under this balancing test, the trial judge must give a limiting instruction upon request, informing the jury that the underlying information may be considered solely as a basis for the expert opinion and must not be used as substantive evidence. Fed.R.Evid. 703, Advisory Committee Note to 2000 amendment; *U.S. v. Gonzales*, 307 F.3d 906 (9th Cir. 2002); *Engebretsen v. Fairchild Aircraft Corp.*, 21 F.3d 721 (6th Cir. 1994).

Whether the facts, data or opinions not admitted in evidence are of a type reasonably relied upon is a preliminary question for the court. Rule 104(a). The requirement that the facts, data or opinions be of a type reasonably relied upon by experts in the field provides a check on the trustworthiness of the opinion and its foundation. In determining whether reliance by the expert is reasonable, the proponent of the evidence must satisfy the court both that such information is of the type customarily relied upon by experts in the field and that the information is sufficiently trustworthy to make such reliance reasonable.

Additional References

Graham, Handbook of Federal Evidence § 703.1 (7th ed. 2012)

Treatises and Practice Aids

Goode and Wellborn, Courtroom Handbook on Federal Evidence Chapter 5, Rule 703 and Obj. 33 (annual ed.)

McCormick, Evidence § 15 (6th ed. 2006)

EXPERT WITNESS: ULTIMATE ISSUE

See:

Fed.R.Evid. 704
Mil.R.Evid. 704

Objection

- Objection [*and move to strike*]. Giving an opinion [*would not be helpful to the jury*], [*is unfairly prejudicial*], [*is improper for this witness*] because [*specify*].

Response

- The [*question/answer*] goes to the ultimate issue in this case and is proper under Rule 704 because [*specify*].

Commentary

Fed.R.Evid. 704 provides that otherwise admissible opinion testimony is not objectionable merely because it reaches an ultimate issue to be decided by the factfinder. This removes the court from the task of determining whether or not an opinion goes to the ultimate issue and eliminates those objections asserting that the testimony "invades the province of the jury" or embraces an "ultimate issue." *See Hygh v. Jacobs*, 961 F.2d 359 (2d Cir. 1992); *U.S. v. Brown*, 7 F.3d 648 (7th Cir. 1993); McCormick, Evidence § 12 (5th ed. 1999).

However, opinion testimony must still be "otherwise admissible." The principal effect of Rule 704 is to shift the inquiry to whether the opinion is admissible under the standards of Rules 701, 702, and 403. Therefore, testimony going to an ultimate issue may be objectionable for any of a number of reasons: because a lay witness is not capable of rendering such an opinion; the opinion is beyond the realm of an expert witness's expertise; the factfinder would not be helped by hearing the opinion; or the probative value of the opinion is outweighed by the danger that it would be unfairly prejudicial, confuse the issues or mislead the jury. *See, e.g., New Mexico v. General Elec. Co.*, 335 F. Supp. 2d 1266 (D.N.M. 2004) (to be helpful to trier of fact, opinion on ultimate issue must take into account the material facts that bear upon the ultimate issue and must adequately explore criteria upon which opinion is based).

Because admissibility of opinions relating to ultimate issues is highly case-specific, the following decisions simply serve to illustrate application of the rule.

Admitted: *U.S. v. Bedford*, 536 F.3d 1148 (10th Cir. 2008) (expert testimony by IRS agent as to the proper tax consequences of a transaction is admissible evidence so long as the expert does not address the ultimate question of whether defendant intended to evade income taxes); *U.S. v. Hatch*, 514 F.3d 145 (1st Cir. 2008) (same); *U.S. v. Moran*, 493 F.3d 1002 (9th Cir. 2007) (testimony that programs promoted by defendants were "shams" permitted); *U.S. v. Dazey*, 403 F.3d 1147 (10th Cir. 2005) (testimony by expert from Federal Reserve that investment program using the word "prime bank" was a fraud; careful not to state, however, that any defendant actually violated the law); *U.S. v. Brown*, 110 F.3d 605 (8th Cir. 1997) (police expert permitted to express opinion that apartment was stash house and defendant's actions were consistent with drug delivery and counter-surveillance activities); *U.S. v. Moore*, 997 F.2d 55 (5th Cir. 1993) (in fraud prosecution, IRS agent appearing as summary expert witness allowed to summarize and analyze facts indicating tax fraud).

Excluded: *Berry v. City of Detroit*, 25 F.3d 1342 (6th Cir. 1994) (in Section 1983 action stemming from fatal shooting by police, error to allow expert to testify that deadly force constituted pattern of gross negligence with deliberate indifference to welfare of citizenry); *U.S. v. Simpson*, 7 F.3d 186 (10th Cir. 1993) (in bank fraud prosecution where court said it was "close question," defense expert not permitted to testify whether transactions amounted to misapplication or concealment of funds); *Owen v. Kerr-McGee Corp.*, 698 F.2d 236 (5th Cir. 1983) (where bulldozer hit pipeline resulting in personal injury, expert not permitted to give opinion as to cause of accident; opinion sought was legal not factual because factual cause was not in dispute and questions which allow expert to tell jury what result to reach are not permitted).

See also Hartzler v. Wiley, 277 F. Supp. 2d 1114

(D. Kan. 2003) (under Rule 704(a), expert may not apply the law to the facts of the case to form legal conclusions but may refer to the law in expressing his opinion).

Opinions About Accused's Mental State

Rule 704(b) prohibits an expert from rendering an opinion as to whether the defendant had or lacked a mental state or condition that constitutes an element of, or defense to, the crime charged. However, testimony that, when combined with other evidence, might imply or otherwise cause a jury to infer this ultimate conclusion is permitted under the Rule. *U.S. v. Liner*, 435 F.3d 920 (8th Cir. 2006) (expert testimony that prospectus contained some indices of fraudulent high-yield investment schemes was admissible; although testimony implied program in question was fraudulent, expert expressed no opinion whether defendant had the requisite mens rea to commit wire fraud or whether the program was, in fact, fraudulent); *U.S. v. Urbina*, 431 F.3d 305 (8th Cir. 2005) (expert testimony that drug traffickers do not typically use couriers who are unaware they are transporting drugs is permissible where one defense theory is that defendant was unaware of the presence of drugs); *U.S. v. Schneiderhan*, 404 F.3d 73 (1st Cir. 2005) (officer properly testified that quantity of drugs found was more indicative of intent to distribute than to keep for personal use; the bar created by Rule 704(b) does not apply to predicate facts from which jury might infer intent); *U.S. v. Younger*, 398 F.3d 1179 (9th Cir. 2005) (same); *U.S. v. Davis*, 397 F.3d 173 (3d Cir. 2005) (no error to admit expert testimony that certain behavior was consistent with possession with intent to deliver narcotics because testimony was given in response to hypothetical question rather than specific questions regarding the intent of individual defendants on trial). It is only as to the last step of the inferential process-a conclusion as to the defendant's mental state-that Rule 704(b) commands the expert to remain silent. *U.S. v. Watson*, 260 F.3d 301 (3d Cir. 2001) (expert testimony is admissible if it merely supports an inference or conclusion that defendant did or did not have requisite *mens rea*, so long as expert does not draw the ultimate inference or conclusion for the jury and the ultimate inference or conclusion does not necessarily follow from the testimony). Rule 704(b) applies to expert opinion about any mental state. It is not restricted to testimony concerning insanity. *See, e.g.*, *U.S. v. Campos*, 217 F.3d 707 (9th Cir. 2000) (defendant's knowledge that vehicle contained drugs).

Additional References

Graham, Handbook of Federal Evidence § 704.1 (7th ed. 2012)

Treatises and Practice Aids

Goode and Wellborn, Courtroom Handbook on Federal Evidence Chapter 5, Rule 704 (annual ed.)

McCormick, Evidence § 12 (6th ed. 2006)

HABIT/ROUTINE PRACTICE

See:

Fed.R.Evid. 406
Mil.R.Evid. 406

Objection

- Objection. Counsel has not established that the conduct qualifies as admissible evidence of habit/routine practice under Rule 406.

Response

- The evidence is admissible because we have established a sufficient pattern of consistent behavior to support the inference of habit/routine practice [*provide specifics*].

Commentary

Fed.R.Evid. 404 embodies the principle that evidence of a person's character *usually* is not admissible for the purpose of proving that the person acted in conformity with his character on a particular occasion. This general rule of exclusion, applicable to both civil and criminal proceedings, is based upon the assumption that such evidence is of slight probative value yet very prejudicial.

Rule 406, however, recognizes the relevance of a person's habit or the routine practice of an organization to prove that conduct on a particular occasion was in conformity with the habit or practice.

Rule 406 provides:

> Evidence of the habit of a person or of the routine practice of an organization, whether corroborated or not and regardless of the presence of eye witnesses, is relevant to prove that the conduct of the person or organization on a particular occasion was in conformity with the habit or routine practice.

Although there is no precise formula for determining when a practice becomes so consistent as to rise to the level of routine, "adequacy of sampling and uniformity of response are controlling considerations." *G.M. Brod & Co., Inc. v. U.S. Home Corp.*, 759 F.2d 1526, 1533 (11th Cir. 1985). These factors focus on whether the behavior at issue "occurred with sufficient regularity making it more probable than not that it would be carried out in every instance or in most instances." *Weil v. Seltzer*, 873 F.2d 1453, 1460 (D.C. Cir. 1989). These requirements help prevent attempts to introduce inadmissible character evidence under Rule 404 in the guise of habit or routine practice evidence. *Simplex, Inc. v. Diversified Energy Systems, Inc.*, 847 F.2d 1290, 1293 (7th Cir. 1988) ("We are cautious in permitting the admission of habit or pattern-of-conduct evidence under Rule 406 because it necessarily engenders the very real possibility that such evidence will be used to establish a party's propensity to act in conformity with its general character, thereby thwarting Rule 404's prohibition against the use of character evidence, except for narrowly prescribed purposes."); *U.S. v. Santos*, 65 F. Supp. 2d 802, 821 (N.D. Ill. 1999).

Habit

A habit is the person's regular practice of meeting a particular kind of situation with a specific type of conduct, such as the habit of going down a particular stairway two stairs at a time, or of giving a hand-signal for a left turn, or of alighting from railway cars while they are moving. Fed.R.Evid. 406 Advisory Committee Note.

Before a court may admit evidence of habit, the offering party must establish the degree of specificity and frequency of uniform response that ensures more than a mere tendency to act in a given manner, but rather, conduct that is semi-automatic in nature. *U.S. v. Al Kassar*, 582 F. Supp. 2d 498 (S.D. N.Y. 2008). *See Pries v. Honda Motor Co., Ltd.*, 31 F.3d 543 (7th Cir. 1994). Evidence that a person had on one or more occasions acted in a particular manner is alone insufficient to establish a regular practice of meeting a particular kind of situation with a specific kind of conduct. *U.S. Football League v. National Football League*, 842 F.2d 1335 (2d Cir. 1988) (three or four episodes over twenty-year period insufficient to conclude that a pattern of behavior exists).

Routine Practice

To obtain a Rule 406 inference of the routine practice of a business, a party must show a sufficient number of specific instances of conduct to support the inference. Evidence of actions on only a few occasions are not enough. It is only when examples offered to establish a pattern of conduct are numerous enough to support an inference of systematic conduct that such evidence is admissible. *Wilson v. Volkswagen of America, Inc.*, 561 F.2d 494, 511 (4th Cir. 1977).

"Courts are inclined to leniency" when it comes to evidence of routine business practice. 2 Weinstein & Berger, Weinstein's Evidence, ¶ 406 [03] at 406–17 (1992). This is because routine business practices are often relied upon by other businesses and because routine business practices are derived from concerted planning activities driven by economic concerns about efficiency, which are, of necessity, more regimented than individual conduct. *Id.*

Evidence of habit or routine practice is to be weighed and considered by the trier of fact in the same manner as any other type of direct or circumstantial evidence. *Meyer v. U.S.*, 638 F.2d 155, 158 (10th Cir. 1980).

Illustrations

Admitted: *Hall v. Arthur*, 141 F.3d 844 (8th Cir. 1998) (testimony by other patients that defendant did not inform them of risks associated with use of ceramic material in spinal fusions and that material did not have FDA approval properly admitted as evidence of routine practice under Rule 406); *Mobil Exploration and Producing U.S., Inc. v. Cajun Const. Services, Inc.*, 45 F.3d 96 (5th Cir. 1995) (error to exclude evidence of party's routine practice of short-loading trucks where over 3,400 invoices and testimony established trucks were loaded in same manner); *Perrin v. Anderson*, 784 F.2d 1040 (10th Cir. 1986) (holding testimony was adequate to establish that plaintiff's decedent had a habit of reacting violently to any contact with a uniformed police officer); *Loughan v. Firestone Tire & Rubber Co.*, 749 F.2d 1519 (11th Cir. 1985) (evidence from three sources regarding plaintiff's drinking practices over six-year period sufficient to establish his habit of drinking on the job); *Meyer*, 638 F.2d at 157 (testimony by dentist and his assistants was sufficient to support trial court's finding that it was dentist's habit and custom to advise patients of potential risks in extraction of molars); *Williams v. Security Nat. Bank of Sioux City, Iowa*, 358 F. Supp. 2d 782 (N.D. Iowa 2005) (occasions on which life beneficiary invaded trust corpus were sufficiently numerous to base inference of systematic conduct necessary to establish "habit"; beneficiary invaded trust on eight occasions when he did not receive overdistributions but not on ten other occasions when he did not receive overdistributions); *Lowry's Reports, Inc. v. Legg Mason, Inc.*, 271 F. Supp. 2d 737 (D. Md. 2003) (where original agreement could not be found but Lowry's could show its routine practice via other contemporaneous agreements, the uniform language of these other agreements allowed trier of fact to conclude Legg had a contract whose terms matched the other agreements); *Beard v. Flying J. Inc.*, 116 F. Supp. 2d 1077, 1097 (S.D. Iowa 2000) aff'd in relevant part, 266 F.3d 792 (8th Cir. 2001) (in Title VII action, testimony by other female employees that supervisor engaged in sexually offensive conduct admissible as habit evidence).

Excluded: *Camfield v. City of Oklahoma City*, 248 F.3d 1214 (10th Cir. 2001) (in civil rights action, five or six incidents of seizing what was allegedly child pornography were insufficient to establish existence of police habit); *U.S. v. West*, 22 F.3d 586 (5th Cir. 1994) (no error excluding defense evidence that FDIC had a routine practice of permitting parties to purchase their own notes through straw purchasers; defendant made no attempt to furnish evidence of other instances where the practice was/was not permitted); *U.S. v. Newman*, 982 F.2d 665, 669 (1st Cir. 1992)("[W]e are aware of no case . . . in which the routine practice of an organization, without more, has been considered probative of the conduct of a particular individual within the organization."); *Jones v. Southern Pacific R.R.*, 962 F.2d 447 (5th Cir. 1992) (evidence of nine violations in the course of 29-year career as train engineer not admissible to show engineer's habit of driving negligently); *Reyes v. Missouri Pac. R. Co.*, 589 F.2d 791 (5th Cir. 1979) (four prior convictions for public intoxication over three and one-half year period were of insufficient regularity to rise to level of habit evidence and, thus, inadmissible in plaintiff's suit for injuries suffered when he was run over by train); *Levin v. U.S.*, 338 F.2d 265 (D.C. Cir. 1964) (in larceny prosecution where portions of crime occurred during Sabbath, no error to refuse to allow rabbi to testify about defendant's habit of observing the Sabbath; religious practices are not the kinds of activities which provide a basis for concluding "invariable regularity" necessary to constitute admissible habit evidence); *Zubulake v. UBS Warburg LLC.*, 382 F. Supp. 2d 536 (S.D. N.Y. 2005) (former employee's alleged deficiencies at prior job were not admissible as habit evidence; each job had its own distinct working environment); *Rivera v. Union Pacific R. Co.*, 868 F. Supp. 294, 299 (D. Colo. 1994) (railroad could not use Rule 406 to show it was its "habit" to be non-negligent).

Additional References

Graham, Handbook of Federal Evidence §§ 406.1 to 406.4 (7th ed. 2012)

Treatises and Practice Aids

Goode and Wellborn, Courtroom Handbook on Federal Evidence Chapter 5, Rule 406 and Obj. 36 (annual ed.)

Mueller & Kirkpatrick, Federal Evidence, §§ 4:44 to 4:81 (3d ed. 2007)

Wright & Graham, Federal Practice and Procedure: Evidence §§ 5271 *et seq.*

McCormick, Evidence § 195 (6th ed. 2006)

Park, Trial Objections Handbook § 2:32 (2nd ed. 2001)

HEARSAY: AUTHOR'S NOTE CONFRONTATION-CRIMINAL CASES

Crawford v. Washington 541 U.S. 36 (2004)

Author's Note

The Confrontation Clause of the Sixth Amendment provides that "[i]n all criminal prosecutions, the accused shall enjoy the right . . . to be confronted with the witnesses against him." U.S. Const. amend. VI. "The central concern of the Confrontation Clause is to ensure the reliability of the evidence against a criminal defendant by subjecting it to rigorous testing in the context of an adversary proceeding before the trier of fact." *Lilly v. Virginia*, 527 U.S. 116, 124, 119 S. Ct. 1887, 144 L. Ed. 2d 117 (1999) (quoting *Maryland v. Craig*, 497 U.S. 836, 845, 110 S. Ct. 3157, 111 L. Ed. 2d 666 (1990)). *See also Davis v. Alaska*, 415 U.S. 308, 315, 94 S. Ct. 1105, 39 L. Ed. 2d 347 (1974) (a primary interest secured by the Confrontation Clause is the right of cross-examination).

Prior to *Crawford v. Washington*, 541 U.S. 36, 124 S. Ct. 1354, 158, 158 L. Ed. 2d 177 (2004), the admissibility of out-of-court statements under the Confrontation Clause was governed by *Ohio v. Roberts*, 448 U.S. 56, 100 S. Ct. 2531, 65 L. Ed. 2d 597 (1980). According to *Roberts*, an unavailable witness's out-of-court statement could be admitted against the accused if the statement had adequate indicia of reliability. *Roberts*, 448 U.S. at 66. A statement was considered to have sufficient indicia of reliability if it either fell within a "firmly rooted hearsay exception" or bore "particularized guarantees of trustworthiness." *Id. Crawford*, however, dramatically alters the interplay between the Confrontation Clause and the law of hearsay.

Crawford involved a tape-recorded statement given by defendant's wife to police describing the stabbing with which defendant was charged. Pursuant to the state marital privilege, the wife did not testify at trial, so defendant had no opportunity to cross-examine her. The wife's statement was admitted at trial over objection because the trial court determined that the statement had "particularized guarantees of trustworthiness." *Roberts*,

448 U.S. at 66.

The *Crawford* Court held that the Confrontation Clause bars the state from introducing out-of-court statements which are *testimonial* in nature, unless the declarant is unavailable as a witness and the defendant had a prior opportunity to cross-examine the declarant. The Court categorically rejected, as inconsistent with the Constitution, hearsay exceptions for statements deemed otherwise "reliable" despite the absence of prior cross-examination:

> [D]ispensing with confrontation because testimony is obviously reliable is akin to dispensing with a jury because a defendant is obviously guilty. This is not what the Sixth Amendment proscribes.

Crawford, 541 U.S. at 62.

The Supreme Court, in *Crawford*, "changed the legal landscape for determining whether the admission of . . . hearsay statements violates the accused's right[s]" under the Confrontation Clause. *Horton v. Allen*, 370 F.3d 75, 83 (1st Cir. 2004). The Second Circuit has observed that "*Crawford* departs from prior Confrontation Clause jurisprudence by establishing a *per se* bar on the admission of out-of-court testimonial statements made by unavailable declarants where there was no prior opportunity for cross-examination." *U.S. v. McClain*, 377 F.3d 219, 221 (2d Cir. 2004).

The *Crawford* Court reaffirmed the importance of the confrontation right and drew a distinction between testimonial and nontestimonial statements for Confrontation Clause purposes: "Where testimonial statements are involved, we do not think the Framers meant to leave the Sixth Amendment's protection to the vagaries of the rules of evidence, much less to amorphous notions of 'reliability.' " *Crawford*, 541 U.S. at 61. The Court overruled *Roberts* as to "testimonial evidence," holding that the Sixth Amendment demands what the common law required: unavailability and prior opportunity for cross-examination. *Id.* at 68. While the Court declined to "spell out a comprehensive definition of 'testimonial,' " it stated that the term "applies at a minimum to prior testimony at a preliminary hearing, before a grand jury, or at a former trial; and to police interrogations. These are the modern practices with closest kinship to the abuses against which Confrontation Clause was directed." *Id.* The Court found that the wife's tape-recorded statement taken by the police was "testimonial under any definition," *id.* at 61, and reversed defendant's conviction, *id.* at 69.

Without endorsing one specific definition, *Crawford* referenced three different "formulations of this core class of 'testimonial' statements": (1) "*ex parte* in-court testimony or its functional equivalent-that is, material such as affidavits, custodial examinations, prior testimony that the defendant was unable to cross-examine, or similar pretrial statements that declarants would reasonably expect to be used prosecutorially," *id.* at 51 (quoting Br. for Pet'r 23); (2) "extrajudicial statements . . . contained in formalized testimonial materials, such as affidavits, depositions, prior testimony or confessions," *id.* at 51–52 (quoting *White v. Illinois*, 502 U.S. 346, 365, 112 S. Ct. 736, 116 L. Ed. 2d 848 (1992) (Thomas, J., concurring)); and (3) "statements that were made under circumstances which would lead an objective witness reasonably to believe that the statement would be available for use at a later trial," *id.* (quoting Br. for Nat'l Assoc. of Criminal Def. Lawyers et al. as Amici Curiae 3). These three definitions, the Court found, "all share a common nucleus and then define the Clause's coverage at various levels of abstraction around it." *Id.*

Admission of non-testimonial hearsay is still governed by *Roberts*. *See* Crawford, 541 U.S. at 68 ("Where nontestimonial hearsay is at issue, it is wholly consistent with the Framer's design to afford the states flexibility in their development of hearsay law-as does *Roberts*, and as would an approach that exempted such statements from Confrontation Clause scrutiny altogether.") *Accord U.S. v. Scheurer*, 62 M.J. 100, 106 (C.A.A.F. 2005) ("We agree with the conclusion of every published appellate court decision that has considered this issue since *Crawford*: the *Ohio v. Roberts* requirement for particularized guarantees of trustworthiness continues to govern confrontation analysis for nontestimonial statements.")

Thus, in criminal cases, the fundamental question with respect to the admissibility of hearsay evidence is whether the out-of-court statements are testimonial or nontestimonial, the former governed by *Crawford* as to confrontation analysis and the latter, by *Roberts*.

"Where testimonial statements are at issue, the only indicium of reliability sufficient to satisfy constitutional demands is the one the Constitution actually prescribes: confrontation." *Crawford*, 541 U.S. at 68–69. Under *Roberts*, a nontestimonial hearsay statement contains "adequate indicia of reliability" if it falls within a "firmly rooted hearsay exception" or if it bears "particularized guarantees of trustworthiness." 448 U.S. at 66. In determining whether a certain statement contains a "particularized guarantee of trustworthiness" sufficient to allow its admission without violating a defendant's Confrontation Clause rights, the court should "consider the totality of those circumstances that surround the making of the statement and that render the declarant particularly worthy of belief." *U.S. v. Dhinsa*, 243 F.3d 635, 655 (2d Cir. 2001) (quoting *Idaho v. Wright*, 497 U.S. 805, 819, 110 S. Ct. 3139, 111 L. Ed. 2d 638 (1990)).

Subsequent Developments

In *Davis v. Washington* and *Hammond v. Indiana*, 547 U.S. 813 (2006), both domestic violence cases, the Court explained that "[s]tatements are nontestimonial when made in the course of police interrogation under circumstances objectively indicating that the [interrogation's] primary purpose... is to enable police assistance to meet an ongoing emergency," but they "are testimonial when the circumstances objectively indicate that there is no such ongoing emergency, and that the [interrogation's] primary purpose is to establish or prove past events potentially relevant to later criminal prosecution." 547 U.S. at 822. See *Michigan v. Bryant*, 562 U.S. ___ 2011 (clarifying *Davis's* "primary purpose" determination).

In *Melendez-Diaz v. Massachussets*, ___*U.S.* ___, 129 S.Ct. 2527, 174 L. Ed. 2d 314 (2009), the trial court had admitted into evidence state laboratory affidavits with forensic analysis results showing material seized from defendant was cocaine. The United States Supreme Court said that the laboratory reports fell within the core class of testimonial statements since they had been created for the sole purpose of providing evidence against a defendant. Acknowledging that the Confrontation Clause may make prosecution of criminals more burdensome, the Court held that crime laboratory reports may not be used against defendants at trial unless the analysts responsible for creating them give testimony and subject themselves to cross-examination.

In *Bullcoming v. New Mexico*, ___ U.S. ___ (2011), a DUI case involving a blood sample analyzed for alcohol, the Supreme Court said the Confrontation Clause does not permit the prosecution to introduce a laboratory report through testimony of an analyst who did not sign the certification or perform or observe the performance of the test reported in the certification. The laboratory report is testimonial in nature created for the very purpose of criminal prosecution.

Since *Crawford*, various courts have wrestled with the definition of "*testimonial*" statements. *See, e.g.*, *Miller v. Stovall*, 608 F.3d 913 (6th Cir. 2010) (policeman's suicide note confessing to murder was testimonial; a reasonable person would have anticipated its use by authorities); *U.S. v. Eagle*, 515 F.3d 794 (8th Cir. 2008) (statements made to forensic interviewer are testimonial); *U.S. v. Moon*, 512 F.3d 359, 362 (7th Cir. 2008) (instruments' readouts are not "statements"; a machine is not a "witness against" anyone); *U.S. v. Jordan*, 509 F.3d 191 (4th Cir. 2007) (statements made by defendant's alleged coconspirator to friend prior to her suicide in which she admitted her involvement in murder were non-testimonial); *U.S. v. Ellis*, 460 F.3d 920 (7th Cir. 2006) (Confrontation Clause does not forbid use of raw data produced by scientific instruments, though interpretation of data may be testimonial); *U.S. v. Brown*, 441 F.3d 1330 (11th Cir. 2006) (excited utterance "you didn't kill that lady" said during private phone conversation between declarant mother and her son while mother was seated in her dining room with only family members present was nontestimonial); *U.S. v. Hagege*, 437 F.3d 943 (9th Cir. 2006) (business records fall outside the core class of "testimonial evidence" and thus are not subject to the absolute requirement of confrontation established in *Craw-*

ford); *U.S. v. Gilbertson*, 435 F.3d 790 (7th Cir. 2006) (in prosecution for knowingly altering odometers of motor vehicles, odometer statements from state certified certificates of title were not testimonial; not made by respective declarants with an eye toward criminal prosecution); *U.S. v. Hansen*, 434 F.3d 92 (1st Cir. 2006) (challenged statements were nontestimonial because they were either co-conspirator statements made during the course of and in furtherance of the conspiracy or casual remarks which the declarant would not reasonably expect to be available for use at a later trial); *U.S. v. Peneaux*, 432 F.3d 882 (8th Cir. 2005) (where statements are made to a physician seeking to give medical aid in the form of diagnosis or treatment, they are presumptively nontestimonial); *U.S. v. Hinton*, 423 F.3d 355 (3d Cir. 2005) (declarant's identification of assailant to police officers while riding in police cruiser in pursuit of suspect was testimonial and, thus, inadmissible; statements made during earlier 911 call, under the circumstances, were nontestimonial); *U.S. v. Pugh*, 405 F.3d 390, 399 (6th Cir. 2005) (declarant's identification of defendant was testimonial because given during police interrogation, made to government officer and because "any reasonable person would assume that a statement that positively identified possible suspects in a picture of the crime scene would be used against those suspects in either investigating or prosecuting the offense"); *U.S. v. Hendricks*, 395 F.3d 173 (3d Cir. 2005) (wiretap recordings are not testimonial for purposes of *Crawford*); *U.S. v. Rodriguez-Marrero*, 390 F.3d 1 (1st Cir. 2004) (signed confession presented under oath to prosecutor is testimonial hearsay); *U.S. v. Cromer*, 389 F.3d 662 (6th Cir. 2004) (statement made knowingly to authorities that describes criminal activity is almost always testimonial; confidential informer's statement to police implicating defendant in criminal activity constituted testimonial hearsay); *Parle v. Runnels*, 387 F.3d 1030 (9th Cir. 2004) (murder victim's diary was admissible evidence; diary not testimonial because not created under circumstances which would lead an objective witness reasonably to believe that it would be available for use at a later trial); *U.S. v. Saget*, 377 F.3d 223 (2d Cir. 2004) (statements to confidential informant, whose true identity was unknown to declarant, did not constitute "testimony" under *Crawford*); *U.S. v. Bruno*, 383 F.3d 65 (2d Cir. 2004) (plea allocution transcript and grand jury testimony of unavailable witnesses constituted testimonial hearsay); *Horton v. Allen*, 370 F.3d 75 (1st Cir. 2004) (statements made in private conversation were within state of mind exception, nontestimonial in nature, and outside *Crawford's* scope; *Roberts* applies to determine admissibility); *U.S. v. Reyes*, 362 F.3d 536 (8th Cir. 2004) (*Crawford* does not apply to co-conspirator statements because they are nontestimonial).

The Supreme Court has said that the right to confrontation is a *trial* right. *Pennsylvania v. Ritchie*, 480 U.S. 39, 52, 107 S. Ct. 989, 999, 94 L. Ed. 2d 40 (1987). It is well established at sentencing that a trial court may use reliable hearsay, *U.S. v. Zlatogur*, 271 F.3d 1025 (11th Cir. 2001) and that the right to confrontation does not apply. *U.S. v. Kirby*, 418 F.3d 621 (6th Cir. 2005). Accordingly, a number of circuits have recognized that *Crawford* does not apply to sentencing proceedings. *U.S. v. Smith*, 253 Fed.Appx. 818 (11th Cir. 2007); *U.S. v. Cantellano*, 430 F.3d 1142 (11th Cir. 2005); *U.S. v. Monteiro*, 417 F.3d 208 (1st Cir. 2005); *U.S. v. Martinez*, 413 F.3d 239 (2d Cir. 2005).

Additional References

Graham, Handbook of Federal Evidence § 802.2 (7th ed. 2012)

Treatises and Practice Aids

Goode and Wellborn, Courtroom Handbook on Federal Evidence Chapter 5, Rule 802 (annual ed.)

HEARSAY: GENERALLY

See:

Fed.R.Evid. 801(c), 802
Mil.R.Evid. 801(c), 802

Objection

- [*To a question*] Objection. The question calls for hearsay.
- [*To an answer*] Objection, hearsay. I move that the answer be stricken and the jury be instructed not to consider it for any purpose.

Response

- The statement is not being offered for the truth of the matter asserted but is only offered:

  [*as circumstantial proof of the speaker's state of mind (e.g., malice, hatred, premeditation, knowledge or notice)*]

  [*to show the effect the statement had on the listener (or reader)*]

  [*to impeach the witness with his or her own prior inconsistent statement*]

  [*because the statement is an operative fact or verbal act offered for its legal significance (e.g., words of an offer or acceptance creating a contract, or defamatory words spoken to establish slander)*]

Commentary

Hearsay is an out-of-court statement offered in evidence to prove the truth of the matter asserted. Rule 801(c); *Anderson v. United States*, 417 U.S. 211, 94 S. Ct. 2253, 41 L. Ed. 2d 20 (1974); *U.S. v. Caraballo*, 595 F.3d 1214 (11th Cir. 2010); *U.S. v. Martinez*, 588 F.3d 301 (6th Cir. 2009); *U.S. v. DeCologero*, 530 F.3d 36 (1st Cir. 2008); *U.S. v. Thomas*, 453 F.3d 838 (7th Cir. 2006); *U.S. v. Wright*, 343 F.3d 849 (6th Cir. 2003); *ACTONet, Ltd. v. Allou Health & Beauty Care*, 219 F.3d 836 (8th Cir. 2000).

An out-of-court statement is any statement (oral or written) except one made by a witness while testifying at trial. Rule 801(c). Thus, face to face communications, telephone conversations, letters, records and reports are all out-of-court statements since they are not made while testifying. *U.S. v. Lewis*, 436 F.3d 939 (8th Cir. 2006) (the fact that past out-of-court statements were made by a witness now testifying at trial does not remove them from the scope of the hearsay rule if they are offered to prove the truth of the matters asserted); *Lust v. Sealy, Inc.*, 383 F.3d 580 (7th Cir. 2004) (a memo normally is hearsay).

There are two elements which must be present before an out-of-court utterance may be rendered inadmissible as hearsay: (1) the out-of-court utterance must be a "statement," i.e. a verbal assertion or conduct intended as an assertion; and (2) the statement must be offered to prove the truth of the matter that it asserts. Rule 801(c); *U.S. v. Lis*, 120 F.3d 28, 30 (4th Cir. 1997); *U.S. v. Arteaga*, 117 F.3d 388, 396 (9th Cir. 1997); *U.S. v. Cruz*, 805 F.2d 1464, 1477–78 (11th Cir. 1986). *See also U.S. v. Hathaway*, 798 F.2d 902 (6th Cir. 1986) (in fraud action, no error allowing customers to testify to statements by defendant's salesmen; statements offered to prove falsity of matter asserted are not hearsay since there is no need to assess credibility of declarant); *U.S. v. Adkins*, 741 F.2d 744, 746 (5th Cir. 1984) (similar).

The hearsay rule "is premised on the theory that out-of-court statements are subject to particular hazards. The declarant might be lying; he might have misperceived the events which he relates; he might have faulty memory; his words might be misunderstood or taken out of context by the listener. And the ways in which these dangers are minimized for in-court statements-the oath, the witness' awareness of the gravity of the proceedings, the jury's ability to observe the witness' demeanor, and, most importantly, the right of the opponent to cross-examine-are generally absent for things said out of court." *Williamson v. United States*, 512 U.S. 594, 598, 114 S. Ct. 2431, 2434, 129 L. Ed. 2d 476 (1994); *U.S. v. Evans*, 216 F.3d 80, 85 (D.C. Cir. 2000) (the problem with hearsay is that it deprives the opponent of the opportunity to cross-examine the person who uttered the statement at issue; "[C]ross-examination may be the greatest legal engine ever invented for the discovery of truth but it is not of much use if there is no one to whom it can be applied" (citation omitted)).

News Media

Courts uniformly hold that newspaper articles are inadmissible hearsay when the article was not written or acknowledged by the referenced party, yet is offered as proof of facts stated in the article. *Boim v. Holy Land Foundation for Relief and Development*, 511 F.3d 707 (7th Cir. 2007); *Eisenstadt v. Centel Corp.*, 113 F.3d 738 (7th Cir. 1997); *Larez v. City of Los Angeles*, 946 F.2d 630 (9th Cir. 1991); *Miles v. Ramsey*, 31 F. Supp. 2d 869 (D. Colo. 1998). But for a nonhearsay use of a news article, *see Martin v. City of Indianapolis*, 192 F.3d 608 (7th Cir. 1999) (news articles commenting on outdoor sculpture admitted not for truth but for limited purpose of showing sculpture was work of recognized stature protected by Visual Artists Rights Act, 17 U.S.C.A. §§ 101 et seq.). *See* Hearsay, Residual Exception, *infra*.

Statements Which Are Not Hearsay

Whether a statement is hearsay and, thus inadmissible, will often hinge on the purpose for which it is offered. If a statement is offered to prove something other than the truth of the fact related in the statement, it is not hearsay. *U.S. v. Colon-Diaz*, 521 F.3d 29 (1st Cir. 2008) (directions from one person to another do not constitute hearsay and nonhearsay includes statements offered to supply a motive for the listener's action); *U.S. v. Quinones*, 511 F.3d 289 (2d Cir. 2007) (murder victim's out-of-court statements were not received for truth but as circumstantial evidence of his state of mind to explain his and defendants' future actions); *U.S. v. Serrano*, 434 F.3d 1003 (7th Cir. 2006) (insurance documents and related correspondence were not hearsay; documents not introduced for truth of matters they assert but simply as circumstantial evidence linking defendant to drug house) (collecting cases); *U.S. v. Bradford*, 246 F.3d 1107 (8th Cir. 2001) (overruled by, U.S. v. Diaz, 296 F.3d 680 (8th Cir. 2002)) (address books not offered for truth of matter asserted but to show associations among the co-defendants); *Lyons Partnership, L.P. v.*

Morris Costumes, Inc., 243 F.3d 789 (4th Cir. 2001) (in trademark infringement case, children's statements as testified to by school principal and newspaper clippings mistaking costume for TV character, Barney, were direct evidence of actual confusion and not hearsay); *Fun-Damental Too, Ltd. v. Gemmy Industries Corp.*, 111 F.3d 993 (2d Cir. 1997); *Medic Alert Foundation U.S., Inc. v. Corel Corp.*, 43 F. Supp. 2d 933 (N.D. Ill. 1999) (similar); *Carson Harbor Village, Ltd. v. Unocal Corp.*, 227 F.3d 1196 (9th Cir. 2000) (prior inconsistent statement is admissible to raise suggestion that if a witness makes inconsistent statements, then his entire testimony may not be credible; since inference does not depend on whether statement is true, there is no hearsay); *U.S. v. Sorrentino*, 72 F.3d 294 (2d Cir. 1995) (confidential informant's statements in tape-recorded conversations with defendant were admissible not for truth but to render defendant's statements intelligible); *Link v. Mercedes-Benz of North America, Inc.*, 788 F.2d 918 (3d Cir. 1986) (publications offered for limited purpose of showing industry practice); *U.S. v. Pheaster*, 544 F.2d 353 (9th Cir. 1976) (hearsay evidence is admissible if it bears on the state of mind of the declarant and if that state of mind is an issue in the case). *U.S. v. Carmichael*, 379 F. Supp. 2d 1299 (M.D. Ala. 2005) (statements introduced not for truth but to show they were false).

Out-of-court statements offered solely to show the statements were made with no issue as to truth can include greetings, pleasantries, expressions of gratitude, questions, verbal acts such as offers, instructions, warnings, demands, exclamations, expressions of emotion, etc. *See, e.g., U.S. v. Moreno*, 233 F.3d 937 (7th Cir. 2000) (utterance of consent to search by police and subsequent retraction are verbal acts, and, as such, are not inadmissible hearsay); *Quartararo v. Hanslmaier*, 186 F.3d 91 (2d Cir. 1999) (a question is not an assertion and cannot be a hearsay statement); *U.S. v. Bellomo*, 176 F.3d 580 (2d Cir. 1999) (statements offered as evidence of commands, threats or rules directed to witness are not hearsay); *Talley v. Bravo Pitino Restaurant, Ltd.*, 61 F.3d 1241 (6th Cir. 1995) (civil rights action alleging race discrimination in employment termination; racial slurs allegedly made by owners offered not for truth but demonstrate their racial attitudes); *Starr v. Pearle Vision, Inc.*, 54 F.3d 1548 (10th Cir. 1995) (in defamation action, witness' testimony that store manager said plaintiff was fired for stealing money was not offered for truth of matter but to prove manager had uttered statement); *Hydrite Chemical Co. v. Calumet Lubricants Co.*, 47 F.3d 887, 892 (7th Cir. 1995) ("It is direct evidence, not hearsay, when a party to a dispute over a contract testifies to the offer or the acceptance made by the other contracting party."); *George v. Celotex Corp.*, 914 F.2d 26 (2d Cir. 1990) (statement offered not for truth but to show defendant was on notice of a danger is not hearsay); *U.S. v. Honken*, 381 F. Supp. 2d 936, 1000–01 (N.D. Iowa 2005) (a question is typically not hearsay because it does not assert the truth or falsity of a fact; a question merely seeks answers and usually has no factual content.)

Some courts have held that "nothing said" by a machine is hearsay. *U.S. v. Moon*, 512 F.3d 359, 362 (7th Cir. 2008) (instruments' readouts are not "statements"; a machine is not a "witness against" anyone; how can one cross-examine a gas chromatograph?); *U.S. v. Hamilton*, 413 F.3d 1138 (10th Cir. 2005) (computer generated "header" information on copies of child pornography images listing information about the person who posted the images was not hearsay; header generated instantaneously by computer without assistance or input of a person); *U.S. v. Khorozian*, 333 F.3d 498 (3d Cir. 2003) (header information automatically generated by fax machine was not hearsay).

An employment discrimination action can frequently put one of the parties in the difficult position of having to prove the state of mind of the person making the employment decision. Where statements are offered not for truth but to prove the state of mind of the decisionmakers, they are not hearsay and may be admitted. *See, e.g., Wright v. Southland Corp.*, 187 F.3d 1287 (11th Cir. 1999); *Bush v. Dictaphone Corp.*, 161 F.3d 363 (6th Cir. 1998); *Blanks v. Waste Management of Arkansas, Inc.*, 31 F. Supp. 2d 673 (E.D. Ark. 1998).

Police Investigations

Courts generally hold that an out-of-court statement is not hearsay if it is offered for the limited purpose of explaining why a police investigation was undertaken. *U.S. v. Eberhart*, 434 F.3d 935 (7th Cir. 2006); *U.S. v. Malik*, 345 F.3d 999 (8th Cir. 2003); *U.S. v. Obi*, 239 F.3d 662 (4th Cir. 2001); *U.S. v. Davis*, 154 F.3d 772 (8th Cir. 1998); *U.S. v. Wilson*, 107 F.3d 774 (10th Cir. 1997). As the Tenth Circuit has explained: "an arresting or investigating officer should not be put in the false position of seeming just to have happened upon the scene and should be allowed some explanation of his or her presence and conduct. However, testimony that the officer acted 'upon information received,' or words to that effect should be sufficient." *U.S. v. Cass*, 127 F.3d 1218, 1223 (10th Cir. 1997) (quoting McCormick on Evidence (4th ed.) § 249 at 104); *U.S. v. Reyes*, 18 F.3d 65 (2d Cir. 1994) (government may be permitted to offer out-of-court statement for purpose of showing investigating agent's state of mind in order to help jury understand agent's subsequent actions); *Munley v. Carlson*, 125 F. Supp. 2d 1117 (N.D. Ill. 2000) (in § 1983 action for use of excessive force, statements that arrestee's wife made to defendant officer at time of arrest were admissible non-hearsay to show effect on officer and how he reacted to them).

However, the "background" rationale should not be used as a pretext to nullify an accused's right to confront and cross-examine the witnesses against him or to inject irrelevant and prejudicial evidence into the trial. *U.S. v. Garcia-Morales*, 382 F.3d 12 (1st Cir. 2004) (criticizing practice of calling government agent as "overview" witness; hearsay does not become admissible merely because it is provided by government agent in the form of an overview of the evidence); *U.S. v. Becker*, 230 F.3d 1224 (10th Cir. 2000) (error to permit police officer to testify to statements made by confidential informer naming defendant as manufacturing and selling drugs; evidence directly implicated issue of guilt and, in its case, government relied on statements as being truthful); *U.S. v. Cass*, 127 F.3d at 1222–24 (error to allow FBI agent to use out-of-court statements to outline the entire prosecution case); *U.S. v. Blake*, 107 F.3d 651 (8th Cir. 1997) (evidence may not be admitted for non-hearsay purpose of explaining police investigation where propriety of investigation is not a relevant issue at trial); *U.S. v. Forrester*, 60 F.3d 52, 59 (2d Cir. 1995) (abuse of discretion to admit through police witnesses background information by informer providing details of defendant's drug smuggling; "The government's identification of a relevant non-hearsay use for such evidence . . . is insufficient to justify its admission if the jury is likely to consider the statement for the truth of what was stated with significant resultant prejudice."); *U.S. v. Evans*, 950 F.2d 187 (5th Cir. 1991) (evidence otherwise admissible as background becomes inadmissible hearsay if it also points directly at defendant and his guilt in the crime charged). For analogous cases, *see U.S. v. Paulino*, 445 F.3d 211 (2d Cir. 2006) (statements introduced not for truth but to aid jury in understanding context of events); *U.S. v. Walter*, 434 F.3d 30 (1st Cir. 2006) (defendant's statements on audiotapes of controlled gun purchases were admissions; cooperating witness's statements admitted not for truth but to place defendant's admissions in context and make them intelligible to jury); *U.S. v. Looking Cloud*, 419 F.3d 781 (8th Cir. 2005) (rumors that victim was informant introduced not for truth but to help jury understand context and circumstances of murder). *Foster-Miller, Inc. v. Babcock & Wilcox Canada*, 210 F.3d 1 (1st Cir. 2000) (notes of outside consultant who did not testify at trial properly admitted and used by witness in his testimony to establish factual context in which his own actions took place). *But see U.S. v. Levine*, 378 F. Supp. 2d 872, 875 (E.D. Ark. 2005) where Judge Wilson wrote:

> Over the years I have carefully reviewed the rules of evidence in an attempt to find the "background" exception to the hearsay rule. Thus far, I haven't been able to locate the rule; but it is firmly established in courthouse lore. . . . The so-called "Background" exception probably reflects the desire of courts to allow witnesses to relate events as they saw or heard them, that is, the urge is to allow the evidence to be presented as a "seamless web" without too much restriction by the exclusionary rules of evidence. . . . [A] little of this background information may be proper to show the effect on the hearer; but more than a little can likely work much mischief. (footnotes and citations omitted).

Crawford v. Washington—Criminal Cases

Until recently, the constitutional admissibility

of hearsay statements in criminal cases was determined according to the two-prong test of *Ohio v. Roberts*, 448 U.S. 56, 100 S. Ct. 2531, 65 L. Ed. 2d 597 (1980). Under this test, a court could admit statements made by a declarant if the prosecution showed that: (1) the declarant was unavailable, and (2) the statements were reliable, either because they fell within a "firmly rooted" hearsay exception or because they bore "particularized guarantees of trustworthiness." *Id.* at 66. Later, the Court refined the *Roberts* test, dispensing with the need to show unavailability when the declarant's statements fell within a firmly rooted exception. *See White v. Illinois*, 502 U.S. 346, 112 S. Ct. 736, 116 L. Ed. 2d 848 (1992).

In *Crawford v. Washington*, 541 U.S. 36, 124 S. Ct. 1354, 158 L. Ed. 2d 177 (2004) (discussed at Commentary under HEARSAY: AUTHOR'S NOTE CONFRONTATION-CRIMINAL CASES), the Supreme Court abandoned twenty-five years of precedent and abrogated *Roberts* with respect to prior *testimonial* statements by holding that *in criminal cases* such statements may never be introduced against the defendant unless the declarant is unavailable to testify and defendant had an opportunity to cross-examine the declarant, regardless of whether the statement falls within a firmly rooted hearsay exception or has particularized guarantees of trustworthiness. As the Third Circuit explained, "The lynchpin of the *Crawford* decision . . . is its distinction between testimonial and nontestimonial hearsay; simply put, the rule announced in *Crawford* applies only to the former category of statements." *U.S. v. Hendricks*, 395 F.3d 173, 179 (3d Cir. 2005).

The admissibility of "nontestimonial" hearsay for purposes of the Confrontation Clause continues to be governed by the standards set forth in *Ohio v. Roberts*. *U.S. v. Jimenez*, 513 F.3d 62 (3d Cir. 2008). Thus, in criminal cases the fundamental question with respect to the admissibility of hearsay evidence is, whether the out-of-court statements are testimonial or nontestimonial, the former governed by *Crawford* as to confrontation analysis and the latter by *Ohio v. Roberts*.

Rule 806

Rule 806 provides, in relevant part, that "[w]hen

a hearsay statement . . . has been admitted in evidence, the credibility of the declarant may be attacked, and if attacked may be supported, by any evidence which would be admissible for those purposes if the declarant had testified as a witness." *See U.S. v. Greenidge*, 495 F.3d 85 (3d Cir. 2007).

Additional References

Graham, Handbook of Federal Evidence §§ 801.1 to 801.10; 802.1 to 802.2 (7th ed. 2012)

Treatises and Practice Aids

Goode and Wellborn, Courtroom Handbook on Federal Evidence Chapter 5, Rules 801, 802 (annual ed.)
Binder, Hearsay Handbook Chapters 1 to 3 (4th ed. 2001)
McCormick, Evidence Chapter 24 (6th ed. 2006)
Park, Trial Objections Handbook §§ 4:1 to 4:19 (2nd ed. 2001)

HEARSAY: MULTIPLE HEARSAY

See:

Fed.R.Evid. 801, 802, 805
Mil.R.Evid. 801, 802, 805

Objection

- [*To a question*] Objection. The question calls for multiple hearsay.
- [*To a proposed exhibit*] Objection. The document is/contains multiple hearsay.
- [*To an answer*] Objection, multiple hearsay. I move the answer be stricken and the jury be instructed not to consider it for any purpose.

Response

- The evidence is admissible; both out-of-court statements qualify as hearsay exceptions [*specify*].

Commentary

Rule 805 makes hearsay within hearsay admissible only if each of the statements involved falls within an exception to the hearsay rule. *U.S. v. Payne*, 437 F.3d 540 (6th Cir. 2006); *Burns v. Board of County Com'rs of Jackson County*, 330 F.3d 1275 (10th Cir. 2003). Rule 805 provides:

> Hearsay included within hearsay is not excluded under the hearsay rule if each part of the combined statements conforms with an exception to the hearsay rule provided in these rules.

While the rule contains no limit on the levels of hearsay, it has been observed that "experience suggests an inverse relationship between the reliability of a statement and the number of hearsay layers it contains." *U.S. v. Fernandez*, 892 F.2d 976 (11th Cir. 1989).

For cases in which each level was found to be either a non-hearsay admission or to fall within a hearsay exception, *see, e.g.*, *Cook v. Arrowsmith Shelburne, Inc.*, 69 F.3d 1235 (2d Cir. 1995) (plaintiff permitted to testify that her supervisors told her she was being dismissed because general manager did not respect women in positions of authority and wanted man as replacement; supervisors' statements were admissions by agents of party opponent under Rule 801(d)(2)(D) and not hearsay); *Munley v. Carlson*, 125 F. Supp. 2d 1117 (N.D. Ill. 2000) (witness' testimony re statements made by plaintiff and his friend about supporting claims of police brutality and splitting proceeds of civil suit were admissible where first level was party admission under Rule 801(d)(2)(A) and second level was adoptive admission under Rule 801(d)(2)(B)); *In re Greenwood Air Crash*, 924 F. Supp. 1511 (S.D. Ind. 1995) (admitting police report of air crash containing statements by spouses of pilot and passenger re purpose for flight; some challenged statements were admissions while others came within Rule 803(3) "state of mind" exception). *See also Mister v. Northeast Illinois Commuter R.R. Corp.*, 571 F.3d 696 (7th Cir. 2009) (investigative report derived from multiple levels of hearsay admissible under hearsay rules but properly excluded under Rule 403 as totally unreliable; hearsay rules do not trump Rule 403); *U.S. v. Eagle*, 515 F.3d 794 (8th Cir. 2008) (by nature of cross-examination defendant opened the door to otherwise inadmissible double hearsay).

The fact that one level of a multi-level statement qualifies as a non-hearsay admission or comes within an exception does not excuse other levels from meeting the Rule 805 requirement that every level must satisfy the hearsay rule. *U.S. v. Kuo*, 2011 WL 145471 (E.D.N.Y 2011) (while 911 reports qualified as business recordings, the recordings contained therein were admissible only if statements made by 911 callers were themselves covered by an independent hearsay exception); *Reed v. Thalacker*, 198 F.3d 1058 (8th Cir. 1999) (in sex abuse case, doctor's testimony contained double hearsay: doctor related what mother told him daughter had said to mother; because the internal hearsay (what daughter told mother) was inadmissible, doctor's testimony was also inadmissible even if medical diagnosis exception applies to conversation between mother and doctor); *Halloway v. Milwaukee County*, 180 F.3d 820 (7th Cir. 1999) (in age discrimination case, plaintiff's statements of what two other persons said defendants told them about forcing plaintiff to retire were not admissible; even if inner layer [defendants' statements] were admissions, outer layer [statements of two other persons who had spoken with plaintiff] did not come within any hearsay exception); *Pittman by Pittman v. Grayson*, 149 F.3d 111 (2d Cir. 1998) (passenger's testimony that flight attendant said she had heard from others that Icelandair helped sneak mother and daughters from U.S. back to Iceland was inadmissible hearsay; content of story attributed to unidentified source was not shown to be non-hearsay or hearsay exception); *Carden v. Westinghouse Elec. Corp.*, 850 F.2d 996, 1001–02 (3d Cir. 1988) (testimony that supervisor said plaintiff did not get job because "he [supervisor] thought they wanted a younger person" was inadmissible; while supervisor's own statement was Rule 801(d)(2)(D) admission, no basis was provided for admitting statement that "they" made).

Double or multiple hearsay is frequently encountered with respect to the contents of business records and other documents.

Where the source of the information and the recorder of that information are not the same person, a business record contains hearsay upon hearsay. If both the source and recorder of the information were acting in the regular course of the organization's business, the double hearsay problem may be excused by the business records exception. Rule 803(6); *see U.S. v. Turner*, 189 F.3d 712 (8th Cir. 1999); *Insignia Systems Inc. v. News America Marketing In-Store, Inc.*, 2011 WL 382964 (D.Minn. 2011); *Larque v. SBC Communications Inc. Disability Income Plan, Core, Inc.*, 2005 WL 3447740 (W.D. Tex. 2005).

If the document is not a business record, other exceptions to the hearsay rule must be satisfied before its contents can be admitted. *See Southern Stone Co., Inc. v. Singer*, 665 F.2d 698 (5th Cir. 1982) (reversible error to admit letter written by plaintiff's attorney containing inculpatory statements allegedly made by one defendant; second level [defendant's statements] might qualify as admission but first level [attorney's statements] was pure hearsay with no applicable exception).

***Crawford v. Washington*—Criminal Cases**

In *Crawford v. Washington*, 541 U.S. 36, 124 S. Ct. 1354, 158 L. Ed. 2d 177 (2004) (discussed at

Commentary under HEARSAY: AUTHOR'S NOTE CONFRONTATION-CRIMINAL CASES), the Supreme Court held that an out-of-court testimonial statement cannot be admitted at trial unless the proponent establishes that: (1) the declarant is unavailable to testify, and (2) the defendant had a prior opportunity to cross-examine the declarant about his or her statement. *See U.S. v. Gibson*, 409 F.3d 325 (6th Cir. 2005) (double hearsay admissible as party opponent admissions; no Confrontation Clause violation since neither statement was testimonial in nature).

Additional References

Graham, Handbook of Federal Evidence § 805.1 (7th ed. 2012)

Treatises and Practice Aids

Goode and Wellborn, Courtroom Handbook on Federal Evidence Chapter 5, Rule 805 (annual ed.)

Mueller & Kirkpatrick, Federal Evidence, §§ 8:141, 8:142 (3d ed. 2007)

McCormick, Evidence § 324.1 (6th ed. 2006)

Park, Trial Objections Handbook §§ 4:82 to 4:84 (2nd ed. 2001)

HEARSAY EXEMPTION: ADMISSION—PARTY'S OWN STATEMENT

See:

Fed.R.Evid. 801(d)(2)(A)
Mil.R.Evid. 801(d)(2)(A)

Objection

- [*To a question*] Objection. The question calls for hearsay.
- [*To an answer*] Objection, hearsay. I move that the answer be stricken and the jury be instructed not to consider it for any purpose.

Response

- Under Rule 801(d)(2), an admission by a party opponent is not hearsay.

Commentary

A party's own statement made in his individual capacity is not hearsay when offered by an opposing party. Rule 801(d)(2)(A).

Perhaps because it is self-evident, a comprehensive definition of admission by party opponent is hard to find in the cases. Therefore, several are offered, as gleaned from the treatises:

1. Admissions are the words or acts of a party or a party's representative that are offered as evidence by the opposing party. They may be express admissions, which are statements of the opposing party . . . or admissions by conduct.*
2. Any relevant statement made by a party is evidence against himself.**
3. Anything the other side ever said or did will be admissible so long as it has something to do with the case.***

A statement need not be inculpatory, against interest or contrary to the trial position of the party

---

[Hearsay etc.]

*McCormick, Evidence § 254.

**Phipson on Evidence, Chapter 24, p. 619.

***Younger, Hearsay: A Practical Guide Through the Thicket § 3.2, p. 75.

to be admissible. *U.S. v. Reed*, 227 F.3d 763, 770 (7th Cir. 2000) (statements need not be incriminating, inculpatory, against interest or inherently damaging to the declarant's case); *U.S. v. McGee*, 189 F.3d 626, 631 (7th Cir. 1999) (rejecting contention that defendant's various accounts of his whereabouts on day of robbery were not admissible since none was inculpatory; "[No] Seventh Circuit case . . . establishes a requirement that admissions by a party-opponent be inculpatory to be admissible as nonhearsay under Rule 801"); *U.S. v. Turner*, 995 F.2d 1357, 1363 (6th Cir. 1993) ("On its face, Rule 801(d)(2) does not limit an admission to a statement against interest. Furthermore, this court has refused to place such a limited construction on the scope of an admission."). Rule 801(d)(2)(A) simply admits those statements made by one party, but offered as evidence by the opposing party.

There is no requirement that a party admission be based on personal knowledge, *Grace United Methodist Church v. City Of Cheyenne*, 451 F.3d 643 (10th Cir. 2006); *Blackburn v. United Parcel Service, Inc.*, 179 F.3d 81 (3d Cir. 1999); *Weinstein v. Siemens*, 2010 WL 4824855 (E.D.Mich. 2010); *S.E.C. v. Merrill Scott & Associates, Ltd.*, 505 F. Supp. 2d 1193 (D. Utah 2007), and the admission may be stated as an opinion. *Washington Public Power Supply System v. Pittsburgh-Des Moines Corp.*, 876 F.2d 690 (9th Cir. 1989); *Owens v. Atchison, T. & S. F. Ry. Co.*, 393 F.2d 77, 79 (5th Cir. 1968) ("[I]t is well settled that the opinion rule does not apply to a party's admissions."); *U.S. v. Bakshinian*, 65 F. Supp. 2d 1104 (C.D. Cal. 1999).

The Rule does not extend to a party's attempt to introduce his or her own statements through the testimony of other witnesses. *U.S. v. McDaniel*, 398 F.3d 540 (6th Cir. 2005) (defendant not permitted to question postal inspector on statements defendant allegedly made to her since that would have effectively allowed defendant to testify without being under oath, without cross-examination, and without direct scrutiny by jury); *U.S. v. Wilkerson*, 84 F.3d 692 (4th Cir. 1996); *see also U.S. ex rel. Fago v. M & T Mortg. Corp.*, 518 F. Supp. 2d 108 (D.D.C. 2007) (letter from lender's counsel to plaintiff's counsel could not be admitted as the admission of a party-opponent where the statement was being offered by the lender, the party that made the statement).

An admission (other than a "Judicial Admission" discussed *infra*) may be denied, explained, contradicted, or otherwise attacked by the party against whom it is offered, just like any other item of evidence introduced against the party. *Huey v. Honeywell, Inc.*, 82 F.3d 327 (9th Cir. 1996); *In re Initial Public Offering Securities Litigation*, 544 F. Supp. 2d 277 (S.D. N.Y. 2008).

It is black letter law that the testimony of one who is merely called as a witness for a party but who does not stand in privity with him may not be considered an admission by the party. *U.S. v. Harwood*, 998 F.2d 91 (2d Cir. 1993) (because co-defendant is not a party opponent, his statement could not be introduced by defendant as an admission; the government is the party opponent of both defendants); *Overstreet v. Kentucky Cent. Life Ins. Co.*, 950 F.2d 931 (4th Cir. 1991) (in suit for entitlement to insurance proceeds, statement of insured's mother that signature on insurance papers was not her son's was not admission; mother was not the plaintiff and her statement cannot bind the administrator, who is the plaintiff); *Vazquez v. National Car Rental System, Inc.*, 24 F. Supp. 2d 197 (D.P.R. 1998) (although a key figure in the facts surrounding the litigation, witness was not a party and his statement was not an admission).

Not all statements made by government agents will be treated as party admissions against the U.S. *U.S. v. Garza*, 448 F.3d 294 (5th Cir. 2006) (Justice Department investigator's report of local police officer's credibility was not a party admission); *U.S. v. Prevatte*, 16 F.3d 767 (7th Cir. 1994) (courts faced with this issue have refused to apply this provision to government employees testifying in criminal trials on grounds that no individual can bind the sovereign). *But see U.S. v. Salerno*, 937 F.2d 797 (2d Cir. 1991) (statements made by prosecutor, rather than some other government employee, are admissible against the government under Rule 801(d)(2)(D) because prosecutors have the power to bind the sovereign); accord *Litif v. U.S.*, 682 F.Supp.2d 60 (D.Mass. 2010).

In a criminal proceeding, statements by an accused prior to arrest are admissible against him as admissions. *U.S. v. Matlock*, 415 U.S. 164, 94 S. Ct. 988, 39 L. Ed. 2d 242 (1974). After arrest, statements must satisfy the requirements of *Miranda v. Arizona*, 384 U.S. 436, 86 S. Ct. 1602, 16 L. Ed. 2d 694 (1966) (prosecution may not use statements, whether exculpatory or inculpatory, stemming from custodial interrogation of defendant unless it demonstrates use of procedural safeguards effective to secure privilege against self-incrimination). *See also Rhode Island v. Innis*, 446 U.S. 291, 100 S. Ct. 1682, 64 L. Ed. 2d 297 (1980) (Miranda protections apply only when statements are made in response to express questioning or its functional equivalent); *U.S. v. Head*, 407 F.3d 925 (8th Cir. 2005) (suspect's statement that is voluntary and not in response to interrogation is admissible with or without the giving of *Miranda* warnings); *U.S. v. Hayes*, 120 F.3d 739 (8th Cir. 1997) (*Miranda* does not protect an accused from a spontaneous admission made under circumstances not induced by the investigating officers or during a conversation not initiated by the officers); *U.S. v. Lawrence*, 952 F.2d 1034 (8th Cir. 1992) (a volunteered statement made by a suspect, not in response to interrogation, is not barred by the Fifth Amendment and is admissible with or without the giving of *Miranda* warnings); *U.S. v. Colon*, 835 F.2d 27 (2d Cir. 1987) (once suspect invokes Miranda right to remain silent, any statements to police must be spontaneous and not the result of interrogation in order to be admissible).

For various types of statements which have been admitted as party admissions, *see: Ruffin v. City of Boston*, 146 Fed. Appx. 501 (1st Cir. 2005) (double-hearsay statements of arrestee in emergency medical technician's contemporaneous patient care report were admissible as non-hearsay statements of party opponent); *U.S. v. Anderson*, 243 F.3d 478 (8th Cir. 2001) (defendant's statements made during wiretapped phone calls, as related at trial by police officer who helped intercept calls); *accord U.S. v. DeAngelo*, 13 F.3d 1228 (8th Cir. 1994); *U.S. v. Ramirez-Cortez*, 213 F.3d 1149 (9th Cir. 2000) (transcript of prior deportation hearing where defendant stated he was a Mexican citizen); *U.S. v. Williams*, 205 F.3d 23 (2d Cir. 2000) (handwritten notation on cash advance receipt giving address at which defendant was staying was party admission contained within a business record); *U.S. v. Billingsley*, 160 F.3d 502 (8th Cir. 1998) (police officer's testimony paraphrasing contents of taped conversation between defendant and his heroin supplier were admissions; defendant's statements were voluntary even though made pursuant to cooperation agreement with police); *U.S. v. Dixon*, 132 F.3d 192 (5th Cir. 1997) (defendant's recorded statements during conversation with government informant); *Tamez v. City of San Marcos, Texas*, 118 F.3d 1085 (5th Cir. 1997) (answers to interrogatories); *Arnold v. Groose*, 109 F.3d 1292 (8th Cir. 1997) (plaintiff prisoner's *pro se* pleadings from earlier § 1983 suit against prison officials); *U.S. v. Williams*, 104 F.3d 213 (8th Cir. 1997) (a guilty plea is admissible in subsequent collateral criminal trial as admission by party opponent); *U.S. v. Haun*, 90 F.3d 1096 (6th Cir. 1996), *U.S. v. Workinger*, 90 F.3d 1409 (9th Cir. 1996) (transcript of defendant's deposition); *Roger Kennedy Const., Inc. v. Amerisure Ins. Co.*, 506 F. Supp. 2d 1185 (M.D. Fla. 2007) (records prepared by plaintiff that were attached to affidavit submitted by defendant in support of summary judgment admissible against plaintiff as admission of party); *Metro-Goldwyn-Mayer Studios, Inc. v. Grokster, Ltd.*, 454 F. Supp. 2d 966 (C.D. Cal. 2006) (documents that bore defendant's trade names, logos, and trademarks); *Samaritan Health Center v. Simplicity Health Care Plan*, 459 F. Supp. 2d 786 (E.D. Wis. 2006) (opponent's expert report, for purposes of getting statements into record for summary judgment); *Vermont Elec. Power Co., Inc. v. Hartford Steam Boiler Inspection and Ins. Co.*, 72 F. Supp. 2d 441 (D. Vt. 1999) (plaintiff company's e-mails); *Guadagno v. Wallack Ader Levithan Associates*, 932 F. Supp. 94 (S.D. N.Y. 1996) (company's formal tax statements of its number of employees were admissions in Title VII action); *U.S. ex rel. Milam v. Regents of University of California*, 912 F. Supp. 868 (D. Md. 1995) (*in qui tam* action, United States is real party in interest and report of its scientific oversight agency is an admission under Rule 801(d)(2)(A)).

See also Keller v. U.S., 58 F.3d 1194, 1199 n.8 (7th Cir. 1995) and *Guadagno v. Wallack Ader Levithan Associates*, 950 F. Supp. 1258, 1261 (S.D. N.Y. 1997) (contrasting the spontaneous and imprecise nature of deposition and trial testimony with answers to contention interrogatories drafted by counsel and discussing why it is generally preferable to treat deposition or trial testimony as an evidentiary admission and not as a judicial admission).

Crawford v. Washington—Criminal Cases

The impact of *Crawford v. Washington*, 541 U.S. 36, 124 S. Ct. 1354, 158 L. Ed. 2d 177 (2004) on the law of hearsay in criminal cases is discussed at Commentary under HEARSAY: AUTHOR'S NOTE CONFRONTATION-CRIMINAL CASES. *See also U.S. v. Tolliver*, 454 F.3d 660, 665–66 (7th Cir. 2006) (when the defendant is the declarant the admission of tape recorded conversations between defendant and an informant did not violate the Confrontation Clause because defendant's statements were 801(d)(2)(A) nonhearsay admissions by a party opponent); *U.S. v. Brown*, 441 F.3d 1330 (11th Cir. 2006) (admitting into evidence the statement of a party-opponent does not violate the Sixth Amendment's Confrontation Clause); *U.S. v. Lafferty*, 387 F. Supp. 2d 500 (W.D. Pa. 2005) (Sixth Amendment does not guarantee defendant right to cross-examine herself as to her own admissions); *see also* 4 Weinstein & Berger, Weinstein's Federal Evidence § 802.05 [3][d] at 802–25 (2d ed. 2005) (noting that "a party cannot seriously claim that his or her own statement should be excluded because it was not made under oath or subject to cross-examination").

Additional References

Graham, Handbook of Federal Evidence § 801.16 (7th ed. 2012)

Treatises and Practice Aids

Goode and Wellborn, Courtroom Handbook on Federal Evidence Chapter 5, Rule 801(d)(2) and Obj. 37 (annual ed.)

Binder, Hearsay Handbook Chapter 35 (4th ed. 2001)

McCormick, Evidence Chapter 25 (6th ed. 2006)

Park, Trial Objections Handbook § 4:12 (2nd ed. 2001)

HEARSAY EXEMPTION: ADOPTIVE ADMISSION

See:

Fed.R.Evid. 801(d)(2)(B)
Mil.R.Evid. 801(d)(2)(B)

Objection

- [*To a question*] Objection. The question calls for hearsay.
- [*To an answer*] Objection, hearsay. I move that the answer be stricken and the jury be instructed not to consider it for any purpose.

Response

- The statement/document is an adoptive admission. The evidence establishes that plaintiff/defendant heard, understood and acquiesced in the statement [*specify*] and manifested adoption by [*specify*].

Commentary

Under Rule 801(d)(2)(B), evidence is not hearsay if it "is offered against a party and is . . . a statement of which the party has manifested an adoption or belief in its truth."

An adoptive admission is dependent upon a showing by the proponent of the evidence that the party-opponent heard, understood and acquiesced in the statement. *U.S. v. Lafferty*, 503 F.3d 293, 306 (3d Cir. 2007) (there must be sufficient foundational facts from which the jury may infer that the defendant heard, understood, and acquiesced in the statement); *U.S. v. Jinadu*, 98 F.3d 239 (6th Cir. 1996); *U.S. v. Jenkins*, 779 F.2d 606 (11th Cir. 1986); *Lear Automotive Dearborn, Inc. v. Johnson Controls. Inc.*, ___ F.Supp.2d ___ (E.D. Mich. 2011) (discussing "adoption by use" of survey results).

Adoption, which may be express or implied, can be manifested by any appropriate means, such as language, conduct or silence. *U.S. v. Magbaleta*, 234 Fed. Appx. 718, 719 (9th Cir. 2007) (National Park Service medical screening form admissible as adoptive admission in criminal prosecution; defendant signed the form, thereby manifesting an adoption or belief in its truth); *Schering Corp. v. Pfizer Inc.*, 189 F.3d 218 (2d Cir. 1999) (in action under Lanham Act for false advertising, where Pfizer employee helped design physician's survey and later wrote report analyzing its results, survey was adoptive admission); *Jinadu*, 98 F.3d at 244 (defendant's reply "yes" to agent's question "you know that's China White heroin" adopted the contents of the question); *U.S. v. Warren*, 42 F.3d 647, 655 (D.C. Cir. 1994) (sworn affidavit submitted to magistrate to obtain search warrant was admissible as nonhearsay statement offered against the government which had "manifested an adoption or belief in its truth."); *Alvord-Polk, Inc. v. F. Schumacher & Co.*, 37 F.3d 996 (3d Cir. 1994) (statements by trade association president and its chief executive in article written by association employee and appearing in its newsletter were adoptive admissions); *Wagstaff v. Protective Apparel Corp. of America, Inc.*, 760 F.2d 1074 (10th Cir. 1985) (by reprinting newspaper articles and distributing them to persons with whom they were doing business, defendants unequivocally manifested their adoption of the inflated financial information contained therein; error to preclude this relevant evidence of fraud); *In re Japanese Electronic Products Antitrust Litigation*, 723 F.2d 238, 300–01 (3d Cir. 1983), decision rev'd on other grounds, 475 U.S. 574, 106 S. Ct. 1348, 89 L. Ed. 2d 538 (1986) (contents of documents referred to by defendants in answering plaintiff's interrogatories pursuant to Fed.R.Civ.P. 33(c) were admissible against defendants as adoptive admissions). *But see Lafferty*, 503 F.3d at 305–07 (silence in the face of questioning after being given *Miranda* warnings cannot be used to establish an adoptive admission on the part of the defendant).

In determining whether adoption of a statement has occurred, an examination must be conducted into the surrounding circumstances to see whether those circumstances indicate approval of the statement. *U.S. v. Missouri*, 535 F.3d 844 (8th Cir. 2008) (where state merely passed survey responses along to federal government with no indication state was adopting their truth, responses were not adoptive admissions). If a party expresses agreement with investigative findings, or implies agreement by taking action in accordance therewith, it may be held to have adopted the findings. *Wright-Simmons v. City of Oklahoma City*, 155 F.3d 1264 (10th Cir. 1998) (where city conducted investigation and prepared report on racial harassment of employee which was then used as basis to force supervisor's resignation, report constituted adoptive admission); *Pilgrim v. Trustees of Tufts College*, 118 F.3d 864 (1st Cir. 1997) (college president's acceptance of contents of grievance committee's report and his implementation of its recommendations without disclaimer served as adoption of report).

Failure to contest an assertion is considered evidence of acquiescence only if it would have been natural under the circumstances to object to the assertion in question. *U.S. v. Duval*, 496 F.3d 64, 76 (1st Cir. 2007) (testimony of informant, who claimed that co-defendant said that he and defendant wanted to sell firearms in their possession was admissible as an adoptive admission, where defendant was in the small room and it could be reasonably inferred that defendant heard co-defendant's statement but did not disassociate himself from statements); *U.S. v. Henke*, 222 F.3d 633 (9th Cir. 2000) (evidence that defendant, as corporation's chief executive officer, responded "next question please" to accusation during press conference that company was "cooking the books" was admissible as adoptive admission in insider trading prosecution; natural response to such accusation would have been to address or deny it); *Southern Stone Co., Inc. v. Singer*, 665 F.2d 698, 703 (5th Cir. 1982) (where only foundation was failure to respond, error to admit letter written by plaintiff's attorney setting forth inculpatory statements allegedly made by addressee about business transactions which contained request for response if contents were inaccurate; "mere failure to respond to a letter does not indicate an adoption unless it was reasonable under the circumstances for the sender to expect the recipient to respond and to correct erroneous assertions."); *Hellenic Lines Limited v. Gulf Oil Corp.*, 340 F.2d 398 (2d Cir. 1965) (failure to respond to letter, under circumstances reasonably calling for reply, constitutes admission by silence).

Although some decisions appear to suggest that

mere possession of incriminating documents is sufficient to constitute adoption, *U.S. v. Marino*, 658 F.2d 1120 (6th Cir. 1981) (possession of airline tickets offered to prove drug defendants traveled in interstate commerce), the view has been criticized. *See* Graham, Handbook of Federal Evidence, § 801. 21. In *U.S. v. Paulino*, 13 F.3d 20, 24 (1st Cir. 1994), the appeals court said the correct approach is "possession plus," *i.e.* so long as the surrounding circumstances tie the possessor and the document together in some meaningful way, the possessor may be found to have adopted the writing and embraced its contents. In *Paulino*, a money order receipt in defendant's name (found along with drugs, drug paraphernalia, and a gun in an apartment which defendant was seen frequenting was an adoptive admission to show defendant paid rent on premises used as a drug distribution center). *Accord, U.S. v. Watters*, 237 Fed. Appx. 376, 382 (10th Cir. 2007) (because the letters admitted at trial were addressed to "John," discussed growing crops, and depicted images of a barn similar to that found on Watters' property, they are tied in a meaningful way to him and were admissible in his prosecution for possessing marijuana plants); *U.S. v. Ospina*, 739 F.2d 448, 451 (9th Cir. 1984) (business cards containing hotel phone number and room of other conspirators and address where cocaine was transferred; "when a person acts on written instructions and the instructions are found in his possession, the instructions are admissible as adopted admissions under Rule 801.") *But see U.S. v. Ramirez*, 479 F.3d 1229, 1246 (10th Cir. 2007) (cell phone receipts possessed by defendant at his arrest did not constitute adoptive admissions where receipts were dated only seven days before defendant's arrest, government did not demonstrate that defendant possessed the two cellular phones, defendant's name was not on the receipts, and the registrants of the phones and the individuals who paid the bills were not identified).

Crawford v. Washington—Criminal Cases

The impact of *Crawford v. Washington*, 541 U.S. 36, 124 S. Ct. 1354, 158 L. Ed. 2d 177 (2004) on the law of hearsay in criminal cases is discussed at Commentary under HEARSAY: AUTHOR'S NOTE

CONFRONTATION-CRIMINAL CASES. *See also Sanchez v. Dexter*, 2008 WL 1766729 (C.D. Cal. 2008) (the Confrontation Clause is not implicated because adoptive admissions are nonhearsay); *U.S. v. Lafferty ("Lafferty II")*, 387 F. Supp. 2d 500 (W.D. Pa. 2005) (adoptive admission can be admitted against a defendant without the right to cross-examination; inherent in Justice Scalia's *Crawford* analysis is the idea that the right of confrontation exists as to accusations of third parties implicating a criminal defendant, not a criminal defendant implicating herself).

Additional References

Graham, Handbook of Federal Evidence §§ 801.20 to 801.21 (7th ed. 2012)

Treatises and Practice Aids

Goode and Wellborn, Courtroom Handbook on Federal Evidence Chapter 5, Rule 801(d)(2) and Obj. 37 (annual ed.)

Mueller & Kirkpatrick, Federal Evidence, §§ 8:35 to 8:49 (3d ed. 2007)

Binder, Hearsay Handbook Chapter 35 (4th ed. 2001)

McCormick, Evidence Chapter 25 (6th ed. 2006)

Park, Trial Objections Handbook §§ 4:12 to 4:13 (2nd ed. 2001)

HEARSAY EXEMPTION: ADMISSION BY AGENT

See:

Fed.R.Evid. 801(d)(2)(D)
Mil.R.Evid. 801(d)(2)(D)

Objection

- [*To a question*] Objection. The question calls for hearsay.
- [*To an answer*] Objection, hearsay. I move that the answer be stricken and the jury be instructed not to consider it for any purpose.

Response

- The statement qualifies as an admission by a party opponent. It was made by [*plaintiff's / defendant's*] agent concerning a matter within the scope of [*agency / employment*] and was made during the existence of that relationship.

Commentary

Rule 801(d)(2)(D) provides that a statement is not hearsay if it "is offered against a party and is . . . a statement by the party's agent or servant concerning a matter within the scope of the agency or employment, made during the existence of that relationship." *Nekolny v. Painter*, 653 F.2d 1164, 1172 (7th Cir. 1981) (such statements are presumably reliable in the absence of cross-examination because an agent "who speaks on any matter within the scope of his agency or employment during the existence of that relationship, is unlikely to make statements damaging to his principal or employer unless those statements are true.").

In order for a statement to be admissible under Rule 801(d)(2)(D), the offering party must make a threefold showing that: (1) an agency or employment relationship existed between the declarant and the party, (2) the statement was made during the agency or employment relationship, and (3) the statement concerned a matter within the declarant's scope of agency or employment. *Marcic v. Reinauer Transp. Companies*, 397 F.3d 120 (2nd Cir. 2005); *Boren v. Sable*, 887 F.2d 1032, 1038

(10th Cir. 1989); *Guzman v. Abbott Laboratories*, 59 F. Supp. 2d 747 (N.D. Ill. 1999) (to be admissible, the statement must concern *matters within the scope of declarant's employment*, not just made during employment). These predicates may be shown by circumstantial evidence, as long as the evidence is more than simply the statement itself. *Aumand v. Dartmouth Hitchcock Medical Center*, 611 F. Supp. 2d 78 (D.N.H. 2009).

Although the rules do not define the term "agent," courts have held that Congress intended Rule 801(d)(2)(D) to describe the traditional master-servant relationship as understood by common law agency doctrine. *City of Tuscaloosa v. Harcros Chemicals, Inc.*, 158 F.3d 548, 557 n.9 (11th Cir. 1998) (at common law, senior officers of corporation normally are agents and servants of corporation); *American Eagle Ins. Co. v. Thompson*, 85 F.3d 327 (8th Cir. 1996); *Lippay v. Christos*, 996 F.2d 1490 (3d Cir. 1993); *Boren v. Sable*, 887 F.2d at 1038.

The existence of agency at the time of the statements and the scope of the employment are preliminary matters for the trial court under Rule 104(a). *See In re Coordinated Pretrial Proceedings in Petroleum Products Antitrust Litigation*, 906 F.2d 432 (9th Cir. 1990).

In determining the agency or employment relationship and its scope, the court must consider the contents of the statement but must also find other supporting evidence independent of the proffered statement. Rule 801(d)(2); *Krause v. City of La Crosse*, 246 F.3d 995, 1002 (7th Cir. 2001) (assistant police chief was not acting within scope of his employment when he discussed alleged motivations of city finance department in dealing with plaintiff; "To hold otherwise would hold a city accountable for statements made by any city employee and Rule 801(d)(2)(D) does not cast such a wide net."); *Hilao v. Estate of Marcos*, 103 F.3d 767 (9th Cir. 1996) (human rights class action; district court properly relied on military members' statements to victims and expert testimony in determining that agency relationship existed between former Philippines president and military members who tortured victims); *Brundidge v. City of Buffalo*, 79 F. Supp. 2d 219 (W.D. N.Y. 1999) (district attorney's statement that arrest was illegal was not admission of party opponent in arrestee's § 1983 action; attorney was not agent of police officers but rather an agent of the state).

This rule (unlike 801(d)(2)(C)) does not require that the agent have the authority to speak for the employer in order to admit the agent's statement into evidence, but only that the statement concern a matter within the scope of agency or employment and be made during the existence of that relationship. *U.S. v. Photogrammetric Data Services, Inc.*, 259 F.3d 229 (4th Cir. 2001) (in fraud prosecution, corporate manager's statements to government informant about his billing practices and procedures were statements concerning matters within scope and during existence of his employment and, thus, admissible against corporate defendant); *U.S. v. Brothers Const. Co. of Ohio*, 219 F.3d 300 (4th Cir. 2000) (grand jury testimony of officer and in-house counsel properly admitted as admission against corporate defendant; because corporation can act only through its employees, statement by corporate official can be admission by corporation); *Big Apple BMW, Inc. v. BMW of North America, Inc.*, 974 F.2d 1358, 1372 (3d Cir. 1992) ("[T]he vicarious admission rule of Federal Rule of Evidence 801(d)(2)(D) does not require that a declarant have the authority to bind its employer."); *Wilkinson v. Carnival Cruise Lines, Inc.*, 920 F.2d 1560 (11th Cir. 1991) (It is not necessary to show that employee or agent declarant possess "speaking authority" tested by usual standards of agency before a statement can be admitted against the principal. It is only necessary that the content of the declarant's statement concern a matter within the scope of his employment or agency.); *Hill v. F.R. Tripler & Co., Inc.*, 868 F. Supp. 593 (S.D. N.Y. 1994).

Not all statements made by government agents will be treated as party admissions against the United States. *U.S. v. Garza*, 448 F.3d 294 (5th Cir. 2006) (Justice Department investigator's report of local police officer's credibility was not a party admission); *U.S. v. Prevatte*, 16 F.3d 767 (7th Cir. 1994) (courts faced with this issue have refused to apply this provision to government employees testifying in criminal trials on rationale that no individual can bind the sovereign). *But see U.S. v.*

Salerno, 937 F.2d 797 (2d Cir. 1991) (statements made by prosecutor, rather than some other government employee, are admissible against the government under Rule 801(d)(2)(D) because prosecutors have the power to bind the sovereign).

Like all admissions, there is no requirement that the speaker had personal knowledge, *Blackburn v. United Parcel Service, Inc.*, 179 F.3d 81 (3d Cir. 1999); *Aumand*, 611 F.Supp.2d at 95, and the statement may be phrased in the form of an opinion. *U.S. v. Bakshinian*, 65 F. Supp. 2d 1104 (C.D. Cal. 1999).

An admission (other than a "Judicial Admission," discussed *infra*) may be denied, explained, contradicted, or otherwise attacked by the party against whom it is offered, just like any other item of evidence introduced against a party. *Huey v. Honeywell, Inc.*, 82 F.3d 327 (9th Cir. 1996).

The hearsay rules do not trump all other Rules of Evidence and statements can be excluded pursuant to Rule 403 where undue prejudice outweighs probative value. *See, e.g., Mister v. Northeast Illinois Commuter R.R. Corp.*, 571 F.3d 696 (7th Cir. 2009) (safety report met requirements of Rule 801(d)(2)(D) but inadmissible under Rule 403).

Employment Discrimination

Some courts hold that an employee's statement regarding a particular action of the employer qualifies as an admission only if the employee-declarant was involved in the decision making process leading up to the employer's action. *Bell v. E.P.A.*, 232 F.3d 546 (7th Cir. 2000) (memo written by member of EPA's promotion selection panel stating that plaintiffs were superior to other applicants for promotion admissible in Title VII action as admission by party opponent); *Pastran v. K-Mart Corp.*, 210 F.3d 1201 (10th Cir. 2000) (K-Mart district manager's statements that failure to promote plaintiff was wrong and unprofessional was party admission since she was K-Mart's agent and the statement concerned a matter within the scope of her employment); *Jacklyn v. Schering-Plough Healthcare Products Sales Corp.*, 176 F.3d 921 (6th Cir. 1999) (supervisor's alleged statement that central regional manager said he did not want "skirts" working for him was not an admission; supervisor was not plaintiff's direct manager at any relevant time and was not involved in any of the critical appraisals of employee's performance that preceded her leaving company); *Moore v. KUKA Welding Systems & Robot Corp.*, 171 F.3d 1073 (6th Cir. 1999) (where evidence indicated that supervisor used one employee to deliver message to coworker that bad stuff was going to happen and he should stay out of it or be fired, court could find that declarant was being used as company's agent and message was non-hearsay admission); *Swanson v. Leggett & Platt, Inc.*, 154 F.3d 730, 733 (7th Cir. 1998) (former CEO's statement that "age" was factor in reductions in force did not constitute an admission attributable to corporation; "[o]nly evidence on the attitudes of employees involved in the decision to fire the plaintiffs is relevant."); *U.S. v. Rioux*, 97 F.3d 648, 661 (2d Cir. 1996) (upholding admission where declarant was an "advisor or other significant participant in the decision making process" that is the subject matter of the statement); *Woodman v. Haemonetics Corp.*, 51 F.3d 1087, 1094 (1st Cir. 1995) (upholding admission where declarant "was directly involved in the reduction in force" leading to plaintiff's termination); *Goss v. George Washington University*, 942 F. Supp. 659 (D.D.C. 1996) (for statement to qualify in employment discrimination action as party admission, declarant must have actually been involved in decision to hire or fire person bringing discrimination charge).

But a number of decisions say it is not necessary that the declarant be an actual decision-maker. Significant involvement, either as advisor or other participant in a process leading to a challenged decision, may be sufficient to establish agency under Rule 801(d)(2)(D). *Talavera v. Shah*, 638 F.3d 303 (D.C.Cir. 2011); *Simple v. Walgreen Co.*, 511 F.3d 668 (7th Cir. 2007) (declarant not involved in employment action but was involved in process that led up to that action); *Marra v. Philadelphia Housing Authority*, 497 F.3d 286 (3d Cir. 2007) (personal involvement in employment decision being litigated is not an absolute prerequisite to admission of employee's statement against his employer); *Williams v. Pharmacia, Inc.*, 137 F.3d 944 (7th Cir. 1998).

Former Employees

Since a former employee is no longer an agent of the corporation, a statement made after employment has ceased is not an admission attributable to the organization. *Cruz v. Aramark Services, Inc.*, 213 Fed. Appx. 329, 333 (5th Cir. 2007); *Walsh v. McCain Foods Ltd.*, 81 F.3d 722 (7th Cir. 1996); *Blanchard v. Peoples Bank*, 844 F.2d 264 (5th Cir. 1988); *Jenkins v. Wal-Mart Stores, Inc.*, 956 F. Supp. 695 (W.D. La. 1997).

Unidentified Declarant

The fact that the declarant is not identified by name does not preclude admission, if it is sufficiently established that he or she was an agent or servant and not an unrelated third party and that the statement concerned a matter with the scope of agency or employment. *Belton v. Washington Metropolitan Area Transit Authority*, 20 F.3d 1197 (D.C. Cir. 1994) (at first trial, investigating police officer testified that bus driver said plaintiff was running alongside bus banging on door but also admitted he really did not know whether statement came from driver, witnesses or fellow officer; on retrial, statement would not be allowable as an admission unless officer could trace it to driver); *Meder v. Everest & Jennings, Inc.*, 637 F.2d 1182 (8th Cir. 1981) (statement does not qualify as admission where witness cannot trace it to party against whom it is offered); *Thomas v. Stone Container Corp.*, 922 F. Supp. 950 (S.D. N.Y. 1996) (where there was no evidence to identify speaker, even by job function, there was nothing to show statement was made by agent concerning matter within scope of his employment); *Hill v. F.R. Tripler & Co., Inc.*, 868 F.Supp. at 593 (in tort action for injuries suffered by customer who walked into glass door, an unidentified speaker asked why there was no warning sign; evidence that declarant wore business attire, used store manager's name and went to find plaintiff's mother in store was sufficient to show he was Tripler's employee).

Deposition Testimony

See Fed.R.Civ.P. 32(a)(2) which provides:

The deposition of a party or of anyone who at the

time of taking the deposition was an officer, director, or managing agent, or a person designated under Rule 30(b)(6) or 31(a) to testify on behalf of a public or private corporation, partnership or association or governmental agency which is a party may be used by an adverse party for any purpose.

Crawford v. Washington—Criminal Cases

The impact of *Crawford v. Washington*, 541 U.S. 36, 124 S. Ct. 1354, 158 L. Ed. 2d 177 (2004), on the law of hearsay in criminal cases is discussed at Commentary under HEARSAY: AUTHOR'S NOTE CONFRONTATION-CRIMINAL CASES. *See also U.S. v. Yi*, 460 F.3d 623, 634 (5th Cir. 2006) (assuming without deciding that rule 801(d)(2)(D) survived *Crawford*); *U.S. v. Petraia Maritime Ltd.*, 489 F. Supp. 2d 90, 95 n.4 (D. Me. 2007) (because 801(d)(2)(D) admissions of defendant are defined as "not hearsay," their admission, even for the truth, does not violate the Confrontation Clause); *U.S. v. Lafferty*, 387 F. Supp. 2d 500 (W.D. Pa. 2005) (Sixth Amendment does not guarantee defendant right to cross-examine herself as to her own admissions); *see also* 4 Weinstein & Berger, Weinstein's Federal Evidence § 802.05 [3][d] at 802–25 (2d ed. 2005) (noting that "a party cannot seriously claim that his or her own statement should be excluded because it was not made under oath or subject to cross-examination").

Additional References

Graham, Handbook of Federal Evidence § 801.23 (7th ed. 2012)

Treatises and Practice Aids

Goode and Wellborn, Courtroom Handbook on Federal Evidence Chapter 5, Rule 801(d)(2) and Obj. 37 (annual ed.)

Mueller & Kirkpatrick, Federal Evidence, §§ 8:53 to 8:57 (3d ed. 2007)

Binder, Hearsay Handbook Chapter 35 (4th ed. 2001)

McCormick, Evidence Chapter 25 (6th ed. 2006)

Park, Trial Objections Handbook § 4:14 (2nd ed. 2001)

HEARSAY EXEMPTION: ADMISSION BY COCONSPIRATOR

See:

Fed.R.Evid. 801(d)(2)(E)
Mil.R.Evid. 801(d)(2)(E)

Objection

- *[To a question]* Objection. The question calls for hearsay.
- *[To an answer]* Objection, hearsay. I move that the answer be stricken and the jury be instructed not to consider it for any purpose.

Response

- The statement is the admission of a coconspirator. As foundation, I have established that: (i) a conspiracy did, in fact, exist; (ii) the declarant and the defendant were members of the conspiracy; and (iii) the statement was made during the course of and in furtherance of the conspiracy.

Commentary

Rule 801(d)(2)(E) provides that "[a] statement is not hearsay if . . . [it] is offered against a party and is . . . a statement by a coconspirator of a party during the course and in furtherance of the conspiracy."

The rationale for the exception is based on principles of agency. During the course of a conspiracy, each conspirator is considered the agent of the other and, thus, a statement by one is an admission by all. *U.S. v. Russo*, 302 F.3d 37 (2d Cir. 2002); *U.S. v. Lampley*, 68 F.3d 1296 (11th Cir. 1995); *U.S. v. Olweiss*, 138 F.2d 798 (C.C.A. 2d Cir. 1943); *Van Riper v. U.S.*, 13 F.2d 961 (C.C.A. 2d Cir. 1926) (Learned Hand, J.). If the statement is made in furtherance of and during the continuance of the common purpose of the conspiracy, it is admissible against all. When a person joins an existing conspiracy, he is deemed to have adopted all prior assertions of the conspirators made during the course and in furtherance of the conspiracy. *See United States v. U.S. Gypsum Co.*, 333 U.S.

364, 68 S. Ct. 525, 92 L. Ed. 746 (1948); *U.S. v. Rodriguez-Gonzalez*, 433 F.3d 165 (1st Cir. 2005).

The admissibility of coconspirators' statements under Rule 801(d)(2)(E) is determined by the trial court pursuant to Rule 104(a), which permits consideration of any non-privileged evidence, regardless of its admissibility. *Qualley v. Clo-Tex Intern., Inc.*, 212 F.3d 1123, 1130 (8th Cir. 2000); *Re/Max Intern., Inc. v. Realty One, Inc.*, 173 F.3d 995, 1012 (6th Cir. 1999).

To admit statements under this rule, the proponent must establish by a preponderance of the evidence that: (1) there was a conspiracy; (2) its members included the declarant and the party against whom the statement is now being offered; and (3) the statement was made both (a) during the course of, and (b) in furtherance of the conspiracy. *Bourjaily v. United States*, 483 U.S. 171, 107 S. Ct. 2775, 97 L. Ed. 2d 144 (1987); *U.S. v. Engler*, 521 F.3d 965 (8th Cir. 2008); *U.S. v. Hall*, 500 F.3d 439 (5th Cir. 2007); *U.S. v. Payne*, 437 F.3d 540 (6th Cir. 2006); *U.S. v. Flemmi*, 402 F.3d 79 (1st Cir. 2005); *U.S. v. Skidmore*, 254 F.3d 635 (7th Cir. 2001); *U.S. v. Dickerson*, 248 F.3d 1036 (11th Cir. 2001); *U.S. v. Heckard*, 238 F.3d 1222 (10th Cir. 2001); *U.S. v. Beckman*, 222 F.3d 512 (8th Cir. 2000); *U.S. v. Ellis*, 156 F.3d 493 (3d Cir. 1998); *U.S. v. Asibor*, 109 F.3d 1023 (5th Cir. 1997). The statement of a conspirator offered for its truth by a co-conspirator is not within this Rule. *U.S. v. Milstein*, 401 F.3d 53 (2d Cir. 2005).

While the trial court may consider the hearsay statement itself to determine the existence of a conspiracy, *Bourjaily*, 483 U.S. at 181, there must be some independent corroborating evidence of the defendant's participation in the conspiracy. *U.S. v. Conrad*, 507 F.3d 424, 429 (6th Cir. 2007) (because hearsay is presumptively unreliable, sufficient independent and corroborating evidence of co-conspirator's knowledge and participation in the conspiracy must be produced to rebut and overcome the presumed unreliability of the proffered out-of-court statement); *U.S. v. Desena*, 260 F.3d 150 (2d Cir. 2001). As the Advisory Committee Note explains: "The contents of the declarant's statement do not alone suffice to establish a conspiracy in which the declarant and the defendant participated. The court must consider in addition the circumstances surrounding the statement, such as the identity of the speaker, the context in which the statement was made, or evidence corroborating the contents of the statement in making its determination as to each preliminary question. Every court of appeals that has resolved this issue requires some evidence in addition to the contents of the statements." Fed.R.Evid. 801 Advisory Committee Note; *see also U.S. v. Aviles-Colon*, 536 F.3d 1 (1st Cir. 2008) (to establish that a conspiracy embracing both the declarant and the defendant existed, extrinsic evidence is needed because coconspirator statements are not deemed self-elucidating); *U.S. v. Payne*, 437 F.3d 540, 544–45 (6th Cir. 2006) (independent and corroborating evidence of defendant's participation in conspiracy provided by another participant in their counterfeiting scheme); *U.S. v. Petty*, 132 F.3d 373 (7th Cir. 1997) (requirement of independent evidence can be satisfied by testimony of nonconspirators or by corroboration of facts contained in conspirators' statements).

In *U.S. v. James*, 590 F.2d 575 (5th Cir. 1979), the Fifth Circuit explained that a court may choose to hold a pre-trial hearing to determine whether each statement that the Government plans to introduce meets the requirements of 801(d)(2)(E). The Sixth Circuit, however, states that a court may choose one of three methods when dealing with 801(d)(2)(E) statements: (1) hold a pretrial mini-hearing; (2) require the Government to meet its initial burden by producing non-hearsay evidence of conspiracy prior to determining admissibility of the hearsay statements; or (3) admit the evidence subject to a ruling on whether the Government has met the standards of 801(d)(2)(E) by a preponderance of the evidence at the close of the prosecution's case-in-chief. *U.S. v. Vinson*, 606 F.2d 149, 152–53 (6th Cir. 1979).

The Confrontation Clause does not require a showing of unavailability as a condition to the admission of out-of-court statements of a nontestifying co-conspirator when those statements otherwise satisfy the requirements of Rule 801(d)(2)(E). *United States v. Inadi*, 475 U.S. 387, 106 S. Ct. 1121, 89 L. Ed. 2d 390 (1986); *U.S. v. Gardner*, 447 F.3d 558

(8th Cir. 2006).

The exception applies in both criminal and civil cases. *World of Sleep, Inc. v. La-Z-Boy Chair Co.*, 756 F.2d 1467 (10th Cir. 1985); *Filco v. Amana Refrigeration, Inc.*, 709 F.2d 1257 (9th Cir. 1983). It also applies even where no party has been formally charged with conspiracy. *U.S. v. Washington*, 434 F.3d 7 (1st Cir. 2006); *U.S. v. Godinez*, 110 F.3d 448 (7th Cir. 1997); *U.S. v. Swidan*, 888 F.2d 1076 (6th Cir. 1989); *U.S. v. Trowery*, 542 F.2d 623 (3d Cir. 1976). Moreover, the conspiracy between the declarant and the defendant need not be identical to any conspiracy that is specifically charged in the indictment. *U.S. v. Gigante*, 166 F.3d 75 (2d Cir. 1999); *U.S. v. Narviz-Guerra*, 148 F.3d 530 (5th Cir. 1998).

"In Furtherance" Requirement

The requirement that the words spoken be "in furtherance of the conspiracy" implies that the statements must, in some way, have been designed to promote or facilitate achievement of the goals of the ongoing conspiracy. *U.S. v. Lopez*, 649 F.3d 1222 (11th Cir. 2011) (statement need not be necessary to the conspiracy but must only further the interests of the conspiracy in some way); *U.S. v. Maldonado-Rivera*, 922 F.2d 934, 958 (2d Cir. 1990) (statements in furtherance of conspiracy prompt the listener to respond in a way that promotes or facilitates the carrying out of a criminal activity). Such statements can take a variety of forms. Examples include comments designed to: assist in recruiting potential members; inform other members about the progress of the conspiracy; control damage to or detection of the conspiracy; hide the criminal objectives of the conspiracy or instill confidence and prevent the desertion of other members. *See, e.g. U.S. v. Townley*, 472 F.3d 1267, 1273 (10th Cir. 2007) (statements that explain events of importance to the conspiracy in order to facilitate its operation, statements between coconspirators which provide reassurance, which serve to maintain trust and cohesiveness among them, or which inform each other of the current status of the conspiracy, and statements of a coconspirator identifying a fellow coconspirator); *U.S. v. Skidmore*, 254 F.3d at 639 (statement made to secure trust and prevent detection of illegal purchase of firearms); *U.S. v. Salgado*, 250 F.3d 438, 450 (6th Cir. 2001) (conversation about car loaded with cocaine being driven from Florida designed to keep coconspirators appraised of progress of conspiracy); *U.S. v. Dickerson*, 248 F.3d at 1049–50 (address book with phone numbers facilitated communication among coconspirators); *U.S. v. Johnson*, 200 F.3d 529, 533 (7th Cir. 2000) (statement conveyed information which helped conspirators perform their designated roles); *U.S. v. SKW Metals & Alloys, Inc.*, 195 F.3d 83 (2d Cir. 1999) (notes containing information relevant to price-fixing conspiracy admissible as statements in furtherance of the conspiracy); *U.S. v. Curry*, 187 F.3d 762 (7th Cir. 1999) (statements made to recruit other conspirators); *U.S. v. Guerra*, 113 F.3d 809 (8th Cir. 1997) (statements of one coconspirator to another identifying a fellow coconspirator as his source of drugs); *U.S. v. Darden*, 70 F.3d 1507, 1529 (8th Cir. 1995) (statements that describe past events are in furtherance of the conspiracy if they are made to keep coconspirators abreast of current developments and problems facing the group); *U.S. v. Lechuga*, 888 F.2d 1472, 1480 (5th Cir. 1989) ("in furtherance" requirement is not to be construed too strictly lest the purpose of the exception be defeated). It is not necessary that the statements actually furthered the conspiracy, only that they were made for that purpose. *U.S. v. Shores*, 33 F.3d 438 (4th Cir. 1994); *U.S. v. Clark*, 18 F.3d 1337 (6th Cir. 1994).

By contrast, conversations that represent "mere idle chatter" or which are just narratives of past conduct are not in furtherance of the conspiracy, regardless of whether an individual coconspirator was implicated in the conversation. *U.S. v. Darwich*, 337 F.3d 645, 657 (6th Cir. 2003) ('mere idle chatter or casual conversation about past events is not considered a statement in furtherance of the conspiracy."); *U.S. v. Maliszewski*, 161 F.3d 992 (6th Cir. 1998); *U.S. v. Urbanik*, 801 F.2d 692 (4th Cir. 1986). *See, e.g., Conrad*, 507 F.3d at 430 (district court erred in failing to make the requisite findings regarding the context and timing of the coconspirator's out-of-court statement before admitting the witness' testimony); *U.S. v. Bowman*, 215

F.3d 951 (9th Cir. 2000) (statement about prior bank robbery that robbers "went in after closing" merely narration of past fact); *Rotec Industries, Inc. v. Mitsubishi Corp.*, 215 F.3d 1246 (Fed. Cir. 2000) (statement that simply informs listener of the declarant's criminal activities is not made in furtherance of the conspiracy); *U.S. v. Cornett*, 195 F.3d 776, 782 (5th Cir. 1999) (idle chatter; "[W]hile the in furtherance requirement is not a strict one, it is a necessary one, and the proponent of admissibility must satisfy it by a preponderance of the evidence."); *U.S. v. Williams*, 87 F.3d 249 (8th Cir. 1996) (statements made to police by one coconspirator incriminating others not made in furtherance of conspiracy); *U.S. v. Santos*, 20 F.3d 280 (7th Cir. 1994) (narrative discussions of past events were not statements made in furtherance of conspiracy); *U.S. v. Lieberman*, 637 F.2d 95, 102 (2d Cir. 1980) ("The conversation . . . smacks of nothing more than casual conversation about past events. It is difficult to envision how it would have furthered the conspiracy.").

The fact that the statement was made to a government informer does not preclude admission. *U.S. v. Bridgeforth*, 441 F.3d 864, 869 (9th Cir. 2006) (statements made to facilitate informant's drug purchase that supplier was arriving and then that he had just left); *U.S. v. Mealy*, 851 F.2d 890 (7th Cir. 1988). The critical question is whether the statement was made "by" a member of the conspiracy, not whether the statement was made "to" a member of the conspiracy. *U.S. v. Tse*, 135 F.3d 200 (1st Cir. 1998).

Unidentified Declarant/Anonymous Documents

While identity of the declarant may be important to admissibility in some situations, it is not always required. *U.S. v. Squillacote*, 221 F.3d 542 (4th Cir. 2000) (only conclusion that could be drawn from information in incriminating documents was they were created by or at direction of East German agents who had knowledge of and were involved in conspiracy with appellants); *U.S. v. Cruz*, 910 F.2d 1072 (3d Cir. 1990) (when the statement itself and the surrounding circumstances provide sufficient evidence of reliability, unidentifiability will not be particularly important).

A number of courts also hold that anonymous documents which record the activities of a criminal conspiracy may be admitted under this rule when there is some independent evidence corroborating the reliability of the document. *U.S. v. Dynalectric Co.*, 859 F.2d 1559 (11th Cir. 1988) (anonymous phone call made during course of antitrust conspiracy); *U.S. v. Mazyak*, 650 F.2d 788 (5th Cir. 1981) (logbooks found on vessel smuggling marijuana); *U.S. v. McGlory*, 968 F.2d 309 (3d Cir. 1992) (handwritten notes found in defendant's garbage); *U.S. v. Helmel*, 769 F.2d 1306, 1313 (8th Cir. 1985) ("we do not believe that positive proof of the declarant's identity, through handwriting analysis or otherwise, is necessarily essential to the invocation of the coconspirator rule."). *But see U.S. v. Gil*, 58 F.3d 1414, 1420 (9th Cir. 1995) (government must prove by preponderance of evidence the author of anonymous documents).

Duration

Hearsay statements made after a conspiracy has terminated are not admissible. *Krulewitch v. United States*, 336 U.S. 440, 69 S. Ct. 716, 93 L. Ed. 790 (1949). But the duration of a conspiracy depends upon the facts of a particular case, i.e., it depends upon the scope of the agreement entered into by its members. *U.S. v. Mayes*, 917 F.2d 457 (10th Cir. 1990); *U.S. v. Hickey*, 360 F.2d 127 (7th Cir. 1966). Generally, a conspiracy is deemed to have ended when the last objective sought is achieved, when all coconspirators have been arrested or when achievement of the objective has been rendered impossible. When acts of concealment are done after the central objectives have been attained, for the purpose only of covering up after the crime, they are inadmissible. *Grunewald v. United States*, 353 U.S. 391, 77 S. Ct. 963, 1 L. Ed. 2d 931 (1957); *U.S. v. Serrano*, 870 F.2d 1 (1st Cir. 1989); *U.S. v. Silverstein*, 737 F.2d 864, 867 (10th Cir. 1984) (the duration of a conspiracy does not extend to attempts to conceal the crime). *But see Payne*, 437 F.3d at 546–47 (statements made as part of a discussion regarding concealment of an ongoing conspiracy were made in furtherance of the conspiracy). But the fact that the central objective of the conspiracy has been nominally attained does not preclude the continuance of the conspiracy. Where there is evidence that the conspirators originally agreed to take certain steps after the principal objective of the conspiracy was reached, or evidence from which such an agreement may reasonably be inferred, the conspiracy may be found to continue. *U.S. v. Medina*, 761 F.2d 12 (1st Cir. 1985) (conspiracy continued as long as coconspirators were acting together to destroy incriminating evidence); *U.S. v. Davis*, 623 F.2d 188 (1st Cir. 1980) (acts of concealment were made in furtherance of main criminal objectives of conspiracy and, thus, admissible). The critical factor is the necessity for some showing that the later activities were part of the original plan.

Crawford v. Washington—Criminal Cases

In *Crawford v. Washington*, 541 U.S. 36, 124 S. Ct. 1354, 158 L. Ed. 2d 177 (2004) (discussed at Commentary under HEARSAY: AUTHOR'S NOTE CONFRONTATION-CRIMINAL CASES, *supra*), the United States Supreme Court held that the Sixth Amendment's Confrontation Clause prohibits the admission of out-of-court statements that are testimonial in nature unless the declarant is unavailable and the defendant had a prior opportunity to cross-examine the declarant concerning the statements. *Id.* at 68; 124 S.Ct. 1354. However, the Court also described statements in furtherance of a conspiracy as "by their nature . . . not testimonial." *Id.* at 56. *See also U.S. v. Farhane*, 634 F.3d 127 (2nd Cir. 2011); *U.S. v. Jenkins*, 419 F.3d 614, 618 (7th Cir. 2005) (*Crawford* inapplicable to nonhearsay statements by a co-conspirator under 801(d)(2)(E)); *U.S. v. Saget*, 377 F.3d 223 (2nd Cir. 2004); *U.S. v. Reyes*, 362 F.3d 536 (8th Cir. 2004) (*Crawford* does not apply to co-conspirator statements because they are nontestimonial).

Additional References

Graham, Handbook of Federal Evidence § 801.25 (7th ed. 2012)

Treatises and Practice Aids

Goode and Wellborn, Courtroom Handbook on Federal Evidence Chapter 5, Rule 801(d)(2) and Obj. 37 (annual ed.)

Mueller & Kirkpatrick, Federal Evidence, §§ 8:54, 8:61, 8:62 (3d ed. 2007)
Binder, Hearsay Handbook Chapter 35 (4th ed. 2001)
McCormick, Evidence § 259 (6th ed. 2006)

HEARSAY EXEMPTION: ADMISSION—PERSONS AUTHORIZED TO SPEAK

See:

Fed.R.Evid. 801(d)(2)(C)
Mil.R.Evid. 801(d)(2)(C)

Objection

- [*To a question*] Objection. The question calls for hearsay.
- [*To an answer*] Objection, hearsay. I move that the answer be stricken and the jury be instructed not to consider it for any purpose.

Response

- The statement is admissible since I have already established the authority of the declarant to speak for [*plaintiff/defendant*] in such matters.

Commentary

Rule 801(d)(2)(C) excludes from the definition of hearsay any statements used against a party which were made by another person "authorized by the party to make a statement concerning the subject."

In order for a statement to be admissible, the proponent must first establish that the declarant is, in fact, the agent of the party opponent, *Merrick v. Farmers Ins. Group*, 892 F.2d 1434 (9th Cir. 1990), and that the scope of the agency included the right to make a statement. *Precision Piping and Instruments, Inc. v. E.I. du Pont de Nemours and Co.*, 951 F.2d 613, 619 (4th Cir. 1991) ("[A]uthority in the context of 801(d)(2)(C) means 'authority to speak' on a particular subject on behalf of someone else."). The declarant's authority can be expressed or implied.

In determining whether the declarant was authorized to speak, the court must consider the contents of the statement but must also find other independent evidence of authorization. Rule 801(d)(2).

Like all admissions, there is no requirement that the speaker have personal knowledge, *Union Mut. Life Ins. Co. v. Chrysler Corp.*, 793 F.2d 1 (1st

Cir. 1986), and the statement may be phrased in the form of an opinion. Furthermore, an admission under Rule 801(d)(2)(C) may be denied, explained, contradicted, or otherwise attacked, just like any other item of evidence introduced against a party. *See* Rule 806; *see also U.S. v. Menendez*, 315 Fed. Appx. 103 (11th Cir. 2008) (slip op.).

For illustrations of the rule, *see*: *Fischer v. Forestwood Co., Inc.*, 525 F.3d 972, 984 (10th Cir. 2008) (taped conversations between former employee and employer's deceased president constituted admissions of a party-opponent where president was authorized to make a statement concerning hiring and firing, and was acting as employer's agent when statements were made); *Kirk v. Raymark Industries, Inc.*, 61 F.3d 147 (3d Cir. 1995) (error to allow plaintiff to introduce prior testimony of expert witness who had testified for defendant in earlier, unrelated case; because expert is not subject to control of party opponent, he cannot be deemed an agent); *U.S. v. Reilly*, 33 F.3d 1396 (3d Cir. 1994) (in prosecution for illegal ocean dumping, radio telegrams sent to ship were admissible under Rule 801(d)(2)(C); messages originated from defendant to his agent and then were relayed by coastal station operators who thus became persons authorized to make statements concerning the subject); *Lightning Lube, Inc. v. Witco Corp.*, 4 F.3d 1153 (3d Cir. 1993) (an attorney has authority to bind the client only with respect to statements directly related to the management of the litigation; defense attorneys' stated threats "to bury" plaintiff for filing suit were inadmissible where evidence did not establish that statements were related to management of case or otherwise authorized); *Michaels v. Michaels*, 767 F.2d 1185 (7th Cir. 1985) (telexes sent by declarant to potential buyers of family business were admissions under Rule 801(d)(2)(C) because defendant had authorized declarant to act as broker and contact potential buyers); *Collins v. Wayne Corp.*, 621 F.2d 777 (5th Cir. 1980) (court erred in restricting plaintiff's use of defense expert's deposition testimony as admission by one authorized to speak; expert was hired to investigate bus accident, had produced report and was deposed by plaintiffs before defendant asserted expert was a consultant whose work was not discoverable/admissible); *Grassmueck v. Bishop*, 2010 WL 1742091 (D.Or. 2010) (statement made by attorney is generally admissible against the cilent); *Zearley v. Ackerman*, 116 F. Supp. 2d 109 (D.D.C. 2000) (where administrator acting as designee of school superintendent had been deposed in unrelated case about district's policy, her statements were authorized and thus admissible in § 1983 suit by emotionally disturbed student because same policy was again in issue).

Generally, where an interpreter is used to translate for a defendant, the interpreter is viewed as an agent of the defendant. Any translation will be attributed to the defendant as an admission under Rule 801(d)(2)(C) or (D). *U.S. v. Sanchez-Godinez*, 444 F.3d 957 (8th Cir. 2006).

A pleading prepared by an attorney is an admission by one presumptively authorized to speak for his principal. When a pleading is amended or withdrawn, the superseded portion ceases to be a conclusive judicial admission. But it still remains as a statement once seriously made by an authorized agent and, as such, is competent evidence of the facts stated, though controvertible like any other admission made by a party or his agent. If the agent made the admission without adequate information, that goes to weight not admissibility. *U.S. v. McKeon*, 738 F.2d 26, 31 (2d Cir. 1984) ("A party . . . cannot advance one version of the facts in its pleadings, conclude that its interests would be better served by a different version, and amend its pleadings to incorporate that version, safe in the belief that the trier of fact will never learn of the change in stories."); *Zitz v. Pereira*, 119 F. Supp. 2d 133 (E.D. N.Y. 1999).

Crawford v. Washington—Criminal Cases

The impact of *Crawford v. Washington*, 541 U.S. 36, 124 S. Ct. 1354, 158 L. Ed. 2d 177 (2004) on the law of hearsay in criminal cases is discussed at Commentary under HEARSAY: AUTHOR'S NOTE CONFRONTATION-CRIMINAL CASES. *See U.S. v. Brown*, 441 F.3d 1330 (11th Cir. 2006) (admitting into evidence the statement of a party-opponent does not violate the Sixth Amendment's Confrontation Clause); *U.S. v. Lafferty*, 387 F.

Supp. 2d 500 (W.D. Pa. 2005) (Sixth Amendment does not guarantee defendant right to cross-examine herself as to her own admissions); *see also* 4 Weinstein & Berger, Weinstein's Federal Evidence § 802.05 [3][d] at 802–25 (2d ed. 2005) (noting that "a party cannot seriously claim that his or her own statement should be excluded because it was not made under oath or subject to cross-examination").

Additional References

Graham, Handbook of Federal Evidence § 801.22 (7th ed. 2012)

Treatises and Practice Aids

Goode and Wellborn, Courtroom Handbook on Federal Evidence Chapter 5, Rule 801(d)(2) and Obj. 37 (annual ed.)

Binder, Hearsay Handbook Chapter 35 (4th ed. 2001)

McCormick, Evidence Chapter 25 (6th ed. 2006)

Park, Trial Objections Handbook § 4:14 (2nd ed. 2001)

HEARSAY EXCEPTION: ANCIENT DOCUMENTS

See:

Fed.R.Evid. 803(16)
Mil.R.Evid. 803(16)

Objection

- I object to the introduction of this document and any testimony about its contents. There has been no foundation to authenticate it and its contents are inadmissible hearsay.

Response

- The document is admissible under the ancient documents exception to the hearsay rule. As foundation, I have established that the document is at least 20 years old, is free from any suspicious alteration and has been in proper custody.

Commentary

The ancient documents exception, Rule 803(16), excepts documents from the hearsay rule when the document is at least 20 years old, is free from suspicious alterations, and has been in proper custody. Authenticity is established pursuant to Rule 901(b)(8), by showing that: (a) its condition creates no suspicion concerning its authenticity, (b) it was in a place where it would likely be found if authentic, and (c) it has been in existence 20 years or more at the time it is offered.

The rule has been applied to a variety of documents, including memoranda and correspondence from the 1940s discussing the dangers of asbestos (*Dartez v. Fibreboard Corp.*, 765 F.2d 456 (5th Cir. 1985)); warranty deeds (*Compton v. Davis Oil Co.*, 607 F. Supp. 1221 (D. Wyo. 1985)); old newspaper articles (*Bell v. Combined Registry Co.*, 397 F. Supp. 1241 (N.D. Ill. 1975) and *Dallas County v. Commercial Union Assur. Co.*, 286 F.2d 388 (5th Cir. 1961)); Soviet interrogation records (*U.S. v. Mandycz*, 447 F.3d 951 (6th Cir. 2006)); documents from Lithuanian archives detailing defendant's Nazi service during World War II (*U.S. v. Stelmo-*

kas, 100 F.3d 302 (3d Cir. 1996)); documents identifying the defendant's service in the Ukrainian Auxiliary Police, a Nazi-backed police force that assisted in the persecution of civilians during World War II (*U.S. v. Firishchak*, 468 F.3d 1015, 1022 (7th Cir. 2006)); witness statements given shortly after World War II (*U.S. v. Hajda*, 135 F.3d 439 (7th Cir. 1998)); maps and surveys (*Koepp v. Holland*, 688 F.Supp.2d 65 (N.D.N.Y. 2010)); payroll book from 1941 (*Fulmer v. Connors*, 665 F. Supp. 1472 (N.D. Ala. 1987)). See also *Langbord v. U.S. Dept. of Treasury*, 2011 WL 2623315 (E.D.Pa. 2011) (statements in 1947 legal opinion qualified under ancient documents exception; however, under Rule 403 analysis, use was limited to establish notice that possession of certain gold coins was illegal).

Additional References

Graham, Handbook of Federal Evidence § 803.16 (7th ed. 2012)

Treatises and Practice Aids

Mueller & Kirkpatrick, Federal Evidence, §§ 8:99, 9:19 (3d ed. 2007)

Binder, Hearsay Handbook Chapter 24 (4th ed. 2001)

McCormick, Evidence § 323 (6th ed. 2006)

Park, Trial Objections Handbook § 4:50 (2nd ed. 2001)

HEARSAY EXCEPTION: BUSINESS RECORDS

See:

Fed.R.Evid. 803(6)
Mil.R.Evid. 803(6)

Objection

- Objection. The records have not been properly authenticated pursuant to Rule 803(6). Therefore, the contents are inadmissible hearsay since they are offered to prove the truth of the matters asserted in them.

Response

- The evidence is admissible under the business records exception to the hearsay rule. As foundation, I have established that:
  1. the record was made at or near the time of the event or transaction described;
  2. the record was made [*by a person with knowledge of the event or transaction described*] [*from information transmitted to the preparer by a person with knowledge*];
  3. the record was made in the course of a regularly conducted business activity;
  4. it was a part of that regularly conducted business activity to make and keep the record; and,
  5. the witness [*is able to identify the document from actual knowledge of its preparation*] [*is the business custodian of the record*] [*is a qualified person to sponsor the records because (specify)*].

Commentary

Rule 803(6) excepts from the hearsay rule records or data compilations in any form of acts, events, conditions, opinions, or diagnoses made at or near the time by a person with knowledge, if kept in the ordinary course of a regularly conducted business activity, and if it was the regular practice of the business to make the record, unless the source of the information or the method or circumstances of preparation indicate lack of trustworthiness. *U.S. v. LeShore*, 543 F.3d 935 (7th Cir. 2008); *U.S. v. Moon*, 513 F.3d 527 (6th Cir. 2008) (in health care fraud prosecution, computer records of purchases from various drug companies were "data compilations" and thus business records under Rule 803(6) and not summaries under Rule 1006); *Collins v. Kibort*, 143 F.3d 331 (7th Cir. 1998); *Monotype Corp. PLC v. International Typeface Corp.*, 43 F.3d 443 (9th Cir. 1994).

The purpose of the exception is to permit the introduction of records that are inherently reliable. *U.S. v. Ary*, 518 F.3d 775 (10th Cir. 2008) (exception's rationale is that business records have high degree of reliability because businesses have incentives to keep accurate records); *U.S. v. Fuchs*, 218 F.3d 957 (9th Cir. 2000); *U.S. v. Morrow*, 177 F.3d 272 (5th Cir. 1999).

Foundation

The sponsoring witness must testify that: (1) the records in question were made contemporaneously with the recorded events; (2) the records were made by, or from information transmitted by, someone with personal knowledge of the events; (3) the records were kept in the course of a regularly conducted business activity; and (4) it was the customary practice of that business activity to prepare such records. *U.S. v. Reilly*, 33 F.3d 1396 (3d Cir. 1994); *Igo v. Coachmen Industries, Inc. (Sportscoach Corp. of America Div.)*, 938 F.2d 650 (6th Cir. 1991).

These foundational elements must be established by testimony of the records custodian or other qualified witness or by certification that complies with Rules 902(11), 902(12) or statute permitting certification.*

Other Qualified Witness

To be an "other qualified witness," it is not nec-

[Hearsay etc.]

*In certain circumstances, a foundation for admissibility may be established by judicial notice of the nature of the business and "the nature of the records as observed by the court, particularly in the case of bank or similar statements." *U.S. v. Johnson*, 971 F.2d 562, 571 (10th Cir. 1992).

essary that the person laying the foundation for the introduction of business records have personal knowledge of their preparation. All that is required is that he or she be familiar with the record-keeping procedures of the organization. *U.S. v. Jenkins*, 345 F.3d 928 (6th Cir. 2003) (custodian of records need not be in control of or have individual knowledge of the particular corporate records, but need only be familiar with company's record-keeping practices); *Dyno Const. Co. v. McWane, Inc.*, 198 F.3d 567 (6th Cir. 1999) (while Federal Express operations manager could not lay foundation as "custodian" of records from geographical area for which he was not responsible, he could lay foundation as "other qualified witness" based on his familiarity with carrier's system for moving and tracking packages and his knowledge that records were generated and kept in regular course of business by carrier in its centralized computer system); *U.S. v. Dixon*, 132 F.3d 192 (5th Cir. 1997) (in drug prosecution, no error to admit pager rental records through business owner who testified that while he did not create records or personally know whether they were accurate, he did assume and rely on their accuracy in the ordinary course of his business); *U.S. v. Console*, 13 F.3d 641 (3d Cir. 1993) (the term "other qualified witness" should be construed broadly and need not be an employee of the record-keeping entity so long as he understands the system); *U.S. v. Hathaway*, 798 F.2d 902 (6th Cir. 1986) (rejecting defendant's contention that government could not lay foundation through testimony of FBI agent for admission of records seized from defendant's business offices). *See also U.S. v. Riley*, 236 F.3d 982 (8th Cir. 2001) (police officers, who had no personal knowledge how state crime lab report was prepared or maintained, could not provide foundational testimony necessary to admission of report analyzing controlled substance); *U.S. v. Dakota*, 197 F.3d 821 (6th Cir. 1999) (similar); *U.S. v. Given*, 164 F.3d 389 (7th Cir. 1999) (witness did not know how or when invoices were prepared and trial court abused its discretion in admitting them); *cf. U.S. v. Ford*, 435 F.3d 204 (2d Cir. 2006) (where witness identified his handwriting and said it was his practice to keep a calendar, his claimed lack of recollection about certain entries was no barrier to calendar's admission as business record).

Trustworthiness

It is essential that no lack of trustworthiness appear in the source of information or the method or circumstances of preparation. Factors to be weighed in evaluating the trustworthiness of business records include whether there was either motive or opportunity to prepare an inaccurate record; the period of delay prior to preparation of the record; systematic checking; whether there was regularity and continuity in maintaining the records, and whether the business relied on them. *See, e.g., U.S. v. Gwathney*, 465 F.3d 1133 (10th Cir. 2006) (the rule is well established that documents made in anticipation of litigation are inadmissible under the business records exception); *Certain Underwriters at Lloyd's, London v. Sinkovich*, 232 F.3d 200 (4th Cir. 2000) (same); *U.S. v. Scholl*, 166 F.3d 964 (9th Cir. 1999) (fact that business records were only rough estimates went to weight of evidence, not admissibility); *In re Balfour MacLaine Intern. Ltd.*, 85 F.3d 68 (2d Cir. 1996) (discrepancy between amount of coffee shown on certificates of deposit versus warehouse receiving reports did not render certificates untrustworthy; discrepancy was precisely the issue in dispute and could not be the basis for challenge to evidence intended to resolve that dispute).

Computer Records

It is not necessary that the computer programmer testify in order to authenticate computer-generated records. *U-Haul Intern., Inc. v. Lumbermens Mut. Cas. Co.*, 576 F.3d 1040 (9th Cir. 2009). A computer printout may be authenticated by one who has knowledge of the particular record system. *U.S. v. Miller*, 771 F.2d 1219, 1237 (9th Cir. 1985). Similarly, a party need not produce expert testimony as to the mechanical accuracy of a computer where it presented evidence that the computer was sufficiently accurate so that the company relied on it in conducting its business. *Id., citing U.S. v. De Georgia*, 420 F.2d 889, 893 n.11 (9th Cir. 1969).

Documents Of Others

Documents prepared by third persons may be

admitted as business records of a party if it is shown that it was the party's regular practice to obtain such information or that these documents were integrated into the party's records and relied upon in its daily operations. *U.S. v. Adefehinti*, 510 F.3d 319 (D.C. Cir. 2007) (loan documentation furnished to and used by bank; collecting cases); *Air Land Forwarders, Inc. v. U.S.*, 172 F.3d 1338 (Fed. Cir. 1999) (in contract action by companies engaged in moving household goods of military personnel, no error to admit as military business records repair shop estimates given to service members; repair estimates were used by military in adjudicating claims for damaged goods) (collecting cases); *MRT Const. Inc. v. Hardrives, Inc.*, 158 F.3d 478 (9th Cir. 1998) (records which business receives from others are admissible under Rule 803(6) when kept in the regular course of that business, relied upon by that business and where that business has a substantial interest in the accuracy of the records); *U.S. v. Bueno-Sierra*, 99 F.3d 375 (11th Cir. 1996) (where testimony showed that ships' agents personally prepared documents submitted to and maintained in port operations office, no error to permit assistant chief of port operations to introduce vessel's berth request form); *U.S. v. Childs*, 5 F.3d 1328 (9th Cir. 1993) (documents prepared by third parties and integrated into records of auto dealership properly admitted based on testimony that such records were kept in the regular course of business and relied upon by dealership); *U.S. v. Jakobetz*, 955 F.2d 786 (2d Cir. 1992) and *Jazz Photo Corp. v. U.S.*, 28 Ct. Int'l Trade 1954, 353 F. Supp. 2d 1327 (2004) (similar).

Courts are divided on whether a financial audit report is admissible as a business record. *U.S. v. Polishan*, 336 F.3d 234 (3d Cir. 2003). *Compare U.S. v. Frazier*, 53 F.3d 1105, 1110 (10th Cir. 1995) (audit report of accountant admitted as business record); *U.S. v. Blackwell*, 954 F. Supp. 944, 973–74 (D.N.J. 1997) (financial audit of bank admitted as business record); *Condus v. Howard Sav. Bank*, 986 F. Supp. 914, 918 (D.N.J. 1997) (report prepared by outside company hired by bank to provide assessment of loss reserves admissible as business record), *with Lamb Engineering & Const. Co. v. Nebraska Public Power Dist.*, 103 F.3d 1422, 1432

n. 5 (8th Cir. 1997) (report prepared by certified public accountant based on audit inadmissible because prepared for litigation); *Paddack v. Dave Christensen, Inc.*, 745 F.2d 1254, 1258 (9th Cir. 1984) (compliance audit inadmissible because company had no regular compliance audit procedure). *CF. Trustees of Chicago Plastering Inst. Pension Trust v. Cork Plastering Co.*, 570 F.3d 890 (7th Cir. 2009) (although audit report derived from company records did not qualify as a business record, it was admissible under Rule 1006 as a summary of employer's payroll data).

Multiple Hearsay

Business records are considered by the part, not the whole, for purposes of this exception. One entry may be excepted from the hearsay rule, and another may not, though both are contained in the same document.

The fact that a business document may contain entries in different forms or from different sources does not necessarily imply that a double hearsay problem exists. When a single business record contains different information recorded directly from multiple sources, or on multiple occasions, there may be several instances of hearsay but there is only one layer of hearsay. For example, if one employee records his time on a time card each day and the supervisor signs the card prior to submitting it to the payroll department, the time card contains hearsay entries from both employee and supervisor, but only one layer of hearsay. *U.S. v. Turner*, 189 F.3d 712 (8th Cir. 1999).

Double hearsay exists when a business record is prepared by one employee from information supplied by another person. If both the source and the recorder of the information as well as every other participant in the chain producing the record are acting in the regular course of the business, the multiple hearsay is excused by Rule 803(6). *U.S. v. Ary*, 518 F.3d at 787 (the essential component of business records exception is that each actor in chain of information is under business duty or compulsion to provide accurate information). However, if the source of the information is an outsider, Rule 803(6) does not, by itself, permit the admission of the business record. *U.S. v. Gurr*, 471 F.3d 144 (D.C. Cir. 2006). The outsider's statement must fall within another hearsay exception to be admissible because it does not have the presumption of accuracy that attaches to statements made during the regular course of business by a person with a business duty to report and/or record. *Koch Industries, Inc. and Subsidiaries v. U.S.*, 564 F. Supp. 2d 1276 (D. Kan. 2008). *See Woods v. City of Chicago*, 234 F.3d 979 (7th Cir. 2000) (statements made by third parties in police report inadmissible under business record exception); *Bemis v. Edwards*, 45 F.3d 1369 (9th Cir. 1995) (911 call not admissible as business record because caller was not under any business duty to report and report did not independently satisfy any other hearsay exception); *Cameron v. Otto Bock Orthopedic Industry, Inc.*, 43 F.3d 14 (1st Cir. 1994) (product failure reports submitted to the manufacturer after plaintiff's accident were inadmissible; reports were submitted by persons who had no business duty to report accurately to the manufacturer); *U.S. v. Baker*, 693 F.2d 183 (D.C. Cir. 1982) (loss forms filled out by intended payees of U.S. Treasury checks sold by defendant did not fall within business records exception since intended payees were not acting in regular course of business and their statements did not fall within any other hearsay exception); *Boca Investerings Partnership v. U.S.*, 128 F. Supp. 2d 16 (D.D.C. 2000) (collecting cases).

Verification Of Third Person Information

Courts have admitted "outsider" statements contained in business records where the standard practice was to verify the information provided. *See, e.g. U.S. v. Reyes*, 157 F.3d 949 (2d Cir. 1998) (admitting prison visitor's logbook after testimony re measures taken to assure its accuracy) (collecting cases); *U.S. v. Sokolow*, 91 F.3d 396 (3d Cir. 1996) (documents properly admitted where proof of claim procedure had been used to verify information provided by outside persons). Where verification is wholly absent, third person information is not covered by this rule. *U.S. v. Vigneau*, 187 F.3d 70 (1st Cir. 1999) (in drug and money laundering case, reversible error to admit Western Union "To Send Money" forms to show defendant was transferring funds to confederates; it was not Western Union's practice to verify any sender information); *U.S. v. Zapata*, 356 F. Supp. 2d 323 (S.D. N.Y. 2005) (same); *U.S. v. Lieberman*, 637 F.2d 95 (2d Cir. 1980) (where hotel employee did not verify information supplied by guests, hotel registry card inadmissible under business records exception).

Operation Of Other Rules

The Rule should not be overread. Rule 803(6) does not make relevant that which is irrelevant nor does it make all business records competent regardless of by whom, in what manner and for what purpose they were compiled. *See, e.g., Weir v. Crown Equipment Corp.*, 217 F.3d 453 (7th Cir. 2000) (no error to exclude certain accident reports collected by forklift manufacturer which trial court found vague, incomplete and confusing); *Vance v. Peters*, 97 F.3d 987 (7th Cir. 1996) (no abuse of discretion in excluding hearing officer's final report that corrections officer used excessive force against inmate; although report qualified as business record, it was excluded as cumulative and because its probative value was outweighed by its prejudicial effect); *Holbrook v. Lykes Bros. S.S. Co., Inc.*, 80 F.3d 777 (3d Cir. 1996) (Rule 403 permits court to redact portions of business records deemed unfairly prejudicial).

The business records exception cannot be used as a 'back door' to introduce evidence that would not be admissible under Rule 803(8). *U.S. v. Blackburn*, 992 F.2d 666, 671 (7th Cir. 1993) ("[I]f a document prohibited under Rule 803(8)(B) or (C) can come into evidence under Rule 803(6), then the 803(8) restrictions are rendered nugatory."); *U.S. v. Cain*, 615 F.2d 380 (5th Cir. 1980).

In criminal proceedings, 18 U.S.C.A. § 3505 allows admission of foreign business records if supported by an affidavit authenticating them. *See U.S. v. Ross*, 33 F.3d 1507 (11th Cir. 1994) (statute does not violate Sixth Amendment confrontation clause).

Note: Rule 803(7) provides that evidence of the absence of an entry in records regularly kept is admissible as affirmative proof of the nonoccurrence or nonexistence of a matter normally recorded. *In re Apex Exp. Corp.*, 190 F.3d 624 (4th Cir. 1999);

Kaiser Aluminum & Chemical Corp. v. Illinois Cent. Gulf R. Co., 615 F.2d 470 (8th Cir. 1980).

Crawford v. Washington—Criminal Cases

The impact of *Crawford v. Washington*, 541 U.S. 36, 124 S. Ct. 1354, 158 L. Ed. 2d 177 (2004) on the law of hearsay in criminal cases is discussed at Commentary under HEARSAY: AUTHOR'S NOTE CONFRONTATION-CRIMINAL CASES. In *Crawford*, the Supreme Court stated that business records are "by their nature . . . not testimonial and not subject to the requirements of the Confrontation Clause," 541 U.S. at 51, 56, 124 S.Ct. 1354; *see also id.* at 76, 124 S.Ct. 1354 (Rehnquist, C.J., concurring in judgment) (noting that "the Court's analysis of 'testimony' excludes some hearsay exceptions, such as business records and official records"); *U.S. v. Mashek*, 606 F.3d 922 (8th Cir. 2010) (business records under Rule 803(6) are nontestimonial statements to which the Confrontation Clause does not apply). Some courts have said that the mere fact a person creating a business record (or other similar record) knows the record might be used for criminal prosecution does not by itself make that record testimonial. *See U.S. v. De La Cruz*, 514 F.3d 121 (1st Cir. 2008) (autopsy report made in ordinary course of business by medical examiner excluded from reach of *Crawford*); *U.S. v. Ellis*, 460 F.3d 920 (7th Cir. 2006) (medical records establishing methamphetamine in defendant's system were nontestimonial business records; admission did not violate right to confrontation; records were created as result of government investigation but were made by professionals recording observations made in the ordinary course of business). But one commentator has cautioned that "[s]ome business records may concern matters that are understood at the time they were made to be destined for litigation or may be clearly accusatory." Mosteller, *Crawford v. Washington*: Encouraging and Ensuring the Confrontation of Witnesses, 39 U.Rich.L.Rev. 511, 548 (2005). In *Melendez-Diaz v. Massachusetts*, 557 U.S. ____, 129 S.Ct. 2527, 174 L. Ed. 2d 314 (2009), the trial court had admitted into evidence state laboratory affidavits with forensic analysis results showing material seized from defendant was cocaine. The Court reiterated that documents kept in the ordinary course of business usually may be admitted at trial despite their hearsay status but said that is not the case if the regularly conducted business activity is the production of evidence for use at trial. 557 U.S. at ___. The United States Supreme Court said that the laboratory reports fell within the core class of testimonial statements since they had been created for the sole purpose of providing evidence against a defendant. Acknowledging that the Confrontation Clause may make prosecution of criminals more burdensome, the Court held that crime laboratory reports may not be used against defendants at trial unless the analysts responsible for creating them give testimony and subject themselves to cross-examination. Accord *Bullcoming v. New Mexico*, ___ U.S. ___ (2011).

Additional References

Graham, Handbook of Federal Evidence § 803.6 (7th ed. 2012)

Treatises and Practice Aids

Goode and Wellborn, Courtroom Handbook on Federal Evidence Chapter 5, Rule 803(6) (annual ed.)

Mueller & Kirkpatrick, Federal Evidence, §§ 8:66, 8:77 *et seq.* (3d ed. 2007)

Binder, Hearsay Handbook Chapter 16 (4th ed. 2001)

McCormick, Evidence Chapter 29 (6th ed. 2006)

Park, Trial Objections Handbook §§ 4:29 to 4:40 (2nd ed. 2001)

HEARSAY EXCEPTION: DYING DECLARATION

See:

Fed.R.Evid. 804(b)(2)
Mil.R.Evid. 804(b)(2)

Objection

- [*To a question*] Objection. The question calls for hearsay.
- [*To an answer*] Objection, hearsay. I move that the answer be stricken and the jury be instructed not to consider it for any purpose.

Response

- The statement is within the dying declaration exception to the hearsay rule. As foundation, I have already established that when the declarant made the statement to this witness: (1) declarant believed his death was imminent; (2) the statement was based on personal knowledge; and (3) the statement addresses what declarant believed to be the cause or circumstances of his imminent death. I have also met the requirement of showing the declarant is unavailable within the definition of Fed.R.Evid. 804(a).

Commentary

In a criminal case of homicide or in any civil proceeding, the statement of a person about the cause or circumstances of what he believes to be his impending death qualifies as a dying declaration if the following conditions are met: (1) declarant believed his death was imminent (whether, in fact, it occurred or not); (2) the statement was based on personal knowledge; and (3) the statement concerns the cause or circumstances of what declarant believed to be his imminent death. Rule 804(b)(2). The offering party must also demonstrate by a preponderance of the evidence that the declarant is unavailable under the definition provided in Rule 804(a).

Admissibility depends initially upon the state of the declarant's mind. *Shepard v. United States*, 290

U.S. 96, 54 S. Ct. 22, 78 L. Ed. 196 (1933). It is sufficient that declarant believed his death was imminent. *Herrera v. Collins*, 904 F.2d 944 (5th Cir. 1990). Death does not actually have to occur. The required sense of imminent death may be shown by the declarant's own statements. It may also be inferred from the surrounding circumstances, including the nature of the injury or the state of declarant's illness. *Mattox v. United States*, 156 U.S. 237, 15 S. Ct. 337, 39 L. Ed. 409 (1895) (sense of imminent death may be inferred from nature and extent of declarant's wounds); *U.S. v. Shields*, 497 F.3d 789, 793 (8th Cir. 2007) (a declarant's serious injuries can support an inference that he believed death was imminent, but the nature and extent of the injuries must be so severe that obviously the declarant must have felt or known that he could not survive); *Webb v. Lane*, 922 F.2d 390 (7th Cir. 1991) (reasonable to infer declarant knew seriousness of his condition because he was attached to life support with six gunshot wounds); *U.S. v. Mobley*, 421 F.2d 345 (5th Cir. 1970) (court looked at gravity of declarant's wounds in determining his awareness of death); *Sternhagen v. Dow Co.*, 108 F. Supp. 2d 1113 (D. Mont. 1999) (where declarant stated he expected to live three to six months and would continue with limited work and eight weeks after statement traveled to religious shrine to 'receive healing' if possible, facts did not support requirement of 'settled hopeless expectation' that his death was at hand).

A dying declaration need not be spontaneous. It may be given in response to a question or phrased in the form of an opinion. *U.S. v. Etheridge*, 424 F.2d 951 (6th Cir. 1970). The declaration can be oral, written, or some combination thereof. It can also be nonverbal such as blinking eyes or squeezing a hand in response to questions. *See Webb*, 922 F.2d at 395 (affirmative nod); Imwinkelried et al, Courtroom Criminal Evidence § 1309 (2d ed. 1993). The statement must, however, relate to the cause or circumstances of declarant's dying condition. *U.S. v. Fernandez*, 892 F.2d 976 (11th Cir. 1989) (testimony about illegal operation of employee-benefit plan inadmissible because no relationship to cause or circumstances of death); *U.S. v. Lemonakis*, 485 F.2d 941 (D.C. Cir. 1973) (rejecting suicide note exonerating defendant from involvement in burglaries).

The rationale for the exception derives from the widely-held notion that the declarant's belief in his own imminent death will eliminate any motive on the part of the declarant to misstate the truth. *Vazquez v. National Car Rental System, Inc.*, 24 F. Supp. 2d 197 (D.P.R. 1998). *But cf. U.S. v. Thevis*, 84 F.R.D. 57 (N.D. Ga. 1979) (more realistically, dying declaration admitted because of compelling need for statement).

Whether the facts and circumstances warrant the admission of a hearsay statement as a dying declaration is decided by the trial judge. Rule 105. The credibility, interpretation and weight to be given to a dying declaration are matters exclusively for the jury.

In *Crawford v. Washington*, 541 U.S. 36, 124 S. Ct. 1354, 158 L. Ed. 2d 177 (2004) (discussed at Commentary under HEARSAY: AUTHOR'S NOTE CONFRONTATION-CRIMINAL CASES), a criminal case involving a Confrontation Clause challenge, the United States Supreme Court held that if a hearsay statement was "testimonial" in nature, it could not be introduced at trial, in the absence of the declarant, unless the defendant had a previous opportunity to cross-examine the declarant. The Court also wrote: "We need not decide in this case whether the Sixth Amendment incorporates an exception for testimonial dying declarations. If this exception must be accepted on historical grounds, it is *sui generis.*" *Id.* at 56 n.6. See *Michigan v. Bryant*, 562 U.S. ___ (2011) ("were the issue properly tendered here, I would take up the question whether the exception for dying declarations survives our recent Confrontation Clause decisions." (Ginsburg, J. dissenting)). One commentator has suggested "[w]hen a statement is accusatory and intended to be conveyed beyond those who would be expected to keep it confidential-to government agents, private agencies that perform government functions, and strangers at arms length from the witness-it should be considered testimonial." Mosteller, *Crawford v. Washington*: Encouraging and Ensuring the Confrontation of Witnesses, 39 U.Rich. L.Rev. 511, 542 (2005). *See also U.S. v. Mayhew*, 380 F. Supp. 2d 961 (S.D.

Ohio 2005) (in dicta, rejecting the argument that dying declarations are an exception to the Confrontation Clause; such statements might be the product of revenge or dislike and lose trustworthiness if the declarant had no religious belief); *U.S. v. Jordan*, 2005 WL 513501 (D. Colo. 2005) (dying declaration inadmissible under *Crawford*; statements made to investigators could not be tested by cross-examination).

Additional References

Graham, Handbook of Federal Evidence § 804.2 (7th ed. 2012)

Treatises and Practice Aids

Mueller & Kirkpatrick, Federal Evidence, § 8:128 (3d ed. 2007)

Binder, Hearsay Handbook Chapter 34 (4th ed. 2001)

McCormick, Evidence Chapter 32 (6th ed. 2006)

Park, Trial Objections Handbook §§ 4:70 to 4:74 (2nd ed. 2001)

HEARSAY EXCEPTION: EXCITED UTTERANCE

See:

Fed.R.Evid. 803(2)
Mil.R.Evid. 803(2)

Objection

- [*To a question*] Objection. The question calls for hearsay.
- [*To an answer*] Objection, hearsay. I move the answer be stricken and the jury be instructed not to consider it for any purpose.

Response

- The statement is admissible as an excited utterance. I have established that the statement relates to a startling event or condition; that it was made under the stress and excitement of the event and that the declarant [witnessed] [participated in] the event.

Commentary

Rule 803(2) provides an exception to the hearsay rule for any "statement relating to a startling event or condition made while the declarant was under the stress of excitement caused by the event or condition."

The rationale for the excited utterance exception is that such statements are given under circumstances which eliminate the possibility of fabrication or coaching. *Idaho v. Wright*, 497 U.S. 805, 110 S. Ct. 3139, 111 L. Ed. 2d 638 (1990); *U.S. v. Clemmons*, 461 F.3d 1057 (8th Cir. 2006) (statement must be spontaneous, excited or impulsive rather than product of reflection and deliberation); *U.S. v. Iron Shell*, 633 F.2d 77 (8th Cir. 1980).

For a hearsay statement to be admitted under this exception, each of the following conditions must be met: (1) a startling event occurred; (2) the declarant observed the event and made the statement under the stress of excitement caused by the startling event; and (3) the statement must relate to the startling event. *Brunsting v. Lutsen Mountains Corp.*, 601 F.3d 813 (8th Cir. 2010); *U.S.*

v. Bercier, 506 F.3d 625 (8th Cir. 2007); *U.S. v. Water*, 413 F.3d 812 (8th Cir. 2005); *U.S. v. Wesela*, 223 F.3d 656 (7th Cir. 2000); *U.S. v. Hall*, 165 F.3d 1095 (7th Cir. 1999); *U.S. v. Mitchell*, 145 F.3d 572 (3d Cir. 1998).

Because the statement need only "relate" to the startling event or condition, an excited utterance is broader in scope than present sense impression which must describe or explain an event or condition. *See* Fed.R.Evid. 803(2) Advisory Committee Note; Weinstein & Berger, Weinstein's Federal Evidence, § 803.04[4] at 803-24.1 (2d ed.1997) ("The statement need not elucidate or explain the occurrence . . .. If the subject matter of the statement is such as would likely be evoked by the event, the statement should be admitted"). Thus, in *David by Berkeley v. Pueblo Supermarket of St. Thomas*, 740 F.2d 230 (3d Cir. 1984), a personal injury case, the court found that the spontaneous statement "I told them to clean it up two hours ago," while not describing the slip and fall, did relate to the event for purposes of Rule 803(2).

The startling event is usually a dramatic occurrence, such as an accident or crime. *U.S. v. Wiseman*, 172 F.3d 1196 (10th Cir. 1999) (robbery); *U.S. v. Phelps*, 168 F.3d 1048 (8th Cir. 1999) (shooting); *Boucher v. Grant*, 74 F. Supp. 2d 444 (D.N.J. 1999) (automobile accident). But it need not be dramatic as long as it has an exciting affect on the declarant. *David by Berkeley v. Pueblo Supermarket of St. Thomas* (witnessing slip and fall by pregnant woman). The existence of a startling event or condition may be inferred from the excited utterance alone, or in combination with surrounding circumstances. *U.S. v. Brown*, 254 F.3d 454 (3d Cir. 2001). *See* McCormick, Evidence § 272 (6th ed. 2006); Graham, Handbook of Federal Evidence § 803.2 (6th ed. 2006).

The excited utterance need not be contemporaneous with the startling event. *U.S. v. Fell*, 531 F.3d 197 (2d Cir. 2008). But the utterance must be contemporaneous with the excitement engendered by the startling event. *U.S. v. Alexander*, 331 F.3d 116 (D.C. Cir. 2003).

To determine whether a declarant was still under the stress of excitement when he or she made a statement, courts will consider the lapse of time between the startling event and the statement; whether the statement was made in response to an inquiry, the age of the declarant, the characteristics of the event, and the subject matter of the statement. *U.S. v. Wilcox*, 487 F.3d 1163 (8th Cir. 2007); *U.S. v. Kenyon*, 481 F.3d 1054 (8th Cir. 2007); *Reed v. Thalacker*, 198 F.3d 1058 (8th Cir. 1999) (two year-old child's allegation of abuse made within 48 hours of incident not admissible primarily because of lapse of time).

There is no set rule as to how much time may elapse between the event and the statement before the statement will cease to qualify as an excited utterance for purposes of Rule 803(2). *U.S. v. Ledford*, 443 F.3d 702 (10th Cir. 2005). If the time interval is long enough to allow the declarant reflective thought, the statement should be excluded, absent some proof that the declarant did not engage in a reflective thought process. McCormick, Evidence § 272 (6th ed. 2006). *See, e.g.*, *U.S. v. Belfast*, 611 F.3d 783 (11th Cir. 2010) (statements made 4–5 hours after torture qualified as excited utterances); *U.S. v. Allen*, 235 F.3d 482 (10th Cir. 2000) (911 tape admissible as excited utterance; caller made statements as defendant was outside her door, trying to get in); *U.S. v. Wesela*, 223 F.3d at 663–64 (wife's statements to police about husband's threatening behavior did not qualify as excited utterances; she had gone to work for a full day after incidents and prior to police interview); *U.S. v. Marrowbone*, 211 F.3d 452 (8th Cir. 2000) (based on lapse of time, age and motive to lie, allegations of sexual abuse made by sixteen-year-old boy three hours after alleged event did not qualify as excited utterances); *U.S. v. Joy*, 192 F.3d 761, 766 (7th Cir. 1999) (statement that defendant had "waved a gun around" made within a few minutes of incident qualified under Rule 803(2)); *U.S. v. Phelps*, 168 F.3d 1048 (8th Cir. 1999) (statement of "visibly distraught" declarant admissible although made 15 to 20 minutes after startling event); *U.S. v. Tocco*, 135 F.3d 116 (2d Cir. 1998) (statement properly admitted as excited utterance by declarant who was "all hyped up" and "nervous" even though made three hours after startling event); *U.S. v. Zizzo*, 120 F.3d 1338 (7th Cir. 1997) (no excited utterance where startling event took place at O'Hare Airport and statement was made at Dirksen Building in downtown Chicago); *U.S. v. Rivera*, 43 F.3d 1291 (9th Cir. 1995) (statements by victim to her mother more than 30 minutes after rape properly allowed).

Some courts allow a longer time period between the event and the statement when a young child is the victim or witness of crime. *U.S. v. Sowa*, 34 F.3d 447 (7th Cir. 1994) (where three-year-old child cried for twenty minutes after witnessing beating, her subsequent statements identifying defendant as perpetrator properly admitted as excited utterances); *U.S. v. Iron Shell*, 633 F.2d 77 (8th Cir. 1980) (given surprise of sexual assault, its shocking nature and fact that victim/declarant was nine-year-old girl, her statements to police were excited utterances even though made somewhere between 45 minutes and an hour fifteen minutes after attack); *but see Reed v. Thalacker*, 198 F.3d at 1058 (habeas corpus proceeding; father's right of confrontation violated by erroneous admission of two-year-old child's statements to mother and babysitter allegedly recollecting events which had happened days or months earlier).

The declarant must personally observe the startling event. *Brown v. Keane*, 355 F.3d 82 (2d Cir. 2004). The burden of establishing perception rests with the proponent of the evidence. *Miller v. Keating*, 754 F.2d 507 (3d Cir. 1985). If the declarant does not have personal knowledge of the event, then the statement describing the event is inadmissible under Rules 803(2) and 602. *See* Fed.R.Evid. 803(2) Advisory Committee Note (stating that firsthand knowledge may appear from declarant's statement or be inferable from circumstances); *U.S. v. Joy*, 192 F.3d 761 (7th Cir. 1999) (personal knowledge includes opinions and inferences grounded in observations or other first-hand experiences; excited utterance about burglaries was reasonable inference for declarant to make); *Coyle v. Kristjan Palusalu Maritime Co., Ltd.*, 83 F. Supp. 2d 535 (E.D. Pa. 2000) (part of statement that declarant fell when he backed up and tripped over wire admissible as excited utterance; part of statement that wire had been replaced by ship's crew inadmissible where there was no evidence to indicate personal knowledge and it was equally plausible declarant simply assumed crew member had done it).

Where the declarant is unidentified, the proponent may have difficulty establishing the requirements of spontaneity and personal knowledge. *See Miller v. Keating*, 754 F.2d at 507 (evidence did not establish unidentified declarant saw accident or was excited when he allegedly spoke); *Meder v. Everest & Jennings, Inc.*, 637 F.2d 1182 (8th Cir. 1981) (impossible to determine whether maker of statement was eyewitness with personal knowledge). If the declarant cannot be identified, there is also the possibility that the declarant never existed. That, however, is really an issue of credibility to be decided by the court or other fact finder.

Crawford v. Washington—Criminal Cases

In *Crawford v. Washington*, 541 U.S. 36, 124 S. Ct. 1354, 158 L. Ed. 2d 177 (2004) (discussed at Commentary under HEARSAY: AUTHOR'S NOTE CONFRONTATION-CRIMINAL CASES), the Supreme Court held the Confrontation Clause requires that out-of-court *testimonial statement* cannot be admitted at trial unless the proponent establishes that: (1) the declarant is unavailable to testify, and (2) the defendant had a prior opportunity to cross-examine the declarant about his or her statement. *See also Whorton v. Bockting*, 549 U.S. 406, 127 S. Ct. 1173, 167, 167 L. Ed. 2d 1 (2007) (the Confrontation Clause has no application to out-of-court nontestimonial statements).

Subsequently, in *Davis v. Washington*, 547 U.S. 813, 126 S. Ct. 2266, 165 L. Ed. 2d 224 (2006) (consolidated appeals involving whether statements made to police during a 911 call or at a crime scene are testimonial), the Court held that statements are nontestimonial when the objective circumstances indicate that the "primary purpose" of police interrogation is to meet an ongoing emergency. They are testimonial when the circumstances objectively indicate that there is no such ongoing emergency, and that the primary purpose of the interrogation is to establish or prove past events potentially relevant to later criminal prosecution. *Id. See also U.S. v. Arnold*, 486 F.3d 177 (6th Cir. 2007) (Davis's assessment of 911 call and the on-the-scene statements indicate the line between testimonial and non-testimonial statements will not always be clear; each statement must be assessed on its own terms and in its own context to determine on which side of the line it falls); *U.S. v. Thomas*, 453 F.3d 838 (7th Cir. 2006) (911 call admissible as present sense impression and excited utterance); *U.S. v. Brown*, 441 F.3d 1330 (11th Cir. 2006) (excited utterance exception applied to testimony that witness overheard defendant's mother's side of phone conversation in which she stated "[Defendant], where you at . . . you didn't kill that lady, no," after which mother began to cry); *U.S. v. Brun*, 416 F.3d 703 (8th Cir. 2005) (adolescent's excited utterances were not testimonial in nature because they were emotional and spontaneous rather than deliberate and calculated).

The First Circuit rejects any per se rule and holds that a case-by-case examination of the totality of the circumstances is needed to determine whether or not a particular excited utterance should be deemed testimonial in nature. *U.S. v. Brito*, 427 F.3d 53 (1st Cir. 2005) (if it is determined that a statement qualifies as excited utterance, then the court must look to attendant circumstances and assess likelihood that a reasonable person would have either retained or regained capacity to make a testimonial statement at time of utterance).

Additional References

Graham, Handbook of Federal Evidence § 803.2 (7th ed. 2012)

Treatises and Practice Aids

Goode and Wellborn, Courtroom Handbook on Federal Evidence Chapter 5, Rule 803(2) and Obj. 36 (annual ed.)

Mueller & Kirkpatrick, Federal Evidence, §§ 8:66, 8:67 (3d ed. 2007)

Binder, Hearsay Handbook Chapter 9 (4th ed. 2001)

McCormick, Evidence § 272 (6th ed. 2006)

Park, Trial Objections Handbook § 4:23 (2nd ed. 2001)

HEARSAY EXCEPTION: FORFEITURE BY WRONGDOING

See:

Fed.R.Evid. 804(b)(6)
M.R.E. 804(b)(6)

Objection

- [*To a question*] Objection. The question calls for hearsay.
- [*To an answer*] Objection, hearsay. I move the answer be stricken and the jury be instructed not to consider it for any purpose.

Response

- The evidence has already established that the absence of the declarant was wrongfully procured; any hearsay objection has been forfeited.
- We intend to prove that the absence of the declarant was wrongfully procured. I ask the court to allow this testimony subject to our fulfilling that condition.

Commentary

As a codification of the long-standing doctrine of waiver by misconduct, Rule 804(b)(6) provides that a party forfeits the right to object to the introduction of hearsay if the party wrongfully causes the declarant to be unavailable to testify at trial. This has been described as a "prophylactic rule to deal with abhorrent behavior which strikes at the heart of the system of justice itself." Fed.R.Evid. 804(b)(6) Advisory Committee Note (internal quotations omitted).

The rule applies to all parties including the government. The wrongdoing that procures the unavailability of the declarant as a witness need not consist of a criminal act. *See* Rule 804(b)(6) Advisory Committee Note; *see also U.S. v. Ochoa*, 229 F.3d 631, 639 n.3 (7th Cir. 2000).

Because evidentiary rules cannot abrogate constitutional rights, it should be noted that the Supreme Court has held repeatedly that a defendant's intentional misconduct can affect a waiver of

Confrontation Clause rights under the Sixth Amendment. *See, e.g. Crawford v. Washington*, 541 U.S. 36, 62, 124 S. Ct. 1354, 1370, 158 L. Ed. 2d 177 (2004) ("[T]he rule of forfeiture by wrongdoing (which we accept) extinguishes confrontation claims on essentially equitable grounds . . ."); *Taylor v. United States*, 414 U.S. 17, 94 S. Ct. 194, 38 L. Ed. 2d 174 (1973); *Illinois v. Allen*, 397 U.S. 337, 90 S. Ct. 1057, 25 L. Ed. 2d 353 (1970). A well-established corollary is that the right of confrontation is forfeited with respect to any witness or potential witness whose absence a defendant wrongfully procures. *Reynolds v. United States*, 98 U.S. 145, 25 L. Ed. 244, 1878 WL 18416 (1878) (The rule has its foundation in the maxim that no one shall be permitted to take advantage of his own wrong); *Hodges v. Attorney General, State of Fla.*, 506 F.3d 1337, 1344 (11th Cir. 2007); *U.S. v. Johnson*, 495 F.3d 951, 970 (8th Cir. 2007); *U.S. v. Martinez*, 476 F.3d 961, 967 (D.C. Cir. 2007); *U.S. v. Montague*, 421 F.3d 1099 (10th Cir. 2005); *U.S. v. Cromer*, 389 F.3d 662 (6th Cir. 2004); *U.S. v. Houlihan*, 92 F.3d 1271 (1st Cir. 1996); *U.S. v. Mastrangelo*, 693 F.2d 269 (2d Cir. 1982); *U.S. v. Carlson*, 547 F.2d 1346 (8th Cir. 1976); *U.S. v. Johnson*, 403 F. Supp. 2d 721 (N.D. Iowa 2005) (exception is applicable to missing witness's statements in trial for murdering that witness, not just in a trial about which defendant allegedly feared that the missing witness would testify); *U.S. v. Lentz*, 384 F. Supp. 2d 934 (E.D. Va. 2005); *U.S. v. Mayhew*, 380 F. Supp. 2d 961 (S.D. Ohio 2005).

In *Giles v. California*, ___ U.S. ___, 128 S.Ct. 2678, 171 L. Ed. 2d 488 (2008), the Supreme Court held that unconfronted testimony is not admissible without a showing that by his conduct, defendant intended to and did prevent declarant from testifying. *See also U.S. v. Lentz*, 524 F.3d 501, 528–29 (4th Cir. 2008) (statements that defendant made to kidnapping victim, who related statements to third parties, were admissible upon trial court's determination, by preponderance of evidence, that defendant engaged in wrongdoing that was intended, at least in part, to procure victim's unavailability as witness); *U.S. v. Gray*, 405 F.3d 227, 242 (4th Cir. 2005) (in applying Rule 804(b)(6) "we have held that a defendant need only intend 'in part' to procure the defendant's unavailability.")

Whether a party has engaged in conduct justifying forfeiture is determined by the preponderance of the evidence standard contained in Rule 104(a). *Id. See Davis v. Washington*, 547 U.S. 813, 833, 126 S. Ct. 2266, 165 L. Ed. 2d 224 (2006) (while not taking a position on the standard necessary to demonstrate that a defendant has procured the unavailability of a witness and forfeited Confrontation Clause rights against that witness, the Supreme Court stated that "federal courts . . . have generally held the Government to the preponderance-of-the-evidence standard."). There is, however, a difference of opinion as to how this determination should be made. *Compare U.S. v. Dhinsa*, 243 F.3d 635 (2d Cir. 2001)* (judge must hold evidentiary hearing outside the presence of jury) *with U.S. v. Emery*, 186 F.3d 921 (8th Cir. 1999) (approving same procedure as is used with respect to hearsay statements of co-conspirators, i.e., trial court admitted hearsay evidence in presence of jury contingent upon proof of underlying murder of declarant by preponderance of evidence).

A number of circuits have held that Rule 804(b)(6) allows the admission of hearsay against a defendant by virtue of his having acquiesced in the acts taken to procure the declarant's unavailability. *Johnson*, 495 F.3d at 971 (forfeiture by wrongdoing doctrine applies when a defendant aids and abets murder of a potential witness against another person); *U.S. v. Rivera*, 412 F.3d 562 (4th Cir. 2005)

[Hearsay etc.]

**Dhinsa* holds that prior to finding defendant waived his confrontation rights with respect to out-of-court statements by an actual or potential witness admitted pursuant to Rule 804(b)(6), the court must hold an evidentiary hearing outside the presence of the jury in which the government has the burden of proving by a preponderance of the evidence that: (1) the defendant (or party against whom the out-of-court statement is offered) was involved in, or responsible for, procuring the unavailability of the declarant through knowledge, complicity, planning or in any other way, and (2) the defendant (or other party) acted with the intent of procuring declarant's unavailability. The government need not show defendant's sole motivation was to procure declarant's absence. It need only show defendant was motivated in part by a desire to silence the witness. 243 F.3d at 653–54.

(rejecting argument that defendant has to personally commit wrongful act which caused declarant's unavailability; Rule 804(b)(6) allows hearsay statements to be admitted against "a party who has engaged or acquiesced in" wrongdoing intended to procure unavailability of declarant); *U.S. v. Thompson*, 286 F.3d 950, 963–64 (7th Cir. 2002) (imputing co-conspirators actions to defendant for purposes of Rule 804(b)(6)); *U.S. v. Cherry*, 217 F.3d 811 (10th Cir. 2000) (same); *U.S. v. Mastrangelo*, 693 F.2d 269, 273–74 (2d Cir. 1982) (bare knowledge of plot to kill victim and failure to give warning to appropriate authorities sufficient to constitute waiver); *Olson v. Green*, 668 F.2d 421, 429 (8th Cir. 1982) (noting that someone acting on defendant's behalf to procure unavailability of witness can operate to waive defendant's hearsay objection). *See also U.S. v. Stewart*, 485 F.3d 666, 671 (2d Cir. 2007) (government was not required to show by direct evidence defendant's involvement in conspiracy to secure absence of witness via murder; defendant's participation with requisite knowledge and criminal intent may be established through circumstantial evidence).

Additional References

Graham, Handbook of Federal Evidence § 804.6 (7th ed. 2012)

Treatises and Practice Aids

Goode and Wellborn, Courtroom Handbook on Federal Evidence Chapter 5, Rule 804(b)(6) (annual ed.)
Binder, Hearsay Handbook Chapter 42 (4th ed. 2001)
McCormick, Evidence § 253 (6th ed. 2006)
Park, Trial Objections Handbook § 4:102 (2nd ed. 2001)

HEARSAY EXCEPTION: FORMER TESTIMONY

See:

Fed.R.Evid. 804(b)(1)
Mil.R.Evid. 804(b)(1)

Objection

- Objection, hearsay. The use of former testimony of the witness is inadmissible here because:
  - [*plaintiff/defendant had no opportunity and/or similar motive to develop this testimony at the prior proceeding (explain)*]
  - [*the prior proceeding did not involve the same subject matter/criminal issue*]
  - [*the witness has not been shown to be unavailable (specify)*]

Response

- The former testimony is admissible because:
- [*plaintiff/defendant was present and had a right to develop the testimony but chose not to*]
- [*the testimony was developed by a prior party who qualifies as plaintiff's/defendant's predecessor in interest*]
  - [*unavailability has been established pursuant to Rule 804(a) (specify details)*]

Commentary

In order for former testimony to be admissible under Rule 804(b)(1): (i) the declarant must be unavailable; (ii) the testimony must have been taken at a hearing or deposition in the same or another proceeding, and (iii) the party against whom the testimony is now offered must have had (or, in a civil action, its predecessor in interest must have had) an opportunity and similar motive to develop the testimony by direct, cross or redirect examination. *U.S. v. Loggins*, 486 F.3d 977 (7th Cir. 2007); *U.S. v. Hunt*, 521 F.3d 636 (6th Cir. 2008) (citing requirements of Rule and holding affidavit given to federal agents did not qualify); *U.S. v. Vartanian*, 245 F.3d 609 (6th Cir. 2001); *New Jersey Turnpike Authority v. PPG Industries, Inc.*,

197 F.3d 96 (3d Cir. 1999); *U.S. v. Mejia*, 376 F. Supp. 2d 460 (S.D. N.Y. 2005); *Tracinda Corp. v. DaimlerChrysler AG*, 362 F. Supp. 2d 487 (D. Del. 2005) (admitting deposition testimony of out-of-state witness where defendants had the opportunity to test the accuracy of her statements).

Predecessor In Interest-Civil Action

Although the rule does not define "predecessor in interest," a number of courts have indicated that privity or a common property interest is not required. *See Supermarket of Marlinton, Inc. v. Meadow Gold Dairies, Inc.*, 71 F.3d 119 (4th Cir. 1995) (in antitrust action by retail store alleging dairies conspired to fix prices, testimony by dairy official who appeared as government witness in prior criminal conspiracy trial admissible in store's case as former testimony notwithstanding that dairies were not defendants in earlier criminal case; privity not required and defendants' motivation in questioning dairy official in prior criminal trial was substantially similar to dairies' motivation here, to show conspiracy never occurred); *Horne v. Owens-Corning Fiberglas Corp.*, 4 F.3d 276, 283 (4th Cir. 1993) (deposition of company witness from earlier asbestos case properly admitted against plaintiff as former testimony since asbestos exposure in both cases was similar; "the party against whom the deposition is offered must point up distinctions in her case not evident in the earlier litigation that would preclude similar motives of witness examination"); *Clay v. Johns-Manville Sales Corp.*, 722 F.2d 1289 (6th Cir. 1983) (similar); *Lloyd v. American Export Lines, Inc.*, 580 F.2d 1179, 1187 (3d Cir. 1978) (testimony of alleged assailant given at prior Coast Guard hearing admissible against plaintiff in subsequent personal injury action against shipowner; "if it appears that in the former suit a party having a like motive to cross-examine about the same matters as the present party would have, was accorded an adequate opportunity for such examination, the testimony may be received against the present party. Under these circumstances, the previous party having like motive to develop the testimony about the same material facts is, in the final analysis, a predecessor in interest to the present party."); *Rule v. International Ass'n of Bridge,*

Structural and Ornamental Ironworkers, Local Union No. 396, 568 F.2d 558 (8th Cir. 1977) (party to second suit need not have been party to prior suit if interest of objecting party in prior suit was calculated to induce cross-examination as thorough as the interest of present opponent). *But see In re Screws Antitrust Litigation*, 526 F. Supp. 1316 (D. Mass. 1981) (witness' testimony from prior trial inadmissible under former testimony exception; predecessor in interest requirement not established where corporate defendants in earlier criminal antitrust action were different from defendants in subsequent civil action arising from same facts).

It should be noted that, while the rule has some flexibility in civil actions, when trial testimony is offered against a criminal defendant, the defendant must have been a party to the prior proceeding with the opportunity for cross-examination. *U.S. v. Deeb*, 13 F.3d 1532 (11th Cir. 1994); *see* McCormick, Evidence § 303.

Opportunity And Similar Motive To Develop The Testimony

In order for testimony from a prior hearing or deposition to be admissible, the party against whom it is offered must have had an opportunity and similar motive to develop or cross-examine that testimony. *United States v. Salerno*, 505 U.S. 317, 320, 112 S. Ct. 2503, 2506, 120 L. Ed. 2d 255 (1992) ("Nothing in the language of Rule 804(b)(1) suggests that a court may admit former testimony absent satisfaction of each of the Rule's elements."); *U.S. v. Lombard*, 72 F.3d 170, 188 (1st Cir. 1995) (codefendant's testimony from prior state murder trial properly admitted in subsequent federal trial on firearms charges because defendant had compelling interest in attacking same testimony in state proceeding; "The party against whom the prior testimony is offered must have had a similar, not necessarily an identical, motive to develop the adverse testimony in the prior proceeding."); *U.S. v. DiNapoli*, 8 F.3d 909, 914–15 (2d Cir. 1993) (prosecutor's lack of similar motive to challenge testimony of witnesses before grand jury precluded defendants from using it against the government at trial; "The proper approach . . . in assessing similarity of motive under Rule 804(b)(1) must consider whether the party resisting the offered testimony at a pending proceeding had at a prior proceeding an interest of substantially similar intensity to prove (or disprove) the same side of a substantially similar issue. The nature of the two proceedings-both what is at stake and the applicable burden of proof-and, to a lesser extent, the cross-examination at the prior proceeding-both what was undertaken and what was available but forgone-will be relevant though not conclusive on the ultimate issues of similarity of motive.") *U.S. v. Deeb*, 13 F.3d at 1532 (fact that other defendants at earlier trial had opportunity to cross-examine witness was not sufficient to admit prior testimony against defendant who was neither present nor represented at earlier trial; "At least as to criminal cases, Rule 804(b)(1) neither states nor implies that it is sufficient that another party with similar interests cross-examine the witness at the prior trial."); *Hill v. City of Chicago*, 2011 WL 3876915 (N.D.Ill. 2011) (the similar motive requirement operates to screen out those statements which although made under oath, were not subject to the scrutiny of a party interested in thoroughly testing their validity); *U.S. v. Zapata*, 357 F. Supp. 2d 667 (S.D. N.Y. 2005) (co-conspirator's earlier plea allocution containing exculpatory testimony in favor of defendant inadmissible as former testimony; in plea proceeding government lacked sufficient opportunity or motive to provide assurance of testimony's accuracy).

But the fact that a party changes counsel or that tactical decisions are made with respect to the extent of questioning does not negate the existence of opportunity and similar motive to develop the testimony. *See, e.g., Battle ex rel. Battle v. Memorial Hosp. at Gulfport*, 228 F.3d 544 (5th Cir. 2000) (error to exclude deposition; fact that defendants' strategy at expert's deposition was motivated by desire to understand plaintiff's case by asking open-ended questions and not cross-examining did not establish lack of similar motive); *U.S. v. Mann*, 161 F.3d 840, 861 (5th Cir. 1998) (upholding admission of deposition testimony and rejecting defendant's argument that deposition he chose not to attend was "mere discovery deposition" where he did not necessarily have motive to conduct cross-examination; "Rule 804(b)(1) . . . does not require that the party against whom the prior testimony is offered had a compelling tactical or strategic incentive to subject the testimony to cross-examination, only that an opportunity and similar motive to develop the testimony existed."); *U.S. v. Tannehill*, 49 F.3d 1049 (5th Cir. 1995) (where defendant made strategic choice to let codefendants conduct almost all cross-examination at first trial, no error to admit prior testimony of deceased government witness in subsequent proceeding where defendant was tried alone; although defendant's trial strategy may have changed, motive for cross-examination was same as initial trial); *Hendrix v. Raybestos-Manhattan, Inc.*, 776 F.2d 1492, 1506 (11th Cir. 1985) ("As a general rule, a party's decision to limit cross-examination in a discovery deposition is a strategic choice and does not preclude his adversary's use of the deposition at a subsequent proceeding.") Fed.R.Evid. 804(b)(1) Advisory Committee's Note ("If the party against whom . . . [the testimony is] now offered is the one against whom the testimony was offered previously, no unfairness is apparent in requiring him to accept his own prior conduct of cross-examination or decision not to cross-examine.").

Unavailability

The Sixth Amendment demands what the common law required: unavailability and a prior opportunity for cross-examination. *Crawford v. Washington*, 541 U.S. 36, 124 S. Ct. 1354, 158, 158 L. Ed. 2d 177 (2004). The constitutional requirement that a witness be "unavailable" before his prior testimony is admissible stands on separate footing that is independent of and in addition to the requirement of a prior opportunity for cross-examination. *See Barber v. Page*, 390 U.S. 719, 724–25, 88 S. Ct. 1318, 20 L. Ed. 2d 255 (1968) (admission of prior testimony that had been subjected to cross-examination violated Confrontation Clause because state did not prove witness was unavailable).

The definition of witness "unavailability" is provided in Rule 804(a) and includes, but is not limited to: assertion of privilege; refusal to testify; loss of memory; death, infirmity, physical or mental illness, or inability to compel attendance by process (subpoena) or other reasonable means. *See U.S. v. Reed*, 227 F.3d 763 (7th Cir. 2000) (refusal to testify); *U.S. v. Kehm*, 799 F.2d 354 (7th Cir. 1986) (privilege against self-incrimination); *U.S. v. Keithan*, 751 F.2d 9 (1st Cir. 1984) (physical disability); *Parrott v. Wilson*, 707 F.2d 1262 (11th Cir. 1983) (mental illness); *McDonnell v. U.S.*, 472 F.2d 1153 (8th Cir. 1973) (lack of memory).

Rule 804(a)(5) provides that in both civil and criminal cases, a declarant is unavailable if his presence cannot be secured by process or other reasonable means. The proponent has the burden of demonstrating unavailability and mere absence of the declarant is insufficient. *U.S. v. Yida*, 498 F.3d 945 (9th Cir. 2007) (government failed to demonstrate witness was unavailable when he refused to return from Israel to testify; government should not have allowed witness to be deported or should have made alternate arrangements; acknowledging split of authority re alien witnesses who leave United States before trial or retrial). *See Kirk v. Raymark Industries, Inc.*, 61 F.3d 147 (3d Cir. 1995) (error to admit expert's testimony from earlier, unrelated trial because nothing in record demonstrated that reasonable efforts were made to have Nebraska expert appear for trial in Philadelphia; witness was never contacted and offered his usual fee to secure attendance); *Angelo v. Armstrong World Industries, Inc.*, 11 F.3d 957 (10th Cir. 1993) (deposition of treating physician excluded because although witness was subpoenaed, no enforcement was requested and no explanation offered of any efforts to persuade him to testify).

Because of the constitutional preference for "face-to-face accusation," *Ohio v. Roberts*, 448 U.S. 56, 65, 100 S. Ct. 2531, 2538, 65 L. Ed. 2d 597 (1980), a witness in a criminal case cannot be found unavailable unless the prosecution has made reasonable good faith efforts to locate and present the witness, *id.* at 74. "Good faith" and "reasonableness" are factual matters to be determined on a case-by-case basis. *Christian v. Rhode*, 41 F.3d 461 (9th Cir. 1994). The central constitutional inquiry is whether or not the government's actions were reasonable given all the circumstances of a particular case. *Roberts*, 448 U.S. at 74; *see, e.g., U.S. v.*

Siddiqui, 235 F.3d 1318 (11th Cir. 2000) (admitting Swiss and Japanese depositions; testimony taken under oath before judicial officer; defense counsel attended and had opportunity for direct and cross-examination with objections preserved); *Whelchel v. Washington*, 232 F.3d 1197 (9th Cir. 2000) (habeas corpus: where state made no effort to seek witness' attendance at trial, introduction of his videotaped deposition violated defendant's rights under Confrontation Clause); *McCandless v. Vaughn*, 172 F.3d 255, 266 (3d Cir. 1999) (habeas corpus: where state's efforts to produce sole eyewitness to murder were casual, belated and slipshod, witness was not constitutionally "unavailable" and use of his preliminary hearing testimony violated petitioner's confrontation rights; "Confrontation Clause concerns are heightened and courts insist on more diligent efforts by the prosecution where a 'key' or 'crucial' witness' testimony is involved."); *U.S. v. Perez-Sosa*, 164 F.3d 1082 (8th Cir. 1998) (deposition testimony admissible where government showed witness had been deported to Mexico and Mexican authorities would not order extradition based on material witness warrant); *U.S. v. Medjuck*, 156 F.3d 916 (9th Cir. 1998) (videotaped depositions admissible where Canadian witnesses were beyond subpoena power of United States and refused to attend trial); *U.S. v. Marchese*, 842 F. Supp. 1307 (D. Colo. 1994) (same).

A party cannot interfere with the testimonial process and profit by his wrongdoing. If a witness is absent or refuses to testify because of the actions of the proponent of a statement, the witness is not unavailable and his statement cannot be used. Rule 804(a). Conversely, if a witness has given a prior statement or testimony but then is silenced by a party for the purpose of excluding his testimony entirely, then the prior testimony is admissible. *See* Hearsay Exception, Forfeiture By Wrongdoing, *supra*; *Magouirk v. Warden, Winn Correctional Center*, 237 F.3d 549 (5th Cir. 2001) (habeas corpus: admitting prior testimony of witness who was threatened at time of trial and refused to testify); *Geraci v. Senkowski*, 211 F.3d 6 (2d Cir. 2000) (habeas corpus: when threats make witness so fearful he will not testify, he is just as unavailable as witness who is dead or cannot be found); *U.S. v. Aguiar*,

975 F.2d 45 (2d Cir. 1992) (where, after hearing, court determines by preponderance of evidence that defendant procured absence of witness, defendant has waived his Sixth Amendment rights and hearsay objection); *U.S. v. Thevis*, 665 F.2d 616, 630 (5th Cir. 1982) (where government established that *Thevis* had principal witness murdered, he waived confrontation rights as well as hearsay objection once prosecution demonstrated need for victim's grand jury testimony and FBI interviews; "The law simply cannot countenance a defendant deriving benefits from murdering the chief witness against him. To permit such subversion of a criminal prosecution would be contrary to public policy, commonsense and the underlying purpose of the confrontation clause . . . and make a mockery of the system of justice that the right was designed to protect." (citation omitted)).

Deposition Rules

In criminal cases, when the government is unable to secure a witness' presence at trial, Fed.R.Crim.P. 15 permits admission of reported or videotaped depositions so long as the government makes diligent efforts to secure the defendant's physical presence at the deposition or, failing that, employs procedures that are adequate to allow the defendant to take an active role in the deposition. *U.S. v. Perez-Sosa*, 164 F.3d 1082 (8th Cir. 1998); *Medjuck*, 156 F.3d at 920. *See also* 8 U.S.C.A. § 1324(d) (West Supp. 1998) (videotaped deposition of witness to transporting of illegal aliens "who has been deported or otherwise expelled from the United States . . . may be admitted into evidence in an action brought for [transporting illegal aliens] if the witness was available for cross-examination and the deposition otherwise complies with the Federal Rules of Evidence.") and Fed.R.Civ.P. 32, use of Depositions in Court Proceedings.

Note: the fact that former testimony satisfies the requirements of Rule 804(b)(1) does not immunize it from exclusion under other rules. *Li v. Canarozzi*, 142 F.3d 83 (2d Cir. 1998) (deposition testimony of unavailable witness excluded under Rule 403 where its probative value was substantially outweighed by danger of unfair prejudice).

Crawford v. Washington—Criminal Cases

In *Crawford v. Washington*, 541 U.S. 36, 124 S. Ct. 1354, 158, 158 L. Ed. 2d 177 (2004) (discussed at Commentary under HEARSAY: AUTHOR'S NOTE CONFRONTATION-CRIMINAL CASES), a criminal case involving a Confrontation Clause challenge, the United States Supreme Court held that if a hearsay statement was "testimonial" in nature, it could not be introduced at trial in the absence of the declarant, unless the proponent establishes: (1) that the declarant is unavailable to testify, and (2) the defendant had a previous opportunity to cross-examine the declarant about his or her statement.

The Confrontation Clause requires that "testimonial" evidence (including former testimony) can only be admitted where the witness is unavailable and the defendant had an opportunity to cross-examine the witness in the prior proceeding. In order for a witness to be unavailable for constitutional purposes, the proponent of the evidence must have undertaken good faith efforts to procure the witness's attendance. *U.S. v. Ozsusamlar*, 428 F. Supp. 2d 161 (S.D. N.Y. 2006) (collecting cases).

Additional References

Graham, Handbook of Federal Evidence § 804.1 (7th ed. 2012)

Treatises and Practice Aids

Goode and Wellborn, Courtroom Handbook on Federal Evidence Chapter 5, Rule 804(b)(1) (annual ed.)

Mueller & Kirkpatrick, Federal Evidence, §§ 8:121 to 8:127 (3d ed. 2007)

Binder, Hearsay Handbook Chapter 33 (4th ed. 2001)

McCormick, Evidence Chapter 31 (6th ed. 2006)

Park, Trial Objections Handbook §§ 4:67 to 4:69 (2nd ed. 2001)

HEARSAY EXCEPTION: LEARNED TREATISE

See:

Fed.R.Evid. 803(18)
Mil.R.Evid. 803(18)

Objection

- [*To a question*] Objection. The question calls for hearsay.
- [*To an answer*] Objection, hearsay. I move that the answer be stricken and the jury be instructed not to consider it for any purpose.
- The witness does not acknowledge the text is authoritative; therefore she cannot be questioned about it.

Response

- The evidence is admissible under the learned treatise exception. I have established that the author of the [*treatise/periodical/pamphlet*] is a recognized expert on the subject and that this publication is considered authoritative.
- I have already established through other witnesses that the text is authoritative. Therefore, the fact that this witness refuses to acknowledge the point does not prevent her from being questioned about it.

Commentary

Rule 803(18) permits statements contained in published treatises, periodicals or pamphlets to be admitted as **substantive evidence** if such statements are established as a reliable authority by the testimony or admission of an expert witness or by judicial notice. *U.S. v. Norman*, 415 F.3d 466, 473 (5th Cir. 2005). If admitted, the statements may be read into evidence **but may not be received as exhibits**. *See* Rule 803(18) Advisory Committee Notes (the rule permits admission of learned treatises as substantive evidence, but only when "an expert is on the stand and available to explain and assist in the application of the treatise . . ..")

Learned treatises are considered trustworthy

because "they are written primarily for professionals and are subject to scrutiny and exposure for inaccuracy, with the reputation of the writer at stake." *Id.* Failure to lay a foundation as to the authoritative nature of a treatise requires its exclusion from evidence because the court has no basis on which to view it as trustworthy. *Schneider v. Revici*, 817 F.2d 987 (2d Cir. 1987) (treatise excluded where defense counsel never asked appropriate foundation questions). *In re Prempro Products Liability Litigation*, 554 F. Supp. 2d 871, 884 (E.D. Ark. 2008), judgment aff'd in part, rev'd in part on other grounds, 586 F.3d 547 (8th Cir. 2009) (expert must establish trustworthiness of a treatise as viewed by professionals in that field before evidence is admissible).

Mere publication does not meet the requirements of the rule. Nor does an article reach the dignity of reliable authority merely because the journal in which it appeared is reputable. The author must also be shown to be an authority before the article can be used as a learned treatise. *Twin City Fire Ins. Co. v. Country Mut. Ins. Co.*, 23 F.3d 1175 (7th Cir. 1994); *Meschino v. North American Drager, Inc.*, 841 F.2d 429 (1st Cir. 1988); *cf. Johnson v. William C. Ellis & Sons Iron Works, Inc.*, 609 F.2d 820 (5th Cir. 1980) (safety codes and standards are admissible when they are prepared by organizations formed for the purpose of promoting safety because they are inherently trustworthy and because of the expense and difficulty involved in assembling at trial those who have compiled such codes).

It is improper to introduce or read from a learned treatise except in conjunction with testimony by an expert witness. *Dartez v. Fibreboard Corp.*, 765 F.2d 456 (5th Cir. 1985); *Lee v. Gurney*, 2011 WL 2681225 (E.D.Va. 2011). The reason for the restriction is to avoid the possibility that the jury will misunderstand and misapply technical language and concepts if they are allowed to consider the publication itself instead of receiving the information through the testimony of an expert in the field. *Id.*

The following cases are illustrative: *Costantino v. David M. Herzog, M.D., P.C.*, 203 F.3d 164, 171 (2d Cir. 2000) (videotape on shoulder dystocia births produced by American College of Obstetricians and Gynecologists admissible as learned treatise; it is "overly artificial to say that information that is sufficiently trustworthy to overcome the hearsay bar when presented in a printed learned treatise loses the badge of trustworthiness when presented in a videotape"); *U.S. v. Turner*, 104 F.3d 217, 221 (8th Cir. 1997) (because Rule 803(18) specifically addresses learned treatises and since there was no expert testimony establishing these medical texts as authoritative, allowing articles into evidence via residual exception [Rule 807] would circumvent general purpose of the rules); *Carroll v. Morgan*, 17 F.3d 787, 790 (5th Cir. 1994) (plaintiff entitled to use treatise in cross-examining cardiologist who refused to recognize it as authoritative since another expert testified it was a reliable authority); *Dawsey v. Olin Corp.*, 782 F.2d 1254, 1264 (5th Cir. 1986) (plaintiffs were not entitled to use government manual to cross-examine defense expert where no witness testified manual was a reliable authority); *Tart v. McGann*, 697 F.2d 75, 78 (2d Cir. 1982) (trial court misunderstood rule when it prohibited use of learned treatise as substantive evidence and stated it could only be used "as a cross-examination tool"); *U.S. v. An Article of Drug*, 661 F.2d 742, 745 (9th Cir. 1981) (trial court correctly applied rule by allowing expert witnesses to read excerpts from treatises into evidence but refusing to admit treatises as exhibits); *Hogge v. Stephens*, 2011 WL 2161100 (E.D.Va. 2011) (because plaintiff failed to present medical articles in conjunction with expert testimony, they were inadmissible).

Additional References

Graham, Handbook of Federal Evidence § 803.18 (7th ed. 2012)

Treatises and Practice Aids

Goode and Wellborn, Courtroom Handbook on Federal Evidence Chapter 5, Rule 803(18) and Obj. 37 (annual ed.)

Mueller & Kirkpatrick, Federal Evidence, § 8:101 (3d ed. 2007)

Binder, Hearsay Handbook Chapter 26 (4th ed. 2001)

McCormick, Evidence § 321 (6th ed. 2006)

Park, Trial Objections Handbook §§ 4:46 to 4:49 (2nd ed. 2001)

HEARSAY EXCEPTION: MARKET REPORTS, COMMERCIAL PUBLICATIONS

See:

Fed.R.Evid. 803(17)
Mil.R.Evid. 803(17)

Objection

- [*To a question*] Objection. The question calls for hearsay.
- [*To a document*] Objection. The document is inadmissible hearsay.
- [*To an answer*] Objection, hearsay, I move that the answer be stricken and the jury be instructed not to consider it for any purpose.

Response

- Market quotations are made admissible when the price or value of items traded in any established market is in issue. Fed.R.Evid. 803(17). The document in question is a(n) [*official publication*] [*trade journal*] [*newspaper*] [*periodical of general circulation*].

Commentary

Rule 803(17) excepts from the hearsay rule market quotations, tabulations, lists, directories or other published compilations generally used and relied upon by the public or by persons in particular occupations. *U.S. v. Masferrer*, 514 F.3d 1158, 1162 (11th Cir. 2008) (historical financial data derived from computerized records of Bloomberg Financial Service fell within exception where financial information from organization was universally relied upon by individuals and institutions involved in financial markets, despite the fact that the Bloomberg information was used to price an illiquid asset); *U.S. v. Cassiere*, 4 F.3d 1006 (1st Cir. 1993) (criminal prosecution arising out of real estate transaction; court approved admission of publication called County Comps, generally used by appraisers to estimate value of properties); *U.S. v. Goudy*, 792 F.2d 664 (7th Cir. 1986) (Polk's Bank Directory); *Level 3 Communications, LLC v. Floyd*, 2011 WL 1106420 (M.D.Tenn. 2011) (telecommunications tariff report and price guide); *Fond du Lac Bumper Exchange, Inc. v. Jui Li Enterprise Co., Ltd.*, 753 F.Supp.2d 792 (E.D.Wis. 2010) (U.S. Customs records); *In re Young*, 390 B.R. 480, 492–93 (Bankr. D. Me. 2008) (Kelley Blue Book values may be accepted as reliable market reports or compilations); *Elliott Associates, L.P. v. Banco de la Nacion*, 194 F.R.D. 116 (S.D. N.Y. 2000) (interest rates obtained from Federal Reserve Board website and Bloomberg reporting service); *In re Byington*, 197 B.R. 130 (Bankr. D. Kan. 1996) (National Automobile Dealers Association "NADA" guide containing wholesale and retail values for new and used cars); *In re Araujo*, 2011 WL 3207371 (Bankr. N.D.Cal. 2011) (recognizing both Kelley Blue Book and NADA Guide as admissible under Rule 803(17)).

The basis for the exception is the necessity for admitting important information not otherwise conveniently available and its inherent trustworthiness (general reliance by public or segment thereof; on information compiled by persons who generally have an economic incentive to be accurate and no motive to deceive). *Conoco Inc. v. Department of Energy*, 99 F.3d 387 (Fed. Cir. 1996) (oil purchase summaries which plaintiff created for its own internal use did not have the same indicia of reliability as commercial publications and were inadmissible under Rule 803(17)); *Rooney v. Sprague Energy Corp.*, 519 F. Supp. 2d 110, 129 (D. Me. 2007) (*dicta,* copies of advertisements downloaded and copied from the internet present a host of potential evidentiary problems); *White Industries, Inc. v. Cessna Aircraft Co.*, 611 F. Supp. 1049 (W.D. Mo. 1985) (exception does not apply to SEC 10-K forms because they are simply filed, not circulated or published, nor to company prospectuses; publications contemplated by the rule are those which deal with compilations of relatively straightforward objective facts not requiring a subjective analysis of other facts in order to create compilations).

A publication may be qualified for this exception by the testimony of a knowledgeable witness. Alternatively, its qualification for the exception may be judicially noticed by the trial judge under Fed.R.Evid. 201.

The Uniform Commercial Code also creates an

exception to the hearsay rule in UCC cases for market quotations of goods regularly bought and sold in any established commodity market. Sec. 2-724, Admissibility of market quotations, provides:

> Whenever the prevailing price or value of any goods regularly bought and sold in any established commodity market is in issue, reports in official publications or trade journals or in newspapers or periodicals of general circulation published as the reports of such market shall be admissible in evidence. The circumstances of the preparation of such a report may be shown to affect its weight but not its admissibility.

Additional References

Graham, Handbook of Federal Evidence § 803.17 (7th ed. 2012)

Hawkland, UCC Series § 2-724 (Art. 2) (annual ed.)

Treatises and Practice Aids

Mueller & Kirkpatrick, Federal Evidence, § 8:100 (3d ed. 2007)

Binder, Hearsay Handbook Chapter 25 (4th ed. 2001)

McCormick, Evidence § 321 (6th ed. 2006)

Park, Trial Objections Handbook § 4:52 (2nd ed. 2001)

HEARSAY EXCEPTION: PERSONAL OR FAMILY HISTORY

See:

Fed.R.Evid. 803(11),(12),(13),(19); Fed.R.Evid. 804(b)(4)
Mil.R.Evid. 803(11)(12)(13)(19); Mil.R.Evid. 804(b)(4)

Objection

- [*To a question*] Objection. The question calls for hearsay.
- [*To a document*] Objection. The document is inadmissible hearsay.
- [*To an answer*] Objection, hearsay. I move the answer be stricken and the jury be instructed not to consider it for any purpose.

Response

The evidence is admissible:

- [*as a record of a religious society / municipality pursuant to* Rule 803(11) or (12)]
- [*as a family record or artifact under* Rule 803(13)]
- [*as a statement of reputation among family members or associates within the community concerning personal or family history under* Rule 803(19)]
- *under Rule 804(b)(4), as a statement by a family member or intimate associate concerning a fact of family history. As a foundation, I have established that declarant is unavailable [specify] as well as his / her status as [a family member] [one who was intimately associated with the family].*

Commentary

One of the oldest exceptions to the hearsay rule is the "pedigree" exception which encompasses statements concerning family history, such as the date and place of birth and death of members of the family and facts about marriage, descent and relationship.

Facts concerning family history may be proven

in three different ways:

1. by documents and artifacts including records of religious organizations, marriage and baptismal certificates, notations in family Bibles, genealogies, charts, engravings on rings, urns, crypts, tombstones and inscriptions on family portraits. Rules 803(11), (12), (13); *see Lewis v. Marshall*, 30 U.S. 470, 5 Pet. 470, 8 L. Ed. 195, 1831 WL 3984 (1831) (entry in family Bible admissible as evidence of date of landowner's death).
2. by evidence of reputation among members of (i) a person's family, (ii) associates, or (iii) in the community. Rule 803(19).
3. where the declarant is unavailable as a witness, by declarant's statements about either his own history or about the history of another person. When the statements concern the history of another person, trustworthiness must first be established by proof that declarant was related to or intimately associated with the other person or family. Rule 804(b)(4).

When proof consists of a public record, such as a civil marriage or birth certificate, a properly authenticated document is sufficient evidence. When the record is not a public record, e.g., a marriage certificate signed by a member of a religious organization, the proponent is required to show that the act to which the certificate relates is one that the maker of the certificate was authorized to perform. *See* Rule 803(12) Advisory Committee's Note.

Whereas the exceptions contained in Rules 803(11), (12) and (13) are directed to documents and artifacts, Rule 803(19) permits the use of reputation evidence to prove personal or family history. *Ramirez v. Clinton*, 2011 WL 2838173 (D.Minn. 2011). This includes testimony by a witness about his or her own history or the history of another person. Id.

A witness who gives reputational testimony concerning another person's history must first demonstrate that he knows of the person and is truly familiar with the family, associates or community in which the reputation has been formed and that the basis of the reputation is likely to be reliable.

Blackburn v. United Parcel Service, Inc., 179 F.3d 81 (3d Cir. 1999); *U.S. v. Jean-Baptiste*, 166 F.3d 102 (2d Cir. 1999) (in prosecution for making false statements in passport application, father should have been permitted to testify defendant daughter was born in Virgin Islands; Rule 803(19) contemplates that family members may testify about common understanding as to birth of family member); *Government of Virgin Islands v. Joseph*, 765 F.2d 394 (3d Cir. 1985) (witness' testimony concerning her own age can be considered reputation concerning personal or family history within Rule 803(19) exception); *McBride on Behalf of McBride v. Heckler*, 619 F. Supp. 1554 (D.N.J. 1985) (in Social Security benefits proceeding, reversible error for ALJ to exclude testimony by paternal family members that deceased father lived with and supported child and openly acknowledged his paternity since such statements fall under Rule 803(19) exception); *Lazovick v. Sun Life Ins. Co. of America*, 586 F. Supp. 918 (E.D. Pa. 1984) (parent's admission that son committed suicide was binding because it was an admission; Rule 803(19) cited as additional support).

Where the alleged reputation is based on nothing more than rumors of unknown origin, or a single instance of "someone told me so," a proper foundation has not been laid for admitting such evidence under Rule 803(19). *Blackburn*, 179 F.3d at 101; *see U.S. v. Ullah*, 282 Fed. Appx. 923 (2d Cir. 2008) (his father told defendant about defendant's own birth does not fall within this exception) (slip op.).

For cases discussing Rule 804(b)(4), *see*: *U.S. v. Farah*, 2007 WL 2309749 at *7 (4th Cir. 2007) (because defendant's father was deceased and, therefore, unavailable at trial, his statements contained within his immigration file concerning his and his family's Somali clan membership are excepted from the hearsay rule) (slip op.); *U.S. v. Pluta*, 176 F.3d 43 (2d Cir. 1999) (border agent's testimony that two women found hiding in brush near Canadian border had said they were Polish citizens admissible under Rule 804(b)(4)(A)); *U.S. v. Hernandez*, 105 F.3d 1330 (9th Cir. 1997) (trial court properly admitted officer's testimony that defendant told him he was born in Mexico; Rule

804(b)(4)(A) makes specific reference to statements concerning declarant's own birth); *U.S. v. Carvalho*, 742 F.2d 146 (4th Cir. 1984) (in prosecution for using false alien registration cards, government could not use affidavits from former spouses reciting reasons why they had married defendants; motive for marriage was not type of fact within Rule 804(b)(4) exception).

Crawford v. Washington—Criminal Cases

The impact of *Crawford v. Washington*, 541 U.S. 36, 124 S. Ct. 1354, 158 L. Ed. 2d 177 (2004) on the law of hearsay in criminal cases is discussed at Commentary under HEARSAY: AUTHOR'S NOTE CONFRONTATION-CRIMINAL CASES. In *U.S. v. Gonzalez-Marichal*, 317 F. Supp. 2d 1200 (S.D. Cal. 2004), defendant was prosecuted for transporting illegal aliens. A material witness who was interrogated by the government admitted to Mexican citizenship. She was then deported back to Mexico. The prosecution argued her statement was admissible under the personal history exception of Rule 804(b)(4). The court excluded the statement in light of *Crawford*, holding that admission of a statement obtained during the course of custodial interrogation concerning the underlying crimes would violate the Confrontation Clause.

Additional References

Graham, Handbook of Federal Evidence §§ 803.11, 803.12, 803.13, 803.19, 804.4 (7th ed. 2012)

Treatises and Practice Aids

Mueller & Kirkpatrick, Federal Evidence, § 8:97 (3d ed. 2007)

Binder, Hearsay Handbook Chapters 19, 20, 21, 27, 37 (4th ed. 2001)

McCormick, Evidence § 311 (6th ed. 2006)

Park, Trial objections Handbook §§ 4:51, 4:59 to 4:61 (2nd ed. 2001)

HEARSAY EXEMPTION: PRIOR CONSISTENT STATEMENT

See:

Rule 801(d)(1)(B)
Mil.R.Evid. 801(d)(1)(B)

Objection

- [*To a question*] Objection. The question calls for hearsay and has no other purpose except to bolster trial testimony with allegedly prior consistent statements.
- [*To an answer*] Objection, hearsay. I move that the answer be stricken and the jury be instructed not to consider it for any purpose.

Response

- The question is proper. My opponent's cross-examination attacked the witness' statement by [*asserting/implying*] it was [*recently fabricated*] [*is the product of improper influence or motive*]. This testimony is offered to rebut that charge.
- The question will elicit prior consistent statements which are not offered for their truth but only for the limited purpose of rehabilitation. The restrictions contained in Rule 801(d)(1)(B) have no application.

Commentary

Under Rule 801(d)(1)(B), a prior consistent statement is excluded from the definition of hearsay and may be admitted as substantive evidence if: (1) the witness testifies at trial and is subject to cross-examination; (2) the prior statement is consistent with the witness' trial testimony; (3) the statement is offered to rebut an express or implied charge of recent fabrication or improper influence or motive; and (4) the statement was made before the witness had a motive to fabricate. *Tome v. U.S.*, 513 U.S. 150, 115 S. Ct. 696, 130 L. Ed. 2d 574 (1995) (adding the temporal requirement that the consistent statement must pre-date the motive to falsify); *U.S. v. Belfast*, 611 F.3d 783 (11th Cir. 2010); *U.S. v. Millbrook*, 553 F.3d 1057 (7th Cir. 2009) (prior consistent statements go beyond rebuttal and constitute substantive evidence in the case); *U.S. v. Frazier*, 469 F.3d 85 (3d Cir. 2006) (there need be only a suggestion that the witness consciously altered his testimony in order to permit the use of earlier statements that are generally consistent with the testimony at trial); *Smith v. Potter*, 445 F.3d 1000 (7th Cir. 2006) (statements did not qualify since they were made long after declarant had motive to fabricate); *U.S. v. Londondio*, 420 F.3d 777 (8th Cir. 2005) (to rebut implied charge that prosecution witness fabricated testimony to receive a more favorable sentence, Rule 801(d)(1)(B) permitted government to introduce witness's prior out-of-court statement to federal agent); *U.S. v. Ruiz*, 249 F.3d 643 (7th Cir. 2001) (where cross-examination implied police testimony was fictional because not contained in written post-incident report, police officer's account of statements made by fellow officer over walkie-talkie who was then observing defendant admissible as prior consistent statement); *U.S. v. Stoecker*, 215 F.3d 788 (7th Cir. 2000) (where voir dire and cross-examination were designed to imply that witness had incentive to testify falsely because of plea agreement, no error to admit consistent statements made to FBI five years before plea agreement); *U.S. v. Powers*, 168 F.3d 741 (5th Cir. 1999) (since prior consistent statements were admissible only to rebut a charge of fabrication, admitting statements made after time when motivation to fabricate arose constitutes error); *U.S. v. Roach*, 164 F.3d 403 (8th Cir. 1998) (a witness other than the declarant is permitted to testify about the statement); *Whitbeck v. Vital Signs, Inc.*, 159 F.3d 1369 (D.C. Cir. 1998) (error to exclude plaintiff's statements to others describing conversation with supervisor who rejected request to use wheelchair at work; plaintiff's credibility had been directly challenged and prior consistent statements were made months before denial of disability benefits, the event which defendant claimed furnished motive to lie); *U.S. v. Street*, 66 F.3d 969 (8th Cir. 1995) (where park ranger was challenged on cross-examination with exaggerating incident because his trial testimony referred to defendant's string of obscenities during violent confrontation whereas his prior grand jury testimony had not, no error on redirect to admit incident report describing defendant's conduct in same terms as trial testimony); *U.S. v. Alzanki*, 54 F.3d 994 (1st Cir. 1995) (in prosecution for involuntary servitude, where defense attacked testimony and impugned motives of domestic worker by suggesting she was trying to sell her story to Hollywood, government was entitled to respond with testimony by nurses and police officer relating her earlier statements of inhuman treatment; prior statements were consistent with trial testimony and made long before motivations attributed to her had arisen); *U.S. v. Reliford*, 58 F.3d 247 (6th Cir. 1995) (where prosecution witness was challenged on cross-examination that 'his memory got better with time', no error to admit his statements given to police shortly after crime since they were consistent with his trial testimony and rebutted any notion of recent fabrication).

Although the witness must testify at trial and be subject to cross-examination, the prior consistent statement may be testified to either by the witness himself or any other person with personal knowledge of the statement. *U.S. v. Caracappa*, 614 F.3d 30 (2nd Cir. 2010) (where declarant has already testified and the prior consistent statement is proffered through the testimony of another witness, the Rule's "subject to cross-examination requirement is satisfied if opposing party is not denied opportunity to recall declarant to the stand for cross-examination regarding the statement"); *U.S. v. Washington*, 434 F.3d 7 (1st Cir. 2006); *U.S. v. Roach*; *U.S. v. Lanier*, 578 F.2d 1246 (8th Cir. 1978).

Several courts of appeal have adopted, at least implicitly, the position that a *Tome* premotive analysis requires the trial court to consider the entire record rather than requiring the proponent of the prior consistent statement to offer a specific date on which the motive arose. *Frazier*, 469 F.3d at 93; *U.S. v. Trujillo*, 376 F.3d 593 (6th Cir. 2004).

Admission of prior consistent statements before impeachment of the declarant may constitute reversible error. *U.S. v. Lowe*, 65 F.3d 1137 (4th Cir. 1995) (corroborative testimony consisting of prior consistent statements is ordinarily inadmissible unless the testimony sought to be bolstered has first been impeached).

When Exception Does Not Apply

Not every impeachment of a witness will permit rehabilitation by means of prior consistent statements. Rehabilitation is not permissible where the witness is impeached by contradiction or by a showing of the implausibility of his testimony. *See U.S. v. Drury*, 396 F.3d 1303 (11th Cir. 2005) (prior consistent statements are admissible non-hearsay only if offered to rebut specific allegation of recent fabrication, not to rehabilitate credibility that has been generally called into question); *Breneman v. Kennecott Corp.*, 799 F.2d 470 (9th Cir. 1986) (mere contradictory testimony cannot give rise to an implied charge of fabrication). The reason for this limitation is that when there is a contradiction between the testimonies of two witnesses, it cannot help the trier of fact in deciding between them merely to show that one of the witnesses said the same thing previously. "If that were an argument, then the witness who had repeated his story to the greatest number of people would be the most credible." 4 Wigmore on Evidence, § 1127 (Chadborn rev. 1972); *Tome*, 513 U.S. at 157–58 ("the Rule speaks of a party rebutting an alleged motive, not bolstering the veracity of the story told."); *U.S. v. Lozada-Rivera*, 177 F.3d 98, 104 (1st Cir. 1999) ("Generally speaking, a charge of improper motive or recent fabrication need not be expressly made or buttressed by concrete evidence. But the proponent of the evidence must point to specific questions during his adversary's examination that suggest recent fabrication or bias. Merely appealing to credibility as a live issue will not do the trick."); *U.S. v. Washington*, 106 F.3d 983, 1001 (D.C. Cir. 1997) (where part of charged conspiracy was providing police protection to drug dealers and defense witness would have testified defendant said he would be doing some private security work, prior statement properly excluded: defendant's credibility was subjected only to "a generalized attack and more than this is required for admission under this rationale"; even if there had been a charge of recent fabrication or improper motive, prior statement had no rebutting force against such a charge.); *Gates v. Rivera*, 993 F.2d 697 (9th Cir. 1993) (In civil rights action against police officer, witness to stand-off testified at trial that he did not see plaintiff's decedent reach into his pockets. Plaintiff was not allowed to ask investigating detective if witness had said very same thing at time of incident. Since there was no express or implied charge that witness' testimony was inaccurate or a fabrication, his prior consistent statement was inadmissible hearsay).

Motive To Fabricate Is A Preliminary Question

At least four circuits agree that whether a witness had a motive to fabricate at the time he made the prior consistent statement is a preliminary question under Rule 104 to be resolved by the trial court based upon the particular circumstances of an individual case. *U.S. v. Prieto*, 232 F.3d 816 (11th Cir. 2000) (collecting cases); *U.S. v. Fulford*, 980 F.2d 1110 (7th Cir. 1992) (rather than attaching automatically on arrest, court recognized that a judge could reasonably find that motive to fabricate did not exist until the witness entered into cooperation agreement with government; reasonable minds can differ as to when a witness may have first possessed a motive to fabricate). *But see U.S. v. Moreno*, 94 F.3d 1453 (10th Cir. 1996) and *U.S. v. Forrester*, 60 F.3d 52 (2d Cir. 1995) (adopting *per se* rule that motive to fabricate necessarily and automatically attaches upon arrest).

Statements Offered Not For Truth But Only As To Credibility

The extent to which a prior consistent statement can be offered into evidence not for its truth but only to rehabilitate the credibility of a witness who has been impeached by prior inconsistent statements has been aptly termed "an extremely complex subject," as perplexing as any in the law of evidence. Graham, Handbook of Federal Evidence, § 801.12.

Broad admissibility has inherent difficulties, including the danger that a party can too easily manufacture evidence with post-motive self-serving statements. Moreover, it is questionable whether the distinction between a prior consistent statement offered for its truth under Rule 801(d)(1)(B) to rebut a charge of recent fabrication versus a prior consistent statement offered not for its truth but for the limited purpose of rehabilitation, has much, if any, meaning to a jury. *See Tome*, 513 U.S. at 171 (Breyer, J. dissenting).

Nonetheless, the majority view is that "where prior consistent statements are not offered for their truth but for the limited purpose of rehabilitation . . . Rule 801(d)(1)(B) and its concomitant restrictions do not apply." *U.S. v. Ellis*, 121 F.3d 908, 919 (4th Cir. 1997) (collecting cases). Use of such evidence has been permitted where the prior consistent statements serve to clarify whether the impeaching statements really were inconsistent when considered in full context. *See U.S. v. Kenyon*, 397 F.3d 1071, 1081 (8th Cir. 2005). This can occur when other consistent statements come from the same document or transcript and pertain to the same supposedly inconsistent statement. *See U.S. v. Simonelli*, 237 F.3d 19, 29 (1st Cir. 2001) (government's rehabilitative use of its witness' prior grand jury testimony improperly went beyond specific inconsistencies in that testimony addressed on cross-examination; "the evidence [introduced on redirect] was an extra helping of what the jury had heard before."); *U.S. v. Pierre*, 781 F.2d 329, 333 (2d Cir. 1986) (prior consistent statements must have some rebutting force "beyond showing that the witness had at an earlier time been consistent with his trial testimony."); *U.S. v. Holland*, 526 F.2d 284 (5th Cir. 1976) (allowing government to use statement made in the same grand jury proceeding to correct an earlier misstatement in grand jury testimony which had been used to impeach witness).

Crawford v. Washington—Criminal Cases

The impact of *Crawford v. Washington*, 541 U.S. 36, 124 S. Ct. 1354, 158 L. Ed. 2d 177 (2004) on the law of hearsay in criminal cases is discussed at Commentary under HEARSAY: AUTHOR'S NOTE CONFRONTATION-CRIMINAL CASES. Here, however, it is a requirement of Rule 801(d)(1)(B) that the witness-declarant be subject to cross-examination concerning the prior statement. *U.S. v. Torrez-Ortega*, 184 F.3d 1128 (10th Cir. 1999).

This would appear to satisfy *Crawford's* mandate that "[w]here testimonial statements are at issue, the only indicium of reliability sufficient to satisfy constitutional demands is the one the Constitution actually prescribes: confrontation." 541 U.S. at 68–69. See *U.S. v. Caracappa*, supra, which addresses the situation where the prior consistent statement is proffered not by the declarant but by testimony of another witness who has firsthand knowledge of the statement.

Additional References

Graham, Handbook of Federal Evidence § 801.12 (7th ed. 2012)

Treatises and Practice Aids

Goode and Wellborn, Courtroom Handbook on Federal Evidence Chapter 5, Rule 801(d)(1)(B) and Obj. 37 (annual ed.)

Mueller & Kirkpatrick, Federal Evidence, §§ 8:38 to 8:40 (3d ed. 2007)

Binder, Hearsay Handbook § 2.12 (4th ed. 2001)

McCormick, Evidence § 47 (6th ed. 2006)

Park, Trial Objections Handbook §§ 4:8, 4:10 (2nd ed. 2001)

HEARSAY EXCEPTION: PUBLIC RECORDS AND REPORTS

See:

Fed.R.Evid. 803(8)
Mil.R.Evid. 803(8)

Objection

- [*To a question*] Objection. The question calls for hearsay.
- [*To an answer*] Objection, hearsay. I move that the evidence be stricken and the jury be instructed not to consider it for any purpose.

Response

- The evidence is admissible under the public records exception to the hearsay rule. As foundation, I have established that the record sets forth [*the activities of a public office or agency*], [*matters observed in the course of official duties*], [(*in civil actions*) *factual findings of a legally authorized investigation*].

Commentary

Under the public records exception, records, reports, statements or data compilations, in any form, of public offices or agencies which set forth:

(A) the activities of the office or agency;
(B) matters observed in the course of official duties; or
(C) in civil actions, factual findings resulting from an investigation made pursuant to authority granted by law may be admitted unless the sources of information or other circumstances indicate lack of trustworthiness. Rule 803(8).

The justification for the exception is the assumption that a public official will perform his duty properly and the unlikelihood that he will remember details independently of the record. *U.S. v. Midwest Fireworks Mfg. Co., Inc.*, 248 F.3d 563 (6th Cir. 2001) (admitting records under 803(8) exception is a practical necessity that must be afforded to government officers who, in the course of their duties, have made thousands of similar written hearsay statements concerning events within their jurisdiction); *U.S. v. Montero-Camargo*, 177 F.3d 1113 (9th Cir. 1999); *Bradford Trust Co. of Boston v. Merrill Lynch, Pierce, Fenner and Smith, Inc.*, 805 F.2d 49 (2d Cir. 1986).

The admissibility of a public record is assumed as a matter of course unless there are sufficient negative factors to indicate a lack of trustworthiness. *English v. District of Columbia*, 651 F.3d 1 (D.C.Cir. 2011); *Kennedy v. Joy Technologies, Inc.*, 269 Fed. Appx. 302 (4th Cir. 2008). The party opposing admission has the burden to establish unreliability. *Maxwell v. Ford Motor Co.*, 160 Fed. Appx. 420 (5th Cir. 2005); *Zeus Enterprises, Inc. v. Alphin Aircraft, Inc.*, 190 F.3d 238 (4th Cir. 1999); *Gilbrook v. City of Westminster*, 177 F.3d 839 (9th Cir. 1999); *Clark v. Clabaugh*, 20 F.3d 1290 (3d Cir. 1994); *Ellis v. International Playtex, Inc.*, 745 F.2d 292 (4th Cir. 1984); Rule 803(8) Advisory Committee Note (rule "assumes admissibility in the first instance but with ample provision for escape if sufficient negative factors are present.")

Law Enforcement Exclusion-Criminal Cases

Rule 803(8)(B) excludes from the scope of the exception "matters observed by police officers and other law enforcement personnel" in criminal cases.* *U.S. v. Sharpe*, 193 F.3d 852 (5th Cir. 1999). The reason for this exclusion is that observations by police officers at the scene of the crime or apprehension of the defendant are not as reliable as observations by public officials in other cases because of the adversarial nature of the confrontation between the police and the defendant in criminal cases. *U.S. v. Pena-Gutierrez*, 222 F.3d 1080

[Hearsay etc.]

*The Military Rules, however, explicitly state that notwithstanding section (B), the following are admissible as a record of a fact or event, if made by a person within the scope of official duty:

> . . . enlistment papers, physical examination papers, outline figure and fingerprint cards, forensic laboratory reports, chain of custody documents, morning reports and other personnel accountability documents, service records, officer and enlisted qualification records, records of court-martial convictions, logs, unit personnel diaries, individual equipment records, guard reports, daily strength records of prisoners, and rosters of prisoners.

(9th Cir. 2000).

Many courts, however, draw a distinction between police records prepared in a routine, nonadversarial setting and those resulting from a more subjective investigation and evaluation of a crime. Where a police report contains factual matter prepared in routine fashion, courts have admitted the record despite the seemingly absolute language of the Rule. *See, e.g., U.S. v. Caraballo*, 595 F.3d 1214 (11th Cir. 2010) (admitting I.N.S. "A" file, a compendium of documents which tracks an alien's status); *U.S. v. Brown*, 9 F.3d 907, 912 (11th Cir. 1993) (no error to admit police property receipt for handgun in weapons possession prosecution; "this is the type of reliable record envisioned by the drafters of Rule 803(8)"); *U.S. v. Quezada*, 754 F.2d 1190, 1194 (5th Cir. 1985) (admission of deportation warrant; "In the case of documents recording routine, objective observations, made as a part of the everyday function of the preparing official or agency, the factors likely to cloud the perception of an official engaged in the more traditional law enforcement functions of observation and investigation of crime are simply not present."). *See also Montero-Camargo*, 177 F.3d at 1124 (drug prosecution, admitting Mexican motor vehicle registration under 803(8)(A); "The registration of automobiles is a bureaucratic, nonadversarial activity undertaken by government employees with no stake in the outcome of criminal prosecutions such as this.").

Investigative Reports—Generally

When an investigation is made pursuant to legal authority, the Supreme Court has interpreted Rule 803(8)(C) to permit admission of opinions and conclusions as well as factual determinations. *Beech Aircraft Corp. v. Rainey*, 488 U.S. 153, 109 S. Ct. 439, 102 L. Ed. 2d 445 (1988) (error to exclude portions of Judge Advocate General report on Navy plane crash which contained opinions and conclusions). Two criteria must be met. First, all statements in such report must be based on factual investigation. *Id.* at 167. Second, any portion of the report admitted into evidence must be sufficiently trustworthy. In making the trustworthiness determination, the court should not focus on questions of credibility, e.g., whether certain witnesses are believable, whether the bases for a conclusion are complete and accurate, all of which are matters for the jury. Instead, the focus is on reliability, that is, whether the report was compiled or prepared in a way that indicates its conclusions can be relied upon. *Anderson v. Westinghouse Savannah River Co.*, 406 F.3d 248 (4th Cir. 2005); *Moss v. Ole South Real Estate, Inc.*, 933 F.2d 1300 (5th Cir. 1991) (collecting cases). The *Rainey* Court approved the following nonexclusive factors in determining whether a report is sufficiently trustworthy: (1) the timeliness of the investigation; (2) the investigator's skill and experience; (3) whether a hearing was held; and (4) possible bias when reports are prepared with a view to possible litigation. *Accord*, *Estate of Edward W. Knoster v. Ford Motor Co.*, 200 Fed. Appx. 106 (3d Cir. 2006); Barry v. Trustees of Intern. Ass'n Full-Time Salaried Officers and Employees of Outside Local Unions and District Counsel's (Iron Workers) Pension Plan, 467 Fed.Supp.2d 91 (D.D.C. 2006).

The following cases are illustrative: *U.S. v. O'Keefe*, 426 F.3d 274 (5th Cir. 2005) (in trial for misconduct or negligence of ship officer, portions of investigative report containing headings stating report's conclusions properly excluded; jury not investigator had to determine whether defendant caused passenger's death and trial judge properly balanced probative value against likelihood of confusion); *U.S. v. Spano*, 421 F.3d 599 (7th Cir. 2005) (when record keeper, rather than being a clerical or professional employee, is a principal with strong motive to falsify records, trial judge may deem records so unreliable as to be unworthy of jury's consideration); *U.S. v. Lopez-Moreno*, 420 F.3d 420 (5th Cir. 2005) (computer printouts from Bureau of Immigration and Customs Enforcement for van passengers, showing dates on which they were deported to Mexico, were admissible as public records); *Bridgeway Corp. v. Citibank*, 201 F.3d 134 (2d Cir. 2000) (in action to enforce Liberian judgment, admitting U.S. State Department Country Report indicating that the Liberian judicial system was corrupt and in disarray); *Desrosiers v. Flight Intern. of Florida Inc.*, 156 F.3d 952 (9th Cir. 1998) (no error to exclude portions of JAG report on crash of military transport plane where report was first ever prepared by investigating officer who: (1) did not attend aviation accident reconstruction school until after completing report; (2) had no formal training in aircraft accident investigation; and (3) never reviewed avionics maintenance records before issuing report); *Complaint of Nautilus Motor Tanker Co., Ltd.*, 85 F.3d 105 (3d Cir. 1996) (no error to admit Coast Guard report containing opinions and conclusions that ship's grounding was fault of docking pilot); *Kehm v. Procter & Gamble Mfg. Co.*, 724 F.2d 613 (8th Cir. 1983) (trial court properly admitted reports of epidemiological studies conducted by Center for Disease Control and various state health departments concerning relationship between tampon use and incidence of toxic shock syndrome).

For cases addressing the issue of double hearsay in investigative reports, *see Reynolds v. Green*, 184 F.3d 589 (6th Cir. 1999) (ombudsman's report not admissible in civil rights action against officer by inmate's estate; report contained numerous hearsay statements by inmate, his mother and field investigators lacking reliability attributable to independent conclusions of public official); *Clark v. Clabaugh*, 20 F.3d at 1290 (no error to admit police report of race riot; although investigating officers interviewed persons who are parties to the litigation, the bias of those interviewed does not render report inherently untrustworthy; representatives of all factions were interviewed and report appears to have achieved some measure of balance between opposing perspectives); *Moss v. Ole South Real Estate, Inc.*, 933 F.2d at 1300 (Many government reports, as with many expert witnesses, have to rely in part on hearsay evidence, and the reports are not generally excluded for this reason. Under Rule 703, experts are allowed to rely on evidence inadmissible in court in reaching their conclusions. There is no reason that government officials preparing reports do not have the same latitude); *Dresser v. Ohio Hempery, Inc.*, 2011 WL 2416595 (E.D.La. 2011) (discussing cases).

EEOC And State Labor Determinations

While prior administrative findings made with respect to an employment discrimination claim *may* be admitted under Rule 803(8)(C), *Chandler v.*

Roudebush, 425 U.S. 840, 96 S. Ct. 1949, 48 L. Ed. 2d 416 (1976), the trial court has broad discretion as to whether such findings *should* be admitted in a particular case. Such evidence may be excluded when the circumstances indicate lack of trustworthiness or where the prejudicial effect of the evidence substantially outweighs its probative value. *Price v. Rosiek Const. Co.*, 509 F.3d 704 (5th Cir. 2007); *Tulloss v. Near North Montessori School, Inc.*, 776 F.2d 150 (7th Cir. 1985). In this connection, *see Paolitto v. John Brown E. & C., Inc.*, 151 F.3d 60 (2d Cir. 1998) (age discrimination case approving exclusion of report of the Connecticut Commission on Human Rights and Opportunities; probative value substantially outweighed by danger of unfair prejudice under Rule 403); *Spruill v. Winner Ford of Dover, Ltd.*, 175 F.R.D. 194 (D. Del. 1997) (similar); *Walker v. NationsBank of Florida N.A.*, 53 F.3d 1548 (11th Cir. 1995) (in the Eleventh Circuit, EEOC determinations are generally admissible in bench trials, but often excludable in jury trials under Rule 403); *Halloway v. Milwaukee County*, 180 F.3d 820 (7th Cir. 1999) (in age discrimination case, no error to disregard state's finding of probable cause; for the most part, finding did not look past the bare allegations of the complaint); *Johnson v. Yellow Freight System, Inc.*, 734 F.2d 1304, 1309 (8th Cir. 1984) ("EEOC determinations are not homogeneous products; they vary greatly in quality and factual detail. The trial judge may correctly perceive a danger of unfair prejudice to the defendant or properly may consider that time spent by the defendant in exposing the weaknesses of the EEOC report would add unduly to the length of the trial. Moreover, the trial judge properly may give weight to the hearsay nature of the EEOC report and to the inability of the defendant to cross-examine the report in the same way that a party can cross-examine an adverse witness. For these reasons, we hold that in an employment discrimination case, the admission of administrative findings . . . is to be left to the sound discretion of the trial court."); *Plummer v. Western Intern. Hotels Co., Inc.*, 656 F.2d 502 (9th Cir. 1981) (plaintiff has right to introduce EEOC probable cause determination in Title VII lawsuit regardless of whether case is tried before a judge or jury); *Noni v. County of*

Chautauqua, 511 F. Supp. 2d 355 (W.D. N.Y. 2007) (EEOC determination letter contained only conclusory findings that failed to describe nature of investigation or basis for conclusions and was of little probative value); *Curry v. District of Columbia*, 9 F. Supp. 2d 1, 3 (D.D.C. 1998), aff'd in part, rev'd in part on other grounds, 195 F.3d 654 (D.C. Cir. 1999), cert. denied, 530 U.S. 1215, 120 S. Ct. 2219, 147 L. Ed. 2d 251 (2000) (sex harassment case admitting EEOC and D.C. Human Rights reports into evidence, not for purpose of proving claim but to rebut defendant's assertion that it took adequate corrective action after receiving notice; "To permit defendant to make this claim but preclude any evidence as to the results of those investigations tells only half of the story."); *Wittenberg v. Wheels, Inc.*, 963 F. Supp. 654 (N.D. Ill. 1997) (decision by Board of Review of Illinois Department of Employment Security that employee had not been discharged for misconduct as defined by state statute was inadmissible hearsay; Illinois act provides that decisions of benefits hearings are not admissible in any other action); *Brom v. Bozell, Jacobs, Kenyon & Eckhardt, Inc.*, 867 F. Supp. 686, 692 (N.D. Ill. 1994) (excluding administrative conclusions but admitting remainder of report; admission of conclusions is "tantamount to saying this has already been decided and here is the decision."); *Abrams v. Lightolier, Inc.*, 841 F. Supp. 584 (D.N.J. 1994) (admitting EEOC Letter of Determination that defendant violated Age Discrimination and Employment Act but with repeated cautionary instructions to jury that: (i) EEOC findings may or may not be correct and were not binding on jury; (ii) EEOC did not conduct hearing and witnesses did not give sworn testimony nor were they cross-examined; and (iii) jury must reach its own decision and not by reliance on EEOC).

The business records exception cannot be used as a 'back door' to introduce evidence that would not be admissible under Rule 803(8). *U.S. v. Blackburn*, 992 F.2d 666, 671 (7th Cir. 1993) ("[I]f a document prohibited under Rule 803(8)(B) or (C) can come into evidence under Rule 803(6), then the 803(8) restrictions are rendered nugatory.")

Crawford v. Washington—Criminal Cases

The impact of *Crawford v. Washington*, 541 U.S.

36, 124, 124 S. Ct. 1354, 158 L. Ed. 2d 177 (2004) on the law of hearsay in criminal cases is discussed at Commentary under HEARSAY: AUTHOR'S NOTE CONFRONTATION-CRIMINAL CASES. In *Crawford*, the Supreme Court stated that business records, which are analogous to public records, are "by their nature . . . not testimonial" and not subject to the requirements of the Confrontation Clause, 541 U.S. at 51, 56, 124 S.Ct. 1354; *see also id.* at 76, 124 S.Ct. 1354 (Rehnquist, C. J., concurring in judgment) (noting that "the Court's analysis of 'testimony' excludes at least some hearsay exceptions, such as business records and official records"). *See U.S. v. De La Cruz*, 514 F.3d 121 (1st Cir. 2008) (autopsy reports are nontestimonial under *Crawford*); *U.S. v. Valdez-Maltos*, 443 F.3d 910 (5th Cir. 2006) (warrants of deportation do not constitute testimonial hearsay under *Crawford*).

In *Melendez-Diaz v. Massachusetts*, 557 U.S. 1256, 129 S.Ct. 2527, 174 L. Ed. 2d 314 (2009), the trial court had admitted into evidence state laboratory affidavits with forensic analysis results showing material seized from defendant was cocaine. The United States Supreme Court said that the laboratory reports fell within the core class of testimonial statements since they had been created for the sole purpose of providing evidence against a defendant. Acknowledging that the Confrontation Clause may make prosecution of criminals more burdensome, the Court held that crime laboratory reports may not be used against defendants at trial unless the analysts responsible for creating them give testimony and subject themselves to cross-examination. Accord, *Bullcoming v. New Mexico*, ___ U.S. ___ (2011). *Cf. U.S. v. Moon*, 512 F.3d 359 (7th Cir. 2008) (relying on data generated by laboratory machines and testing done by others, DEA chemist testified as expert that substance was cocaine; Confrontation Clause did not bar testimony because facts or data need not be admissible for expert witness opinion to be admitted); *U.S. v. Ellis*, 460 F.3d 920 (7th Cir. 2006) (Rule 902(11) certification of medical records was not testimonial; court did not find as controlling fact that Rule 902(11) certification of authenticity is made in anticipation of litigation).

Hearsay Exception: Public Records and Reports

Additional References

Graham, Handbook of Federal Evidence § 803.8 (7th ed. 2012)

Treatises and Practice Aids

Goode and Wellborn, Courtroom Handbook on Federal Evidence Chapter 5, Rule 803(8) (annual ed.)

Mueller & Kirkpatrick, Federal Evidence, § 8:91 (3d ed. 2007)

Binder, Hearsay Handbook Chapter 17 (4th ed. 2001)

McCormick, Evidence Chapter 30 (6th ed. 2006)

Park, Trial Objections Handbook §§ 4:41 to 4:43 (2nd ed. 2001)

HEARSAY EXCEPTION: PRESENT SENSE IMPRESSION

See:

Fed.R.Evid. 803(1)
Mil.R.Evid. 803(1)

Objection

- [*To a question*] Objection. The question calls for hearsay.
- [*To an answer*] Objection, hearsay. I move that the answer be stricken and the jury be instructed not to consider it for any purpose.

Response

- The statement is admissible under Rule 803(1) as a present sense impression. I have established that the statement concerns [*an event*] [*a condition*] which the declarant was witnessing at the time she made the statement to this witness.

Commentary

The three criteria for admission of a statement as a present sense impression are: (1) the statement must describe an event or condition without calculated narration; (2) the speaker must have personally perceived the event or condition described; and (3) the statement must have been made while the speaker was perceiving the event or condition, or immediately thereafter. *Cody v. Harris*, 409 F.3d 853 (7th Cir. 2005); *Greene v. B.F. Goodrich Avionics Systems, Inc.*, 409 F.3d 784 (6th Cir. 2005) (pilot's statement "I think my gyro just quit" seconds before his fatal helicopter crash was admissible as present sense impression); *U.S. v. Ruiz*, 249 F.3d 643 (7th Cir. 2001) (police officer could testify to description of suspect and his actions prior to drug transaction as relayed to him by fellow officer through walkie-talkie; statements were made while declarant was perceiving events); *U.S. v. Mitchell*, 145 F.3d 572 (3d Cir. 1998) (anonymous note linking defendant to robbery getaway car not admissible as present sense impression because government could not establish personal knowledge of declarant or amount of time between event and statement); *People of Territory of Guam v. Ignacio*, 10 F.3d 608 (9th Cir. 1993) (child victim's statement to older sister about not washing victim's vaginal area because it hurt admissible as present sense impression in sex abuse case); *U.S. v. Kuo*, 2011 WL 145471 (E.D.N.Y. 2011) (statements of 911 caller admissible as both present sense impression and excited utterance); *Tracinda Corp. v. DaimlerChrysler AG*, 362 F. Supp. 2d 487 (D. Del. 2005) (notes of meetings re the Daimler Benz-Chrysler merger qualified as present sense impression); *U.S. v. Hamilton*, 948 F. Supp. 635, 639 (W.D. Ky. 1996) (photographic identification of alleged perpetrator falls outside exception; identification requires reflection back as to who was seen and "[w]ith reflection some reliability, which goes to the very essence of the present sense impression hearsay exception is lost.").

Under this exception, a startling occurrence or accident is not required. *U.S. v. Parker*, 936 F.2d 950 (7th Cir. 1991) (no error admitting baggage handler's statement that certain luggage had been given to him by defendant); *Michaels v. Michaels*, 767 F.2d 1185 (7th Cir. 1985) (admitting into evidence telex sent immediately after business discussion summarizing contents of conversation). *Solomon v. Waffle House, Inc.*, 365 F. Supp. 2d 1312 (N.D. Ga. 2004) (diner's statement "the food was not very good.").

The underlying rationale of the present sense impression exception is that substantial contemporaneity of event and statement minimizes unreliability due to defective recollection or conscious fabrication. *U.S. v. Green*, 541 F.3d 176 (3d Cir. 2008); *U.S. v. Ruiz*, 249 F.3d at 647; *Rock v. Huffco Gas & Oil Co., Inc.*, 922 F.2d 272 (5th Cir. 1991); *U.S. v. Honken*, 378 F. Supp. 2d 970 (N.D. Iowa 2004). There is no *per se* rule indicating what time interval is too long under Rule 803(1). *Parker*, 936 F.2d at 954; *U.S. v. Santos*, 65 F. Supp. 2d 802 (N.D. Ill. 1999).

However, given the clear language of the rule and its underlying rationale, courts consistently require substantial contemporaneity. *See, e.g., U.S. v. Shoup*, 476 F.3d 38, 42 (1st Cir. 2007) (911 phone call made "only one or two minutes . . . immediately following" event admissible); *U.S. v. Danford*, 435 F.3d 682, 687 (7th Cir. 2006) (statement made "less then 60 seconds" after witnessing robbery qualified as present-sense impression); *U.S. v. Jackson*, 124 F.3d 607, 618 (4th Cir. 1997) (statement by witness to police upon their arrival at scene that defendant was threatening to kill her family was admissible as "description of ongoing events"); *U.S. v. Blakey*, 607 F.2d 779, 785–86 (7th Cir. 1979) (not error to admit statement made at most 23 minutes after event); *cf. U.S. v. Manfre*, 368 F.3d 832, 840 (8th Cir. 2004) (statement made after "an intervening walk or drive" following event not admissible; "The present-sense-impression exception . . . is rightfully limited to statements made while a declarant perceives an event or immediately thereafter, and we decline to expand it to cover a declarant's relatively recent memories."); *Hilyer v. Howat Concrete Co., Inc.*, 578 F.2d 422, 426 n.7 (D.C. Cir. 1978) (excluding statement made between 15 and 45 minutes following event). The Third Circuit expressed skepticism that a statement made some 40 minutes after the fact could be properly admitted as a present-sense impression. *Mitchell*, 145 F.3d at 577 (where robbery occurred between 9:00 a.m. and 9:15 a.m. and notes were found in getaway car a mile from the crime scene at approximately 10:00 a.m., intervening lapse was "probably too long for applicability of the present-sense impression . . . which requires the statement to be made virtually contemporaneously with the event being perceived"); *see also Miller v. Keating*, 754 F.2d 507 (3d Cir. 1985) (concluding it was "not necessarily an abuse of discretion" to admit statement made "several minutes" after the fact as excited utterance, but noting courts have recognized that the length of time separating the event from the statement [for admission as an excited utterance] *may be considerably longer* than for statements qualifying under the present sense impression exception of Rule 803(1)).

Time for reflection lessens or removes the assurance of trustworthiness. *See U.S. v. Green*, at 180 (statement made 50 minutes after perceiving transaction, and after declarant was searched, driven to DEA office and debriefed not properly admitted as present-sense impression); *Chan v. S*

& C Elec. Co., 2011 WL 2581971 (N.D.Ill. 2011) (personal journal entries on working conditions made at home after work not admissible as present sense impressions); *U.S. v. Narciso*, 446 F. Supp. 252, 287–88 (E.D. Mich. 1977) (note written two hours after event and in response to questions not present-sense impression because declarant "not only had time to reflect on what had transpired [but] was intentionally encouraged to reflect on those events before answering").

A common use of this exception has been to permit a witness to testify about assertions that a declarant made immediately after participating in a telephone conversation concerning what was said on the phone. *First State Bank of Denton v. Maryland Cas. Co.*, 918 F.2d 38 (5th Cir. 1990); *U.S. v. Portsmouth Paving Corp.*, 694 F.2d 312 (4th Cir. 1982); *Phoenix Mut. Life Ins. Co. v. Adams*, 828 F. Supp. 379 (D.S.C. 1993).

Unidentified Declarant

Nothing in the language of Rule 803(1) requires that the declarant be identified. An unidentified declarant, however, can present two possible problems: (1) the declarant did not exist and the statement was invented by the witness, or (2) the declarant did not have personal knowledge of the event.

The possibility that the declarant never existed is not a hearsay problem but rather an issue of credibility to be decided by the fact finder. But where the declarant did not have personal knowledge of the event, any statement purporting to describe the event is inadmissible. *Bemis v. Edwards*, 45 F.3d 1369 (9th Cir. 1995) ("911" tape describing altercation with police inadmissible as present sense impression because caller was relating descriptions of what other people were observing); *Kornicki v. Calmar S.S. Corp.*, 460 F.2d 1134 (3d Cir. 1972) (Rule 602 personal knowledge requirement applies with equal force to hearsay statements).

Direct proof of perception is not always required. The substance of the statement itself or circumstantial evidence may create a sufficient inference that the declarant perceived the event. *U.S. v. Thomas*,

453 F.3d 838 (7th Cir. 2006) (anonymous caller's tape-recorded hearsay statements to 911 operator were admissible both as a present sense impression and excited utterance; caller was describing events related to shooting as they were happening); *U.S. v. Medico*, 557 F.2d 309 (2d Cir. 1977) (admitting as present sense impression getaway car description relayed from unidentified eyewitness and bank customer to security guard; brief time frame of events reduced possibility of inaccuracy, speculation or fabrication).

Crawford v. Washington—Criminal Cases

The impact of *Crawford v. Washington*, 541 U.S. 36, 124 S. Ct. 1354, 158 L. Ed. 2d 177 (2004), on the law of hearsay in criminal cases is discussed at Commentary under HEARSAY: AUTHOR'S NOTE CONFRONTATION-CRIMINAL CASES. The *Crawford* Court held that the Confrontation Clause categorically bars the admission of testimonial hearsay unless the declarant is unavailable and the accused has had a prior opportunity to cross-examine the declarant. But Justice Scalia did say that "[a]n accuser who makes a formal statement to government officers bears testimony in a sense that a person who makes a casual remark to an acquaintance does not." *Id.* at 51. *See also U.S. v. Danford*, 435 F.3d 682 (7th Cir. 2006) (employee's testimony that she was told by manager that manager had just shown defendant how to disarm store's alarm admissible under present sense impression; employee laid foundation that she saw the two talking in front of alarm and less than 60 seconds later, she asked manager what happened. The court said this conversation was more akin to casual remark than it was to testimony in the *Crawford* sense.).

Davis v. Washington, 547 U.S. 813, 126 S. Ct. 2266, 165 L. Ed. 2d 224 (2006), considered admissibility of statements made to police by a victim of domestic violence. Although the assault had ended, the statements were sufficiently close in time to the incident that the trial court admitted her affidavit as a present sense impression. Notwithstanding that the statements were nearly contemporaneous with the reported events, the Supreme Court held they could not be admitted absent opportunity to confront the witness.

Additional References

Graham, Handbook of Federal Evidence § 803.1 (7th ed. 2012)

Treatises and Practice Aids

Goode and Wellborn, Courtroom Handbook on Federal Evidence Chapter 5, Rule 803(1) and Obj. 37 (annual ed.)

Mueller & Kirkpatrick, Federal Evidence, § 8:67 (3d ed. 2007)

Binder, Hearsay Handbook Chapter 8 (4th ed. 2001)

McCormick, Evidence § 271 (6th ed. 2006)

Park, Trial Objections Handbook § 4:22 (2nd ed. 2001)

HEARSAY EXCEPTION: RECORDED RECOLLECTION

See:

Fed.R.Evid. 803(5)
Mil.R.Evid. 803(5)

Objection

- Objection. The document is hearsay and a proper foundation cannot be established. It has not been shown that this witness, after reviewing the document, lacks sufficient memory. Moreover, there has been no proof that the witness made the record at a time when the matter was still fresh in her memory and that it accurately reflects her knowledge.

Response

- I have established that the contents of this writing are admissible under Rule 803(5). As foundation, I have demonstrated:
  (1) the record pertains to a matter about which the witness once had personal knowledge;
  (2) the witness now has an insufficient recollection about the matter to testify fully and accurately;
  (3) the record was made [or adopted] by the witness when the matter was fresh in the witness's memory; and,
  (4) the record reflects the witness's prior knowledge accurately.

Commentary

If a witness cannot testify from unaided or refreshed memory, Rule 803(5) allows a memorandum or record of an event to be read into evidence where: (1) the witness once had personal knowledge about the matters in the document; (2) the witness now has insufficient recollection to testify fully and accurately; and (3) the record was made or adopted by the witness at a time when the matter was fresh in his memory and reflected his knowledge. *U.S. v. Garcia*, 282 Fed. Appx. 14 (2d

Cir. 2008) (police officers permitted to read from arrest reports and booking sheets under recorded recollection exception; no violation of Confrontation Clause because officers were also witnesses subject to cross-examination by defendants); *U.S. v. Mornan*, 413 F.3d 372 (3d Cir. 2005) (statement given to authorities and attested to by Canadian official inadmissible as recorded recollection where there was no showing witness either reviewed or adopted recording and she could not attest to its accuracy at trial); *U.S. v. Cash*, 394 F.3d 560 (7th Cir. 2005) (exception applied where witness testified defendant phoned her directly and while she could not remember his statements verbatim, her notes recorded defendant's exact words during course of conversation); *Collins v. Kibort*, 143 F.3d 331 (7th Cir. 1998) (error to allow witness to read from diary as recorded recollection where there was no foundation that he could not recall events contained in the document); *U.S. v. Collicott*, 92 F.3d 973 (9th Cir. 1996) (police report not admissible as recorded recollection of witness' conversation with officer; no foundation that witness had adopted report or vouched for its accuracy); *Hynes v. Coughlin*, 79 F.3d 285 (2d Cir. 1996) (in § 1983 suit for unreasonable use of force, incident report did not qualify as recorded recollection since prison guard who prepared document did not see beginning of incident); *U.S. v. Gans*, 32 M.J. 412 (C.M.A. 1991) (where child testified she was truthful when she gave statement about sex abuse to military police, her contradictory testimony about accuracy of certain facts went to weight of evidence and not to its admissibility as recorded recollection); *Rock v. Huffco Gas & Oil Co., Inc.*, 922 F.2d 272 (5th Cir. 1991) (supervisors' reports containing deceased employee's statements about his alleged accident inadmissible as recorded recollection since they had no personal knowledge of facts); *In re Acceptance Ins. Companies, Inc. Securities Litigation*, 352 F. Supp. 2d 940 (D. Neb. 2004) (meeting notes comprised of what author considered to be "significant points" not admissible as recorded recollection); *Steinberg v. Obstetrics-Gynecological & Infertility Group, P.C.*, 260 F. Supp. 2d 492 (D. Conn. 2003) (letter written by attorney prior to her death inadmissible as recorded recollection; necessary predicate of Rule is that there be witness with insufficient recollection).

Although the rule permits the document to be read to the jury, it may not be received as an exhibit unless offered by an adverse party. Rule 803(5); *Collins*, 143 F.3d at 338; *U.S. v. Judon*, 567 F.2d 1289 (5th Cir. 1978); *Tracinda Corp. v. DaimlerChrysler AG*, 362 F. Supp. 2d 487 (D. Del. 2005) (rationale behind requirement that document be read into evidence rather than admitted as exhibit is to prevent trier of fact from being overly impressed by the writing).

A showing that the witness lacks all recollection of the event or condition described is not required; it is enough that the witness lacks sufficient recollection to testify fully and completely. *Gans*, 32 M.J. at 416.

It is not necessary that the document itself be prepared or written by the witness so long as he reviewed and adopted the statement while the event was fresh in his memory. *Mornan*, 413 F.3d at 377; *U.S. v. Wimberly*, 60 F.3d 281 (7th Cir. 1995) (sexual abuse victim's written statement to military police should have been admitted as recorded recollection where victim read statement, made and initialed corrections and signed attestation clause. Although trial court found report lacked sufficient indicia of credibility because interview took place late at night and victim was young and tired, those factors go to weight of evidence, not admissibility); *U.S. v. Severson*, 49 F.3d 268 (7th Cir. 1995) (where policewoman denied making some statements and accuracy of others, U.S. Attorney's memo of their conversation did not constitute recorded recollection under Rule 803(5); also inadmissible under residual exception (Rule 807) since document lacked circumstantial guarantees of trustworthiness); *U.S. v. Schoenborn*, 4 F.3d 1424 (7th Cir. 1993) (requirement that report be adopted by witness not satisfied where witness testified he told the truth in interview but that FBI agent's report was not an accurate representation of his statement); *U.S. v. Benson*, 961 F.2d 707 (8th Cir. 1992) (error to admit FBI interviews of defendant where reports were not verbatim and were unsigned and unsworn); *U.S. v. Almonte*, 956 F.2d 27 (2d Cir. 1992) (burden of proving notes reflect witness' own words rather than notetaker's characterization falls on party seeking to introduce notes; third party's characterization does not constitute recorded recollection of witness unless witness has subscribed to that characterization); *U.S. v. Williams*, 571 F.2d 344 (6th Cir. 1978) (statement prepared by Secret Service agent but signed and sworn to by witness properly admitted even though witness subsequently disputed certain portions on cross-examination; however, subjective impressions were redacted).

Rule 803(5) does not have specific constraints on the timing of the preparation and adoption of the memorandum or record. *U.S. v. Lewis*, 954 F.2d 1386 (7th Cir. 1992). The Advisory Committee's Note states that "[n]o attempt is made in the exception to spell out . . . the contemporaneity and accuracy of the record, leaving them to be dealt with as the circumstances of the particular case might indicate." *See U.S. v. Smith*, 197 F.3d 225 (6th Cir. 1999) (admitting statement given fifteen months after events it described); *U.S. v. Patterson*, 678 F.2d 774 (9th Cir. 1982) (holding delay of ten months satisfied freshness requirement); *U.S. v. Senak*, 527 F.2d 129 (7th Cir. 1975) (three-year delay satisfied rule); *U.S. v. Kortright*, 2011 WL 4406352 (S.D.N.Y. 2011) (transcript of police officers grand jury testimony given two months after arrest qualified as recorded recollection).

This exception to the hearsay rule has proved useful to the prosecution in criminal cases dealing with a "turncoat witness," *i.e.* one who makes a statement implicating the defendant prior to trial, but who, at trial, testifies to a loss of memory concerning the crime. *See, e.g., U.S. v. Porter*, 986 F.2d 1014 (6th Cir. 1993) (insufficient recollection established by fact that witness was being disingenuous and evasive); *Williams*, 571 F.2d at 349 (appropriate to admit statement because witness was exercising selective memory).

Note: Although Rule 803(8)(B) bars admission *in criminal cases* of records, reports or statements of matters observed by police officers and other law enforcement personnel under the public records exception, some courts have admitted such documents as recorded recollection in cases where the officer takes the stand to testify. *U.S. v. Sawyer*,

607 F.2d 1190 (7th Cir. 1979) (stating that restrictions of Rule 803(8) were intended to bar the use of law enforcement reports as a substitute for the testimony of the officer but declining to disqualify the recorded recollections of a *testifying* law enforcement officer otherwise admissible under Rule 803(5)). *Accord, U.S. v. Picciandra*, 788 F.2d 39 (1st Cir. 1986).

Crawford v. Washington—Criminal Cases

In *Crawford v. Washington*, 541 U.S. 36, 124 S. Ct. 1354, 158, 158 L. Ed. 2d 177 (2004) (discussed at Commentary under HEARSAY: AUTHOR'S NOTE CONFRONTATION-CRIMINAL CASES), a criminal case involving a Confrontation Clause challenge, the United States Supreme Court held that if a hearsay statement was "testimonial" in nature, it could not be introduced at trial in the absence of the declarant, unless the defendant had a previous opportunity to cross-examine the declarant. *See also Whorton v. Bockting*, 549 U.S. 406, 127 S. Ct. 1173, 167 L. Ed. 2d 1 (2007) (the Confrontation Clause has no application to out-of-court nontestimonial statements.)

For whatever guidance may be provided at present, counsel can consult the following decisions: *U.S. v. Owens*, 484 U.S. 554, 108 S. Ct. 838, 98 L. Ed. 2d 951 (1988) (even when a witness has no present memory of a prior out-of-court statement, the right of confrontation is satisfied if the accused has the opportunity to cross-examine the witness at trial); *California v. Green*, 399 U.S. 149, 90 S. Ct. 1930, 26 L. Ed. 2d 489 (1970) (upholding admission of witness' preliminary hearing testimony since truth-seeking purpose of Confrontation Clause is satisfied if declarant is present and testifying at trial); *State v. Gorman*, 2004 ME 90, 854 A.2d 1164 (Me. 2004) (where defendant's mother claimed no memory of her grand jury testimony about her son's murder confession, the Supreme Judicial Court held there was no Confrontation Clause violation admitting such testimony as recorded recollection. The Maine court cited to *Crawford* (when declarant appears for cross-examination at trial, Confrontation Clause places no constraints at all on use of his prior testimonial statements)); and *Clark v. State*, 808 N.E.2d 1183

(Ind. 2004) and *Government of Virgin Islands v. George*, 2004 WL 3546285 (V.I. Terr. Ct. 2004) (Terr.V.I.). *But see* Ruebner & Seahill, *Crawford v. Washington*, the Confrontation Clause, and Hearsay: A New Paradigm for Illinois Evidence Law, 36 Loy. U. Chi. L.J. 703, 778 (2005):

> The presence of the declarant at trial as a witness will likely not cure Confrontation Clause problems. One essential condition for the admissibility under this exception is that the witness has no present recollection of the event recorded. This foundational requirement negates a constitutional condition for the admissibility of an out-of-court statement and will deny the accused a sufficient opportunity to cross-examine the witness concerning the out-of-court statement in violation of the Confrontation Clause and *Crawford*.

Additional References

Graham, Handbook of Federal Evidence § 803.5 (7th ed. 2012)

Treatises and Practice Aids

Goode and Wellborn, Courtroom Handbook on Federal Evidence Chapter 5, Rule 803(5) and Obj. 37 (annual ed.)

Mueller & Kirkpatrick, Federal Evidence, § 8:103 (3d ed. 2007)

Binder, Hearsay Handbook Chapter 15 (4th ed. 2001)

McCormick, Evidence §§ 279 to 283 (6th ed. 2006)

Park, Trial Objections Handbook §§ 4:26 to 4:28 (2nd ed. 2001)

HEARSAY EXCEPTION: REPUTATION CONCERNING BOUNDARIES OR GENERAL HISTORY

See:

Fed.R.Evid. 803(20)
Mil.R.Evid. 803(20)

Objection

- [*To a question*] Objection. The question calls for hearsay.
- [*To a document*] Objection. The document constitutes inadmissible hearsay.
- [*To an answer*] I move that the answer be stricken and the jury be instructed not to consider it for any purpose.

Response

- The [*question*] [*document*] is proper. Reputation evidence with respect to [*boundaries*] [*general history*] is admissible as one of the recognized exceptions to the hearsay rule.

Commentary

While real estate boundaries are typically established by reference to deeds and other documentary evidence, Rule 803(20) furnishes an alternative method of proof by permitting testimony of reputation in the community as to land boundaries. The reputation must antedate the controversy. The rule also permits reputation evidence with respect to events of general history "important to the community or state or nation in which located." Rule 803(20); *U.S. v. Belfast*, 611 F.3d 783 (11th Cir. 2010) (State Department officer's testimony re background and political structure of Liberia). To have significant probative value, the matter in question "must be one of general interest, so that it can accurately be said that there is a high probability that the matter underwent general scrutiny as the community reputation was formed." McCormick, Evidence § 322 (6th ed. 2006); *accord Connecticut Light & Power Co. v. Federal Power Com'n*, 557 F.2d 349 (2d Cir. 1977) (in determining its jurisdiction to regulate certain hydroelectric projects, Commission had right to rely on historical data dating back to colonial era with respect to navigability of Housatonic River); *Ariel Land Owners, Inc. v. Dring*, 2008 WL 189644 *8 (M.D. Pa. 2008) (slip op.) (testimony from witnesses at trial who indicated that the reputation in the community was that a lake was owned by the plaintiff up to the high water mark admissible to support boundary); *Ute Indian Tribe v. State of Utah*, 521 F. Supp. 1072, 1149 (D. Utah 1981), judgment aff'd in part, rev'd in part on other grounds, 716 F.2d 1298 (10th Cir. 1983) (court reached its conclusions on tribal reservation status of certain lands based on overall sense of historical record discounting evidence of reputation in the non-Indian community, given lack of interaction between whites and Indians on the issue; "While a long-standing reputation may serve as important evidence of the status of a boundary of immediate personal importance, e.g., a private property line among neighbors, or of more universal importance, such as a national or state boundary, reputation in a non-Indian community as to Indian boundaries, rights, etc., is indeed a treacherous ground for decision.").

Additional References

Graham, Handbook of Federal Evidence § 803.20 (7th ed. 2012)

Treatises and Practice Aids

Mueller & Kirkpatrick, Federal Evidence, § 8:103 (3d ed. 2007)

Binder, Hearsay Handbook Chapter 29 (4th ed. 2001)

McCormick, Evidence § 322 (6th ed. 2006)

Park, Trial Objections Handbook § 4:53 (2nd ed. 2001)

HEARSAY EXCEPTION: RESIDUAL EXCEPTION

See:

Fed.R.Evid. 807
Mil.R.Evid. 807

Objection

- [*To a question*] Objection. The question calls for hearsay.
- [*To an answer*] Objection, hearsay. I move that the answer be stricken and the jury be instructed not to consider it for any purpose.

Response

- The requirements for admissibility under the residual exception are: (1) circumstantial guarantees of trustworthiness; (2) materiality; (3) probative value; (4) the interests of justice; and (5) notice. [*Plaintiff/Defendant*] has met these by [*specify*].

Commentary

Rule 807 provides a residual or catchall exception to the hearsay rule, granting admissibility to trustworthy statements that are "not specifically covered by" other exceptions.* *U.S. v. Peneaux*, 432 F.3d 882, 893 (8th Cir. 2005) ("Congress added Rule 803(24), the predecessor to Rule 807, because it could not foresee every possible evidentiary scenario.") The rule may permit admission of an out-of-court statement that: (1) is offered as evidence of a material fact; (2) is more probative on the point for which it is offered than any other evidence which the proponent can procure through

[Hearsay etc.]

*Prior to 1997, the residual hearsay exceptions were contained in Rules 803(24) and 804(b)(5). In 1997, the Rules were amended and the two residual exceptions were combined and transferred to new Rule 807. "This was done to facilitate new additions to Rule 803 and 804. No change in meaning is intended." Rule 807 advisory committee's note. Decisions interpreting either Rule 803(24) or Rule 804(b)(5) are thus authority with respect to Rule 807 as well. *U.S. v. Hall*, 165 F.3d 1095, 1110 n.8 (7th Cir. 1999).

reasonable efforts; (3) serves the general purpose of the rules of evidence and the interests of justice by its admission; (4) has circumstantial guarantees of trustworthiness equivalent to the listed hearsay exceptions; and if, (5) notice is given to the adverse party sufficiently in advance of trial. *Tome v. United States*, 513 U.S. 150, 166, 115 S. Ct. 696, 705, 130 L. Ed. 2d 574 (1995) (residual exception exists for the circumstance "[w]hen a party seeks to introduce out-of-court statements that contain strong circumstantial indicia of reliability that are highly probative on the material questions at trial, and that are better than other evidence otherwise available."); *U.S. v. White Bull*, 646 F.3d 1082 (8th Cir. 2011); *U.S. v. Ochoa*, 229 F.3d 631 (7th Cir. 2000); *U.S. v. Rodriguez*, 218 F.3d 1243 (11th Cir. 2000); *U.S. v. Sanchez-Lima*, 161 F.3d 545 (9th Cir. 1998). Rule 807 is to be used rarely and only in exceptional circumstances. *See, e.g. U.S. v. Ingram*, 501 F.3d 963, 967 (8th Cir. 2007); *U.S. v. Bailey*, 581 F.2d 341, 347 (3d Cir. 1978).

Application of this exception in criminal cases must take into account that *Crawford v. Washington*, 541 U.S. 36, 124 S. Ct. 1354, 158 L. Ed. 2d 177 (2004) has established a *per se* bar on the admission of out-of-court testimonial statements made by unavailable declarants where there was no prior opportunity for cross-examination. *See also U.S. v. Jamieson*, 427 F.3d 394 (6th Cir. 2005) (in order to admit evidence under Rule 807, district court must consider the independent restrictions on the admission of certain evidence contained in the Confrontation Clause of the Sixth Amendment).

The rule is not limited to aspects of hearsay evidence not specifically addressed by Rules 803 and 804 but may also be available when the proponent fails to meet the standards set forth in those other exceptions. *U.S. v. Wilson*, 249 F.3d 366, 375 n.5 (5th Cir. 2001); *U.S. v. Earles*, 113 F.3d 796, 799–800 (8th Cir. 1997) (most courts construe the term "not specifically covered" by another hearsay exception to mean "not admissible under" another hearsay exception; collecting cases); *U.S. v. Valdez-Soto*, 31 F.3d 1467 (9th Cir. 1994) (almost fitting within one of the enumerated exceptions cuts in favor of admission, not against); *U.S. v. Deeb*, 13 F.3d 1532, 1536 (11th Cir. 1994) (rejecting what has been called the "near miss" argument, which maintains that a hearsay statement that is close to, but that does not fit precisely into, a recognized hearsay exception is not admissible under Rule 807); *U.S. v. Furst*, 886 F.2d 558, 573 (3d Cir. 1989). In either event, the courts construe the residual exception narrowly to prevent it from swallowing the hearsay rule. *U.S. v. Sinclair*, 74 F.3d 753 (7th Cir. 1996); *U.S. v. Collins*, 66 F.3d 984 (8th Cir. 1995) (the rule applies only in rare and exceptional circumstances); *U.S. v. Tome*, 61 F.3d 1446 (10th Cir. 1995) (exception is extremely narrow and requires testimony to be very important and very reliable); *U.S. v. Benavente Gomez*, 921 F.2d 378 (1st Cir. 1990) (Congress did not intend to authorize major judicial revisions of the hearsay rule); *U.S. v. Walker*, 410 F.3d 754, 757 (5th Cir. 2005) (the exception is to be "used only rarely in truly exceptional cases."), accord *U.S. v. Jayyousi*, 657 F.3d 1085 (11th Cir. 2011).

Trustworthiness

Criminal cases must take into account the testimonial/nontestimonial dichotomy created by the *Crawford* decision, discussed more fully at Commentary under HEARSAY: AUTHOR'S NOTE CONFRONTATION-CRIMINAL CASES. For nontestimonial out-of-court statements still governed by *Ohio v. Roberts*, 448 U.S. 56, 100 S. Ct. 2531, 65 L. Ed. 2d 597 (1980), the essential requirement is a finding by the trial court that the statement has circumstantial guarantees of trustworthiness equivalent to that of hearsay excepted under the other federal rules. *U.S. v. Dunford*, 148 F.3d at 393; *Braun v. Lorillard Inc.*, 84 F.3d 230 (7th Cir. 1996) (no error excluding journalist's testimony about 1980 interview with now deceased tobacco company employee about scientific work she had done in 1954 on cigarette filters; statements were too remote in time and there were too many unanswered questions about declarant's activities); *Larez v. City of Los Angeles*, 946 F.2d 630, 642 (9th Cir. 1991) ("The touchstone of this exception is trustworthiness equivalent to that of the other specific hearsay exceptions."); *F.D.I.C. v. Inmuebles Metropolitanos, Inc.*, 32 F. Supp. 2d 485, 489 (D.P.R. 1998) (while all requirements must be satisfied, the most significant is that the statement possess circumstantial guarantees of trustworthiness).

While there is no mechanical test for determining trustworthiness in all cases, the focus must be on the circumstances that "surround the making of the statement and that render the declarant particularly worthy of belief." *Idaho v. Wright*, 497 U.S. 805, 819, 110 S. Ct. 3139, 3148, 111 L. Ed. 2d 638 (1990). *See, e.g., In re Slatkin*, 525 F.3d 805, 812 (9th Cir. 2008) (plea agreement admissible under residual exception to demonstrate that debtor operated Ponzi scheme with intent to defraud; offered as evidence of material fact, debtor's admissions were more probative than any other evidence trustee could procure; admission of agreement furthered the general purposes of the Rules of Evidence and served the interests of justice; agreement had equivalent circumstantial guarantees of trustworthiness, as it was made under oath with advice of counsel and after debtor was advised of his constitutional rights; it subjected debtor to severe criminal penalties, and was accepted by the court only after determination that plea was knowing and voluntary); *U.S. v. Banks*, 514 F.3d 769, 777 (8th Cir. 2008) (ATF purchase form obtained from pawn shop that sold gun had circumstantial guarantee of trustworthiness since firearms dealers were required by federal regulation to record all of their sales on this type of form); *U.S. v. Hunt*, 521 F.3d 636, 644 (6th Cir. 2008) ("[A] statement is not rendered trustworthy simply by the fact that it tends to exculpate one other than the declarant").

The trial court may not consider the fact that other evidence in the case corroborates the truth of the matter asserted in the statement. *Idaho v. Wright*, 497 U.S. at 819 ("We agree that 'particularized guarantees of trustworthiness' must be shown from the totality of the circumstances, but we think the relevant circumstances include only those that surround the making of the statement and that render the declarant particularly worthy of belief."). *Accord Lilly v. Virginia*, 527 U.S. 116, 137–138, 119 S. Ct. 1887, 1900, 144 L. Ed. 2d 117 (1999) (plurality opinion) ("We have squarely rejected the notion that evidence corroborating the truth of a hearsay statement may properly support a finding that the statement bears particularized guarantees of trustworthiness."); *Swan v. Peterson*, 6 F.3d 1373 (9th Cir. 1993) (trial court engaged in impermissible bootstrapping by referencing other evidence in finding cross-corroboration of each child's statements).

Given that the outcome in cases is highly fact-specific, the following decisions simply serve to illustrate the rule.

Admitted: *U.S. v. Wilson*, 249 F.3d at 374–76 (foreign bank records with a chain of custody but inadmissible under Rule 803(6) for lack of custodian testimony); *Bohler-Uddeholm America, Inc. v. Ellwood Group, Inc.*, 247 F.3d 79 (3d Cir. 2001) (affidavit of plaintiff's deceased president offered as evidence on a material fact, namely, parties' course of dealings; highly probative since it was only evidence available to plaintiff to counter defense claims re operation of joint venture contract); *U.S. v. Rodriguez*, 218 F.3d at 1246 (testimony by motel clerks that they had registered guests from outside Florida; purpose was to establish Hobbs Act requirement of effect on commerce in prosecution for robbery); *Schering Corp. v. Pfizer Inc.*, 189 F.3d 218 (2d Cir. 1999) (indicating survey evidence may be sufficiently trustworthy to be admitted under the residual exception and remanding to trial court for determination whether plaintiff's surveys were sufficiently trustworthy and necessary to be admitted under Rule 807); *John Paul Mitchell Systems v. Quality King Distributors, Inc.*, 106 F. Supp. 2d 462 (S.D. N.Y. 2000) (where custodian invoked Fifth Amendment privilege, court admitted third party business records that appeared regular on their face and which were implicitly authenticated by the act of production); *In re Screws Antitrust Litigation*, 526 F. Supp. 1316 (D. Mass. 1981) (corporate officer's testimony in criminal antitrust action admissible in subsequent civil suit brought against parent company).

Excluded: *U.S. v. McCraney*, 612 F.3d 1057 (8th Cir. 2010) (post-arrest statement to police lacked trustworthiness where defendant had motivation to present himself as unwilling participant in crimes); *U.S. v. Patrick*, 248 F.3d 11 (1st Cir. 2001) (police notes of anonymous calls from tipsters about who committed murder); *U.S. v. Ochoa*, 229

F.3d at 638–39 (accomplice statements incriminating defendant which court also rejected as statements against penal interest under Rule 804(b)(3)); *U.S. v. Perez*, 217 F.3d 323 (5th Cir. 2000) (informal statements made by deported aliens to INS agents; statements were not under oath and there was no cross-examination); *Sweet v. Delo*, 125 F.3d 1144, 1158 (8th Cir. 1997) ("[A] denial of guilt made by a criminal defendant to a friend contains no indicia whatsoever of reliability."); *Eisenstadt v. Centel Corp.*, 113 F.3d 738 (7th Cir. 1997) (newspaper article proffered in § 10(b) action as evidence of false representations by corporation; inadmissible because of doubt about what article meant, whether it was an accurate report of what Centel said and because author was available to be deposed and clear up these questions); *U.S. v. Turner*, 104 F.3d 217 (8th Cir. 1997) (medical texts where defendant offered no expert testimony that texts were authoritative; admission would circumvent general purpose of the rules since Rule 803(18) specifically deals with learned treatises); *Conoco Inc. v. Department of Energy*, 99 F.3d 387 (Fed. Cir. 1996) (crude oil purchase summaries prepared by Conoco's customers long after events in issue); *Collins*, 66 F.3d at 987 (taped statements between defendant and alleged drug dealer; defendant did not explain why dealer did not testify at trial nor did he show why statements which were vague and susceptible to multiple interpretations were the most probative evidence reasonably available to him); *Kirk v. Raymark Industries, Inc.*, 61 F.3d 147 (3d Cir. 1995) (interrogatory answer of former co-defendant seeking to avoid liability lacks circumstantial guarantees of trustworthiness); *U.S. v. Trenkler*, 61 F.3d 45 (1st Cir. 1995) (ATF computer database of bomb and arson incidents compiled from federal, state and local law enforcement agencies; reports were not required by law, followed no set procedures nor were there specific standards for collecting or recording information); *Rock v. Huffco Gas & Oil Co., Inc.*, 922 F.2d 272 (5th Cir. 1991) (statements made by deceased oil platform employee to family members and insurance agent as to how he injured ankle; employee realized statements would be used in litigation and evidence suggested motive to fabricate); *U.S. v. Munoz Franco*, 124 F. Supp. 2d 32

(D.P.R. 2000) (civil depositions inadmissible in criminal prosecution; government did not point out the material facts it intended to establish or show why deposition testimony was more probative than any other evidence which it could procure through reasonable efforts); *In re Cirrus Logic Securities Litigation*, 946 F. Supp. 1446 (N.D. Cal. 1996) (stock analyst's notes and reports of statements allegedly made by company executives).

News Media

News accounts, unsupported by corroborating evidence and offered to prove that certain statements were made, will usually lack the circumstantial guarantees of trustworthiness that Rule 807 requires. *Eisenstadt v. Centel Corp*, 113 F.3d at 738; *Larez*, 946 F.2d at 630; *May v. Cooperman*, 780 F.2d 240 (3d Cir. 1985) (Becker, J., dissenting on other grounds). Courts admitting evidence under Rule 807 require some showing that the declarant's perception, memory, narration, or sincerity are reliable. *May*, 780 F.2d at 263. Unsupported newspaper articles will normally fail on all of these grounds. Unless the author is available for cross-examination, newspaper stories give little clue as to the reliability of the reporter's perception, memory, narration, or sincerity and also fail to disclose how the article was changed in the editing process. *Id.* News articles, however, may be introduced if they are bolstered by supporting evidence that confers circumstantial guarantees of trustworthiness upon them. *See, e.g. Larez*, 946 F.2d at 643–44 (finding trustworthiness requirement met when three independent newspapers attributed similar quotations to defendant but excluding articles as not the "best evidence" since reporters could have been called to testify in person); *In re Columbia Securities Litigation*, 155 F.R.D. 466 (S.D. N.Y. 1994) (admitting articles from Forbes Magazine and Reuters news service in securities fraud action).

Notice

The rule requires the proponent to give notice to the adverse party that the proponent intends to introduce the statement into evidence. The Third Circuit has interpreted this to mean that the proponent must give notice of the hearsay statement itself as well as the intention to rely on the rule as grounds for admissibility of the hearsay statement. *Kirk*, 61 F.3d at 167.

No particular form of notice is specified. *U.S. v. Munoz*, 16 F.3d 1116 (11th Cir. 1994) (as long as party against whom evidence is offered has notice of its existence and the proponent's intention to introduce it-and thus has opportunity to counter it and protect himself against surprise-the notice requirement is satisfied); *U.S. v. Musal*, 421 F. Supp. 2d 1153 (S.D. Iowa 2006) (excluding evidence because government did not provide defendant with name and address of declarant sufficiently in advance of trial which is part of the notice requirement under the rule).

Some courts have interpreted the requirement strictly, refusing to admit evidence unless the adverse party was notified prior to trial. *U.S. v. Ruffin*, 575 F.2d 346, 357–58 (2d Cir. 1978). Others have been more flexible, particularly with respect to evidence that proponent was not aware of prior to the start of trial. *U.S. v. Bailey*, 581 F.2d 341 (3d Cir. 1978). *See Furtado v. Bishop*, 604 F.2d 80, 92 (1st Cir. 1979) (Most courts interpret pretrial notice requirement somewhat flexibly, in light of its express policy of providing opposing party with a fair opportunity to meet the evidence. Failure to give pretrial notice has been excused if proffering party was not at fault-because he could not have anticipated the need to use the evidence-and if adverse party had sufficient opportunity (for example, via continuance) to prepare for and contest the use of the evidence).

Additional References

Graham, Handbook of Federal Evidence § 807.1 (7th ed. 2012)

Treatises and Practice Aids

Goode and Wellborn, Courtroom Handbook on Federal Evidence Chapter 5 Rule 807 and Obj. 37)

Binder, Hearsay Handbook Chapter 47 (4th ed. 2001)

McCormick, Evidence § 324 (6th ed. 2006)

Park, Trial Objections Handbook § 4:78 (2nd ed. 2001)

HEARSAY EXCEPTION: STATEMENT AGAINST INTEREST

See:

Fed.R.Evid. 804(b)(3)
Mil.R.Evid. 804(b)(3)

Objection

- [*To a question*] Objection. The question calls for hearsay. The evidence cannot qualify as a statement against interest since it has not been shown that:
- [*the statement was against the declarant's pecuniary / penal interest*]
- [*the declarant had any personal knowledge of these facts and is unavailable to testify*]
- [*the declarant was exposed to any criminal liability*].
- [*To an answer*] Objection, hearsay. I move the answer be stricken and the jury be instructed not to consider it for any purpose.

Response

- The evidence is admissible as a statement against [*pecuniary*] [*proprietary*] interest. As foundation, I have established that declarant: (i) knew the statement was contrary to his interest; (ii) had personal knowledge of the facts; and (iii) is unavailable to testify.
- The evidence qualifies as a statement against penal interest: the declarant is unavailable to testify at trial; the statement was against declarant's penal interest; and corroborating circumstances bolster the statement's trustworthiness [*specify*].

Commentary

An oral or written statement of fact which a person knew to be against his own pecuniary, proprietary or penal interest when made is excepted from the hearsay rule, provided that the declarant had personal knowledge of the fact and is now unavailable to testify as a witness. Rule 804(b)(3).

To introduce a hearsay statement under Rule 804(b)(3), the proponent must establish that: (1)

the declarant is unavailable as a witness, (2) the statement was against the declarant's interest, when made, and in criminal cases, (3) corroborating circumstances clearly suggest that the statement is trustworthy. *U.S. v. Halk*, 634 F.3d 482 (8th Cir. 2011); *U.S. v. Loggins*, 486 F.3d 977 (7th Cir. 2007).

Statements against interest by an unavailable declarant are admissible as a hearsay exception because their trustworthiness is safeguarded by the improbability that a declarant would fabricate a statement that is contrary to his own interest. *See Williamson v. United States*, 512 U.S. 594, 599, 114 S. Ct. 2431, 2434, 129 L. Ed. 2d 476 (1994) (exception is "founded on the commonsense notion that reasonable people, even reasonable people who are not especially honest, tend not to make self-inculpatory statements unless they believe them to be true."); *Carson v. Squirrel Inn Corp.*, 298 F. Supp. 1040, 1047 (D.S.C. 1969) (exception is based on the assumption that no man will speak falsely to his own hurt and will not make a statement against his interest unless truth compels it).

The proponent of the evidence bears the burden of showing that the declarant is unavailable. *Elnashar v. Speedway SuperAmerica, LLC*, 484 F.3d 1046 (8th Cir. 2007) (where plaintiff served one subpoena returned undeliverable and made no other efforts apart from motion to compel FBI to disclose agent's location, agent was not unavailable as required by Rule 804(b)(3)); *U.S. v. Ochoa*, 229 F.3d 631 (7th Cir. 2000) (burden met where FBI spent several days trying to locate witness through employer, landlord and others and obtained a material witness arrest warrant); *U.S. v. Reed*, 227 F.3d 763, 767 (7th Cir. 2000) (the rule is not that the government must do everything it can to get a witness to testify, only that it make a reasonable, good faith effort to get the witness into court; "the lengths to which the prosecution must go to produce a witness . . . is a question of reasonableness," quoting *Ohio v. Roberts*, 448 U.S. 56, 74, 100 S. Ct. 2531, 2543, 65 L. Ed. 2d 597 (1980)). Unavailability based on Fifth Amendment privilege satisfies the rule. Rule 804(a)(1); *U.S. v. Jackson*, 335 F.3d 170 (2d Cir. 2003); *U.S. v. Thomas*, 62 F.3d 1332 (11th Cir. 1995). *See also U.S. v. Hughes*, 535

F.3d 880 (8th Cir. 2008) (for purposes of statement against interest exception, when defendant invokes his Fifth Amendment privilege, he has made himself unavailable to any other party, but he is not unavailable to himself); *U.S. v. Kimball*, 15 F.3d 54, 55–56 (5th Cir. 1994) (concluding that a defendant may not create the condition of unavailability and then benefit therefrom).

An assertion against interest, though excepted from the hearsay rule, may be excluded if it appears that declarant lacked personal knowledge of the facts related. *U.S. v. Lanci*, 669 F.2d 391 (6th Cir. 1982) (the requirement of firsthand knowledge has always been inherent in the statement against interest exception); *U.S. v. Lang*, 589 F.2d 92 (2d Cir. 1978) (same).

Pecuniary or Proprietary Interest

In a civil context, the application of the rule is illustrated in such cases as *Donovan v. Crisostomo*, 689 F.2d 869, 877 (9th Cir. 1982) (in action by Labor Department for cheating foreign workers by failing to pay overtime and charging kickbacks, trial court properly excluded as untrustworthy testimony that certain workers told Guam officials they did not work overtime; "[a] reasonable man in the position of an H-2 worker, who could be sent back to the Philippines at his employer's discretion, might feel it was in his interest to state he was paid properly to avoid the wrath of his employer."); *Gichner v. Antonio Troiano Tile & Marble Co.*, 410 F.2d 238 (D.C. Cir. 1969) (error to exclude testimony that defendant's employee told fire inspector on morning of fire that he and others had been smoking in warehouse that night; a statement is against pecuniary and proprietary interest when it threatens the loss of employment, or reduces the chances for future employment, or entails possible civil liability); *U.S. v. Musal*, 421 F. Supp. 2d 1153 (S.D.Iowa 2006) (in excise tax collection case, accountant's worksheet was inadmissible hearsay under 804(b)(3); worksheet was not against accountant's pecuniary or proprietary interest nor did it subject him to civil or criminal liability—accountant merely hired to examine company's books and had no stake or interest in that accounting); *Carson*, 298 F.Supp. at 1048 (excluding witness from testifying to assertion by former motel manager that similar accident had occurred previously; no evidence former employee's pecuniary or penal interest could possibly be jeopardized).

Penal Interest

A defendant offering hearsay evidence under Rule 804(b)(3) to exculpate himself must show: (1) an unavailable declarant; (2) from the perspective of the average, reasonable person, the statement must have been truly adverse to the declarant's penal interest, considering when it was made; and (3) sufficient corroboration to indicate the trustworthiness of the statement. *U.S. v. Westry*, 524 F.3d 1198 (11th Cir. 2008); *U.S. v. Leahy*, 464 F.3d 773 (7th Cir. 2006) (a statement is against penal interest if it subjects the declarant to criminal liability; exception does not include statements that could "possibly" subject declarant to prosecution); *U.S. v. Andreas*, 216 F.3d 645 (7th Cir. 2000); *U.S. v. Maliszewski*, 161 F.3d 992 (6th Cir. 1998); *U.S. v. Spring*, 80 F.3d 1450 (10th Cir. 1996); *U.S. v. Butler*, 71 F.3d 243, 253 (7th Cir. 1995) ("The hearsay exception does not provide that any statement which 'possibly could' or 'maybe might' lead to criminal liability is admissible.").

A 2009 amendment to Rule 804(b)(3) makes clear that in criminal cases, the corroborating circumstances requirement applies when either the defendant or the government offers a statement as one that tends to expose the declarant to criminal liability. A number of courts had already imposed the corroborating circumstances requirement to statements offered by the prosecution, even though the text of the former rule did not so provide.

The rule does not allow admission of self-exculpatory statements incriminating others, even if they are made within a broader narrative that is generally self-inculpatory. *Williamson*, 512 U.S. at 600–01. Those portions of a statement which are not in and of themselves against the declarant's penal interest are not admissible. *Id.* at 604; *U.S. v. Chase*, 451 F.3d 474 (8th Cir. 2006) (only the portions of an unavailable witness's statement that genuinely inculpate her are admissible).

An Inculpatory Statement Offered to Exculpate the Accused

A statement tending to expose the unavailable declarant to criminal liability which is offered to exculpate the accused is not admissible unless corroborating circumstances clearly indicate the trustworthiness of the statement. Rule 804(b)(3). *U.S. v. Jackson*, 540 F.3d 578 (7th Cir. 2008); *U.S. v. Jordan*, 509 F.3d 191 (4th Cir. 2007) (as 804(b)(3) makes clear, corroborating circumstances are only required if statement is offered to exculpate accused). The purpose of the corroboration requirement is to protect against the possibility that a statement would be fabricated to exculpate the accused. *U.S. v. Paulino*, 445 F.3d 211 (2d Cir. 2006) (declarant had obvious motive to lie to protect his son); *U.S. v. Brainard*, 690 F.2d 1117, 1124 (4th Cir. 1982) (rule requires not a determination that declarant is credible but a finding that the circumstances clearly indicate that statement was not fabricated; it is the statement rather than the declarant which must be trustworthy).

Corroboration of the trustworthiness of the out-of-court statement should generally focus on the circumstances of the making of the statement and the motivation of the declarant. McCormick, Evidence § 319. *See, e.g., U.S. v. Bumpass*, 60 F.3d 1099, 1102 (4th Cir. 1995) (although precise nature of corroboration required cannot be fully described, several factors are relevant in determining whether sufficient corroboration exists, including: (1) whether declarant at the time of making statement had pled guilty or was still exposed to prosecution; (2) declarant's motive in making statement and whether there was a reason to lie; (3) whether declarant had repeated statement and did so consistently; (4) the party to whom the statement was made; (5) the relationship of the declarant with the accused; (6) nature and strength of independent evidence relevant to the conduct in question); *U.S. v. Nagib*, 56 F.3d 798 (7th Cir. 1995) (to determine whether corroborating circumstances exist, court must consider: (1) the relationship between the confessing party and the exculpated party; (2) whether statement was made voluntarily after Miranda warnings; (3) whether there is any evidence that the statement was made to curry favor with the authorities).

The Rule 804(b)(3) corroborating circumstances requirement is applicable to civil cases. *American Automotive Accessories, Inc. v. Fishman*, 175 F.3d 534 (7th Cir. 1999).

Statements That Inculpate The Accused

Analysis of whether a co-conspirator's or accomplice's statements against penal interest are admissible *against a defendant* has two components, one statutory and the other constitutional.

First, the testimony must be admissible under Rule 804(b)(3). Under *Williamson*, the district court must consider whether each statement, not just the confession as a whole, was truly self-inculpatory. 512 U.S. at 604.

Second, because co-conspirator statements incriminating the defendant do not fall within a firmly rooted hearsay exception, the Confrontation Clause requires that such evidence contain particularized guarantees of trustworthiness such that cross-examination would be of marginal utility in determining the truthfulness of the statements. *Lilly v. Virginia*, 527 U.S. 116, 119 S. Ct. 1887, 144 L. Ed. 2d 117 (1999) (plurality opinion rejecting accomplice's custodial confession to law enforcement agents as a statement against penal interest because it was largely self-exculpatory, i.e., declarant minimized his own criminal responsibility and shifted blame to defendant). Such guarantees must be shown by the circumstances of the statements themselves and cannot be proven by other evidence produced at trial. *Lilly*, 527 U.S. at 137–38; *Idaho v. Wright*, 497 U.S. 805, 820, 110 S. Ct. 3139, 3149, 111 L. Ed. 2d 638 (1990) (guarantees of trustworthiness must "be drawn from the totality of circumstances that surround the making of the statement and that render the declarant particularly worthy of belief"); *U.S. v. Castelan*, 219 F.3d 690, 695 (7th Cir. 2000) (guarantees must be inherent in the circumstances of the testimony itself; the fact that other evidence corroborates the testimony in question does not suffice). A very strong presumption of unreliability attaches to non-self-inculpatory statements of co-conspirators made while in police custody. *Lilly*, 527 U.S. at 137.

Notwithstanding the concerns articulated in *Williamson* and *Lilly* that portions of a confession that do not inculpate the declarant are not reliable enough for prosecutors to use against anyone other than the declarant, lower courts regularly admit accomplice statements inculpating the defendant using various rationales, e.g., statement was not an effort to shift blame; statements to close family members have requisite trustworthiness; exculpatory and inculpatory portions are completely intertwined, etc. For cases post-*Lilly*, *see U.S. v. Jordan*, 509 F.3d at 201 ("to our knowledge no court has extended *Crawford* to statements made by a declarant to friends or associates"; collecting cases); *U.S. v. Manfre*, 368 F.3d 832, 842 (8th Cir. 2004) (sustaining admission of statement made "casually to an intimate confidante in a setting that does not raise the same concerns as" statements made to police officers under incentive to curry their favor); *U.S. v. Saget*, 377 F.3d 223 (2d Cir. 2004) (sustaining admission of statements made by declarant to someone he thought was his friend and confidant but turned out to be a confidential informant); *U.S. v. Westmoreland*, 240 F.3d 618 (7th Cir. 2001) (unavailable co-conspirator's statements implicating both himself and defendant in murder and drug conspiracy were statements against interest; however, statements made to police fail to survive Confrontation Clause analysis while those made to his son and to his cell mate have particularized guarantees of trustworthiness); *U.S. v. Ochoa*, 229 F.3d 631 (7th Cir. 2000) (error to allow FBI agent to relate contents of cooperating witness' statement that defendant arranged to have his own car stolen; facts established strong incentive to curry favor with police so declarant would not be charged); *U.S. v. Boone*, 229 F.3d 1231 (9th Cir. 2000) (no error to admit taped conversation implicating defendant in armed robbery; conversation took place in private setting in which accomplice was confiding to girlfriend, inculpating himself while making no effort to mitigate his own conduct); *Castelan*, 219 F.3d at 696 (where statements implicating defendant were made to police during custodial interview in which declarant asked if he would receive any benefit for cooperation, court concluded statements lacked particularized guarantees of trustworthiness sufficient to satisfy Confrontation Clause); *U.S. v. Moskowitz*, 215 F.3d 265 (2d Cir. 2000) (no error admitting co-defendant's plea allocution as statement against penal interest; blame-shifting portion of allocution was redacted and court gave immediate limiting instruction that jury could only use plea to determine whether a conspiracy existed and not whether defendant was a participant); *U.S. v. Tocco*, 200 F.3d 401 (6th Cir. 2000) (statements made to son in confidence by Mafia member who died before trial implicating himself and others in organized crime survives *Lilly* analysis); *Varela v. U.S.*, 364 F. Supp. 2d 720 (N.D. Ill. 2005) (although naming defendant as one of the perpetrators, challenged statements were otherwise self-inculpatory, made to relatives in a noncustodial setting and sufficiently trustworthy to pass muster under Confrontation Clause); *Bruton v. Phillips*, 64 F. Supp. 2d 669 (E.D. Mich. 1999) (habeas corpus: admission of nontestifying codefendant's statements did not violate Confrontation Clause; spontaneous statements acknowledging declarant's active role in crime made to friends and acquaintances shortly after murders and prior to arrest with no attempt to shift blame to petitioner).

Crawford v. Washington—Criminal Cases

Evidence that is otherwise admissible under a hearsay exception may nonetheless be barred if it violates the defendant's Sixth Amendment right to confront witnesses against him. For a discussion of the impact of *Crawford v. Washington*, 541 U.S. 36, 124 S. Ct. 1354, 158 L. Ed. 2d 177 (2004) on the law of hearsay evidence in criminal cases, see Commentary under HEARSAY: AUTHOR'S NOTE CONFRONTATION-CRIMINAL CASES. *See U.S. v. Udeozor*, 515 F.3d 260 (4th Cir. 2008); *Jordan*, 509 F.3d at 201; *U.S. v. Franklin*, 415 F.3d 537 (6th Cir. 2005) and *U.S. v. Savoca*, 335 F. Supp. 2d 385 (S.D. N.Y. 2004) for an analysis of statements against penal interest in the context of the *Crawford/Roberts* decisions, to wit:

(i) does the hearsay statement qualify as a statement against penal interest;

(ii) if the statement does qualify under this exception, is it testimonial or nontestimonial in nature;

(iii) if testimonial, is the declarant unavailable as a witness and has defendant had the opportunity to cross-examine the declarant; and

(iv) if nontestimonial, is the statement sufficiently trustworthy for admission under Rule 804(b)(3).*

Additional References

Graham, Handbook of Federal Evidence § 804.3 (7th ed. 2012)

Treatises and Practice Aids

Goode and Wellborn, Courtroom Handbook on Federal Evidence Chapter 5, Rule 804(b)(3) and Obj. 37 (annual ed.)

Mueller & Kirkpatrick, Federal Evidence, §§ 8:129 to 8:136 (3d ed. 2007)

Binder, Hearsay Handbook Chapter 36 (4th ed. 2001)

McCormick, Evidence Chapter 33 (6th ed. 2006)

Park, Trial Objections Handbook §§ 4:75 to 4:77 (2nd ed. 2001)

[Hearsay etc.]

*In *U.S. v. Jordan*, 509 F.3d 191, 201 n.5 (4th Cir. 2007), the Fourth Circuit said:

> We note that any doubt left by Crawford as to the applicability of the Confrontation Clause to non-testimonial hearsay statements was dispelled by the Supreme Court's unanimous decision in *Whorton v. Bockting*, 549 U.S. 406, 127 S.Ct. 1173, 167 L.Ed.2d 1 (2007). The *Whorton* Court made clear that *Crawford* overruled *Ohio v. Roberts,* 448 U.S. 56, 100 S.Ct. 2531, 65 L.Ed.2d 597 (1980), and that "under *Crawford*, the Confrontation Clause has no application to [out-of-court-non-testimonial] statements and therefore permits their admission even if they lack indicia of reliability." *Wharton*, 127 S.Ct. at 1183.

This may be a limited point of view.

HEARSAY EXCEPTION: STATEMENTS FOR PURPOSES OF MEDICAL DIAGNOSIS OR TREATMENT

See:

Fed.R.Evid. 803(4)
Mil.R.Evid. 803(4)

Objection

- [*To a question*] Objection. The question calls for hearsay.
- [*To an answer*] Objection, hearsay. I move that the answer be stricken and the jury be instructed not to consider it for any purpose.

Response

- The statement is admissible as a hearsay exception under Fed.R.Evid. 803(4) because I have established it was made to this witness for the purpose of medical diagnosis and treatment.

Commentary

Rule 803(4) excepts from the hearsay rule "[s]tatements made for purposes of medical diagnosis or treatment and describing medical history, or past or present symptoms, pain or sensations, or the inception or general character of the cause or external source thereof insofar as reasonably pertinent to diagnosis or treatment."

Admissibility is governed by a two-part test: (1) the declarant's motive in making the statement must be consistent with the purposes of promoting treatment; and (2) the content of the statement must be such as is reasonably relied on by a physician in treatment or diagnosis. *Willingham v. Crooke*, 412 F.3d 553 (4th Cir. 2005).

The rationale for the exception is that a person seeking medical assistance has a strong, self-interested motivation to give the doctor truthful information. *U.S. v. Pacheco*, 154 F.3d 1236 (10th Cir. 1998); *People of Territory of Guam v. Ignacio*, 10 F.3d 608 (9th Cir. 1993); *U.S. v. Bowdoin*, 770 F.Supp.2d 133, 141 n 4 (D.D.C. 2011); Fed.R.Evid. 803(4), Advisory Committee's Note; *see also White v. Illinois*, 502 U.S. 346, 112 S. Ct. 736, 116 L. Ed. 2d 848 (1992) ("a statement made in the course of procuring medical services, where the declarant knows that a false statement may cause misdiagnosis or mistreatment, carries special guarantees of credibility.")

Rule 803(4) eliminates the distinction between examining and treating physicians: an examining physician may now testify to statements made for the purpose of medical diagnosis to the same extent as the treating physician, even though the only purpose of the examination was to enable him to testify. *U.S. v. Iron Shell*, 633 F.2d 77 (8th Cir. 1980).

The assertion need not be made by the patient. It may be made by someone on the patient's behalf, such as a parent concerning its child, or a policeman concerning an unconscious victim of an accident or crime. *Danaipour v. McLarey*, 386 F.3d 289 (1st Cir. 2004) (mother's statements to doctor, recounting minor daughter's prior statements, were made for purposes of medical treatment within meaning of this exception); *U.S. v. Yazzie*, 59 F.3d 807 (9th Cir. 1995) (plain language of Rule does not limit its application to patient-declarants; in most instances, statements to doctor by parent of injured child could easily qualify as statement for purpose of obtaining proper medical diagnosis).

The assertion need not be made to a doctor. For example, it may be made to a nurse, ambulance attendant or hospital admitting clerk. *U.S. v. Tome*, 61 F.3d 1446 (10th Cir. 1995); *U.S. v. Gonzalez*, 533 F.3d 1057 (9th Cir. 2008) (victim's statement to nurse that she had been sexually assaulted); *U.S. v. Bercier*, 506 F.3d 625 (8th Cir. 2007); *Smith v. Pfizer Inc.*, 688 F.Supp.2d 735 (M.D.Tenn. 2010) (statements to pharmacist admissible under medical diagnosis exception). It is the purpose of the assertion, i.e., to aid in medical treatment or diagnosis leading to treatment, and not the identity of its immediate recipient, that qualifies the statement for exception to the hearsay rule.

The exception also applies to statements made to a psychiatrist or psychologist. *U.S. v. Kappell*, 418 F.3d 550 (6th Cir. 2005) (collecting cases). However, there is a recognized distinction between the types of information pertinent to a psychiatrist as opposed to a physician. *See Swinton v. Potomac Corp.*, 270 F.3d 794 (9th Cir. 2001) (in suit against employer alleging racial harassment, no abuse of discretion admitting employee's statements to his psychologists regarding harassment); *Guzman v. Abbott Laboratories*, 59 F. Supp. 2d 747 (N.D. Ill. 1999) (Title VII case applying exception to statements to plaintiff's psychiatrist that she was being harassed and was the subject of discrimination and persecution); *U.S. ex rel. Gacy v. Welborn*, 1992 WL 211018 at *23 (N.D. Ill. 1992) ("The psychiatrist has no temperature or pulse to take, no x-rays to read and no open wound to examine. What he has for the most part is what he learns from the mouth of the patient, together with what little there may be in the way of visually observable signs."). *See also U.S. v. Running Horse*, 175 F.3d 635 (8th Cir. 1999) (exception applied to testimony by clinical psychologist).

A declarant's statement to a physician that assigns fault or identifies the person responsible for the declarant's injuries is generally inadmissible under Rule 803(4) because fault and identity are usually unnecessary either for accurate diagnosis or effective treatment. *Bercier*, 506 F.3d at 632 (doctor's testimony improperly bolstered victim's earlier account; no evidence that assailant's identity was pertinent to diagnosis and treatment); *Rock v. Huffco Gas & Oil Co., Inc.*, 922 F.2d 272, 278 (5th Cir. 1991) (doctors only needed to know that plaintiff had twisted his ankle; they did not need to know additional details that injury occurred while stepping through rusted-out or defective step or by slipping in grease in order to diagnose or treat the injury); *Cook v. Hoppin*, 783 F.2d 684 (7th Cir. 1986) (where plaintiff was injured in fall on stairway, statements in medical records relating to alleged wrestling match were not type of statements medical personnel generally rely on when making diagnosis and providing treatment); *U.S. v. Renville*, 779 F.2d 430 (8th Cir. 1985) (physicians rarely rely on statements of identity in treatment or diagnosis); *Iron Shell*, 633 F.2d at 84 (statements of fault would seldom be pertinent); *Johnson v. Tuffey*, 2011 WL 4345285 (N.D.N.Y. 2011) (plaintiff's statement to doctors that he was beaten by the Albany Police Dept. went to fault and was inadmissible);

Fed.R.Evid. 803(4) Advisory Committee Notes (statements of fault "not ordinarily admissible"). *But see* discussion of sex abuse victims, especially young children *infra*.

Testimony by the patient regarding medical opinions, diagnoses, and statements made by doctors who have examined the patient is not admissible under Rule 803(4). *Field v. Trigg County Hosp., Inc.*, 386 F.3d 729 (6th Cir. 2004) (exception applies only to statements made by patient to doctor and not to statements by doctor to patient); *Bombard v. Fort Wayne Newspapers, Inc.*, 92 F.3d 560 (7th Cir. 1996); *Gong v. Hirsch*, 913 F.2d 1269 (7th Cir. 1990); *Holt v. Olmsted Tp. Bd. of Trustees*, 43 F. Supp. 2d 812 (N.D. Ohio 1998).

Children and Family Victims of Sexual Abuse

Some courts have adopted a special rule that a hearsay statement revealing the identity of a sexual abuser who is a member of the victim's family or household can be admissible under Rule 803(4) where the abuser has such an intimate relationship with the victim that the abuser's identity becomes reasonably pertinent to the victim's proper treatment. *Pacheco*, 154 F.3d at 1236 (child sex abuse by mother's former boyfriend); *Tome*, 61 F.3d at 1446 (child sex abuse by father); *Ignacio*, 10 F.3d at 608 (child sex abuse by family member); *U.S. v. Joe*, 8 F.3d 1488 (10th Cir. 1993) (rape of wife by estranged husband).

Such information is pertinent to treatment because the physician must be attentive to the need to remove the victim from the abusive environment as well as to the emotional and psychological injuries, the nature and extent of which often depend upon the identity of the abuser. *U.S. v. Peneaux*, 432 F.3d 882 (8th Cir. 2005); *U.S. v. George*, 960 F.2d 97 (9th Cir. 1992).

In the Fourth and Eighth Circuits there is a presumption that young children do not necessarily understand the medical importance of being truthful. These circuits utilize a two-part test to determine whether the out-of-court statements were reasonably pertinent to diagnosis or treatment. First, the declarant's motive in making the statements must be consistent with the purpose of obtaining treatment; and, second, the statement must be the type that a physician reasonably could rely on when engaged in diagnosis or treatment. *Lovejoy v. U.S.*, 92 F.3d 628 (8th Cir. 1996); *Morgan v. Foretich*, 846 F.2d 941 (4th Cir. 1988); *Renville*, 779 F.2d at 430; *see U.S. v. Sumner*, 204 F.3d 1182 (8th Cir. 2000) (statements excluded because doctor failed to discuss with six-year-old girl why questions he asked were important to diagnosis and treatment and why it was important for child to tell the truth regarding identity of abuser); *U.S. v. Beaulieu*, 194 F.3d 918, 921 (8th Cir. 1999) (child's statements of identity to nurse practitioner and psychologist excluded because they failed to explain that identity of abuser was important to diagnosis or treatment and child testified purpose of visits was "just to get evidence."); *Olesen v. Class*, 164 F.3d 1096 (8th Cir. 1999) (statements excluded because failure to show that child understood medical significance of being truthful, i.e, role of medical health professional in trying to help or heal her, which triggers motivation to be truthful). The Tenth Circuit specifically rejects the presumption and preconditions imposed by the Fourth and Eighth circuits. *See*, for example, *Joe*, 8 F.3d at 1494 n.5 ("This two-part test is not contemplated by the rule and is not necessary to ensure that the rule's purpose is carried out. The first prong . . . inquires into the declarant's motive. Such inquiries . . . were not contemplated by the rule; the rule itself has built-in guarantees that assure the trustworthiness of a statement made for purposes of medical diagnosis or treatment . . .. The second prong . . . merely rephrases the Rule 803(4) requirement that the statement be 'reasonably pertinent to diagnosis or treatment.' "). *See also U.S. v. Edward J.*, 224 F.3d 1216 (10th Cir. 2000); *U.S. v. Norman T.*, 129 F.3d 1099 (10th Cir. 1997); *Government of the Virgin Islands v. Morris*, 191 F.R.D. 82, 85–86 (D.V.I. 1999) ("There is no presumption that a child is any less aware that visiting a doctor is for the purpose of seeking medical treatment.")

Crawford v. Washington—Criminal Cases

The impact of *Crawford v. Washington*, 541 U.S. 36, 124 S. Ct. 1354, 158, 158 L. Ed. 2d 177 (2004) on the law of hearsay in criminal cases is discussed at Commentary under HEARSAY: AUTHOR'S NOTE CONFRONTATION-CRIMINAL CASES.

In *U.S. v. Peneaux*, where a three-year-old girl was the alleged victim of sex abuse, the government presented testimony from the victim, a pediatrician and a foster parent. Finding no *Crawford* violation, the court said "[w]here statements are made to a physician seeking to give medical aid in the form of diagnosis or treatment, they are presumptively nontestimonial." 432 F.3d at 896. The court also rejected the argument that a foster parent is an agent of the state and that the child's statement to the foster mother was testimonial under *Crawford*.

In *U.S. v. Kappell*, 418 F.3d 550 (6th Cir. 2005), the trial witnesses included the victims, then aged eight and five, and a psychotherapist who had interviewed the children about sexual abuse for the purpose of making a medical diagnosis. The court distinguished *Crawford*, as a case involving the admissibility under the Confrontation Clause of recorded testimonial statements of a person who did not testify at trial. Here the testimony was deemed admissible because victims and psychotherapist testified and were subjected to cross-examination.

Additional References

Graham, Handbook of Federal Evidence § 803.4 (7th ed. 2012)

Treatises and Practice Aids

Goode and Wellborn, Courtroom Handbook on Federal Evidence Chapter 5 and Obj. 36 (annual ed.)

Mueller & Kirkpatrick, Federal Evidence, § 8:75 (3d ed. 2007)

Binder, Hearsay Handbook Chapter 13 (4th ed. 2001)

McCormick, Evidence Chapter 27 (6th ed. 2006)

Park, Trial Objections Handbook § 4:25 (2nd ed. 2001)

HEARSAY EXCEPTION: STATEMENTS IN DOCUMENTS AFFECTING AN INTEREST IN PROPERTY

See:

Fed.R.Evid. 803(15)
Mil.R.Evid. 803(15)

Objection

- I object to the introduction of this document and any testimony about its contents. It is inadmissible hearsay.

Response

- The evidence is admissible under Rule 803(15) which creates an exception for statements in a document affecting an interest in property. As a foundation, I have established (*specify*).

Commentary

Rule 803(15) creates an exception to the rule against hearsay for:

> A statement contained in a document purporting to establish or affect an interest in property if the matter stated was relevant to the purpose of the document, unless dealings with the property since the document was made have been inconsistent with the truth of the statement or the purport of the document.

The requirements for admissibility under Rule 803(15) are that the document has been authenticated and is trustworthy, that it affects an interest in property, and that the dealings with the property since the document was made have been consistent with the truth of the statement. *Silverstein v. Chase*, 260 F.3d 142 (2d Cir. 2001) (remanding for the trial court to consider whether statements contained in a document labeled 'Cancellation of Indebtedness' came within exception); *Enbridge Pipelines (Illinois) LLC v. Burris*, 2010 WL 3038501 (S.D.Ill. 2010) and *Kelly v. Enbridge (U.S.) Inc.*, 2008 WL 2123755 at *7 (C.D. Ill. 2008) (assignment agreements evidenced name changes and, therefore, the chain of title to easement in dispute); *U.S. v. Weinstock*, 863 F. Supp. 1529 (D. Utah 1994) (affidavit made by stock owner and furnished to transfer agent to obtain replacement stock certificate); *Compton v. Davis Oil Co.*, 607 F. Supp. 1221 (D. Wyo. 1985) (warranty deeds).

Additional References

Graham, Handbook of Federal Evidence § 803.15 (7th ed. 2012)

Treatises and Practice Aids

Mueller & Kirkpatrick, Federal Evidence, § 8:97 (3d ed. 2007)

Binder, Hearsay Handbook Chapter 23 (4th ed. 2001)

McCormick, Evidence § 323 (6th ed. 2006)

Park, Trial Objections Handbook § 4:63 (2nd ed. 2001)

HEARSAY EXCEPTION: THEN EXISTING MENTAL, EMOTIONAL CONDITION (STATE OF MIND)

See:

Fed.R.Evid. 803(3)
Mil.R.Evid. 803(3)

Objection

- [*To a question*] Objection. The question calls for hearsay.
- [*To an answer*] Objection, hearsay. I move that the answer be stricken and the jury be instructed not to consider it for any purpose.

Response

- The statement comes within Rule 803(3), the state of mind exception to the hearsay rule. As foundation, I have established that the declarant made the statement to this witness contemporaneously with the event in question and that the statement referred to declarant's [*then existing state of mind*] [*intent*] [*motive*] [*emotion*].

Commentary

Rule 803(3) creates a hearsay exception for a statement of the declarant's "then existing state of mind, emotion, sensation or physical condition* (such as intent, plan, motive, design, mental feeling, pain and bodily health*)." The exception does not include a statement of memory or belief to prove the fact remembered or believed unless it relates to the execution, revocation, identification or terms of the declarant's will. Rule 803(3); *see U.S. v. Tome*, 61 F.3d 1446, 1453 (10th Cir. 1995) (child abuse victim's statement that she did not want to go back to her father "because my father gets drunk and thinks I'm his wife" was inadmissible under state of mind exception because it fell within express prohibition against admitting statement of memory to prove fact remembered); *U.S. v. Fontenot*,

---

**See* Hearsay Exception: Then Existing Physical Condition, *infra*.

14 F.3d 1364 (9th Cir. 1994) (testimony that defendant told witness "they are going to kill Kathy" [his wife] and that he had to go to San Francisco, that his life was in danger by going but was in even more danger if he did not go, properly excluded as statements of belief-not condition).

For a statement to be admissible, it must have been contemporaneous with the state of mind sought to be proved and the declarant must not have had an opportunity to reflect and possibly fabricate or misrepresent his thoughts. *U.S. v. Reyes*, 239 F.3d 722 (5th Cir. 2001); *U.S. v. LeMaster*, 54 F.3d 1224 (6th Cir. 1995); *U.S. v. Neely*, 980 F.2d 1074 (7th Cir. 1992).

The exception applies only to a statement describing a state of mind expressed by the declarant. Such statements, however, cannot be used to prove the cause of that state of mind. *U.S. v. Joe*, 8 F.3d 1488 (10th Cir. 1993) (declarant's explanation of why she was afraid of her husband not encompassed by Rule 803(3)); *U.S. v. Liu*, 960 F.2d 449 (5th Cir. 1992) (declarant's explanation of why he feared for his life inadmissible); *U.S. v. Emmert*, 829 F.2d 805, 810 (9th Cir. 1987) ("'If the reservation in the text of the rule is to have any effect, it must be understood to narrowly limit those admissible statements to declarations of condition'-'I'm scared'-and not belief-'I'm scared because [someone] threatened me.'") (quoting *U.S. v. Cohen*, 631 F.2d 1223, 1225 (5th Cir. 1980)). Rule 803(3) also does not permit receipt of a statement by one person as proof of another's state of mind. *Hong v. Children's Memorial Hosp.*, 993 F.2d 1257 (7th Cir. 1993) (in Title VII case claiming discharge because of national origin, no error to exclude plaintiff's testimony that her deceased brother-in-law told her supervising doctor said plaintiff should move back to Korea; applying rule to testimony, declarant was brother-in-law whose state of mind was irrelevant to case).

Offering evidence under the state of mind *exception* to the hearsay rule is different than offering it for a non-hearsay purpose—for example, to show declarant's state of mind. The *exception* to the hearsay rule is invoked when the statement is offered for the truth of the matter asserted *and* shows the declarant's state of mind (e.g. "I hate X"). By contrast, the mere utterance of a statement, without regard to its truth, may indicate circumstantially the state of mind of the declarant and is *not hearsay* (e.g. "I am Napoleon"). *U.S. v. Quinones*, 511 F.3d 289 (2d Cir. 2007); *Smith v. Duncan*, 411 F.3d 340, 346 n.4 (2d Cir. 2005); *Tierney v. Davidson*, 133 F.3d 189, 192 n.1 (2d Cir. 1998); *see also U.S. v. Johnson*, 354 F. Supp. 2d 939, 962–63 (N.D. Iowa 2005); *Cary Oil Co., Inc. v. MG Refining & Marketing, Inc.*, 257 F. Supp. 2d 751 (S.D. N.Y. 2003).

Statements of Memory and Belief Excluded

Statements of memory and belief are expressly excluded from the ambit of the exception. *Boyce v. Eggers*, 513 F. Supp. 2d 139 (D.N.J. 2007); *U.S. v. Zapata*, 369 F. Supp. 2d 454 (S.D. N.Y. 2005). Almost any statement used to describe events that a speaker has experienced in the past can be characterized as a "memory," which is a presently-existing state of mind when it is conveyed. If such statements were admissible under Rule 803(3) to prove the facts remembered, parties could offer hearsay to establish almost any past fact, a result that would mark "the virtual destruction of the hearsay rule." Fed.R.Evid. 803(3) Advisory Committee's Note.

The exclusion of statements of memory or belief grew out of Justice Cardozo's opinion in *Shepard v. United States*, 290 U.S. 96, 54 S. Ct. 22, 78 L. Ed. 196 (1933), where the Supreme Court refused to admit, under the state of mind exception, a statement by defendant's wife that "Dr. Shepard has poisoned me." The court said that, "[t]he testimony now questioned faced backward and not forward . . .. What is even more important, it spoke to a past act, and even more than that, to an act by someone not the speaker." *Id.* at 104.

Credibility

Since credibility is a matter for the jury, the fact that a statement is self-serving is not a basis for exclusion. *U.S. v. Cardascia*, 951 F.2d 474, 487 (2d Cir. 1991) (self-serving nature of statement is considered when the jury weighs evidence at conclusion of trial); *U.S. v. DiMaria*, 727 F.2d 265

(2d Cir. 1984) (although prosecution argued defendant's statement was classic false exculpatory statement, if it fell within Rule 803(3), its truth or falsity was for jury to determine); *U.S. v. Dellinger*, 472 F.2d 340 (7th Cir. 1972) (exclusion of declarations of party on grounds they are self-serving, even though otherwise free from objection under the hearsay rule and exceptions, detracts from relevant information which should be available to jury).

Relevance

The declarant's state of mind must be relevant to the case. *U.S. v. Tokars*, 95 F.3d 1520 (11th Cir. 1996) (murder victim's state of mind regarding her desire for divorce relevant to husband's motive for planning to kill her); *Morris Jewelers, Inc. v. General Elec. Credit Corp.*, 714 F.2d 32 (5th Cir. 1983) (suit against collection agency alleging improper practices causing plaintiff to lose of profit and goodwill; customers' letters and verbal statements to plaintiff indicating angry state of mind admissible because angry state of mind was core of case); *KW Plastics v. U.S. Can Co.*, 130 F. Supp. 2d 1297 (M.D. Ala. 2001) (state of mind exception is valuable in tortious interference cases; evidence bearing on third party's contractual plans around time of defendant's interference is relevant to whether defendant's conduct caused injury to plaintiff).

Contemporaneous Statements as to State of Mind or Emotion

Evidence of a declarant's out-of-court assertion of his or her then existing state of mind or emotional feeling was recognized as a hearsay exception in the following illustrative cases: *D.J.M. ex rel. D.M. v. Hannibal Public School Dist. No. 60*, 647 F.3d 754 (8th Cir. 2011) (emails relating threats received from plaintiff to commit violent acts at school); *U.S. v. Hyles*, 479 F.3d 958 (8th Cir. 2007) (co-conspirator's statement that he planned to kill victim admissible as his "then existing state of mind"); *Citizens Financial Group, Inc. v. Citizens Nat. Bank of Evans City*, 383 F.3d 110 (3d Cir. 2004) (bank tellers' testimony about customer confusion re similarly named banks); *U.S. v. Serafini*, 233

F.3d 758 (3d Cir. 2000) (perjury prosecution; statements by company executive to witnesses indicating he intended certain checks to be reimbursement for illegal campaign contributions); *U.S. v. Dolan*, 120 F.3d 856, 869 (8th Cir. 1997) (in prosecution of attorney for conspiracy to conceal bankruptcy property, bankrupt's statement that he "had [Dolan] by the balls" admissible to show bankrupt's then existing state of mind indicating a plan, motive and design concerning relationship with Dolan); *Talley v. Bravo Pitino Restaurant, Ltd.*, 61 F.3d 1241 (6th Cir. 1995) (in case of race discrimination in terminating plaintiff's employment, alleged racist comments would be admissible under state of mind exception to demonstrate owners' racial attitudes); *U.S. v. Alzanki*, 54 F.3d 994 (1st Cir. 1995) (prosecution for involuntary servitude; statements by domestic worker to nurses and policeman that she was afraid, hungry and exhausted were admissible but rule did not permit out-of-court statements elaborating on underlying reasons for declarant's state of mind); *Story v. Sunshine Foliage World, Inc.*, 120 F. Supp. 2d 1027 (M.D. Fla. 2000) (assuming that nonverbal conduct was intended as an assertion, co-worker's testimony that plaintiff acted "in a very angry manner" fell under state of mind exception); *Hirsch v. Corban Corporations, Inc.*, 949 F. Supp. 296 (E.D. Pa. 1996) (NLRB could offer union representative's testimony under state of mind exception that, when asked to join union, employees expressed fear of losing jobs; same statements could not be offered to prove what caused fear and additional evidence would be required); *Lightner for and on Behalf of N.L.R.B. v. Dauman Pallet, Inc.*, 823 F. Supp. 249 (D.N.J. 1992) (similar).

For cases where the exception was held not to apply, see: *Reyes*, 239 F.3d at 743 (prosecution for bribery and mail fraud; recorded conversation made by defendant in which he described his illegal acts as secret plan to "scam the scammers" was self-serving hearsay and not contemporaneous statement of then existing mental state because his last criminal act occurred months earlier and he now suspected person called was working with police); *U.S. v. Hernandez*, 176 F.3d 719, 726–27 (3d Cir. 1999) (testimony that when police approached hijacked truck, defendant said "he was unloading truck and expected to be paid for his labor" not admissible as state of mind evidence inferring that he did not know goods were stolen; it is simply hearsay, explaining what he was doing at location where truck was parked); *Colasanto v. Life Ins. Co. of North America*, 100 F.3d 203 (1st Cir. 1996) (in suit over life insurance proceeds, letters written by decedent in March and April, 1994 were not evidence of state of mind several months earlier when he gave policies to his former companion); *LeMaster*, 54 F.3d at 1231 (where defendant was charged with knowingly making false statements during FBI interview, statement made next day not admissible to prove state of mind on prior day because there was opportunity to reflect and fabricate).

Survey Evidence

Pursuant to Rule 803(3), a number of courts have admitted survey evidence of instances of customer confusion in trademark infringement and Lanham Act false advertising cases. See, e.g., *Doctor's Associates, Inc. v. QIP Holder LLC*, 2010 WL 669870 (D.Conn. 2010). In order to establish actual confusion or secondary meaning, typically such surveys poll individuals about their presently-existing states of mind to establish facts about the group's mental impressions. *Schering Corp. v. Pfizer Inc.*, 189 F.3d 218 (2d Cir. 1999) (reversing trial court for abuse of discretion in excluding evidence; two of five physician surveys were admissible under Rule 803(3) to show pattern of implied falsehood while others upon analysis could prove admissible under Rule 807 catch-all exception to establish literal falsehoods; collecting cases and discussing whether survey methodology goes to weight or is proper ground for exclusion); *Sterling Drug, Inc. v. Bayer AG*, 14 F.3d 733 (2d Cir. 1994) (admitting survey evidence to prove confusion); *Bristol-Myers Squibb Co. v. McNeil-P.P.C., Inc.*, 973 F.2d 1033 (2d Cir. 1992) (admitting survey evidence to prove secondary meaning). There is, however, no general rule allowing surveys into evidence in all cases for all purposes. *Compare U.S. v. Pryba*, 900 F.2d 748 (4th Cir. 1990) (in obscenity case excluding survey offered to demonstrate community's attitude concerning sexually explicit materials) *with Keith v. Volpe*, 858 F.2d 467 (9th Cir. 1988) (race discrimination case to force city to construct housing for residents displaced by highway construction; admitting survey to show statistics concerning respondents' race, income and housing preferences).

Conduct of Declarant and Others

A declarant's out-of-court statement as to his intent to perform a certain act in the future is not excludable on hearsay grounds. *See* Rule 803(3) ("A statement of the declarant's then existing state of mind . . . such as intent" is "not excluded by the hearsay rule.") If relevant, such a statement may be introduced to prove that the declarant thereafter acted in accordance with the stated intent. *See Mutual Life Ins. Co. of New York v. Hillmon*, 145 U.S. 285, 12 S. Ct. 909, 36 L. Ed. 706 (1892). As the Eighth Circuit has explained, "A declarant's out-of-court statement of intention is admissible to prove that the declarant subsequently acted in conformity with that intention, if the doing of that act is a disputed material fact." *Firemen's Fund Ins. Co. v. Thien*, 8 F.3d 1307, 1312 (8th Cir. 1993) (quoting *U.S. v. Calvert*, 523 F.2d 895, 910 (8th Cir. 1975)).

There is, however, a difference of opinion as to whether out-of-court statements of intent are admissible only to prove the declarant's future conduct or whether such statements can also be used to prove the future conduct of another person—a nondeclarant. *See Coy v. Renico*, 414 F. Supp. 2d 744, 765–74 (E.D. Mich. 2006) (collecting cases). Some courts hold such statements are admissible to prove subsequent conduct of another person without any other corroborating evidence. *U.S. v. Pheaster*, 544 F.2d 353 (9th Cir. 1976) (in kidnapping prosecution, court did not err in admitting testimony of victim's friend that, shortly before victim disappeared, he said he was going to meet person with same name as defendant); *U.S. v. Houlihan*, 871 F. Supp. 1495, 1501–02 (D. Mass. 1994) (witness allowed to testify that, as her brother left her apartment shortly before his murder, he said he "was going to meet Billy Hurd;" statement of intent only circumstantial evidence that he actually met Hurd, but admissible as part of larger array of evidence before the jury). By contrast, in *U.S. v. Jenkins*, 579 F.2d 840 (4th Cir. 1978), the court relied on a House Judiciary Committee Report to conclude that the portion of *Hillmon* dealing with statements introduced to show the future conduct of a nondeclarant did not survive the adoption of Rule 803(3). *See also U.S. v. Smallwood*, 299 F. Supp. 2d 578 (E.D. Va. 2004) (statements of intent admissible only to prove declarant's future conduct, not future conduct of others; collecting cases). The Second Circuit, however, holds that admissibility turns on whether there is independent corroborating evidence connecting the declarant's statement with the non-declarant's subsequent conduct. *U.S. v. Best*, 219 F.3d 192 (2d Cir. 2000) (testimony that company officer stated he intended to ask defendant to prepare fraudulent Medicare documents sufficiently corroborated by other evidence to be admissible).

Crawford v. Washington—Criminal Cases

In *Crawford v. Washington*, 541 U.S. 36, 124 S. Ct. 1354, 158 L. Ed. 2d 177 (2004) (discussed at Commentary under HEARSAY: AUTHOR'S NOTE CONFRONTATION-CRIMINAL CASES), the Supreme Court "introduced a fundamental re-conception of the Confrontation Clause." *U.S. v. Cromer*, 389 F.3d 662, 671 (6th Cir. 2004). *Crawford* held that "testimonial" out-of-court statements offered against an accused to establish the truth of the matter asserted may only be admitted where the declarant is unavailable and where the defendant has had a prior opportunity to cross-examine the declarant.

The Court left for another day any effort to spell out a comprehensive definition of "testimonial," *Crawford*, 541 U.S. at 68, but did say it "applies at a minimum to prior testimony at a preliminary hearing, before a grand jury, or at a former trial; and to police interrogations." *Id.* Although the Court did not provide a precise line between "testimonial" and "nontestimonial" statements, Justice Scalia said that "[a]n accuser who makes a formal statement to government officers bears testimony in a sense that a person who makes a casual remark to an acquaintance does not." *Id.* at 51. *See Horton v. Allen*, 370 F.3d 75, 84 (1st Cir.

2004) (holding statements made on the day of the murders recounting that defendants' accomplice told witness that he needed money and that victim refused to give him drugs on credit were properly admitted under state of mind exception and were nontestimonial); *Coy v. Renico* (victim's statement of future intent or plan to meet with defendant on the night of her murder admissible as state of mind and not precluded by *Crawford*); *U.S. v. Honken*, 378 F. Supp. 2d 970 (N.D. Iowa 2004) (victim's statements that he was to pick up drugs from defendant and that defendant's accomplice owed him $2,400 for drugs were admissible per Rule 803(3) and were nontestimonial because made in private conversation with acquaintances and not under circumstances where one would reasonably believe statements would be available to use at a trial).

Additional References

Graham, Handbook of Federal Evidence § 803.3 (7th ed. 2012)

Treatises and Practice Aids

Goode and Wellborn, Courtroom Handbook on Federal Evidence Chapter 5 and Obj. 37 (annual ed.)

Mueller & Kirkpatrick, Federal Evidence, § 8:71 (3d ed. 2007)

Binder, Hearsay Handbook Chapter 11 (4th ed. 2001)

McCormick, Evidence §§ 273 to 276 (6th ed. 2006)

Park, Trial Objections Handbook § 4:24 (2nd ed. 2001)

HEARSAY EXCEPTION: THEN EXISTING PHYSICAL CONDITION

See:

Fed.R.Evid. 803(3)
Mil.R.Evid. 803(3)

Objection

- [*To a question*] Objection. The question calls for a hearsay answer.
- [*To an answer*] Objection, hearsay. I move the answer be stricken and the jury be instructed not to consider it for any purpose.

Response

- The statement is admissible as an exception to the hearsay rule under Rule 803(3) since it was a declaration as to then existing physical condition. I have established as foundation that the declarant made the statement to this witness contemporaneously with the event in question and that, at that time, it referred to the declarant's then existing physical condition.

Commentary

A declaration as to then existing physical condition is one of the hearsay exceptions that was formerly considered under the *"res gestae"* label but now is codified at 803(3). McCormick, Evidence § 268. As with the other *"res gestae"* exceptions, such statements (typically expressing pain or bodily harm) are considered trustworthy because of their spontaneous nature. *Id.* § 273.

The exception was firmly recognized prior to codification. *Nuttall v. Reading Co.*, 235 F.2d 546 (3d Cir. 1956) (error not to admit decedent's statement to co-worker that he was not feeling well and had requested day off but was refused). Case law, however, was and is sparse. In *Sana v. Hawaiian Cruises, Ltd.*, 181 F.3d 1041 (9th Cir. 1999), the issue was whether plaintiff, a seaman, fell ill with viral encephalitis while still in the service of his vessel, thus entitling him to maintenance and cure. At the time of trial, he remained in a coma. Although Sana had told co-workers that he had bumped his head at work and felt sick, the trial court held the statements to be inadmissible hearsay and the claim was denied. Reversing, the Ninth Circuit held that the statements were admissible under Rule 803(3).

The exception does not include statements of past medical conditions.

As with Rule 803(4) (concerning statements for purposes of medical diagnosis or treatment), there is no requirement that statements of present physical condition be made to a physician. Such statements can be made to family members, friends or other persons. *Sana*, 181 F.3d at 1045 (statements made to co-workers admissible).

Crawford v. Washington—Criminal Cases

The impact of *Crawford v. Washington*, 541 U.S. 36, 124 S. Ct. 1354, 158, 158 L. Ed. 2d 177 (2004) on the law of hearsay in criminal cases is discussed at Commentary under HEARSAY: AUTHOR'S NOTE CONFRONTATION-CRIMINAL CASES. The *Crawford* Court held that the Confrontation Clause categorically bars the admission of testimonial hearsay unless the declarant is unavailable and the accused has had a prior opportunity to cross-examine the declarant. But Justice Scalia did say that "[a]n accuser who makes a formal statement to government officers bears testimony in a sense that a person who makes a casual remark to an acquaintance does not." *Id.* at 51.

Additional References

Graham, Handbook of Federal Evidence § 803.3 (7th ed. 2012)

Treatises and Practice Aids

Goode and Wellborn, Courtroom Handbook on Federal Evidence Chapter 5 and Obj. 37 (annual ed.)

Mueller & Kirkpatrick, Federal Evidence, § 8:70 (3d ed. 2007)

Binder, Hearsay Handbook Chapter 12 (4th ed. 2001)

McCormick, Evidence § 273 (6th ed. 2006)

Park, Trial Objections Handbook § 4:24 (2nd ed. 2001)

IMPEACHMENT: BIAS, INTEREST, MOTIVE

See:

Fed.R.Evid. 607, 611(b)
Mil.R.Evid. 607, 611(b)

Objection

- Objection. The question has no relevance to or bearing on the witness' testimony or credibility. It is nothing more than an attempt to [*smear the witness*] [*place unfairly prejudicial evidence before the jury*].

Response

- The line of inquiry is proper. I am entitled to impeach the witness by showing that his direct testimony was colored by [*bias*] [*prejudice*] [*interest*] [*corrupt motive*].

Commentary

Although cross-examination ordinarily is limited to those matters brought out on direct examination, an exception exists where the cross-examiner seeks to impeach the witness by showing bias, prejudice, interest, corrupt/ulterior motive or defects in his ability to observe, remember or recount the matter about which he has testified. Rules 607 and 611(b); *Pennsylvania v. Ritchie*, 480 U.S. 39, 51–52, 107 S. Ct. 989, 94 L. Ed. 2d 40 (1987) (the right to cross-examination includes the opportunity to show that a witness is biased, or that the testimony is exaggerated or unbelievable); *Delaware v. Van Arsdall*, 475 U.S. 673, 678–79, 106 S. Ct. 1431, 89 L. Ed. 2d 674 (1986) (exploring possible bias is a proper and important function of right of cross-examination); *U.S. v. Lyons*, 403 F.3d 1248 (11th Cir. 2005) (cross-examination of government "star" witness is important and presumption favors free cross-examination on possible bias, motive, ability to perceive and remember and general character for truthfulness); *Bui v. DiPaolo*, 170 F.3d 232, 242 (1st Cir. 1999) (the threshold requirement imposed by Confrontation Clause is satisfied so long as defendant is given a fair chance to inquire into a witness' bias); *Schledwitz v. U.S.*,

169 F.3d 1003, 1015 (6th Cir. 1999) (defendant entitled to expose bias pursuant to Rule 607); *U.S. v. Lynn*, 856 F.2d 430, 432 n.3 (1st Cir. 1988) (bias is always relevant in assessing a witness' credibility).

Bias has been defined as "the relationship between a party and a witness which might lead the witness to slant, unconsciously or otherwise, his testimony in favor of or against a party." *United States v. Abel*, 469 U.S. 45, 52, 105 S. Ct. 465, 83 L. Ed. 2d 450 (1984).

Bias is not limited to personal animosity against a party or pecuniary gain. Courts have found bias in a wide variety of situations, including familial or sexual relationships, friendships, common organizational memberships and situations in which the witness has a litigation claim against another party or witness. *See* Graham, Handbook of Federal Evidence, §§ 607.7 at 110 to 113 (5th ed. 2001) (collecting cases); *U.S. v. Schoneberg*, 396 F.3d 1036 (9th Cir. 2005) (where plea agreement allows for some benefit or detriment to flow to witness as result of his testimony, defendant must be permitted to cross-examine witness sufficiently to make clear to jury what benefit or detriment will flow and what will trigger benefit or detriment to show why witness might testify falsely to gain benefit or avoid detriment).

Because objectivity is always material to the assessment of credibility, "federal courts have been hospitable to the point of liberality in admitting evidence relevant to a witness' bias." *U.S. v. Akitoye*, 923 F.2d 221 (1st Cir. 1991).

Cross-examination as to bias, interest or corrupt motive may incidentally expose otherwise inadmissible facts to the jury. This alone is not a basis for excluding impeachment evidence. *Abel*, 469 U.S. at 56 ("[T]here is no rule of evidence which provides that testimony admissible for one purpose and inadmissible for another purpose is thereby rendered inadmissable; quite the contrary is the case.") This is not to say that all evidence of an impeaching nature offered to attack the credibility of a witness is admissible. The trial court has discretion to limit or exclude such evidence where its unfairly prejudicial impact outweighs its impeachment value. Fed.R.Evid. 403. *U.S. v. Jimenez*,

513 F.3d 62 (3d Cir. 2008) (marginal relevance and risk of delay and confusion support trial judge's decision to limit cross-examination); *U.S. v. McCarty*, 82 F.3d 943 (10th Cir. 1996) (trial court correctly prohibited particularly invasive, injurious line of questioning concerning serious and unsubstantiated allegations of sexual impropriety).

Impeachment may not be used merely as a pretext to place inadmissible evidence before the fact-finder. *U.S. v. Gilbert*, 57 F.3d 709 (9th Cir. 1995). Impeaching evidence may also be disallowed because it is not relevant to the witness' credibility or because it is based on speculation. *See U.S. v. Martinez-Vives*, 475 F.3d 48, 53 (1st Cir. 2007) (defendant does not have the right to cross-examine on every conceivable theory of bias and court may limit cross-examination if defendant is unable to lay a proper evidentiary foundation or when the theory of bias is inherently speculative); *U.S. v. Zaccaria*, 240 F.3d 75, 81 (1st Cir. 2001) (a party who seeks to cross-examine a witness for the purpose of impeaching his credibility cannot base his queries solely on hunch or innuendo.)

In criminal cases, the accused is constitutionally entitled to explore a witness' motivation in testifying against him. *Delaware v. Van Arsdall*, 475 U.S. at 678–79; *Knight v. Spencer*, 447 F.3d 6 (1st Cir. 2006); *U.S. v. Schoneberg, supra* (constitutional violation; defendant not permitted to adequately explore that star witness' plea bargain reserved possibility of sentence reduction after testimony against co-conspirators). The Confrontation Clause of the Sixth Amendment guarantees the reliability of "evidence against a criminal defendant by subjecting it to rigorous testing in the context of an adversary proceeding before the trier of fact." *Maryland v. Craig*, 497 U.S. 836, 845, 110 S. Ct. 3157, 111 L. Ed. 2d 666 (1990). Cross-examination of a witness testifying against the accused allows the jury to observe the witness' demeanor so they may assess her credibility and evaluate the truth of her testimony. *California v. Green*, 399 U.S. 149, 158, 90 S. Ct. 1930, 26 L. Ed. 2d 489 (1970). A defendant's right of confrontation is violated when he is prohibited from pursuing areas of cross-examination that may undermine the credibility of the witness. *Olden v. Kentucky*, 488

U.S. 227, 233, 109 S. Ct. 480, 102 L. Ed. 2d 513 (1988). However, the Confrontation Clause is satisfied "when the defense is given a full and fair opportunity to probe and expose . . . infirmities through cross-examination, thereby calling to the attention of the factfinder the reasons for giving scant weight to the witness' testimony." *Delaware v. Fensterer*, 474 U.S. 15, 22, 106 S. Ct. 292, 295, 88 L. Ed. 2d 15 (1985); *U.S. v. Baptista-Rodriguez*, 17 F.3d 1354, 1371 (11th Cir. 1994). But the Supreme Court has also said that the Confrontation Clause only "guarantees an *opportunity* for effective cross-examination, not cross-examination that is effective in whatever way, and to whatever extent, the defense might wish." *Delaware v. Fensterer,* 474 U.S. at 20 (emphasis in original); *U.S. v. Contreras*, 536 F.3d 1167 (10th Cir. 2008); *U.S. v. Ghilarducci*, 480 F.3d 542, 548 (7th Cir. 2007).

Additional References

Graham, Handbook of Federal Evidence §§ 607.7, 611.11 (7th ed. 2012)

Treatises and Practice Aids

Goode and Wellborne, Courtroom Handbook on Federal Evidence Chapter 5, Rules 607, 611 and Obj. 41 (annual ed.)

Wright & Gold, Federal Practice and Procedure: Evidence 2d § 6095

McCormick, Evidence § 39(6th ed. 2006)

Park, Trial Objections Handbook § 7:18 (2nd ed. 2001)

IMPEACHMENT: CREDIBILITY-SPECIFIC CONDUCT

See:

Fed.R.Evid. 608(b)
Mil.R.Evid. 608(b)

Objection

- Objection. The question is improper; that subject has nothing to do with truthfulness.
- Objection. Counsel must take the witness' answer; Rule 609(b) forbids the use of extrinsic evidence.

Response

- The conduct is probative of truthfulness [*explain*].
- The witness' answer does not end cross-examination; I am entitled to explore the matter.

Commentary

In order to cast doubt on the veracity of testimony, any witness, including a character witness, may be cross-examined concerning specific instances of conduct if that conduct is probative of untruthfulness. *Rahn v. Hawkins*, 464 F.3d 813 (8th Cir. 2006). The limited use of specific conduct is governed by Rule 608(b) which provides in relevant part:

> (b) Specific instances of conduct. Specific instances of the conduct of a witness, for the purpose of attacking or supporting the witness' credibility, other than conviction of crime as provided in rule 609, may not be proved by extrinsic evidence. They may, however, in the discretion of the court, if probative of truthfulness or untruthfulness, be inquired into on cross-examination of the witness (1) concerning the witness' character for truthfulness or untruthfulness, or (2) concerning the character for truthfulness or untruthfulness of another witness as to which character the witness being cross-examined has testified.

If the witness denies the conduct, such acts may not be proved by extrinsic evidence and the questioning party must take the witness' answer as is.

U.S. v. Thomas, 467 F.3d 49 (1st Cir. 2006); *U.S. v. Matthews*, 168 F.3d 1234 (11th Cir. 1999). "Taking the witness' answer" simply means that the cross-examiner cannot call other witnesses to prove the discrediting acts. It does not mean that the cross-examiner cannot continue to press the witness for an admission. *Carter v. Hewitt*, 617 F.2d 961, 969 (3d Cir. 1980); McCormick, Evidence, § 41 at 155 (5th ed. 1999).

Limitations on the use, scope and extent of cross-examination are expressly committed to the discretion of the trial judge. *U.S. v. Shinderman*, 515 F.3d 5, 16 (1st Cir. 2008). In addition to the terms of Rule 608(b), Rules 403 and 611 govern this discretionary authority. *U.S. v. Schuler*, 458 F.3d 1148 (10th Cir. 2006) (under Rule 608(b), court has discretion to decide whether defendant may be cross-examined about prior conduct concerning her character for truthfulness subject to balancing test of Rule 403); *Firemen's Fund Ins. Co. v. Thien*, 63 F.3d 754, 759–60 (8th Cir. 1995).

The purpose of Rule 608(b)'s prohibition of extrinsic evidence is to avoid holding mini trials on irrelevant or collateral matters. *U.S. v. Riddle*, 193 F.3d 995 (8th Cir. 1999); *Palmer v. City of Monticello*, 31 F.3d 1499, 1507 n.11 (10th Cir. 1994); *U.S. v. Beauchamp*, 986 F.2d 1, 3 n.1 (1st Cir. 1993).

Extrinsic Evidence

While the rule does not define "extrinsic evidence," the courts have indicated it is a reference to testimony by other witnesses or use of documentation. *See U.S. v. Balsam*, 203 F.3d 72, 87 n.18 (1st Cir. 2000) (Rule 608(b) which allows specific instances of conduct to be inquired into, does not provide for the admission of physical evidence); *U.S. v. Murray*, 103 F.3d 310, 321 (3d Cir. 1997) (extrinsic evidence is evidence offered through other witnesses rather than through cross-examination of the witness himself); *U.S. v. Martz*, 964 F.2d 787, 789 (8th Cir. 1992) (while documents may be admissible on cross-examination to prove a material fact, they are not admissible under Rule 608(b) merely to show a witness' general character for truthfulness or untruthfulness); *U.S. v. Peterson*, 808 F.2d 969, 972–73 (2d Cir. 1987) (holding admission of check that defendant denied forging was error under Rule 608(b)); *Carter v. Hewitt*, 617 F.2d at 969 ("The principal concern of the rule is to prohibit impeachment of a witness through extrinsic evidence of his bad acts when this evidence is to be introduced by calling other witnesses to testify."); *U.S. v. Herzberg*, 558 F.2d 1219, 1222–23 (5th Cir. 1977) (having witness read last few lines of an opinion affirming civil fraud judgment was error). Cross-examination questions alone are not extrinsic evidence. *U.S. v. Olivo*, 80 F.3d 1466, 1471 (10th Cir. 1996).

Unlike evidence of prior convictions under Rule 609 which covers a wide spectrum of conduct (see Impeachment: Prior Convictions, *infra*, conduct probative of untruthfulness is more narrowly defined* for purposes of Rule 608(b)). Such conduct has been held to include the following: use of false names or false identities (*Turner v. White*, 443 F. Supp. 2d 288 (E.D. N.Y. 2005)); altering time cards, inflating bills, hiding job records (*U.S. v. Simonelli*, 237 F.3d 19 (1st Cir. 2001)); suspension from the Kansas Highway Patrol for falsifying a police report (*Hampton v. Dillard Dept. Stores, Inc.*, 247 F.3d 1091 (10th Cir. 2001)); embezzlement (*Elcock v. Kmart Corp.*, 233 F.3d 734 (3d Cir. 2000)); prior frauds (*U.S. v. Munoz*, 233 F.3d 1117 (9th Cir. 2000)); intimidating other witnesses to get them either to testify falsely or refuse to testify at all, (*U.S. v. Manske*, 186 F.3d 770 (7th Cir. 1999)); receipt of stolen goods (*U.S. v. Zizzo*, 120 F.3d 1338, 1355 (7th Cir. 1997)); theft (*U.S. v. Smith*, 80 F.3d 1188, 1193 (7th Cir. 1996)); false statements made on bankruptcy and loan documents (*U.S. v. Jensen*, 41 F.3d 946 (5th Cir. 1994)); fraudulently obtaining fake driver's license and using it to cash stolen checks (*U.S. v. Williams*, 986 F.2d 86, 88–89 (4th Cir. 1993)); failure to file federal income tax returns

---

[Impeachment etc.]

*The 1972 Advisory Committee Notes observe that "the possibilities of abuse are substantial" when counsel cross-examines a witness about "[p]articular instances of conduct, though not the subject of criminal conviction," and stress that "[c]onsequently safeguards are erected in the form of specific requirements that the instances inquired into be probative of truthfulness or its opposite and not remote in time."

and bribery (*U.S. v. Wilson*, 985 F.2d 348, 351 (7th Cir. 1993)); false statements made on application for employment, an apartment, driver's license, a loan, membership in NASD and on tax returns (*U.S. v. Jones*, 900 F.2d 512, 520–21 (2d Cir. 1990)); loss of professional license because of deceptive practices (*U.S. v. Fulk*, 816 F.2d 1202, 1206 (7th Cir. 1987)); use of false names or false identities, (*U.S. v. Mansaw*, 714 F.2d 785, 789 (8th Cir. 1983)); (*Fletcher v. City of New York*, 54 F. Supp. 2d 328, 333 (S.D. N.Y. 1999)).

Evidence of prior bad acts has been recognized as so prejudicial that it should only be admitted when clearly probative of a witness's credibility. *Tri-State Hosp. Supply, Inc. v. U.S.*, 471 F. Supp. 2d 170 (D.D.C. 2007). For cases restricting cross-examination or finding error where the evidence was not probative of veracity, see *U.S. v. Holt*, 486 F.3d 997 (7th Cir. 2007) (prohibiting cross-examination of police officers regarding disciplinary actions unrelated to veracity); *U.S. v. McGee*, 408 F.3d 966, 982 (7th Cir. 2005) (excluding recording of defendant's telephone conversations regarding lie he told to a third party after his arrest; government's attempt to characterize the statement as a prior inconsistent statement would amount to an end-run around 608(b)); *U.S. v. Wilson*, 244 F.3d 1208 (10th Cir. 2001) (drug crimes have no relation to truth or untruth); *Samson v. Apollo Resources, Inc.*, 242 F.3d 629 (5th Cir. 2001) (no error to exclude evidence of environmental violations, improper tax deductions and violation of local building codes); *U.S. v. McHorse*, 179 F.3d 889 (10th Cir. 1999) (questions regarding alleged child molestation were unrelated to witness' veracity); *U.S. v. Young*, 567 F.2d 799, 803 (8th Cir. 1977) (precluding cross-examination into witness' alleged offer to pay $10,000 to have her ex-husband killed as irrelevant to veracity and highly prejudicial); *U.S. v. Willis*, 43 F. Supp. 2d 873, 879 (N.D. Ill. 1999) (slipshod investigative work by DEA agents amounts to specific instances of conduct not obviously probative of veracity); *U.S. v. Gonzalez*, 938 F. Supp. 1199 (D. Del. 1996) (showing witness to be racist or sexist is not probative of character for truthfulness or untruthfulness); *Mischalski v. Ford Motor Co.*, 935 F. Supp. 203, 207–08 (E.D. N.Y.

1996) ("Ford has cited no authority, and the court is aware of none, to support the conclusion that the status of being an illegal alien impugns one's credibility. Thus, by itself, such evidence is not admissible for impeachment purposes."); *U.S. v. Devery*, 935 F. Supp. 393 (S.D. N.Y. 1996) (cross-examination concerning immoral acts and acts of sexual perversion may be properly excluded by a trial judge who determines they are not probative of the witness' veracity); *Eng v. Scully*, 146 F.R.D. 74 (S.D. N.Y. 1993) (murder is not necessarily indicative of truthfulness, and the probative value of a murder conviction is substantially outweighed by the danger of unfair prejudice).

Rule 608(b) should not be overread. It does not address other forms of impeachment (such as for bias or interest). Nor, for example, does it address whether extrinsic evidence is admissible under the theory of impeachment by contradiction. *U.S. v. Higa*, 55 F.3d 448, 452 (9th Cir. 1995). *See, e.g., U.S. v. Scott*, 243 F.3d 1103, 1107 (8th Cir. 2001) (while impeachment by contradiction is a well-recognized way of attacking a witness' credibility, contradiction offered through the testimony of another witness is customarily excluded unless it is independently relevant or admissible); *U.S. v. Kozinski*, 16 F.3d 795, 806 (7th Cir. 1994) (one may not contradict for the sake of contradiction by proffering testimony that relates only to collateral matters).

Additional References

Graham, Handbook of Federal Evidence §§ 608.3 to 608.5 (7th ed. 2012)

Treatises and Practice Aids

Goode and Wellborne, Courtroom Handbook on Federal Evidence Chapter 5, Rule 608 and Obj. 42 (annual ed.)

McCormick, Evidence §§ 41, 47 to 48 (6th ed. 2006)

Park, Trial Objections Handbook § 7:10 (2nd ed. 2001)

IMPEACHMENT: PRIOR CONVICTIONS

See:

Fed.R.Evid. 609
Mil.R.Evid. 609

Objection

- Objection. [*request sidebar*] Counsel's attempt to impeach the witness is improper because [*examples*]:
- this is a stale conviction, with no probative value and we were not given advance written notice of intent to use;
- it was a misdemeanor with a maximum sentence of one year or less;
- [*witness is the accused*] the prejudicial effect outweighs any probative value [*explain*];
- [*any other witness*] the probative value is substantially outweighed by the danger of unfair prejudice [*explain*].

Response [examples]

- the conviction is less than ten years old; there is no notice requirement;
- it was a crime of dishonesty committed within the ten-year period, and
  - therefore, it does not matter whether it was a felony or a misdemeanor;
  - there is no balancing test to be applied;
- the conviction is highly probative here because [*explain*].

Commentary

Evidence of prior conviction is subject to careful scrutiny and use at trial "because of the inherent danger that a jury may convict a defendant because he is a bad person instead of because the evidence of the crime with which he is charged proves him guilty." *U.S. v. Holloway*, 1 F.3d 307, 311 (5th Cir. 1993). *See Schmude v. Tricam Industries, Inc.*, 556 F.3d 624 (7th Cir. 2009) (allowing a prior conviction to be used to impeach a witness's testimony is in tension with the most elementary conception of the rule of "corrective justice," i.e., judging the case rather than the parties).

Absent exceptional circumstances, evidence of a prior conviction admitted for impeachment purposes may not include collateral details and circumstances surrounding the conviction. *U.S. v. Sine*, 493 F.3d 1021, 1036 n.14 (9th Cir. 2007). Generally, only the prior conviction, its general nature and punishment of felony range are fair game for testing the defendant's credibility. *U.S. v. Albers*, 93 F.3d 1469 (10th Cir. 1996). *See U.S. v. Gordon*, 780 F.2d 1165 (5th Cir. 1986) (limiting cross-examination to the number of convictions, the nature of the crimes and the dates and times of the convictions and excluding the particular facts of defendant's previous offenses); *Campbell v. Greer*, 831 F.2d 700 (7th Cir. 1987) (same limitations applied in civil case).

A witness may not be impeached by evidence that he or she was indicted for a crime, since indictment is not any evidence of guilt. *U.S. v. Chance*, 306 F.3d 356 (6th Cir. 2002).

General Principles

All Witnesses Other Than A Criminal Defendant

Rule 609 provides that evidence of prior convictions of all witnesses other than a criminal defendant "shall be admitted" if: (1) the convictions are for crimes punishable by death or imprisonment in excess of one year (or, under the Mil.R.Evid., dishonorable discharge), (2) the convictions are less than ten years old, and (3) the evidence is being used to attack the witness's credibility. Fed.R.Evid. 609(a),(b). By incorporating Rule 403 by reference, this part of the rule also requires that the probative value of the evidence not be substantially outweighed by unfair prejudice, confusion or delay created by admission of the evidence. *See, e.g. U.S. v. Raplinger*, 555 F.3d 687 (8th Cir. 2009) (in prosecution for sex crimes, defendant's request to offer evidence of his own prior sex offenses rejected; purpose was not to attack his own character for truthfulness but to confuse and mislead jury and perhaps cause them to think the federal charges would punish him twice).

The Criminal Defendant

If, however, the witness is the accused, evidence

of prior felony convictions "shall be admitted" so long as the court first finds that the probative value of the conviction as credibility evidence outweighs the prejudicial effect to the accused. Rule 609(a)(1); *U.S. v. Greenidge*, 495 F.3d 85, 97 n.9 (3d Cir. 2007) (when accused is witness, prejudice from use of prior conviction need only exceed probative value to be excluded; with any other witness, the Rule 403 considerations apply, i.e., the prejudice must substantially outweigh the probative value of the conviction).

Rule 609 embodies the common sense proposition that one who has transgressed society's norms by committing a felony is less likely than most to be deterred from lying under oath. *U.S. v. Collier*, 527 F.3d 695 (8th Cir. 2008). As the Seventh Circuit has noted, this empirical proposition may or may not be true; nevertheless, the premise of Rule 609 "that crookedness and lying are correlated," is not for the court to question. *Campbell*, 831 F.2d at 707; *accord U.S. v. Cavender*, 578 F.2d 528, 534 (4th Cir. 1978) (purpose of impeachment is not to demonstrate that witness is bad person "but rather to show background facts which bear directly on whether jurors ought to believe him."); *U.S. v. Ortega*, 561 F.2d 803, 806 (9th Cir. 1977) (explaining that prior convictions involving dishonesty are peculiarly probative of credibility).

Federal, state or foreign convictions that meet the requirements of this Rule can be used. *See U.S. v. Wilson*, 556 F.2d 1177 (4th Cir. 1977) (court permitted German felony conviction to impeach defendant accused of rape; no showing that German legal system lacked fundamental fairness).

In balancing the probative value of evidence of prior convictions against the danger of unfair prejudice, some courts, in the context of criminal cases, have adopted a five-part test. *See U.S. v. Hursh*, 217 F.3d 761 (9th Cir. 2000); *U.S. v. Hernandez*, 106 F.3d 737 (7th Cir. 1997); *U.S. v. Pritchard*, 973 F.2d 905 (11th Cir. 1992); *U.S. v. Sloman*, 909 F.2d 176 (6th Cir. 1990); *Gordon v. U.S.*, 383 F.2d 936 (D.C. Cir. 1967); *U.S. v. Brown*, 606 F. Supp. 2d 306 (E.D. N.Y. 2009). Moreover, the first and second factors relate to an assessment of probative value and can be applied in civil cases. *See also East Coast Novelty Co., Inc. v. City of New York*, 842 F.

Supp. 117 (S.D. N.Y. 1994). The five factors are:

1. The impeachment value of the prior crime. *See, e.g., Elcock v. Kmart Corp.*, 233 F.3d 734 (3d Cir. 2000) (*in dicta*, amount of money misappropriated by expert witness and exact way it was done are relevant to prove extent of witness's dishonesty; juror could rationally conclude one who embezzles a million dollars over a period of time has less veracity than person who steals five dollars once); *U.S. v. Lugo*, 170 F.3d 996 (10th Cir. 1999) (no error to admit prior drug conviction in drug case when defendant claimed lack of involvement with drugs based on father's admonitions); *U.S. v. Rowe*, 92 F.3d 928, 933 (9th Cir. 1996) (in car-jacking case, fact that victim had conviction for car theft seven years earlier "had a lot of prejudice and almost no probative value" especially because jury might improperly infer victim had stolen car she was driving on night of crime).
2. The point in time of the conviction and the witness's subsequent history. *See, e.g., U.S. v. Alexander*, 48 F.3d 1477 (9th Cir. 1995) (where crime charged occurred in 1992, prior convictions in 1987 and 1988 were sufficiently recent to satisfy this part of test).
3. The similarity between the past crime and the charged crime. *See, e.g., U.S. v. Footman*, 33 F. Supp. 2d 60, 62 (D. Mass. 1998) (in prosecution for interstate transportation of minors for prostitution, defendant's prior rape conviction not admissible for impeachment; similarity of conduct, coercing women to have sex, would create unfair prejudice). *But see U.S. v. Alexander*, 48 F.3d at 1488 (9th Circuit has held prior bank robbery conviction not automatically inadmissible merely because prior offense was identical to that for which defendant was on trial; "[w]hat matters is the balance of all five factors").
4. The importance of defendant's testimony. *See, e.g., U.S. v. Smith*, 131 F.3d 685 (7th Cir. 1997) (where offense charged was bank robbery by intimidation and defense was bank teller was not intimidated, two major witnesses would be teller and defendant; defendant's testimony

was crucial to case and use of prior convictions was appropriate).

5. The overall centrality of the credibility issue. *See, e.g., U.S. v. Cavender*, 228 F.3d 792 (7th Cir. 2000) (error to exclude evidence of prior narcotics conviction when prosecution witness was linchpin of government's case and such evidence would have strongly impeached his credibility); *U.S. v. Payton*, 159 F.3d 49 (2d Cir. 1998) (no error to admit witness's thirteen-year old food stamp convictions based on deceit where even defendant admitted witness's credibility was "critical"); *U.S. v. Browne*, 829 F.2d 760 (9th Cir. 1987) (when defendant testifies and denies having committed charged offense, he places his credibility directly at issue). *But see U.S. v. Bensimon*, 172 F.3d 1121 (9th Cir. 1999); *American Home Assur. Co. v. American President Lines, Ltd.*, 44 F.3d 774 (9th Cir. 1994) (rejecting centrality of credibility as relevant factor; probative value of witness's conviction is measured by how well it demonstrates lack of trustworthiness, not how badly opposing party wants to impeach him).

Crimes Of Dishonesty or False Statement

Crimes of dishonesty or false statement, regardless of the punishment (whether felony or misdemeanor), can be used to impeach *any* witness. Rule 609(a)(2). Unless the conviction is more than ten years old, the cross-examiner has an absolute right to introduce a conviction involving dishonesty or false statement for impeachment purposes. 4 Weinstein & Berger, Weinstein's Federal Evidence § 609.03[1] (2d ed. 1998).

Crimes of dishonesty and false statement are characterized by an element of misrepresentation, deceit or other indicium of a propensity to lie and have been held to include the following: bank fraud, *U.S. v. Osazuwa*, 564 F.3d 1169 (9th Cir. 2009); embezzlement, *Elcock*, 233 F.3d at 734; false statements to government officials, *S.E.C. v. Sargent*, 229 F.3d 68 (1st Cir. 2000); failure to file tax return, *Dean v. Trans World Airlines, Inc.*, 924 F.2d 805 (9th Cir. 1991) and *U.S. v. Yang*, 887 F. Supp. 95

(S.D. N.Y. 1995); false and misleading statements in sale of securities, *U. S. v. O'Connor*, 635 F.2d 814 (10th Cir. 1980); and making false claims to U.S. government, *U.S. v. Wolf*, 561 F.2d 1376 (10th Cir. 1977). *But see Cree v. Hatcher*, 969 F.2d 34 (3d Cir. 1992) (failure to file tax return not crime of dishonesty).

There is general agreement that crimes of violence typically do not involve dishonesty. In addition, neither dishonesty nor deceit was found with respect to the following crimes: *U.S. v. Galati*, 230 F.3d 254 (7th Cir. 2000) and *U.S. v. Owens*, 145 F.3d 923 (7th Cir. 1998) (petty shoplifting); *Gust v. Jones*, 162 F.3d 587 (10th Cir. 1998) (smuggling drugs into prison, possession of methamphetamine); *U.S. v. Begay*, 144 F.3d 1336 (10th Cir. 1998) (marijuana possession); *U.S. v. Brackeen*, 969 F.2d 827 (9th Cir. 1992) (bank robbery); *Czajka v. Hickman*, 703 F.2d 317 (8th Cir. 1983) (rape); *U.S. v. Cox*, 536 F.2d 65 (5th Cir. 1976) (prostitution); *U.S. v. Grandmont*, 680 F.2d 867 (1st Cir. 1982) (robbery per se not crime of dishonesty); *U.S. v. Millings*, 535 F.2d 121 (D.C. Cir. 1976) (possession of drugs, carrying gun without a license); *Fletcher v. City of New York*, 54 F. Supp. 2d 328 (S.D. N.Y. 1999) (attempted robbery). However, property crimes (burglary, theft, shoplifting, etc.) will qualify under Rule 609(a)(2) if the crime was committed by fraudulent or deceitful means. *See U.S. v. Foster*, 227 F.3d 1096 (9th Cir. 2000) (receipt of stolen property is not *per se* crime of dishonesty and trial court erred in treating it as such without inquiry into facts underlying conviction).

Note, however, that Rule 609(a)(2) was amended, effective December 1, 2006, to provide for automatic impeachment with any conviction "if it readily can be determined that establishing the elements of the crime required proof or admission of an act of dishonesty or false statement by the witness." This language permits some limited inquiry behind the conviction, but would provide for automatic admissibility only where it is clear that the jury had to find, or the defendant had to admit, that an act of dishonesty or false statement occurred that was material to the conviction. The new language specifically encompasses convictions that resulted from guilty pleas. The amendment does not envision mini-trials into the facts of a conviction but is limited to instances where *crimin falsi* can be determined easily and efficiently.

Whether a crime involved dishonesty or false statement is a determination for the trial judge. *Compare Payton*, 159 F.3d at 49 (conviction for possession of food stamps acquired by filing false statement is crime of dishonesty) *with U.S. v. Mejia-Alarcon*, 995 F.2d 982 (10th Cir. 1993) (acquiring food stamps by trading truck wheels to undercover agent not crime of deceit and should not have been admitted under Rule 609(a)(2)). The proponent of the evidence bears the burden of demonstrating that the conviction was for a crime that involved dishonesty or false statement. *U.S. v. Rodriguez-Andrade*, 62 F.3d 948 (7th Cir. 1995) (defendant's obligation); *U.S. v. Hayes*, 553 F.2d 824 (2d Cir. 1977) (prosecutor's burden).

Ten Year Time Limit

When any conviction is more than ten years old, it is not admissible unless the court first determines that its probative value substantially outweighs its prejudicial effect. Rule 609(b); *U.S. v. Nguyen*, 542 F.3d 275 (1st Cir. 2008) (Rule 609(b) creates strong presumption against use of stale convictions for impeachment purpose); *U.S. v. Heath*, 447 F.3d 535 (7th Cir. 2006) (conviction older than ten years only admissible if probative value supported by specific facts and circumstances substantially outweigh its prejudicial effect); *U.S. v. Tisdale*, 817 F.2d 1552, 1555 (11th Cir. 1987) (convictions older than ten years should be admitted for impeachment purposes only very rarely). The ten year time limit runs from the date of the conviction or release from prison (whichever is later) to the date on which the witness testifies. Time spent on probation or parole is not considered a confinement and is not taken into account. *U.S. v. Daniel*, 957 F.2d 162 (5th Cir. 1992); *Bizmark, Inc. v. Kroger Co.*, 994 F. Supp. 726 (W.D. Va. 1998); *THK America, Inc. v. NSK, Ltd.*, 917 F. Supp. 563 (N.D. Ill. 1996).

Under Mil.R.Evid. 609(f), there is a "conviction" in a court-martial case when a sentence has been adjudged.

Where a party intends to introduce evidence of

a conviction that is more than ten years old, Rule 609(b) requires the proponent to give the adverse party sufficient advance written notice in order to provide the adverse party with a fair opportunity to contest use of such evidence.

Where evidence of a prior conviction is admitted for purposes of impeachment, cross-examination is usually restricted to the essential facts, i.e., nature, time, place of and punishment for each conviction rather than the surrounding details of the conviction. *U.S. v. Burston*, 159 F.3d 1328 (11th Cir. 1998); *Gora v. Costa*, 971 F.2d 1325 (7th Cir. 1992); *James v. Tilghman*, 194 F.R.D. 402 (D. Conn. 1999). Where, however, a defendant attempts to explain away the prior conviction during direct examination by giving his own version of events, he has "opened the door" to impeachment by the prosecution on the details of the conviction. *U.S. v. White*, 222 F.3d 363 (7th Cir. 2000); *U.S. v. Baylor*, 97 F.3d 542 (D.C. Cir. 1996) (government witness opened door to more extensive cross-examination by attempting to minimize conduct for which he was convicted; usual need for protection from unfair prejudice diminished since witness is not on trial). But the "open door" does not give license to dwell on the details of a prior conviction and shift the focus of the trial to the prior bad acts. *U.S. v. Robinson*, 8 F.3d 398 (7th Cir. 1993); *Geitz v. Lindsey*, 893 F.2d 148 (7th Cir. 1990); *Tri-State Hosp. Supply, Inc. v. U.S.*, 471 F. Supp. 2d 170 (D.D.C. 2007); *Edwards v. Thomas*, 31 F. Supp. 2d 1069 (N.D. Ill. 1999); *Charles v. Cotter*, 867 F. Supp. 648 (N.D. Ill. 1994) (cautioning that in civil rights cases, which serve a useful deterrent function, but which often pit unsympathetic plaintiffs against the guardians of community safety, it is easy (albeit unfairly prejudicial) to use prior convictions to transform the claim into an attack on plaintiff's character).

A witness may not be impeached by any conviction which has been pardoned, annulled or has been the subject of a certificate of rehabilitation. Rule 609(c); *cf. U.S. v. Hourihan*, 66 F.3d 458 (2d Cir. 1995) (New York certificate of relief from disabilities does not qualify). Likewise, once a conviction has been reversed, it cannot be used for impeachment purposes. *U.S. v. Russell*, 221 F.3d

615 (4th Cir. 2000).

Juvenile adjudications can never be used to impeach a criminal defendant, *U.S. v. Harvey*, 588 F.2d 1201 (8th Cir. 1978), but they can be used against a witness in a criminal case if the conviction is of a type that would be admissible to attack the credibility of an adult. *Id.*; Rule 609(d). The pendency of an appeal does not render a conviction inadmissible. Rule 609(e).

Note: Where a motion *in limine* to exclude use of convictions has failed, it is a common defense strategy to introduce a defendant's prior convictions on direct examination to try to reduce the damage from anticipated cross-examination disclosing the convictions. However, a defendant who preemptively introduces evidence of a prior conviction on direct examination waives her objection and may not challenge on appeal the admission of such evidence. *Ohler v. United States*, 529 U.S. 753, 120 S. Ct. 1851, 146 L. Ed. 2d 826 (2000); *U.S. v. Decoud*, 456 F.3d 996 (9th Cir. 2006).

Additional References

Graham, Handbook of Federal Evidence §§ 609.1 *et seq.* (7th ed. 2012)

Treatises and Practice Aids

Goode and Wellborn, Courtroom Handbook on Federal Evidence Chapter 5, Rule 609 (annual ed.)

Mueller & Kirkpatrick, Federal Evidence, §§ 94, 273 to 88 (2nd ed. 1994)

Wright, Federal Practice and Procedure: Criminal 3d § 405

Wright & Graham, Federal Practice and Procedure: Evidence §§ 5003, 5213

Wright & Gold, Federal Practice and Procedure: Evidence §§ 6131 *et seq.*

McCormick, Evidence § 42 (6th ed. 2006)

Park, Trial Objections Handbook §§ 7:11 to 7:17 (2nd ed. 2001)

INSURANCE

See:

Fed.R.Evid. 411
Mil.R.Evid. 411

Objection

- Objection. [*Request sidebar**] This evidence is irrelevant and highly prejudicial. [*I move for a mistrial / request an immediate cautionary instruction.*]

Response

- [*The question is proper / the answer is admissible*] because the purpose is to show [*bias or prejudice of the witness*] [*agency*] [*ownership or control*] [*other, specify*].

Commentary

Rule 411 provides that evidence of liability insurance is not admissible to prove negligence or other wrongdoing. *Palmer v. Krueger*, 897 F.2d 1529 (10th Cir. 1990) Two concerns account for the rule: one is that the evidence is irrelevant because possessing liability insurance does not make one more or less careful on a given occasion. The other is the risk that the jury will be tempted to return a verdict against an insured defendant, regardless of the strength or weakness of the evidence of fault, in the belief that the defendant will not have to pay a judgment from his own resources. McCormick, Evidence § 201. *See Garnac Grain Co., Inc. v. Blackley*, 932 F.2d 1563 (8th Cir. 1991) (in suit against accountants for failure to discover employee embezzlement, abuse of discretion to admit evidence of purchase and recovery on fidelity bond to show plaintiff acted negligently); *Ouachita Nat. Bank v. Tosco Corp.*, 686 F.2d 1291 (8th Cir. 1982) (jury's knowledge that plaintiff is receiving insurance benefits, or that defendant is carrying liability insurance, might serve to decrease or increase the

---

[Insurance]

*Any argument about the admissibility of insurance evidence should not take place within the hearing of the jury.

amount of damages awarded); *Higgins v. Hicks Co.*, 756 F.2d 681 (8th Cir. 1985) (the concern of Rule 411 is that knowledge of the presence or absence of liability insurance will induce juries to decide cases on improper grounds); *City of Cleveland v. Peter Kiewit Sons' Co.*, 624 F.2d 749 (6th Cir. 1980) (prejudicial error for plaintiff to interject into trial idea that defendant had insurance which would cover any award of damages).

Rule 411 contemplates that evidence of insurance may be admissible on issues other than liability. *Conde v. Starlight I, Inc.*, 103 F.3d 210 (1st Cir. 1997); *Pinkham v. Burgess*, 933 F.2d 1066 (1st Cir. 1991). The existence of insurance may be shown in connection with matters such as agency, ownership or control, or bias or prejudice of a witness. *DSC Communications Corp. v. Next Level Communications*, 107 F.3d 322 (5th Cir. 1997) (evidence of indemnity agreement properly admitted to show full extent of relationship between parties); *Charter v. Chleborad*, 551 F.2d 246 (8th Cir. 1977) (fact that defendant's insurer employed witness admissible to show possible bias); *Posttape Associates v. Eastman Kodak Co.*, 537 F.2d 751 (3d Cir. 1976) (evidence of liability insurance relevant to establish trade custom of limiting liability to replacement of defective movie film); *see also Hunziker v. Scheidemantle*, 543 F.2d 489 (3d Cir. 1976) (suggesting that necessary foundation for evidence of insurance should be presented outside presence of jury so that court may determine admissibility without prejudice to rights of parties); *Williams v. Security Nat. Bank of Sioux City, Iowa*, 358 F. Supp. 2d 782 (N.D. Iowa 2005) (former trustee's letter to liability insurer admissible in beneficiaries' action not to show trustee had insurance but to show trustee's efforts to legitimize erroneous distributions). The exceptions listed in Rule 411 are illustrative only and not all inclusive. Even when offered for such purpose, the trial judge may, nonetheless, exclude the evidence under Rule 403 if its probative value is outweighed by the risk that the jury would misuse the evidence.

Inadvertent reference to insurance is generally not grounds for mistrial. *Rios v. Bigler*, 67 F.3d 1543 (10th Cir. 1995) (remark about insurance was careless and court offered to give limiting instruction which was refused); *Raybestos Products Co. v. Younger*, 54 F.3d 1234 (7th Cir. 1995) (holding that "to constitute reversible error, references to insurance coverage must be due to some misconduct or improper remarks or questions of counsel, ofttimes repeated, and calculated to influence or prejudice the jury") (*citing Adams Laboratories, Inc. v. Jacobs Engineering Co., Inc.*, 761 F.2d 1218, 1226–27 (7th Cir. 1985)). In other words, many courts hold that there must have been a prejudicial intent, as well as a prejudicial effect in order for a reference to the adverse party's insurance to give rise to grounds for mistrial. *Younger*, 54 F.3d at 1240.

Additional References

Graham, Handbook of Federal Evidence § 411.1 (7th ed. 2012)

Treatises and Practice Aids

Goode and Wellborn, Courtroom Handbook on Federal Evidence Chapter 5, Rule 411 (annual ed.)

Mueller & Kirkpatrick, Federal Evidence, § 5:26 (3d ed. 2007)

Wright & Graham, Federal Practice and Procedure: Evidence §§ 5365 to 5368

McCormick, Evidence § 201 (6th ed. 2006)

Park, Trial Objections Handbook §§ 2:56 to 2:57 (2nd ed. 2001)

JUDGE'S QUESTIONS

See:

Fed.R.Evid. 614(b),(c)
Mil.R.Evid. 614(b),(c)

Objection

- [*Request sidebar*] I object to the court's question. Your Honor, that question goes well beyond seeking clarification; [*it is cross-examination of the witness*], [*you are improperly questioning the witness' credibility*], [*the jury will fairly interpret your (questions / conduct) as indicating a distinct bias against my client*].

Response

- [*Although the court will defend itself, opposing counsel, if asked, should be prepared to argue the correctness of the court's questions*].

Commentary

Federal judges have wide discretion to determine the role that they will play during the course of a trial. *U.S. v. McCray*, 437 F.3d 639 (7th Cir. 2006). A judge is generally free to interrogate witnesses to ensure that issues are clearly presented to the jury. Fed.R.Evid. 614(b); *U.S. v. Martin*, 189 F.3d 547, 553 (7th Cir. 1999); *U.S. v. Bellomo*, 176 F.3d 580, 596–97 (2d Cir. 1999) ("Intelligent questioning by the trial judge is the judge's prerogative; he need not be a silent spectator"); *Pescatore v. Pan American World Airways, Inc.*, 97 F.3d 1, 20 (2d Cir. 1996) (judge "need not sit like a bump on a log" but has active responsibility to ensure that issues are clearly presented to jury).

The judge may also comment on the evidence, bring out facts not yet adduced and maintain the pace of the trial by interrupting or setting time limits on counsel. *U.S. v. Washington*, 417 F.3d 780 (7th Cir. 2005) (judge free to interject during direct or cross to clarify issue, to require attorney to lay foundation or to encourage counsel to get to the point); *U.S. v. Sanchez*, 325 F.3d 600 (5th Cir. 2003) (court's efforts to move trial along may not come at cost of strict impartiality); *U.S. v. Pratt*, 239 F.3d 640 (4th Cir. 2001); *U.S. v. Thayer*, 201 F.3d 214 (3d Cir. 1999); *U.S. v. Montas*, 41 F.3d 775 (1st Cir. 1994); *U.S. v. Wallace*, 32 F.3d 921 (5th Cir. 1994).

Because trial judges have substantial influence over juries, a judge's discretion to question witnesses is not unlimited. *See Starr v. United States*, 153 U.S. 614, 626, 14 S. Ct. 919, 923, 38 L. Ed. 841 (1894) ("the influence of the trial judge on the jury is necessarily and properly of great weight, and . . . his lightest word or intimation is received with deference and may prove controlling."); *McMillan v. Castro*, 405 F.3d 405 (6th Cir. 2005) (actual impartiality as well as the appearance of impartiality is critical because the judge's every action is likely to have a great influence on the jury). A judge cannot assume the role of advocate for either side. *U.S. v. Villarini*, 238 F.3d 530 (4th Cir. 2001) (court should not by its questions give appearance of partiality or undermine the legitimate efforts of any party to present case); *Herman v. U.S.*, 289 F.2d 362, 365 (5th Cir. 1961), overruled on other grounds, U.S. v. Zuniga-Salinas, 952 F.2d 876 (5th Cir. 1992)) ("The trial judge has a duty to conduct the trial carefully, patiently and impartially. He must be above even the appearance of being partial to the prosecution."). While a judge can question a witness in an effort to make the testimony clear for the jury, this should not include questions which indicate the judge's belief about a witness's honesty, *see U.S. v. Tilghman*, 134 F.3d 414 (D.C. Cir. 1998), especially when a criminal defendant testifies on his own behalf. *U.S. v. Cantu*, 167 F.3d 198 (5th Cir. 1999). *See generally Shah v. Pan American World Services, Inc.*, 148 F.3d 84 (2d Cir. 1998) (although asking numerous and probing questions of witnesses is unquestionably proper, trial judge should limit questioning to inquiries necessary to clarify ambiguities, correct misstatements, or obtain information necessary to make rulings).

Rule 614(c) requires a party to object to the court's interrogation of a witness "at the time or at the next available opportunity when the jury is not present."

The Second Circuit has adopted a rule which presumes that once a judge's actions create an impression of partisanship, curative instructions generally will not save the day. *U.S. v. Matt*, 116 F.3d 971 (2d Cir. 1997). The Seventh and Ninth Circuits, by contrast, have said that in most instances the potential for prejudice from judicial questions can be removed with an appropriate instruction. *U.S. v. Morgan*, 376 F.3d 1002 (9th Cir. 2004); *U.S. v. Parker*, 241 F.3d 1114 (9th Cir. 2001); *Martin*, 189 F.3d at 555 n.5.

In the following cases, the trial judge's questions and/or conduct departed from the required impartiality to such an extent as to deny a fair trial: *U.S. v. Nickl*, 427 F.3d 1286 (10th Cir. 2005) (court did not summarize testimony, it reshaped it; it converted equivocations into a definite answer and improperly addressed an ultimate factual issue to be decided by jury); *Wang v. Attorney General of U.S.*, 423 F.3d 260 (3d Cir. 2005) (immigration judges cautioned repeatedly against making intemperate or humiliating remarks during immigration proceedings; a disturbing pattern of misconduct repeatedly echoed by sister circuits); *U.S. v. Saenz*, 134 F.3d 697 (5th Cir. 1998) (court's extensive questioning of witnesses done in manner that appeared to convey partiality toward prosecution); *Rivas v. Brattesani*, 94 F.3d 802 (2d Cir. 1996) (by its comments, court conveyed impression to jury that it held fixed and unfavorable opinion of defendants, their counsel and their position); *Santa Maria v. Metro-North Commuter R.R.*, 81 F.3d 265 (2d Cir. 1996) (court displayed antipathy to plaintiff's claim that went beyond judicial skepticism; defense attempt to put plaintiff's lawyer on trial was aided by court's conduct); *U.S. v. Segines*, 17 F.3d 847 (6th Cir. 1994) (attitude and comments of trial judge violated defendants' due process rights to fair trial and presumptively had chilling effect on defense counsels' conduct of trial); *U.S. v. Van Dyke*, 14 F.3d 415 (8th Cir. 1994) (one-sided and distracting comments indicating judge was not paying attention to defense, interrupting defense questioning by inviting prosecutor to object, over-involvement with prosecution questioning, all giving impression that judge and prosecutor were working toward common goal); *U.S. v. Singer*, 710 F.2d 431 (8th Cir. 1983) (inappropriate judicial intervention designed to clarify government testimony, help government counsel make objections, indicate when to stop witness examination, what to write on blackboard to illustrate government's point as well as taking over questioning of government witnesses); *U.S. v. Coke*, 339 F.2d 183 (2d Cir. 1964) (judge's excessive interference in examination of witnesses, repeated rebukes and disparaging remarks directed at defense counsel and denial of motion for judgment of acquittal in front of the jury violated defendant's due process rights).

No abuse of discretion: *Chlopek v. Federal Ins. Co.*, 499 F.3d 692 (7th Cir. 2007) (court's criticism of plaintiff's attorney would have been better done when jury was not present but did not impair the lawyer's credibility in eyes of jury or deprive client of fair trial); *U.S. v. Lizon-Barias*, 252 Fed. Appx. 976 (11th Cir. 2007) (court had right to interrupt opening statement to exclude irrelevant facts and stop argument); *Ferguson v. Bombardier Services Corp.*, 244 Fed. Appx. 944 (11th Cir. 2007) (air crash case involved several experts and complex questions of fact; therefore entirely proper for court to question witnesses in order to clarify evidence presented); *U.S. v. Smith*, 452 F.3d 323 (4th Cir. 2006) (court's *sua sponte* objections permissible; court spoke up when counsel posed questions that were difficult to understand, that had already been asked and answered or that were irrelevant); *U.S. v. Simpson*, 337 F.3d 905 (7th Cir. 2003) (similar); *U.S. v. Cisneros*, 203 F.3d 333 (5th Cir. 2000) (court has discretion to clarify testimony even if that elicits facts harmful to defendant); *U.S. v. Lankford*, 196 F.3d 563 (5th Cir. 1999) (majority of exchanges occurred because court legitimately sought clarifications and attempted to move proceedings along; mere fact of more interruptions on one side or other does not suggest, without more, that judge has predetermined guilt of defendant or is assisting prosecution); *U.S. v. Reynolds*, 189 F.3d 521 (7th Cir. 1999) (court's numerous interruptions were to clarify testimony or have counsel lay proper foundation for questions); *U.S. v. Candelaria-Silva*, 166 F.3d 19 (1st Cir. 1999) (judge's frustration displayed at sidebar did not deprive defendant of fair trial because jury could not hear exchanges); *U.S. v. Duran*, 96 F.3d 1495 (D.C. Cir. 1996) (no unfair prejudice but noting that two of judge's questions were problematic in that they tended to veer away from clarification and towards cross-examination); *U.S. v. Webb*, 83 F.3d 913 (7th Cir. 1996) (in non-jury proceedings, questioning by judge will rarely be prejudicial to defendant); *U.S. v. Hammer*, 25 F. Supp. 2d 518 (M.D. Pa. 1998) (if comments made during closing argument are not supported by record, judge has right, and often obligation, to interrupt counsel to ensure fair trial).

Additional References

Graham, Handbook of Federal Evidence § 614.2 (7th ed. 2012)

Treatises and Practice Aids

Goode and Wellborn, Courtroom Handbook On Federal Evidence Chapter 5, Rule 614 (annual ed.)

Mueller & Kirkpatrick, Federal Evidence, § 6:106 (3d ed. 2007)

Wright & Gold, Federal Practice and Procedure: Evidence §§ 5235 to 6236

McCormick, Evidence § 8 (6th ed. 2006)

Park, Trial Objections Handbook § 1:18 (2nd ed. 2001)

JUDGMENT AS A MATTER OF LAW-MOTION

See:

Fed.R.Civ.P. 50

Illustration

- Pursuant to Rule 50 I move for judgment as a matter of law in favor of [*plaintiff/defendant*] on grounds that [*here state specific reasons supporting the motion*].

Commentary

Pursuant to Fed.R.Civ.P. 50, a court should render judgment as a matter of law when a party has been fully heard on an issue and there is no legally sufficient evidentiary basis for a reasonable jury to find for that party on that issue. Rule 50(a); *see also Weisgram v. Marley Co.*, 528 U.S. 440, 447–48, 120 S. Ct. 1011, 1016–17, 145 L. Ed. 2d 958 (2000); *Taylor v. TECO Barge Line, Inc.*, 517 F.3d 372 (6th Cir. 2008); *Wilson v. Morgan*, 477 F.3d 326 (6th Cir. 2007); *Harris Corp. v. Ericsson Inc.*, 417 F.3d 1241 (Fed. Cir. 2005). In making this determination, the court must draw all reasonable inferences in favor of the nonmoving party without making credibility assessments or weighing the evidence. *See Lytle v. Household Mfg., Inc.*, 494 U.S. 545, 554–555, 110 S. Ct. 1331, 1337–38, 108 L. Ed. 2d 504 (1990); *see also Kinserlow v. CMI Corp*, 217 F.3d 1021, 1025 (8th Cir. 2000); *Johnson v. Clark*, 484 F. Supp. 2d 1242, 1245 (M.D. Fla. 2007); *Calderone v. Kent County Memorial Hosp.*, 360 F. Supp. 2d 397 (D.R.I. 2005). "Credibility determinations, the weighing of the evidence, and the drawing of legitimate inferences from the facts are jury functions, not those of a judge." *Reeves v. Sanderson Plumbing Products, Inc.*, 530 U.S. 133, 150–51, 120 S. Ct. 2097, 2110, 147 L. Ed. 2d 105 (2000) (quoting *Anderson v. Liberty Lobby, Inc.*, 477 U.S. 242, 250–51, 106 S. Ct. 2505, 2511, 91 L. Ed. 2d 202 (1986)).

> . . . although the court should review the record as a whole, it must disregard all evidence favorable to the moving party that the jury is not required to believe. That is, the court should give credence to

the evidence favoring the nonmovant as well as that evidence supporting the moving party that is uncontradicted and unimpeached, at least to the extent that that evidence comes from disinterested witnesses.

Reeves, 530 U.S. at 151. It is "[w]hen the record contains no proof beyond speculation to support the verdict, [that] judgment as a matter of law is appropriate." *Kinserlow*, 217 F.3d at 1026 (internal quotations omitted); *First Union Nat. Bank v. Benham*, 423 F.3d 855 (8th Cir. 2005). Weakness of the evidence does not justify judgment as a matter of law. As in the case of a grant of summary judgment, the evidence must be such that a reasonable juror would have been compelled to accept the view of the moving party. *Ganthier v. North Shore-Long Island Jewish Health System, Inc.*, 345 F. Supp. 2d 271 (E.D. N.Y. 2004). If reasonable persons could differ in their interpretations of the evidence, then the motion should be denied. *Bryant v. Compass Group USA Inc.*, 413 F.3d 471 (5th Cir. 2005).

Nothing in Rule 50 requires that a motion for judgment as a matter of law be made at a specific time. It can be made at the close of plaintiff's case or at the close of the evidence, but it also may be raised at any other point before the jury retires. *Karam v. Sagemark Consulting, Inc.*, 383 F.3d 421 (6th Cir. 2004); *American & Foreign Ins. Co. v. General Elec. Co.*, 45 F.3d 135 (6th Cir. 1995).

Note that a post-verdict motion under Rule 50(b) for judgment as a matter of law cannot be made unless a previous motion for judgment as a matter of law under Rule 50(a) was made by the moving party at the close of all of the evidence. *Desrosiers v. Flight Intern. of Florida Inc.*, 156 F.3d 952 (9th Cir. 1998).* The rationale for this rule is two-fold: first to protect the Seventh Amendment right to trial by jury, and second ensure that the opposing party has enough notice of the alleged error to permit an attempt to cure it before resting.

[Judgment etc.]

*As the Third Circuit has explained, without preservation of objections to sufficiency, the trial court would be asked to reexamine the facts already tried by the jury and this the court may not do without violating the Seventh Amendment. *DeMarines v. KLM Royal Dutch Airlines*, 580 F.2d 1193, 1195 n.4 (3d Cir. 1978).

Marshall v. Columbia Lea Regional Hosp., 474 F.3d 733 (10th Cir. 2007).**

Although better practice suggests that the motion be in writing, the rule contains no such requirement, and an oral motion made on the record will suffice. *Wolfgang v. Mid-America Motorsports, Inc.*, 111 F.3d 1515 (10th Cir. 1997); *U. S. Industries, Inc. v. Semco Mfg., Inc.*, 562 F.2d 1061 (8th Cir. 1977). Regardless of the form chosen, the motion must "specify the judgment sought and the law and facts on which the moving party is entitled to judgment." Rule 50(a)(2).

Rule 50 applies only to binding jury cases. The appropriate motion in non-jury trials and trials with an advisory jury is a motion for judgment on partial findings under Rule 52(c). *Federal Ins. Co. v. HPSC, Inc.*, 480 F.3d 26 (1st Cir. 2007).

Treatises and Practice Aids

Baicker-McKee, Janssen, Corr, Federal Civil Rules Handbook, Rule 50 (annual ed.)

Wright & Miller, Federal Practice and Procedure: Civil 3d §§ 2521 to 2540

**In 2006 Rule 50(b) was amended. Previous versions of the rule had required that a motion under Rule 50(a) be made at the close of all of the evidence as a predicate for a Rule 50(b) motion. The 2006 amendment to the rule allows the renewal of any motion for judgment as a matter of law made under Rule 50(a). However, a Rule 50(b) motion can be granted only on grounds raised in the preverdict motion; therefore, it usually will be desirable to make a Rule 50(a) motion at the close of all the evidence regardless so as not to forfeit any grounds for argument when the motion is reviewed. *See Wright & Miller, Federal Practice & Procedure: Civil 2d § 2521.*

JUDICIAL ADMISSIONS

Objection

- [*To a question*] Objection. The question is directed to facts judicially admitted by the [*specify source, e.g., complaint, answer, stipulation, answers to requests for admission, or, by counsel's own statement*]. Those judicially admitted facts cannot be contradicted.
- [*To an answer*] Objection, the response contradicts a judicially admitted fact. I move the answer be stricken and the jury be instructed not to consider it for any purpose.

Response

- The potential responses are limited because a judicially admitted fact cannot be contradicted by the party who made the admission. If there are grounds, counsel might argue the fact was not admitted or that the alleged admission was not unequivocal and, therefore, the evidence should be received. Fed.R.Civ.P. 36(b) does allow the court to permit withdrawal or amendment of an admission, "when the presentation of the merits of the action will be subserved thereby and the party who obtained the admission fails to satisfy the court that withdrawal or amendment will prejudice that party in maintaining the action or defense on the merits."

Commentary

A judicial admission is a formal concession made in court or prior to trial by a party or its attorney, conceding for purposes of trial, the truth of the admitted fact. *Medcom Holding Co. v. Baxter Travenol Laboratories, Inc.*, 106 F.3d 1388 (7th Cir. 1997) (binding judicial admissions are any deliberate, clear and unequivocal statement, either written or oral, made in the course of judicial proceedings); *Guidry v. Sheet Metal Workers Intern. Ass'n, Local No. 9*, 10 F.3d 700 (10th Cir. 1993); *In re Cendant Corp. Securities Litigation*, 109 F. Supp. 2d 225 (D.N.J. 2000) (a party will be held to its unambiguous and plainly worded statements, deliberately drafted by counsel for the express purpose of limiting and defining the facts at issue; however, to be binding, judicial admissions must be unequivocal). As Professor Graham has written: "Judicial admissions are not evidence at all but rather have the effect of withdrawing a fact from contention." Handbook of Federal Evidence, § 801. 26.

Unless the court allows it to be withdrawn, a judicial admission is binding on the party making it and cannot be subsequently contradicted at trial or on appeal. *Keller v. U.S.*, 58 F.3d 1194 (7th Cir. 1995); *Banks v. Yokemick*, 214 F. Supp. 2d 401, 405 (S.D. N.Y. 2002).

Judicial admissions may arise from: a party's statement in its pleadings, *Hughes v. Vanderbilt University*, 215 F.3d 543 (6th Cir. 2000); *Taylor v. Monsanto Co.*, 150 F.3d 806 (7th Cir. 1998); *Schott Motorcycle Supply, Inc. v. American Honda Motor Co., Inc.*, 976 F.2d 58 (1st Cir. 1992); attorney's statement at deposition, *Martinez v. Bally's Louisiana, Inc.*, 244 F.3d 474 (5th Cir. 2001); answers to requests for admission, *Brasure v. Optimum Choice Ins. Co.*, 37 F. Supp. 2d 340 (D. Del. 1999); answers to interrogatories, *Circuit Systems, Inc. v. Mescalero Sales, Inc.*, 925 F. Supp. 546 (N.D. Ill. 1996); legal briefs, *Purgess v. Sharrock*, 33 F.3d 134 (2d Cir. 1994); stipulations, *Wheeler v. John Deere Co.*, 935 F.2d 1090 (10th Cir. 1991); written statements submitted to court, *In re Lefkas General Partners No. 1017*, 153 B.R. 804 (N.D. Ill. 1993); opening statement, *U.S. v. McKeon*, 738 F.2d 26 (2d Cir. 1984); a statement of fact made at trial by the party's attorney, *U.S. v. Cravero*, 530 F.2d 666 (5th Cir. 1976); closing statement, *Childs v. Franco*, 563 F. Supp. 290 (E.D. Pa. 1983). *See also Keller v. U.S.*, 58 F.3d 1194, 1199 n.8 (7th Cir. 1995) and *Guadagno v. Wallack Ader Levithan Associates*, 950 F. Supp. 1258, 1261 (S.D. N.Y. 1997) (contrasting the spontaneous and imprecise nature of deposition and trial testimony with answers to contention interrogatories crafted by counsel and discussing why it is generally preferable to treat deposition or trial testimony as an evidentiary admission and not as a judicial admission).

The scope of judicial admissions is restricted to matters of fact which otherwise would require evidentiary proof. It does not include statements by counsel as to what a party intends to prove at trial. *Pivirotto v. Innovative Systems, Inc.*, 191 F.3d 344 (3d Cir. 1999). A legal conclusion, for example, that a party was negligent or caused an injury-does not qualify as a judicial admission. *New York State Nat. Organization for Women v. Terry*, 159 F.3d 86, 97 n.7 (2d Cir. 1998); *MacDonald v. General Motors Corp.*, 110 F.3d 337 (6th Cir. 1997); *Glick v. White Motor Co.*, 458 F.2d 1287 (3d Cir. 1972). When a pleading is amended or withdrawn, the superceded portion ceases to be considered as a binding judicial admission. It does, however, continue in force and effect as an evidentiary admission which may be controverted or explained by the party who made it. *Huey v. Honeywell, Inc.*, 82 F.3d 327 (9th Cir. 1996); *White v. ARCO/Polymers, Inc.*, 720 F.2d 1391 (5th Cir. 1983); *Zitz v. Pereira*, 119 F. Supp. 2d 133 (E.D. N.Y. 1999); *In re Commercial Tissue Products*, 183 F.R.D. 589 (N.D. Fla. 1998); *Bank One, Texas, N.A. v. Prudential Ins. Co. of America*, 939 F. Supp. 533 (N.D. Tex. 1996).

Fed.R.Civ.P. 8(e)(2) specifically permits alternative and hypothetical pleading. Accordingly, judicial admissions should not be applied to undermine the right to allege inconsistent facts in alternative pleadings. *Schott Motorcycle Supply, Inc.*, 976 F.2d at 61–62.

A judicial admission is binding only in the litigation in which it is made. *Kohler v. Leslie Hindman, Inc.*, 80 F.3d 1181 (7th Cir. 1996). In any other suit, it operates merely as an evidentiary admission. *Higgins v. Mississippi*, 217 F.3d 951 (7th Cir. 2000). *See also National Spiritual Assembly of Baha'is of U.S. Under Hereditary Guardianship, Inc. v. National Spiritual Assembly of Baha'is of U.S., Inc.*, 547 F. Supp. 2d 879, 898 (N.D. Ill. 2008)

Additional References

Graham, Handbook of Federal Evidence § 801.26 (7th ed. 2012)

Treatises and Practice Aids

Wright & Graham, Federal Practice and Procedure: Evidence § 5194

McCormick, Evidence Chapter 25 (6th ed. 2006)

JUDICIAL NOTICE

See:

Fed.R.Evid. 201
Mil.R.Evid. 201

Form

- I request that the court take judicial notice of the fact that [*specify*].

Response

- Objection. The fact in question is not generally known nor is it verifiable with certainty. Therefore, it is not the proper subject of judicial notice.

Commentary

Certain facts are beyond any serious dispute because they are of such common knowledge or accurate determination that evidence of their existence is unnecessary. The doctrine of judicial notice is intended to avoid the necessity for the formal introduction of evidence where there is no real need for it. *See York v. American Tel. & Tel. Co.*, 95 F.3d 948 (10th Cir. 1996) (judicial notice is adjudicative device that alleviates parties' evidentiary duties at trial, serving as substitute for conventional method of taking evidence to establish facts). **The scope of Rule 201 is limited to adjudicative facts** which are simply facts about the events, persons and places involved in the lawsuit. *Qualley v. Clo-Tex Intern., Inc.*, 212 F.3d 1123 (8th Cir. 2000) (adjudicative facts are facts that normally go to the jury, relating to the parties, their activities, their properties, their business); *U.S. v. Gould*, 536 F.2d 216 (8th Cir. 1976) (adjudicative facts concern who did what, where, when, how and with what motive or intent).

The fact to be noticed must be one not subject to reasonable dispute either because it is: (1) generally known within the territorial jurisdiction of the court or (2) is capable of accurate and ready determination by resort to reliable sources. Rule 201(b); *U.S. v. Husein*, 478 F.3d 318 (6th Cir. 2007); *Walker v. Woodford*, 454 F. Supp. 2d 1007 (S.D.

Cal. 2006) (Rule is intended to obviate need for formal fact-finding as to facts that are undisputed and easily verified).

If the fact to be noticed is not generally known, the court may take notice if the existence of the fact can be ascertained by resort to sources whose accuracy cannot reasonably be questioned. Such sources include historical works, science and art books, language and medical journals, dictionaries, calendars, encyclopedias, commercial lists, maps, charts, statutes and legislative reports. *U.S. v. Neill*, 964 F. Supp. 438, 445 (D.D.C. 1997).

The court must take judicial notice if a party makes a request and provides the necessary information. Rule 201(d). The court may also take judicial notice on its own motion. Rule 201(c).

When judicial notice is invoked, the opposing party must be accorded the due process right to disprove the fact sought to be noticed if he believes it disputable. Rule 201(e).

Because a decision on whether to take judicial notice is one for the court alone pursuant to Rule 104(a), the rules of evidence, except for privilege, do not apply. *U.S. v. Bello*, 194 F.3d 18 (1st Cir. 1999); 21 Wright & Graham, "Federal Practice and Procedure: Evidence" § 5108. Information supplied to the court in support of or in opposition to a request for judicial notice need not be in a form that would be admissible as evidence. Once the judge has judicially noticed a fact in a civil case, no evidence is admissible to rebut it and the jury must be instructed to accept the fact as conclusively established. *Hardy v. Johns-Manville Sales Corp.*, 681 F.2d 334 (5th Cir. 1982). In criminal cases, the court must tell the jury that it may, but is not required to, accept as conclusive any fact judicially noticed. Rule 201(g).

Note: Judicial notice of legislative facts (i.e., facts which relate to legal reasoning and the law making process) is not subject to the requirements of Rule 201. Advisory Committee's Note; *Qualley*, 212 F.3d at 1128. Judicial notice of matters of foreign law is governed by Fed.R.Civ.P. 44.1 and Fed.R.Crim.P. 26.1.

The following cases illustrate the application of the doctrine of judicial notice: (1) **historical facts,**

sufficiently notorious: *Gafoor v. I.N.S.*, 231 F.3d 645 (9th Cir. 2000) (political upheaval in Fiji with attendant dangers for persons of Indian descent); *In re Sealed Case No. 99-3091*, 192 F.3d 995 (D.C. Cir. 1999) (President Clinton's status as a grand jury witness); *Ivezaj v. I.N.S.*, 84 F.3d 215 (6th Cir. 1996) (persecution of Albanians by Serbs); *Kaczmarczyk v. I.N.S.*, 933 F.2d 588 (7th Cir. 1991) (changes in Polish politics); *Cochran v. NYP Holdings, Inc.*, 58 F. Supp. 2d 1113 (C.D. Cal. 1998) (notoriety of the O.J. Simpson criminal trial); (2) **geographical facts**: *U.S. v. Byrne*, 171 F.3d 1231 (10th Cir. 1999) (City of Clovis is located within Curry County, New Mexico); *Tucker v. Outwater*, 118 F.3d 930 (2d Cir. 1997) (counties did not adjoin but were, in fact, separated by over 100 miles and several large lakes); *Patterson v. Dahlsten Truck Line, Inc.*, 130 F. Supp. 2d 1228 (D. Kan. 2000) (map of Kansas); *Volk v. U.S.*, 57 F. Supp. 2d 888 (N.D. Cal. 1999) (Presidio in San Francisco was under federal jurisdiction); *Chung v. Chrysler Corp.*, 903 F. Supp. 160 (D.D.C. 1995) (one can easily drive from North Tonawanda, New York to the federal courthouse in Buffalo in thirty minutes); (3) **science/medicine**: *H2O Houseboat Vacations Inc. v. Hernandez*, 103 F.3d 914 (9th Cir. 1996) (carbon monoxide emissions must be contained within enclosed space to be injurious); *Harris v. H & W Contracting Co.*, 102 F.3d 516 (11th Cir. 1996) (Graves' disease is condition that is capable of substantially limiting major life activities if left untreated by medication); *McGraw v. Sears, Roebuck & Co.*, 21 F. Supp. 2d 1017 (D. Minn. 1998) (menopause is entirely normal consequence of human aging); *Adams v. U.S.*, 964 F. Supp. 511 (D. Mass. 1996) (Xanax is antianxiety medication); (4) **facts capable of accurate determination**: *Ieradi v. Mylan Laboratories, Inc.*, 230 F.3d 594 (3d Cir. 2000) (opening and closing stock prices relevant to securities fraud suit); *Levan v. Capital Cities/ABC, Inc.*, 190 F.3d 1230 (11th Cir. 1999) (prime interest rate on February 14, 1989 as provided by Federal Reserve Board); *Witter v. Delta Air Lines, Inc.*, 138 F.3d 1366 (11th Cir. 1998) (in ADA case, that Hartsfield Atlanta International Airport was one of busiest airports in country with available non-piloting jobs); *U.S. v. Bailey*, 97 F.3d 982 (7th Cir.

1996) (average, 65-year-old white male U.S. citizen in 1992 could expect to live 15.4 more years); *Roe v. Unocal Corp.*, 70 F. Supp. 2d 1073 (C.D. Cal. 1999) (State Law and Order Restoration Council constitutes government of Burma); *Bridgeway Corp. v. Citibank*, 45 F. Supp. 2d 276 (S.D. N.Y. 1999) (political conditions in Liberia); *Marcus v. AT & T Corp.*, 938 F. Supp. 1158 (S.D. N.Y. 1996) (long distance phone company's tariffs); (5) **public records**: *U.S. v. City of St. Paul*, 258 F.3d 750 (8th Cir. 2001) (HUD handbook entitled to judicial notice as agency's interpretation of its own regulations); *Furnari v. Warden, Allenwood Federal Correctional Inst.*, 218 F.3d 250 (3d Cir. 2000) (decisions of administrative agency); *Dionne v. Shalala*, 209 F.3d 705 (8th Cir. 2000) (new qualification standards in Indian Health Service); *Bryant v. Avado Brands, Inc.*, 187 F.3d 1271 (11th Cir. 1999) and *Shurkin v. Golden State Vintners Inc.*, 471 F. Supp. 2d 998 (N.D. Cal. 2006) (documents legally required by and publicly filed with SEC but only to determine what statements are contained therein and not for truth of statements); *Zimomra v. Alamo Rent-A-Car, Inc.*, 111 F.3d 1495 (10th Cir. 1997) (municipal ordinances); *U.S. v. Jones*, 29 F.3d 1549 (11th Cir. 1994) (court may take notice of another court's order only for limited purpose of recognizing "judicial act" that order represents or the subject matter of the litigation); *U.S. ex rel. Robinson Rancheria Citizens Council v. Borneo, Inc.*, 971 F.2d 244 (9th Cir. 1992) (federal courts may take notice of proceedings in other courts, both within and without the federal judicial system, if those proceedings have a direct relation to the matters at issue); *Trevino v. Merscorp, Inc.*, 583 F. Supp. 2d 521 (D. Del. 2008) and *Sea Tow Services Intern., Inc. v. Pontin*, 472 F. Supp. 2d 349 (E.D. N.Y. 2007) (court may take judicial notice of a document filed in another court, not for truth of matters asserted in other litigation, but rather to establish fact of such litigation and related filings); *Gargano v. Belmont Police Dept.*, 476 F. Supp. 2d 39 (D. Mass. 2007) (official records of the state registry of motor vehicles); *Daghlian v. DeVry University, Inc.*, 461 F. Supp. 2d 1121 (C.D. Cal. 2006) (records and reports of administrative bodies are proper subjects of judicial notice as long as their authenticity or accuracy is not disputed); *Associated General Contractors of Ohio, Inc. v. Drabik*, 50 F. Supp. 2d 741 (S.D. Ohio 1999) (Census Bureau reports); *Cerasani v. Sony Corp.*, 991 F. Supp. 343 (S.D. N.Y. 1998) (in defamation action, judicial notice of plaintiff's criminal record); *Menominee Indian Tribe of Wisconsin v. Thompson*, 922 F. Supp. 184 (W.D. Wis. 1996) (Annual Report of the Commissioner of Indian Affairs for 1851); (6) **miscellaneous**: *Andrews v. TRW, Inc.*, 225 F.3d 1063 (9th Cir. 2000) (persons are required to make their social security numbers available in many ways so that they are no longer private but open to scrutiny and copying); *U.S. v. Parise*, 159 F.3d 790 (3d Cir. 1998) (union movement exists of, by, and for workers and dedicates itself to their welfare and recognition of their rights); *Goldblatt v. F.D.I.C.*, 105 F.3d 1325 (9th Cir. 1997) (interest bearing nature of money market accounts); *Cassirer v. Kingdom of Spain*, 461 F. Supp. 2d 1157 (C.D. Cal. 2006), aff'd in part, rev'd in part on other grounds, 580 F.3d 1048 (9th Cir. 2009) (Nazi citizenship laws); *Virtual Countries, Inc. v. Republic of South Africa*, 148 F. Supp. 2d 256 (S.D. N.Y. 2001) (financial hardship experienced by dot-coms following decline of technology-laden NASDAQ stock market in 2000); *U.S. v. Ryan*, 128 F. Supp. 2d 232 (E.D. Pa. 2000) (inspection sticker must be affixed to front driver's side portion of windshield); *Jackson v. Apfel*, 105 F. Supp. 2d 1220 (N.D. Ala. 2000) (contrary to human nature for worker's surviving family members to falsely acknowledge worker's paternity of child seeking social security survivor's benefits if worker were not child's father); *Winfield Collection, Ltd. v. McCauley*, 105 F. Supp. 2d 746 (E.D. Mich. 2000) (function of auction is to permit highest bidder to purchase property offered for sale and choice of highest bidder is beyond control of seller); *Greene v. Brown & Williamson Tobacco Corp.*, 72 F. Supp. 2d 882 (W.D. Tenn. 1999) (in relevant ten-year period preceding filing of case, consumers were generally aware that cigarette smoking posed serious health risks); *U.S. v. Tuitt*, 68 F. Supp. 2d 4 (D. Mass. 1999) (racial make-up of four western counties in court's jurisdiction); *Watts v. Organogenesis, Inc.*, 30 F. Supp. 2d 101 (D. Mass. 1998) (most nurses spend at least some of their time doing unskilled tasks such as helping patients move, get comfortable, eat, clean themselves, etc.); *African-American Voting Rights Legal Defense Fund, Inc. v. State of Mo.*, 994 F. Supp. 1105 (E.D. Mo. 1997) (value of standard deviation analysis).

Judicial notice **was refused** in the following cases because the fact sought to be noticed was not indisputable in that it either was not a matter of common knowledge or was not capable of accurate and ready determination: *Lozano v. Ashcroft*, 258 F.3d 1160 (10th Cir. 2001) (presumed receipt date of EEOC findings which was contested); *Abdille v. Ashcroft*, 242 F.3d 477 (3d Cir. 2001) (South African law; foreign law is treated as a fact that must be proven by the parties); *Cabberiza v. Moore*, 217 F.3d 1329 (11th Cir. 2000) (that jury of twelve is better for a defendant than jury of six); *Frehling Enterprises, Inc. v. International Select Group, Inc.*, 192 F.3d 1330 (11th Cir. 1999) (incidents of alleged confusion in service mark infringement case); *Stouffer v. Reynolds*, 168 F.3d 1155 (10th Cir. 1999) ("the apparent insularity of the Oklahoma legal community"); *Knox County Educ. Ass'n v. Knox County Bd. of Educ.*, 158 F.3d 361 (6th Cir. 1998) (that teachers hold safety-sensitive positions); *McMahon v. Bunn-O-Matic Corp.*, 150 F.3d 651 (7th Cir. 1998) (179° F is abnormally hot for brewed coffee); *International Star Class Yacht Racing Ass'n v. Tommy Hilfiger U.S.A., Inc.*, 146 F.3d 66 (2d Cir. 1998) (trademark search practices in 1993 as determined in an earlier case; fact proved in one case does not enable courts to take judicial notice of it in other cases); *York v. American Tel. & Tel. Co.*, 95 F.3d at 948 (few, if any, women in the Oklahoma City area would be able to satisfy two-year engineering experience requirement); *Cantrell v. Knoxville Community Development Corp.*, 60 F.3d 1177 (6th Cir. 1995) (mental instability of plaintiff's attorney); *Ruiz v. Gap, Inc.*, 540 F. Supp. 2d 1121 (N.D. Cal. 2008) (studies from internet sites regarding identity theft and data breach incidents); *Long v. City of Leawood, Kan.*, 6 F. Supp. 2d 1249 (D. Kan. 1998) (in ADA lawsuit that worker's job duties would require repetitive grasping and lifting with both hands); *Stone v. Galaxy Carpet Mills, Inc.*, 841 F. Supp. 1181 (N.D. Ga. 1993) (employer made assumption that plaintiff, as a woman, would not be able to take position involving travel). *See also U.S. v. Berber-Tinoco*, 510 F.3d 1083 (9th Cir. 2007) (judge improperly used his own background knowledge of roads, speed limits, stop sign locations; a trial judge is prohibited from relying on his personal experience to support the taking of judicial notice).

Documents that are not proper subjects of judicial notice may still be admissible as evidence if they are properly authenticated, i.e., if the proponent introduces evidence to support a finding that the document is what the proponent claims. Fed.R.Evid. 901(a); *Pavone v. Citicorp Credit Services, Inc.*, 60 F. Supp. 2d 1040 (S.D. Cal. 1997).

Additional References

Graham, Handbook of Federal Evidence §§ 201.1 to 201.9 (7th ed. 2012)

Treatises and Practice Aids

Goode and Wellborn, Courtroom Handbook on Federal Evidence Chapter 5, Rule 201 (annual ed.)

Mueller & Kirkpatrick, Federal Evidence, §§ 2:1 to 2:14 (3d ed. 2007)

Wright & Graham, Federal Practice and Procedure: Evidence 2d §§ 5101 *et seq.*

McCormick, Evidence §§ 328 to 335 (6th ed. 2006)

JUROR QUESTIONING

See:

Fed.R.Evid. 611(a)
Mil.R.Evid. 614(b),(c)

Objection

- [*At sidebar*] The question does not seek factual clarification. It is [*cross-examination directed to credibility*], [*improper advocacy (because . . .)*] [*speculation (specifics)*].

Response

- The question is proper. It is specific, factual in nature and seeks clarification of (*give details*).

Commentary

The trial judge has discretion to allow jurors to question witnesses. *U.S. v. Rawlings*, 522 F.3d 403 (D.C. Cir. 2008); *U.S. v. Richardson*, 233 F.3d 1285 (11th Cir. 2000); *U.S. v. Collins*, 226 F.3d 457 (6th Cir. 2000); *U.S. v. Hernandez*, 176 F.3d 719 (3d Cir. 1999); *U.S. v. Feinberg*, 89 F.3d 333 (7th Cir. 1996); *U.S. v. Thompson*, 76 F.3d 442 (2d Cir. 1996); *U.S. v. Cassiere*, 4 F.3d 1006 (1st Cir. 1993); *U.S. v. Groene*, 998 F.2d 604 (8th Cir. 1993); *DeBenedetto by DeBenedetto v. Goodyear Tire & Rubber Co.*, 754 F.2d 512 (4th Cir. 1985); *U.S. v. Callahan*, 588 F.2d 1078 (5th Cir. 1979); *U.S. v. Gonzales*, 424 F.2d 1055 (9th Cir. 1970).

The rationale for permitting jurors to ask questions is that it helps the jury to clarify and understand factual issues, especially in complex or lengthy trials that involve expert witness testimony or financial or technical evidence. *U.S. v. Richardson*, 233 F.3d at 1289–90. "Juror-inspired questions may serve to advance the search for truth by alleviating uncertainties in the jurors' minds, clearing up confusion or alerting the attorneys to points that bear further elaboration." *U.S. v. Sutton*, 970 F.2d 1001, 1005 n.3 (1st Cir. 1992).

There are, however, certain inherent risks, including impairing juror neutrality, encouraging premature deliberations and undermining litigation strategies, all of which have caused some appellate courts to express serious reservations about the practice. *See, e.g., Collins*, 226 F.3d at 461 (routine practice of juror questioning should be discouraged); *Thompson*, 76 F.3d at 448 ("we have strongly discouraged the practice except in extraordinary or compelling circumstances"); *Cassiere*, 4 F.3d at 1018 (juror questioning should be reserved for exceptional situations, and should not become routine, even in complex cases); *U.S. v. Johnson*, 892 F.2d 707, 713 (8th Cir. 1989) (Lay, C.J., concurring) ("The fundamental problem with juror questions lies in the gross distortion of the adversary system and the misconception of the role of the jury.").

When juror questioning is permitted, the following procedural safeguards should be used: (1) jurors should be instructed to submit their questions in writing to the judge; (2) the judge should review the questions *in camera* with counsel who may then object; and (3) the court itself should put the approved questions to the witnesses. *Richardson*, 233 F.3d at 1290–91; *Hernandez*, 176 F.3d at 726; *U.S. v. Bush*, 47 F.3d 511, 516 (2d Cir. 1995); *Sutton*, 970 F.2d at 1005–06 (suggesting that counsel be alerted to court's intention to allow juror questioning at earliest practicable time and given opportunity to object). *Cf. U.S. v. Ajmal*, 67 F.3d 12 (2d Cir. 1995) (abuse of discretion to permit extensive juror questioning in simple drug conspiracy case; regardless of safeguards utilized, trial court may not exercise its discretion without regard to balance of potential benefits and disadvantages of juror questioning).

In addition, before any questioning begins, the court should instruct the jurors about the function of the questioning procedure in clarifying factual (not legal) issues and should direct them to remain neutral and, if the judge fails to ask a particular question, not to take offense or to speculate as to the reasons or what answer might have been given. Then, after a particular witness has responded to the questions, the court should permit counsel to requestion the witness. *Rawlings*, 522 F.3d at 408 (citations omitted).

The military rules give the courts-martial the explicit right to interrogate witnesses. Mil.R.Evid. 614(b). Members must submit their questions to the military judge in writing so that a ruling may be made as to propriety. The military judge asks all acceptable questions. *Id.* Objections to such questions may be made at the time or at the next available opportunity when the members are not present. Mil.R.Evid. 614(c).

A.L.R. Library

Propriety of Jurors Asking Questions During Open Court During Course of Trial, 31 ALR 3d 872

Treatises and Practice Aids

Goode and Wellborn, Courtroom Handbook on Federal Evidence Chapter 5, Rule 611 (annual ed.)

Wright & Graham, Federal Practice and Procedure: Evidence 2d § 5013

JURY INSTRUCTIONS

See:

Fed.R.Civ.P. 51
Fed.R.Crim.P. 30
R.C.M. 920(f)

Illustration

- [*at sidebar*] I object.
- The instruction misstates the law because [*specify citing controlling legal authority*].
- There is no factual support in the record for the instruction [*specify*].
- The court's instruction will mislead or confuse the jury because [*specify*].
- The [*plaintiff/defendant*] is entitled to the instruction which I submitted on the issue [*specify issue citing controlling legal authority*], and it is error to have omitted it.

Commentary

In a civil trial, objections to jury instructions are governed by Rule 51 of the Federal Rules of Civil Procedure. The Rule provides:

> At the close of the evidence or at such earlier time during the trial as the court reasonably directs, any party may file written requests that the court instruct the jury on the law set forth in the requests. The court shall inform counsel of its proposed action upon the requests prior to their arguments to the jury. The court, at its election, may instruct the jury before or after argument, or both. *No party may assign as error the giving or the failure to give an instruction unless that party objects thereto before the jury retires to consider its verdict, stating distinctly the matter objected to and the grounds of the objection.* Opportunity shall be given to make the objection out of the hearing of the jury. [emphasis added]

The analogue to Rule 51 in a criminal trial is Fed.R.Crim.P. 30 and Rule 920(f) of the Rules for Courts-Martial.*

By requiring parties *to object with specificity*

[Jury etc.]

*Rule 30 provides:

At the close of the evidence or at such earlier time dur-

before the jury retires, the rule ensures that the trial court is made aware of and given an opportunity to correct any error in the charge, including special interrogatories, before the jury begins its deliberations. *Schobert v. Illinois Dept. of Transp.*, 304 F.3d 725 (7th Cir. 2002) (specificity requirement is not a game of "gotcha"; it is a rule that allows judge to be made aware of error prior to instructing jury so that the judge can fix the problem); *Smith v. Biomet, Inc.*, 384 F. Supp. 2d 1241 (N.D. Ind. 2005). *See DeCaro v. Hasbro, Inc.*, 580 F.3d 55 (1st Cir. 2009); *Cal-Agrex, Inc. v. Tassell*, 258 F.R.D. 340 (N.D. Cal. 2009) (failure to object to jury instructions at time and in manner specified by Rule 51 forfeits any objection); *Millenkamp v. Davisco Foods Intern., Inc.*, 562 F.3d 971 (9th Cir. 2009); *Thompson v. Connick*, 553 F.3d 836 (5th Cir. 2008); *Houskins v. Sheahan*, 549 F.3d 480 (7th Cir. 2008); *Foradori v. Harris*, 523 F.3d 477 (5th Cir. 2008); *Fashauer v. New Jersey Transit Rail Operations, Inc.*, 57 F.3d 1269 (3d Cir. 1995) (if party fails to raise specific objection in trial court to form or content of an interrogatory, it cannot raise that objection for the first time on appeal; issue limited to plain error review). With respect to Fed.R.Crim.P. 30, *see U.S. v. Skilling*, 554 F.3d 529 (5th Cir. 2009); *U.S. v. Rodriguez*, 525 F.3d 85 (1st Cir. 2008); *U.S. v. Roberson*, 459 F.3d 39 (1st Cir. 2006) (defendant must object to court's refusal to give proposed tendered instruction to preserve issue for appeal); *U.S. v. Sirang*, 70 F.3d 588 (11th Cir. 1995) (under Rule 30, counsel must object with specificity to instructions); *U.S. v. Weintraub*, 273 F.3d 139 (2d Cir. 2001); *U.S. v. Boruff*, 909 F.2d

---

ing the trial as the court reasonably directs, any party may file written requests that the court instruct the jury on the law as set forth in the requests. At the same time copies of such requests shall be furnished to all parties. The court shall inform counsel of its proposed action upon the requests prior to their arguments to the jury. The court may instruct the jury before or after the arguments are completed or at both times. *No party may assign as error any portion of the charge or omission therefrom unless that party objects thereto before the jury retires to consider its verdict, stating distinctly the matter to which that party objects and the grounds of the objection.* Opportunity shall be given to make the objection out of the hearing of the jury and, on request of any party, out of the presence of the jury. [emphasis added]

111 (5th Cir. 1990) (objection should be sufficiently specific to give court chance to correct errors before case goes to jury).

Objections must "bring into focus the precise nature of the alleged error." *Palmer v. Hoffman*, 318 U.S. 109, 119, 63 S. Ct. 477, 483, 87 L. Ed. 645 (1943); *accord Horstmyer v. Black & Decker, (U.S.), Inc.*, 151 F.3d 765 (8th Cir. 1998). A general objection stating no grounds is insufficient, as is an objection that attempts to state grounds but fails to do so with specificity. *Dupre v. Fru-Con Engineering Inc.*, 112 F.3d 329 (8th Cir. 1997) (general objection to instruction coupled with statement that instruction should not be given are insufficient to preserve objection for appeal absent plain error); *Chemical Leaman Tank Lines, Inc. v. Aetna Cas. and Sur. Co.*, 89 F.3d 976 (3d Cir. 1996) (objection lacked sufficient clarity to give judge notice of possible error where objection was difficult to understand because of convoluted grammar and did not specify legal authority); *U.S. v. Starke*, 62 F.3d 1374 (11th Cir. 1995) (to preserve objection to jury instructions for appellate review, party must object before jury retires, stating distinctly specific grounds for objection); *U.S. v. Dorri*, 15 F.3d 888 (9th Cir. 1994) (same); *U.S. v. Zannino*, 895 F.2d 1, 17 (1st Cir. 1990) ("Judges are not expected to be mindreaders. Consequently, a litigant has an obligation to spell out its arguments squarely and distinctly, or else forever hold its peace."); *U.S. v. Kehm*, 799 F.2d 354, 362–63 (7th Cir. 1986) ("The objection must point to something particular in the instruction and identify what, particularly, is wrong and why; nothing else alerts the judge to what is at stake.")

So long as the trial judge is appraised of the grounds for the objection, a litigant is not required to adhere to " 'formalities of language and style.' " *Guerts v. Barth*, 892 F.2d 622, 624 (7th Cir. 1989) (applying Rule 51) (quoting *Willits v. Yellow Cab Co.*, 214 F.2d 612, 616 (7th Cir. 1954)).

Because there is some difference of opinion amongst the circuits as to the requirements for preserving objections for full appellate review, prudent counsel will make objections at the charging conference and then renew all objections to the instructions at the close of the charge. On both occasions, objections must be made on the record and outside the hearing of the jury. These differing approaches are illustrated in the following cases: *U.S. v. Blood*, 435 F.3d 612 (6th Cir. 2006) (general objection made by defense counsel at charging conference incorporating all objections made by codefendant was insufficient to preserve for appeal particular objection to one instruction where objection to that instruction was later renewed by codefendant but not mentioned by defense counsel); *Smith v. Borough of Wilkinsburg*, 147 F.3d 272 (3d Cir. 1998) (where counsel submitted charge with legal authorities and objected to its omission at charge conference, court was fully appraised of position and it would serve no purpose to require formal objection after charge was given to jury); *Dawson v. New York Life Ins. Co.*, 135 F.3d 1158 (7th Cir. 1998) (parties should not be penalized for relying on court's assurance that record adequately contained their objections, although more prudent practice is to restate in exacting language precise objections and reasons therefor after instruction given to jury); *Elliott v. S.D. Warren Co.*, 134 F.3d 1 (1st Cir. 1998) (court expects strict compliance with Rule 51; objection raised in chambers before delivery of charge with only general reference thereto after charge will not preserve objection for appellate review); *Jones Truck Lines, Inc. v. Full Service Leasing Corp.*, 83 F.3d 253, 256 (8th Cir. 1996) ("In this circuit . . . concern that the trial judge would prefer no objection or the view that an objection would be futile does not relieve parties from making an objection [after court's charge] to preserve errors for review"); *Bath & Body Works, Inc. v. Luzier Personalized Cosmetics, Inc.*, 76 F.3d 743, 749 (6th Cir. 1996) (party must make formal objection both before and after instruction is given to jury; sole exception occurs when record clearly indicates that judge was aware of dissatisfaction with instruction and specific basis for claimed error or omission).

Treatises and Practice Aids

Wright & Miller, Federal Practice and Procedure: Civil 3d §§ 2553 to 54

LAY WITNESS OPINION

See:

Fed.R.Evid. 701
Mil.R.Evid. 701

Objection

- Objection. The witness is being asked to give an opinion [*that is not based on personal knowledge*], [*that would not be helpful to the jury because (explain)*], [*that can only be given by an expert.*]

Response

- The question does not seek an expert opinion. The witness has firsthand knowledge and his opinion will be helpful because (*explain*).

Commentary

Lay opinion testimony is admissible when it is: (a) rationally based on the perception of the witness, (b) helpful to a clear understanding of the witness's testimony or the determination of a fact in issue, and (c) not based on scientific, technical, or other specialized knowledge within the scope of Rule 702. Rule 701; *U.S. v. Contreras*, 536 F.3d 1167 (10th Cir. 2008) (probation officer's familiarity with defendant made her identification of him as bank robber in surveillance video helpful to jury); *U.S. v. Kaplan*, 490 F.3d 110 (2d Cir. 2007); *MCI Telecommunications Corp. v. Wanzer*, 897 F.2d 703 (4th Cir. 1990) (Rule 701 permits lay witnesses to offer an opinion on the basis of relevant historical or narrative facts that the witness has perceived); *Hampton v. Dillard Dept. Stores, Inc.*, 18 F. Supp. 2d 1256 (D. Kan. 1998).

The witness also must meet the "personal knowledge" requirements set forth in Rule 602. *See* 29 Wright & Gold, Federal Practice And Procedure § 6254 at 126 (1997) (There is no evidence that the Advisory Committee intended to eliminate the requirements that the witness "have perceived with his senses the matters on which his opinion is based" and satisfy the court that there is some "rational connection between the witness' opinion and his perceptions."); *Woodman v. WWOR-TV, Inc.*, 411 F.3d 69 (2d Cir. 2005) (excluding plaintiff's testimony that her age was well known throughout the broadcast industry; plaintiff not competent to testify how others perceived her age); *see also Kaplan* (lay opinion inadmissible in absence of evidence that it was based on first-hand knowledge); *U.S. v. Durham*, 464 F.3d 976 (9th Cir. 2006) (opinion testimony of lay witnesses must be predicated upon concrete facts within their own observation and recollection); *U.S. v. Garcia*, 413 F.3d 201 (2d Cir. 2005) (rule governing admissibility of lay opinion testimony simply recognizes lay opinion as an acceptable "shorthand" for the rendition of facts that the witness personally perceived).

A lay witness may testify as to an ultimate issue of fact, *so long as the testimony is otherwise admissible*. Fed.R.Evid. 704; *Haun v. Ideal Industries, Inc.*, 81 F.3d 541 (5th Cir. 1996) (proper to admit evidence that employer was phasing out older workers because it was based on perception and helped jury determine whether there was discrimination). *Cf. Hirst v. Inverness Hotel Corp.*, 544 F.3d 221 (3d Cir. 2008); *Mitroff v. Xomox Corp.*, 797 F.2d 271 (6th Cir. 1986) (seldom will a lay opinion on an ultimate issue meet the test of being helpful to the trier of fact since the jury's opinion is as good as the witness's and the witness turns into little more than an "oath helper"). The lay witness may not testify as to a legal conclusion, such as the correct interpretation of a contract. *Evangelista v. Inlandboatmen's Union of Pacific*, 777 F.2d 1390, 1398 n.3 (9th Cir. 1985); *see also U.S. v. Crawford*, 239 F.3d 1086 (9th Cir. 2001); *Kivalina Relocation Planning Committee v. Teck Cominco Alaska, Inc.*, 227 F.R.D. 523 (D. Alaska 2004); *Quiksilver, Inc. v. Kymsta Corp.*, 247 F.R.D. 579 (C.D. Cal. 2007).

The Rule 701(a) requirement that a lay witness's opinion be rationally based on the perception of the witness simply means that the opinion or inference is based on firsthand knowledge and is one which a normal person would form on the basis of observed facts. *U.S. v. Yanez Sosa*, 513 F.3d 194 (5th Cir. 2008); *U.S. v. Rea*, 958 F.2d 1206 (2d Cir. 1992); *Torres v. County of Oakland*, 758 F.2d 147 (6th Cir. 1985); *Ligon v. Triangle Pacific Corp.*, 935 F. Supp. 936 (M.D. Tenn. 1996).

The helpfulness requirement (Rule 701(b)) is designed to guard against the admission of opinions which merely tell the jury what result to reach. *Hester v. BIC Corp.*, 225 F.3d 178 (2d Cir. 2000) (co-workers' testimony equating supervisor's condescension with racial discrimination improperly admitted; Rule 701(b) bars opinion testimony amounting to naked speculation). If attempts are made to introduce meaningless assertions which amount to little more than choosing up sides, such evidence should be excluded for lack of helpfulness. *U.S. v. Samet*, 466 F.3d 251, 255 (2d Cir. 2006) (lay witness opinion improper when jury is equally capable of making the same comparisons); *Garcia,* 413 F.3d at 213 (opinion as to culpability failed to qualify as "helpful" under Rule 701(b)); *U.S. v. Henke*, 222 F.3d 633, 642 (9th Cir. 2000) (testimony that defendant "must have known" fails to meet helpfulness requirement); *U.S. v. Anderskow*, 88 F.3d 245 (3d Cir. 1996) (same); *Rea*, 958 F.2d at 1215 (quoting Advisory Committee Note); *see* Weinstein and Berger, Weinstein's Federal Evidence § 701.05 (2d ed. 2000) ("[L]ay testimony generally is not helpful on matters that *are* essentially a jury question, such as credibility issues.")

Lay opinion is appropriate where it is difficult for a witness to explain through factual testimony the combination of circumstances that led him to formulate the opinion. *Wilburn v. Maritrans GP Inc.*, 139 F.3d 350 (3d Cir. 1998) (Rule 701 permits evidence that constitutes shorthand renditions of total situation or statements of collective facts); *Fireman's Fund Ins. Companies v. Alaskan Pride Partnership*, 106 F.3d 1465 (9th Cir. 1997) (claims manager's testimony that claim was a legitimate loss in his opinion and that he was upset about denial of coverage was admissible lay opinion); *U.S. v. Skeet*, 665 F.2d 983 (9th Cir. 1982) (lay opinion may be admitted when data observed by witness are difficult to reproduce, or facts are difficult to explain or complex or combine circumstances in a manner that cannot be adequately described and presented with force and clarity as they appeared to witness).

In *Asplundh Mfg. Div., a Div. of Asplundh Tree Expert Co. v. Benton Harbor Engineering*, 57 F.3d 1190, 1196–98 (3d Cir. 1995), the court summarized the "prototypical" or "core area" examples of opinions routinely admitted under Rule 701 as including: appearance of persons and things, identity, the manner of conduct, competency of a person, degrees of light or darkness, sound, size, weight, distance, speed, value of property, and other situations in which the differences between fact and opinion blur and it is difficult or cumbersome to elicit an answer from the witness that will not be expressed in the form of an opinion.

Rule 701 was amended in December, 2000 in order to distinguish more precisely between opinions that may be rendered by lay persons and those that may be rendered only by experts. Rule 701(c) provides that scientific, technical or other specialized knowledge may not form the basis for opinions and inferences of lay witnesses. The amendment is intended to eliminate the risk that the reliability requirements for admissibility of scientific, technical or specialized knowledge under Rule 702 and the disclosure requirements of Fed.R.Civ.P. 26 and Fed.R.Crim.P. 16 will be evaded by offering an expert as a lay witness under Rule 701. *See Certain Underwriters at Lloyd's, London v. Sinkovich*, 232 F.3d 200 (4th Cir. 2000) (insurance claim for ship wreck; error to allow lay witness to testify to conclusions that could only be drawn by experienced seaman or marine engineer); *U.S. v. Riddle*, 103 F.3d 423 (5th Cir. 1997) (bank examiner exceeded scope of proper lay testimony by purporting to describe sound banking practice); *Doddy v. Oxy USA, Inc.*, 101 F.3d 448 (5th Cir. 1996) (person may testify as lay witness only if his opinions and inferences do not require specialized knowledge and could be reached by ordinary person); *Hilgraeve Corp. v. McAfee Associates, Inc.*, 70 F. Supp. 2d 738 (E.D. Mich. 1999) (party cannot use Rule 701 as back door attempt to admit testimony of expert nature under guise of lay opinion and thus strip court of its "*Daubert*" gatekeeping functions).

The following cases are also instructive. **Lay opinion excluded:** *U.S. v. Mock*, 523 F.3d 1299 (11th Cir. 2008) (lay witness excluded from testifying that she "believed" someone else committed two fires; not based on first-hand knowledge or observation); *Stagman v. Ryan*, 176 F.3d 986 (7th Cir. 1999) (lack of personal knowledge; mere speculation); *U.S.*

v. Marshall, 173 F.3d 1312 (11th Cir. 1999) (lack of personal knowledge as to source of cocaine); *U.S. v. Montalvo*, 20 F. Supp. 2d 270 (D.P.R. 1998) (opinion on veracity of another witness not admissible). **Lay opinion admitted:** *U.S. v. Hoffecker*, 530 F.3d 137 (3d Cir. 2008) (lay witness testimony that defendant's action was a "scam" was admissible; statement was based on first-hand knowledge and observation, rational perceptions, defendant's statements, and witnesses interactions with defendant, not on specialized knowledge); *U.S. v. Hogan*, 253 Fed. Appx. 889 (11th Cir. 2007) (admission of testimony by victims, as lay witnesses, to similarity between robber's clothing and clothing seized by police from him); *U.S. v. Durham*, 464 F.3d 976 (9th Cir. 2006) (opinion of lay witness that burnt residue given to infant to smoke was, or contained marijuana was admissible); *U.S. v. Dulcio*, 441 F.3d 1269 (11th Cir. 2006) (federal agents could offer lay opinion testimony as to whether people transporting shipments of illegal drugs know they are transporting illegal drugs); *Texas A&M Research Foundation v. Magna Transp., Inc.*, 338 F.3d 394 (5th Cir. 2003) (Rule 701 does not preclude testimony by business owners or officers on matters relating to their business affairs; here industry practices and pricing); *U.S. v. Marsalla*, 164 F.3d 1178 (8th Cir. 1999) (former dealer could identify crack cocaine); *U.S. v. Sheffey*, 57 F.3d 1419 (6th Cir. 1995) (testimony that defendant was driving recklessly with extreme disregard for human life; terms used in question had same meaning in ordinary speech as in law); *Schlier v. Rice*, 2008 WL 4922435 (M.D. Pa. 2008) (plaintiff owner permitted to give lay opinion testimony as to damages as it was based on his knowledge and participation in the day-to-day affairs of the business); *U.S. v. Giampa*, 904 F. Supp. 235 (D.N.J. 1995) (witness' interpretation of "mob talk", i.e., code words used in abbreviated and unfinished sentences); *U.S. v. Novaton*, 867 F. Supp. 1023 (S.D. Fla. 1994) (same).

A treating physician is a fact witness (not an expert) when describing the diagnosis or treatment of a person. *Principi v. Survivair, Inc.*, 231 F.R.D. 685 (M.D. Fla. 2005) (a doctor's lay opinions are analyzed pursuant to Rule 701). However, when a doctor goes beyond observations and opinions observed by treating the individual and expresses opinions as to causation or prognosis, then the treating physician steps into the shoes of an expert. *Indemnity Ins. Co. of North America v. American Eurocopter LLC*, 227 F.R.D. 421 (M.D. N.C. 2005).

Additional References

Graham, Handbook of Federal Evidence § 701.1 (7th ed. 2012)

Treatises and Practice Aids

Goode and Wellborn, Courtroom Handbook on Federal Evidence Chapter 5, Rule 701 and Obj. 52 (annual ed.)
Mueller & Kirkpatrick, Federal Evidence, §§ 7:1 to 7:6 (3d ed. 2007)
Wright & Gold, Federal Practice and Procedure: Evidence §§ 6254 to 6255
McCormick, Evidence § 11 (6th ed. 2006)
Park, Trial Objections Handbook § 8:4 (2nd ed. 2001)

LEADING QUESTION

See:

Fed.R.Evid. 611(c)
Mil.R.Evid. 611(c)

Objection

- Objection. Counsel is leading the witness.
- I object to the question as leading.

Response

- Your Honor, I request permission to lead [because these are only uncontested preliminary matters] [given the young age of the witness] [because the witness is having difficulty in answering any questions] [because of this witness's handicap] [because this witness is hostile].

Commentary

A leading question is one which puts the desired answer in the mouth of the witness by suggesting the desired answer. *See Roy v. Austin Co.*, 194 F.3d 840 (7th Cir. 1999). The problem with leading questions is that the attorney is really the one who is testifying (telling the story) and the witness is merely affirming the lawyer's testimony, often by responding with "yes" or "no" answers. *See generally Stine v. Marathon Oil Co.*, 976 F.2d 254, 266 (5th Cir. 1992) (any good trial advocate who is allowed leading questions can both testify for witness and argue his client's case); *U.S. v. McGovern*, 499 F.2d 1140, 1142 (1st Cir. 1974) (the evil of leading a friendly witness is that information conveyed in questions may supply false memory).

Rule 611(c) follows the traditional common law rule that leading questions ordinarily should be confined to cross-examination and should not be asked on direct examination. The trial court, however, has discretion to allow leading questions, *U.S. v. Castro-Romero*, 964 F.2d 942 (9th Cir. 1992), and may allow them in a variety of situations if helpful to develop testimony. Leading questions have been deemed permissible: (i) with child witnesses, *U.S. v. Rojas*, 520 F.3d 876, 881 (8th Cir.

2008) (prosecutor permitted to ask leading questions of ten-year-old victim of aggravated sexual abuse); *U.S. v. Archdale*, 229 F.3d 861 (9th Cir. 2000) (twelve-year-old victim of abusive sexual contact); *U.S. v. Wright*, 119 F.3d 630 (8th Cir. 1997) (four-year-old child victim); *U.S. v. Boyles*, 57 F.3d 535 (7th Cir. 1995) (leading questions helped to elicit difficult testimony from four-year-old boy); *U.S. v. Butler*, 56 F.3d 941 (8th Cir. 1995) (nine-year-old witness); (ii) where, because of physical or mental limitations, a witness is experiencing difficulty in answering questions, *U.S. v. Goodlow*, 105 F.3d 1203 (8th Cir. 1997) (mentally retarded victim); (iii) where the witness is hostile, biased, reluctant to testify or exhibits lack of understanding, *U.S. v. Cisneros-Gutierrez*, 517 F.3d 751, 761 (5th Cir. 2008) (leading questions permitted where witness was hostile and had extensive "memory problems" which appeared to have been feigned); *U.S. v. Hernandez-Albino*, 177 F.3d 33 (1st Cir. 1999); *U.S. v. Mulinelli-Navas*, 111 F.3d 983 (1st Cir. 1997) (leading questions assisted in developing coherent testimony because witness was unresponsive or showed a lack of understanding); *Bingham v. Zolt*, 66 F.3d 553 (2d Cir. 1995) (hostile witness who persisted in giving non-responsive answers); *U.S. v. Rossbach*, 701 F.2d 713 (8th Cir. 1983) (fifteen-and seventeen-year-old victims who were hesitant to answer questions and who had been threatened). *See also U.S. v. Ajmal*, 67 F.3d 12 (2d Cir. 1995) (court did not abuse discretion in allowing witness who spoke little English and testified in Urdu through translator, to testify almost entirely by way of leading questions); *U.S. v. Rodriguez-Garcia*, 983 F.2d 1563 (10th Cir. 1993) (similar).

When a party calls a hostile witness, an adverse party or a witness identified with an adverse party, interrogation may be by leading questions. Rule 611(c); *U.S. v. Reddix*, 106 F.3d 236 (8th Cir. 1997). The court may, however, prohibit leading questions when the line of questioning is cross-examination *in form only* and not in fact. An example of such sham cross-examination is the "cross-examination" of a party by his own counsel after being called and questioned by the opponent. Fed.R.Evid. 611(c) Advisory Committee Notes; *Woods v. Lecureux*, 110

F.3d 1215 (6th Cir. 1997) (trial court should be hesitant to blindly authorize use of leading questions when it is cross-examination in form only).

With respect to the use of deposition transcripts, if a party fails to object to the form of a leading question during the deposition, the party waives its ability to raise the objection at trial. *Roy v. Austin Co.*, 194 F.3d 840 (7th Cir. 1999) (depositions as trial evidence would quickly lose their value if party could strategically withhold objection during deposition and later exclude testimony that could have been elicited if objection raised promptly); *Oberlin v. Marlin American Corp.*, 596 F.2d 1322 (7th Cir. 1979) (same).

Leading questions are a standard technique of impeachment. Fed.R.Evid. 607 allows the credibility of a witness to be impeached by *any party*, including the party calling the witness. Rule 607 abolishes the voucher rule (i.e., the traditional view that a party vouched for the credibility of the witnesses it called) and its corollaries, such as having to declare the witness adverse before cross-examining him or having to show that his testimony was a surprise. *U.S. v. Ienco*, 92 F.3d 564 (7th Cir. 1996) (serious error was committed when trial judge refused to let defense counsel impeach his own witness by leading questions; there was no need for advance notice to court of adverse witness or claim of surprise).

Additional References

Graham, Handbook of Federal Evidence § 611.8 (7th ed. 2012)

Treatises and Practice Aids

Goode and Wellborn, Courtroom Handbook on Federal Evidence Chapter 5, Rule 611 and Obj. 8 (annual ed.)

Mueller & Kirkpatrick, Federal Evidence, §§ 6:60, 6:65, 6:68, 6:93 (3d ed. 2007)

Wright & Gold, Federal Practice and Procedure: Evidence § 6168

McCormick, Evidence Chapter 2 (6th ed. 2006)

Park, Trial Objections Handbook §§ 6:2 to 6:5 (2nd ed. 2001)

LEGAL CONCLUSION

See:

Fed.R.Evid. 701
Mil.R.Evid. 701

Objection

- Objection. The question calls for a legal conclusion which this witness is not competent to render.

Response

- The question is proper. I am using the term [*specify*] only in its established lay meaning and not as a legal term of art.
- I shall rephrase the question.

Commentary

Under Rule 701, a witness, not testifying as an expert, is limited in testimony in the form of opinions and inferences to those which are based on his perception and helpful to a clear understanding of his testimony or the determination of a fact in issue. As the Seventh Circuit has explained, when a witness is asked whether conduct was "unlawful" or "willful" or whether the defendants "conspired", terms that demand an understanding of the nature and scope of the law, the trial court may properly conclude that any response would not be helpful to the trier of fact. *U.S. v. Baskes*, 649 F.2d 471, 478 (7th Cir. 1980). The witness, unfamiliar with the contours of the law, may erroneously feel that the legal standard is either higher or lower than it really is. In either event, a jury may give too much weight to such a legal conclusion. *Baskes*, 649 F.2d at 478; *accord, U.S. v. Wantuch*, 525 F.3d 505 (7th Cir. 2008) (asking witness to opine as to defendant's knowledge of whether his actions were legal demanded legal conclusion unhelpful to jury per Rule 701; jury was just as capable as witness of inferring that defendant knew he was committing a crime); *U.S. v. Espino*, 32 F.3d 253 (7th Cir. 1994).

In *Torres v. County of Oakland*, 758 F.2d 147 (6th Cir. 1985), the court held that the question of whether plaintiff had been discriminated against because of her national origin called for an improper legal conclusion. But a more carefully phrased question (such as whether the witness believed plaintiff's national original motivated the hiring decision) could have elicited similar information and avoided the problem of testimony containing a legal conclusion. *See also Figgins v. Advance America Cash Advance Centers of Michigan, Inc.*, 482 F. Supp. 2d 861 (E.D. Mich. 2007) (whether plaintiff's coworkers could be asked about discrimination or retaliation because plaintiff was overweight depended upon their personal knowledge and how questions were phrased).

However, where words have an established lay meaning, they can be used in that context rather than as legal terms of art. *U.S. v. Levine*, 180 F.3d 869, 872 (7th Cir. 1999) (no error in allowing prosecutor to ask defendant if he had "forged" signatures on checks; " 'Forgery' was an apt description of the acts Levine performed; that the crime is also called 'forgery' does not close the subject to inquiry."); *U.S. v. Standard Oil Co.*, 316 F.2d 884 (7th Cir. 1963) (trial court erred in not permitting defense witnesses to answer questions as to whether there had been an "agreement", "understanding", "promise", or "commitment" concerning prices; such words have well-established lay meanings and do not demand a conclusion as to the legal implications of conduct). By the same reasoning, the *Levine* court noted: "Witnesses can't insist that the prosecutor use euphemisms when inquiring into conduct that the indictment labels a crime. A prosecutor may ask an accused thief whether he stuck up the teller and robbed the bank; he may ask an accused drug peddler whether he sold drugs to an undercover agent; he may ask an accused price-fixer whether he joined a cartel; he may ask an accused killer whether he murdered the deceased . . .. all are proper subjects of cross examination, provided only that the judge makes it clear to the jury that neither the questioner nor the witness defines the elements of the offense." 180 F.3d at 872.

Treatises and Practice Aids

Mueller & Kirkpatrick, Federal Evidence, § 7:4 (3d ed. 2007)

Legal Conclusion

Wright & Gold, Federal Practice and Procedure: Evidence § 6255
Park, Trial Objections Handbook § 8:28 (2nd ed. 2001)

LIMITING (CAUTIONARY) INSTRUCTIONS

See:

Fed.R.Evid. 105
Mil.R.Evid. 105

Form

- [*At sidebar*] Your Honor, in light of your ruling that you are going to admit this evidence for a limited purpose, I request that the jury be given the following cautionary instruction:
  1. Evidence Admissible Against One Party But Not Others. The testimony of this witness [*summarize substance*] is only admissible against [*name of party*]. You must not consider this evidence in connection with any other party.
  2. Evidence Admissible On One Claim But Not Others. The testimony of this witness [*summarize substance*] is only admissible in connection with [*count 1 of the indictment/the claim of negligence*]. You must not consider this evidence in connection with [*any other count of the indictment/any other claim in the case*].
  3. Evidence Admissible On One Issue But Not Others. The testimony of this witness is only admissible in connection with one issue in this case, namely [*state issue*]. You must not use this evidence for any other purpose.

Commentary

When evidence is admitted for a limited purpose, or against only one party, the judge must instruct the jury as to the proper scope of the evidence if requested to do so. Rule 105; *see, e.g., U.S. v. Fraser*, 448 F.3d 833 (6th Cir. 2006) (duty to provide instruction arises only upon request of one of the parties); *Sherman v. Burke Contracting, Inc.*, 891 F.2d 1527 (11th Cir. 1990) (taped conversation admissible only for impeachment of witness who denied having conversation; in all other respects it was inadmissible hearsay); *U.S. v. Ferguson*, 478 F. Supp. 2d 220 (D. Conn. 2007) (limiting instruction can be appropriate remedy even in cases where evidence is presented against one defendant that would not be admissible in a separate trial of a co-defendant). Normally, the opponent of the evidence will request a limiting instruction. Rule 105, however, has no restrictions, and a proponent of evidence who is satisfied with limited use and wishes to protect the record against a possible appeal can also make the request. While the rule speaks only of instructions to the jury, on request in a bench trial, the court should rule on how it intends to limit the use of the evidence.

Although Rule 105 obligates the trial judge to restrict the evidence to its proper scope, it does not specify the time at which a limiting instruction should be given. The better practice is a specific instruction at the time the evidence is admitted followed by a general instruction at the end of the case reminding the jurors that some evidence may be used only for limited purposes. Wright & Graham, Federal Practice and Procedure: Evidence § 5066. Failure to request a limiting instruction at the time the evidence is introduced does not bar a party from making a later request at the time of the general charge to the jury. Fed.R.Civ.P. 51; Fed.R.Crim.P. 30.

The judge may give a limiting instruction *sua sponte* but has no such duty under Rule 105 in the absence of a request. *U.S. v. Miranda*, 197 F.3d 1357 (11th Cir. 1999) (in absence of request, no duty to give limiting instruction with respect to prior bad acts evidence admitted under Rule 404(b)); *U.S. v. Fraza*, 106 F.3d 1050 (1st Cir. 1997) (defendants' responsibility to request instruction limiting deposition testimony to the particular defendant/deponent). *But see U.S. v. Sauza-Martinez*, 217 F.3d 754 (9th Cir. 2000) (where incriminating hearsay evidence was admissible only to impeach one party in joint trial, failure to give limiting instruction *sua sponte* was reversible error).

However, there is authority for the proposition that, if a district court chooses to give a deliberating jury transcribed testimony, or chooses to read testimony to that jury, the court must give an instruction cautioning the jury on the proper use of such testimony. *U.S. v. Smith*, 419 F.3d 521 (6th

Cir. 2005); *U.S. v. Rodgers*, 109 F.3d 1138 (6th Cir. 1997). For example, the Ninth Circuit holds that a district court must take four precautions before allowing a deliberating jury to read trial testimony: (1) provide counsel with an opportunity to note inaccuracies in the transcript; (2) caution the jury that the transcript is merely an aid and is not to serve as a substitute for their own memories of live testimony and assessments of credibility; (3) admonish the jury to weigh all the evidence and not to focus on any isolated portion of the trial; and (4) instruct the jury that the transcript is not authoritative and should not prevail over the jurors' memories. *U.S. v. Lujan*, 936 F.2d 406, 411–12 (9th Cir. 1991).

Counsel occasionally will choose not to request limiting instructions for strategic reasons; where, for example, it might focus the jury's attention on the damaging evidence. *U.S. v. Brawner*, 32 F.3d 602 (D.C. Cir. 1994). A party who makes it clear he does not want a limiting instruction cannot later complain that the failure to give one was error. *U.S. v. Haukaas*, 172 F.3d 542 (8th Cir. 1999).

The Rule is illustrated in the following cases: *U.S. v. Mangual-Santiago*, 562 F.3d 411 (1st Cir. 2009) (limiting instruction adequately addressed any prejudice that might arise from improperly admitted evidence); *U.S. v. Morena*, 547 F.3d 191 (3d Cir. 2008) (where government repeatedly injected highly prejudicial evidence into trial, court's instruction to jury did not cure prosecutor's misconduct); *U.S. v. Bell*, 516 F.3d 432 (6th Cir. 2008) (limiting instruction will minimize to some degree the prejudicial nature of other criminal acts evidence; it is not, however, a sure-fire panacea for the prejudice resulting from needless admission of such evidence); *U.S. v. Lopez-Medina*, 461 F.3d 724 (6th Cir. 2006) (where federal agents would be testifying as both fact and expert witnesses, court should inform jury of duel roles so jury could give proper weight to each type of testimony); *U.S. v. Chance*, 306 F.3d 356 (6th Cir. 2002) (defendant waived claim as to adequacy of limiting instruction regarding evidence of improper conduct by third parties when he did not request trial court to give a more specific instruction tailored to testimony at issue).

Additional References

Graham, Handbook of Federal Evidence § 105.1 (7th ed. 2012)

Treatises and Practice Aids

Goode and Wellborn, Courtroom Handbook on Federal Evidence Chapter 5, Rule 105 (annual ed.)

Mueller & Kirkpatrick, Federal Evidence, § 1:41 (3d ed. 2007)

Wright & Graham, Federal Practice and Procedure: Evidence 2d § 5066

McCormick, Evidence § 59 (6th ed. 2006)

Park, Trial Objections Handbook § 1:17 (2nd ed. 2001)

MISTRIAL-MOTION

Illustration

- Objection, your Honor. Counsel has referred to evidence that the court previously ruled inadmissible. I now move for a mistrial on grounds that this misconduct is so unfairly prejudicial that my client is denied a fair trial. A curative instruction will not remove from the minds of the jurors what they have heard. This inadmissible and unduly prejudicial information which counsel has presented prevents them from considering the evidence in a fair and impartial manner.

Response

- Nothing in this isolated remark was so prejudicial as to require a new trial. A curative instruction will remedy any alleged harm.
- A new trial is not required unless the unavoidable effect of the evidence would be to prejudice the jury by creating such bias and hostility that they cannot weigh the evidence and render a true verdict. That has not happened here.

Commentary

A mistrial is a trial which has been terminated prior to its normal conclusion because of some extraordinary event or prejudicial error that cannot be corrected at trial. A mistrial "may be granted upon the initiative of either party or upon the court's own initiative." *United States v. Scott*, 437 U.S. 82, 92, 98 S. Ct. 2187, 57 L. Ed. 2d 65 (1978). Grounds that support a mistrial motion include statements or conduct by counsel, witnesses, jurors, court officials or the judge that:

- are substantially and unfairly prejudicial to such an extent that a fair and impartial trial has been impaired;
- constitute gross misconduct;
- intentionally violate a court order;
- deliberately and unfairly attempt to influence the judge or jury;
- provide false evidence;

- improperly and adversely affect the substantial rights of a party;
- result in substantial irregularities in the trial proceedings;
- or otherwise make a fair trial impossible.

Examples of errors that can support a motion for mistrial are illustrated in the following cases: *Illinois v. Somerville*, 410 U.S. 458, 93, 93 S. Ct. 1066, 35 L. Ed. 2d 425 (1973) (when error certain to result in reversal occurs, trial court properly exercises its discretion in declaring mistrial); *U.S. v. Brown*, 426 F.3d 32 (1st Cir. 2005) (deadlocked jury); *Hardnett v. Marshall*, 25 F.3d 875, 879 (9th Cir. 1994) (error to refuse mistrial in face of egregious prosecutorial misconduct; "[t]he prosecutor's remarks instilled a poison which the defense could not draw from the case."); *U.S. v. Randle*, 966 F.2d 1209 (7th Cir. 1992) (defendant entitled to mistrial based on court's failure to allow poll of jury); *U.S. v. Spears*, 89 F. Supp. 2d 891 (W.D. Mich. 2000) (potential juror bias because of conduct of defense counsel); *Finley v. National R.R. Passenger Corp.*, 1 F. Supp. 2d 440 (E.D. Pa. 1998) (in FELA action for injuries suffered by railroad employee, references to plaintiff's receipt of pension benefits); *U.S. v. Kanahele*, 951 F. Supp. 928 (D. Haw. 1996) (juror performed independent legal research during deliberations); *Littlewind v. Rayl*, 839 F. Supp. 1369 (D.N.D. 1993) (error to refuse mistrial in civil rights case where defendant's opening statement referred to plaintiff as suspect in murder investigation); *Hodge v. American Home Assur. Co.*, 150 F.R.D. 25 (D.P.R. 1993) (violation of Rule 408 and judge's admonitions by references during opening statement to defendant's refusal to settle claim); *Vance v. Texas A & M University System*, 117 F.R.D. 93 (S.D. Tex. 1987) (plaintiff lacked competent counsel because attorney was totally unprepared, completely disorganized and ineffective; court required to intervene in interests of justice and integrity of legal system).

The grounds for mistrial must be so severe and uncorrectable that a party is denied a fair trial. *U.S. v. Mannie*, 509 F.3d 851, 856 (7th Cir. 2007) (where courtroom intimidation, outbursts and violence caused appeals court to observe "certain courtroom situations are so beyond the pale, so prejudicial, that no amount of *voir dire* and cautionary instructions can remedy the defect."); *U.S. v. Clarke*, 227 F.3d 874 (7th Cir. 2000); *U.S. v. O'Dell*, 204 F.3d 829 (8th Cir. 2000); *U.S. v. Chastain*, 198 F.3d 1338 (11th Cir. 1999); *U.S. v. Clarke*, 24 F.3d 257 (D.C. Cir. 1994). The mere occurrence of misconduct is not sufficient to require the granting of the motion because the adverse effect usually can be reduced by providing the jurors with a curative instruction to disregard the misconduct, by admonishing the offending person and/or by granting a continuance. *U.S. v. Wadlington*, 233 F.3d 1067 (8th Cir. 2000); *U.S. v. Talley*, 194 F.3d 758 (6th Cir. 1999); *U.S. v. Nelson*, 137 F.3d 1094 (9th Cir. 1998); *Phea v. Benson*, 95 F.3d 660 (8th Cir. 1996); *U.S. v. Sepulveda*, 15 F.3d 1161 (1st Cir. 1993); *U.S. v. Scala*, 487 F. Supp. 2d 454 (S.D. N.Y. 2007).

In criminal cases, the circumstances surrounding a mistrial dictate whether the Double Jeopardy Clause bars retrial. *U.S. v. Givens*, 88 F.3d 608 (8th Cir. 1996); *U.S. v. Allen*, 984 F.2d 940 (8th Cir. 1993); *U.S. v. Bates*, 917 F.2d 388 (9th Cir. 1990); *U.S. v. Dixon*, 913 F.2d 1305 (8th Cir. 1990) (retrial barred by Double Jeopardy Clause where trial court abused its discretion in declaring mistrial).

If the defendant gives consent, express or implied, to the mistrial, retrial is allowed. *United States v. Scott*, 437 U.S. at 100 (ordinarily where defendant seeks mistrial, no interest protected by the Double Jeopardy Clause is invaded); *U.S. v. Gaytan*, 115 F.3d 737 (9th Cir. 1997); *U.S. v. Smith*, 621 F.2d 350 (9th Cir. 1980). If the defendant does not consent, retrial will be permitted only if the mistrial was justified by "manifest necessity." *United States v. Jorn*, 400 U.S. 470, 481, 91 S. Ct. 547, 555, 27 L. Ed. 2d 543 (1971);* *U.S. v. Rivera*, 384 F.3d 49 (3d Cir. 2004) (barring subsequent prosecu-

[Mistrial-Motion]

*The Supreme Court has repeatedly declined to define "manifest necessity" with rigid precision, explaining that "those words do not describe a standard that can be applied mechanically or without attention to the particular problem confronting the trial judge." *Arizona v. Washington*, 434 U.S. 497, 506, 98 S. Ct. 824, 830, 54 L. Ed. 2d 717 (1978). The level of necessity

tion where trial judge *sua sponte* declared mistrial due to unavailability of key government witness without considering available alternatives; he did not act under manifest necessity). Even if mistrial is declared at defendant's request, the Double Jeopardy Clause will still bar retrial if defendant can show that the "conduct giving rise to the successful motion for mistrial was intended to provoke . . . [him] into moving for a mistrial." *Oregon v. Kennedy*, 456 U.S. 667, 679, 102 S. Ct. 2083, 2091, 72 L. Ed. 2d 416 (1982). The federal rules now provide a procedure to reduce the possibility of erroneously ordered mistrial. Fed.R.Crim.P. 26.3 states:

> Before ordering a mistrial, the court shall provide an opportunity for the government and for each defendant to comment on the propriety of the order, including whether each party consents or objects to a mistrial, and to suggest any alternatives.

The dialogue fostered by Rule 26.3 ensures that only those mistrials that are truly necessary are ultimately granted. *Crawford v. Fenton*, 646 F.2d 810 (3d Cir. 1981).

The trial court can reconsider its intention to declare a mistrial until the jury is actually excused. *U.S. v. Smith*, 621 F.2d at 352 n.2.

Treatises and Practice Aids

Wright, Federal Practice and Procedure: Criminal 4th § 440

Wright & Graham, Federal Practice and Procedure: Evidence 2d §§ 5039 *et seq.*, 5193

Park, Trial Objections Handbook § 1:16 (2nd ed. 2001)

---

must be of a "high degree" before mistrial may be declared. *Id.* "Under [this] rule, a trial can be discontinued when particular circumstances manifest a necessity for so doing, and when the failure to discontinue would defeat the ends of justice." *Wade v. Hunter*, 336 U.S. 684, 690, 69 S. Ct. 834, 837, 93 L. Ed. 974 (1949). The manifest necessity standard does not require the court to look at the mistrial dilemma from a single point of view. *U.S. v. Givens*, 88 F.3d at 613. It is a flexible standard which seeks fairness to the defendant, the government and the public interest alike. *Wade*, 336 U.S. at 691.

MODELS, MAPS, CHARTS AND OTHER VISUAL AIDS

See:

Fed.R.Evid. 611(a), 901.

Objection

- Objection. This [*chart*] [*diagram*] [*map*] is not supported by the evidence; it is inaccurate and misleading.
- Objection. This model is so dissimilar to the actual object that it will only serve to mislead the jury.

Response

- The necessary foundation has been established to show that this visual aid [*is a fair representation*] [*correctly summarizes the testimony*].
- It is accepted practice to use [*models*] [*drawings*] to illustrate testimony and argument; we are not seeking to mark this visual aid as an exhibit and the stricter standard of authentication for exhibits has no application here.

Commentary

In contrast with those charts admitted as substantive evidence under Rule 1006 (*see* Summaries), charts that summarize documents or testimony, **already admitted in evidence,** may be shown to the jury under Rule 611(a) as demonstrative aids in the discretion of the trial court.* *U.S. v. Stiger*, 413 F.3d 1185 (10th Cir. 2005); *U.S. v. Johnson*, 54 F.3d 1150 (4th Cir. 1995) (collecting cases); *U.S. v. Pinto*, 850 F.2d 927 (2d Cir. 1988); *U.S. v. Possick*, 849 F.2d 332 (8th Cir. 1988); *U.S. v. Gardner*, 611 F.2d 770 (9th Cir. 1980); *U.S. v. Scales*, 594 F.2d 558 (6th Cir. 1979). Some courts have said such charts are not admitted into evi-

---

[Models etc.]

*As discussed in the Advisory Committee Note to Rule 611, the rule covers such matters as the presentation of evidence, "the use of demonstrative evidence . . . and the many other questions arising during the course of a trial which can be solved only by the judge's common sense and fairness in view of the particular circumstances."

dence, *U.S. v. Boulware*, 470 F.3d 931 (9th Cir. 2006), and should not go to the jury room absent consent of the parties. *U.S. v. Meshack*, 225 F.3d 556 (5th Cir. 2000); *U.S. v. Taylor*, 210 F.3d 311 (5th Cir. 2000); *but see U.S. v. Johnson*, 54 F.3d at 1159 (no error admitting summary chart into evidence; "Whether or not the chart is technically admitted into evidence, we are more concerned that the district court ensure the jury is not relying on that chart as 'independent' evidence but rather is taking a close look at the evidence upon which that chart is based."); *U.S. v. Pinto*, 850 F.2d at 935; *U.S. v. Scales*, 594 F.2d at 564. When Rule 611 charts are used, many courts *sua sponte* will give a limiting instruction which informs the jury of the summary's purpose and that it does not constitute evidence. *Wipf v. Kowalski*, 519 F.3d 380 (7th Cir. 2008) (limiting instruction lessened possibility that evidence would have prejudicial effect); *U.S. v. Bakke*, 942 F.2d 977 (6th Cir. 1991) (jury instructed charts were not independent evidence and were no better than the testimony or documents on which they were based); *U.S. v. Paulino*, 935 F.2d 739 (6th Cir. 1991); *U.S. v. Blackwell*, 954 F. Supp. 944 (D.N.J. 1997).

Demonstrative exhibits may be admitted, at the trial court's discretion, as educational tools for the jury. *U.S. v. Martinez*, 588 F.3d 301 (6th Cir. 2009) (demonstrative evidence is admissible to assist jurors in understanding basic principles); *U.S. v. Two Elk*, 536 F.3d 890 (8th Cir. 2008). A visual aid such as a drawing, chart, diagram or animation will be admitted **as an exhibit** if it: (1) is properly authenticated under Rule 901 as a fair and accurate representation of the evidence it purports to portray (or summarizes correctly evidence of record); (2) is relevant under Rules 401 and 402; and (3) has probative value that is not outweighed by the danger of unfair prejudice *See, e.g., Johnson*, 54 F.3d at 1158–1159; *U.S. v. Fauls*, 65 F.3d 592 (7th Cir. 1995) (in securities fraud case, defense chart showing trades by others properly excluded; trading strategies were dissimilar and there was distinct risk chart would confuse jury); *U.S. v. Gaskell*, 985 F.2d 1056 (11th Cir. 1993) (expert's demonstration of shaken baby syndrome using rubber doll not sufficiently similar to circumstances of infant's death to afford fair comparison; unfairly prejudicial and reversible error); *U.S. v. Johnson*, 362 F. Supp. 2d 1043 (N.D. Iowa 2005).

Use of models, maps, charts, diagrams and other visual aids **simply as illustrations** is also a matter within the discretion of the trial judge. *U.S. v. Crockett*, 49 F.3d 1357 (8th Cir. 1995); *U.S. v. Downen*, 496 F.2d 314 (10th Cir. 1974).

The First Circuit has addressed the proper use of the various evidentiary rules governing the introduction of document summaries. In a case where voluminous underlying records are involved, the key difference between these various approaches appears to be the purpose for which the summaries are offered. Charts admitted under Rule 1006 are explicitly intended to reflect the contents of the documents they summarize and typically are substitutes in evidence for the voluminous originals. Consequently, they must fairly represent the underlying documents and be accurate and nonprejudicial.

By contrast, a pedagogical aid that is allowed under Rule 611(a) to illustrate or clarify a party's position, or allowed under Rule 703 to assist expert testimony, may be less neutral in its presentation. Record support is necessary because such devices tend to be more akin to argument than evidence and may reflect to some extent, through captions or other organizational devices or descriptions, the inferences and conclusions drawn from the underlying evidence by the summary's proponent. In some cases, however, such pedagogical devices may be sufficiently accurate and reliable that they, too, are admissible in evidence, even though they do not meet specific requirements of Rule 1006. *U.S. v. Milkiewicz*, 470 F.3d 390 (1st Cir. 2006) (citations omitted).

Additional References

Graham, Handbook of Federal Evidence § 401:6 (7th ed. 2012)

Treatises and Practice Aids

McCormick, Evidence § 214 (6th ed. 2006)

MOTION TO STRIKE

See:

Fed.R.Evid. 103(a)(1)
Mil.R.Evid. 103(a)(1)

Illustration

- I move to strike the witness's last statement on two grounds: first, it is inadmissible hearsay; secondly, it was not responsive to the question asked. I also ask the court to instruct the jury to disregard this last answer and caution them not to consider it for any purpose in this case.

Commentary

To preserve an issue for appeal, Rule 103(a)(1) provides that a party objecting to the admission of evidence must make "a timely objection or motion to strike . . . stating the specific ground of objection . . . "

Occasionally the jury will hear inadmissible evidence when counsel did not object to a question because:

1. while the question was proper, the witness' answer was not;
2. the witness answered so quickly, opposing counsel did not have time to object; or,
3. the ground for objection was not apparent at the time the evidence was offered (e.g. where subsequent cross-examination demonstrates that the witness lacked personal knowledge and was relating hearsay).

When this occurs, counsel must move to strike the testimony and request the court to instruct the jury that the answer constitutes no evidence whatsoever and is to be disregarded, *see* Curative Instructions, *supra*; *U.S. v. Hutcher*, 622 F.2d 1083, 1087 (2d Cir. 1980) ("Motions to strike and limiting instructions exist to curb the jury's attention to improper evidence.").

In *Jones v. Lincoln Elec. Co.*, 188 F.3d 709, 727 (7th Cir. 1999), the court said:

> . . . we do not believe it to always be the case that an objection has to be perfectly contemporaneous

> with the challenged testimony in order to satisfy Rule 103(a) and be considered "timely." Instead, an objection can still be deemed "timely" if it is raised within a sufficient time after the proffer of testimony so as to allow the district court an adequate opportunity to correct any error. How contemporaneous an objection must be to the challenged testimony in order to be considered "timely" under Rule 103(a) is a question of degree. Asking a court to strike testimony introduced at trial three weeks earlier would, by all accounts, be unreasonable-such an objection cannot be considered "timely" by any stretch of the imagination. On the other hand, petitioning the court to strike testimony offered by a witness at the close of that witness's testimony or prior to the start of the proceedings on the very next day when the witness was the last to testify on the preceding day, is a much closer question. In such a situation, the district court can certainly correct any error by issuing a limiting or curative instruction while the testimony is still relatively fresh in the mind of the jurors.

A motion to strike can be used to challenge documentary evidence. *See New York v. Solvent Chemical Co., Inc.*, 225 F. Supp. 2d 270 (W.D. N.Y. 2002). A trial judge may also strike a witness's direct testimony if he refuses to answer cross-examination questions related to the details of his direct testimony, thereby undermining the opposing party's ability to test the truth of his direct testimony. *U.S. v. Baskin*, 424 F.3d 1 (1st Cir. 2005).

Additional References

Graham, Handbook of Federal Evidence § 103.3 (7th ed. 2012)

Treatises and Practice Aids

Goode and Wellborn, Courtroom Handbook on Federal Evidence Chapter 5, Rule 103 (annual ed.)

Mueller & Kirkpatrick, Federal Evidence, § 5 (2nd ed. 1994)

Wright & Graham, Federal Practice and Procedure: Evidence § 5042

McCormick, Evidence § 52 (6th ed. 2006)

Park, Trial objections Handbook § 1:16 (2nd ed. 2001)

NON-RESPONSIVE ANSWER

See:

Fed.R.Evid. 611(a)
Mil.R.Evid. 611(a)

Objection

- Objection. The answer was not responsive to my question. I move the answer be stricken and the jury be instructed not to consider it for any purpose. I further request the court to admonish the witness and direct her to answer the questions specifically without volunteering further information.
- Objection. I move for a mistrial. The answer was non-responsive and so unfairly prejudicial that a curative instruction cannot possibly remove the harm because [*specify reasons.*]

Response

- The answer was not unresponsive. The witness is entitled to [explain][qualify] her answer.
- A curative instruction will remedy any alleged harm.

Commentary

A non-responsive or volunteered answer occurs when a witness provides information not required by the attorney's question. Any response that extends beyond the specific information sought by the question is objectionable. It is often sufficient for the court to strike the non-responsive answer and to give the jury clear instructions to disregard it. *U.S. v. Carr*, 5 F.3d 986 (6th Cir. 1993). But when the non-responsive answer injects unfairly prejudicial information, mistrial may be warranted. *See U.S. v. Rivera*, 61 F.3d 131 (2d Cir. 1995) (non-responsive answers disclosing that defendant previously was in prison combined with incriminating hearsay information warranted mistrial); *Silbergleit v. First Interstate Bank of Fargo, N.A.*, 37 F.3d 394 (8th Cir. 1994) (new trial ordered in age discrimination case where non-responsive references to plaintiff as rich, Jewish and receiving unemployment compensation were designed to impassion and prejudice jury). When non-responsive answers deny a party effective cross-examination, striking all of that witness's testimony may be required. *U.S. v. McKneely*, 69 F.3d 1067 (10th Cir. 1995) (no error striking witness's direct testimony that defendant was not his source of drugs when he refused on cross-examination to answer questions about where he got drugs; drug source was central issue and government was denied ability to test his assertion); *Denham v. Deeds*, 954 F.2d 1501, 1503 (9th Cir. 1992) (where a witness precludes inquiry into the details of direct testimony and the defense is deprived of the right to test the truth of his direct testimony, the witness's testimony may be stricken in whole, or in part). Striking the testimony of a witness is a drastic remedy not lightly invoked. But when refusal to answer the questions of the cross-examiner frustrates the purpose of the process, striking all of the testimony of the witness may be the only appropriate remedy. *Lawson v. Murray*, 837 F.2d 653 (4th Cir. 1988).

The objection that the answer is unresponsive and a motion to strike are available only to the questioner. Unresponsiveness is not a matter of concern to the opposite party if the evidence is otherwise admissible. Graham, Handbook of Federal Evidence § 611.23 (4th ed. 1996); *see also Charlton Memorial Hosp. v. Sullivan*, 816 F. Supp. 50, 59 (D. Mass. 1993).

Additional References

Graham, Handbook of Federal Evidence § 611.23 (7th ed. 2012)

Treatises and Practice Aids

Goode and Wellborn, Courtroom Handbook on Federal Evidence Chapter 5, Rule 611 (annual ed.)

Wright & Gold, Federal Practice and Procedure: Evidence § 6163

Park, Trial Objections Handbook § 6:16 (2nd ed. 2001)

OFFER OF PROOF

See:

Fed.R.Evid. 103(a)(2)
Mil.R.Evid. 103(a)(2)

Form

- Your Honor, in light of your ruling sustaining my opponent's objection, may I approach the bench to make an offer of proof. I offer to prove by this [*witness/document*] that [*state evidence which the witness/document will present*]. This proof is offered for the purpose of establishing [*state purpose of evidence*].

Commentary

When an objection is sustained and evidence is excluded as a result, the examining attorney *must* make an offer of proof to preserve the error for appellate review unless the substance of the evidence is apparent from the context within which questions were asked. Fed.R.Evid. 103(a)(2); *U.S. v. Kay*, 513 F.3d 432 (5th Cir. 2007); *Faigin v. Kelly*, 184 F.3d 67 (1st Cir. 1999); *Williams v. Drake*, 146 F.3d 44, 49 (1st Cir. 1998) ("It is a bedrock rule of trial practice that, to preserve for appellate review a claim of error premised on the exclusion of evidence, the aggrieved party must ensure that the record sufficiently reflects the content of the proposed evidence"); *Dupre v. Fru-Con Engineering Inc.*, 112 F.3d 329 (8th Cir. 1997); *Holst v. Countryside Enterprises, Inc.*, 14 F.3d 1319 (8th Cir. 1994). An offer of proof serves two purposes: (1) it informs the court and opposing counsel of the substance of the excluded evidence, enabling them to take appropriate action; and (2) it provides the appellate court with a record allowing it to determine whether the exclusion was erroneous and whether the offering party was prejudiced by the exclusion. *U.S. v. Baptista-Rodriguez*, 17 F.3d 1354 (11th Cir. 1994); *Christinson v. Big Stone County Co-op.*, 13 F.3d 1178 (8th Cir. 1994). *See also U.S. v. King*, 75 F.3d 1217 (7th Cir. 1996); *Stockstill v. Shell Oil Co.*, 3 F.3d 868 (5th Cir. 1993) (while formal proffer is not required, the proponent of the evidence must show in some fashion the substance of the proposed testimony).

The offer of proof must be sufficiently detailed to alert the trial judge to the purpose for which the evidence is being offered. *U.S. v. Crockett*, 435 F.3d 1305 (10th Cir. 2006) (proponent of excluded evidence does not satisfy his burden to make an offer of proof merely by telling the court the content of the proposed testimony; rather he must explain what he expects the evidence to show and the grounds for which the party believes the evidence to be admissible). The appellate court must evaluate the trial court's exclusion of evidence by reviewing the contents of the offer at the time it was made. *U.S. v. Hudson*, 970 F.2d 948 (1st Cir. 1992) (in making offer of proof, counsel must be careful to articulate every purpose for which evidence is admissible; any purpose not identified at trial level will not provide basis for reversal on appeal). Once an offer of proof is made, specifying the purpose for which evidence is admissible, all other grounds for admission are waived. A party cannot later complain on appeal that the evidence was admissible for still another purpose because other reasons not raised below are waived. *Tate v. Robbins & Myers, Inc.*, 790 F.2d 10 (1st Cir. 1986) (if evidence is excluded as inadmissible for its only articulated purpose, proponent of evidence cannot challenge ruling on appeal by arguing that evidence could have been rightly admitted for another purpose); *U.S. v. Barrett*, 766 F.2d 609 (1st Cir. 1985) (accused may not substitute new claim on appeal for the one advanced at trial).

The offer of proof provides an opportunity for the examining lawyer to explain why the evidence is admissible. The offer of proof also provides an opportunity for the judge to reconsider the original ruling. *U.S. v. Graves*, 5 F.3d 1546 (5th Cir. 1993). Sometimes, after hearing the proposed evidence, the judge understands why it is admissible and overrules the objection.

Offers of proof must conform to the rules of evidence, and opposing counsel may make other new objections after the offer has been made.

There are several ways to make an offer of proof, each of which occurs *on the record* but outside the hearing of the jury. *See* Fed.R.Evid. 103(c). All these involve an explanation to the judge of the anticipated testimony and the grounds for its admissibility. In making an offer: (1) counsel may narrate the intended testimony for the record; (2) the testimony may be elicited from the witness; (3) the offering attorney may submit a written statement of the proffered testimony; or (4) if the evidence is contained in a document, the document may be incorporated in the record.

A party opposed to the admission of certain evidence may make a request for an offer of proof prior to the testimony of a specific witness, in order to head off the presentation of prejudicial evidence. *See, e.g., U.S. v. Jackson*, 208 F.3d 633 (7th Cir. 2000) (precluding testimony which could not have aided defendant's case).

When an offer of proof contains evidence, part of which is admissible and part of which is not, the court may reject the entire offer since it is not the duty of the court to separate the good from the bad. *Angelo v. Armstrong World Industries, Inc.*, 11 F.3d 957 (10th Cir. 1993); *U.S. v. Willie*, 941 F.2d 1384 (10th Cir. 1991).

Failure to make an offer of proof can be excused if the offer would have been redundant, unnecessary or futile. *Beech Aircraft Corp. v. Rainey*, 488 U.S. 153, 109 S. Ct. 439, 102 L. Ed. 2d 445 (1988) (nature of proposed testimony abundantly apparent from question asked; trial judge and defense counsel cut off explanation); *U.S. v. Jimenez*, 256 F.3d 330 (5th Cir. 2001) (failure to make offer of proof regarding proposed impeachment excused where court sealed witness's mental health records and repeatedly stated that defense objections were preserved for appeal); *R.B. Matthews, Inc. v. Transamerica Transp. Services, Inc.*, 945 F.2d 269 (9th Cir. 1991) (purpose of excluded evidence was obvious; attempts to make offer were denied).

Because of disagreement amongst the circuits about whether a trial court's ruling on a motion in limine preserves error in the admission or exclusion of evidence without a renewed objection or offer of proof at trial.* Rule 103(a) was amended in 2000 to provide:

> Once the court makes a definitive ruling on the record admitting or excluding evidence, either at or before trial, a party need not renew an objection or offer of proof to preserve a claim of error for appeal.

The amendment is intended to govern all evidentiary rulings regardless of when made.

However, the court's ruling must be "definitive", meaning there must be "no suggestion that [the trial court] would reconsider the matter at trial." *Walden v. Georgia-Pacific Corp.*, 126 F.3d 506, 518 (3d Cir. 1997). *See also U.S. v. Carpenter*, 494 F.3d 13 (1st Cir. 2007) (in applying Rule 103, appeals court must pay particular attention to whether the trial court made definitive rulings on the motion in limine); *Wilson v. Williams*, 182 F.3d 562, 565 (7th Cir. 1999) (a definitive ruling is one that is not conditional, contingent or tentative; it "does not invite reconsideration").

Even a definitive ruling extends only to those reasons which a party specifies or the court uses for its ruling. *Walden*, 126 F.3d at 518–19. If new facts or circumstances emerge at trial, the party must renew its offer of proof in order to preserve the issue for appeal.

If there is any doubt that the record reflects a definitive ruling, the safest course is to renew the offer of proof on the record at trial.

[Offer etc.]

**Compare U.S. v. Graves*, 5 F.3d 1546 (5th Cir. 1993) *and U.S. v. Estes*, 994 F.2d 147 (5th Cir. 1993) (if motion in limine is granted, party against whom exclusion operates still must make offer of proof to preserve error) *with Unit Drilling Co. v. Enron Oil & Gas Co.*, 108 F.3d 1186 (10th Cir. 1997) (offer of proof not necessary if the offer in response to a motion in limine adequately explained reasons supporting admissibility and court unconditionally excluded evidence by granting motion). Even in those circuits utilizing the more flexible approach, an offer of proof could still be necessary to preserve the issue for appeal if a motion in limine was granted but: (1) the offer of proof in response to the motion was inadequate; (2) the court's ruling granting the motion in limine was "tentative or qualified"; or (3) if circumstances had changed. 1 Weinstein & Berger, Weinstein's Federal Evidence § 103.21[2] at p. 103-40 (Joseph M. McLaughlin, 2d ed. 1999).

OFFER OF PROOF

Treatises and Practice Aids

Goode and Wellborn, Courtroom Handbook on Federal Evidence Chapter 5, Rule 103 (annual ed.)

Mueller & Kirkpatrick, Federal Evidence, §§ 13 to 16 (2nd ed. 1994)

Wright & Graham, Federal Practice and Procedure: Evidence §§ 5036, 5040

Graham, Handbook of Federal Evidence § 103.8 (6th ed. 2006)

Park, Trial Objections Handbook §§ 1:9 to 1:14 (2nd ed. 2001)

OPENING THE DOOR: CURATIVE ADMISSIBILITY

Objection

- I object; this evidence is inadmissible.

Response

- My opponent opened the door on this matter and I am permitted to introduce this evidence under the doctrine of curative admissibility.

Commentary

The doctrine of curative admissibility can arise in the following way. One party offers evidence which is inadmissible. Because the adversary fails to object or because he has no opportunity to do so, or because the judge erroneously overrules his objection, the inadmissible evidence comes in. Is the adversary entitled to fight fire with fire, that is, to rebut this evidence by testimony in denial or explanation of the facts so admitted? Case law suggests that this is a matter within the discretion of the trial court.* *Beech Aircraft Corp. v. Rainey*, 488 U.S. 153, 177 n.2, 109 S. Ct. 439, 102 L. Ed. 2d 445 (1988) (Rehnquist, J. dissenting) (curative admissibility an "exercise of judicial discretion"); *Tanberg v. Sholtis*, 401 F.3d 1151 (10th Cir. 2005) (when a party opens the door to a topic, the admission of rebuttal evidence on that topic becomes permissible; permissible does not mean mandatory, however; the decision to admit or exclude rebuttal evidence remains within court's sound discretion).

Under the rule of curative admissibility, or the "opening the door" doctrine, the introduction of inadmissible evidence by one party allows an opponent, in the court's discretion, to introduce evidence on the same issue to rebut any false impression that might have resulted from the earlier admission. *Jerden v. Amstutz*, 430 F.3d 1231, 1239 n.9 (9th Cir. 2005). Courts have also said that

---

[Opening etc.]

*When a party is found to have "opened the door", the cases also seem to use interchangeably the phrases "invited error" and "invited response."

where cross-examination has been used to elicit an incomplete picture which gives a distorted impression of a witness's credibility, the opponent should generally be allowed to set the record straight on redirect. *U.S. v. Panebianco*, 543 F.2d 447 (2d Cir. 1976); *U.S. v. Gonzalez*, 407 F. Supp. 2d 375 (D. Conn. 2005).

Many federal courts have used a variety of theories to hold that admission of inadmissible evidence does allow the opponent to reply with what would otherwise be inadmissible evidence. For example, in *U.S. v. Martinez*, 988 F.2d 685, 702 (7th Cir. 1993), the court explained that the "opened door" or "invited error" doctrine provides that, where a proponent introduces inadmissible evidence, the court in its discretion may permit the opponent to introduce similarly inadmissible evidence in rebuttal or engage in otherwise improper cross-examination in order to neutralize or cure any prejudice incurred. *See U.S. v. Acosta*, 475 F.3d 677 (5th Cir. 2007) (defendant opened door for admission of government witness's written statement by discrediting statement during cross-examination of that witness); *Mattenson v. Baxter Healthcare Corp.*, 438 F.3d 763 (7th Cir. 2006) (in ADEA case, employer opened door to what ordinarily would be irrelevant evidence of emotional distress by contending that employee had quit voluntarily); *U.S. v. Burns*, 432 F.3d 856 (8th Cir. 2005) (when defense counsel leaves a false impression after cross-examining witness, court may allow use of otherwise inadmissible evidence on redirect to clarify the issue); *U.S. v. Weisser*, 417 F.3d 336 (2d Cir. 2005) (evidence of defendant's prior conviction for child molestation admissible on cross-examination to impeach defendant's credibility in child sex prosecution, where defendant opened door by testifying he was not sexually interested in minors); *U.S. v. Banks*, 405 F.3d 559 (7th Cir. 2005) (government allowed to elicit testimony re defendant's prior practice of storing cocaine in witness's apartment after defense had questioned her about where she got cocaine she personally used); *U.S. v. Beason*, 220 F.3d 964 (8th Cir. 2000) (by cross-examination of FBI agent which created misleading inference, defendant opened door on redirect to admission of statements by non-testifying codefendant (usually inadmissible under *Bruton*) naming defendant as source of drug money hidden in vehicle); *U.S. v. Hanley*, 190 F.3d 1017 (9th Cir. 1999) (defense opened door to evidence that fraud scheme targeted elderly by asking FBI agent if it was illegal to make cold calls on people, some of whom happened to be elderly); *Reilly v. Natwest Markets Group Inc.*, 181 F.3d 253 (2d Cir. 1999) (evidence of wealth, generally inadmissible in trials not involving punitive damages, admitted to impeach testimony of witness who opened door); *Textile Deliveries, Inc. v. Stagno*, 52 F.3d 46 (2d Cir. 1995) (same); *U.S. v. McHorse*, 179 F.3d 889, 902 (10th Cir. 1999) (defendant's cross-examination testimony that he "was good to everyone" opened door to question about specific wrongdoing against family members); *Spencer v. Stuart Hall Co., Inc.*, 173 F.3d 1124 (8th Cir. 1999) (in age discrimination claim, defense questions opened door for plaintiff on redirect to explain why he felt conspiracy existed to get rid of him); *Griffin v. Washington Convention Center*, 142 F.3d 1308 (D.C. Cir. 1998) (although subordinate's bias is generally not relevant in Title VII case, where defendant submitted evidence of lack of discriminatory intent, court erred in precluding rebuttal; once door is opened, other party can introduce otherwise irrelevant evidence to extent necessary to remove any unfair prejudice); *U.S. v. Roper*, 135 F.3d 430 (6th Cir. 1998) (defendant's testimony that he had not previously engaged in drug transactions permitted government to offer specific evidence of such prior activities); *U.S. v. Baron*, 94 F.3d 1312 (9th Cir. 1996) (although drug courier profile evidence is unfairly prejudicial and inadmissible, government allowed to use such evidence where defendant opened door); *U.S. v. Segines*, 17 F.3d 847 (6th Cir. 1994) (evidence otherwise inadmissible as too prejudicial under Rule 403 may become admissible to rebut testimony that creates a false impression).

The unifying thread of these cases is that the rule of curative admissibility may permit an opponent to introduce similar evidence to combat any prejudice which may result from the original inadmissible evidence.

That one party opened the door, however, does not provide the other party with an excuse to introduce whatever irrelevant evidence it wishes. Once a subject is opened up, evidence by the other party must be within the scope of the evidence originally offered. *See Bearint ex rel. Bearint v. Dorell Juvenile Group, Inc.*, 389 F.3d 1339 (11th Cir. 2004) (the extent to which otherwise inadmissible evidence is permitted must correspond to the unfair prejudice created); *U.S. v. Bursey*, 85 F.3d 293, 296 (7th Cir. 1996) (the Rules of Evidence do not simply evaporate when one party opens door on a specific issue).

A number of courts hold that counsel in a criminal case may waive a client's Sixth Amendment right of confrontation by opening the door. *U.S. v. Lopez-Medina*, 596 F.3d 716 (10th Cir. 2010); *Ko v. Burge*, 2008 WL 552629 (S.D.N.Y. 2008). But see *U.S. v. Cromer*, 389 F.3d 662 (6th Cir. 2004) (a foolish decision to open the door will not cause defendant to forfeit his rights under the Confrontation Clause).

The invited response doctrine was examined in *United States v. Young*, 470 U.S. 1, 105 S. Ct. 1038, 84 L. Ed. 2d 1 (1985) in the context of improper closing argument. The Court said the preferred course is timely objection and control by the trial court but declined to find plain error. The doctrine was roundly criticized by Judge Kozinski in his dissenting opinion in *U.S. v. Wales*, 977 F.2d 1323, 1328 (9th Cir. 1992), where he noted that "[t]his 'opening the door' doctrine has a certain commonsense appeal, but where is it to be found in the Rules of Evidence? I'm aware of no authority for admitting inadmissible evidence just because we think turnabout is fair play."

For cases in which a defendant's "limited but accurate testimony" did not open the door to otherwise inadmissible evidence, *see U.S. v. Osazuwa*, 564 F.3d 1169 (9th Cir. 2009) and *U.S. v. Sine*, 493 F.3d 1021 (9th Cir. 2007).

See also Rule of Completeness, *infra*; *U.S. v. Sutton*, 801 F.2d 1346, 1368–69 (D.C. Cir. 1986) ("Rule 106 can adequately fulfill its function only by permitting the admission of some otherwise inadmissible evidence when the court finds in fairness that the proffered evidence should be considered contemporaneously.")

Certain federal rules explicitly recognize "the

opened door" albeit triggered by admissible evidence introduced by the opposing party.

A prior consistent statement which might otherwise be inadmissible hearsay becomes admissible as substantive evidence under Rule 801(d)(1)(B) when consistent with the declarant's trial testimony and offered to rebut a charge of recent fabrication, improper influence or motive. *Tome v. United States*, 513 U.S. 150, 115 S. Ct. 696, 130 L. Ed. 2d 574 (1995). Where the requirements of Rule 801(d)(1)(B) are not met, a number of courts will allow a party to rehabilitate the witness's credibility by introducing prior statements which were part of the same conversation or document from which impeaching statements were drawn. *U.S. v. Ellis*, 121 F.3d 908 (4th Cir. 1997); *U.S. v. Collicott*, 92 F.3d 973 (9th Cir. 1996) (collecting cases).

Evidence of bad character may be introduced once a defendant has introduced evidence of good character. Rule 404(a)(1); *see Michelson v. United States*, 335 U.S. 469, 479, 69 S. Ct. 213, 220, 93 L. Ed. 168 (1948) ("The price a defendant must pay for attempting to prove his good name is to throw open the entire subject which the law has kept closed for his benefit and to make himself vulnerable where the law otherwise shields him."); *U.S. v. Holt*, 170 F.3d 698 (7th Cir. 1999) (where crime charged was sale of illegal firearm, government allowed to ask witnesses about allegations of sex harassment and failure to pay child support; by calling witnesses to testify to his reputation as law-abiding, defendant opened door for prosecution to examine witnesses' familiarity with his reputation). Evidence of "other bad acts" has been held admissible in an entrapment case because the defendant's predisposition to commit the charged crime is legitimately at issue. *U.S. v. Emerson*, 501 F.3d 804 (7th Cir. 2007) (by asserting entrapment defense in a case involving robbing drug dealers, defendant opened door to evidence of prior involvement in other drug robberies).

Treatises and Practice Aids

Mueller & Kirkpatrick, Federal Evidence, § 12 (2nd ed. 1994)

Wright & Graham, Federal Practice and Procedure: Evidence § 5039

Opening the Door: Curative Admissibility

Graham, Handbook of Federal Evidence § 103.4 (6th ed. 2006)
Park, Trial Objections Handbook § 1:6 (2nd ed. 2001)

OPENING STATEMENT

Objection

- Objection. It is improper in opening statement for counsel to be [*arguing the case*] [*arguing the law*][*mentioning inadmissible or unprovable evidence*] [*giving personal opinions*] [*speculating about our case*] [*making disparaging comments*].

Response

- Your Honor, my comments are proper. I am entitled to [*review the facts and opinions which will be introduced as evidence*] [*discuss the theories of the case and issues presented*] [*refer to the legal issues presented*].

Commentary

The purpose of an opening statement "is to state what evidence will be presented, to make it easier for the jurors to understand what is to follow, and to relate parts of the evidence and testimony to the whole." *United States v. Dinitz*, 424 U.S. 600, 612, 96 S. Ct. 1075, 1082, 47 L. Ed. 2d 267 (1976); *U.S. v. Lizon-Barias*, 252 Fed. Appx. 976 (11th Cir. 2007). The scope and extent of opening statements are within the discretion of the trial judge. See *U.S. v. Salovitz*, 701 F.2d 17 (2d Cir. 1983); *U.S. v. Hershenow*, 680 F.2d 847 (1st Cir. 1982); *U.S. v. Freeman*, 514 F.2d 1184 (10th Cir. 1975).

The opening is not to be used as a subterfuge to present inadmissible or nonexistent evidence to the jury or to circumvent the rules of evidence and professional responsibility. *See, e.g., Government of Virgin Islands v. Turner*, 409 F.2d 102, 103 (3d Cir. 1968) ("The purpose of an opening is to give the broad outlines of the case to enable the jury to comprehend it. It is not to poison the jury's mind against the defendant"); ABA Standards for Criminal Justice 3-5.5, commentary at 100 (3d ed. 1993) ("[T]he prosecutor should scrupulously avoid any utterance that he or she believes cannot and will not later actually be supported with [competent and reliable] evidence.").

What Can Be Presented

1. Facts and opinions which will be introduced as evidence. The facts that can be described include direct and circumstantial evidence and reasonable inferences drawn from the evidence. *Rodriguez v. Scillia*, 193 F.3d 913 (7th Cir. 1999) (prosecutor allowed to invite jury to draw inferences from evidence to be presented to jury); *U.S. v. Roberts*, 185 F.3d 1125 (10th Cir. 1999) (government's opening statement was appropriate prediction of testimony).
2. Case theories and issues.
3. The law. In a jury trial, the judge explains the law to the jury. The attorney, however, can refer concisely to the legal issues in the case, the elements that comprise a claim or defense, and the burden of proof.

What Cannot Be Presented

1. Referring to inadmissible or unprovable evidence. Counsel must not refer to inadmissible evidence or unprovable facts during opening statement. This prohibition extends to evidence excluded by pretrial rulings, or likely to be excluded by the rules of evidence, as well as facts, opinions or inferences that are not supported by the evidence. *See U.S. v. Moore*, 104 F.3d 377 (D.C. Cir. 1997), quoting *U.S. v. Small*, 74 F.3d 1276, 1280 (D.C. Cir. 1996) ("the government must take care to ensure that statements made in opening and closing . . . are supported by evidence introduced at trial,"); *U.S. v. Williams-Davis*, 90 F.3d 490 (D.C. Cir. 1996) (same); *U.S. v. Adams*, 74 F.3d 1093 (11th Cir. 1996). *Cf. Frazier v. Cupp*, 394 U.S. 731, 736, 89 S. Ct. 1420, 1423, 22 L. Ed. 2d 684 (1969) ("many things might happen during the course of the trial which would prevent the presentation of all the evidence described in advance. Certainly not every variance between the advance description and the actual presentation constitutes reversible error, when a proper limiting instruction has been given.")
2. Explaining details of the law or giving jury instructions. While making brief explanatory references regarding the law in the case is

proper, counsel should not give lengthy descriptions of the law or give instructions to the jury.

3. Making argumentative statements. The opening is the opportunity to present the evidence that will be introduced and not to argue the facts, the law or the case. *U.S. v. Gladfelter*, 168 F.3d 1078 (8th Cir. 1999); *U.S. v. Zielie*, 734 F.2d 1447 (11th Cir. 1984) (court can exclude irrelevant facts and stop argument if it occurs).
4. Stating personal beliefs and opinions. The attorney should not give the jurors a personal opinion or belief concerning the evidence or the case.
5. Speculating about the other side's case. A prosecutor in a criminal case cannot suggest what the defense will prove because the defense has no obligation to prove anything. Speculation about the other side's case in a civil matter is argumentative, does not represent what the evidence will show, and is usually improper.
6. Making disparaging remarks. Counsel may not make remarks during opening statement which disparage opposing counsel, the opposing case, the opposing party, or witnesses. Such conduct is improper, unfairly prejudicial and unethical, and may be grounds for mistrial. *James v. Bowersox*, 187 F.3d 866, 870 (8th Cir. 1999) (habeas corpus proceeding where defendant had been called "slime"; "We strongly disapprove of such epithets . . . it is beneath the dignity of an officer of the court to engage in such back-alley name calling.")

While cautionary instructions are generally found to be sufficient to address any prejudice, this is not always the case. *See U.S. v. Steinkoetter*, 593 F.2d 747 (6th Cir. 1979) (where defendant was charged with possession of unregistered firearm, judgment and sentence reversed because of prosecutorial misconduct in opening statement which referred to bombings and resulting murders that were not charged and were not part of prosecution's evidence at trial; cautionary instruction insufficient to cure misconduct because jury could not possibly obliterate such comments from memory in weighing evidence).

Although introduction of plea agreements with truth-telling requirements between the government and its cooperating witnesses typically must await attack on the witnesses' credibility, there are exceptions. If, in opening statement, defense counsel attacks the character and credibility of government witnesses, the prosecutor may rehabilitate those witnesses on direct examination. Specifically, a prosecutor may elicit testimony regarding the truth-telling portion of a cooperation agreement during direct examination. *U.S. v. Delgado*, 56 F.3d 1357 (11th Cir. 1995); *U.S. v. Cruz*, 805 F.2d 1464 (11th Cir. 1986).

Treatises and Practice Aids

Wright & Graham, Federal Practice and Procedure: Evidence §§ 5034, 5036, 5084

Jeans, Trial Advocacy Chapter 10 (2nd ed. 1993)

Park, Trial Objections Handbook Chapter 10 (2nd ed. 2001)

Additional References

Haydock and Sonsteng's Trial: Advocacy Before Judges, Jurors and Arbitrators Chapter 6 (3d ed. 2004)

OTHER CRIMES, WRONGS OR ACTS

See:

Fed.R.Evid. 404(b)
Mil.R.Evid. 404(b)

Objection

- Objection. [*request sidebar*] The question seeks to elicit improper character evidence for the purpose of showing propensity or disposition. The evidence is immaterial to any issue in this case and is highly prejudicial to defendant.

Response

- I am not attempting to cause unfair prejudice to the defendant by showing him to be a person of bad character. Evidence of other crimes is admissible here because [*state specific exception which permits the use of this evidence*]. The probative value of this evidence clearly outweighs any potential for prejudice and a cautionary instruction by the court will insure that the jury does not misunderstand the purpose for which this evidence is offered.

Commentary

Rule 404(b) is a rule both of exclusion and inclusion.

As a rule of exclusion, it expresses the traditional principle that prior misconduct is inadmissible to show criminal propensity, i.e., that the defendant is a bad person likely to have committed the crime for which he or she is presently charged. *U.S. v. Campa*, 419 F.3d 1219 (11th Cir. 2005) (rule is intended to prevent conviction based on theory of "give a dog an ill name and hang him"); *U.S. v. Andreas*, 216 F.3d 645, 664 (7th Cir. 2000) ("Rule 404(b) guards against the impermissible inference that because a defendant committed Crime A at some time in the past, he is more likely to have committed Crime B, the crime charged in the present").

In *Michelson v. United States*, 335 U.S. 469, 475–76, 69 S. Ct. 213, 218, 93 L. Ed. 168 (1948), Justice Jackson wrote:

> The State may not show defendant's prior trouble with the law, specific criminal acts, or ill name among his neighbors, even though such facts might logically be persuasive that he is by propensity a probable perpetrator of the crime. The inquiry is not rejected because character is irrelevant; on the contrary, it is said to weigh too much with the jury and to so over persuade them as to prejudge one with a bad general record and deny him a fair opportunity to defend against a particular charge.

See also U.S. v. Holloway, 1 F.3d 307, 311 (5th Cir. 1993) ("evidence of a prior conviction has long been the object of careful scrutiny and use at trial because of the inherent danger that a jury may convict a defendant because he is a 'bad person' instead of because the evidence . . . proves him guilty").

As a rule of inclusion, evidence of "other crimes, wrongs or acts" may be admitted under Rule 404(b) for purposes other than demonstrating criminal propensity, including, but not limited to, proving defendant's motive, opportunity, intent, preparation, plan, knowledge, identity, or absence of mistake or accident. *Huddleston v. United States*, 485 U.S. 681, 108 S. Ct. 1496, 99 L. Ed. 2d 771 (1988); *U.S. v. Siegel*, 536 F.3d 306 (4th Cir. 2008); *U.S. v. Cruz*, 343 F. Supp. 2d 226 (S.D. N.Y. 2004).

The rule applies in civil as well as criminal cases. *Huddleston,* 485 U.S. at 685–86; *Brunet v. United Gas Pipeline Co.*, 15 F.3d 500 (5th Cir. 1994) (evidence of prior convictions admissible to show towboat company was negligent in hiring crew); *Zubulake v. UBS Warburg LLC.*, 382 F. Supp. 2d 536 (S.D. N.Y. 2005) (defendant employer could not use evidence of plaintiff's prior employment to show she had a propensity for certain performance deficiencies). Evidence is not limited to criminal convictions, but can consist of uncharged crimes, wrongs, or other acts, *U.S. v. Ozuna*, 129 F. Supp. 2d 1345 (S.D. Fla. 2001), which occurred before or after the facts at issue. *U.S. v. Peterson*, 244 F.3d 385, 392 (5th Cir. 2001) ("Our prior decisions clearly allow for evidence of 'bad acts' subsequent to the subject matter of the trial for the purpose of demonstrating intent."); *U.S. v. Germosen*, 139 F.3d 120, 128 (2d Cir. 1998) ("The fact that the evidence involved a subsequent rather than a prior act is of no moment").

The threshold inquiry a court must make before admitting other acts evidence under Rule 404(b) is whether that evidence is probative of a material issue other than character. *Huddleston*, 485 U.S. at 686; *U.S. v. Daraio*, 445 F.3d 253 (3d Cir. 2006); *U.S. v. Bowie*, 232 F.3d 923, 930 (D.C. Cir. 2000) ("A proper analysis under Rule 404(b) begins with the question of relevance: is the other crime or act relevant and, if so, relevant to something other than the defendant's character or propensity? If yes, the evidence is admissible unless excluded under other rules of evidence such as Rule 403."); *U.S. v. Gonzalez*, 110 F.3d 936, 941 (2d Cir. 1997) (To be relevant, evidence need only tend to prove the government's case, and evidence that adds context and dimension to the government's proof of the charges can have that tendency. Relevant evidence is not confined to that which directly establishes an element of the crime). But in *U.S. v. Morley*, 199 F.3d 129, 133 (3d Cir. 1999), the court issued the following caution:

> [T]here is no alchemistic formula by which 'bad act' evidence that is not relevant for a proper purpose under Rule 404(b) is transformed into admissible evidence. Thus, a proponent's incantation of the proper uses of such evidence under the rule does not magically transform inadmissible evidence into admissible evidence. 'Relevance is not an inherent characteristic,' *Huddleston*, 485 U.S. at 689, 108 S.Ct. 1496, 'nor are prior bad acts intrinsically relevant to 'motive, opportunity, intent, preparation, plan, knowledge, identity or absence of mistake.' *United States v. Sampson*, 980 F.2d 883, 888 (3d Cir. 1992). Thus, when prior bad act evidence is both relevant and admissible for a proper purpose, 'the proponent must clearly articulate how that evidence fits into a chain of logical inferences, no link of which may be the inference that the defendant has the propensity to commit the crime charged.' *United States v. Himelwright*, 42 F.3d 777, 782; *United States v. Jemal*, 26 F.3d 1267 (3d Cir. 1994).

Admissibility—Generally

For prior bad acts evidence to be admissible, the Supreme Court has directed that: (1) the evidence must have a proper purpose under Rule 404(b); (2) it must be relevant under Rule 402; (3) its probative value must outweigh its prejudicial effect under Rule 403; and (4) the court must instruct the jury to consider the evidence only for the limited purpose for which it is admitted. *Huddleston,* 485 U.S. at 691–92. Once a legitimate purpose has been identified, the district court must determine whether the identified purpose (e.g., motive, intent, identity, etc.) is material, that is whether it is "in issue" in the case. *U.S. v. Newsom*, 452 F.3d 593 (6th Cir. 2006) (finding absence of mistake not a permissible purpose in felon-in-possession case where defendant's only defense was that gun was not his and that he did not know it was under his seat).

The admissibility of other crimes evidence is, in the first instance, a question of conditional relevancy under Rule 104(b). The trial judge need only find that the jury could reasonably conclude by a preponderance of the evidence that defendant committed or is responsible for the other crime, wrong or act. *Huddleston*, 485 U.S. at 689–90; *Johnson v. Elk Lake School Dist.*, 283 F.3d 138 (3d Cir. 2002).

The standards governing the admissibility of such evidence, while generally uniform in ultimate application, are variously expressed by the different circuits. For example, the Third Circuit has a "four-factor standard governing admissibility of evidence pursuant to Rule 404(b) which requires: (1) a proper evidentiary purpose; (2) relevance under Rule 402; (3) a weighing of the probative value of the evidence against its prejudicial effect under Rule 403, and (4) a limiting instruction concerning the purpose for which the evidence may be used." *U.S. v. Butch*, 256 F.3d 171, 175 (3d Cir. 2001).*

[Other etc.]

*The Sixth Circuit states that the Rule 404(b) inquiry consists of three parts: "First, the trial court must make a preliminary determination as to whether sufficient evidence exists that the prior act occurred. Second, the district court must make a determination as to whether the 'other act' is admissible for a proper purpose under Rule 404(b). Third, the district court must determine whether the 'other acts' evidence is more prejudicial than probative under Rule 403." *U.S. v. Bell*, 516 F.3d 432, 441 (6th Cir. 2008).

In the First Circuit, "[a] two-pronged framework implementing Federal Rule of Evidence 404(b) governs the admissibility of 'bad act' evidence. First, the proffered evidence must not merely show a defendant's reprehensible character or predisposition

Admissibility to Show Intent and Knowledge

Evidence of other misconduct may be admissible to prove both intent and knowledge. *U.S. v. Jones*, 248 F.3d 671 (7th Cir. 2001) (in prosecution for cocaine distribution, no error admitting evidence of prior drug dealing by defendants five years earlier; intent to distribute drugs and knowledge that particular substance is narcotic often are proven through testimony about prior sales of controlled substances); *U.S. v. Hawthorne*, 235 F.3d 400 (8th Cir. 2000) (in prosecution for possession with intent to distribute cocaine, prior felony drug convictions were admissible where defendant's "mere presence defense" put his knowledge and intent at issue.); *U.S. v. Mathis*, 216 F.3d 18 (D.C. Cir. 2000) (evidence of other uncharged crimes or bad acts tending to demonstrate intent, plan, preparation and motive is particularly probative where the government has alleged conspiracy); *U.S. v. Himelwright*, 42 F.3d 777, 782 (3d Cir. 1994) (to admit evidence under the "intent" component of Rule 404(b), intent must be an element of the crime charged and the evidence offered must cast light upon the defendant's intent to commit the crime); *U.S. v. Puckett*, 405 F.3d 589 (7th Cir. 2005) (it is well settled specific intent cases that evidence of past action is probative if used to establish an essential element of the crime charged); *U.S. v. Lattner*, 385 F.3d 947 (6th Cir. 2004) (similar).

---

towards knavery, but, rather, must possess some special relevance to a disputed issue in the case. Even if the evidence so qualifies, it must still run a second gauntlet; Rule 404(b) incorporates *sub silentio* the prophylaxis of Federal Rule of Evidence 403. This means that the evidence, although relevant, nonetheless must be rejected if its likely prejudicial impact substantially outweighs its likely probative worth." *U.S. v. Sebaggala*, 256 F.3d 59, 67 (1st Cir. 2001) (Footnotes and citations omitted).

For standards in other circuits, *see U.S. v. Farish*, 535 F.3d 815 (8th Cir. 2008); *U.S. v. Banks*, 506 F.3d 756 (9th Cir. 2007); *U.S. v. Lombardozzi*, 491 F.3d 61 (2d Cir. 2007); *U.S. v. Simpson*, 479 F.3d 492 (7th Cir. 2007); *U.S. v. Becker*, 230 F.3d 1224, 1232 (10th Cir. 2000); *U.S. v. Chavez*, 204 F.3d 1305 (11th Cir. 2000); *U.S. v. Guerrero*, 169 F.3d 933 (5th Cir. 1999); *U.S. v. Van Metre*, 150 F.3d 339 (4th Cir. 1998).

Admissibility to Show Motive

Evidence of other misconduct may be admissible to show defendant's motive in performing certain actions related to the commission of the crime charged. *U.S. v. Sebolt*, 460 F.3d 910 (7th Cir. 2006) (prior instances of sexual misconduct with child victim may establish defendant's interest in children and serve as evidence of motive to commit charged offense involving sexual exploitation of children); *U.S. v. Kosth*, 257 F.3d 712 (7th Cir. 2001) (in prosecution for making false statements in connection with loans from Small Business Administration, prior fraud conviction and terms of defendant's supervised release were admissible to establish his motive for establishing sham ownership arrangement with wife); *U.S. v. Rush*, 240 F.3d 729 (8th Cir. 2001) (evidence of prior conviction for amphetamine possession helped explain defendant's motive for entering into conspiracy to manufacture and distribute methamphetamine); *U.S. v. Phillips*, 219 F.3d 404 (5th Cir. 2000) (evidence of subsequent vote-buying scheme relevant to establish motive for why defendant put political supporter and his wife on parish payroll in positions where they did little or no work).

Admissibility to Show Identity/Distinctive Modus Operandi

Evidence of other misconduct may be introduced to show a system or course of conduct that connects the defendant to the crime charged. *U.S. v. Price*, 516 F.3d 597 (7th Cir. 2008) (in evaluating probative value of modus operandi evidence, focus is on commonalities between charged crime and other act — not on their differences); *Mack*, 258 F.3d at 553–54 (prior robbery and robberies charged in the indictment were sufficiently similar for Rule 404(b) purposes when trial court found that elements, viewed in combination, constituted a "signature" due to their uniqueness: (i) use of ski mask in conjunction with hooded sweatshirt, (ii) by a person who always burst into bank and leaped over teller counter, and (iii) then leaped over counter to leave; all robberies occurred within short time period in same neighborhood at small banks by perpetrator who used similar commands, collecting the money himself and appearing not to use getaway car); *U.S. v. Murillo*, 255 F.3d 1169 (9th Cir. 2001) (evidence of multiple prior car rentals covering long distances in short times relevant to show defendant's knowledge that drugs were secreted in rental car through demonstration of his *modus operandi* and to rebut defense that purpose of trip was to pick up his mother); *U.S. v. Mills*, 895 F.2d 897, 907–08 (2d Cir. 1990) (indicating trial court permissibly could have allowed proof that process used to make counterfeit bills was a unique one that had been encountered only once before by Secret Service and that on that occasion, the perpetrator was the defendant); *U.S. v. Sliker*, 751 F.2d 477, 486–87 (2d Cir. 1984) (allowing proof of similar fraud where both schemes depended upon use of fraudulent bank checks issued by the same non-existent offshore bank as well as a prearrangement with an "officer" of the bank to confirm the validity of the checks despite the fact that victims (a bank and a diamond seller) were different); *U.S. v. Decicco*, 370 F.3d 206 (1st Cir. 2004) (evidence of prior arson admitted to show common plan or scheme to commit insurance fraud).

Admissibility to Rebut a Material Assertion

Prior misconduct may be admissible for the purpose of rebutting a material assertion by defendant regardless of whether the evidence fits into one of the traditional categories such as motive, intent, or identity. *See, e.g.*, *U.S. v. Verduzco*, 373 F.3d 1022 (9th Cir. 2004) (prior acts used to rebut defense of duress); *U.S. v. Houle*, 237 F.3d 71, 78 (1st Cir. 2001) (in prosecution for conspiracy to distribute drugs, the fact that defendant provided security to same individuals for collection of gambling debt four days before he provided security for cocaine shipment relevant to rebut entrapment defense); *U.S. v. Moore*, 97 F.3d 561 (D.C. Cir. 1996) (prior acts could be used to negate claimed mistake of fact).

Other Uses

The list of permissible uses of evidence of other crimes or acts set forth in Rule 404(b) is neither exhaustive nor conclusive. *U.S. v. Wesevich*, 666

F.2d 984 (5th Cir. 1982). Although not listed in Rule 404(b), spoliation evidence, including evidence that a defendant attempted to bribe, intimidate or threaten a witness, is admissible to show consciousness of guilt. *See U.S. v. Blackwell*, 459 F.3d 739 (6th Cir. 2006); *U.S. v. Copeland*, 321 F.3d 582 (6th Cir. 2003); *U.S. v. Gatto*, 995 F.2d 449 (3d Cir. 1993); *U.S. v. Mendez-Ortiz*, 810 F.2d 76 (6th Cir. 1986) (collecting cases).

Reverse 404(b)

Under what has come to be known as "reverse 404(b) evidence," a defendant can introduce evidence of someone else's conduct if it tends to negate the defendant's guilt. *U.S. v. Della Rose*, 403 F.3d 891 (7th Cir. 2005). *See* 2 Wigmore on Evidence § 304, at 252 (J. Chadbourn rev. ed. 1979); *U.S. v. Stevens*, 935 F.2d 1380 (3d Cir. 1991) (error to exclude reverse Rule 404(b) evidence of similar robbery; evidence offered to show identity, i.e., same person committed both robberies and because defendant was not identified as perpetrator of first robbery, he was not perpetrator of second crime). The same prohibition against using bad acts evidence to show propensity applies regardless of whether offered against a defendant or a third party. *U.S. v. Williams*, 458 F.3d 312 (3d Cir. 2006); *U.S. v. Lucas*, 357 F.3d 599 (6th Cir. 2004) (prior bad acts are not considered proof of any person's likelihood to commit bad acts in future; such evidence must demonstrate something more than propensity); *U.S. v. Reed*, 259 F.3d 631 (7th Cir. 2001) (acknowledging use of evidence in appropriate circumstances but finding no error in excluding defendant's proffered evidence that his brother had manufactured methamphetamine on numerous occasions when brother had not been on defendant's property in many months and drug residue collected at time of arrest indicated recent manufacture); *U.S. v. Walton*, 217 F.3d 443 (7th Cir. 2000) (no error precluding defendants charged with ATM theft from offering evidence of another unsolved ATM theft as reverse 404(b) evidence since it neither tended to prove or disprove defendants' involvement in charged offense); *Agushi v. Duerr*, 196 F.3d 754 (7th Cir. 1999) (Rule 404(b) applies to third parties as well as to defendants) (collecting cases).

Inextricably Intertwined Conduct

Evidence of uncharged criminal activity is not considered other crimes evidence under Rule 404(b) if it arose out of the same transaction or series of transactions and, thus, is inextricably intertwined with the evidence regarding the charged offense. *U.S. v. Parker*, 553 F.3d 1309 (10th Cir. 2009); *U.S. v. Hoffecker*, 530 F.3d 137 (3d Cir. 2008); *U.S. v. Quinones*, 511 F.3d 289 (2d Cir. 2007). *See, e.g., U.S. v. McGuire*, 389 F.3d 225 (1st Cir. 2004) (where bad act is direct proof of crime charged, evidence need not satisfy Rule 404(b)'s special relevance requirement); *Elliot v. Turner Const. Co.*, 381 F.3d 995 (10th Cir. 2004) (in negligence action by worker injured on bridge, prior acts permitted to prove that contractor was ill-prepared for bridge launch); *U.S. v. Maynie*, 257 F.3d 908 (8th Cir. 2001) (evidence that co-conspirator participated in acts which furthered conspiracy [here, shooting colleague who was taking more than his share of drug proceeds] constitutes substantive evidence of conspiracy's existence and does not fall within Rule 404(b)'s exclusion of "other crimes, wrongs or acts"); *U.S. v. Lipford*, 203 F.3d 259 (4th Cir. 2000); *U.S. v. Gibbs*, 190 F.3d 188 (3d Cir. 1999) (similar); *U.S. v. Carrasco*, 257 F.3d 1045 (9th Cir. 2001) (in prosecution for being felon in possession of a firearm, no error admitting evidence of drug paraphernalia seized at time of arrest; firearms are known tools of narcotics trade and evidence of possession of drug paraphernalia is relevant in determining whether defendant knowingly possessed weapon found in close proximity); *U.S. v. Peoples*, 250 F.3d 630 (8th Cir. 2001) (in prosecution for aiding and abetting murder of federal witness, evidence was not "other acts" where other burglaries established motive for murder while robbery evidence showed how killers were paid); *U.S. v. Arney*, 248 F.3d 984 (10th Cir. 2001) (where bank loans were secured by cattle, no error admitting false cattle inventory reports since they were intrinsic to the charged crime of bank fraud; evidence is direct or intrinsic to the crime charged if both acts are part of a single criminal episode or the other acts were necessary preliminaries to the crime charged); *Bowie*, 232 F.3d at 927

(D.C. Cir. 2000) ("Every circuit now applies some formulation of the inextricably intertwined 'test'.") (collecting cases); *U.S. v. Andreas*, 216 F.3d 645, 665 (7th Cir. 2000) (other crimes or acts do not include those acts that are part and parcel of the charged crime itself; they simply are not "other"). *See also U.S. v. Miranda*, 248 F.3d 434 (5th Cir. 2001) (testimony about earlier drug purchases served as background information establishing the connection between witness and defendant); *U.S. v. Angle*, 234 F.3d 326, 343 (7th Cir. 2000) (in prosecution for attempted receipt of child pornography and attempted solicitation of minor, evidence that defendant possessed other child pornography admissible since it "helped complete the story" behind the charged offenses); *but see U.S. v. Harris*, 536 F.3d 798, 807 (7th Cir. 2008) ("inextricably intertwined formula . . . is unhelpfully vague; almost all evidence admissible under the inextricably interwoven doctrine is admissible under one of the specific exceptions in Rule 404(b)").

Rule 403

Compliance with Rule 404(b) does not itself assure admission of other crimes evidence. Pursuant to Rule 403, the court may exclude such evidence on the basis that it is "unfairly prejudicial, cumulative or the like, its relevance notwithstanding." *Old Chief v. United States*, 519 U.S. 172, 179, 117 S. Ct. 644, 649, 136 L. Ed. 2d 574 (1997); *U.S. v. Varoudakis*, 233 F.3d 113 (1st Cir. 2000) (reversible error where testimony that defendant burned his restaurant came from girlfriend/coconspirator who was also permitted to testify defendant confided he earlier had burned his leased auto; government did not need car fire evidence to establish close relationship between witness and defendant because other evidence established romantic relationship); *U.S. v. Gilbert*, 229 F.3d 15, 22 (1st Cir. 2000) (in prosecution of nurse for murdering patients, evidence that she also attempted to murder her husband properly excluded as "too powerful for any juror to ignore, any attorney to leave unanswered, or any judge to guard against."); *Duran v. City of Maywood*, 221 F.3d 1127 (9th Cir. 2000) (in § 1983 suit by parents for shooting of son, evidence of subsequent shooting by same officer excluded since marginal probative value was substantially outweighed by danger of unfair prejudice and evidence would create full-blown trial within a trial). *See also U.S. v. Evans*, 216 F.3d 80, 88 n.6 (D.C. Cir. 2000) (noting that 404(b) evidence of prior acts can only be proven by admissible evidence and not by use of hearsay).

Time of Prior Acts

While courts have said the length of time between incidents affects the relevance of the offered evidence, there is no *per se* rule to determine when a prior bad act is too old to be admissible. *U.S. v. Franklin*, 250 F.3d 653 (8th Cir. 2001); *U.S. v. Rodriguez*, 215 F.3d 110 (1st Cir. 2000) (collecting cases). *See, e.g., United States v. Cotton*, 535 U.S. 625, 629, 122 S. Ct. 1781, 152 L. Ed. 2d 860 (2002) (three to five years between prior fraudulent transactions and charged offense does not diminish probative value); *U.S. v. Cook*, 454 F.3d 938 (8th Cir. 2006) (in prosecution for cocaine distribution, mere possession offense six years earlier was too remote and functionally dissimilar to the charged distribution offense); *U.S. v. Becker*, 230 F.3d 1224, 1232 (10th Cir. 2000) (prior narcotics involvement is relevant when conduct is close in time but four to six years "transcends our conception of 'close in time' . . . "); *U.S. v. Hernandez-Guevara*, 162 F.3d 863 (5th Cir. 1998) (affirming admission of eighteen-year-old conviction under 404(b) to show intent); *U.S. v. Robinson*, 110 F.3d 1320 (8th Cir. 1997) (acts committed within three years prior to charged crime are sufficiently close in time); *U.S. v. Shoffner*, 71 F.3d 1429 (8th Cir. 1995) (approving admission of other crimes evidence for acts committed up to thirteen years before crime charged); *U.S. v. Wint*, 974 F.2d 961 (8th Cir. 1992) (five years is sufficiently close).

Notice

Rule 404(b) requires the prosecution to provide reasonable notice in advance of trial of its intention to present 'other acts' evidence if the accused has requested such notice. The policy behind this requirement is to reduce surprise and promote early resolution on the issue of admissibility. *See*

Rule 404 Advisory Committee Note.

The rule also provides that notice to the defense may be provided during trial if the court excuses pretrial notice on good cause shown. *U.S. v. Lopez-Gutierrez*, 83 F.3d 1235 (10th Cir. 1996) (court held that because evidence was not made available to government until night before trial, there was good cause to excuse the pretrial notice requirement).

The rule imposes no specific time limits beyond requiring reasonable pretrial notice. The Advisory Committee's Note explains that "what constitutes a reasonable . . . disclosure will depend largely on the circumstances of each case."

U.S. v. Perez-Tosta, 36 F.3d 1552, 1562 (11th Cir. 1994) lists three factors to be considered in determining the reasonableness of pretrial notice: (1) when the government, through timely preparation for trial, could have learned of the availability of the witness; (2) the extent of prejudice to the opponent of the evidence from a lack of time to prepare; and (3) how significant the evidence is to the prosecution's case.

Other illustrative cases include: *U.S. v. Spinner*, 152 F.3d 950 (D.C. Cir. 1998) (providing such evidence to the defense in discovery does not satisfy notice requirements; government must specifically disclose the general nature of any such evidence it intends to introduce at trial); *U.S. v. Holmes*, 111 F.3d 463 (6th Cir. 1997) (claim of unfair surprise sufficiently addressed by court ordering prosecution not to call witness for five days, giving defense time to prepare); *U.S. v. Tuesta-Toro*, 29 F.3d 771 (1st Cir. 1994) (defense must present timely request sufficiently clear and particular to alert government that defense is invoking its right to pretrial notification of Rule 404(b) evidence; general discovery request is insufficient); *U.S. v. Matthews*, 20 F.3d 538 (2d Cir. 1994) (notice requirement does not require prosecution to disclose names and addresses of its witnesses); *U.S. v. DiStefano*, 129 F. Supp. 2d 342 (S.D. N.Y. 2001) (government directed to give notice of 404(b) evidence at least ten working days before trial); *U.S. v. Jackson*, 850 F. Supp. 1481 (D. Kan. 1994) (notice requirement is not a tool for open-ended discovery).

Limiting Instruction

When the prosecution introduces evidence of prior bad acts and the defendant requests a limiting instruction, a trial court must immediately provide one. *U.S. v. Hemphill*, 514 F.3d 1350 (D.C. Cir. 2008).

Additional References

Graham, Handbook of Federal Evidence § 404.5 (7th ed. 2012)

Treatises and Practice Aids

Goode and Wellborne, Courtroom Handbook on Federal Evidence Chapter 5, Rule 404(b), and Objs. 62 to 65 (annual ed.)

Mueller & Kirkpatrick, Federal Evidence, §§ 6:42 *et seq.* (3d ed. 2007)

Wright, Federal Practice and Procedure: Criminal 3d §§ 5239 *et seq.*

McCormick, Evidence § 190 (6th ed. 2006)

Park, Trial Objections Handbook Chapter 2 (2nd ed. 2001)

OTHER SEXUAL BEHAVIOR

See:

Fed.R.Evid. 412, 413, 414, 415
Mil.R.Evid. 412, 413, 414

Objection

- Objection. Evidence of other sexual behavior [*or sexual predisposition*] is not admissible. It is wholly irrelevant and unfairly prejudicial. [*The motion required by Rule 412(c) was never filed / the disclosure required by Rule (413, 414, 415) was never made.*]

Response

- [*The responsibility of another person for the act*] [*consent*] is in issue; the appropriate motion was filed and a ruling of relevance and admissibility has been made.
- Prior false accusations by the alleged victim are not considered instances of previous sexual conduct.
- The [*Government / Plaintiff / Defendant*] made the required disclosure under Rule [413, 414, 415].

Commentary

Rule 412, commonly known as the "rape shield law," creates a privacy shield for a complaining witness by restricting the examination of a person's sexual past.

Rule 412 applies to all criminal and civil cases involving sexual misconduct, without regard to whether the alleged victim or person accused is a party to the litigation.

The rule's fundamental premise is that evidence of a victim's past sexual behavior generally is irrelevant to the credibility of her testimony, and that her prior sexual activity with third parties has no bearing on the issue of whether she consented to the sexual violence charged. *Truong v. Smith*, 183 F.R.D. 273 (D. Colo. 1998) (applying Rule 412 and denying discovery request re plaintiff's history of extramarital affairs in action for unwelcome sexual contacts under Violence Against Women Act, 42

U.S.C.A. § 13981).

With certain limited exceptions, Rule 412 bars the admission of evidence "offered to prove that any alleged victim engaged in other sexual behavior." Rule 412(a)(1). "Sexual behavior" includes all activities that involve sexual intercourse or sexual contact or that imply such physical contact. *See* Advisory Committee Note. The Rule is designed to safeguard the alleged victim against the invasion of privacy, potential embarrassment and sexual stereotyping that is associated with public disclosure of intimate sexual details. *U.S. v. Elbert*, 561 F.3d 771 (8th Cir. 2009).

Rule 412 also generally precludes introduction of evidence "offered to prove any alleged victim's sexual predisposition." Rule 412(a)(2). This provision is designed to exclude evidence "relating to the alleged victim's mode of dress, speech or lifestyle," and other evidence that "does not directly refer to sexual activities or thoughts, but that the proponent believes may have a sexual connotation for the factfinder." *See* Advisory Committee Note.

Criminal Cases Under Rule 412

In a criminal case, evidence may be admissible under the exceptions listed in Rule 412(b)(1), provided that the evidence also satisfies other requirements for admissibility specified in the rules of evidence, including Rule 403. The Rule 412(b)(1) exceptions are:

(i) the accused may offer evidence of specific instances of an alleged victim's sexual behavior to prove that someone other than the accused was the source of semen, injury or other physical evidence. Rule 412(b)(1)(A); *see U.S. v. Begay*, 937 F.2d 515 (10th Cir. 1991) (error to exclude evidence of earlier sexual assaults on child victim where, *inter alia*, prosecution expert conceded those assaults could have caused injuries for which defendant was now charged); *U.S. v. Torres*, 937 F.2d 1469 (9th Cir. 1991) (trial court correctly held "source of semen" exception did not apply and properly excluded evidence of subsequent sexual assault which occurred six months after charged crime and at a time when victim's semen stained panties were in police custody; exclusion of past sexual behavior of alleged victim includes all sexual behavior which precedes date of trial).

(ii) the accused may offer evidence of specific instances of sexual behavior by the alleged victim to prove consent. Rule 412(b)(1)(B); *see also U.S. v. Platero*, 72 F.3d 806 (10th Cir. 1995) (where defense was consent and that complainant fabricated rape charge to protect her romantic relationship with another man, jury should be permitted to determine if such relationship existed and to consider such evidence in determining guilt or innocence); *U.S. v. Johns*, 15 F.3d 740 (8th Cir. 1994) (rejecting evidence that victim had in past consented to sex with persons other than defendant); *U.S. v. Saunders*, 943 F.2d 388 (4th Cir. 1991) (defendant could testify to his own prior sexual relations with victim to establish consent but cannot base belief of consent on victim's past sexual experiences with third persons nor submit such evidence; rejecting suggested inference that, because victim is prostitute, she automatically is assumed to have consented with anyone at any time). *See U.S. v. Raplinger*, 555 F.3d 687 (8th Cir. 2009) (consent evidence of prior sexual behavior properly excluded since consent was not a defense to crime of sexual exploitation of a child); *U.S. v. Street*, 531 F.3d 703 (8th Cir. 2008) (same).

(iii) the prosecution may offer evidence of specific instances of sexual behavior between the alleged victim and the accused. Rule 412(b)(1)(B).

(iv) Evidence of other sexual behavior is admissible when exclusion would violate the constitutional rights of the defendant. Rule 412 (b)(1)(C); *U.S. v. Powers*, 59 F.3d 1460 (4th Cir. 1995) (evidence of victim's sexual relations with boyfriend that occurred long after acts for which defendant was charged properly excluded as irrelevant because they could not provide reasonable alternative explanation to defendant's guilt; Fifth and Sixth Amendments require only that accused be permitted to introduce all *relevant* and admissible evidence); *U.S. v. Bear Stops*, 997 F.2d 451 (8th Cir. 1993) (evidence that victim was sexually assaulted by other boys was required under Sixth Amendment to be admitted where these assaults occurred at about the same time as alleged assault by defendant and potentially provided alternative explanation to prosecution evidence that victim exhibited behavior of sexually abused child).

Evidence of consent or that another person was responsible requires proof in the form of specific instances of sexual behavior since reputation or opinion testimony relating to past sexual behavior of the alleged victim is inadmissible. Advisory Committee Note (reputation/opinion evidence has limited probative value and dubious reliability).

Evidence offered to prove allegedly false prior claims is not barred by Rule 412. Advisory Committee Note; *see U.S. v. Bartlett*, 856 F.2d 1071 (8th Cir. 1988).

Civil Cases Under Rule 412

In any civil case, evidence offered to prove the sexual behavior or predisposition of any alleged victim of sexual misconduct may be admitted if the proponent satisfies the balancing test articulated in Rule 412(b)(2). The proponent must demonstrate: (1) that the proffered evidence is otherwise admissible under the Federal Rules of Evidence; and (2) that the probative value substantially outweighs the danger of harm to any victim and of unfair prejudice to any party (a reverse Rule 403 balancing test). Additionally, the rule specifies that evidence of an alleged victim's reputation is admissible only if it has been placed in controversy by the victim.

The following civil cases are instructive: *Meritor Sav. Bank, FSB v. Vinson*, 477 U.S. 57, 69, 106 S. Ct. 2399, 2406, 91 L. Ed. 2d 49 (1986) (employee's workplace behavior highly relevant to question of whether alleged harassment was welcome); *Wolak v. Spucci*, 217 F.3d 157 (2d Cir. 2000) (evidence that female police officer viewed pornography outside workplace inadmissible in hostile work environment case; whether sexual advance was welcome or whether alleged victim perceived environment to be offensive does not turn on private sexual behavior of alleged victim); *Excel Corp. v. Bosley*, 165 F.3d 635 (8th Cir. 1999) (in Title VII suit, no error to refuse to admit evidence of plaintiff's sexual activity which occurred outside workplace); *Judd v. Rodman*, 105 F.3d 1339 (11th Cir. 1997) (in civil case of wrongful transmission of sexually transmitted disease, no error to admit evidence of prior sexual relationships and employment as nude dancer because former was relevant to defendant's liability and latter to damages); *Beard v. Flying J, Inc.*, 266 F.3d 792 (8th Cir. 2001) (in Title VII case alleging sexually hostile work environment, no error to admit evidence of plaintiff's workplace sexual behavior; evidence related to non-intimate behavior in public place that plaintiff did not hide from others, citing *Meritor*, 477 U.S. at 69 ("sexually provocative speech or dress" is "obviously relevant" in sexual harassment cases)); *Socks-Brunot v. Hirschvogel Inc.*, 184 F.R.D. 113 (S.D. Ohio 1999) (in Title VII case, supervisor entitled to show that plaintiff initiated explicit sexual speech with him but not permitted to submit evidence of: (i) sexual conversations with other employees to which supervisor was not party; (ii) allegations of flirting which not even supervisor claimed occurred; or (iii) generalized, undifferentiated testimony that plaintiff used profanity in workplace; new trial ordered); *Blackmon v. Buckner*, 932 F. Supp. 1126 (S.D. Ind. 1996) (in prisoner's civil rights case alleging injuries caused by deliberate indifference of prison official, court ruled certain evidence of sexual conduct admissible, including dispute involving transfer of plaintiff's sexual partner to another cellblock because it created motive for plaintiff to lie and concoct claim).

Notice

Rule 412(c) establishes procedures to be followed in order to determine the admissibility of evidence proffered under the rule.

When a party seeks to introduce evidence of sexual behavior or predisposition of an alleged victim, that party must file a written motion at least fourteen (14) days before trial specifically describing the evidence and purpose for which it is offered. Rule 412(c)(1)(A). The party must serve the motion on all other parties and notify the alleged victim, or when appropriate, the guardian or representative of the alleged victim. Rule 412(c)(1)(B). Before admitting evidence under Rule 412, the trial court must conduct an *in camera* hearing and afford the victim and parties a right to attend and be heard. Rule 412(c)(2). The motion and any related papers and the record of the in camera hearing must be placed under seal unless otherwise ordered by the court. Id. Finally, Rule 412(c)(1)(A) also provides that the court may "for good cause," require a different time for filing or permit filing during trial. See *U.S. v. Seymour*, 468 F.3d 378, 387 (6th Cir. 2006) (testimony of defendant's friend regarding relationship of defendant and victim properly excluded where defendant did not comply with the notice requirement); *U.S. v. Ramone*, 218 F.3d 1229 (10th Cir. 2000) (exclusion of evidence for failure to comply with notice requirement); *U.S. v. Eagle*, 137 F.3d 1011 (8th Cir. 1998) (same); *U.S. v. Rouse*, 111 F.3d 561, 569 (8th Cir. 1997) (upholding exclusion for lack of notice); *U.S. v. Boyles*, 57 F.3d 535 (7th Cir. 1995) (failure to comply with notice requirements); *Sheffield v. Hilltop Sand & Gravel Co., Inc.*, 895 F. Supp. 105, 109 (E.D. Va. 1995) (where defendant filed motion not under seal as required by Rule 412(c), court sanctioned this "callous disregard" by excluding testimony from all employees other than alleged harasser that plaintiff engaged in sexually explicit discussions in workplace); *but see Johnson v. Elk Lake School Dist.*, 283 F.3d 138 (3d Cir. 2002) (despite lack of any formal notice, Rule 415 disclosure requirements not offended because defendant attended deposition and questioned witness about alleged prior incident); *Beard*, 266 F.3d at 801 (failure to follow procedural requirements for admission harmless given plaintiff's knowledge that defendant intended to introduce the evidence); *LaJoie v. Thompson*, 217 F.3d 663 (9th Cir. 2000) (habeas corpus; exclusion of evidence due to defendant's failure to comply with Oregon rape shield notice requirement violated defendant's constitutional rights).

The procedure to determine admissibility under the Military Rules of Evidence is by written motion at least five (5) days prior to the entry of pleas. Mil.R.Evid. 412(c).

Rules 413, 414, 415

Evidence of prior bad acts is generally not admissible to prove a defendant's character or propensity to commit crime. However, in certain cases involving sexual assault or child molestation, Rules 413, 414 and 415 create an exception to the general bar against propensity evidence contained in Rule 404(b). *See U.S. v. Gabe*, 237 F.3d 954 (8th Cir. 2001).

Rules 413 and 414 apply to criminal proceedings, while Rule 415 applies to civil trials. Rule 413 permits prosecutors to introduce evidence that a criminal defendant accused of sexual assault previously committed a similar offense and allows the evidence, once admitted, to be "considered for its bearing on any matter to which it is relevant." *U.S. v. Guidry*, 456 F.3d 493 (5th Cir. 2006). Rule 414 applies the same rule to cases of criminal child molestation. Rule 415 allows plaintiffs to introduce evidence of past sexual assaults in civil cases in which the claim of damages is predicated on the defendant's alleged commission of a sexual assault. These other instances of conduct need not have resulted in conviction. *Johnson*, 283 F.3d at 151–153 (legislative history of Rules 413 to 15 indicates Congress intended to allow admission not only of prior convictions for sexual offenses, but also of uncharged conduct).

The trial court may admit such evidence pursuant to Rule 104(b) if it is satisfied that a reasonable jury could find by a preponderance of the evidence that the past act was an "offense of sexual assault under Rule 413(d)'s definition and that it was committed by the defendant." *Johnson*, 283 F.3d at 154–155; *U.S. v. Dillon*, 532 F.3d 379 (5th Cir. 2008); *U.S. v. Enjady*, 134 F.3d 1427 (10th Cir. 1998).

In considering whether to admit evidence under

Rules 413, 414 and 415,* the trial court must still apply the balancing test of Rule 403, which calls for the exclusion of evidence whose probative value is substantially outweighed by its potential for unfair prejudice. *U.S. v. Kelly*, 510 F.3d 433 (4th Cir. 2007) (admitting evidence that defendant had been convicted of sexual conduct similar to the offense in question); *U.S. v. Withorn*, 204 F.3d 790 (8th Cir. 2000) (no error to admit evidence of prior forcible rape which bore similarities to charged offense); *U.S. v. Sumner*, 204 F.3d 1182 (8th Cir. 2000) (admitting evidence of prior acts of child molestation relatively recent in time and substantially similar to charged assaults); *U.S. v. Guardia*, 135 F.3d 1326, 1331 (10th Cir. 1998) (noting that "the similarity of the prior acts" to the acts at issue is a factor to be considered in determining their probative value). In doing so, however, courts must balance probative value against the potential for unfair prejudice "in such a way as to allow the new rules their intended effect." *U.S. v. Mound*, 149 F.3d 799, 800 (8th Cir. 1998). In *Enjady*, 134 F.3d at 1433, the appeals court said: "Rule 403 balancing in the sexual assault context requires the [trial] court to consider: (1) how clearly the prior act has been proved; (2) how probative the evidence is of the material fact it is admitted to prove; (3) how seriously disputed the material fact is; and (4) whether the government can avail itself of any less prejudicial evidence. When analyzing the probative dangers, a court considers: (1) how likely is it such evidence will contribute to an improperly based jury verdict; (2) the extent to which such evidence will distract the jury from the central issues of the trial; and (3) how time consuming it will be to prove

---

[Other etc.]

*In the context of applying Rule 415, the Third Circuit has said that in cases where the past act is demonstrated with specificity and is substantially similar to the acts for which the defendant is being sued, it is Congress's intent that the probative value of the similar act be presumed to outweigh Rule 403's concerns. However, when the evidence of the past act of sexual offense is equivocal and the past act differs from the charged act, there is no presumption of admissibility and the trial court retains significant authority to exclude the evidence under Rule 403. *Johnson v. Elk Lake School Dist.*, 283 F.3d 138 (3d Cir. 2002).

the prior conduct." *Accord U.S. v. Benally*, 500 F.3d 1085 (10th Cir. 2007); *see also Frank v. County of Hudson*, 924 F. Supp. 620 (D.N.J. 1996) (civil suit for sex harassment applying Rule 403 balancing test to Rule 415).

Noting that Congress expressly rejected imposing any time limit on prior sex offense evidence, a number of courts have held that this evidence is often probative and properly admitted notwithstanding very substantial lapses in time in relation to the charged offense. *See, e.g., U.S. v. Bentley*, 561 F.3d 803 (8th Cir. 2009) (time lapse between prior acts (1994–1998) and criminal conduct here (2003) not so long to require its exclusion); *U.S. v. Hollow Horn*, 523 F.3d 882 (8th Cir. 2008) (testimony of prosecution witness that defendant raped her eleven years prior to current offenses was relevant); *U.S. v. Kelly*, *supra* (although defendant's prior conviction was twenty-two years prior to crimes charged, that fact alone, given factual similarities in the offenses, does not render conviction inadmissible); *U.S. v. Drewry*, 365 F.3d 957 (10th Cir. 2004) (finding sufficient factual similarity between 25-year-old uncharged child molestation and charged offense merited admission of evidence that might otherwise be inadmissible due to staleness); *U.S. v. Gabe*, *supra* (no abuse of discretion in allowing witness to testify under Rule 414 that defendant, on trial for child molestation, had molested her twenty years earlier); *U.S. v. Meacham*, 115 F.3d 1488 (10th Cir. 1997) (similarity of prior acts to charged offense may outweigh concerns of remoteness in time); *cf. U.S. v. Dillon*, *supra* (admitting evidence of conduct close in time; excluding evidence of sexual assaults more than seven years old).

Additional References

Graham, Handbook of Federal Evidence §§ 412 to 415 (7th ed. 2012)

Treatises and Practice Aids

Goode and Wellborn, Courtroom Handbook on Federal Evidence Rules 412 to 415 and Objs. 85 to 86 (annual ed.)

Wright & Graham, Federal Practice and Procedure: Evidence §§ 5239, 5248,5381 *et seq.*, 5411 *et seq.*

McCormick, Evidence §§ 189 to 193 (6th ed. 2006)

Park, Trial Objections Handbook § 2:13 (2nd ed. 2001)

PAROL EVIDENCE RULE

Objection

- Objection. The question seeks to elicit testimony which violates the parol evidence rule.

Response

- The rule does not apply. Extrinsic evidence is admissible: to prove the meaning of ambiguous terms; to show fraud, misrepresentation, accident or mutual mistake; to show by custom and usage the meaning of these terms in this particular industry.

Commentary

When a contract is expressed in an unambiguous writing which is intended to be the complete and final expression of the rights and duties of the parties, evidence of prior or contemporaneous oral or written agreements, negotiations or understandings that varies or contradicts the written contract is not admissible. *MediaNews Group, Inc. v. McCarthey*, 494 F.3d 1254 (10th Cir. 2007) (applying Utah law); *Cagin v. McFarland Clinic, P.C.*, 456 F.3d 903 (8th Cir. 2006) (Iowa law); *Cherokee Nation Of Oklahoma v. Norton*, 389 F.3d 1074 (10th Cir. 2004); *Webb v. National Union Fire Ins. Co. of Pittsburgh, Pa.*, 207 F.3d 579 (9th Cir. 2000) (Oregon law); *Gebreyesus v. F.C. Schaffer & Associates, Inc.*, 204 F.3d 639 (5th Cir. 2000) (Louisiana law); *Union Elec. Co. v. Consolidation Coal Co.*, 188 F.3d 998 (8th Cir. 1999) (Missouri law); *In re Cambridge Biotech Corp.*, 186 F.3d 1356 (Fed. Cir. 1999) (Massachusetts law); *Horton v. Metropolitan Life Ins. Co.*, 459 F. Supp. 2d 1246 (M.D. Fla. 2006) (established rules of contract interpretation); *Borough of Lansdale v. PP & L, Inc.*, 426 F. Supp. 2d 264 (E.D. Pa. 2006) (Pennsylvania law); *Miller v. Liberty Mut. Ins. Co.*, 393 F. Supp. 2d 399 (S.D. W. Va. 2005) (West Virginia law); *Holloway v. King*, 361 F. Supp. 2d 351 (S.D. N.Y. 2005) (New York law); *In re Sulzer Orthopedics, Inc. Hip Prosthesis and Knee Prosthesis Products Liability Litigation*, 335 F. Supp. 2d 830 (N.D. Ohio 2004) (Oklahoma law). The primary purpose of the rule is to preserve the integrity of written contracts by preventing the contracting parties from changing the meaning of the contract through extraneous information. *North American Sav. Bank v. Resolution Trust Corp.*, 65 F.3d 111 (8th Cir. 1995) (Missouri law); *Iconix, Inc. v. Tokuda*, 457 F. Supp. 2d 969 (N.D. Cal. 2006) (California law). Despite its name, the parol evidence rule is not a discretionary rule of evidence but rather an element of substantive state contract law. *See Glazer v. Lehman Bros., Inc.*, 394 F.3d 444 (6th Cir. 2005) (Ohio law); *Electrical Distributors, Inc. v. SFR, Inc.*, 166 F.3d 1074 (10th Cir. 1999) (Colorado law); *Johnson Enterprises of Jacksonville, Inc. v. FPL Group, Inc.*, 162 F.3d 1290 (11th Cir. 1998) (Florida law); *Crockett & Myers, Ltd. v. Napier, Fitzgerald & Kirby, LLP*, 440 F. Supp. 2d 1184 (D. Nev. 2006) (Nevada law); *Fourth Toro Family Ltd. Partnership v. PV Bakery, Inc.*, 88 F. Supp. 2d 188 (S.D. N.Y. 2000) (New York law); *Lincoln Ben. Life Co. v. Edwards*, 45 F. Supp. 2d 722 (D. Neb. 1999) (Nebraska law). The parol evidence rule does not preclude the admission of evidence to establish whether the parties *intended* the writing to be a complete embodiment of their agreement. *Cook v. Little Caesar Enterprises, Inc.*, 210 F.3d 653 (6th Cir. 2000) (Michigan law); *Brantley Venture Partners II, L.P. v. Dauphin Deposit Bank and Trust Co.*, 7 F. Supp. 2d 936 (N.D. Ohio 1998) (Ohio law).

There are, however, fairly well-defined situations in which parol evidence is admissible and the rule excluding it does not apply:

- Ambiguity — where the agreement is ambiguous, parol evidence is admissible to explain the agreement and resolve ambiguities in order to determine the meaning of the parties. *Ms. Liberty Inc. v. Eyelematic Mfg. Co., Inc.*, 931 F. Supp. 264 (S.D. N.Y. 1996) (Connecticut law).

  Whether an ambiguity exists is to be determined by the court as a question of law. *Scrivner v. Sonat Exploration Co.*, 242 F.3d 1288 (10th Cir. 2001) (Oklahoma law); *Nautilus Ins. Co. v. Jabar*, 188 F.3d 27 (1st Cir. 1999) (Maine law); *Michalski v. Bank of America Arizona*, 66 F.3d 993 (8th Cir. 1995) (Minnesota law); *Command Cinema Corp. v. VCA Labs, Inc.*, 464 F. Supp. 2d 191 (S.D. N.Y. 2006)

(New York law); *Kay-Cee Enterprises, Inc. v. Amoco Oil Co.*, 45 F. Supp. 2d 840 (D. Kan. 1999) (Kansas law). To determine whether a contract is ambiguous, the court must look at the contract as a whole and not at isolated portions of it. *PlaNet Productions, Inc. v. Shank*, 119 F.3d 729 (8th Cir. 1997) (Missouri law); *Mustang Tractor & Equipment Co. v. Liberty Mut. Ins. Co.*, 76 F.3d 89 (5th Cir. 1996) (Texas law). A contract will be found to be ambiguous if, and only if: (i) it is reasonably or fairly susceptible of different constructions and is capable of being understood in more senses than one or (ii) it is obscure in meaning through indefiniteness of expression. *In re Heine Feedlot Co.*, 107 F.3d 622 (8th Cir. 1997) (South Dakota law); *Duquesne Light Co. v. Westinghouse Elec. Corp.*, 66 F.3d 604 (3d Cir. 1995) (Pennsylvania law); *Constellation Power Source, Inc. v. Select Energy, Inc.*, 467 F. Supp. 2d 187 (D. Conn. 2006) (New York law); *Brown v. Holy Name Church*, 80 F. Supp. 2d 1261 (D. Wyo. 2000) (Wyoming law); *MAN Roland Inc. v. Quantum Color Corp.*, 57 F. Supp. 2d 568 (N.D. Ill. 1999) (Illinois law). A contract is not ambiguous if the court can determine its meaning without any guide other than a knowledge of the facts on which, from the nature of the language in general, its meaning depends. A contract is not rendered ambiguous by the mere fact that the parties do not agree upon the proper construction. *McNamara v. Tourneau, Inc.*, 464 F. Supp. 2d 232 (S.D. N.Y. 2006) (New York law); *Deal v. Consumer Programs, Inc.*, 458 F. Supp. 2d 970 (E.D. Mo. 2005) (Missouri law); *Barnes v. Forest Hills Inv., Inc.*, 11 F. Supp. 2d 699 (E.D. Tex. 1998) (Texas law). One party's unilateral subjective impressions or private intentions, without more, are insufficient to create an ambiguity in light of clear contract language. *Bonham v. Indemnity Ins. Co. of North America*, 507 F. Supp. 2d 1196 (D.N.M. 2007) (New Mexico law).

Note: A number of jurisdictions recognize the doctrine of latent ambiguity which allows consideration of extrinsic evidence "to demonstrate that although the contract looks clear, anyone who understood the context of its creation would understand that it doesn't mean what it seems to mean." *Mathews v. Sears Pension Plan*, 144 F.3d 461, 466 (7th Cir. 1998). *See, e.g.*, *Texas v. American Tobacco Co.*, 463 F.3d 399 (5th Cir. 2006); *Bock v. Computer Associates Intern., Inc.*, 257 F.3d 700 (7th Cir. 2001) (extrinsic evidence can, in some circumstances, be admissible to establish an ambiguity when it is objective and does not depend on the credibility of the testimony of an interested party); *Lincoln Elec. Co. v. St. Paul Fire and Marine Ins. Co.*, 210 F.3d 672, 684 n.12 (6th Cir. 2000) (discussing latent ambiguity and collecting cases); *National Utility Service, Inc. v. Chesapeake Corp.*, 45 F. Supp. 2d 438 (D.N.J. 1999) (extrinsic evidence may reveal ambiguity that was not evident from face of contract because it may demonstrate that from the linguistic reference point of the parties, contract is susceptible of different meanings).

- Fraud and misrepresentation — the parol evidence rule does not exclude evidence offered to prove that one of the parties was induced to enter the contract through a fraudulent misstatement of fact or misrepresentation of the other party. *Philips Medical Capital, LLC v. Medical Insights Diagnostics Center, Inc.*, 471 F. Supp. 2d 1035 (N.D. Cal. 2007) (California law); *Ramada Franchise Systems, Inc. v. Tresprop, Ltd.*, 188 F.R.D. 610 (D. Kan. 1999) (Kansas law); *Alphagraphics Franchising, Inc. v. Whaler Graphics, Inc.*, 840 F. Supp. 708 (D. Ariz. 1993) (Arizona law).
- Accident or mutual mistake — parol evidence is admissible to show that contract terms were omitted from the agreement by accident or mutual mistake. *Lawyers Title Ins. Co. v. Golf Links Development Corp.*, 87 F. Supp. 2d 505 (W.D. N.C. 1999) (North Carolina law).
- Custom and usage — by custom and usage in particular trades and businesses, certain words acquire a meaning different from their dictionary definition or the meaning as used generally. Parol evidence of custom and usage is admissible to show that even ordinary words

in common use were included in the written contract to designate a performance other than that which would ordinarily be ascribed to them. *Adobe Systems Inc. v. One Stop Micro, Inc.*, 84 F. Supp. 2d 1086 (N.D. Cal. 2000) (California law: evidence of trade usage demonstrates that sales terminology is frequently used in connection with what are actually software licensing agreements); *Brammer-Hoelter v. Twin Peaks Charter Academy*, 492 F.3d 1192 (10th Cir. 2007) (Colorado law: if the relevant contract provision is unambiguous, the course of dealing may not override the document's plain meaning); *Roy F. Weston Services, Inc. v. Halliburton NUS Environmental Corp.*, 839 F. Supp. 1144 (E.D. Pa. 1993) (Pennsylvania law: custom and practice may be admitted to assist in contract interpretation but such evidence may not prevail over unambiguous language of contract).

Treatises and Practice Aids

Wright & Graham, Federal Practice and Procedure: Evidence §§ 5001 *et seq.*, 5200 *et seq.*

Park, Trial Objections Handbook § 9:14 (2nd ed. 2001)

PERSONAL KNOWLEDGE

See:

Fed.R.Evid. 602
Mil.R.Evid. 602

Objection

- [*To a question*] Objection. It has not been established that the witness has the personal knowledge to be able to answer that question. Any answer will be purely speculative.
- [*To an answer*] Objection. The answer demonstrates that the witness lacks personal knowledge and that her response was purely speculative. I move the answer be stricken and the jury be instructed not to consider it for any purpose.

Response

- The witness does have firsthand knowledge. To the extent that she has expressed any hesitancy or uncertainty, that goes only to the weight of the evidence and not its admissibility.

Commentary

A witness may not testify to any matter unless evidence is introduced which is sufficient to support a finding that the witness has personal knowledge of the matter. The threshold for admitting testimony under Rule 602 is low. *U.S. v. Franklin*, 415 F.3d 537 (6th Cir. 2005). Evidence to prove personal knowledge may, but need not, consist of the witness's own testimony. Fed.R.Evid. 602; *Hilgraeve, Inc. v. Symantec Corp.*, 271 F. Supp. 2d 964 (E.D. Mich. 2003) (personal knowledge may be proved by witness's own testimony but he must still set forth a factual basis for his claim of personal knowledge). "Personal knowledge" means a present recollection of an impression derived from the exercise of the witness's own senses. 2 Wigmore, Evidence § 657 at 762 (3d ed. 1940). Because most knowledge is inferential, personal knowledge includes opinions and inferences grounded in observations or other first-hand experiences. *U.S.*

v. Joy, 192 F.3d 761 (7th Cir. 1999) (portion of 911 call referring to burglaries was supported by sufficient circumstantial evidence to make caller's inference reasonable); *U.S. v. Cantu*, 167 F.3d 198 (5th Cir. 1999) (no error for witness to testify that defendant was boss of drug operation based on her personal observations of his interaction with others); *Bohannon v. Pegelow*, 652 F.2d 729 (7th Cir. 1981) (permitting witness who observed arrest to testify she believed it was motivated by racial prejudice); *PAS Communications, Inc. v. Sprint Corp.*, 139 F. Supp. 2d 1149, 1181 (D. Kan. 2001) (inferences and opinions must be grounded in observation or other first-hand personal experience; they must not be flights of fancy, speculations, hunches, intuitions, or rumors about matters remote from that experience).

"Absolute certainty either of observation or of recollection is not required to establish personal knowledge. All that is required is an opportunity to observe and a belief that what is related depicts the perception." Graham, Handbook of Federal Evidence § 602.02 at 28 (5th ed. 2001); *M. B. A. F. B. Federal Credit Union v. Cumis Ins. Soc., Inc.*, 681 F.2d 930 (4th Cir. 1982). Thus, where a witness has observed an occurrence and formed an impression of it, the fact that, at the trial, due to the passage of time and the fading of memory, she is not able to state with positive or absolute certainty exactly what she observed, but only what "I think" or "I vaguely remember" occurred, will not preclude the introduction of the witness's testimony. *See, e.g., Sheek v. Asia Badger, Inc.*, 235 F.3d 687 (1st Cir. 2000) (the fact that witness was unable to specify the dates on which he saw work being done may affect weight, but not admissibility of his testimony); *U.S. v. Sinclair*, 109 F.3d 1527 (10th Cir. 1997) (fact that witness had been under influence of drugs did not render her incompetent; reliability of memory was jury question); *Barto v. Armstrong World Industries, Inc.*, 923 F. Supp. 1442 (D.N.M. 1996) (although witness's heavily medicated state and occasionally uncertain testimony raised questions of credibility, those questions go to weight and not to admissibility).

Opinion testimony by a lay witness may be admissible only if it is based on first-hand knowledge or observation. Rule 701(a); *U.S. v. Espino*, 317 F.3d 788 (8th Cir. 2003); *Stagman v. Ryan*, 176 F.3d 986 (7th Cir. 1999); *U.S. v. Marshall*, 173 F.3d 1312 (11th Cir. 1999); *U.S. v. Wirtz*, 357 F. Supp. 2d 1164 (D. Minn. 2005).

Testimony should not be excluded for lack of personal knowledge unless the court first finds that no reasonable juror could believe the witness had the ability and opportunity to perceive the event or matter in question. *U.S. v. Franklin*, 415 F.3d at 549.

When opposing counsel believes the witness lacks personal knowledge, she should object pursuant to Rule 602 and request voir dire of the witness to establish that the witness is not competent. When lack of personal knowledge is established by cross-examination, a motion to strike the witness's testimony should be made.

Treatises and Practice Aids

Goode and Wellborn, Courtroom Handbook on Federal Evidence Chapter 5, Rule 602 and Obj. 64 (annual ed.)

Wright & Graham, Federal Practice and Procedure: Evidence §§ 6021 *et seq.*

Graham, Handbook of Federal Evidence §§ 602.1 to 602.2 (6th ed. 2006)

McCormick, Evidence Chapter 3 (6th ed. 2006)

Park, Trial Objections Handbook § 6:20 (2nd ed. 2001)

PHOTOGRAPHS

See:

Fed.R.Evid. 901, 1001 to 1004, 403
Mil.R.Evid. 901, 1001 to 1004, 403

Objection

- Objection. The photographs violate Rule 901 in that they do not fairly and accurately represent the particular condition at the time of the accident.
- The photographs will necessarily have an inflammatory and prejudicial impact which cannot be adequately addressed by a cautionary instruction. They should be excluded under Rule 403. Moreover, they are cumulative of the testimonial evidence and cannot be shown to have essential evidentiary value.

Response

- The law does not require that every object depicted in photographs remain unchanged from the time of the accident until the photographs are taken. Where there is a change, it can be specifically pointed out. These photographs are readily capable of being understood by the jury and will assist them in evaluating the facts; or,
- Photographs are not excluded merely because they are gruesome. *Government of Virgin Islands v. Albert*, 241 F.3d 344 (3d Cir. 2001). We have limited the photographs to those necessary to illustrate the witness's testimony; their evidentiary value clearly outweighs the likelihood that they will inflame the passions of the jurors. A cautionary instruction can be given.

Commentary

Demonstrative evidence such as photographs and motion pictures must be authenticated by other evidence sufficient to support a finding that the pictorial evidence fairly and accurately represents that which it purports to depict. Rule 901(a); *Banghart v. Origoverken, A.B.*, 49 F.3d 1302 (8th

Cir. 1995). Admission of photographs is a matter largely within the discretion of the trial judge. *U.S. v. Macklin*, 104 F.3d 1046 (8th Cir. 1997). As a foundation, in both civil and criminal cases, a photograph can be authenticated by the testimony of the person who took it. *Young v. Illinois Cent. Gulf R. Co.*, 618 F.2d 332 (5th Cir. 1980). It may also be verified by a person with sufficient knowledge to state that it fairly and accurately represents the object or place as it existed at the time of the event. *U.S. v. Englebrecht*, 917 F.2d 376 (8th Cir. 1990) (elements of authentication established by various witnesses); *Mauldin v. Upjohn Co.*, 697 F.2d 644 (5th Cir. 1983) (admitting photos of tissue slides which pathologist could not say with absolute certainty came from plaintiff but the numbers matched and there was no indication of mix-up); *Rogers v. Ingersoll-Rand Co.*, 971 F. Supp. 4 (D.D.C. 1997) (so long as scenes depicted accurately represent what they are alleged to portray, there is no requirement that individual who actually took pictures testify at trial to lay foundation). If there is a difference or change, the difference or change should be specifically identified and made capable of being clearly understood and appreciated by the factfinder. *U.S. v. Tirrell*, 120 F.3d 670 (7th Cir. 1997) (differences pointed out to jury); *U.S. v. Crockett*, 49 F.3d 1357 (8th Cir. 1995) (same).

Photographs are subject to the best evidence requirement of production of the original. Rule 1002. This is usually of no significance since a duplicate is also admissible to the same extent as an original unless: (1) a genuine question is raised as to the authenticity of the original, or (2) under the circumstances it would be unfair to admit the duplicate in lieu of the original. Rule 1003.

Videotape evidence is categorized as photographic evidence under Rule 1001(2). *See, e.g., Deters v. Equifax Credit Information Services, Inc.*, 202 F.3d 1262 (10th Cir. 2000).

In civil and criminal matters, and especially with regard to photographs of a corpse or gruesome injuries, the court must balance whether the probative value of the evidence is substantially outweighed by the danger of unfair prejudice. Rule 403. *See, e.g., Wilson v. Sirmons*, 536 F.3d 1064 (10th Cir. 2008) (where victim was beaten to death, photos of bloody head allowed medical examiner to show injuries caused by baseball bat and were probative of defendant's intent to kill); *Rousan v. Roper*, 436 F.3d 951 (8th Cir. 2006) (photos of severely decomposed bodies corroborated testimony of key witness, aided jury in understanding pathologist's testimony and assisted proof that killing was deliberate); *U.S. v. Sarracino*, 340 F.3d 1148 (10th Cir. 2003) (photos of victim's bloodied head and face assisted medical expert's description of fatal injuries and showed victim's appearance at end of fight when defendants abandoned him); *U.S. v. Allen*, 247 F.3d 741 (8th Cir. 2001) (no error admitting graphic autopsy photos showing victim's gunshot wounds that aided testimony of medical examiner and were probative of intent); *U.S. v. Velazquez*, 246 F.3d 204 (2d Cir. 2001) (no abuse of discretion admitting autopsy photos in civil rights action for death of prisoner; extent of injuries established cruel and unusual punishment and addressed whether prisoner's signature on cover-up report was coerced); *Government of Virgin Islands v. Albert*, 241 F.3d at 344 (despite videotape's gruesome depictions of crime scene, admission was not abuse of discretion because probative of issues at trial); *U.S. v. Salameh*, 152 F.3d 88, 122–23 (2d Cir. 1998) (no abuse of discretion to admit "significant" numbers of "graphic" and "disturbing" photos of World Trade Center bombing victims, including corpse of pregnant woman, despite defendants' stipulation offer); *U.S. v. Hall*, 152 F.3d 381 (5th Cir. 1998) (notwithstanding defendant's offer to stipulate, photos of decomposed body relevant to victim's identity and cause of death; the fact to which evidence is directed need not be in dispute; unless trials are to be conducted on scenarios, on unreal facts tailored and sanitized for the occasion, application of Rule 403 must be cautious and sparing); *Campbell v. Keystone Aerial Surveys, Inc.*, 138 F.3d 996 (5th Cir. 1998) (excluding photos of decapitated and badly burned body where oral testimony could establish family's mental anguish); *U.S. v. Davidson*, 122 F.3d 531 (8th Cir. 1997) (admitting graphic autopsy photos of victim to explain testimony of pathologist); *Ferrier v. Duckworth*, 902 F.2d 545 (7th Cir. 1990) (district court erred in admitting enlarged color photos of pool of victim's blood where only conceivable reason for introducing them was to inflame jury against defendant); *Alley v. Bell*, 101 F. Supp. 2d 588 (W.D. Tenn. 2000) (habeas corpus proceeding; prosecution virtually forced to introduce photographs of murder scene and numerous wounds on victim's brutalized body to meet its burden of proof on elements of malice, deliberation and aggravating factor of torture; use of graduation photo to remind jury victim was a human being and not just a corpse was entirely proper).

Trial courts approach the admissibility of photographs and films on a case-by-case basis, with the paramount concerns being relevance and the avoidance of unfair prejudice. Courts have accepted: photos of genitalia of small female child which aided doctors in explaining results of their examinations, in sex abuse prosecution, *U.S. v. Two Elk*, 536 F.3d 890 (8th Cir. 2008); surveillance videos of plaintiff where his post-accident quality of life was hotly disputed, *Baker v. Canadian National / Illinois Cent. R.R.*, 536 F.3d 357 (5th Cir. 2008); photos of defendants' tattoos and gold tooth to demonstrate gang affiliation and provide evidentiary support for existence of a conspiracy, *U.S. v. Suggs*, 374 F.3d 508 (7th Cir. 2004); pornographic images, *U.S. v. Hay*, 231 F.3d 630 (9th Cir. 2000) and *U.S. v. Campos*, 221 F.3d 1143 (10th Cir. 2000); computer animation of shooting incident, *Byrd v. Guess*, 137 F.3d 1126 (9th Cir. 1998); still photographs prepared from surveillance videotape, *U.S. v. Triplett*, 104 F.3d 1074 (8th Cir. 1997); photographs of burned prison cell and charred body of inmate in civil rights action charging officials with deliberate indifference to plaintiff's safety, *Haley v. Gross*, 86 F.3d 630 (7th Cir. 1996); day-in-the-life films depicting injuries/ disabilities, *Bannister v. Town of Noble, Okl.*, 812 F.2d 1265 (10th Cir. 1987);* posed photographic reconstruction of accident, *Johnson v.*

[Photographs]

*The Tenth Circuit developed the following four prong test for determining whether day-in-the-life depictions of physical injury should be admitted: (1) whether the tape fairly represents the facts about the impact of the injury or condition of the party; (2) whether the party was aware that he was being videotaped such that he might have been engaging in self-serving behavior; (3) the risk that the jury might give greater weight to videotape evidence because it is more

Matlock, 771 F.2d 1432 (10th Cir. 1985); edited and enhanced copy of videotape, *U.S. v. Beeler*, 62 F. Supp. 2d 136 (D. Me. 1999); photographs of injuries to show nature and extent and to illuminate pain and suffering claim, *Nakajima v. General Motors Corp.*, 894 F. Supp. 18 (D.D.C. 1995).

Excluded were: photographs for which no foundation had been established, *Acosta-Mestre v. Hilton Intern. of Puerto Rico, Inc.*, 156 F.3d 49 (1st Cir. 1998); *U.S. v. Abayomi*, 820 F.2d 902 (7th Cir. 1987); gruesome photographs of victim's decapitated body, *Campbell v. Keystone Aerial Surveys, Inc.*, 138 F.3d at 996; *Gomez v. Ahitow*, 29 F.3d 1128 (7th Cir. 1994); photograph allegedly simulating how truck was loaded at time of accident where truck driver disputed accuracy, *McDaniel v. Frye*, 536 F.2d 625 (5th Cir. 1976); photographs of rejected equipment taken on eve of trial which did not indicate condition of equipment at time of shipment many months earlier, *A-Cal Copiers, Inc. v. North American Van Lines, Inc.*, 180 F.R.D. 183 (D. Mass. 1998).

Treatises and Practice Aids

Goode & Wellborn, Courtroom Handbook on Federal Evidence Chapter 5, Rules 901, 1001, 1002 and Objs. 65 and 66 (annual ed.)

Mueller & Kirkpatrick, Federal Evidence, §§ 551 *et seq.* (2nd ed.1994)

Wright & Gold, Federal Practice and Procedure: Evidence §§ 7161 *et seq.*

Graham, Handbook of Federal Evidence § 401.7 (6th ed. 2006)

McCormick, Evidence § 214 (6th ed. 2006)

Park, Trial Objections Handbook §§ 9:23 to 9:25 (2nd ed. 2001)

---

memorable; and (4) whether the benefit of cross-examination is lost. 812 F.2d at 1269–70.

POLLING THE JURY

See:

Fed.R.Crim.P. 31(d)

Form

- I respectfully request that the court poll the jurors individually.

Commentary

Although not a constitutional right, the right to have the jury polled is of ancient origin and basic importance. *Humphries v. District of Columbia*, 174 U.S. 190, 19 S. Ct. 637, 43 L. Ed. 944 (1899); *U.S. v. Shepherd*, 576 F.2d 719 (7th Cir. 1978). It applies in both civil and criminal cases.

A verdict is not valid and final until the result is announced in open court and no dissent by a juror is registered. *U.S. v. Graham*, 484 F.3d 413 (6th Cir. 2007); *Government of the Virgin Islands v. Hercules*, 875 F.2d 414 (3d Cir. 1989); *U. S. v. Love*, 597 F.2d 81 (6th Cir. 1979).

A jury poll gives each juror an opportunity, before the verdict is recorded, to declare in open court assent to the verdict that the foreman has returned. This enables the court and the parties to ascertain with certainty that no juror has been coerced or induced to agree to a verdict to which he or she has not fully assented. *U.S. v. Sturman*, 49 F.3d 1275 (7th Cir. 1995); *U.S. v. August*, 984 F.2d 705 (6th Cir. 1992); *U.S. v. Gambino*, 951 F.2d 498 (2d Cir. 1991); *Miranda v. U S*, 255 F.2d 9 (1st Cir. 1958).

The right to a jury poll is codified in Rule 31(d) of the Federal Rules of Criminal Procedure. Denial of a timely request for a poll under Rule 31(d) is reversible error. It is also reversible error not to allow the defendant a reasonable opportunity to make such a request. *U.S. v. Harlow*, 444 F.3d 1255 (10th Cir. 2006) (defendant had sufficient time to request poll); *U.S. v. Randle*, 966 F.2d 1209 (7th Cir. 1992) (insufficient time or opportunity); *U.S. v. Hiland*, 909 F.2d 1114 (8th Cir. 1990). A poll under Rule 31(d), however, is not required unless requested by a party and is waived if the request is not timely. *U.S. v. Beldin*, 737 F.2d 450 (5th Cir. 1984). Silence constitutes a waiver if adequate time is allowed for a request. *Id.* Except for the mandate that jurors be polled individually, the method of polling the jury is left to the judge's discretion, so long as the polling process does not coerce any juror. *Gambino,* 951 F.2d at 501.

Polling the jury is not addressed in the civil rules and thus, in civil cases, appears to be a matter which rests within the sound discretion of the trial court. *See Audette v. Isaksen Fishing Corp.*, 789 F.2d 956 (1st Cir. 1986).

The longstanding preference of the appellate courts and most district courts has been for an individual jury poll. *U.S. v. Miller*, 59 F.3d 417 (3d Cir. 1995); *U.S. v. Carter*, 772 F.2d 66 (4th Cir. 1985); *U.S. v. Sexton*, 456 F.2d 961 (5th Cir. 1972). *See also* ABA Standards Relating to Trial by Jury, § 5.5; ABA Standards for Criminal Justice § 15-4.5. In criminal cases, Fed.R.Crim.P. 31(d) now provides that "the court shall, on a party's request, or may on its own motion, poll the jurors *individually*." [emphasis added] A verdict form signed by all jurors does not constitute or substitute for a poll pursuant to Rule 31(d). *U.S. v. Marinari*, 32 F.3d 1209 (7th Cir. 1994) (each juror's signature on verdict form cannot substitute for oral poll in open court because signing verdict form in jury room does not demonstrate uncoerced unanimity, which is the purpose of Rule 31(d)). *Cf. U.S. v. Causor-Serrato*, 56 F. Supp. 2d 1092 (N.D. Iowa 1999) (requiring all jurors to sign verdict form is not substitute for jury poll but is another procedural guarantee that 6th Amendment right to unanimous jury verdict has been protected).

The request for a poll must come between the return of the verdict and the time the verdict is recorded. *U.S. v. Marr*, 428 F.2d 614 (7th Cir. 1970). Once the jury is discharged, it is too late to request a poll. *See Baker v. Sherwood Const. Co.*, 409 F.2d 194 (10th Cir. 1969); 9 C. Wright & A. Miller, Federal Practice and Procedure: Civil 2d § 2504.

In *U.S. v. Singer*, 345 F. Supp. 2d 230 (D. Conn. 2004), the court said while Fed.R.Crim.P. 31(d) creates a procedure by which the judge can test the unanimity of the jury, the procedure is not an evidentiary hearing; the jurors are not witnesses; the judge is not finding facts and the Rules of Evidence do not apply. Moreover, although a judge is not bound by Fed.R.Evid. 606(b) (prohibiting jurors from testifying about deliberations), the judge should refrain from probing into the deliberative process of the jury. *Id.* at 234.

In a criminal case, if the poll reveals a lack of unanimity, the court may direct the jury to deliberate further or may declare a mistrial and discharge the jury. Fed.R.Crim.P. 31(d). The choice is a matter within the discretion of the trial judge, even if a motion for mistrial is made. *U.S. v. Aimone*, 715 F.2d 822 (3d Cir. 1983); *U.S. v. Warren*, 594 F.2d 1046 (5th Cir. 1979).

Treatises and Practice Aids

Wright, Federal Practice and Procedure: Criminal 2d § 517

POLYGRAPH

See:

Fed.R.Evid. 403, 608, 702
Mil.R.Evid. 707

Objection

- [*To a question*] Objection. The question seeks inadmissible evidence.
- [*To an answer*] Objection. I move for a mistrial; or, I move the answer be stricken and request a cautionary instruction.

Response

- The fact that the witness took [or, refused to take] a polygraph test is relevant here because [specify].
- The remark was an isolated one and was not so prejudicial as to merit mistrial. A curative instruction will remedy any alleged harm.

Commentary

Polygraph tests require the examiner to measure and interpret a set of physiological correlates of anxiety in order to offer an opinion about whether the witness was deceptive in answering questions about matters at issue in a trial. Such evidence continues to be generally disfavored throughout the federal court system. *See, e.g., U.S. v. Gill*, 513 F.3d 836 (8th Cir. 2008); *U.S. v. Benavidez-Benavidez*, 217 F.3d 720 (9th Cir. 2000). A few courts, however, have acknowledged certain limited exceptions. *Gibbs v. Gibbs*, 210 F.3d 491, 500 (5th Cir. 2000) (polygraph evidence properly admitted in bench trial on insurance claim; "Most of the safeguards provided for in *Daubert* are not as essential in a case . . . where a district judge sits as the trier of fact in place of a jury.").

The Supreme Court addressed the admissibility of polygraph evidence in *United States v. Scheffer*, 523 U.S. 303, 118 S. Ct. 1261, 140 L. Ed. 2d 413 (1998). In upholding the *per se* ban on polygraph evidence under the Military Rules of Evidence, the principal opinion noted that "there is simply no consensus that polygraph evidence is reliable." *Id.*

at 309. The four member concurrence agreed: "The continuing good-faith disagreement among experts and courts on the subject of polygraph reliability counsels against our invalidating a *per se* exclusion of polygraph results . . . " *Id.* at 318. The Supreme Court indicated that trial courts must look to the rule in their own circuit. "Individual jurisdictions . . . may reasonably reach differing conclusions as to whether polygraph evidence should be admitted." *Id.* at 312.; *cf. Wood v. Bartholomew*, 516 U.S. 1, 116 S. Ct. 7, 133 L. Ed. 2d 1 (1995) (holding that prosecution's failure to disclose polygraph results to defense did not violate disclosure rule of *Brady v. Maryland*, 373 U.S. 83, 83 S. Ct. 1194, 10 L. Ed. 2d 215 (1963) because polygraph results are not "evidence."); *Ortega v. U.S.*, 270 F.3d 540 (8th Cir. 2001).

A Fourth Circuit case holds that the *per se* ban continues in that circuit. *U.S. v. Ruhe*, 191 F.3d 376 (4th Cir. 1999). *But see U.S. v. Posado*, 57 F.3d 428, 432 (5th Cir. 1995) (polygraph tests are no longer *per se* inadmissible; "flexible inquiry" approach as used in *Daubert* should be utilized in deciding admissibility of future polygraph results).

A number of courts have held that polygraph evidence does not survive *Daubert* scrutiny. *See U.S. v. Cordoba*, 194 F.3d 1053 (9th Cir. 1999) (affirming exclusion of polygraph evidence due to lack of known error rate, controversy in relevant scientific community, and paucity of controlling standards); *accord U.S. v. Orians*, 9 F. Supp. 2d 1168 (D. Ariz. 1998); *U.S. v. Pitner*, 969 F. Supp. 1246 (W.D. Wash. 1997); *Meyers v. Arcudi*, 947 F. Supp. 581 (D. Conn. 1996); *U.S. v. Bellomo*, 944 F. Supp. 1160 (S.D. N.Y. 1996); *Miller v. Heaven*, 922 F. Supp. 495 (D. Kan. 1996). *But see U.S. v. Galbreth*, 908 F. Supp. 877 (D.N.M. 1995) (expert testimony re polygraph results met *Daubert* standard).

Other courts have used a Rule 403 analysis as the basis for exclusion. *U.S. v. Robbins*, 197 F.3d 829 (7th Cir. 1999) (danger of causing confusion and speculation requires exclusion of polygraph evidence); *U.S. v. Waters*, 194 F.3d 926 (8th Cir. 1999) (affirming exclusion of polygraph results under Rule 403 as collateral matter); *U.S. v. Thomas*, 167 F.3d 299 (6th Cir. 1999) (unilaterally obtained polygraph evidence almost never admissible under Rule

403); *U.S. v. Bishop*, 64 F. Supp. 2d 1149 (D. Utah 1999) (finding substantial risk that jury would place undue weight on test results).

Polygraph test results have also been rejected as inadmissible extrinsic evidence of character for truthfulness under Rule 608(b). *Maddox v. Cash Loans of Huntsville II*, 21 F. Supp. 2d 1336 (N.D. Ala. 1998); *Pitner*, 969 F.Supp. at 1246 (polygraph result purports to be measure of specific instance of dishonesty which is inadmissible extrinsic evidence).

There is some authority that polygraph-related evidence may be admissible if relevant for a purpose other than the correctness of the test result. *See U.S. v. Allard*, 464 F.3d 529 (5th Cir. 2006) (testimony concerning polygraph examination admissible for limited purpose of rebutting defendant's assertion that her confession was coerced); *Murphy v. Cincinnati Ins. Co.*, 772 F.2d 273 (6th Cir. 1985) (in a suit against insurance company, plaintiff's willingness to take polygraph requested by insurer was relevant to substantive issue of insurer's bad faith denial of claim). In *U.S. v. Piccinonna*, 885 F.2d 1529 (11th Cir. 1989) ("*Piccinonna I*"), the Eleventh Circuit said polygraph evidence "may be admitted": (1) pursuant to stipulation of the parties, or (2) to corroborate or impeach a witness where three conditions are satisfied: (i) opponent has adequate notice of this evidence; (ii) reasonable opportunity for opposing party to administer its own polygraph test; and (iii) admissibility is governed by the Federal Rules of Evidence dealing with corroboration or impeachment testimony (Rules 608 and 403). *But see U.S. v. Sanchez*, 118 F.3d 192 (4th Cir. 1997) (polygraph evidence is never admissible to impeach credibility of a witness); *U.S. v. Wright*, 22 F. Supp. 2d 751 (W.D. Tenn. 1998) (trial court is the final arbiter of the evidence which the jury will consider and cannot be pre-empted by parties' pre-trial stipulation to admit polygraph test results).

Once polygraph evidence has been excluded, disregarding that order can result in mistrial. *U.S. v. Gantley*, 172 F.3d 422 (6th Cir. 1999) (where entire case hinged on whether jury believed defendant's version of facts, deliberately inserting polygraph evidence created unfair bias against government); *Ferby v. Blankenship*, 501 F. Supp. 89 (E.D. Va. 1980) (curative instructions could not preserve integrity of the verdict); *Pettigrew v. Hardy*, 403 F. Supp. 869 (D. Ariz. 1975) (no abuse of discretion declaring mistrial in murder prosecution after defendant gave unresponsive answer indicating he had successfully passed polygraph test).

Additional References

Graham, Handbook of Federal Evidence § 702.6 (7th ed. 2012)

Treatises and Practice Aids

Goode and Wellborn, Courtroom Handbook on Federal Evidence Chapter 5, Rule 702 (annual ed.)

Mueller & Kirkpatrick, Federal Evidence, § 360 (2nd ed. 1994)

Wright & Graham, Federal Practice and Procedure: Evidence § 5169

McCormick, Evidence § 206 (6th ed. 2006)

Park, Trial Objections Handbook § 8:13 (2nd ed. 2001)

PRETRIAL EXPERIMENTS

See:

Fed.R.Evid. 401, 402, 403
Mil.R.Evid. 401, 402, 403

Objection

- Objection. The [*test/experiment*] was not made under conditions sufficiently similar to those of the actual event and, therefore, is irrelevant, misleading and unduly prejudicial.

Response

- Similarity has been established. Any differences between the [*test/experiment*] and the event go only to the weight to be given the experimental evidence.
- Similarity is not required here because the purpose of the test is simply to illustrate the principle of [*specify*].

Commentary

A party seeking to admit tests or experiments for the purpose of showing how a particular event did or did not occur must first demonstrate a substantial similarity of circumstances and conditions between the tests and the event in question. *Jones v. Ralls*, 187 F.3d 848 (8th Cir. 1999); *Pandit v. American Honda Motor Co., Inc.*, 82 F.3d 376 (10th Cir. 1996); *Four Corners Helicopters, Inc. v. Turbomeca, S.A.*, 979 F.2d 1434 (10th Cir. 1992); *Jackson v. Fletcher*, 647 F.2d 1020 (10th Cir. 1981). Perfect identity between experimental and actual conditions is neither attainable nor required. But conditions must be sufficiently similar to provide a fair comparison. *U.S. v. Norris*, 217 F.3d 262 (5th Cir. 2000). When substantial similarity is established, any differences affect the weight of the evidence, not its admissibility. *Randall v. Warnaco, Inc., Hirsch-Weis Div.*, 677 F.2d 1226 (8th Cir. 1982). Although more often addressed in civil cases, the "substantially similar" requirement also applies in the criminal context. *U.S. v. Jackson*, 479 F.3d 485 (7th Cir. 2007); *U.S. v. Baldwin*, 418 F.3d 575 (6th Cir. 2005).

But where the experiment is not intended to recreate the incident but simply to illustrate general physical principles, the similarity requirement is relaxed. *U.S. v. Jackson*, 479 F.3d at 489 (where purpose of experiment is not to recreate events but simply to rebut or falsify the opposing party's sweeping hypothesis, the substantial similarity requirement is relaxed); *Nachtsheim v. Beech Aircraft Corp.*, 847 F.2d 1261 (7th Cir. 1988) (experiments used to illustrate principles underlying expert opinion do not require strict re-creation of prior conditions).

If the experiment is admitted merely to show physical principles, there can be no suggestion that it simulates actual events and the jury should receive an appropriate instruction as to the limited purpose of the tests. *Robinson v. Audi Nsu Auto Union Aktiengesellschaft*, 739 F.2d 1481 (10th Cir. 1984).

Courts have found probative value in the tests and experiments presented in the following cases: *U.S. v. Norris* (in prosecution for false declarations in bankruptcy where defendant claimed he burned $490,000 in currency, no error admitting expert's videotape re-creation; while there were some deviations from actual event, re-creation was conducted under substantially similar conditions); *Jones v. Ralls* (courtroom demonstration of technique used by police in applying a kneeling wrist lock); *Byrd v. Guess*, 137 F.3d 1126 (9th Cir. 1998) (computer animation of shooting incident; all facial expressions removed); *Montag by Montag v. Honda Motor Co., Ltd.*, 75 F.3d 1414 (10th Cir. 1996) (videotape depicting collision between train and auto admitted for limited purpose of demonstrating physical forces at work in accident); *Kehm v. Procter & Gamble Mfg. Co.*, 724 F.2d 613 (8th Cir. 1983) (courtroom demonstration that tampon's cellulose component reacted with vaginal enzyme to promote growth of bacterium causing toxic shock syndrome; dissimilarities with human body environment merely slowed speed of reaction); *Voohries-Larson v. Cessna Aircraft Co.*, 177 F.R.D. 462 (D. Ariz. 1998) (mock-up of aircraft wing permitted to illustrate opinion that plane's fuel system was defective).

For cases in which test evidence was inadmissible, *see*: *Fireman's Fund Ins. Co. v. Canon U.S.A.*,

Inc., 394 F.3d 1054 (8th Cir. 2005) (excluding tests purporting to show that copy machine was cause of fire; tests were not conducted according to recognized national standards and were sufficiently dissimilar to actual accident conditions); *Williams v. Briggs Co.*, 62 F.3d 703 (5th Cir. 1995) (test performed on water heater two years after accident and after subsequent repairs); *Finchum v. Ford Motor Co.*, 57 F.3d 526 (7th Cir. 1995) (although offered only to illustrate principles, sled test was similar enough to actual accident to confuse jury and leave prejudicial suggestion as to how events took place); *Four Corners Helicopters, Inc. v. Turbomeca, S.A.* (experiment conducted on a three horsepower lathe purporting to show that 800 horsepower helicopter engine would not be affected by screw-impeller contact properly excluded); *Gladhill v. General Motors Corp.*, 743 F.2d 1049 (4th Cir. 1984) (accident reenactment so dissimilar it was misleading; in dicta, party cannot evade foundation requirement of similarity simply by labeling test as "a demonstration of principles.").

The Fourth Circuit has cautioned that because videotape simulation evidence has such dramatic power, the trial judge should first view the tape *in camera* to assess its foundation, relevance and potential for undue prejudice. *Hinkle v. City of Clarksburg, W.Va.*, 81 F.3d 416 (4th Cir. 1996).

For cases addressing the issue of the jury conducting experiments with the trial evidence, *see Konkel v. Bob Evans Farms Inc.*, 165 F.3d 275 (4th Cir. 1999) (jury experiments that constitute more intensive examinations of exhibits than examinations made during trial are not objectionable); *U.S. v. Beach*, 296 F.2d 153 (4th Cir. 1961) (remanded for determination; reversible error where such experiments have the effect of putting the jury in possession of evidence not offered at trial).

Courtroom Demonstrations

For a courtroom demonstration to be admissible as evidence, the proponent of the demonstration must show that the demonstration is relevant. *U.S. v. Williams*, 461 F.3d 441 (4th Cir. 2006) (requiring defendant to try on fanny pack in court which police said he was wearing at time of arrest). A courtroom demonstration that purports to recreate events at issue is relevant if performed under conditions substantially similar to the actual events. *Hinkle v. City of Clarksburg, W.Va.*, 81 F.3d 416 (4th Cir. 1996). If there is substantial similarity, any differences between the demonstration and the actual event ordinarily are regarded as affecting the weight of the test evidence and not its admissibility. However, the differences between the demonstration and the actual occurrence may be such that the trial judge is justified in concluding either that the evidence is totally lacking in probative value as to any material issue or that the probative value of the evidence is exceeded by the danger that introduction of the evidence will tend to confuse the issues, unnecessarily prolong the trial, or create a likelihood of unfair prejudice.

Additional References

Graham, Handbook of Federal Evidence § 401.10 (7th ed. 2012)

Treatises and Practice Aids

Goode and Wellborn, Courtroom Handbook on Federal Evidence Chapter 5, Rule 401 (annual ed.)

McCormick, Evidence § 202 (6th ed. 2006)

PRIVILEGE: ATTORNEY-CLIENT

See:

Fed.R.Evid. 501
Mil.R.Evid. 502

Objection

- Objection. The question calls for disclosure of a privileged communication between the witness and his attorney.

Response

- The evidence is not privileged because [the communication took place in the presence of a third party] [the privilege has been waived (specify)] [the communication was made with the expectation that it would be revealed to others] [the attorney was acting in a nonlegal capacity].

Commentary

The attorney-client privilege, the oldest of the privileges for confidential communications known to the common law, *Upjohn Co. v. United States*, 449 U.S. 383, 101 S. Ct. 677, 66 L. Ed. 2d 584 (1981), rests on the need for the advocate and counselor to know all that relates to the client's reasons for seeking representation if the professional mission is to be carried out. *Swidler & Berlin v. United States*, 524 U.S. 399, 118 S. Ct. 2081, 141 L. Ed. 2d 379 (1998); *Trammel v. United States*, 445 U.S. 40, 100 S. Ct. 906, 63 L. Ed. 2d 186 (1980); *Gomez v. Vernon*, 255 F.3d 1118 (9th Cir. 2001). The central concern of this privilege is to encourage full and frank communication between attorneys and their clients. *In re Grand Jury Subpoena*, 419 F.3d 329 (5th Cir. 2005); *In re Grand Jury Proceedings #5 Empanelled January 28, 2004*, 401 F.3d 247 (4th Cir. 2005). The privilege exists to protect not only the giving of professional advice to those who can act on it but also the giving of information to the lawyer to enable him to give sound and informed advice. *Upjohn*, 449 U.S. at 390–91; *U.S. v. Rowe*, 96 F.3d 1294 (9th Cir. 1996). When the privilege applies, it affords confidential communications between lawyer and client absolute protection from disclosure. *See U.S. v. Edwards*, 39 F. Supp. 2d 716 (M.D. La. 1999); *Arcuri v. Trump Taj Mahal Associates*, 154 F.R.D. 97 (D.N.J. 1994). The privilege applies to communications made by the client to the attorney and by the attorney to the client, *In re Spalding Sports Worldwide, Inc.*, 203 F.3d 800 (Fed. Cir. 2000); *Westinghouse Elec. Corp. v. Republic of Philippines*, 951 F.2d 1414 (3d Cir. 1991); *U.S. v. Defazio*, 899 F.2d 626 (7th Cir. 1990), and survives the client's death, *Swidler & Berlin v. United States*, 524 U.S. at 407, 118 S.Ct. at 2086 (1998).

The shelter afforded by the privilege "only protects disclosure of communications; it does not protect disclosure of the underlying facts by those who communicated with the attorney," *Upjohn*, 449 U.S. at 395, unless such disclosure would reveal confidential communications. The client cannot be compelled to answer the question, "What did you say or write to the attorney?", but may not refuse to disclose any relevant fact within his knowledge merely because he incorporated such fact into his communication to his attorney. *Savoy v. Richard A. Carrier Trucking, Inc.*, 176 F.R.D. 10 (D. Mass. 1997); *City of Philadelphia, Pa. v. Westinghouse Elec. Corp.*, 205 F. Supp. 830 (E.D. Pa. 1962). The scope of the attorney-client privilege is fact sensitive and must be addressed on a case-by-case basis. *Upjohn*, 449 U.S. at 396–97.

The party invoking the privilege must prove: (1) the asserted holder of the privilege is or sought to become a client; (2) the person to whom the communication was made (a) is a member of the bar of a court, or his subordinate, and (b) in connection with the communication is acting as a lawyer; (3) the communication relates to a fact of which the attorney was informed (a) by his client, (b) without the presence of strangers, (c) for the purpose of securing primarily either (i) an opinion on law or (ii) legal services or (iii) assistance in some legal proceeding, and not (d) for the purpose of committing a crime or tort; and (4) the privilege has been (a) claimed and (b) not waived by the client. *U.S. v. Lentz*, 524 F.3d 501 (4th Cir. 2008); *In re Grand Jury Subpoena*, 341 F.3d 331 (4th Cir. 2003); *In re Lindsey*, 158 F.3d 1263 (D.C. Cir. 1998); *Hawkins v. Stables*, 148 F.3d 379 (4th Cir. 1998); *U.S. v. Jones*, 696 F.2d 1069, 1072 (4th Cir. 1982); *U.S. v. United Shoe Machinery Corp.*, 89 F. Supp. 357, 358–59 (D. Mass. 1950); *Rivera v. Kmart Corp.*, 190 F.R.D. 298 (D.P.R. 2000).

The content of the communication determines whether the privilege applies. The privilege protects only communications made for the purpose of rendering professional legal services. *U.S. v. Gray*, 876 F.2d 1411 (9th Cir. 1989). If a lawyer is acting in a non-legal capacity, such as a business advisor or accountant, the attorney-client privilege does not apply. *U.S. v. Bisanti*, 414 F.3d 168 (1st Cir. 2005); *U.S. v. Rowe*, 96 F.3d 1294 (9th Cir. 1996); *In re Grand Jury Subpoena GJ2/00-345*, 132 F. Supp. 2d 776 (S.D. Iowa 2000); *ConAgra, Inc. v. Arkwright Mut. Ins. Co.*, 32 F. Supp. 2d 1015 (N.D. Ill. 1999); *Boca Investerings Partnership v. U.S.*, 31 F. Supp. 2d 9 (D.D.C. 1998); *Massachusetts School of Law at Andover, Inc. v. American Bar Ass'n*, 895 F. Supp. 88 (E.D. Pa. 1995). Where business and legal advice are intertwined, the legal advice must predominate for the communication to be protected. *Moore v. Bd of Trustees of Illinois Community College Dist. No. 508*, 2010 WL 4703859 (N.D.Ill. 2010); *Neuder v. Battelle Pacific Northwest Nat. Laboratory*, 194 F.R.D. 289 (D.D.C. 2000).

Several courts have held that, where the client reasonably but mistakenly believes that his or her confidential communication was with a licensed attorney, the privilege still applies. *In re Grand Jury Subpoena Duces Tecum*, 112 F.3d 910 (8th Cir. 1997); *U.S. v. Rivera*, 837 F. Supp. 565 (S.D. N.Y. 1993); *U.S. v. Mullen & Co.*, 776 F. Supp. 620 (D. Mass. 1991); *U.S. v. Tyler*, 745 F. Supp. 423 (W.D. Mich. 1990); *U.S. v. Boffa*, 513 F. Supp. 517 (D. Del. 1981).

The client is the holder of the privilege and he alone may waive it. *U.S. v. Doe*, 429 F.3d 450 (3d Cir. 2005) (privilege belongs to client, not the attorney); *Knorr-Bremse Systeme Fuer Nutzfahrzeuge GmbH v. Dana Corp.*, 383 F.3d 1337 (Fed. Cir. 2004). A client may be an individual or any kind of entity, including a governmental unit, corporation or unincorporated association. *See, e.g., Ross v. City of Memphis*, 423 F.3d 596 (6th Cir. 2005) (municipal corporation can invoke attorney-client privilege in civil litigation; collecting cases and authorities); *U.S. v. Zingsheim*, 384 F.3d 867 (7th Cir. 2004) (privilege covers conversations between prosecutors and client agencies within the government); *Town of Norfolk v. U.S. Army Corps of Engineers*, 968 F.2d 1438, 1457–58 (1st Cir. 1992) (protecting communications between U.S. Attorney and Corps of Engineers); *see also U.S. v. Martin*, 278 F.3d 988 (9th Cir. 2002) (privilege enjoyed by corporation does not extend automatically to corporate officer in his individual capacity); *U.S. v. Toliver*, 972 F. Supp. 1030 (W.D. Va. 1997)(fact that attorney represents union does not establish attorney-client privilege with individual union member). Even if the person or entity does not actually become a client of the attorney, the privilege attaches to communications made while the potential client was consulting the lawyer with a view toward obtaining legal services. *In re Auclair*, 961 F.2d 65, 70 (5th Cir. 1992). Communications made after the attorney has declined employment are not privileged. *U.S. v. Dennis*, 843 F.2d 652 (2d Cir. 1988).

The question of whether an attorney-client relationship exists does not necessarily depend upon who pays the fees. *See Westinghouse Elec. Corp. v. Kerr-McGee Corp.*, 580 F.2d 1311 (7th Cir. 1978) (a professional relationship is not dependent upon payment of fees); *Allman v. Winkelman*, 106 F.2d 663 (9th Cir. U.S. Ct. China 1939) (a lawyer's advice to his client establishes professional relationship though it be gratis); *Hillerich & Bradsby Co. v. MacKay*, 26 F. Supp. 2d 124 (D.D.C. 1998); *E. F. Hutton & Co. v. Brown*, 305 F. Supp. 371 (S.D. Tex. 1969). The identity of the client, fee amount, and general purpose of work performed are usually not protected from disclosure because such information ordinarily reveals no confidential communications between attorney and client. *Reiserer v. U.S.*, 479 F.3d 1160 (9th Cir. 2007); *O'Neal v. U.S.*, 258 F.3d 1265 (11th Cir. 2001); *Chaudhry v. Gallerizzo*, 174 F.3d 394 (4th Cir. 1999). However, some circuits have held that a client's identity or fee information is protected when disclosure would implicate the client in the very criminal activity for which legal advice was sought, *see, e.g., U. S. v. Strahl*, 590 F.2d 10 (1st Cir. 1978), would reveal the client's motive for seeking legal advice, *In re*

Subpoenaed Grand Jury Witness, 171 F.3d 511 (7th Cir. 1999), *Baird v. Koerner*, 279 F.2d 623 (9th Cir. 1960) or would supply the "last link" in an existing chain of incriminating evidence likely to lead to the client's indictment, *In re Grand Jury Proceedings (GJ90-2)*, 946 F.2d 746 (11th Cir. 1991). A number of courts, including the Fourth Circuit, reject the last link rationale. *In re Grand Jury Subpoena*, 204 F.3d 516 (4th Cir. 2000) (client's identity is privileged only if disclosure would in essence reveal a confidential communication, citing *N. L. R. B. v. Harvey*, 349 F.2d 900 (4th Cir. 1965)).

Presence and Activities of Third Persons

The presence of certain third parties, if essential to and in furtherance of the communication, does not destroy the privilege. *von Bulow by Auersperg v. von Bulow*, 811 F.2d 136 (2d Cir. 1987) (law clerks, secretaries and paralegals). Some courts have held that the privilege can attach to reports of third parties (such as non-testifying experts) made at the request of the attorney or the client where the purpose of the report is to put in usable form information obtained from the client. Privilege recognized: *Jenkins v. Bartlett*, 487 F.3d 482 (7th Cir. 2007) (police liaison officer considered agent of shooting officer's attorney); *U.S. v. Schwimmer*, 892 F.2d 237 (2d Cir. 1989) (in RICO case, reports of accountant hired by defense counsel to analyze financial transactions); *U.S. v. Alvarez*, 519 F.2d 1036 (3d Cir. 1975) (psychiatrist hired to aid in insanity defense); *U.S. v. Cote*, 456 F.2d 142 (8th Cir. 1972) (audit of client prepared by accountant to aid attorney in advising whether to file amended tax return); *U.S. v. Kovel*, 296 F.2d 918 (2d Cir. 1961) (accountant, who was employed by tax law firm and sat in on conversations with client, properly refused to answer questions before grand jury). Privilege refused: *U.S. v. Ackert*, 169 F.3d 136 (2d Cir. 1999) (communication between in-house tax counsel and third party investment banker is not privileged solely because conversation proves important to attorney's ability to represent client); *F.T.C. v. TRW, Inc.*, 628 F.2d 207 (D.C. Cir. 1980) (research institute report lies at outer and indistinct boundary of privilege law; where there are insufficient facts to state with reasonable certainty that privilege applies, burden of proof is not met); *Occidental Chemical Corp. v. OHM Remediation Services Corp.*, 175 F.R.D. 431 (W.D. N.Y. 1997) (no privilege where work performed by environmental remediation consultant served purposes other than to assist attorneys in litigation); *U.S. Postal Service v. Phelps Dodge Refining Corp.*, 852 F. Supp. 156 (E.D. N.Y. 1994) (same).

Common Interest/Joint Defense Doctrine

Communications between or among a client or the client's lawyer and a lawyer representing another client in a matter of common legal interest are also privileged. In *In re Teleglobe Communications Corp.*, 493 F.3d 345 (3d Cir. 2007); *U.S. v. BDO Seidman, LLP*, 492 F.3d 806 (7th Cir. 2007); Restatement (Third) of the Law Governing Lawyers § 76. Depending upon the circumstances, this is variously referred to as the "common interest," "pooled information" or "joint defense" privilege. *U.S. v. Austin*, 416 F.3d 1016 (9th Cir. 2005) (joint defense privilege is an extension of attorney-client privilege); *In re Grand Jury Subpoenas, 89-3 and 89-4, John Doe 89-129*, 902 F.2d 244 (4th Cir. 1990) (common interest—civil proceeding); *U.S. v. Schwimmer*, 892 F.2d 237 (2d Cir. 1989) (common interest—criminal case); *U.S. v. Bay State Ambulance and Hosp. Rental Service, Inc.*, 874 F.2d 20 (1st Cir. 1989). *See also U.S. v. Gotti*, 771 F. Supp. 535 (E.D. N.Y. 1991) (privilege did not apply to conversations between defendants in the absence of any lawyer).

The doctrine creates an exception to the requirement that a communication must be made in confidence, and prevents a waiver of the privilege to the extent that confidential communications are shared between parties with a common interest. *U.S. v. Agnello*, 135 F. Supp. 2d 380 (E.D. N.Y. 2001); *Griffith v. Davis*, 161 F.R.D. 687 (C.D. Cal. 1995).

To establish the right to the privilege, the party asserting it must show that: (1) the communications were made in the course of a common legal effort; (2) the statements were made to further that legal effort, and (3) the privilege has not been waived. *U.S. v. Weissman*, 195 F.3d 96 (2d Cir.

1999); *Matter of Bevill, Bresler & Schulman Asset Management Corp.*, 805 F.2d 120 (3d Cir. 1986); *Ageloff v. Noranda, Inc.*, 936 F. Supp. 72 (D.R.I. 1996).

When the same attorney acts for two different clients who each have a common interest, communications of either party to the attorney are not necessarily privileged in subsequent litigation between the two clients. *F.D.I.C. v. Ogden Corp.*, 202 F.3d 454 (1st Cir. 2000); *Opus Corp. v. International Business Machines Corp.*, 956 F. Supp. 1503 (D. Minn. 1996); *Central Nat. Ins. Co. of Omaha v. Medical Protective Co. of Fort Wayne, Indiana*, 107 F.R.D. 393 (E.D. Mo. 1985). If, however, the joint clients consult separately with their joint attorney on matters about which they clearly do not share a common interest, the communication enjoys a separate privilege protection that may be asserted against the other client in order to preserve the confidentiality. *Eureka Inv. Corp., N.V. v. Chicago Title Ins. Co.*, 743 F.2d 932 (D.C. Cir. 1984).

Waiver

The privilege may be waived by (1) communication of privileged information to third persons, *Maday v. Public Libraries of Saginaw*, 480 F.3d 815 (6th Cir. 2007); *U.S. v. Rockwell Intern.*, 897 F.2d 1255 (3d Cir. 1990); *U.S. v. Jackson*, 969 F. Supp. 881 (S.D. N.Y. 1997); (2) placing advice given by counsel or counsel's performance "at issue," *In re Lott*, 424 F.3d 446 (6th Cir. 2005); *Worthington v. Endee*, 177 F.R.D. 113 (N.D. N.Y. 1998); *Steelcase Inc. v. Haworth, Inc.*, 954 F. Supp. 1195 (W.D. Mich. 1997) (patent case); (3) bringing suit or raising an affirmative defense that makes one's knowledge of the law relevant, *Recycling Solutions, Inc. v. District of Columbia*, 175 F.R.D. 407 (D.D.C. 1997); (4) use of privileged material in a manner inconsistent with maintaining confidentiality, *U.S. v. Mejia*, 655 F.3d 126 (2nd Cir. 2011) (where inmate is aware his calls are being recorded, those calls not protected by privilege); *McCafferty's, Inc. v. The Bank of Glen Burnie*, 179 F.R.D. 163 (D. Md. 1998) (collecting cases; finding no waiver re privileged document retrieved by private detective from opposing party's dumpster); *Local 851 of Intern. Broth. of Teamsters v. Kuehne & Nagel Air Freight,*

Inc., 36 F. Supp. 2d 127 (E.D. N.Y. 1998) (finding inadvertent disclosure so careless as to warrant waiver). *See also In re Seagate Technology, LLC*, 497 F.3d 1360 (Fed. Cir. 2007) (asserting advice of counsel defense and disclosing opinions of opinion counsel does not waive attorney-client privilege for communications with trial counsel; but acknowledging varying results in other courts); *In re Grand Jury*, 475 F.3d 1299 (D.C. Cir. 2007) (courts will grant no greater protection to those who assert the privilege than their own precautions warrant; privilege is lost even if disclosure is inadvertent); *U.S. v. Massachusetts Institute of Technology*, 129 F.3d 681 (1st Cir. 1997) (rejecting selective waiver theory; voluntary disclosure of documents per Defense Department regulation waived any later claim of privilege with respect to IRS).

Crime Fraud Exception

Communications between an attorney and a client in furtherance of the commission of a crime or fraud are not protected. *In re Grand Jury Subpoenas*, 561 F.3d 408 (5th Cir. 2009); *In re Impounded*, 241 F.3d 308 (3d Cir. 2001).

The attorney need not have been aware that the client harbored an improper purpose. Conversely, the privilege is not lost solely because the client's lawyer is corrupt. *In re Grand Jury Proceedings*, 417 F.3d 18 (1st Cir. 2005). Because both the legal advice and the privilege are for the benefit of the client, it is the client's knowledge and intent that are relevant. *In re Napster, Inc. Copyright Litigation*, 479 F.3d 1078 (9th Cir. 2007). The planned crime or fraud need not have succeeded for the exception to apply. The client's abuse of the attorney-client relationship, not his or her successful criminal or fraudulent act, vitiates the privilege. *In re Grand Jury Proceedings*, 87 F.3d 377, 382 (9th Cir. 1996).

To obtain an in camera review of allegedly privileged communications, the party attacking the claim of privilege must first present prima facie evidence that the client was engaged in or was planning the criminal or fraudulent conduct when he sought the assistance of counsel, that the assistance was obtained in furtherance of the conduct, and that the crime or fraud was carried out. *See In re Grand Jury Subpoenas*, 144 F.3d 653 (10th Cir. 1998); *In re Sealed Case*, 107 F.3d 46 (D.C. Cir. 1997). This showing must be made through the use of non-privileged materials.

The exception does not apply if assistance is sought only to disclose past wrongdoing, *United States v. Zolin*, 491 U.S. 554, 109 S. Ct. 2619, 105 L. Ed. 2d 469 (1989), but it does apply if the assistance was used to cover up and perpetuate the crime or fraud, *In re Grand Jury Proceedings*, 102 F.3d 748 (4th Cir. 1996) (applying exception where client used lawyers, without their knowledge, to misrepresent or conceal what the client had already done); *In re Richard Roe, Inc.*, 68 F.3d 38 (2d Cir. 1995) (exception applies where communication with counsel or attorney work product was intended to facilitate or conceal criminal activity); *U.S. v. Keys*, 67 F.3d 801 (9th Cir. 1995) (announced plans to engage in future criminal conduct not protected); *U.S. v. Sutton*, 732 F.2d 1483 (10th Cir. 1984) (privilege not applicable to client's statements to attorney that he intended to destroy records sought by government); *Matter of Doe*, 551 F.2d 899 (2d Cir. 1977) (plan to bribe juror not protected); *U.S. v. Gordon-Nikkar*, 518 F.2d 972 (5th Cir. 1975) (plans to commit perjury not protected).

Although the amount of proof necessary to meet the prima facie standard has not been decided by the Supreme Court, *see U.S. v. Zolin*, 491 U.S. at 563–64, several circuits have attempted to define this requirement. *See, e.g., U.S. v. Al-Shahin*, 474 F.3d 941 (7th Cir. 2007) (standard for prima facie evidence is not whether the evidence supports a verdict but whether it calls for inquiry); *In re Grand Jury Investigation*, 445 F.3d 266 (3d Cir. 2006) (evidence that if believed by fact finder would be sufficient to support finding that elements of crime-fraud exception were met); *In Re Grand Jury Proceedings*, 417 F.3d at 23 (it is enough to overcome the privilege that there is a reasonable basis to believe that the lawyer's services were used by the client to foster a crime or fraud); *In re Sealed Case*, 107 F.3d at 50 (exception requires evidence that if believed by trier of fact would establish elements of ongoing or imminent crime or fraud); *In re Grand Jury Proceedings*, 87 F.3d at 381 (9th Cir.

1996) (exception requires reasonable cause to believe attorney was used in furtherance of ongoing scheme); *In re Richard Roe, Inc.*, 68 F.3d at 40 (exception requires probable cause to believe a crime or fraud has been committed); *In re Grand Jury Investigation*, 842 F.2d 1223, 1226 (11th Cir. 1987) (exception requires evidence that if believed by trier of fact would establish elements of some violation that was ongoing or about to be committed).

Additional References

Graham, Handbook of Federal Evidence § 503 (7th ed. 2012)

Treatises and Practice Aids

Rice, Attorney-Client Privilege In The United States (annual ed.)

Goode and Wellborn, Courtroom Handbook on Federal Evidence Chapter 5 and Obj. 74 (annual ed.)

Mueller & Kirkpatrick, Federal Evidence, §§ 5:7, 5:13 *et seq.* (3d ed. 2007)

Wright & Graham, Federal Practice and Procedure: Evidence §§ 5001, 5421 *et seq.*, 5471 *et seq.*

Rothstein and Crump, Federal Testimonial Privileges Chapter 2 (annual ed.)

McCormick, Evidence Chapter 10 (6th ed. 2006)

Park, Trial Objections Handbook §§ 5:1 to 5:18 (2d ed. 2001)

PRIVILEGE: CLERGY

See:

Fed.R.Evid. 501
Mil.R.Evid. 503

Objection

- Objection. The question seeks information communicated to a clergyman which is privileged under Fed.R.Evid. 501.

Response

- This evidence is not privileged and is admissible because [*the statements made were not in the context of religious counseling*] [*the circumstances in which the statements were made were such that they were not religious, in that nothing spiritual or in the nature of forgiveness was ever discussed*] [*the statements were made in the presence of a third person who was not an agent for one of the parties to the privilege*].

Commentary

The clergy-communicant privilege protects communications to a member of the clergy, in his or her spiritual or professional capacity, by persons who seek spiritual counseling and who reasonably expect that their words will be kept in confidence. *In re Grand Jury Investigation*, 918 F.2d 374 (3d Cir. 1990); *WebXchange Inc. v. Dell Inc.*, 264 F.R.D. 123 (D.Del. 2010) (emails from inventor to Hindu gurus protected); *U.S. v. Mohanlal*, 867 F. Supp. 199 (S.D. N.Y. 1994); *see also Trammel v. United States*, 445 U.S. 40, 100 S. Ct. 906, 63 L. Ed. 2d 186 (1980) (in dicta, acknowledging existence of privilege). As with the attorney-client privilege, the presence of third parties, if essential to and in furtherance of the communication, does not vitiate the clergy-communicant privilege. *In re Grand Jury Investigation*, supra.

The privilege does not prohibit all testimony by members of the clergy. Rather, the privilege is limited to information told in confidence to them in their role as confessors or spiritual counselors.

Mullen v. U.S., 263 F.2d 275 (D.C. Cir. 1958) (concurring opinion). The trial court will look at the circumstances to determine whether a person's statements were made in secrecy and confidence to a member of the clergy in the course and context of the member's religious duties. *See, e.g.*, *U.S. v. Dube*, 820 F.2d 886 (7th Cir. 1987) (privilege did not apply to communications made to minister to obtain assistance in avoiding tax obligations); *U.S. v. Gordon*, 655 F.2d 478 (2d Cir. 1981) (defendant's business communications to priest he employed in nonreligious capacity were not protected).

Although the question of who may assert the privilege has rarely arisen, at least one federal court has held that only the clergy member can waive the privilege, thereby "safeguarding [a] clergyman's status as a secure repository for the confessant's confidences." *Eckmann v. Board of Educ. of Hawthorn School Dist. No. 17*, 106 F.R.D. 70 (E.D. Mo. 1985); *see also In re Grand Jury Investigation*, 918 F.2d at 385, n.15 (acknowledging authority for proposition that privilege can be asserted by clergyperson on behalf of communicant).

Additional References

Graham, Handbook of Federal Evidence § 506.1 (7th ed. 2012)

Treatises and Practice Aids

Goode and Wellborn, Courtroom Handbook on Federal Evidence Chapter 5 (annual ed.)

Mueller & Kirkpatrick, Federal Evidence, §§ 5:4, 5:7 (3d ed. 2007)

Wright & Graham, Federal Practice and Procedure: Evidence 2d § 5013

Rothstein and Crump, Federal Testimonial Privileges Chapter 10, § 10.03[4] (annual ed.)

McCormick, Evidence § 76.2 (6th ed. 2006)

Park, Trial Objections Handbook § 5:31 (2nd ed. 2001)

PRIVILEGE: CONFIDENTIAL INFORMER

See:

Fed.R.Evid. 501
Mil.R.Evid. 507

Objection

- [*Request sidebar*] I object on grounds of privilege. The question seeks [*the identity of*][*information which will lead to the identity of*] the government's informant.

Response

- Your Honor, we believe the informant was the only eyewitness to the event and since we are asserting a defense of mistaken identity, the right to call or cross-examine him is vital to the defense.

Commentary

What is commonly referred to as the informer's privilege is, in reality, the federal government's qualified privilege to refuse to disclose the identity of persons who furnish information concerning crimes to law enforcement officers. The privilege extends only to the identity of the informer. If the contents of a communication would not disclose the informant's identity, then the privilege is not applicable to the communication. *Roviaro v. United States*, 353 U.S. 53, 77 S. Ct. 623, 1 L. Ed. 2d 639 (1957); *U.S. v. Mendoza-Salgado*, 964 F.2d 993 (10th Cir. 1992); *U.S. v. D'Armond*, 65 F. Supp. 2d 1189 (D. Kan. 1999). By preserving the informer's anonymity, the privilege is designed to encourage cooperation and to protect government sources from retaliation. *U.S. v. Robinson*, 144 F.3d 104 (1st Cir. 1998). Because of these policy considerations, the government is granted the privilege as of right and need not make a threshold showing that reprisal is likely. *Dole v. Local 1942, Intern. Broth. of Elec. Workers, AFL-CIO*, 870 F.2d 368 (7th Cir. 1989).

The privilege, however, is not absolute and must yield to fairness if the informer's identity is relevant and helpful to the defense of an accused or is essential to a fair determination of a case.

Roviaro, 353 U.S. at 60–61. The trial court must balance the public interest in protecting the flow of information against the individual's right to prepare his or her case. *Id.*, at 62; *U.S. v. Harris*, 531 F.3d 507, 514 (7th Cir. 2008). There are no fixed rules with respect to disclosure; the fundamental concern is one of fairness. Striking a proper balance depends on the particular circumstances of each case, taking into consideration the crime charged, the possible defenses, the possible significance of the informer's testimony and other relevant factors. *Id.*; *U.S. v. Vincent*, 611 F.3d 1246 (10th Cir. 2010).

It is the defendant's burden to come forward with evidence establishing that the *Roviaro* criteria favor disclosure. *U.S. v. Lewis*, 40 F.3d 1325 (1st Cir. 1994); *U.S. v. Bender*, 5 F.3d 267 (7th Cir. 1993); *U.S. v. Blevins*, 960 F.2d 1252 (4th Cir. 1992); *U.S. v. Ortiz*, 2010 WL 4622529 (D.Utah 2010); *U.S. v. Carino-Torres*, 549 F. Supp. 2d 151, 152 (D.P.R. 2007). More than suspicion or speculation is needed to meet this burden. *U.S. v. Rowland*, 464 F.3d 899, 909 (9th Cir. 2006); *U.S. v. Williams*, 898 F.2d 1400 (9th Cir. 1990); *U.S. v. Brown*, 178 F.R.D. 88 (W.D. Va. 1998). Although a criminal defendant cannot be expected to predict exactly what the informer would say if called as a witness, he must at least suggest a reasonable possibility that the informer could give testimony that would be relevant to the defendant's case, so that justice would be best served by disclosure. *U.S. v. Roberson*, 439 F.3d 934 (8th Cir. 2006); *U.S. v. Reardon*, 787 F.2d 512 (10th Cir. 1986); *U.S. v. Smith*, 780 F.2d 1102 (4th Cir. 1985).

An *in camera* hearing will preserve necessary secrecy while allowing the parties to demonstrate whether the informer can provide such testimony.* There is, however, no mandatory procedure for ad-

---

[Privilege etc.]

*This is consistent with longstanding federal procedure for handling disputes involving claims of privilege in the context of criminal cases where the constitutional due process rights of a defendant must be weighed against the privilege of another. *See Pennsylvania v. Ritchie*, 480 U.S. 39, 107 S. Ct. 989, 94 L. Ed. 2d 40 (1987) (suggesting that in camera review by court of state records pertaining to a child abuse investiga-

dressing disclosure requests. *See, e.g., U.S. v. Spires*, 3 F.3d 1234 (9th Cir. 1993) (*in camera* hearing required); *Matter of Search of 1638 E. 2nd Street, Tulsa, Okl.*, 993 F.2d 773 (10th Cir. 1993) (*in camera* hearing useful but not mandatory); *U.S. v. Mendoza-Burciaga*, 981 F.2d 192 (5th Cir. 1992) (suggesting presence of all counsel at *in camera* hearing in conjunction with use of a gag order as a way to protect defendant's confrontation rights); Proposed Rule 510(c)(2) (mandating *in camera* inspection with "no counsel or party" present).

In ruling on disclosure requests, the court examines: (1) the informer's degree of involvement in the alleged crime; (2) the helpfulness of the disclosure to the asserted defense; and (3) the government's interest in nondisclosure. *U.S. v. Ibarra*, 493 F.3d 526, 531 (5th Cir. 2007); *U.S. v. Sanchez*, 988 F.2d 1384 (5th Cir. 1993); *U.S. v. Singh*, 922 F.2d 1169 (5th Cir. 1991).

Disclosure has been ordered where the informer was an active participant in the crime, *U.S. v. Mendoza-Salgado*, 964 F.2d 993 (10th Cir. 1992), or was the only witness in a position to amplify or contradict the testimony of government witnesses. *U.S. v. Martinez*, 922 F.2d 914 (1st Cir. 1991); *U.S. v. Saa*, 859 F.2d 1067 (2d Cir. 1988). Where the court orders disclosure pursuant to *Roviaro*, it may require the government to exercise reasonable diligence in locating the informer and producing him at trial. *See, e.g., U.S. v. Suarez*, 939 F.2d 929 (11th Cir. 1991).

The request for identity has been denied where the informer: was merely a source or a tipster, *Harris*, 531 F3d at 515; *U.S. v. Gordon*, 173 F.3d 761 (10th Cir. 1999); *U.S. v. Robinson*, 144 F.3d 104 (1st Cir. 1998); *U.S. v. Stewart*, 353 F. Supp. 2d 703 (E.D. La. 2004); instigated the investigation of defendant but was not present at the transactions, *U.S. v. Valles*, 41 F.3d 355 (7th Cir. 1994); *U.S. v. Andrus*, 775 F.2d 825 (7th Cir. 1985); acted as a

---

tion would properly accommodate state's compelling interest in protecting child-abuse information and defendant's compelling due process interest in information that may change outcome of trial); *U.S. v. Wilson*, 798 F.2d 509 (1st Cir. 1986) (affirming *in camera* review of documents protected under attorney-client privilege to determine if any were exculpatory).

middleman who introduced an undercover agent to the defendant, *U.S. v. Mabry*, 953 F.2d 127 (4th Cir. 1991); *U.S. v. Brinkman*, 739 F.2d 977 (4th Cir. 1984); or, at best, had only cumulative testimony, *U.S. v. Sinclair*, 109 F.3d at 1527.

A confidential informant's statements to a law enforcement officer are clearly testimonial under the Confrontation Clause of the Sixth Amendment. *U.S. v. Lopez-Medina*, 596 F.3d 716 (10th Cir. 2010); *U.S. v. Cromer*, 389 F.3d 662 (6th Cir. 2004).

The privilege is also available in civil cases. *Elnashar v. Speedway SuperAmerica, LLC*, 484 F.3d 1046, 1052 (8th Cir. 2007); *Matter of Search of 1638 E. 2nd St., Tulsa, Okl.*, 993 F.2d at 773; *Hoffman v. Reali*, 973 F.2d 980 (1st Cir. 1992); *Holman v. Cayce*, 873 F.2d 944 (6th Cir. 1989); *Dole v. Local 1942, IBEW, AFL-CIO*, 870 F.2d at 368. In civil cases, the privilege is arguably stronger and more difficult to overcome because not all constitutional guarantees which inure to criminal defendants are similarly available to civil litigants. *In re Kleberg County, Texas*, 86 Fed. Appx. 29, 32 (5th Cir. 2004); *Dole*, 870 F.2d at 372.

Additional References

Graham, Handbook of Federal Evidence § 510.1 (7th ed. 2012)

Treatises and Practice Aids

Goode and Wellborn, Courtroom Handbook on Federal Evidence Chapter 5, Prop. Rule 510 and Obj. 75 (annual ed.)

Mueller & Kirkpatrick, Federal Evidence, §§ 5:4, 5:62 *et seq.* (3d ed. 2007)

Wright & Graham, Federal Practice and Procedure: Evidence §§ 5701 *et seq.*

Rothstein and Crump, Federal Testimonial Privileges Chapter 7 (annual ed.)

McCormick, Evidence § 111 (6th ed. 2006)

Park, Trial Objections Handbook § 5:34 (2nd ed. 2001)

PRIVILEGE: DELIBERATIVE PROCESS

See:

Fed.R.Evid. 501
Mil.R.Evid. 501(a)(4)

Objection

- [*At sidebar*] The court earlier ruled that the deliberative process privilege applies in this case. This question now seeks to elicit privileged information.

Response

- The privilege does not apply to factual information and that is all the question asks for.

Commentary

One of the traditional evidentiary privileges available to the government is the common law deliberative process privilege. This qualified privilege protects the consultative functions of government by maintaining the confidentiality of advisory opinions, recommendations and deliberations comprising part of a process by which governmental decisions and policies are formulated. *Department of Interior v. Klamath Water Users Protective Ass'n*, 532 U.S. 1, 121 S. Ct. 1060, 149 L. Ed. 2d 87 (2001); *Loving v. Department of Defense*, 550 F.3d 32 (D.C. Cir. 2008); *Dow Jones & Co., Inc. v. Department of Justice*, 917 F.2d 571, 573 (D.C. Cir. 1990) (privilege "predicated on the recognition that the quality of administrative decisionmaking would be seriously undermined if agencies were forced to operate in a fish bowl"). The privilege attaches to inter- and intra-agency communications that are part of the deliberative process *preceding* the adoption and promulgation of an agency policy. *Rein v. U.S. Patent & Trademark Office*, 553 F.3d 353 (4th Cir. 2009); *Missouri Coalition for Environment Foundation v. U.S. Army Corps of Engineers*, 542 F.3d 1204 (8th Cir. 2008); *U.S. v. Farley*, 11 F.3d 1385 (7th Cir. 1993); *F.T.C. v. Warner Communications Inc.*, 742 F.2d 1156 (9th Cir. 1984); *Arizona Rehabilitation Hosp., Inc. v. Shalala*, 185 F.R.D. 263 (D. Ariz. 1998); *U.S. v. Rozet*, 183 F.R.D. 662 (N.D. Cal.

1998). The deliberative process privilege may include materials generated by agency employees as well as consultants. *Stewart v. U.S. Dept. of Interior*, 554 F.3d 1236 (10th Cir. 2009).

The three primary purposes of the privilege are: (1) to assure that subordinates within an agency will feel free to provide the decisionmaker with their uninhibited opinions and recommendations without fear of criticism; (2) to protect against premature disclosure of proposed policies before they have been adopted; and (3) to protect against confusing the issues and misleading the public by dissemination of documents suggesting reasons and rationales for a course of action which were not in fact the ultimate reasons for the agency's action. *Coastal States Gas Corp. v. Department of Energy*, 617 F.2d 854, 866 (D.C. Cir. 1980).

Only predecisional deliberative communications are protected. *U.S. v. Fernandez*, 231 F.3d 1240 (9th Cir. 2000) (death penalty evaluation form and prosecution memorandum are predecisional and deliberative because designed to help Attorney General decide whether death penalty is appropriate in a given case); *Chevron U.S.A., Inc. v. U.S.*, 80 Fed. Cl. 340, 356 (2008); *Hopkins v. U.S. Dept. of Housing and Urban Development*, 929 F.2d 81 (2d Cir. 1991); *Access Reports v. Department of Justice*, 926 F.2d 1192, 1194 (D.C. Cir. 1991); *Judicial Watch, Inc. v. U.S. Dept. of Justice*, 800 F.Supp.2d 202 (D.D.C. 2011) (a document is 'predecisional' if it precedes, in temporal sequence, the 'decision' to which it relates). The privilege does not apply to communications made subsequent to the agency's decision. *Elkem Metals Co. v. U.S.*, 24 Ct. Int'l Trade 1395, 126 F. Supp. 2d 5672, 574 (2000) Subjective materials that "reflect the personal opinion of the writer, rather than the policy of the agency", are also privileged because they are considered predecisional. *Lee v. F.D.I.C.*, 923 F. Supp. 451, 456 (S.D. N.Y. 1996).

The privilege usually does not extend to factual or objective material or to documents that the agency adopts as its position on an issue. *Hopkins*, 929 F.2d at 84; *Arthur Andersen & Co. v. I. R. S.*, 679 F.2d 254 (D.C. Cir. 1982); *Doe v. Nebraska*, 788 F.Supp.2d 975 (D.Neb. 2011); *K.L. v. Edgar*, 964 F. Supp. 1206 (N.D. Ill. 1997). However, factual information that reflects or reveals the deliberative processes of an agency is protected by the privilege. *In re U.S.*, 321 Fed. Appx. 953 (Fed. Cir. 2009) (collecting cases); *Miccosukee Tribe of Indians of Florida v. U.S.*, 516 F.3d 1235 (11th Cir. 2008) (factual material in a deliberative document may be withheld where disclosure of factual material would reveal deliberative process or where the factual material is so inextricably intertwined with deliberative material that meaningful segregation is not possible); *Mapother v. Department of Justice*, 3 F.3d 1533 (D.C. Cir. 1993); *but see Trentadue v. Integrity Committee*, 501 F.3d 1215, 1229 (10th Cir. 2007) ("To the extent that *Mapother* allows an agency to withhold factual material simply because it reflects a choice as to which facts to include in a document, we reject that approach.").

The government must bear the initial burden of showing that the privilege applies. *Schreiber v. Society for Sav. Bancorp, Inc.*, 11 F.3d 217 (D.C. Cir. 1993). Three procedural requirements must be satisfied: (1) there must be a formal claim of privilege made by the head of the department or his designated subordinate which has control over the matter, after actual consideration by that officer, *United States v. Reynolds*, 345 U.S. 1, 73 S. Ct. 528, 97 L. Ed. 727 (1953); *Landry v. F.D.I.C.*, 204 F.3d 1125 (D.C. Cir. 2000) (assertion of privilege by highest official not required; lesser officials may assert privilege); (2) the responsible agency official must provide precise and certain reasons for asserting confidentiality with respect to the information, *U. S. v. O'Neill*, 619 F.2d 222 (3d Cir. 1980); *Mobil Oil Corp. v. Department of Energy*, 520 F. Supp. 414 (N.D. N.Y. 1981); and (3) the government information or documents must be identified and described, *Resident Advisory Bd. v. Rizzo*, 97 F.R.D. 749 (E.D. Pa. 1983).

Once the government makes a *prima facie* showing of entitlement, the trial court must then balance the competing interests of the parties, including: (1) the relevance of the evidence sought to be protected; (2) the availability of other relevant evidence; (3) the seriousness of the litigation and the issues involved; (4) the government's role in the litigation; and, (5) the extent to which disclosure would chill future deliberations within agencies. *Ford Motor Co. v. U.S.*, 94 Fed.Cl. 211 (Fed.Cl. 2010); *Dairyland Power Co-op. v. U.S.*, 77 Fed. Cl. 330, 338 (2007); *First Eastern Corp. v. Mainwaring*, 21 F.3d 465 (D.C. Cir. 1994); *Redland Soccer Club, Inc. v. Department of Army of U.S.*, 55 F.3d 827 (3d Cir. 1995); *see Ferrell v. U.S. Dept. of Housing and Urban Development*, 177 F.R.D. 425 (N.D. Ill. 1998) (in contempt action against HUD for violation of consent decree, plaintiffs' need for information overcame privilege).

The privilege is not absolute. It "disappears altogether when there is any reason to believe government misconduct occurred." *In re Sealed Case*, 121 F.3d 729, 746 (D.C. Cir. 1997). Documents also will not be protected from disclosure if their content reflects an attempt by an agency to establish "secret law" or policies that are not subject to public scrutiny. *Sterling Drug, Inc. v. F.T.C.*, 450 F.2d 698, 708 (D.C. Cir. 1971) ("[T]o prevent the development of secret law within the Commission, we must require it to disclose orders and interpretations which it actually applies in cases before it").

Some courts have severely restricted the use of the privilege by government agencies when those agencies are seeking affirmative judicial relief. These decisions hold that when the government seeks affirmative relief, fundamental fairness requires the government to disclose materials that a private plaintiff would have to reveal. *E.E.O.C. v. Airborne Express*, 1999 WL 124380 *22 (E.D. Pa. 1999); *U.S. v. Ernstoff*, 183 F.R.D. 148 (D.N.J. 1998); *F.D.I.C. v. Hatziyannis*, 180 F.R.D. 292 (D. Md. 1998); *E.E.O.C. v. Citizens Bank*, 117 F.R.D. 366 (D. Md. 1987); *see also* Wright & Graham, Federal Practice and Procedure: Evidence § 5690 (1992) (noting that courts have rejected qualified deliberative process privilege when government acts as plaintiff); *In re Subpoena Duces Tecum Served on Office of Comptroller of Currency*, 145 F.3d 1422 (D.C. Cir. 1998) (privilege does not apply when cause of action is directed at the agency's subjective motivation; also noting that the privilege has no place in Title VII actions or constitutional claims for discrimination because when the Constitution or a statute makes the nature of governmental deliberations the issue, the privilege is a non sequitur).

Even if the privilege is found to apply, a court may still order disclosure if the party seeking the information can demonstrate that its need for disclosure of such material is greater than the government's interest in non-disclosure. *See Elkem Metals Co. v. U.S.*, 24 Ct. Int'l Trade 1395, 126 F. Supp. 2d 567, 574 (2000); *Star-Kist Foods, Inc. v. U.S.*, 8 Ct. Int'l Trade 305, 600 F. Supp. 212, 217 (1984) ("Once the proponent of privilege has complied with the established criteria for asserting privilege, the opposing party must demonstrate clearly and persuasively that the need for disclosure outweighs the harm that could result from disclosure.") (citing *Melamine Chemicals, Inc. v. U.S.*, 1 Ct. Int'l Trade 65, 66, 1980 WL 2224 (1980)).

There is no deliberative process privilege for private entities. *Wilstein v. San Tropai Condominium Master Ass'n*, 189 F.R.D. 371 (N.D. Ill. 1999) (privilege not available to condominium association sued under federal Fair Housing Act).

Law Enforcement Privilege

There is support in a number of circuits for a "law enforcement" privilege. *In re U.S. Dept. of Homeland Sec.*, 459 F.3d 565 (5th Cir. 2006) (collecting cases). The purpose of this qualified privilege is to "prevent disclosure of law enforcement techniques and procedures, to preserve the confidentiality of sources, to protect witness and law enforcement personnel, to safeguard the privacy of individuals involved in an investigation, and otherwise to prevent interference with an investigation." *In re Department of Investigation of City of New York*, 856 F.2d 481, 484 (2d Cir. 1988) (citations omitted). "[T]he privilege is designed not only to facilitate investigations, but also to protect individuals whose reputation may be damaged by disclosure of investigative leads or statements from witnesses developed during the investigation." *Id.* at 486; *National Congress for Puerto Rican Rights ex rel. Perez v. City of New York*, 194 F.R.D. 88 (S.D. N.Y. 2000) (discussing operation of privilege and collecting cases); *Morrissey v. City of New York*, 171 F.R.D. 85 (S.D. N.Y. 1997) (privilege recognized in civil rights action to protect information relating to police investigations). The privilege may only be invoked by government law enforcement authorities. *Sterling Merchandising, Inc. v. Nestle, S.A.*, 470 F. Supp. 2d 77 (D.P.R. 2006). The privilege requires that: (1) a formal claim of privilege is made by the head of the department in control of the requested information; (2) the assertion of privilege is based on actual personal consideration by the official raising the claim of privilege, and (3) the information for which the privilege is claimed is specified and an explanation given as to why the information falls within the scope of the privilege. *In re Sealed Case*, 856 F.2d 268, 271–72 (D.C. Cir. 1988). The government must make a clear showing of harm if the information is disclosed. *MacWade v. Kelly*, 230 F.R.D. 379 (S.D. N.Y. 2005). However, when the information at issue is relevant and essential to the presentation of the case on the merits and the need for disclosure of the information outweighs the need for secrecy, the privilege is overcome and the information may be revealed. *Miller v. Mehltretter*, 478 F. Supp. 2d 415, 424 (W.D. N.Y. 2007).

Treatises and Practice Aids

Goode and Wellborn, Courtroom Handbook on Federal Evidence Chapter 5 and Obj. 73 (annual ed.)

Wright & Graham, Federal Practice and Procedure: Evidence § 5680

Larkin, Federal Testimonial Privileges Chapter 5, § 5.02[2] (2001 ed.)

Graham, Handbook of Federal Evidence § 509.1 (6th ed. 2006)

McCormick, Evidence § 108 (6th ed. 2006)

PRIVILEGE: HUSBAND AND WIFE

See:

Fed.R.Evid. 501
Mil.R.Evid. 504

Objection

- Objection: As the spouse of the defendant, the witness invokes the privilege not to furnish any testimony adverse to defendant's interest.
- Objection: Privilege, the question calls for disclosure of a confidential communication between husband and wife.

Response

- The question will not elicit any testimony adverse to defendant's interests.
- Any testimonial privilege ended with the parties' divorce/spouse's death.
- The testimony is not privileged because [the privilege has been waived] [the evidence does not touch or concern a confidential communication] [there is no confidentiality since a third party was present].

Commentary

The federal common law rules of testimonial privilege recognize two distinct marital privileges: (1) the adverse spousal testimony privilege, and, (2) the confidential marital communications privilege. *U.S. v. Bad Wound*, 203 F.3d 1072 (8th Cir. 2000). The former allows a spouse called as a witness against his or her spouse in a criminal proceeding to refuse to testify, *Trammel v. United States*, 445 U.S. 40, 53, 100 S. Ct. 906, 913, 63 L. Ed. 2d 186 (1980), while the latter protects from disclosure private communications between the spouses in the confidence of the marital relationship. *Blau v. United States*, 340 U.S. 332, 333, 71 S. Ct. 301, 302, 95 L. Ed. 306 (1951); *In re Reserve Fund Securities and Derivative Litigation*, 275 F.R.D. 154 (S.D.N.Y. 2011) (collecting cases).

Adverse Spousal Testimony

The adverse spousal testimony privilege permits

an individual to refuse to testify in a criminal proceeding against his or her spouse, subject to certain exceptions and waiver. *U.S. v. Espino*, 317 F.3d 788 (8th Cir. 2003) (privilege rests with testifying spouse who may waive privilege without consent of other spouse); *Bad Wound*, 203 F.3d at 1075 (an individual cannot be compelled to testify nor foreclosed from testifying against the person to whom he or she is married at the time of trial); *S.E.C. v. Lavin*, 111 F.3d 921 (D.C. Cir. 1997). *See also Trammel*, 445 U.S. at 40 (ruling that the privilege can be asserted only by the testifying spouse); *U.S. v. Morris*, 988 F.2d 1335, 1338 (4th Cir. 1993) (noting that privilege "has been a feature of the common law for centuries"); *U.S. v. James*, 128 F. Supp. 2d 291 (D. Md. 2001) (tracing history of privilege).

Because the privilege is rooted in a dual desire to protect marital harmony and to avoid the unseemliness of compelling one spouse to testify against the other in a criminal proceeding, the scope of the privilege is limited to any testimony that is adverse to the legal interests of the defendant-spouse. *Trammel*; *U.S. v. Yerardi*, 192 F.3d 14 (1st Cir. 1999). Questions which do not tend to incriminate the non-testifying spouse do not jeopardize the marriage. *In re Grand Jury Proceedings*, 664 F.2d 423 (5th Cir. 1981).

A spouse may voluntarily testify against the other since, as *Trammel* recognized, "[w]hen one spouse is willing to testify against the other in a criminal proceeding . . . their relationship is almost certainly in disrepair; there is probably little in the way of marital harmony to preserve." 445 U.S. at 52.

A person asserting either of the marital privileges has the burden of establishing the existence of a valid marriage. *U.S. v. Acker*, 52 F.3d 509 (4th Cir. 1995) (no privilege where state of residence did not recognize common law marriage). Whether a couple is married is a matter determined by state law. *Id.* Once a court determines that a valid marriage exists, the testimonial privilege should apply to all matters whether they occurred before or during the marriage. *A.B. v. U.S.*, 24 F. Supp. 2d 488 (D. Md. 1998). The testimonial privilege ceases to exist if the parties do not remain married. *U.S. v.*

Marashi, 913 F.2d 724 (9th Cir. 1990) (no privilege after divorce).

Because the privilege operates only to block adverse testimony, once the government grants immunity which eliminates the possibility that the testimony will be used to prosecute the witness's spouse, the witness cannot invoke the testimonial privilege. *In re Grand Jury*, 111 F.3d 1083 (3d Cir. 1997); *In re Snoonian*, 502 F.2d 110 (1st Cir. 1974).

Confidential Marital Communications

In civil and criminal cases, the confidential marital communications privilege protects statements or actions intended as a communication by one spouse to the other, made during the existence of a valid marriage, and that are intended as confidential by the spouse who makes the communication. *U.S. v. Strobehn*, 421 F.3d 1017 (9th Cir. 2005); *Caplan v. Fellheimer Eichen Braverman & Kaskey*, 162 F.R.D. 490 (E.D. Pa. 1995).

The purpose of the privilege is to foster intimate communication between spouses by assuring that their statements will never be subjected to forced disclosure. *U.S. v. Byrd*, 750 F.2d 585 (7th Cir. 1984); *see also U.S. v. Neal*, 532 F. Supp. 942, 946 (D. Colo. 1982) (privilege preserves "some small island of privacy as a refuge for the human spirit").

The privilege may be asserted against the production of evidence when four prerequisites are met: (1) there must have been a communication, *Pereira v. United States*, 347 U.S. 1, 6–7, 74 S. Ct. 358, 361–62, 98 L. Ed. 435 (1954); (2) there must have been a valid marriage at the time of the communication, *U.S. v. Evans*, 966 F.2d 398, 401 (8th Cir. 1992); (3) the communication must have been made in confidence, *Marashi*, 913 F.2d at 724; *In re Grand Jury Proceedings (86-2)*, 640 F. Supp. 988 (E.D. Mich. 1986); and (4) the privilege must not have been waived, *U.S. v. Figueroa-Paz*, 468 F.2d 1055, 1057 (9th Cir. 1972).

While the party asserting the communications privilege bears the burden of establishing that answering the question would require disclosure of words or acts intended as communication to/from the other spouse, and that the communication was made during a valid marriage, the final element of confidentiality is presumed. *U.S. v. Byrd, supra* (communications intended to be private are often made without a request for secrecy; the difficult matter of proving the intent to keep the communications confidential is avoided by the presumption).

Although marital communications are presumed confidential, the presumption may be overcome by proof of facts that they were not intended to be private. The presence of a third party negates the presumption of privacy as does the intention that the information conveyed be transmitted to a third person. *U.S. v. Montgomery*, 384 F.3d 1050 (9th Cir. 2004) (prosecution failed to show wife's letter to husband was not intended to be confidential); *U.S. v. Barefoot*, 2011 WL 3678152 (E.D.N.C. 2011).

The communications privilege survives termination of the marriage by annulment, divorce or death. *Pereira*, 347 U.S. at 6 (divorce); *U.S. v. Lea*, 249 F.3d 632 (7th Cir. 2001) (divorce); *U.S. v. Burks*, 470 F.2d 432 (D.C. Cir. 1972) (death).

The privilege belongs to both spouses and either may invoke it to avoid interrogation or to prevent the other spouse from testifying about protected communications. *U.S. v. Premises Known as 281 Syosset Woodbury Road, Woodbury, N.Y.*, 71 F.3d 1067 (2d Cir. 1995); *U.S. v. Espino*, 317 F.3d at 796 (trial court properly preserved marital confidential communications privilege by prohibiting wife from testifying about conversations with her husband but, pursuant to her waiver of adverse spousal testimony privileges, allowed her to testify to observations of his conduct and actions involving drug trade).

A number of circuits hold that communications about crimes in which the spouses are jointly participating are not deemed worthy of protection and thus do not fall within the protection of the marital communications privilege. *U.S. v. Howard*, 216 Fed. Appx. 463 (6th Cir. 2007) (wife permitted to testify about letter received from husband discussing how they could obstruct justice and commit perjury); *U.S. v. Bey*, 188 F.3d 1 (1st Cir. 1999) (wife could testify to confidential marital communications that took place after she became joint participant in husband's drug smuggling activities); *U.S. v. Short*, 4 F.3d 475 (7th Cir. 1993) (noting spouse's "minor role" in aiding and abetting husband's conspiracy sufficient to admit testimony); *U.S. v. Parker*, 834 F.2d 408 (4th Cir. 1987) (limitation of privilege reflects belief greater public good will result from permitting spouse of an accused to testify willingly concerning joint criminal activities than would come from permitting accused to erect roadblock against search for truth); *U.S. v. Picciandra*, 788 F.2d 39 (1st Cir. 1986) (wife could testify about conversations with husband; she was a co-conspirator and conversations were in furtherance of conspiracy to evade income tax); *U.S. v. Ammar*, 714 F.2d 238 (3d Cir. 1983) (co-conspirator wife could testify to conversations with husband in furtherance of drug conspiracy); *U.S. v. Price*, 577 F.2d 1356 (9th Cir. 1978) (tape recordings between husband and wife concerning their prostitution ring admissible); *U.S. v. Mendoza*, 574 F.2d 1373 (5th Cir. 1978) (similar). The government must produce evidence of complicity; a spouse's knowledge or suspicion are insufficient. *U.S. v. Cooper*, 85 F. Supp. 2d 1 (D.D.C. 2000). The spouse's participation in the criminal activity need not be substantial. *U.S. v. Short; but see Appeal of Malfitano*, 633 F.2d 276 (3d Cir. 1980) (rejecting limitation of privilege).

The marital communications privilege has been held not to apply to statements relating to crimes committed against a spouse, child, stepchild or the functional equivalent of a child, such as a foster child. *U.S. v. White*, 974 F.2d 1135 (9th Cir. 1992); *U.S. v. Allery*, 526 F.2d 1362 (8th Cir. 1975) (exception needed to protect children of either spouse from abuse by the other spouse); *U.S. v. Banks*, 556 F.3d 967 (9th Cir. 2009) (violence against functional equivalent of child subject to the exception but grandchild who was only an occasional visitor was not the functional equivalent of a birth or stepchild; therefore privilege applied to defendant's admission to spouse of acts committed against their grandchild). The Tenth Circuit extends the exception to testimony relating to the abuse of any minor child in the marital household, whether residing there or visiting, *U.S. v. Bahe*, 128 F.3d 1440 (10th Cir. 1997), but will not compel such testimony); *U.S. v. Jarvison*, 409 F.3d 1221 (10th Cir. 2005) (where wife did not wish to testify against her husband, trial court correctly declined government's invitation to create new exception allowing courts to compel adverse spousal testimony in cases involving allegations of child abuse).

Statements between spouses that are made in the presence of third parties are not privileged. *Wolfle v. United States*, 291 U.S. 7, 54 S. Ct. 279, 78 L. Ed. 617 (1934); *U.S. v. Taylor*, 92 F.3d 1313 (2d Cir. 1996); *U.S. v. Klayer*, 707 F.2d 892 (6th Cir. 1983).

Additional References

Graham, Handbook of Federal Evidence § 505.2 (7th ed. 2012)

Treatises and Practice Aids

Goode and Wellborn, Courtroom Handbook on Federal Evidence Chapter 5 and Objs. 76 and 77 (annual ed.)

Mueller & Kirkpatrick, Federal Evidence, §§ 5:7, 5:39 to 5:40 (3d ed. 2007)

Wright & Graham, Federal Practice and Procedure: Evidence §§ 5421 *et seq.*

Rothstein and Crump, Federal Testimonial Privileges Chapter 4 (annual ed.)

McCormick, Evidence Chapter 9 (6th ed. 2006)

Park, Trial Objections Handbook §§ 5:25 to 5:27 (2nd ed. 2001)

PRIVILEGE: JOURNALIST

See:

Rule 501
Mil.R.Evid. 501

Objection

- Objection. [*Request sidebar*] The First Amendment and Rule 501 confer upon the news media a privilege against disclosure of [*their confidential sources*] [*nonconfidential information such as notes, outtakes and other unused information*].

Response

- The privilege is only a qualified one and does not apply here because the [*testimony/information*] sought to be withheld is highly relevant [*specify*]; cannot be obtained by alternate means [*explain*]; and there is a compelling interest in the information [*specify*].

Commentary

The qualified journalist's privilege allows reporters in some instances to decline to disclose information about their sources. Derived from the First Amendment, the privilege recognizes society's interest in protecting the integrity of the news gathering process and in ensuring the free flow of information to the public.* It is an interest of "sufficient social importance to justify some incidental

---

[Privilege etc.]

*In *Branzburg v. Hayes*, 408 U.S. 665, 92 S. Ct. 2646, 33 L. Ed. 2d 626 (1972), the Supreme Court addressed whether requiring newsmen to appear and testify before state or federal grand juries abridges the freedom of speech and the press guaranteed by the First Amendment and held that it does not. But the Court did acknowledge the existence of First Amendment protection for newsgathering, also referred to as the qualified privilege. Justice Powell, in a concurrence, said the claim to privilege should be judged on its facts by the striking of a proper balance between freedom of the press and the obligation of all citizens to give relevant testimony with respect to criminal conduct. *Id.* at 710. Justice Powell also said that the proper balance should be struck on a case-by-case basis by the interest of society in a free press on one hand and in

sacrifice of sources of facts needed in the administration of justice." *Herbert v. Lando*, 441 U.S. 153, 183, 99 S. Ct. 1635, 1652, 60 L. Ed. 2d 115 (1979) (Brennan, J. dissenting); *see also U.S. v. Cutler*, 6 F.3d 67 (2d Cir. 1993); *Zerilli v. Smith*, 656 F.2d 705 (D.C. Cir. 1981); *Riley v. City of Chester*, 612 F.2d 708 (3d Cir. 1979); *Baker v. F and F Inv.*, 470 F.2d 778 (2d Cir. 1972); *U.S. Commodity Futures Trading Com'n v. McGraw-Hill Companies, Inc.*, 390 F. Supp. 2d 27 (D.D.C. 2005); *Wright v. F.B.I.*, 385 F. Supp. 2d 1038 (C.D. Cal. 2005).

The privilege is not absolute and will be overcome whenever society's need for the confidential information outweighs the intrusion on the reporter's First Amendment interests. *The New York Times Co. v. Gonzales*, 459 F.3d 160 (2d Cir. 2006); *Ashcraft v. Conoco, Inc.*, 218 F.3d 282 (4th Cir. 2000); *U.S. Commodity Futures Trading Com'n v. Whitney*, 441 F. Supp. 2d 61 (D.D.C. 2006); *In Re Grand Jury Subpoenas*, 438 F. Supp. 2d 1111 (N.D. Cal. 2006).

Courts faced with the journalist's privilege have proceeded on a case-by-case basis, balancing the potential harm to the free flow of information that might result against the asserted need for the requested information. *In re Grand Jury Subpoena, Judith Miller*, 438 F.3d 1141 (D.C. Cir. 2006) (no First Amendment privilege protecting journalists from providing evidence to grand jury); *see also Cusumano v. Microsoft Corp.*, 162 F.3d 708 (1st Cir. 1998); *U.S. v. Caporale*, 806 F.2d 1487 (11th Cir. 1986); *U.S. v. Criden*, 633 F.2d 346 (3d Cir. 1980); *U.S. v. Cuthbertson*, 630 F.2d 139 (3d Cir. 1980) (*Cuthbertson I*); *Miller v. Transamerican Press, Inc.*, 621 F.2d 721 (5th Cir. 1980); *Palandjian v. Pahlavi*, 103 F.R.D. 410 (D.D.C. 1984); *Continental Cablevision, Inc. v. Storer Broadcasting Co.*, 583 F. Supp. 427 (E.D. Mo. 1984). As a result of this analysis, the courts have fashioned a three-part test, first articulated in *Garland v. Torre*,

---

a fair and complete trial on the other. *Id.* A number of courts have limited the applicability of the *Branzburg* precedent to the circumstances considered by that Court, i.e. the context of a criminal proceeding, or even more specifically, a grand jury subpoena. *Lee v. Department of Justice*, 413 F.3d 53, 58 (D.C. Cir. 2005).

259 F.2d 545 (2d Cir. 1958) to resolve privilege cases: the reporter's privilege is overridden only if: (1) the information sought is relevant, (2) it cannot be obtained by alternative means, and (3) there is a compelling interest in the information. *See, e.g., In re Petroleum Products Antitrust Litigation*, 680 F.2d 5 (2d Cir. 1982); *U.S. v. Sterling*, 2011 WL 4852226 (E.D.Va. 2011); *Criden*; *Cuthbertson*; *Sanders v. Alabama State Bar*, 887 F. Supp. 272 (M.D. Ala. 1995); *Continental Cablevision*; *but see In re Grand Jury Proceedings*, 810 F.2d 580 (6th Cir. 1987) (rejecting privilege); *U.S. v. King*, 194 F.R.D. 569, 584 (E.D. Va. 2000) ("[A] survey of the decisions in this circuit teaches that our Court of Appeals has recognized that *Branzburg* does not create a reportorial privilege, but that it entitles reporters to protection under certain circumstances").

The showing that the information sought is relevant and material must be specific. *U.S. v. Bingham*, 765 F. Supp. 954 (N.D. Ill. 1991). "Relevant" means the information goes to the heart of, or is crucial to, the claims made by the requesting party. *Neal v. City of Harvey, Ill.*, 173 F.R.D. 231 (N.D. Ill. 1997).

In addition to traditional journalists, the privilege has been extended to: academic investigators, *Cusumano*, 162 F.3d at 708; a documentary film maker, *Silkwood v. Kerr-McGee Corp.*, 563 F.2d 433 (10th Cir. 1977); the author of a technical publication, *Apicella v. McNeil Laboratories, Inc.*, 66 F.R.D. 78 (E.D. N.Y. 1975); an investigative book author, *Shoen v. Shoen*, 5 F.3d 1289 (9th Cir. 1993). *But see In re Madden*, 151 F.3d 125 (3d Cir. 1998) (privilege not available to pro wrestling publicist).

The critical question in determining if an individual falls within the protected class is whether the person at the inception of the investigatory process had the intent to disseminate to the public the information obtained through the investigation. *von Bulow by Auersperg v. von Bulow*, 811 F.2d 136 (2d Cir. 1987).

A number of courts hold that the qualified privilege applies to nonconfidential, as well as to confidential, information. *Gonzales v. National Broadcasting Co., Inc.*, 194 F.3d 29 (2d Cir. 1999); *Shoen v. Shoen*, 48 F.3d 412 (9th Cir. 1995) (routine court-compelled disclosure of nonconfidential research materials poses a serious threat to the vitality of the news gathering process); *U.S. v. LaRouche Campaign*, 841 F.2d 1176 (1st Cir. 1988) (discerning subtle threat to journalists and their employers if disclosure of outtakes, notes and other unused information, even if non-confidential, is routinely compelled); *Cuthbertson*, 630 F.2d at 139 (compelled production of reporter's resource materials can constitute significant intrusion into news gathering and editorial processes); *Penland v. Long*, 922 F. Supp. 1080 (W.D. N.C. 1995) (subpoenas quashed because privilege outweighed plaintiffs' need for reporters' notes; at issue was defendant's words as published in media and not his unpublished words as they appeared in journalists' notes or memories).

In *Gonzales v. National Broadcasting Co.*, the Second Circuit said that, while nonconfidential press materials are protected, the showing needed to overcome the privilege is less demanding than the showing required where confidential materials are sought. In the case of nonconfidential materials, the privilege is overcome if the materials are of likely relevance to a significant issue in the case and are not reasonably obtainable from other sources.

Additional References

Graham, Handbook of Federal Evidence § 501.1 (7th ed. 2012)

Treatises and Practice Aids

Goode and Wellborn, Courtroom Handbook on Federal Evidence Chapter 5, Rule 501 and Obj. 73 (annual ed.)

Wright & Graham, Federal Practice and Procedure: Evidence §§ 5005, 5426

Rothstein and Crump, Federal Testimonial Privileges Chapter 8 (annual ed.)

McCormick, Evidence § 76.2 (6th ed. 2006)

Park, Trial Objections Handbook § 5:32 (2nd ed. 2001)

PRIVILEGE: MILITARY AND STATE SECRETS PRIVILEGE

See:

Fed.R.Civ.P. 501

Mil.R.Evid. 505, Classified information, and 506, Government information other than classified information

Objection

- [*At sidebar*] The court previously ruled the military secrets privilege applies in this case. The question seeks to elicit privileged information.

Response

- If opposing counsel's objection is well founded, there is no response because the privilege is absolute.

Commentary

The military and state secrets privilege is an evidentiary privilege that allows the United States to withhold from disclosure military or state secrets when disclosure would be harmful to national security. *Tenet v. Doe*, 544 U.S. 1, 125 S. Ct. 1230, 161 L. Ed. 2d 82 (2005); *United States v. Reynolds*, 345 U.S. 1, 73 S. Ct. 528, 97, 97 L. Ed. 727 (1953); *In re Sealed Case*, 494 F.3d 139 (D.C. Cir. 2007); *Crater Corp. v. Lucent Technologies, Inc.*, 423 F.3d 1260 (Fed. Cir. 2005); *Frost v. Perry*, 919 F. Supp. 1459 (D. Nev. 1996); *Bentzlin v. Hughes Aircraft Co.*, 833 F. Supp. 1486 (C.D. Cal. 1993). Although the state secrets privilege was developed at common law, it performs a function of constitutional significance because it allows the executive branch to protect information whose secrecy is necessary to its military and foreign-affairs responsibilities. *El-Masri v. U.S.*, 479 F.3d 296 (4th Cir. 2007) (dismissal of claims that plaintiff was illegally detained as part of CIA's rendition program because claims and defenses could not be litigated without disclosure of protected secrets).

The privilege has been held to apply to information that would result in impairment of the nation's defense capabilities, disclosure of intelligence-gathering methods or capabilities, and disruption of diplomatic relations with foreign governments or where disclosure would be inimical to national security. *Black v. U.S.*, 62 F.3d 1115 (8th Cir. 1995); *In re U.S.*, 872 F.2d 472 (D.C. Cir. 1989); *Virtual Defense and Development Intern., Inc. v. Republic of Moldova*, 133 F. Supp. 2d 9 (D.D.C. 2001).

To properly invoke the military and state secrets privilege: (1) the head of the department which has control over the matter, after personal consideration, must formally claim the privilege on the public record (generally in the form of affidavit), and (2) either (a) publicly explain in detail the kinds of injury to national security he or she seeks to avoid and the reason those harms would result from revelation of the information or (b) indicate why such an explanation would itself endanger national security. *Reynolds*, 345 U.S. at 7–8; *Monarch Assur. P.L.C. v. U.S.*, 244 F.3d 1356 (Fed. Cir. 2001); *In re United States*, 872 F.2d at 472; *Ellsberg v. Mitchell*, 709 F.2d 51 (D.C. Cir. 1983); *Halkin v. Helms*, 690 F.2d 977 (D.C. Cir. 1982); *Linder v. Calero-Portocarrero*, 183 F.R.D. 314 (D.D.C. 1998).

Once the privilege has been formally claimed, the court must balance the "executive's expertise in assessing privilege on the grounds of military or diplomatic security" against the mandate that a court "not merely unthinkingly ratify the executive's assertion of absolute privilege, lest it inappropriately abandon its important judicial role." *In re United States*, 872 F.2d at 475–76 (internal citations omitted). "Judicial control over the evidence in a case cannot be abdicated to the caprice of executive officials." *Id.* (quoting *Reynolds*, 345 U.S. at 9–10).

When properly invoked, the privilege is absolute. *Halkin v. Helms*, 598 F.2d 1 (D.C. Cir. 1978) ("*Halkin 1*"). The military and state secrets privilege alone can be the basis for dismissal of part or an entire case. See, e.g., *General Dynamics Corp. v. U.S.*, ___ U.S. ___, 131 S.Ct. 1900, 179 L.Ed.2d 957 (2011) (special circumstances dictated a refusal to enforce a government contract, leaving the parties where they are) and *Al-Haramain Islamic Foundation, Inc. v. Bush*, 507 F.3d 1190

(9th Cir. 2007) (where very subject matter of lawsuit is matter of state secret, action must be dismissed without reaching question of evidence); *American Civil Liberties Union v. National Sec. Agency*, 493 F.3d 644, 650 n.2 (6th Cir. 2007) ("the state secrets doctrine has two applications: a rule of evidentiary privilege and a rule of non-justiciability"); *Sterling v. Tenet*, 416 F.3d 338 (4th Cir. 2005) (Title VII litigation centering around covert agents' assignments, evaluations and colleagues meets tests for dismissal under state secrets privilege); *Kasza v. Browner*, 133 F.3d 1159 (9th Cir. 1998) (if plaintiff cannot prove *prima facie* elements of claim without resort to privileged information, court may dismiss); *Bareford v. General Dynamics Corp.*, 973 F.2d 1138 (5th Cir. 1992); *Zuckerbraun v. General Dynamics Corp.*, 935 F.2d 544 (2d Cir. 1991); *Weston v. Lockheed Missiles & Space Co.*, 881 F.2d 814 (9th Cir. 1989); *Edmonds v. U.S. Dept. of Justice*, 323 F. Supp. 2d 65 (D.D.C. 2004) (case dismissed where plaintiff could not establish her claims and defendant could not establish its defenses without disclosure of privileged information).

Additional References

Graham, Handbook of Federal Evidence § 509.1 (7th ed. 2012)

Treatises and Practice Aids

Goode and Wellborn, Courtroom Handbook on Federal Evidence Chapter 5 and Obj. 73 (annual ed.)

Mueller & Kirkpatrick, Federal Evidence, § 5:55 (3d ed. 2007)

Wright & Graham, Federal Practice and Procedure: Evidence 2d § 5006

Rothstein and Crump, Federal Testimonial Privileges Chapter 5, §§ 5.02[1], 5.03[1] (annual ed.)

McCormick, Evidence § 107 (6th ed. 2006)

Park, Trial Objections Handbook § 5:34 (2nd ed. 2001)

PRIVILEGE: PSYCHOTHERAPIST-PATIENT

See:

Fed.R.Evid. 501
Mil.R.Evid. 513

Objection

- Objection. [*Request sidebar*] The question seeks information communicated to a [*psychiatrist*] [*psychologist*] [*clinical social worker*] which is privileged under Rule 501.

Response

- This evidence is not privileged because [*the statements were made in the presence of a third person who was not an agent for one of the parties to the privilege*] [*there was no confidential relationship nor any confidential communications*] [*the witness has placed her mental condition in issue by (specify)*].

Commentary

In *Jaffee v. Redmond*, 518 U.S. 1, 116 S. Ct. 1923, 135 L. Ed. 2d 337 (1996), the Supreme Court recognized a psychotherapist-patient privilege that protects confidential communications made by a patient to a licensed psychiatrist or psychologist in the course of diagnosis and treatment. The privilege extends to licensed clinical social workers whose "clients often include the poor and those of modest means who could not afford the assistance of a psychiatrist or psychologist . . . but whose counseling sessions serve the same public goals." *Id.* at 16.

The privilege is rooted in the imperative need for confidence and trust by the patient and to encourage full disclosure to the psychotherapist. By preventing the latter from divulging information which could cause embarrassment or disgrace, the privilege is designed to promote effective treatment and to insulate the patient's private thoughts from involuntary disclosure. The privilege shields both testimony and records from discovery, absent the consent of the patient. *Jaffee*.

Although *Jaffee* did not attempt to flesh out the

full contours of the privilege, it held that decisions regarding the privilege should not be made by balancing the interests of the patient against the value of the evidence. *Id.* at 17–18.

The Court recognized the privilege can be waived, *Id.* at 15 n.14, but did not elaborate on what would constitute waiver. The Court did suggest one instance in which the privilege would not apply—when a serious threat of harm to the patient or to others can be averted only by means of a disclosure by the therapist. *Id.* at 18 n.19. *Compare U.S. v. Glass*, 133 F.3d 1356 (10th Cir. 1998) (recognizing dangerous patient exception to the privilege) with *U.S. v. Hayes*, 227 F.3d 578, 586 (6th Cir. 2000) ("dangerous patient" exception should not become part of federal common law).

Post *Jaffee*, there is division in the courts on the issue of waiver. Some courts hold that a claim of emotional distress alone is sufficient to put a plaintiff's medical condition "at issue." *Doe v. Oberweis Dairy*, 456 F.3d 704 (7th Cir. 2006) (by placing medical condition at issue, plaintiff waived privilege); *Schoffstall v. Henderson*, 223 F.3d 818 (8th Cir. 2000) (same); *Fox v. Gates Corp.*, 179 F.R.D. 303 (D. Colo. 1998); *Sarko v. Penn-Del Directory Co.*, 170 F.R.D. 127 (E.D. Pa. 1997); *but see Koch v. Cox*, 489 F.3d 384 (D.C. Cir. 2007) (employee did not put mental state in issue by acknowledging depression for which he was not seeking damages). Other courts hold that the privilege is waived only where the patient either calls the therapist as a witness or introduces in evidence the substance of any therapist-patient communication. *Vanderbilt v. Town of Chilmark*, 174 F.R.D. 225 (D. Mass. 1997); *Fritsch v. City of Chula Vista*, 187 F.R.D. 614, 629 (S.D. Cal. 1999) (following the analysis in *Vanderbuilt*).

The privilege does not apply where there is actual notice or indication due to the circumstances, that the communications will not be kept confidential, as is frequently the case with employer, agency or court-ordered psychiatric or psychological examinations. *U.S. v. Auster*, 517 F.3d 312 (5th Cir. 2008) (where defendant knew his therapist had duty to, and would warn targets of his death threats; confidentiality requirement not met and privilege did not apply); *Barrett v. Vojtas*, 182

F.R.D. 177 (W.D. Pa. 1998) (no privilege where police officer was ordered to undergo counseling and reports were submitted to employer); *accord Phelps v. Coy*, 194 F.R.D. 606 (S.D. Ohio 2000); *Kamper v. Gray*, 182 F.R.D. 597 (E.D. Mo. 1998); *but see James v. Harris County*, 237 F.R.D. 606, 611 (S.D. Tex. 2006) (psychotherapist-patient privilege applies to mandatory post-shooting counseling sessions for law enforcement officer if officer had reasonable expectation of privacy before starting therapy). Accord, *Barrios-Barrios v. Clipps*, 2011 WL 4550205 (E.D.La. 2011).

Some courts have held that a defendant's constitutional rights of confrontation, cross-examination and due process outweigh this privilege. *U.S. v. Lindstrom*, 698 F.2d 1154 (11th Cir. 1983) (society's interest in guarding confidentiality of communications between therapist and patient who was key prosecution witness outweighed by defendant's constitutional right to effectively prepare and cross-examine witness); *Bassine v. Hill*, 450 F. Supp. 2d 1182 (D. Or. 2006) (same); *U.S. v. Mazzola*, 217 F.R.D. 84 (D. Mass. 2003) (same); *but see Newton v. Kemna*, 354 F.3d 776 (8th Cir. 2004) (trial judge's refusal to allow defendant to discover psychiatric records of prosecution witness who asserted privilege, not abuse of discretion).

Borrowing its analysis from attorney-client privilege, the First Circuit, in a case of first impression, has held that the crime-fraud exception applies where the therapist's services are sought to further a criminal or fraudulent endeavor. *In re Grand Jury Proceedings (Gregory P. Violette)*, 183 F.3d 71 (1st Cir. 1999). Even if the criminal intent is solely that of the patient and not the therapist, the exception applies and the communication is not privileged. *Id.* The party seeking to take advantage of the exception has the burden of proof and must make out a prima facie case sufficient to satisfy the court that the patient was engaged in an ongoing crime or fraud or was seeking to commit a crime or fraud at the time the communication was made. *Id.* The court may conduct an *in camera* review of allegedly privileged communications to determine whether the crime-fraud exception applies. The party seeking review must first show a factual basis adequate to support a good faith belief by a reasonable person that an *in camera* review may reveal evidence that would establish the crime-fraud exception to the psychotherapist-patient privilege. This showing must be made through the use of non-privileged materials. *See United States v. Zolin*, 491 U.S. 554, 109 S. Ct. 2619, 105 L. Ed. 2d 469 (1989).

Cf. Oleszko v. State Compensation Ins. Fund, 243 F.3d 1154 (9th Cir. 2001) (privilege extends to unlicensed counselors in employee assistance programs); *Speaker ex rel. Speaker v. County of San Bernardino*, 82 F. Supp. 2d 1105 (C.D. Cal. 2000) (privilege applies where police officer patient reasonably but mistakenly believed that mental health counselor was psychotherapist); *U.S. v. Lowe*, 948 F. Supp. 97 (D. Mass. 1996) (client of rape counseling center holds some form of a federal privilege for communications with rape crisis counselor); *Ziemann v. Burlington County Bridge Com'n*, 155 F.R.D. 497 (D.N.J. 1994) (declining to recognize marriage counselor privilege under federal common law but opining in dicta that it should receive protection as outgrowth of psychotherapist-patient privilege); *U.S. v. Hansen*, 955 F. Supp. 1225 (D. Mont. 1997) (homicide defendant's need for privileged material outweighed interests against disclosure where patient was dead and his mental and emotional condition was central element of defendant's claim of self-defense).

Note: With certain enumerated exceptions, the Public Health Service Act, 42 U.S.C.A. §§ 290dd-2 et seq. and regulations (42 C.F.R. §§ 2.1 to 2.67) prohibit release of medical records disclosing treatment for drug and alcohol abuse in federally funded programs and declare such records confidential. As one court noted, Congress felt the strictest adherence to the confidentiality provision was needed lest individuals in need of treatment be dissuaded from seeking help. *Ellison v. Cocke County, Tenn.*, 63 F.3d 467, 470 (6th Cir. 1995) (drug abuse records); *Whyte v. Connecticut Mut. Life Ins. Co.*, 818 F.2d 1005 (1st Cir. 1987) (alcoholism). For discussion of the exceptions, *see U.S. v. Hughes*, 95 F. Supp. 2d 49 (D. Mass. 2000) and *Fannon v. Johnston*, 88 F. Supp. 2d 753 (E.D. Mich. 2000).

Additional References

Graham, Handbook of Federal Evidence § 504.1 (7th ed. 2012)

Treatises and Practice Aids

Goode and Wellborn, Courtroom Handbook on Federal Evidence Chapter 5 and Obj. 79 (annual ed.)

Mueller & Kirkpatrick, Federal Evidence, §§ 5:7, 5:42, 5:43 (3d ed. 2007)

Wright & Graham, Federal Practice and Procedure: Evidence §§ 5521 *et seq.*

Rothstein and Crump, Federal Testimonial Privileges, Chapter 8 (annual ed.)

McCormick, Evidence § 98 (6th ed. 2006)

Park, Trial Objections Handbook § 5:24 (2nd ed. 2001)

PRIVILEGE: SELF-INCRIMINATION

See:

U.S. Const., Amend. V
Fed.R.Evid. 501
Mil.R.Evid. 501

Objection

- [*At sidebar*] The question is one that the witness cannot be compelled to answer because of the privilege against self-incrimination, which is hereby invoked.

Response

- [*Opposing counsel should demand an offer of proof on the validity of the claim of privilege. Where the trial court determines the requested evidence would tend to incriminate the witness, there is no response since the privilege is absolute.*]

Commentary

The Fifth Amendment provides that "[n]o person . . . shall be compelled in any criminal case to be a witness against himself." U.S. Const. Amend. V. The privilege may be invoked not only at trial but also at the pleading stage and in the course of discovery proceedings. *Nutramax Laboratories, Inc. v. Twin Laboratories, Inc.*, 32 F. Supp. 2d 331 (D. Md. 1999). It can be asserted in any proceeding, whether civil, criminal, administrative, or investigatory (including a grand jury) in which the witness reasonably believes that the information sought, or the evidence discovered as a result of that information, could be used against him in a subsequent criminal proceeding. *Lefkowitz v. Turley*, 414 U.S. 70, 94 S. Ct. 316, 38 L. Ed. 2d 274 (1973); *Kastigar v. United States*, 406 U.S. 441, 92 S. Ct. 1653, 32 L. Ed. 2d 212 (1972); *Sher v. U.S. Dept. of Veterans Affairs*, 488 F.3d 489 (1st Cir. 2007); *U.S. v. Bodwell*, 66 F.3d 1000 (9th Cir. 1995); *U.S. v. Penrod*, 609 F.2d 1092 (4th Cir. 1979). The privilege extends not only to disclosures that would support a conviction but also to those that might lead to the discovery of evidence needed to prosecute the witness for a crime. *Ohio v. Reiner*, 532 U.S. 17, 121 S. Ct. 1252, 149 L. Ed. 2d 158 (2001) (privilege not only extends to answers that would support a conviction but embraces those which would furnish a link in the chain of evidence needed to prosecute the witness); *Doe v. United States*, 487 U.S. 201, 108 S. Ct. 2341, 101 L. Ed. 2d 184 (1988); *Hoffman v. United States*, 341 U.S. 479, 71 S. Ct. 814, 95 L. Ed. 1118 (1951); *Blau v. United States*, 340 U.S. 159, 71 S. Ct. 223, 95 L. Ed. 170 (1950); *U.S. v. Rendahl*, 746 F.2d 553 (9th Cir. 1984); *U.S. v. Bourdet*, 477 F. Supp. 2d 164 (D.D.C. 2007).

The privilege protects a witness as fully as it does one who is a party. *National Life Ins. Co. v. Hartford Acc. and Indem. Co.*, 615 F.2d 595 (3d Cir. 1980). To invoke Fifth Amendment protection, the person must be confronted with substantial and real, and not merely trifling or imaginary, hazards of incrimination. *United States v. Apfelbaum*, 445 U.S. 115, 100, 100 S. Ct. 948, 63 L. Ed. 2d 250 (1980); *Zicarelli v. New Jersey State Commission of Investigation*, 406 U.S. 472, 92 S. Ct. 1670, 32 L. Ed. 2d 234 (1972); *California v. Byers*, 402 U.S. 424, 91 S. Ct. 1535, 29 L. Ed. 2d 9 (1971) (privilege does not protect against remote and speculative possibilities); *U.S. v. Bowling*, 239 F.3d 973 (8th Cir. 2001) (where witness was under indictment, possibility of self-incrimination was not remote or speculative); *U.S. v. Gecas*, 120 F.3d 1419 (11th Cir. 1997) (witness' fear of conviction because of his testimony must be reasonable, real and appreciable); *U.S. v. Madrzyk*, 990 F. Supp. 1004 (N.D. Ill. 1998). Fear of public disgrace, personal danger or civil liability are not adequate constitutional grounds to invoke the privilege. McCormick, Evidence, § 120 (5th ed. 1999).

When an individual is called to testify in a judicial proceeding, he or she is not excused from answering questions merely by declaring that to do so would be self-incriminating. It is always for the court to determine if silence is justified, *U.S. v. Gaitan-Acevedo*, 148 F.3d 577 (6th Cir. 1998), and an illusory claim should be rejected. To sustain the invocation of the privilege, the trial judge must determine only whether there is a reasonable basis for believing a risk of prosecution might arise from answering a particular question, for "if the witness

. . . were required to prove the hazard . . . he would be compelled to surrender the very protection which the privilege is designed to guarantee." *Hoffman*, 341 U.S. at 486; *U.S. v. Allen*, 491 F.3d 178 (4th Cir. 2007) (because requiring a witness to prove the necessity of the privilege would often vitiate the privilege itself, it need only be evident from the implications of the question, in the setting in which it is asked, that a responsive answer to the question or explanation of why it cannot be answered might be dangerous because injurious disclosure could result). When the witness refuses to answer a particular question, the trial judge has a duty to determine whether a narrower privilege would suffice to protect the witness from danger while permitting the government or other opposing party to elicit desired testimony. *U.S. v. Reese*, 561 F.2d 894 (D.C. Cir. 1977). Usually, a trial court cannot speculate whether all relevant questions would or would not tend to incriminate the witness. Accordingly, the court normally requires the privilege to be asserted in response to specific questions. *Vazquez-Rijos v. Anhang*, 654 F.3d 122 (1st Cir. 2011); *U.S. v. Bright*, 596 F.3d 683 (9th Cir. 2010); *U.S. v. Gibbs*, 182 F.3d 408 (6th Cir. 1999). In unusual cases, however, the trial judge may sustain a blanket assertion of privilege after determining that there is a reasonable basis for believing a risk to the witness might arise from answering any relevant question. *Anton v. Prospect Cafe Milano, Inc.*, 233 F.R.D. 216 (D.D.C. 2006); *U.S. v. Reese*, 561 F.2d at 894; *U.S. v. Tsui*, 646 F.2d 365, 367–68 (9th Cir. 1981) (trial court may accept blanket privilege where, "based on its knowledge of the case and of the testimony expected from the witnesses, [it] can conclude that the witness could legitimately refuse to answer all relevant questions") (quoting *U.S. v. Goodwin*, 625 F.2d 693, 701 (5th Cir. 1980)).

For a court properly to overrule a claim of privilege, it must be clear from a careful consideration of all of the circumstances, that the witness is mistaken in the belief of self-incrimination and the answer demanded cannot possibly pose a risk of prosecution. *Hoffman*, 341 U.S. at 487–88.

The Fifth Amendment's protection applies only when the accused is compelled to make a *testimonial* communication that is incriminating. *Baltimore*

City Dept. of Social Services v. Bouknight, 493 U.S. 549, 110 S. Ct. 900, 107 L. Ed. 2d 992 (1990). Various types of evidence may be testimonial in nature, including the act of producing materials in response to a summons and subpoena. *United States v. Hubbell*, 530 U.S. 27, 120 S. Ct. 2037, 147 L. Ed. 2d 24 (2000) (act of producing incriminating documents previously unknown to government was sufficiently testimonial for purposes of Fifth Amendment). However, the Fifth Amendment does not offer protection from the compelled production of demonstrative, physical or real evidence such as fingerprints, photographs, measurements, writing or speaking for identification, appearing in court, standing, walking or making a particular gesture. *See Pennsylvania v. Muniz*, 496 U.S. 582, 110 S. Ct. 2638, 110 L. Ed. 2d 528 (1990) (field sobriety test); *U.S. v. Dionisio*, 410 U.S. 1, 93 S. Ct. 764, 35 L. Ed. 2d 67 (1973) (voice exemplar); *U.S. v. Wade*, 388 U.S. 218, 87 S. Ct. 1926, 18 L. Ed. 2d 1149 (1967) (same); *Gilbert v. California*, 388 U.S. 263, 87 S. Ct. 1951, 18 L. Ed. 2d 1178 (1967) (handwriting sample); *Schmerber v. California*, 384 U.S. 757, 87, 86 S. Ct. 1826, 16 L. Ed. 2d 908 (1966) (blood sample); *Wilson v. Collins*, 517 F.3d 421 (6th Cir. 2008) (collection of DNA specimen does not implicate Fifth Amendment privilege); *U.S. v. Williams*, 461 F.3d 441 (4th Cir. 2006) (Fifth Amendment does not protect a person from having to try on clothing); *U.S. v. Montgomery*, 100 F.3d 1404 (8th Cir. 1996) (same); *U.S. v. Clark*, 847 F.2d 1467 (10th Cir. 1988) (handwriting sample); *U.S. v. Holloway*, 906 F. Supp. 1437 (D. Kan. 1995) (no violation to extract drugs from defendant's mouth). *See In re Grand Jury Subpoena to John Doe*, 475 F. Supp. 2d 1185 (M.D. Fla. 2006) (discussing at what point providing handwriting exemplar ceases to be mere physical act and becomes testimonial and communicative, thus invoking Fifth Amendment protections).

The privilege is purely personal and cannot be utilized by a corporation or other collective entity. *Bellis v. United States*, 417 U.S. 85, 94 S. Ct. 2179, 40 L. Ed. 2d 678 (1974) (law partnership); *United States v. White*, 322 U.S. 694, 64 S. Ct. 1248, 88 L. Ed. 1542 (1944) (labor union); *Hale v. Henkel*, 201 U.S. 43, 26 S. Ct. 370, 50 L. Ed. 652 (1906); *U.S. v.*

Feng Juan Lu, 248 Fed. Appx. 806 (9th Cir. 2007) (single member limited liability company (LLC) not protected by privilege); *U.S. v. Maxey & Co., P.C.*, 956 F. Supp. 823 (N.D. Ind. 1997) (corporation); *U.S. v. Kennedy*, 122 F. Supp. 2d 1195 (N.D. Okla. 2000) (trust). Because corporate document custodians hold corporate records in a representative rather than a personal capacity, those records cannot be the subject of the custodian's personal privilege against self-incrimination. *Braswell v. United States*, 487 U.S. 99, 108 S. Ct. 2284, 101 L. Ed. 2d 98 (1988); *In re Grand Jury Witnesses*, 92 F.3d 710 (8th Cir. 1996); *F.T.C. v. Pacific First Ben., LLC*, 361 F. Supp. 2d 751 (N.D. Ill. 2005) (an individual cannot rely on a personal privilege of self-incrimination to avoid producing records of a collective entity which are in his possession in a representative capacity, even if those records might incriminate him personally). Notwithstanding that the custodian asserts a Fifth Amendment privilege in his/her individual capacity, testimony that may be compelled consists generally of: (1) the identity of the documents produced; (2) the nature and scope of the search performed; and (3) the authenticity of the documents within the meaning of Rule 901. By contrast, testimony qualifying the documents as business records under Rule 803(6) and substantive testimony cannot be compelled. *In Re Grand Jury Proceedings*, 473 F. Supp. 2d 201 (D.Mass. 2007) (collecting cases).

A witness who asserts his Fifth Amendment privilege may be compelled to testify if he is granted statutory immunity. Statutory immunity prohibits the government from using any "testimony or other information compelled under the order (or any information directly or indirectly derived from such testimony or other information) . . . against the witness in any criminal case." 18 U.S.C.A. § 6002; *see U.S. v. Pagnotti*, 507 F. Supp. 2d 494 (M.D. Pa. 2007) (Section 6002 provides "a sweeping proscription of any use, direct or indirect, of the compelled testimony and any information derived therefrom," *citing Kastigar*, 406 U.S. at 460). Statutory immunity, however, does not completely insulate an individual from prosecution. The government may prosecute a witness who has been granted statutory immunity if the government proves "that the evidence it proposes to use is derived from a legitimate source wholly independent of the compelled testimony." *Kastigar v. United States*, 406 U.S. 441, 460, 92 S. Ct. 1653, 1664, 32 L. Ed. 2d 212 (1972).

If a witness asserts the privilege on cross-examination regarding collateral matters, the witness' direct testimony need not be stricken. *U.S. v. Cardillo*, 316 F.2d 606 (2d Cir. 1963). But if the witness' assertion of privilege precludes inquiry into the details of his direct testimony so that the opponent is deprived of the right to test its truth, the court should strike it. *Id*; *U.S. v. Henry*, 472 F. Supp. 2d 649 (E.D.Pa. 2007) (collecting cases).

The Fifth Amendment applies to proceedings conducted in a court or other governmental forum and not to those conducted in a private forum. *U.S. v. International Broth. of Teamsters*, 945 F. Supp. 96 (S.D. N.Y. 1996) (Fifth Amendment unavailable to union member called to sworn examination before internal union disciplinary body); *Nuzzo v. Northwest Airlines, Inc.*, 887 F. Supp. 28 (D. Mass. 1995) (internal company investigation); *Cohen v. President and Fellows of Harvard College*, 568 F. Supp. 658 (D. Mass. 1983) (university employment decision).

If an accused has been convicted but not sentenced or has been sentenced but is appealing, he or she usually may invoke the privilege. *See, e.g., Mitchell v. United States*, 526 U.S. 314, 119 S. Ct. 1307, 143 L. Ed. 2d 424 (1999) (defendant could assert Fifth Amendment right not to testify at sentencing); *U.S. v. Lumpkin*, 192 F.3d 280 (2d Cir. 1999) (witness who pleaded guilty but had not yet been sentenced could assert privilege not to testify at co-defendant's trial); *U.S. v. Bahadar*, 954 F.2d 821 (2d Cir. 1992) (same).

Criminal Proceedings

The privilege against self-incrimination operates differently in civil and criminal proceedings.

In a criminal case, the jury is not permitted to draw any inference from the decision of a witness to exercise his constitutional privilege. *Rhode v. Olk-Long*, 84 F.3d 284 (8th Cir. 1996); *U.S. v. Duran*, 884 F. Supp. 573 (D.D.C. 1995). The prosecution is not permitted to call a witness to the stand for the purpose of having him exercise his privilege since this invites the jury to make an improper inference. *U.S. v. Rivas-Macias*, 537 F.3d 1271 (10th Cir. 2008); *U.S. v. Reese*, 561 F.2d 894 (D.C. Cir. 1977) (defendant has no right to put witness on stand simply to require him to assert privilege); *U.S. v. Quinn*, 543 F.2d 640 (8th Cir. 1976) (mistrial may be warranted when prosecutor calls witness to stand with advance knowledge that witness will invoke Fifth Amendment); *Bowles v. U.S.*, 439 F.2d 536 (D.C. Cir. 1970); *San Fratello v. U.S.*, 340 F.2d 560 (5th Cir. 1965) (reversible error in permitting prosecution to call witness so as to require her to claim Fifth Amendment privilege in presence of jury).

It is a fundamental principle of due process that the government cannot use, at trial, a defendant's post-*Miranda* silence as substantive evidence of guilt. *Doyle v. Ohio*, 426 U.S. 610, 96 S. Ct. 2240, 49 L. Ed. 2d 91 (1976) (government may not impeach defendant's exculpatory story told for first time at trial by cross-examining defendant about failure to have told that story after receiving Miranda warnings at time of arrest);* *U.S. v. O'Keefe*, 461 F.3d 1338 (11th Cir. 2006). A prosecutor may

---

[Privilege etc.]

*The rule does not apply when a defendant testifies at trial that he told his exculpatory story at the time of his arrest. *Doyle*, 426 U.S. at 619 n.11. In such a case, the prosecution may introduce defendant's post-arrest silence to impeach his trial testimony that upon arrest, he did not remain silent but told his exculpatory story. *Id.*, *U.S. v. Martinez-Larraga*, 517 F.3d 258 (5th Cir. 2008). While the government may use a defendant's post-arrest silence to impeach testimony about the circumstances of an arrest, it cannot proceed to argue that defendant's silence was inconsistent with his claim of innocence. *U.S. v. Rodriguez*, 260 F.3d 416 (5th Cir. 2001) (permissible to impeach defendant's testimony about exculpatory story with post-arrest silence but error to urge jury in closing argument to infer guilt from that silence).

Circuits that have considered whether the government may comment on a defendant's *prearrest* silence in its case in chief are divided.

Four circuits have held that such use violates the privilege against self-incrimination, relying principally upon *Griffin v. California*, 380 U.S. 609, 85 S. Ct. 1229, 14 L. Ed. 2d 106 (1965) (Fifth Amendment forbids either comment by prosecution on accused's refusal to testify at trial or instructions by

not comment directly or indirectly on a defendant's failure to testify. *Griffin v. California*, 380 U.S. 609, 85 S. Ct. 1229, 14 L. Ed. 2d 106 (1965); *U.S. v. Bey*, 188 F.3d 1 (1st Cir. 1999); *U.S. v. Griffith*, 118 F.3d 318 (5th Cir. 1997); *U.S. v. Cotnam*, 88 F.3d 487 (7th Cir. 1996); *U.S. v. Andreas*, 23 F. Supp. 2d 855 (N.D. Ill. 1998). Comment is impermissible if it is manifestly intended to call attention to the defendant's failure to testify, or is of such a character that the jury would naturally and necessarily take it to be a comment on the failure to testify. *U.S. v. Mietus*, 237 F.3d 866 (7th Cir. 2001); *Lincoln v. Sunn*, 807 F.2d 805 (9th Cir. 1987) (prosecutor commits "*Griffin*" error by referring to absence of testimony that only defendant could have provided); *Lesko v. Lehman*, 925 F.2d 1527 (3d Cir. 1991) ("*Griffin*" error where prosecutor implied that capital defendant had moral or legal obligation to apologize for his crimes).

Civil Proceedings

The Fifth Amendment does not forbid adverse inferences against parties to civil actions when they refuse to testify in response to probative evidence offered against them. *Mitchell v. United States*, 526 U.S. 314, 119 S. Ct. 1307, 143 L. Ed. 2d 424 (1999); *Baxter v. Palmigiano*, 425 U.S. 308, 96 S. Ct. 1551, 47 L. Ed. 2d 810 (1976); *Greviskes v. Universities Research Ass'n, Inc.*, 417 F.3d 752 (7th Cir. 2005)

---

court that silence is evidence of guilt). *See Combs v. Coyle*, 205 F.3d 269 (6th Cir. 2000); *U.S. v. Burson*, 952 F.2d 1196 (10th Cir. 1991); *Coppola v. Powell*, 878 F.2d 1562 (1st Cir. 1989); *U.S. ex rel. Savory v. Lane*, 832 F.2d 1011 (7th Cir. 1987).

Three other circuits have reached the opposite conclusion. *U.S. v. Oplinger*, 150 F.3d 1061 (9th Cir. 1998) (overruled on other grounds by, U.S. v. Katie Sue Contreras, 2010 WL 348004 (9th Cir. 2010)) (privilege irrelevant to citizen's decision to remain silent when he is under no official compulsion to speak); *U.S. v. Zanabria*, 74 F.3d 590 (5th Cir. 1996); *U.S. v. Rivera*, 944 F.2d 1563 (11th Cir. 1991).; *U.S. v. Kallin*, 50 F.3d 689 (9th Cir. 1995) (prosecutor's line of questioning and closing remarks not inadvertent but calculated so that inappropriate inference of guilt from silence was stressed to jury); *U.S. v. Harris*, 956 F.2d 177 (8th Cir. 1992) (reference at trial to silence of accused impermissible because fundamentally unfair for government to induce silence through *Miranda* warnings and then use silence against accused).

(Fifth Amendment does not forbid inferences against parties to civil actions when they refuse to testify in response to probative evidence offered against them); *Central States, Southeast and Southwest Areas Pension Fund v. Wintz Properties, Inc.*, 155 F.3d 868 (7th Cir. 1998) (invoking Fifth Amendment in civil context permits inference that witness' testimony would be adverse to his interests); *see also LiButti v. U.S.*, 107 F.3d 110 (2d Cir. 1997) (circumstances of case made nonparty witness' invocation of privilege admissible against plaintiff). And in certain civil cases, a party may call a witness to the stand even when that witness has made known his intention to invoke the Fifth Amendment. Courts evaluate these situations on a case-by-case basis and subject to the Rule 403 balancing test, weighing the probative value of the evidence against its prejudicial effect. *See F.D.I.C. v. Fidelity & Deposit Co. of Maryland*, 45 F.3d 969 (5th Cir. 1995) (in fidelity bond claim where loss discovery date and activities of chief lending officer were in issue, jury could determine that witness took Fifth Amendment to avoid disclosing collusion with lending officer); *Cerro Gordo Charity v. Fireman's Fund American Life Ins. Co.*, 819 F.2d 1471 (8th Cir. 1987) (where insured was murdered and beneficiary was charity founded by half brother, insurance company permitted to call half brother who invoked privilege as to all questions concerning death); *Rad Services, Inc. v. Aetna Cas. and Sur. Co.*, 808 F.2d 271 (3d Cir. 1986) (coverage case where insurance company was permitted to introduce depositions of plaintiff's former employees who had claimed Fifth Amendment re crucial facts at issue); *Brink's Inc. v. City of New York*, 717 F.2d 700 (2d Cir. 1983) (in action by city against armored-car carrier for negligent hiring and supervision, refusal by past and present Brink's employees on Fifth Amendment grounds to answer questions about theft of parking meter revenues was admissible evidence).

In appropriate cases, courts may bar litigants from testifying later about matters previously hidden from discovery through improper invocation of the Fifth Amendment. *Nationwide Life Ins. Co. v. Richards*, 541 F.3d 903 (9th Cir. 2008) (witness precluded at trial from testifying about her lack of involvement in insured's murder because she refused to answer questions on this subject during deposition); *Bourgal v. Robco Contracting Enterprises, Ltd.*, 969 F. Supp. 854 (E.D. N.Y. 1997) (collecting cases); *S.E.C. v. Softpoint, Inc.*, 958 F. Supp. 846 (S.D. N.Y. 1997); *F.T.C. v. Sharp*, 782 F. Supp. 1445 (D. Nev. 1991) (trial courts generally will not permit a party to invoke the privilege against self-incrimination with respect to deposition questions and then later testify about the same subject matter at trial). When a claimant in a civil case invokes the privilege to refuse to answer relevant and necessary questions during discovery, it is within the court's discretion to dismiss his claims. *See Trustees of Boston University v. ASM Communications, Inc.*, 33 F. Supp. 2d 66 (D. Mass. 1998) (citing, *inter alia, Serafino v. Hasbro, Inc.*, 893 F. Supp. 104 (D. Mass. 1995)).

Most courts hold that waiver of the privilege in one proceeding does not affect the right of a witness to invoke the privilege as to the same subject matter in another independent proceeding. *U.S. v. James*, 609 F.2d 36 (2d Cir. 1979); *In re Vitamins Antitrust Litigation*, 120 F. Supp. 2d 58 (D.D.C. 2000).

Treatises and Practice Aids

Goode and Wellborn, Courtroom Handbook on Federal Evidence Chapter 5 (annual ed.)

Wright & Graham, Federal Practice and Procedure: Evidence §§ 5723, 5752

McCormick, Evidence Chapter 13 (6th ed. 2006)

Park, Trial Objections Handbook §§ 5:28 to 5:30 (2nd ed. 2001)

REFRESHING PRESENT RECOLLECTION

See:

Fed.R.Evid. 612
Mil.R.Evid. 612

Technique

[*After demonstrating that the witness needs to review a document (or thing) to revive his recollection, the attorney for the proponent shows the writing (or object) to the witness and asks him to review it silently. Counsel then asks the witness if his memory is refreshed. If so, the document (or object) is put aside and the witness can testify*].

Objection

- Objection. There is no foundation showing that the witness' present memory was inadequate. The witness never testified that he could not recall specific details and, in fact, admitted to having an independent present recollection of events.

Response

- I have established that: (1) the witness' present memory is inadequate; (2) the writing could refresh the witness' present memory; and (3) after reviewing the writing, the witness has indicated this writing actually does refresh his present memory.

Commentary

It is not uncommon for a witness at trial to forget information or to recollect information only partially or inaccurately. A witness whose memory is shown to be inadequate or exhausted may use a writing or other aid to refresh or revive his present recollection of past events. Rule 612; *U.S. v. Cisneros-Gutierrez*, 517 F.3d 751 (5th Cir. 2008); *U.S. v. Cardales*, 168 F.3d 548 (1st Cir. 1999) (where officer inaccurately testified that his report did not mention field testing seized marijuana, his recollection could be refreshed by showing him his report indicating field test was performed); *U.S. v. Muhammad*, 120 F.3d 688 (7th Cir. 1997) (FBI agent could refresh her own recollection from report prepared by another agent).

To use a writing to refresh memory, the following foundation must first be established: (1) the witness' present memory is inadequate; (2) the writing could refresh the witness' present memory; and (3) reference to the writing actually does refresh the witness' present memory. *U.S. v. Thompson*, 708 F.2d 1294, 1299 (8th Cir. 1983); *U.S. v. Jimenez*, 613 F.2d 1373 (5th Cir. 1980).

The proper procedure for a party to refresh his own witness' recollection is with a request that the witness read the document to himself; after the witness' recollection is refreshed, the direct examination may proceed with the witness testifying from present recollection. Graham, Handbook of Federal Evidence § 612.1 (5th ed. 2001).

While Rule 612 permits a witness to use a prior writing to refresh his present memory of past events, the witness must testify from present, albeit refreshed memory and not from the writing itself. *U.S. v. Weller*, 238 F.3d 1215 (10th Cir. 2001) (court has discretion to withhold writing from witness where the judge believes document will be source of direct testimony rather than key to refreshing witness' independent recollection); *Strickland Tower Maintenance, Inc. v. AT & T Communications, Inc.*, 128 F.3d 1422 (10th Cir. 1997) (same); *Hall v. American Bakeries Co.*, 873 F.2d 1133, 1136 (8th Cir. 1989) ("It is error to allow a witness to testify at trial from prepared notes under the guise of refreshing recollection"); *U.S. v. Scott*, 701 F.2d 1340 (11th Cir. 1983) (where defendant was charged with making false statements to banks, witnesses were allowed to use credit applications to refresh recollection but instructed by court not to testify to any statement in documents for which they did not have independent recollection).

Once the writing has refreshed the witness' present memory, it has served its purpose and may not be introduced into evidence except by the opposing party. Therefore, a witness may use a memorandum or other aid for the purpose of refreshing memory even though the writing itself may be inadmissible evidence. *U.S. v. Shinderman*, 515 F.3d 5 (1st Cir. 2008); *U.S. v. Weller*, 238 F.3d at 1221. *See U.S. v. Rappy*, 157 F.2d 964, 967 (C.C.A.

2d Cir. 1946) where Judge Learned Hand wrote: "Anything may in fact revive a memory: a song, a scent, a photograph, an allusion, even a past statement known to be false." In commenting upon prior writings used to refresh the memory of a witness, Professor Wigmore has said that "[i]t follows from the nature of the purpose for which the paper is used that it is in no strict sense evidence" and "that the offering party has not the right to treat it as evidence by reading it or showing it or handing it to the jury, is well established." 3 J. Wigmore, Evidence § 763 (Chadbourn rev. 1972). The reason such writings are not admitted into evidence is that they are only a repetition of the witness' courtroom testimony.

It is improper to use the rubric of refreshing recollection as a guise to present inadmissible evidence to the jury. *U.S. v. Zackson*, 12 F.3d 1178 (2d Cir. 1993) (in drug prosecution where witness had previously given statements to F.B.I. but then said he would not testify, error to allow government to ask series of questions re whether his recollection was refreshed by contents of statements where real purpose was to get hearsay into evidence).

Once a witness has resorted to a writing or other object to refresh recollection, the adverse party has an absolute right to inspect the writing and to have it available for reference in cross-examining the witness. The opposing party may also introduce into evidence those portions of the writing which relate to the testimony of the witness. Rule 612. However, the right of inspection and use is not unlimited. The rule only requires disclosure of the passage actually used by the witness, and other portions relating to the same subject matter. *U.S. v. Larranaga*, 787 F.2d 489 (10th Cir. 1986); *U.S. v. Costner*, 684 F.2d 370 (6th Cir. 1982); Rule 612 advisory committee note. Rule 612 confers no rights on the adverse party where a witness reviews a writing before or while testifying but does not rely on it to refresh memory. *U.S. v. Sheffield*, 55 F.3d 341, 343 (8th Cir. 1995) (trial court acted within its discretion to deny defendant's request for case file which detective said he had reviewed but did not need to aid his recollection or testimony; "Rule 612 is not a vehicle for a plenary search for contradictory or rebutting evidence that may be in a file but rather is a means to reawaken recollection of the witness to the witness's past perception about a writing.") Moreover, the right conferred by Rule 612 to introduce in evidence those portions which relate to the testimony of the witness simply means the writing may be admitted on the question of the witness' credibility and is not thereby made admissible for other purposes. If offered for some other purpose, different rules would be applicable, such as those regulating hearsay and the use of copies. *U.S. v. Hugh*, 236 Fed. Appx. 796 (3d Cir. 2007).

Depositions

Although Rule 612 is a rule of evidence and not a rule of discovery, *Hiskett v. Wal-Mart Stores, Inc.*, 180 F.R.D. 403 (D. Kan. 1998), it has been held applicable to depositions pursuant to Fed.R.Civ.P. 30(c). *Sporck v. Peil*, 759 F.2d 312 (3d Cir. 1985); *Magee v. Paul Revere Life Ins. Co.*, 172 F.R.D. 627 (E.D. N.Y. 1997); *Sauer v. Burlington Northern R. Co.*, 169 F.R.D. 120 (D. Minn. 1996).

Three foundational elements must be met before Rule 612 is applicable to documents reviewed by a witness to prepare for a deposition: (1) a witness must use a writing to refresh his or her memory; (2) for the purpose of testifying; and (3) the court must determine that, in the interest of justice, the adverse party is entitled to see the writing. *Sporck*, 759 F.2d at 317; *Nutramax Laboratories, Inc. v. Twin Laboratories Inc.*, 183 F.R.D. 458 (D. Md. 1998).

The first element ensures that the writing is relevant to an attempt to test deponent's credibility. *Id.* The second element safeguards against the use of Rule 612 "as a pretext for wholesale exploration of an opposing party's files" and ensures "that access is limited only to those writings which may fairly be said in part to have an impact upon the testimony of the witness," since only writings which actually influenced a witness' testimony are of utility in impeachment and cross-examination. *Sporck*, 759 F.2d at 317–18; *see also In re Rivastigmine Patent Litigation (MDL No. 1661)*, 486 F. Supp. 2d 241 (S.D. N.Y. 2007) and *Berkey Photo, Inc. v. Eastman Kodak Co.*, 74 F.R.D. 613, 615 (S.D. N.Y.

1977) (for Rule 612 to apply, it must be shown "at least to a strongly arguable degree" that documents had impact on the testimony of witness).

If the first two elements are not met, the inquiry ends because Rule 612 is not applicable. But when these elements are met, the court will determine whether disclosure is mandated by balancing the policies underlying the work product doctrine or other asserted privilege against the need for disclosure to promote effective cross-examination and impeachment. *See Burns v. Exxon Corp.*, 158 F.3d 336 (5th Cir. 1998); *Audiotext Communications Network, Inc. v. US Telecom, Inc.*, 164 F.R.D. 250 (D. Kan. 1996); *Redvanly v. NYNEX Corp.*, 152 F.R.D. 460 (S.D. N.Y. 1993); *In re Joint Eastern and Southern Dist. Asbestos Litigation*, 119 F.R.D. 4 (E.D. N.Y. 1988); *James Julian, Inc. v. Raytheon Co.*, 93 F.R.D. 138 (D. Del. 1982).

Note: With respect to criminal cases, Professor Wright and other commentators have concluded that amendments to Fed.R.Crim.P. 26.2 and 17(h) effectively supercede the Jencks Act, 18 U.S.C.A. § 3500. Therefore, the significance of the Jencks Act exception referenced in Rule 612 is a matter of controversy. *See* 28 Wright and Gold, Federal Practice and Procedure, § 6186 (1993).

Additional References

Graham, Handbook of Federal Evidence §§ 612.1 to 612.2 (7th ed. 2012)

Treatises and Practice Aids

Goode and Wellborn, Courtroom Handbook on Federal Evidence Chapter 5, Rule 612 (annual ed.)

Mueller & Kirkpatrick, Federal Evidence, §§ 6:92 to 6:97 (3d ed. 2007)

Wright & Gold, Federal Practice and Procedure: Evidence §§ 6181 *et seq.*

McCormick, Evidence § 9 (6th ed. 2006)

Park, Trial Objections Handbook § 9:30 (2nd ed. 2001)

RELEVANCE

See:

Fed.R.Evid. 401, 402
Mil.R.Evid. 401, 402

Objection

- [*To a question*] Objection. The information sought by the question is irrelevant to any issue in this case.
- [*To an answer*] Objection, irrelevant. I move the answer be stricken and the jury be instructed not to consider it for any purpose.

Response

- The evidence sought by the question has a logical bearing on an issue in this case because [*explain*].
- The testimony goes to the weight or credibility of the evidence.

Commentary

"Relevant evidence" means evidence having any tendency to make the existence of any fact that is of consequence to the determination of the action more probable or less probable than it would be without the evidence. Rule 401; *United States v. Abel*, 469 U.S. 45, 105 S. Ct. 465, 83 L. Ed. 2d 450 (1984); *Millenkamp v. Davisco Foods Intern., Inc.*, 562 F.3d 971 (9th Cir. 2009); *U.S. v. Bailey*, 510 F.3d 726 (7th Cir. 2007); *U.S. v. Jimenez*, 507 F.3d 13 (1st Cir. 2007); *U.S. v. Trala*, 386 F.3d 536 (3d Cir. 2004). Although the rule makes no reference to credibility, evidence relating to credibility falls under the definition of "relevant evidence" because the outcome of an action is often determined by the jurors' assessment of the credibility of the witnesses.

Relevance is comprised of two fundamental components: materiality and probative value. Materiality looks to the relation between the propositions for which the evidence is offered and the issues in the case. If the evidence is offered to help prove a proposition which is not a matter in issue, the evidence is immaterial. Probative value, on the other hand, deals with the tendency of the evidence to establish the proposition that it is offered to prove. McCormick, Evidence, § 185 (6th ed. 2006).

The threshold for relevance is very low under Rule 401. *Iacobucci v. Boulter*, 193 F.3d 14 (1st Cir. 1999); *U.S. v. Tutiven*, 40 F.3d 1 (1st Cir. 1994). The degree of materiality and probativity necessary for evidence to be relevant is minimal and must only provide a factfinder with a basis for making some inference or chain of inferences. *U.S. v. Jordan*, 485 F.3d 1214, 1218 (10th Cir. 2007). While the burden is low, it does not sanction the *carte blanche* admission of whatever evidence a party would like. *Id.*

Satisfying Rule 401 involves three basic questions: (1) What is the issue for which the evidence is offered? (2) Is that issue material to the case? and, (3) Is the evidence probative of the issue? *Straley v. U.S.*, 887 F. Supp. 728 (D.N.J. 1995).

Relevance of Mental History

A witness' mental history is relevant to credibility if it bears on the witness' ability to perceive or to recall events or to testify accurately. *U.S. v. Moore*, 923 F.2d 910 (1st Cir. 1991); *U.S. v. Lindstrom*, 698 F.2d 1154 (11th Cir. 1983) (during relevant time period, witness suffered from mental illness which caused her to misperceive and misinterpret the words and actions of others and which seriously affected ability to know, comprehend and relate truth). The modern trend is not to allow cross-examination into a witness' psychiatric background where the probative value is minimal and the only real effect would be to stigmatize the witness. *U.S. v. Jones*, 213 F.3d 1253 (10th Cir. 2000); *U.S. v. Lopez*, 611 F.2d 44 (4th Cir. 1979); *U.S. ex rel. Kline v. Lane*, 707 F. Supp. 368 (N.D. Ill. 1989). Before admitting such evidence, the court should consider three factors: (1) the witness' mental condition must relate to the time period about which he is attempting to testify; (2) the witness' mental condition must bear on the capacity to observe the events in question, to testify about those observations accurately and truthfully, or to maintain a clear recollection of those observations;

and (3) the witness' mental condition must not introduce into the case a collateral issue which would confuse the jury and must not lead to lengthy testimony that is extraneous to the essential facts and issues of the case. *U.S. v. Jackson*, 155 F.R.D. 664 (D. Kan. 1994).

Relevance of Similar Incidents

Under Rule 401, evidence of similar occurrences may be relevant to establish such elements as discriminatory intent, notice, the standard of care and causation, magnitude of danger, ability to correct a known defect, and lack of safety for intended use. *E.E.O.C. v. Farmer Bros. Co.*, 31 F.3d 891 (9th Cir. 1994); *Kehm v. Procter & Gamble Mfg. Co.*, 724 F.2d 613 (8th Cir. 1983). Admission of other similar accidents or occurrences is governed by the federal "substantial similarity" doctrine and not state law. *Heath v. Suzuki Motor Corp.*, 126 F.3d 1391 (11th Cir. 1997).

Employment Discrimination — "Me Too" Evidence

The testimony of other employees regarding their treatment by an employer under similar circumstances and close in time to the circumstances alleged by plaintiff can be relevant to the question of an employer's discriminatory intent. *Spulak v. K Mart Corp.*, 894 F.2d 1150 (10th Cir. 1990); *Waterson v. Plank Road Motel Corp.*, 43 F. Supp. 2d 284 (N.D. N.Y. 1999) (co-worker's testimony relevant to show defendant's discriminatory attitude toward women as well as demonstrating a generally hostile work environment permeated with ridicule and insult); *but see Mooney v. Aramco Services Co.*, 54 F.3d 1207 (5th Cir. 1995) (testimony of anecdotal witnesses with different supervisors, working in different parts of company too attenuated to relate to alleged pattern and practice of age discrimination). Recognizing that there will seldom be eyewitness testimony as to the employer's mental processes, the Supreme Court has held that evidence of the employer's discriminatory attitude *in general* is relevant and admissible to prove race discrimination. *U.S. Postal Service Bd. of Governors v. Aikens*, 460 U.S. 711, 103 S. Ct. 1478, 75 L. Ed.

2d 403 (1983); *Estes v. Dick Smith Ford, Inc.*, 856 F.2d 1097 (8th Cir. 1988) (evidence of prior acts of discrimination relevant to employer's motive in discharging plaintiff). The Supreme Court has also said that "me too" evidence is neither *per se* admissible nor *per se* inadmissible. In *Sprint / United Management Co. v. Mendelsohn*, 552 U.S. 379, 128 S. Ct. 1140, 170 L. Ed. 2d 1 (2008), an age discrimination case, the Court said whether evidence of other discrimination is relevant is fact based and depends upon many factors, including how closely related the evidence is to plaintiff's circumstances and theory of the case.

Occurrence or Absence of Other Accidents

Evidence of similar accidents involving the same product is admissible in negligence or product liability actions to establish notice, the existence of a defect, or to refute testimony by the defense that a given product was designed without safety hazards. *Torbit v. Ryder System, Inc.*, 416 F.3d 898 (8th Cir. 2005); *Smith v. Ingersoll-Rand Co.*, 214 F.3d 1235 (10th Cir. 2000); *Ponder v. Warren Tool Corp.*, 834 F.2d 1553 (10th Cir. 1987) (collecting cases); *Reid v. BMW of North America*, 464 F. Supp. 2d 1267 (N.D. Ga. 2006); *Cardenas v. Dorel Juvenile Group, Inc.*, 230 F.R.D. 611 (D. Kan. 2005). Admission of other accidents or complaints is predicated on a showing that the circumstances surrounding them were substantially similar to those involved in the present case. *Bitler v. A.O. Smith Corp.*, 400 F.3d 1227 (10th Cir. 2004); *Gibson v. Ford Motor Co.*, 510 F. Supp. 2d 1116 (N.D. Ga. 2007). The rationale for this rule is simple. In such cases, the jury is invited to infer from the presence of other accidents: (1) that a dangerous condition existed, (2) which caused the accident. As the circumstances and conditions of the other accidents become less similar to the accident under consideration, the probative force of such evidence decreases. But the danger that the evidence will be unfairly prejudicial remains. "[T]he jury might infer from evidence of the prior accident alone that ultra-hazardous conditions existed . . . and were the cause of the later accident without those issues ever having been proved." *Gardner v. Southern Ry. Systems*, 675 F.2d 949 (7th Cir. 1982). Evidence of other injuries may also raise extraneous controversial points, lead to a confusion of issues, and present undue prejudice disproportionate to its usefulness. *Crump v. Versa Products, Inc.*, 400 F.3d 1104 (8th Cir. 2005).

Whether accidents are substantially similar depends largely on the theory of the case. *Four Corners Helicopters, Inc. v. Turbomeca, S.A.*, 979 F.2d 1434 (10th Cir. 1992). "Differences in the nature of the defect alleged may affect a determination whether the accidents are substantially similar . . .. How substantial the similarity must be is in part a function of the proponent's theory of proof." *Ponder*, 834 F.2d at 1560. To show the existence of a dangerous condition requires a high degree of similarity. *Chlopek v. Federal Ins. Co.*, 499 F.3d 692 (7th Cir. 2007); *Smith v. Ingersoll-Rand Co.*; *Nachtsheim v. Beech Aircraft Corp.*, 847 F.2d 1261 (7th Cir. 1988). The requirement is relaxed, however, when the evidence of other accidents is offered to prove notice or awareness of the potential defect. *Wheeler v. John Deere Co.*, 862 F.2d 1404 (10th Cir. 1988); *Exum v. General Elec. Co.*, 819 F.2d 1158 (D.C. Cir. 1987); *Bado-Santana v. Ford Motor Co.*, 364 F. Supp. 2d 79 (D.P.R. 2005) (collecting cases). Any differences in the accidents not affecting a finding of substantial similarity go to the weight of the evidence. *Jackson v. Firestone Tire & Rubber Co.*, 788 F.2d 1070 (5th Cir. 1986).

Relevant evidence encompasses evidence tending to establish negative as well as positive facts. *Michetti v. Linde Baker Material Handling Corp.*, 969 F. Supp. 286 (E.D. Pa. 1997).

In general, courts have recognized that the absence of prior accidents may be admissible to show: (1) absence of defect or other condition alleged; (2) lack of causal connection between the injury and the alleged defect or condition; and (3) the nonexistence of an unduly dangerous situation. *Espeaignnette v. Gene Tierney Co., Inc.*, 43 F.3d 1 (1st Cir. 1994); *DeMarines v. KLM Royal Dutch Airlines*, 580 F.2d 1193 (3d Cir. 1978) (in personal injury action where plaintiff claimed injury caused by pressurization of aircraft, error to exclude evidence of absence of any other claims arising from that flight; proof of absence of claims makes existence of alleged defect less probable than it would be without evidence).

Evidence of the absence of prior accidents may not be admitted unless the offering party first establishes that the lack of accidents was with regard to a product substantially identical to the one at issue and used in settings and circumstances sufficiently similar to those surrounding the product at issue at the time of the accident. *Klonowski v. International Armament Corp.*, 17 F.3d 992 (7th Cir. 1994).

Conditional Relevance—Admission Subject to Connection

Under Rule 104(b), the trial judge has discretion to admit evidence on the condition that the proponent later establish relevance by supplying other evidence as foundation or connecting facts. *U.S. v. Gambino*, 926 F.2d 1355 (3d Cir. 1991) (admitting hearsay statements subject to later connection of declarant's participation in conspiracy); *Dresser v. Cradle of Hope Adoption Center, Inc.*, 421 F. Supp. 2d 1024 (E.D. Mich. 2006) (judge may conditionally admit evidence subject to proof of connecting facts, and if connecting facts are not proven, strike the evidence from the record). Conditional admission is an exceptional rather than routine procedure. *U.S. v. Ferra*, 900 F.2d 1057 (7th Cir. 1990). Evidence admitted on a promise to establish relevance should be excluded on a motion to strike if appropriate connection has not been established. *U.S. v. Gilbreath*, 445 F.2d 810 (10th Cir. 1971); *Baker v. Lane County*, 33 F. Supp. 2d 1291 (D. Or. 1999) (reversible error where evidence of alleged sexual misconduct by psychiatric patient was never connected to decision to continue medication despite symptoms of adverse reaction). The burden rests with objecting party to renew his objection or move to strike. *U.S. v. Dougherty*, 895 F.2d 399 (7th Cir. 1990); *Peterson v. Gaughan*, 404 F.2d 1375 (1st Cir. 1968).

Remoteness

The question of remoteness is basically one of relevance. Remoteness relates not only to the passage of time, alone, but also requires the court to consider the possible invalidity of reasonable inferences due to supervening factors. *U.S. v. Hankey*, 203 F.3d 1160 (9th Cir. 2000).

Exclusion of Relevant Evidence

Relevant evidence may be excluded if its probative value is substantially outweighed by the danger of unfair prejudice, confusion of the issues, misleading the jury, waste of time, or needless presentation of cumulative evidence. Fed.R.Evid. 403; *Gierlinger v. Gleason*, 160 F.3d 858 (2d Cir. 1998). Because virtually all evidence is prejudicial to one party or another, the prejudice must be *unfair* to justify exclusion under Rule 403. *Costantino v. David M. Herzog, M.D., P.C.*, 203 F.3d 164 (2d Cir. 2000) (unfairness contemplated involves some adverse effect beyond tending to prove fact or issue that justifies admission); *U.S. v. Marrero-Ortiz*, 160 F.3d 768 (1st Cir. 1998); *Nesbitt v. Sears, Roebuck and Co.*, 415 F. Supp. 2d 530 (E.D. Pa. 2005) (in products liability action involving radial saw, where there was no claim of any impairment at time of accident, plaintiff's juvenile criminal conduct and previous use of marijuana and alcohol years prior was irrelevant and even if marginally relevant would unfairly prejudice jury against plaintiff). Unfair prejudice includes "the possibility that the evidence will excite the jury to make a decision on the basis of a factor unrelated to the issues properly before it." *Heyne v. Caruso*, 69 F.3d 1475, 1481 (9th Cir. 1995). In the context of criminal cases, unfair prejudice speaks to the capacity of some relevant evidence to lure the fact-finder into declaring guilt on a ground different from the proof specific to the offense charged. *Old Chief v. United States*, 519 U.S. 172, 117 S. Ct. 644, 136 L. Ed. 2d 574 (1997); *U.S. v. Noe*, 411 F.3d 878 (8th Cir. 2005); *U.S. v. Christians*, 200 F.3d 1124 (8th Cir. 1999).

The following cases are instructive on the issue of relevance: *U.S. v. Harris*, 536 F.3d 798 (7th Cir. 2008) (unexplained wealth admissible as relevant circumstantial evidence of drug trafficking if government also establishes wealth not obtained through legitimate means); *U.S. v. Curtin*, 489 F.3d 935 (9th Cir. 2007) (where intent was in issue, evidence that defendant possessed material describing sexual acts between adults and children was relevant to his intent to have sexual encounter with juvenile); *U.S. v. Abdul-Aziz*, 486 F.3d 471 (8th Cir. 2007) (defendant's statement that he could not be locked up forever and when he got out, somebody would be sorry relevant to show consciousness of guilt); *U.S. v. Sells*, 477 F.3d 1226 (10th Cir. 2007) (evidence of methamphetamine manufactured in another home on same property as defendant's residence irrelevant when no evidence connected defendant with other home); *U.S. v. Lopez-Medina*, 461 F.3d 724 (6th Cir. 2006) (evidence that demonstrates only guilt by association such as family member's criminal history irrelevant to question of defendant's actual guilt); *U.S. v. Newsom*, 452 F.3d 593 (6th Cir. 2006) (where defendant was charged with being a felon in possession of a firearm, evidence of his tattoos depicting firearms and negative messages irrelevant to issue of whether he actually possessed gun); *U.S. v. Mitchell*, 172 F.3d 1104 (9th Cir. 1999) (evidence that person is poor irrelevant to establish commission of crime to obtain more money); *U.S. v. Hawkins*, 360 F. Supp. 2d 689 (E.D. Pa. 2005) (same); *U.S. v. Catalfo*, 64 F.3d 1070 (7th Cir. 1995) (evidence that defendant's mother was very rich irrelevant in wire fraud prosecution of options trader since she had no legal obligation to cover losses); *U.S. v. Elliott*, 62 F.3d 1304 (11th Cir. 1995) (evidence of certain satisfied customers irrelevant to charge of operating fraudulent Ponzi scheme); *Wilson v. Union Pacific R. Co.*, 56 F.3d 1226, 1231 (10th Cir. 1995) (in FELA case for injuries sustained by railroad brakeman, no error to exclude evidence of subsequent conviction for drug possession; in addition to being highly prejudicial, "[e]vidence of a conviction for drug possession alone is not highly relevant to the issue of veracity."); *Black v. Ryder/P.I.E. Nationwide, Inc.*, 15 F.3d 573, 587 (6th Cir. 1994) (in hybrid claim by employee under § 301 of Labor Management Relations Act, 29 U.S.C.A. § 185, fact that NLRB elected not to issue complaint "probative of almost nothing"); *U.S. v. Whorley*, 400 F. Supp. 2d 880 (E.D. Va. 2005) (in prosecution for receipt of obscene materials involving children, expert's comparison of these materials to paintings, statues and other works of art excluded as irrelevant, confusing and misleading to jury); *Skultin v. Bushnell*, 82 F. Supp. 2d 1258 (D. Utah 2000) (evidence that two plaintiffs were adult entertainers and third worked in legal brothel irrelevant in civil rights action); *U.S. v. Han*, 66 F. Supp. 2d 362 (N.D. N.Y. 1999) (reputation as law-abiding citizen who did not exploit others not relevant to criminal charge of travel with intent to engage in sexual act with minor); *DeRoche v. All American Bottling Corp.*, 57 F. Supp. 2d 791 (D. Minn. 1999) (comment made one year after applicant denied position too remote to support age discrimination claim).

Additional References

Graham, Handbook of Federal Evidence §§ 401.1 to 402.1 (7th ed. 2012)

Treatises and Practice Aids

Goode and Wellborn, Courtroom Handbook on Federal Evidence Chapter 5, Rules 401, 402 and Obj. 48 (annual ed.)

Mueller & Kirkpatrick, Federal Evidence, §§ 4:1 to 4:82 (3d ed. 2007)

Wright & Graham, Federal Practice and Procedure: Evidence §§ 5161 *et seq.*

McCormick, Evidence Chapter 16, §§ 184 *et seq.* (6th ed. 2006)

Park, Trial Objections Handbook §§ 2:1 to 2:4 (2nd ed. 2001)

RELIGIOUS BELIEF

See:

Fed.R.Evid. 610
Mil.R.Evid. 610

Objection

- Objection. The question is irrelevant, prejudicial and directly violates Rule 610 which excludes evidence of religious belief.

Response

- The question has nothing to do with credibility; it is aimed at demonstrating bias.
- Religious beliefs are relevant to the merits of the case because *(explain)*.

Commentary

Rule 610 bars evidence of a witness' religious beliefs for the purpose of showing that his credibility is impaired or enhanced as a result of those beliefs. *U.S. v. Darui*, 545 F. Supp. 2d 108 (D.D.C. 2008). The purpose of the rule is to guard against any prejudice which may result from the disclosure of a witness' faith. *Malek v. Federal Ins. Co.*, 994 F.2d 49 (2d Cir. 1993) (error to permit questions where it was apparent from cross-examination that defense counsel was attempting to show witness' truthfulness was affected by his religious beliefs); *Munn v. Algee*, 924 F.2d 568 (5th Cir. 1991) (in wrongful death case where plaintiff was Jehovah's witness, abuse of discretion to permit cross-examination about teachings of that faith other than prohibition on blood transfusions, which was relevant to the claim).

The scope of the prohibition includes unconventional or unusual religions. *See U.S. v. Sampol*, 636 F.2d 621 (D.C. Cir. 1980) (government witness could not be examined about his adherence to the Luceme religion); *Government of Virgin Islands v. Petersen*, 553 F.2d 324 (3d Cir. 1977) (defense counsel could not elicit testimony that alibi witness was Rastafarian); *see also Bains v. Cambra*, 204 F.3d 964 (9th Cir. 2000) (habeas corpus; evidence of Sikh religious beliefs properly admitted to show motive and intent in murder case but then used in a clearly inflammatory fashion in closing argument).

The rule's prohibition is not a per se rule of exclusion under all circumstances and occasionally such evidence will be relevant to other issues in the case. *Mauldin v. Upjohn Co.*, 697 F.2d 644 (5th Cir. 1983) (in products liability case, evidence about difficulty in attending church relevant to injuries allegedly caused by adverse reaction to defendant's antibiotic drugs).

Inquiry into religious beliefs is proper for the purpose of showing interest or bias. Rule 610, Advisory Committee Note; *Firemen's Fund Ins. Co. v. Thien*, 63 F.3d 754 (8th Cir. 1995) (trial court properly admitted testimony that two witnesses were members of church where defendant served as pastor for purpose of showing possible bias); *U.S. v. Teicher*, 987 F.2d 112 (2d Cir. 1993) (witness' views about Jewish people not probative of bias).

Evidence of a person's beliefs, superstitions or affiliation with a religious group is properly admissible when probative of an issue in a criminal prosecution. *Aliwoli v. Carter*, 225 F.3d 826 (7th Cir. 2000) (habeas corpus; no error in prosecutor's questions where references to defendant's black Muslim faith were meant to show motive for shooting police officers and to rebut insanity defense); *U.S. v. Beasley*, 72 F.3d 1518 (11th Cir. 1996) (religious teachings of Yahweh religion were used to justify, rationalize and promote crime; Yahweh named in indictment as the racketeering enterprise); *U.S. v. Hoffman*, 806 F.2d 703 (7th Cir. 1986) (court may receive evidence of religious belief when relevant to defendant's motive for committing crime); *U.S. v. Sun Myung Moon*, 718 F.2d 1210 (2d Cir. 1983) (inevitable that some Unification Church practices would creep into trial in order to illustrate defendant's control over actions of other church officials); *U.S. v. Simmons*, 431 F. Supp. 2d 38 (D.D.C. 2006) (evidence of religious conversion properly elicited to show witness' motive for cooperating with law enforcement); *U.S. v. Kennedy*, 29 F. Supp. 2d 662 (D. Colo. 1998) (evidence that Ponzi scheme targeted individuals with conservative religious beliefs provided *modus operandi* context for alleged crimes).

Additional References

Graham, Handbook of Federal Evidence § 610.1 (7th ed. 2012)

Treatises and Practice Aids

Goode and Wellborn, Courtroom Handbook on Federal Evidence Chapter 5, Rule 610 and Obj. 81 (annual ed.)

Mueller & Kirkpatrick, Federal Evidence, §§ 6:58 to 6:59 (3d ed. 2007)

Wright & Graham, Federal Practice and Procedure: Evidence §§ 5161 *et seq.*

McCormick, Evidence § 46 (6th ed. 2006)

REOPENING THE CASE—MOTION

See:

Fed.R.Evid. 611(a)
Mil.R.Evid. 611(a)

Form

- I respectfully request leave of court to reopen [*plaintiff's*] [*defendant's*] case for the purpose of introducing evidence on the issue of [*state specifically*].
- I respectfully request leave of court to reopen [*plaintiff's*] [*defendant's*] case for the purpose of allowing the witness to correct her testimony with respect to [*state specifically*].

Objection

- Objection. To reopen the case at this point will cause unfair prejudice [*explain*]; this is a belated attempt to reverse an earlier tactical decision [*specify*]; the "new" evidence has no/little probative value because [*specify*].

Commentary

The rules of evidence give the trial court broad discretion over the mode and order of the interrogation of witnesses. *See* Rule 611(a). This discretion extends to granting or denying motions to reopen. *Zenith Radio Corp. v. Hazeltine Research, Inc.*, 401 U.S. 321, 91 S. Ct. 795, 28 L. Ed. 2d 77 (1971); *U.S. v. Abbas*, 74 F.3d 506 (4th Cir. 1996); *Rivera-Flores v. Puerto Rico Telephone Co.*, 64 F.3d 742 (1st Cir. 1995).

While the particular criteria that guide a trial court's decision to reopen are necessarily flexible and fact-specific, it is generally understood that a trial court abuses its discretion if the refusal to reopen creates an injustice in the particular circumstances. *Rivera-Flores*, 64 F.3d at 746.

The specific factors to be assessed include: (i) the timeliness of the motion to reopen, (ii) the probative value of the evidence sought to be introduced, (iii) the proponent's explanation for failing to offer the evidence earlier, and (iv) the likelihood of undue prejudice to the opposing party. *United*

States v. Bayer, 331 U.S. 532, 67 S. Ct. 1394, 91 L. Ed. 1654 (1947); *U.S. v. Medina*, 430 F.3d 869 (7th Cir. 2005); *U.S. v. Peay*, 972 F.2d 71 (4th Cir. 1992).

The party moving to reopen should provide a reasonable explanation for failure to present the evidence in its case-in-chief. *U.S. v. Thetford*, 676 F.2d 170 (5th Cir. 1982). The evidence proffered should be relevant, admissible and helpful to the jury in reaching its determination. *U.S. v. Larson*, 596 F.2d 759 (8th Cir. 1979). The belated receipt of testimony should not give the evidence a distorted importance, prejudice the opposing party's case, or preclude an adversary from having an adequate opportunity to meet the additional evidence offered. *U.S. v. Walker*, 772 F.2d 1172 (5th Cir. 1985).

Although the cases take a liberal and flexible approach, reopening arguably does afford the opportunity to color or manufacture testimony to remedy deficiencies in the reopening party's case. Any such request must be considered carefully by the court, and counsel should be prepared to explain fully the necessity for reopening.

The following cases are illustrative. **Motion granted**: *U.S. v. Boone*, 437 F.3d 829 (8th Cir. 2006) (testimony was highly probative and came directly after government rested so "orderly flow" of evidence was not disrupted; defendants had opportunity to cross-examine and did not request continuance); *Buziashvili v. Inman*, 106 F.3d 709 (6th Cir. 1997) (reopening occurred immediately after plaintiff rested; evidence was documentary and defendants did not have to deal with unanticipated testimony from surprise witness); *Blinzler v. Marriott Intern., Inc.*, 81 F.3d 1148 (1st Cir. 1996) (after plaintiff rested and parties argued motion for directed verdict, plaintiff allowed to reopen for additional evidence on causation when new evidence was only two witnesses, there was no unfair surprise or delay and defendant was offered continuance); *Walker*, 772 F.2d at 1183–84 (finding not unreasonable defendant's explanation that during case-in-chief he was too emotionally distraught to testify). **Motion denied**: *U.S. v. Peterson*, 233 F.3d 101 (1st Cir. 2000) (defendant gave no excuse for not testifying in case-in-chief; attorney's statement that he could not put defendant on the stand strongly suggested defendant intended to commit perjury); *Gathright v. St. Louis Teacher's Credit Union*, 97 F.3d 266 (8th Cir. 1996) (in age discrimination case, plaintiff's surprise at defendant resting without calling witnesses was not grounds to reopen to permit additional evidence of pretext); *Filipowicz v. American Stores Ben. Plans Committee*, 56 F.3d 807 (7th Cir. 1995) (proffered testimony would have contributed little to defendants' case); *Joseph v. Terminix Intern. Co.*, 17 F.3d 1282 (10th Cir. 1994) (new evidence would have been cumulative); *U.S. v. Paz*, 927 F.2d 176 (4th Cir. 1991) (no abuse of discretion when motion was made after verdict was reached); *Simon v. Shearson Lehman Bros., Inc.*, 895 F.2d 1304 (11th Cir. 1990) (reopening not permitted when party had earlier elected not to put document into evidence for tactical reasons); *Thomas v. SS Santa Mercedes*, 572 F.2d 1331 (9th Cir. 1978) (new evidence would have provided little additional probative force); *John v. Sotheby's, Inc.*, 858 F. Supp. 1283 (S.D. N.Y. 1994) (reopening not permitted to correct earlier tactical decision not to put document into evidence).

See also U.S. v. Nunez, 432 F.3d 573 (4th Cir. 2005) (error to reopen evidence for prosecution after jury had retired for deliberations; evidence took on distorted importance, prejudiced defendants' case and denied them fair opportunity to respond to this additional evidence); *U.S. v. Santana*, 175 F.3d 57 (1st Cir. 1999) (by permitting jury during deliberations to see defendant's ears because relevant to police identification, trial court did not reopen case but instead improperly permitted jury to consider information extrinsic to closed record without formalities attendant to reopening); *Lussier v. Runyon*, 50 F.3d 1103 (1st Cir. 1995) (when parties had rested, error for trial court to order them to submit additional documentary evidence without affording trial protections of rights to object, cross-examine, impeach and contradict evidence).

Treatises and Practice Aids

Wright & Gold, Federal Practice and Procedure: Evidence § 6164

REPETITION

See:

Fed.R.Evid. 611(a)(3)
Mil.R.Evid. 611(a)(3)

Objection

- Objection. The question is repetitive.
- Objection. The question has been asked and answered.

Response

- The witness has not answered this question.
- I have not asked this question previously.

Commentary

Fed.R.Evid. 611(a)(3) provides that the court shall exercise reasonable control over the mode of interrogating witnesses to protect them from harassment. If a question has been asked and answered, the trial court has broad discretion to limit or preclude repetitive and unduly harassing interrogation. *Delaware v. Van Arsdall*, 475 U.S. 673, 106 S. Ct. 1431, 89 L. Ed. 2d 674 (1986); *Davis v. Alaska*, 415 U.S. 308, 94 S. Ct. 1105, 39 L. Ed. 2d 347 (1974); *U.S. v. Skelton*, 514 F.3d 433 (5th Cir. 2008); *Haynes v. Haviland*, 267 Fed. Appx. 422 (6th Cir. 2008); *Hargrave v. McKee*, 248 Fed. Appx. 718 (6th Cir. 2007); *U.S. v. Blackwell*, 459 F.3d 739 (6th Cir. 2006); *U.S. v. Laboy-Delgado*, 84 F.3d 22 (1st Cir. 1996) (cross examiners should be given reasonable latitude, especially in criminal cases, but they are not at liberty endlessly to cover the same ground when they are dissatisfied with witness' answers); *U.S. v. Adames*, 56 F.3d 737 (7th Cir. 1995) (disallowing repetitive questions well within court's discretion). Repetition wastes time and places undue emphasis on evidence through cumulative testimony. The form of the question does not have to be absolutely identical in order to raise this objection. If a new question calls for an answer previously given, the question is objectionable as repetitious. The objection applies not only when an answer already has been given but also when a witness testifies that he does not know about or remember a matter. The same principles apply with respect to the introduction of exhibits. *See International Minerals and Resources, S.A. v. Pappas*, 96 F.3d 586 (2d Cir. 1996) (letters properly excluded as repetitive where same evidence already had been given by party and expert witness).

Additional References

Graham, Handbook of Federal Evidence § 611.17 (7th ed. 2012)

Treatises and Practice Aids

Goode and Wellborn, Courtroom Handbook on Federal Evidence Chapter 5, Rule 611 and Obj. 11 (annual ed.)
Wright & Gold, Federal Practice and Procedure: Evidence § 6164
McCormick, Evidence Chapter 2 (6th ed. 2006)
Park, Trial Objections Handbook § 6:21 (2nd ed. 2001)

RULE OF COMPLETENESS (REMAINDER OF OR RELATED WRITINGS OR RECORDED STATEMENTS)

See:

Fed.R.Evid. 106
Mil.R.Evid. 106

Form

- Your Honor, for the witness to read only the first paragraph of the document leaves the jury with a very misleading impression because [*specify*]. Pursuant to Rule 106, I ask that the witness be directed to read the second and third paragraphs also.
- Your Honor, my opponent has indicated she intends at this time to read into the record the deposition of John Doe at page 20, lines 13–17. I would ask under the rule of completeness, set forth in Fed.R.Evid. 106 and Fed.R.Civ.P. 32(a)(4), that she also be required to read lines 5–12 and 18–25 since they are relevant to the issue and place the portion being offered in proper context.

Commentary

Whenever fragmentary statements are introduced or other written matters are taken out of context, misleading impressions can be created. Rule 106 provides:

> When a writing or recorded statement or part thereof is introduced by a party, an adverse party may require the introduction at that time of any other part or any other writing or recorded statement which ought in fairness to be considered contemporaneously with it.

The rule is based on two considerations. The first is the misleading impression created by taking matters out of context. The second is the inadequacy of repair work when delayed to a point later in the trial. Rule 106, Advisory Committee Notes; *Beech Aircraft Corp. v. Rainey*, 488 U.S. 153, 172, 109 S. Ct. 439, 451, 102 L. Ed. 2d 445 (1988) ("[W]hen one party has made use of a portion of a document, such that misunderstanding or distortion can be averted only through presentation of another portion, the material required for completeness is *ipso facto* relevant and therefore admissible . . . .. "); *U.S. v. Moussaoui*, 382 F.3d 453 (4th Cir. 2004) and *Echo Acceptance Corp. v. Household Retail Services, Inc.*, 267 F.3d 1068 (10th Cir. 2001) (Rule 106 functions as defensive shield against potentially misleading evidence proffered by opposing party); *U.S. v. Branch*, 91 F.3d 699 (5th Cir. 1996) (assuming that government used recorded statement at trial in manner that would bring it under Rule 106, rule did not require admission of excluded portions since they did not qualify, explain or place in context portions that were admitted); *U.S. v. Washington*, 12 F.3d 1128 (D.C. Cir. 1994) (proper exercise of discretion to condition admission of impeaching portions of police officers' prior statements on admission of full statements); *U.S. v. LeFevour*, 798 F.2d 977, 981 (7th Cir. 1986) (rule gives trial judge authority to avoid misleading impression "on the spot"); *cf. U.S. v. Wilkerson*, 411 F.3d 1 (1st Cir. 2005) (there is interplay between rule of completeness and common law doctrine re prior consistent statements: both allow prior consistent statements which tend to show that a statement used to impeach a witness is not really inconsistent when understood in its proper context); *U.S. v. Yevakpor*, 419 F. Supp. 2d 242 (N.D. N.Y. 2006) (government cannot make use of cherry-picked video segments when remainder of recording has been erased subsequent to defendant's arrest).

Where there is no attempt to admit the writing into evidence but a party uses the document in such a way that it is "tantamount" to introduction of the document itself, Rule 106 should apply because the same concerns about fairness and completeness are present. *U.S. v. Ramirez-Perez*, 166 F.3d 1106, 1113 (11th Cir. 1999).

To determine whether an omitted portion is necessary, the trial court considers whether it: (1) is relevant to the issue and explains the admitted evidence; (2) places the admitted evidence in context; (3) avoids misleading the jury; and (4) ensures fair and impartial understanding of the evidence. *U.S. v. Hoffecker*, 530 F.3d 137 (3d Cir. 2008) (stating the rule and finding defendant failed to show tape recording was necessary to explain or place in context other evidence); *U.S. v. Rivera*, 61 F.3d 131

(2d Cir. 1995) (where plea agreement admitted as impeachment evidence, error to introduce attachment containing inadmissible hearsay which added nothing to jury's understanding); *U.S. v. Velasco*, 953 F.2d 1467 (7th Cir. 1992); *U.S. v. Gutierrez-Chavez*, 842 F.2d 77 (5th Cir. 1988) (statements on tape recording admissible for limited purpose of putting defendant's responses in context and making them intelligible to jury and recognizable as admissions).

In criminal cases where multiple defendants are involved and statements have been redacted to avoid *Bruton** problems, the rule of completeness is violated only when the statement in its edited form effectively distorts the meaning of the statement or excludes information substantially exculpatory of the non-testifying defendant. *U.S. v. Range*, 94 F.3d 614 (11th Cir. 1996); *U.S. v. Lopez*, 898 F.2d 1505 (11th Cir. 1990) (citing *U.S. v. Smith*, 794 F.2d 1333 (8th Cir. 1986)). When it appears that literal compliance with *Bruton* may abridge the rule of completeness, a district court must decide whether a severance for separate trials is necessary. That determination must be based on whether admission of the edited statement would distort the meaning of the original in a way that gives rise to a serious risk that a joint trial would compromise a specific trial right of one of the defendants, or prevent the jury from making a reliable judgment about guilt or innocence. *Zafiro v. United States*, 506 U.S. 534, 113 S. Ct. 933, 122 L. Ed. 2d 317 (1993); *U.S. v. Burns*, 162 F.3d 840 (5th Cir. 1998).

Whether Rule 106 permits the admission of otherwise inadmissible evidence is a matter of some disagreement. *Compare U.S. v. Houlihan*, 92 F.3d 1271 (1st Cir. 1996) (Rule 106 can serve its proper function only if trial court from time to time is prepared to permit the introduction of some otherwise inadmissible evidence) *and U.S. v. Sutton*, 801 F.2d

---

[Rule etc.]

*In *Bruton v. United States*, 391 U.S. 123, 88 S. Ct. 1620, 20 L. Ed. 2d 476 (1968), the Supreme Court held that, when the prosecution seeks to admit the statement of a non-testifying defendant and portions of the statement incriminate a co-defendant, then those portions must be omitted to protect the co-defendant's right of confrontation.

1346 (D.C. Cir. 1986) (same) *with U.S. v. Lentz*, 524 F.3d 501 (4th Cir. 2008) (Rule 106 does not render admissible evidence which otherwise is inadmissible under hearsay rules) *and U.S. v. Collicott*, 92 F.3d 973 (9th Cir. 1996) (same) *and U.S. v. Costner*, 684 F.2d 370 (6th Cir. 1982) (Rule 106 addresses order of proof problem; it is not designed to make something admissible that should be excluded).

A number of courts agree that inadmissible evidence sometimes can be admitted under Rule 106 by the principle of waiver known as "opening the door" or "curative admissibility". Graham, Handbook of Federal Evidence § 106.1 (4th ed. 1996). *See* OPENING THE DOOR: CURATIVE ADMISSIBILITY, *supra*.

Some circuits hold that Rule 106 is limited to writings and recorded statements and does not apply to oral statements such as conversations. *U.S. v. Ramos-Caraballo*, 375 F.3d 797 (8th Cir. 2004); *U.S. v. Ortega*, 203 F.3d 675, 683 (9th Cir. 2000). However, other courts say that Rule 611(a) grants district courts the same authority regarding oral statements which Rule 106 grants regarding written and recorded statements. *U.S. v. Lopez-Medina*, 596 F.3d 716, 734 (10th Cir. 2010) (we have held the rule of completeness embodied in Rule 106 is substantially applicable to oral testimony as well as by virtue of Fed.R.Evid. 611(a) which obligates the court to make the interrogation and presentation effective for the ascertainment of the truth); *U.S. v. Price*, 516 F.3d 597 (7th Cir. 2008); *U.S. v. Johnson*, 507 F.3d 793 (2d Cir. 2007); *U.S. v. Li*, 55 F.3d 325 (7th Cir. 1995).

Note: Fed.R.Civ.P. 32(a)(4) which applies to deposition testimony also incorporates a form of the "rule of completeness" and substantially restates the evidentiary rule:

> If only a part of a deposition is offered in evidence by a party, then an adverse party may require the offeror to introduce any other part which ought in fairness to be considered with the part introduced, and any party may introduce other parts.

See U.S. v. Paladino, 401 F.3d 471 (7th Cir. 2005) (error to allow prosecution to use severely cropped version of deposition but harmless under circumstances where defendant testified but did not address government's misleading editing). For a case in which Judge Weinstein refused to order the use of deposition counter-designations, *see Blue Cross and Blue Shield of New Jersey, Inc. v. Philip Morris, Inc.*, 199 F.R.D. 487 (E.D. N.Y. 2001) (potential prejudice defendants faced by presenting video clips later in trial outweighed by importance to plaintiff of manageably presenting evidence to jury).

Additional References

Graham, Handbook of Federal Evidence § 106.1 (7th ed. 2012)

Treatises and Practice Aids

Goode and Wellborn, Courtroom Handbook on Federal Evidence Chapter 5, Rule 106 (annual ed.)

Mueller & Kirkpatrick, Federal Evidence, §§ 1:42 to 1:46 (3d ed. 2007)

Wright & Graham, Federal Practice and Procedure: Evidence 2d § 5077

McCormick, Evidence § 56 (6th ed. 2006)

SEQUESTER WITNESSES—MOTION

See:

Fed.R.Evid. 615
Mil.R.Evid. 615

Form

- I respectfully request the Court pursuant to Fed.R.Evid. 615 to order that all witnesses for [plaintiff] [defendant] be excluded from the courtroom until they are actually called to the witness stand; and that the witnesses be ordered not to discuss the case with one another, not to read any trial transcripts and not to talk with any witness who has already testified. I would further ask that once a witness has testified, he be ordered not to relate his testimony or to discuss what occurred in the courtroom. I also ask that opposing counsel be instructed to advise his witnesses as to the purpose and effect of the Court's sequestration order.

Commentary

In some cases, counsel may wish to request that fact witnesses be sequestered: that is, that they not be present in the courtroom while other witnesses testify. The purpose of sequestration is to prevent witnesses from altering their testimony in light of what they have heard from prior witnesses or observed from counsel's cross-examination or trial tactics. *Geders v. United States*, 425 U.S. 80, 87, 96 S. Ct. 1330, 1334, 47 L. Ed. 2d 592 (1976); *U.S. v. Collins*, 340 F.3d 672 (8th Cir. 2003); *Opus 3 Ltd. v. Heritage Park, Inc.*, 91 F.3d 625, 628 (4th Cir. 1996); *Government of Virgin Islands v. Edinborough*, 625 F.2d 472, 475 (3d Cir. 1980).

Fed.R.Evid. 615 makes witness exclusion mandatory at the request of any party, except that the court may not exclude: (1) a party who is a natural person; (2) the designated representative of a corporate party; or (3) a person whose presence is shown by a party to be essential to the presentation of the party's case (typically, an expert witness). In criminal cases these exceptions are applied to allow the prosecution's case agent to remain at counsel table with the prosecutor, hear the other witnesses testify, and nevertheless testify on behalf of the prosecution. *U.S. v. Avalos*, 506 F.3d 972 (10th Cir. 2007); *U.S. v. Turner*, 203 F.3d 1010 (7th Cir. 2000); *U.S. v. Crabtree*, 979 F.2d 1261 (7th Cir. 1992); *U.S. v. Parodi*, 703 F.2d 768 (4th Cir. 1983). There is disagreement as to whether the rule permits the government to designate more than one agent-witness to represent it. *Compare U.S. v. Jackson*, 60 F.3d 128 (2d Cir. 1995) (while it might be a rare case when trial court exempts more than one witness under a particular subprovision of Rule 615, judge has discretion to do so) *with U.S. v. Pulley*, 922 F.2d 1283, 1286 (6th Cir. 1991) (finding no reason to "convert the singular into the plural" in interpreting Rule 615).

While the text of Rule 615 is clear, its scope is not. Circuits have split on the question of whether the scope of Rule 615 extends beyond the courtroom to preclude out-of-court communication between witnesses about the case during trial. Wright & Gold, 29 Federal Practice & Procedure § 6243, at 61 (1997); *Compare U.S. v. Sepulveda*, 15 F.3d 1161 (1st Cir. 1993) (Rule 615 authorizes court to order witnesses excluded only from the courtroom proper) *with U.S. v. Prichard*, 781 F.2d 179 (10th Cir. 1986) (Rule 615 sequestration order requires not only that witnesses be excluded from courtroom but also refrain from discussing their testimony outside the courtroom). Even if Rule 615 only applies to in-court communications between witnesses, trial courts would still retain discretion to preclude such out-of-court communications between witnesses as a function of the court's general powers to manage the conduct of the trial. Wright & Gold, 29 Federal Practice & Procedure § 6243, at 62 (1997). *See U.S. v. Ortiz*, 10 F. Supp. 2d 1058 (N.D. Iowa 1998) (In addition to exclusion, the court may take further measures of separation designed to prevent communication between witnesses, such as ordering them to remain physically apart, ordering them not to discuss the case with one another or with any other person and ordering them not to read a transcript of the trial testimony of other witnesses). To avoid any misunderstandings about the scope of a Rule 615 order, these additional measures should be clearly set forth in the court's order. *See U.S. v.*

Buchanan, 787 F.2d 477 (10th Cir. 1986) (holding that trial court erred in failing to state clearly in sequestration order that witnesses were not to discuss the case); *U.S. v. Johnston*, 578 F.2d 1352 (10th Cir. 1978) (admonishing trial courts to instruct sequestered witnesses not to discuss testimony with other witnesses).

The Victim Rights Clarification Act, 18 U.S.C.A. § 3510 provides that, in criminal cases, victims may not be excluded from the trial because they intend to give victim impact testimony at any sentencing hearing. *See U.S. v. McVeigh*, 958 F. Supp. 512 (D. Colo. 1997) (the Oklahoma City bombing). A victim for purposes of this statute includes a person "that has suffered direct physical, emotional, or pecuniary harm as a result of the commission of a crime . . .", 42 U.S.C. § 106.7(e)(2); *see also* 18 U.S.C. § 3510(c); *U.S. v. Visinaiz*, 428 F.3d 1300 (10th Cir. 2005) (son of murder victim qualified as "victim" and could remain in courtroom after his testimony). Similarly, the Justice For All Act, 18 U.S.C.A. § 3771 provides that unless the court determines, by clear and convincing evidence that the victim's testimony would be materially altered if the victim heard other testimony, a crime victim may not be excluded from a trial. *See, e.g., In re Mikhel*, 453 F.3d 1137, 1139 (9th Cir. 2006) (court must find that it is "highly likely" that victim-witness will alter testimony); *U.S. v. Johnson*, 362 F. Supp. 2d 1043 (N.D. Iowa 2005).

Ideally, the sequestration motion should be made *in limine* or at the start of trial, but no rule precludes a party from making such motion at any other time.

Sequestration orders prohibiting discussions between witnesses do permit witnesses to discuss the case with counsel for either party. *U.S. v. Rhynes*, 218 F.3d 310, 317 (4th Cir. 2000) (collecting cases and authorities). However, occasionally during trial, counsel may wish to request a limited sequestration order applicable to a particular witness to cover recess or lunch periods. *See Perry v. Leeke*, 488 U.S. 272, 109 S. Ct. 594, 102 L. Ed. 2d 624 (1989) (court order directing accused not to consult his attorney during brief recess, called while accused was on witness stand, did not violate 6th Amendment right to counsel). In *Perry*, the Supreme Court held only that witnesses may be prohibited from speaking with lawyers between direct and cross-examination to prevent unethical coaching; it did not generally prohibit lawyer-witness contact as a part of a sequestration order. *Rhynes*, 218 F.3d at 317 n.7.

Because not all witnesses may be present when a sequestration order is entered, it is good practice to request that counsel be ordered to advise all of their witnesses of the sequestration order and its effect.

Whether a witness is essential and thus exempt from an order of exclusion is a matter committed to the trial court's discretion. *See Jackson*, 60 F.3d at 135; *U.S. v. Payan*, 992 F.2d 1387 (5th Cir. 1993). A party seeking to exempt a witness from a sequestration order must show that the witness has such specialized expertise or intimate knowledge of the facts that the party could not effectively function in the witness' absence. *U.S. v. Klaphake*, 64 F.3d 435 (8th Cir. 1995); *Oliver B. Cannon and Son, Inc. v. Fidelity and Cas. Co. of New York*, 519 F. Supp. 668 (D. Del. 1981). A showing that the witness' presence would be "helpful" is not enough. The party seeking an exemption from sequestration must demonstrate that the witness' presence is "essential" to his cause. *Opus 3 Ltd.*, 91 F.3d at 629.

Drawing on case law from various circuits, the Second Circuit developed a list of six considerations for the district court in exercising its discretion to grant or deny an exemption from a witness sequestration order: (1) how critical the testimony in question is, i.e., whether it will involve controverted and material facts; (2) whether the testimony is such that it could be subject to tailoring in light of the testimony of other witnesses; (3) whether the testimony is likely to cover the same issues as other witnesses; (4) the order in which the witnesses will testify; (5) any potential for bias that might motivate the witness to tailor his testimony; and (6) whether the witness' presence is essential or simply desirable. *Jackson*, 60 F.3d at 135; *see, e.g., Bruneau ex rel. Schofield v. South Kortright Cent. School Dist.*, 163 F.3d 749 (2d Cir. 1998) (in Title IX and § 1983 sexual harassment suit filed by 6th grade student, no error refusing to exclude administrator with Title IX responsibility and 6th grade teacher who was only adult witnessing events in classroom); *Opus 3 Ltd. v. Heritage Park Inc.* (acknowledging that Rule 615 is addressed to fact witnesses and does not mandate exclusion of expert witnesses but declining to adopt per se rule exempting expert witnesses); *U.S. v. Ortiz* (exempting court-appointed investigator who would testify primarily to objective facts ordinarily not subject to tailoring).

Additional References

Graham, Handbook of Federal Evidence § 615.1 (7th ed. 2012)

Treatises and Practice Aids

Goode and Wellborn, Courtroom Handbook on Federal Evidence Chapter 5, Rule 615 and Obj. 29 (annual ed.)
Wright & Gold, Federal Practice and Procedure: Evidence §§ 6241 *et seq.*
McCormick, Evidence § 50 (6th ed. 2006)
Park, Trial Objections Handbook § 11:5 (2nd ed. 2001)

SEQUESTRATION: VIOLATION OF ORDER

See:

Fed.R.Evid. 615
Mil.R.Evid. 615

Objection

- I object to this witness testifying. The Court previously granted my motion to have all witnesses sequestered. This witness intentionally disobeyed that order [*explain how, e.g. read the daily transcript*]. She has learned what earlier witnesses have testified to for purposes of tailoring her own testimony. I ask that the Court preclude this witness from testifying.

Response

- The sequestration order was unintentionally violated. [*Plaintiff/Defendant*] was not the cause of the violation. The violation was not serious and will have no impact on the testimony of the witness. A less drastic sanction is all that is warranted under the circumstances.

Commentary

Rule 615 gives parties the right to exclude prospective witnesses from the courtroom in order to prevent them from hearing the testimony of other witnesses. The Rule, a codification of common law, seeks to prevent the tailoring of a witness's testimony to evidence given earlier in the trial and is designed to discourage and expose fabrication, inaccuracy and collusion. *Geders v. United States*, 425 U.S. 80, 96 S. Ct. 1330, 47 L. Ed. 2d 592 (1976); *Holder v. U.S.*, 150 U.S. 91, 14 S. Ct. 10, 37 L. Ed. 1010 (1893); *U.S. v. Collins*, 340 F.3d 672 (8th Cir. 2003) (although government's witnesses discussed case while waiting in holding cell, no violation of Rule 615 because neither had testified prior to this conversation); *U.S. v. Vallie*, 284 F.3d 917 (8th Cir. 2002); *U.S. v. Jackson*, 60 F.3d 128 (2d Cir. 1995); *U.S. v. Ortiz*, 10 F. Supp. 2d 1058 (N.D. Iowa 1998) (collecting cases). Except for the three categories of witnesses exempted by the Rule and persons covered by the Victim Rights Clarification Act of

1997, 18 U.S.C.A. § 3510 and the Justice For All Act, 18 U.S.C. § 3771 *(see* "Sequester Witnesses—Motion," *supra)* the court, on request, must exclude all witnesses from the courtroom.

Once a sequestration order has been issued and a possible violation is brought to the court's attention, the trial judge must determine as a question of fact, whether there has been a violation and, if so, the sanction required. *U.S. v. Arruda*, 715 F.2d 671 (1st Cir. 1983).

In determining a sanction, if any, the trial court will consider: (1) the seriousness of the violation; (2) its impact on the testimony of the witness; (3) its probable impact on the outcome of the trial; (4) whether the witness intentionally disobeyed the order so that he could determine the content of other testimony; and (5) whether the party calling the witness had knowledge of, procured or consented to his disobedience. *See generally* 75 Am. Jur.2d, "Trial" § 245; *U.S. v. Hobbs*, 31 F.3d 918 (9th Cir. 1994).

Depending upon the circumstances of the violation, the court may: (1) declare a mistrial, *U.S. v. Wodtke*, 711 F.2d 86 (8th Cir. 1983); (2) preclude the witness from testifying, *U.S. v. Cropp*, 127 F.3d 354 (4th Cir. 1997); *U.S. v. Wilson*, 103 F.3d 1402 (8th Cir. 1997); (3) strike testimony already given, *Jerry Parks Equipment Co. v. Southeast Equipment Co., Inc.*, 817 F.2d 340 (5th Cir. 1987); (4) allow the testimony but permit cross-examination about the sequestration violation and any coaching, *U.S. v. Posada-Rios*, 158 F.3d 832 (5th Cir. 1998); (5) permit the testimony but instruct the jury it can consider the violation in evaluating the credibility of the witness, *Hill v. Porter Memorial Hosp.*, 90 F.3d 220 (7th Cir. 1996); *U.S. v. Riggs*, 184 Fed. Appx. 651 (9th Cir. 2006); and/or (6) hold the offender in contempt, *U.S. v. McMahon*, 104 F.3d 638 (4th Cir. 1997); and/or (7) admit the testimony if the court determines the violation does not affect the testimony of other witnesses or prejudice the defendant. *U.S. v. Samuels*, 493 F.3d 1187 (10th Cir. 2007); *U.S. v. Carvajal*, 206 Fed. Appx. 391, 395 (5th Cir. 2006).

Some courts have said that the remedy of witness exclusion, especially in criminal cases, is so severe that it should only be used when there has been a showing that a party or his attorney caused the violation and the right to a fair trial was prejudiced. *See U.S. v. Smith*, 441 F.3d 254, 263 (4th Cir. 2006); *U.S. v. Solorio*, 337 F.3d 580 (6th Cir. 2003) (where government did not arrange or know about violation, court prevented prejudice by limiting questions that could be asked by prosecutor, instructing jury about violation, allowing defense to cross-examine regarding the violation and to raise it in closing argument); *U.S. v. Rhynes*, 218 F.3d 310 (4th Cir. 2000); *U.S. v. Cropp* (expressing concern for the constitutionally based right of a defendant to present evidence in his favor); *U.S. v. Hobbs, supra.*

Additional References

Graham, Handbook of Federal Evidence § 615.1 (7th ed. 2012)

Treatises and Practice Aids

Goode and Wellborn, Courtroom Handbook on Federal Evidence Chapter 5, Rule 615 and Obj. 29 (annual ed.)

Wright & Gold, Federal Practice and Procedure: Evidence § 6246

McCormick, Evidence § 50 (6th ed. 2006)

Park, Trial Objections Handbook § 11:5 (2nd ed. 2001)

SETTLEMENT: OFFERS TO COMPROMISE

See:

Fed.R.Evid. 408
Mil.R.Evid. 408

Objection

- Objection. [*Request sidebar*] The question is improper under Rule 408 because it relates to an offer to settle or compromise a disputed claim.

Response

- The "other purpose" exception set forth in Rule 408 applies here because [*specify why exclusion is not required*].

Commentary

Fed.R.Evid. 408 excludes any evidence of settlement or settlement offers when offered to prove liability for or invalidity of a claim or its amount. Evidence of conduct or statements made in settlement negotiations is also inadmissible except when offered in a subsequent criminal case and the negotiations related to a claim by the government in the exercise of regulatory, investigative or enforcement authority. The exclusion applies regardless of which party attempts to offer the evidence. *Pierce v. F.R. Tripler & Co.*, 955 F.2d 820 (2d Cir. 1992).

The purpose of the rule is to promote the public policy favoring compromise and settlement of disputes and to encourage honesty and candor in settlement negotiations. *Stockman v. Oakcrest Dental Center, P.C.*, 480 F.3d 791 (6th Cir. 2007); *Olin Corp. v. Insurance Co. of North America*, 603 F. Supp. 445 (S.D. N.Y. 1985); *see Alcan Intern. Ltd. v. S.A. Day Mfg. Co., Inc.*, 179 F.R.D. 403 (W.D. N.Y. 1998) (rule recognizes that in give and take of settlement negotiations, offers and concessions are made which are inconsistent with legal and factual positions maintained by parties).

If an offer to settle a dispute could be used as evidence of the weakness of a claim or defense, parties would seldom come to the negotiating table. The rule, therefore, provides wide protection to both an actual settlement or offer to settle and to negotiations and conduct associated with the settlement or offer to settle. *Dimino v. New York City Transit Authority*, 64 F. Supp. 2d 136 (E.D. N.Y. 1999).

A number of courts have said that the spirit of Rule 408 supports the exclusion of work product, internal memos and other materials created specifically for the purpose of conciliation, even if not communicated to the other party. *E.E.O.C. v. UMB Bank Financial Corp.*, 558 F.3d 784 (8th Cir. 2009); *Affiliated Mfrs., Inc. v. Aluminum Co. of America*, 56 F.3d 521 (3d Cir. 1995) (Rule 408 applies to internal memos regarding compromise negotiations even though not communicated to opposing party). The protections of Rule 408 cannot be waived unilaterally because the rule, by definition, protects both parties from having the fact of negotiation disclosed to the jury.

The trigger for application of Rule 408 is the existence of an actual dispute as to an existing claim. *Affiliated Mfrs., Inc. v. Aluminum Co. of America*, 56 F.3d 521 (3d Cir. 1995) (meaning of "dispute" in Rule 408 includes both litigation and less formal stages of dispute). This requires more than discussions or business negotiations, *National Presto Industries, Inc. v. West Bend Co.*, 76 F.3d 1185 (Fed. Cir. 1996), but can be less than the point of actual or threatened litigation. *See Bradbury v. Phillips Petroleum Co.*, 815 F.2d 1356 (10th Cir. 1987) (if application of Rule 408 exclusion is doubtful, better practice is to exclude evidence of compromise negotiations).

Rule 408 applies to consent decrees executed with government agencies. *See, e.g., U.S. v. Austin*, 54 F.3d 394 (7th Cir. 1995) (consent decree with Federal Trade Commission); *Johnson v. Hugo's Skateway*, 974 F.2d 1408 (4th Cir. 1992) (Department of Justice); *U.S. v. Gilbert*, 668 F.2d 94 (2d Cir. 1981) (Securities and Exchange Commission); *New Jersey Turnpike Authority v. PPG Industries, Inc.*, 16 F. Supp. 2d 460 (D.N.J. 1998) (New Jersey Department of Environmental Protection); *Cannon v. Durham County Bd. of Elections*, 959 F. Supp. 289 (E.D. N.C. 1997) (proposed consent agreement in voting rights case).

There has been disagreement whether Rule 408 precludes admission in a criminal case of evidence that the accused settled or attempted to settle a related civil claim. *Compare U.S. v. Roti*, 484 F.3d 934 (7th Cir. 2007), *U.S. v. Hays*, 872 F.2d 582 (5th Cir. 1989) *and U.S. v. Skeddle*, 176 F.R.D. 254 (N.D. Ohio 1997) (Fed.R.Evid. 1101(b) explicitly states that rules of evidence apply generally to criminal cases and proceedings; nothing in Rule 408 limits its application to civil litigation) *with Manko v. U.S.*, 87 F.3d 50 (2d Cir. 1996) (clear reading of Rule 408 suggests it should apply only in civil proceedings; public interest in prosecution of crime is greater than public interest in settlement of civil disputes).

Note, however, that Rule 408 was amended, effective December 1, 2006, to permit introduction *in a criminal case of statements or conduct* during compromise negotiations regarding a civil dispute by a government regulatory, investigative or enforcement agency. These new provisions remain subject to Rule 403. The offer or acceptance of the settlement itself remains inadmissible in a subsequent criminal case if offered to prove liability for, invalidity of, or amount of the claim.

Evidence of settlement negotiations with respect to a different dispute has been held to be admissible. *Towerridge, Inc. v. T.A.O., Inc.*, 111 F.3d 758 (10th Cir. 1997) (to prove it was not at fault for any construction delay, subcontractor permitted to introduce evidence of delay claims settlement between general contractor and government); *Broadcort Capital Corp. v. Summa Medical Corp.*, 972 F.2d 1183 (10th Cir. 1992); *Vulcan Hart Corp. (St. Louis Div.) v. N.L.R.B.*, 718 F.2d 269 (8th Cir. 1983); *Rico v. American Family Ins. Group*, 267 F. Supp. 2d 554 (E.D. La. 2002) (to establish that plaintiff claimed same injuries in earlier lawsuit); *see also* 2 Weinstein & Berger, Weinstein's Federal Evidence § 408.08[5] (Joseph M. McLaughlin ed., Matthew Bender 2d ed. 2001) ("If the settlement negotiations and terms explain and are part of another dispute they must often be admitted if the trier is to understand the case."). But where the same parties are involved, or the same set of facts gives rise to a claim, these factors weigh in favor of a determination that the cases are too closely related to permit a settlement proposed in one to be admitted in the other. *Fiberglass Insula-*

tors, Inc. v. Dupuy, 856 F.2d 652 (4th Cir. 1988) (evidence of settlement discussions in prior lawsuits excluded since present action was latest in series of related lawsuits between former business partners); *Branch v. Fidelity & Cas. Co. of New York*, 783 F.2d 1289 (5th Cir. 1986) (error to admit evidence of earlier settlements in multiparty maritime accident case); *McInnis v. A.M.F., Inc.*, 765 F.2d 240 (1st Cir. 1985) (settlement agreement entered into between plaintiff and a third party joint tortfeasor could not be used by defendant because policies underlying exclusionary rule are applicable to such situation); *Quad/Graphics, Inc. v. Fass*, 724 F.2d 1230 (7th Cir. 1983) (evidence of plaintiff's settlement with two defendants in contract action not admissible at trial of remaining defendants); *Lo Bosco v. Kure Engineering Ltd.*, 891 F. Supp. 1035 (D.N.J. 1995) (former husband's settlement offer in divorce action not admissible in suit against father-in-law for breach of contract and fraud because of close relationship between cases); *but cf. Kennon v. Slipstreamer, Inc.*, 794 F.2d 1067 (5th Cir. 1986) (while it was proper to tell jury fact of settlement to explain why certain defendants were now absent, it was error to disclose the amount of the settlement).

Other Purposes Exception

Rule 408 does not exclude use of compromise evidence when it is offered to prove something other than liability for, or invalidity of, a claim or its amount. For example, compromise evidence can be admitted to prove the bias or prejudice of a witness, to show knowledge and intent, to show a continuing course of reckless conduct, to prove estoppel, to negate a contention of undue delay in pursuing a claim, to prove agency, ownership or control, or to support a claim that an illegal act occurred during the course of settlement negotiations. *Zurich American Ins. Co. v. Watts Industries, Inc.*, 417 F.3d 682 (7th Cir. 2005); *U.S. v. J.R. LaPointe & Sons, Inc.*, 950 F. Supp. 21 (D. Me. 1996). The following is an illustrative, not an exhaustive, list of exceptions to the Rule 408 prohibition: *Bankcard America, Inc. v. Universal Bancard Systems, Inc.*, 203 F.3d 477 (7th Cir. 2000) (to show state of mind and to rebut claim of contract violation); *Starter*

Corp. v. Converse, Inc., 170 F.3d 286 (2d Cir. 1999) (to prove estoppel); *Cochenour v. Cameron Savings and Loan, F.A.*, 160 F.3d 1187 (8th Cir. 1998) *and Freidus v. First Nat. Bank of Council Bluffs*, 928 F.2d 793 (8th Cir. 1991) (for purposes of rebuttal); *Westchester Specialty Ins. Services, Inc. v. U.S. Fire Ins. Co.*, 119 F.3d 1505 (11th Cir. 1997) (to resolve factual dispute re meaning of settlement agreement terms); *U.S. v. Hauert*, 40 F.3d 197 (7th Cir. 1994) (to show knowledge and intent re tax law requirements); *Eli Lilly and Co. v. Emisphere Technologies, Inc.*, 408 F. Supp. 2d 668 (S.D. Ind. 2006) and *eAcceleration Corp. v. Trend Micro, Inc*, 408 F. Supp. 2d 1110 (W.D. Wash. 2006) (to rebut a contention of undue delay); *Becker v. Kroll*, 340 F. Supp. 2d 1230 (D. Utah 2004) (Rule 408 inapplicable to suits seeking to vindicate wrongs committed during settlement discussions); *Seafarers Intern. Union of North America v. Thomas*, 42 F. Supp. 2d 547 (D.V.I. 1999) (to show union breached duty of fair representation); *Chemtall, Inc. v. Citi-Chem, Inc.*, 992 F. Supp. 1390 (S.D. Ga. 1998) (party is estopped from invoking evidentiary exclusion when real purpose of settlement communication was to commit fraud).

When evidence concerning statements or conduct occurring during settlement negotiations is not barred under Rule 408, the trial court still must perform a balancing test under Rule 403, weighing the probative value of the proffered evidence against its potential for unfair prejudice to the objecting party. *Weir v. Federal Ins. Co.*, 811 F.2d 1387 (10th Cir. 1987); *Southwest Nurseries, LLC v. Florists Mut. Ins., Inc.*, 266 F. Supp. 2d 1253 (D. Colo. 2003); *Scott v. Goodman*, 961 F. Supp. 424 (E.D. N.Y. 1997).

Additional References

Graham, Handbook of Federal Evidence § 408.1 (7th ed. 2012)

Treatises and Practice Aids

Goode and Wellborn, Courtroom Handbook on Federal Evidence Chapter 5, Rule 408 and Obj. (annual ed.)

Mueller & Kirkpatrick, Federal Evidence, §§ 4:56 to 4:60 (3d ed. 2007)

Wright & Graham, Federal Practice and Procedure: Evidence §§ 5301 *et seq.*

McCormick, Evidence § 266 (6th ed. 2006)

Park, Trial Objections Handbook §§ 2:47 to 2:53 (2nd ed. 2001)

SPECULATION

See:

Fed.R.Evid. 602
Mil.R.Evid. 602

Objection

- [*To a question*] Objection. The question calls for speculation by the witness.
- [*To an answer*] Objection. The answer is pure speculation and should be striken.

Response

- The question is based on facts of record and this witness has the ability to respond based upon personal knowledge.

Commentary

No witness is permitted to guess or to state an opinion based on mere conjecture. Rule 602. Any question that asks the witness to guess or engage in conjecture is objectionable since speculation as to what could have happened is usually of little probative value. Technically, this objection falls within the realm of competency since the rule is simply an application of the general principle that a witness' testimony must be based on personal knowledge. Rule 602. *See U.S. v. Lucas*, 499 F.3d 769 (8th Cir. 2007) (speculative evidence may also be excluded under Rule 403 to avoid confusing or misleading jury); *Chapa v. U.S.*, 497 F.3d 883 (8th Cir. 2007) (testimony re what action witness would have taken if she had known grandchild was being abused properly excluded as speculative); *Lust v. Sealy, Inc.*, 383 F.3d 580 (7th Cir. 2004) (hypothetical question called for speculation); *Cooper v. Smith & Nephew, Inc.*, 259 F.3d 194, 200 (4th Cir. 2001) (no error to exclude expert's opinion which was little more than speculation; "A reliable expert opinion must be based on scientific, technical, or other specialized knowledge and not on belief or speculation, and inferences must be derived using scientific or other valid methods.") (*citing Oglesby v. General Motors Corp.*, 190 F.3d 244, 250 (4th Cir. 1999)); *U.S. v. Stewart*, 104 F.3d 1377, 1384

(D.C. Cir. 1997) (where police officer had no relevant knowledge of events surrounding the chain of custody of seized drugs, he could not be questioned about time gap before drugs reached DEA laboratory for analysis; "the district court does not abuse its discretion in cutting off examination of a witness where the question would call for a speculative answer."); *U.S. v. Morrison*, 98 F.3d 619 (D.C. Cir. 1996) (where prosecution witness had not yet been sentenced, she could not be asked on cross-examination whether the only way she could keep her children was to testify against defendant because she would only be speculating about what the sentencing judge might do and/or what might happen had she refused to testify); *Burton v. Wyeth-Ayerst Laboratories Div. of American Home Products Corp.*, 513 F. Supp. 2d 708 (N.D. Tex. 2007) (court cannot allow random speculation to be presented to jury under guise of expert testimony); *Athridge v. Aetna Cas. and Sur. Co.*, 474 F. Supp. 2d 102 (D.D.C. 2007) (testimony by witnesses as to what they *would have done* is purely speculative); *Feit v. Great-West Life and Annuity Ins. Co.*, 460 F. Supp. 2d 632 (D.N.J. 2006) (expert's opinion must be based on methods and procedures of science rather than on subjective belief and unsupported speculation); *Medalen v. Tiger Drylac U.S.A., Inc.*, 269 F. Supp. 2d 1118 (D. Minn. 2003) (expert testimony that is speculative is not competent proof and contributes nothing to a legally sufficient evidentiary basis).

Additional References

Graham, Handbook of Federal Evidence §§ 602.1 to 602.2 (7th ed. 2012)

Treatises and Practice Aids

Goode and Wellborn, Courtroom Handbook on Federal Evidence Chapter 5, Rule 602 and Obj. 87 (annual ed.)

Mueller & Kirkpatrick, Federal Evidence, §§ 6:5, 6:6 (3d ed. 2007)

Wright & Gold, Federal Practice and Procedure: Evidence §§ 6021 *et seq.*

McCormick, Evidence § 10 (6th ed. 2006)

Park, Trial Objections Handbook § 6:11 (2nd ed. 2001)

SUBSEQUENT REMEDIAL MEASURES

See:

Fed.R.Evid. 407
Mil.R.Evid. 407

Objection

- Objection. The question relates to remedial measures taken after the accident and that evidence is inadmissible.

Response

- The question is proper under the circumstances because the evidence is being offered [*for the limited purpose of showing ownership, control, feasibility of precautionary measures*] [*to impeach the credibility of the witness*].

Commentary

Rule 407 excludes evidence of remedial actions taken after an injury or harm which, if taken previously, would have made the injury or harm less likely to occur if the evidence is offered for the purpose of proving negligence, culpable conduct, product defect, design defect, or failure to warn. The rule states:

> When, after an injury or harm allegedly caused by an event, measures are taken that, if taken previously, would have made the injury or harm less likely to occur, evidence of the subsequent measures is not admissible to prove negligence, culpable conduct, a defect in a product, a defect in a product's design, or a need for a warning or instruction. This rule does not require the exclusion of evidence of subsequent measures when offered for another purpose, such as proving ownership, control, or feasibility of precautionary measures, if controverted, or impeachment.

Henning v. Union Pacific R. Co., 530 F.3d 1206 (10th Cir. 2008); *Specialty Products Intern., Ltd. v. Con-Way Transp. Services, Inc.*, 410 F. Supp. 2d 423 (M.D. N.C. 2006); *Benedict v. Zimmer, Inc.*, 405 F. Supp. 2d 1026 (N.D. Iowa 2005); *Rivera Pomales v. Bridgestone Firestone, Inc.*, 224 F.R.D. 50 (D.P.R. 2004).

In addition to repairs, design changes, installation of safety devices or firing a culpable employee, subsequent remedial measures have been held to include changes in rules and policies. *See Baker v. Canadian National/Illinois Cent. R.R.*, 536 F.3d 357 (5th Cir. 2008) (where plaintiff could not show railroad's flagman policy existed at time of accident, any reference to policy at trial would violate Rule 407); *Maddox v. City of Los Angeles*, 792 F.2d 1408, 1417 (9th Cir. 1986) (police internal affairs investigation and measures taken by defendant city were remedial measures taken after alleged incident of police misconduct); *Luera v. Snyder*, 599 F. Supp. 1459, 1463 (D. Colo. 1984) (testimony of changes in police department's policies inadmissible as evidence of a subsequent remedial measure).

The justification for Rule 407 is twofold. First, as an admission of fault, the probative value of subsequent remedial measures is limited. Second, exclusion is important to foster a social policy of encouraging persons to take steps in furtherance of added safety. Fed.R.Evid. 407 advisory committee's note; *Lust v. Sealy, Inc.*, 383 F.3d 580 (7th Cir. 2004); *Petree v. Victor Fluid Power, Inc.*, 831 F.2d 1191 (3d Cir. 1987) (*"Petree I"*); *Hull v. Chevron U.S.A., Inc.*, 812 F.2d 584 (10th Cir. 1987); *Seyler v. Burlington Northern Santa Fe Corp.*, 102 F. Supp. 2d 1226 (D. Kan. 2000).

Exceptions

Rule 407 is not a general rule of exclusion. The rule explicitly provides that subsequent remedial measures may be admissible when offered for some purpose other than to prove culpable conduct such as when ownership, control or the feasibility of precautionary measures are controverted or for impeachment. An opposing party "controverts" feasibility when that party testifies, in effect, that a device or procedure was not capable of being utilized or dealt with successfully. *Williams v. Security Nat. Bank of Sioux City, Iowa*, 358 F. Supp. 2d 782 (N.D. Iowa 2005). Illustrative cases include: *Hull*, 812 F.2d at 587 (evidence offered to show control inadmissible where control was not disputed); *Donahue v. Phillips Petroleum Co.*, 866 F.2d 1008 (8th Cir. 1989) (feasibility contested); *Swans v. City of Lansing*, 65 F. Supp. 2d 625 (W.D. Mich. 1998) (same).

Impeachment

Unrestricted use of subsequent remedial measures to impeach a witness carries with it the distinct danger that the exception will undermine or nullify the Rule. Therefore, pursuant to Rule 403, courts generally limit the use of such evidence to situations where it is offered for impeachment by direct contradiction, or as one commentator has said: "cases in which defense witnesses have made extravagant claims of safety." Prof. Daniel J. Capra, Case Law Divergence from the Federal Rules of Evidence, 197 F.R.D. 531, 536 (2000). *See, e.g., Wood v. Morbark Industries, Inc.*, 70 F.3d 1201 (11th Cir. 1995) (post-accident design change admissible for impeachment where defense witness testified that original design was safest possible design); *Harrison v. Sears, Roebuck and Co.*, 981 F.2d 25 (1st Cir. 1992) (a desire merely to undercut an expert's credibility is not sufficient to trigger the impeachment exception to Rule 407); *Kelly v. Crown Equipment Co.*, 970 F.2d 1273 (3d Cir. 1992) (where expert did not say that forklift design was the best or the only one possible but did testify it was an excellent and proper design, evidence of subsequent changes could not be offered to contradict him); *Petree v. Victor Fluid Power, Inc.*, 887 F.2d 34 (3d Cir. 1989) ("Petree II") (where expert opined that hydraulic press posed no inherent danger and warning labels were unnecessary, error to exclude evidence that company had begun using warning labels because such evidence would have directly impeached expert); *Muzyka v. Remington Arms Co., Inc.*, 774 F.2d 1309 (5th Cir. 1985) (design change should have been admitted for impeachment where defense witnesses testified that the product was the best and safest product of its kind); *Kirkland v. Marriott Intern., Inc.*, 416 F. Supp. 2d 480 (E.D. La. 2006) (impeachment may include proving defendants' knowledge of the alleged dangerous condition at the time of the accident).

Measures Not Within the Scope of the Rule

By its terms, Rule 407 has no application to the following kinds of evidence:

1. subsequent remedial measures taken by a third person who is not a party to the

litigation. *See e.g., Millennium Partners, L.P. v. Colmar Storage, LLC*, 494 F.3d 1293 (11th Cir. 2007) (Rule 407 only applies to a defendant's voluntary actions, it does not apply to subsequent remedial measures by non-defendants); *Diehl v. Blaw-Knox*, 360 F.3d 426 (3d Cir. 2004) (seven other circuits have concluded Rule 407 does not apply to subsequent remedial measures taken by non-party); *Dixon v. International Harvester Co.*, 754 F.2d 573 (5th Cir. 1985) (repair by tractor owner after an accident not excluded when offered against tractor manufacturer).

2. measures taken prior to the occurrence of the event. *See, e.g., Trull v. Volkswagen of America, Inc.*, 187 F.3d 88 (1st Cir. 1999) (change in design of van several years prior to accident from rear to front engine with longer front end did not implicate Rule 407; evidence excluded, however, as unduly prejudicial under Rule 403 since claim turned on seat belt design and not lack of front crumple zone); *Bogosian v. Mercedes-Benz of North America, Inc.*, 104 F.3d 472 (1st Cir. 1997) (similar); *In re Air Crash Disaster*, 86 F.3d 498, 531 (6th Cir. 1996) (Rule 407 does not apply to post-manufacture, pre-accident measures); *Misener v. General Motors*, 924 F. Supp. 130 (D. Utah 1996) (language of Rule 407 excluding measures taken "after the event" refers to the date of the accident).
3. post-event reports and investigations. *See, e.g., Prentiss & Carlisle Co., Inc. v. Koehring-Waterous Div. of Timberjack, Inc.*, 972 F.2d 6, 10 (1st Cir. 1992) (Rule prohibits evidence of subsequent measures, not evidence of a party's analysis of its product); *Dow Chemical Corp. v. Weevil-Cide Co., Inc.*, 897 F.2d 481 (10th Cir. 1990) (Rule 407 is not a basis to exclude a report on what corrective action might be taken); *Rocky Mountain Helicopters, Inc. v. Bell Helicopters Textron, a Div. of Textron, Inc.*, 805 F.2d 907, 918 (10th Cir. 1986) (upholding admission of post-accident tests of allegedly defective product because "[i]t would strain the spirit of the remedial measure prohibition in Rule 407 to extend its shield to evidence

contained in post-event tests or reports"); *Hochen v. Bobst Group, Inc.*, 193 F.R.D. 22 (D. Mass. 2000) (admitting cause and origin report of mechanical explosion).

4. measures compelled by the government. *See, e.g., In re Aircrash in Bali, Indonesia*, 871 F.2d 812, 817 (9th Cir. 1989) (report of airline's safety record and procedures did not qualify as subsequent remedial measure because it was prepared by FAA without the voluntary participation of Pan Am; "where the defendant has not voluntarily participated in the subsequent measure at issue, the admission of that measure into evidence does not 'punish' the defendant for his efforts to remedy his safety problems.").

A number of courts have also held that Rule 407 has no application in breach of contract actions. *See Mowbray v. Waste Management Holdings, Inc.*, 45 F. Supp. 2d 132 (D. Mass. 1999) (collecting cases); *but see Pastor v. State Farm Mut. Auto. Ins. Co*, 487 F.3d 1042, 1045 (7th Cir. 2007) (to use a revision in a contract to argue the meaning of the original version would violate Rule 407 which is not limited to "repair" in the literal sense).

Additional References

Graham, Handbook of Federal Evidence § 407.1 (7th ed. 2012)

Treatises and Practice Aids

Goode and Wellborn, Courtroom Handbook on Federal Evidence Chapter 5, Rule 407 and Obj. 88 (annual ed.)

Mueller & Kirkpatrick, Federal Evidence, §§ 4:49 to 4:55 (3d ed. 2007)

Wright & Graham, Federal Practice and Procedure: Evidence §§ 5281 *et seq.*

McCormick, Evidence § 267 (6th ed. 2006)

SUMMARIES

See:

Fed.R.Evid. 1006
Mil.R.Evid. 1006

Objection

- The evidence on which this summary is based is inadmissible and, therefore, the summary is inadmissible.
- The summary does not fairly and accurately represent the underlying evidence because [*explain*].
- My opponent cannot meet the foundational requirements since he/she never made the underlying evidence available.

Response

- The underlying evidence is admissible [*explain*].
- The summary is an accurate representation of the underlying evidence [*explain*].
- The underlying evidence was made available [*explain*].

Commentary

Summary exhibits are explicitly authorized by Fed.R.Evid. 1006 and are particularly useful to help triers of fact understand complex factual issues. *U.S. v. Lewis*, 759 F.2d 1316 (8th Cir. 1985).

Rule 1006 provides:

> The contents of voluminous writings, recordings, or photographs which cannot conveniently be examined in court may be presented in the form of a chart, summary or calculation. The originals, or duplicates, shall be made available for examination or copying, or both, by other parties at reasonable time and place. The court may order that they be produced in court.

Because the summaries themselves are the evidence, there is no need to introduce the underlying voluminous material into evidence. *U.S. v. Schuler*, 458 F.3d 1148 (10th Cir. 2006); *U.S. v. Samaniego*, 187 F.3d 1222 (10th Cir. 1999); *U.S. v. Bakker*, 925 F.2d 728 (4th Cir. 1991).

Admission of summaries as substantive evidence is conditioned, however, on the requirement that the evidence upon which they are based must be admissible. *U.S. v. Moon*, 513 F.3d 527 (6th Cir. 2008); *U.S. v. Johnson*, 594 F.2d 1253, 1255 (9th Cir. 1979) ("We do not believe that Congress intended that counsel could abrogate other restrictions on . . . admissibility-like the hearsay rule-by the use of summaries . . ..."). Although proper foundation also requires that summary charts fairly represent and summarize the evidence on which they are based, *U.S. v. Ogba*, 526 F.3d 214 (5th Cir. 2008), *U.S. v. Koskerides*, 877 F.2d 1129 (2d Cir. 1989), courts have also said that the inaccuracy of a summary goes to the weight, rather than the admissibility of the evidence. *BD ex rel. Jean Doe v. DeBuono*, 193 F.R.D. 117 (S.D. N.Y. 2000) (*citing In re Richardson-Merrell, Inc. Bendectin Products Liability Litigation*, 624 F. Supp. 1212 (S.D. Ohio 1985)). The summary must be introduced through the testimony of a witness who supervised its preparation. *U.S. v. Jamieson*, 427 F.3d 394 (6th Cir. 2005).

"Made Available" Requirement

The First Circuit has said that to satisfy the "made available" requirement, a party seeking to use a summary under Rule 1006 must identify its exhibit, provide a list or description of the documents supporting the exhibit and state when and where the documents can be reviewed. *Air Safety, Inc. v. Roman Catholic Archbishop of Boston*, 94 F.3d 1, 8 (1st Cir. 1996). This gives the opponent the ability to check the summary's accuracy and prepare for cross-examination. The court also said Rule 1006 operates independently of the discovery rules and that failure to request or obtain the documents during discovery does not negate a party's absolute right to subsequent production of material under Rule 1006 should that material become incorporated in a chart, summary or calculation. *Id; cf. Coates v. Johnson & Johnson*, 756 F.2d 524, 549–50 (7th Cir. 1985) (rule requires that the underlying material, not the summary itself, be made available to adverse party before trial).

The following cases illustrate the operation of the Rule: *U.S. v. Harms*, 442 F.3d 367 (5th Cir.

2006) (in prosecution for mail fraud and perjury in connection with receipt of workers comp, timeline and summary testimony were admissible); *U.S. v. Richardson*, 233 F.3d 1285 (11th Cir. 2000) (court will permit use of summary charts [here, transactional histories of bank accounts] incorporating certain assumptions so long as supporting evidence has been presented previously to jury and court makes it clear it is jury's decision as to what weight should be given to evidence); *U.S. v. Leon-Reyes*, 177 F.3d 816 (9th Cir. 1999) (in prosecution for perjury, summaries of testimony from prior trial offered not for truth but to show materiality of defendant's allegedly false testimony); *U.S. v. Samaniego*, 187 F.3d at 1224–25 (in prosecution for drug trafficking, reversible error to allow FBI agent to testify from summaries of subpoenaed telephone records without first establishing admissibility of underlying records); *Air Safety v. Roman Catholic Archbishop of Boston*, 94 F.3d at 8 (no error excluding summary exhibits where offering party failed to identify and make available underlying documents); *Herman v. Davis Acoustical Corp.*, 21 F. Supp. 2d 130, 135–36 (N.D. N.Y. 1998) rev'd on other grounds, 196 F.3d 354 (2d Cir. 1999) (in wage violations case, no error to admit summary exhibit constructed from contractors' payroll records).

The fact that a non-expert witness prepares a summary or testifies about it does not make the summary inadmissible. *U.S. v. Hemphill*, 514 F.3d 1350, 1359 (D.C. Cir. 2008).

Demonstrative Evidence Under Rule 611 Distinguished

In contrast with those charts admitted as substantive evidence under Rule 1006, charts that summarize documents or testimony, **already admitted in evidence**, may be shown to the jury under Rule 611(a) as demonstrative aids.* *U.S. v. Johnson*, 54 F.3d 1150 (4th Cir. 1995) (collecting

---

[Summaries]

*As discussed in the Advisory Committee Note to Rule 611, the rule covers such matters as the presentation of evidence, "the use of demonstrative evidence . . . and the many other questions arising during the course of a trial which can be solved only by the judge's common sense and fairness in view of the partic-

cases); *U.S. v. Pinto*, 850 F.2d 927 (2d Cir. 1988); *U.S. v. Possick*, 849 F.2d 332 (8th Cir. 1988); *U.S. v. Gardner*, 611 F.2d 770 (9th Cir. 1980); *U.S. v. Scales*, 594 F.2d 558 (6th Cir. 1979).

The Rules of Evidence are silent on the use and admissibility of "demonstrative" exhibits. The Eighth Circuit has said that district courts have "virtually unfettered discretion to regulate the use of . . . non-evidentiary devices, either generally or to achieve procedural fairness and regularity in a particular case." *U.S. v. Crockett*, 49 F.3d 1357, 1362 (8th Cir. 1995) (considering the use of transparencies to help jurors recall the testimony of witnesses). Exercising that discretion, courts have used a balancing test, balancing probative value against potential prejudice, as Rule 403 provides, to determine whether "demonstrative" exhibits may be used at trial. *U.S. v. Fauls*, 65 F.3d 592, 596 (7th Cir. 1995) (applying such a balancing test); *U.S. v. Gaskell*, 985 F.2d 1056, 1061 n.2 (11th Cir. 1993) (same, also noting that "[s]everal circuits have recognized that demonstrative exhibits tend to leave a particularly potent image in the jurors' minds"). The Tenth Circuit has also used a balancing of probative value and potential for unfair prejudice to determine whether demonstrative exhibits could be used *during deliberations*, as well as during trial. The court reiterated its prior holdings "that it is within the discretion of the Trial Court, absent abuse working to the clear prejudice of the defendant, to permit the display of demonstrative or illustrative exhibits admitted in evidence *both in the courtroom during trial and in the jury room during deliberations*." *U.S. v. Downen*, 496 F.2d 314, 320 (10th Cir. 1974) (emphasis added) (citing *Taylor v. Reo Motors, Inc.*, 275 F.2d 699 (10th Cir. 1960); *Ahern v. Webb*, 268 F.2d 45 (10th Cir. 1959); *Millers' Nat. Ins. Co., Chicago, Ill. v. Wichita Flour Mills Co.*, 257 F.2d 93 (10th Cir. 1958); *Carlson v. U.S.*, 187 F.2d 366 (10th Cir. 1951)). The court held that the submission of papers, documents or articles, whether or not admitted in evidence, to the jury for view during trial or jury deliberations, accompanied by careful cautionary instructions as to their use and limited significance, is within the

---

ular circumstances."

discretion accorded the trial court in order that it may guide and assist the jury in understanding and judging the factual controversy. *Id.* at 321; *see also U.S. v. Johnson*, 54 F.3d at 1159 (no error admitting summary chart into evidence; "Whether or not the chart is technically admitted into evidence, we are more concerned that the district court ensure the jury is not relying on that chart as 'independent' evidence but rather is taking a close look at the evidence upon which that chart is based."); *U.S. v. Pinto*, 850 F.2d at 935; *U.S. v. Scales*, 594 F.2d at 564. When Rule 611 charts are used, many courts *sua sponte* will give a limiting instruction which informs the jury of the summary's purpose and that it does not constitute evidence. *U.S. v. Bakke*, 942 F.2d 977 (6th Cir. 1991); *U.S. v. Blackwell*, 954 F. Supp. 944 (D.N.J. 1997).

Summary Witnesses Distinguished

In exceptional cases involving complicated facts and/or numerous records, and in exercise of the trial court's discretion under Rule 611(a), summary witnesses may testify at trial to summarize the testimony of other witnesses and documents or charts previously admitted into evidence. *U.S. v. Nguyen*, 504 F.3d 561 (5th Cir. 2007); *U.S. v. Bishop*, 264 F.3d 535 (5th Cir. 2001) (allowing IRS agent to testify as summary witness where summary had foundation in evidence already admitted and was accompanied by a limiting instruction); *U.S. v. Johnson*, 54 F.3d at 1150; *U.S. v. Moore*, 997 F.2d 55 (5th Cir. 1993) (permitting IRS agent to selectively summarize where facts fell within his expertise); *U.S. v. Osum*, 943 F.2d 1394 (5th Cir. 1991); *U.S. v. Caswell*, 825 F.2d 1228 (8th Cir. 1987); *U.S. v. Lemire*, 720 F.2d 1327 (D.C. Cir. 1983). Among the dangers inherent in the use of a summary witness are that such testimony improperly might serve to bolster the credibility of earlier witnesses or provide what really amounts to a mid-trial summation, more properly the function of closing argument. *U.S. v. Fullwood*, 342 F.3d 409 (5th Cir. 2003) (error to allow Special Agent as last witness in rebuttal and without justification, to recap substantial portions of Government's case-in-chief); *U.S. v. Castillo*, 77 F.3d 1480 (5th Cir. 1996) (without good reason or real need, summary witness testimony unfairly allowed one prosecution witness merely to repeat or paraphrase in-court testimony of another); *Johnson,* 54 F.3d at 1162 (summary witness testimony inappropriate in normal case given inherent dangers, including confusion); *U.S. v. Baker*, 10 F.3d 1374 (9th Cir. 1993) (summary witnesses should only be allowed in exceptional cases because credibility of summary witness may be substituted for credibility of evidence summarized).

Additional References

Graham, Handbook of Federal Evidence § 1006.1 (7th ed. 2012)

Treatises and Practice Aids

Goode and Wellborn, Courtroom Handbook on Federal Evidence Chapter 5, Rule 1006 (annual ed.)
Mueller & Kirkpatrick, Federal Evidence, §§ 10:33 to 10:35 (3d ed. 2007)
Wright & Gold, Federal Practice and Procedure: Evidence §§ 8041 *et seq*
McCormick, Evidence § 233 (6th ed. 2006)
Park, Trial Objections Handbook §§ 9:9 to 9:13 (2nd ed. 2001)

UNFAIR PREJUDICE

See:

Fed.R.Evid. 403
M.R.E. 403

Objection

- Objection. May we approach the bench to discuss my objection? [*At sidebar*] This evidence has little probative value, if any, and is unfairly prejudicial to my client for the following reasons [*specify*]. The evidence warrants a mistrial if the jury hears it, and, therefore, I ask that the evidence be excluded.

Response

- The probative value of this evidence and its importance to the case justify its admission [*explain*]. A cautionary instruction to the jury will avoid any unfair prejudice.

Commentary

Rule 403 codifies the court's power to exclude otherwise relevant evidence whose probative value "is substantially outweighed by the danger of unfair prejudice." *U.S. v. Massino*, 546 F.3d 123 (2d Cir. 2008); *accord, e.g., U.S. v. W.R. Grace*, 504 F.3d 745 (9th Cir. 2007); *U.S. v. Christians*, 200 F.3d 1124 (8th Cir. 1999); *U.S. v. Marrero-Ortiz*, 160 F.3d 768 (1st Cir. 1998). Because virtually all evidence is prejudicial to one party or another, to justify exclusion under Rule 403, the prejudice must be *unfair*. *Costantino v. David M. Herzog, M.D., P.C.*, 203 F.3d 164 (2d Cir. 2000); *U.S. v. Guerrero-Cortez*, 110 F.3d 647 (8th Cir. 1997) (unfair prejudice does not include damage that occurs to a party's case because of the legitimate probative force of the evidence).

"Unfair prejudice" means an undue tendency to suggest decision on an improper basis, which is commonly, though not necessarily, an emotional one. *Old Chief v. United States*, 519 U.S. 172, 180, 117 S. Ct. 644, 650, 136 L. Ed. 2d 574 (1997); *U.S. v. Nevels*, 490 F.3d 800 (10th Cir. 2007) (evidence is unfairly prejudicial if it tends to affect adversely jury's attitude toward defendant wholly or apart from its judgment as to his guilt or innocence of crime charged); *U.S. v. Frost*, 234 F.3d 1023, 1025 (8th Cir. 2000) (unfair prejudice as to criminal defendant means the capacity of some concededly relevant evidence to lure the fact-finder into declaring guilt on basis different from proof specific to offense charged); *U.S. v. Nichols*, 169 F.3d 1255 (10th Cir. 1999) (same); *Sutkiewicz v. Monroe County Sheriff*, 110 F.3d 352 (6th Cir. 1997) (relevant evidence may be excluded if it serves to inflame jury's passions); *Nickerson v. G.D. Searle & Co.*, 900 F.2d 412 (1st Cir. 1990) (affirming exclusion of questions of medical expert on his work in abortion clinics because of danger of emotional reaction).

Unlike some other evidentiary exclusions which may bar evidence for one purpose only to have it admitted for another purpose, exclusion under Rule 403 is absolute. Once the probative value of a piece of evidence is found to be substantially outweighed by the danger of unfair prejudice, there is no other evidentiary rule that can operate to make that same evidence admissible. *U.S. v. Benavidez-Benavidez*, 217 F.3d 720 (9th Cir. 2000).

The following criminal cases illustrate the rule: *U.S. v. Jackson*, 549 F.3d 963 (5th Cir. 2008) (murder witness could not be impeached by evidence he was registered sex offender because of risk jury would discount testimony out of revulsion for sex offenses); *U.S. v. Morales-Aldahondo*, 524 F.3d 115, 119 (1st Cir. 2008) (probative value of child pornography images taken from defendant's computer was not substantially outweighed by danger of unfair prejudice); *U.S. v. Stout*, 509 F.3d 796 (6th Cir. 2007) (in prosecution for receipt of sexually explicit images of children, court properly excluded prior conviction for surreptitiously videotaping a showering 14-year-old girl; jury would be more alarmed and disgusted by prior acts than actual conduct charged); *U.S. v. Sine*, 493 F.3d 1021 (9th Cir. 2007) (unfair prejudice outweighed probative value of prosecutor's cross examination incorporating another judge's adverse findings in related civil suit concerning defendant's credibility); *U.S. v. Cabrera*, 222 F.3d 590 (9th Cir. 2000) (repeated references to defendants and others as Cuban drug dealers together with comments about drug practices in

Cuban community constituted reversible error; appeals to racial, ethnic or religious prejudice violate right to fair trial); *U.S. v. Gordon*, 173 F.3d 761 (10th Cir. 1999) (where charge was drug possession with intent to distribute, improper to question defendant whether paycheck was garnished to provide child support); *U.S. v. Neill*, 166 F.3d 943 (9th Cir. 1999) (reference that bank robbery defendant lived at work release center indirectly allowed into evidence damaging fact that defendant had been convicted of prior crime); *U.S. v. Vue*, 13 F.3d 1206 (8th Cir. 1994) (reference to tendency of Hmong people to smuggle opium into Twin Cities unfairly prejudicial); *U.S. v. Cruz*, 981 F.2d 659 (2d Cir. 1992) (references to Hispanic drug dealers and Hispanic neighborhood as prime source of drugs created substantial danger of unfair prejudice); *U.S. v. Doe*, 903 F.2d 16 (D.C. Cir. 1990) (trial testimony and closing argument about Jamaicans taking over Washington, D.C. crack cocaine market unfairly prejudicial); *U.S. v. Beltran-Rios*, 878 F.2d 1208 (9th Cir. 1989) (drug courier profiles are inherently prejudicial because of the potential for including innocent citizens as profiled drug couriers); *U.S. v. Gillespie*, 852 F.2d 475 (9th Cir. 1988) (reversing sex abuse conviction due to admission of evidence suggesting homosexuality); *Cohn v. Papke*, 655 F.2d 191 (9th Cir. 1981) (requiring new trial in § 1983 action where evidence of prior homosexual relationships had been admitted); *U.S. v. Birrell*, 421 F.2d 665 (9th Cir. 1970) (reversing theft conviction due to evidence of homosexuality).

For operation of the rule in civil cases, *see Schmude v. Tricam Industries, Inc.*, 556 F.3d 624 (7th Cir. 2009) (in products liability case for injuries in ladder collapse, portions of vocational report properly excluded wherein plaintiff indicated dislike of other humans and that he had thrived in prison environment; prejudicial effect obvious, probative value nil); *Tidemann v. Nadler Golf Car Sales, Inc.*, 224 F.3d 719 (7th Cir. 2000) (where golf car was not examined until four years after accident and had been used for two of those years, plaintiff's expert testimony properly excluded; minimal probative value outweighed by danger of unfair prejudice); *Duran v. City of Maywood*, 221 F.3d 1127 (9th Cir. 2000) (evidence that policeman was involved in second shooting three days after shooting at issue in § 1983 suit excluded as unfairly prejudicial and requiring trial within a trial); *Lathem v. Department of Children and Youth Services*, 172 F.3d 786 (11th Cir. 1999) (although EEOC determinations are admitted in bench trials, liberal admissibility does not apply to jury trials; in Title VII action where plaintiff claimed EEOC did not interview certain witnesses or review all documents, agency determination properly excluded); *BE &K Const. Co. v. Will & Grundy Counties Bldg. Trades Council*, 156 F.3d 756 (7th Cir. 1998) (labor law violation case precluding union from showing videotape to jury which included such highly prejudicial statements as "BE & K is a parasite in the life of the community"); *Nichols v. American Nat. Ins. Co.*, 154 F.3d 875 (8th Cir. 1998) (in sex harassment case, abuse of discretion to admit highly prejudicial evidence that plaintiff was practicing Catholic who had obtained abortion; such evidence increased likelihood that jury would view her as immoral and not worthy of trust); *Goulah v. Ford Motor Co.*, 118 F.3d 1478 (11th Cir. 1997) (in products liability action, proper to exclude proffered testimony of ex-Ford employee who would have testified a supervisor told him it was acceptable to kill people); *Pouliot v. Paul Arpin Van Lines, Inc.*, 235 F.R.D. 537 (D. Conn. 2006) (no error allowing treating physician to point out injuries on plaintiff's body, colostomy and catheter bags; demonstration was useful in illustrating and explaining doctor's verbal testimony); *Niver v. Travelers Indem. Co. of Illinois*, 433 F. Supp. 2d 968 (N.D. Iowa 2006) (evidence of plaintiff's sexual promiscuity properly excluded in action for bad faith failure to pay workers compensation benefits); *Spruill v. Winner Ford of Dover, Ltd.*, 175 F.R.D. 194 (D. Del. 1997) (collecting cases as to prejudice *vel non* of findings by administrative agencies).

Rule 403 balancing is a quintessentially fact-sensitive enterprise. *Udemba v. Nicoli*, 237 F.3d 8, 15 (1st Cir. 2001). In weighing the probative value of evidence against the dangers and considerations enumerated in Rule 403, the balance should be struck in favor of admissibility. *U.S. v. Johnson*, 199 F.3d 123 (3d Cir. 1999); *Jacques v. Clean-Up Group, Inc.*, 96 F.3d 506 (1st Cir. 1996); *U.S. v.*

Dennis, 625 F.2d 782 (8th Cir. 1980). Exclusion of evidence based upon its prejudicial effect should occur only sparingly. *Mendelsohn v. Sprint/United Management Co.*, 466 F.3d 1223 (10th Cir. 2006), cert. granted, 551 U.S. 1113, 127 S. Ct. 2937, 168 L. Ed. 2d 261 (2007) and judgment vacated on other grounds and remanded, 552 U.S. 379, 128 S. Ct. 1140, 170 L. Ed. 2d 1 (2008). *See, e.g.*, *U.S. v. Gartmon*, 146 F.3d 1015, 1021 (D.C. Cir. 1998) (in fraud and money laundering case, proper to admit evidence that defendant threatened his reluctant confederate by putting gun into her vagina). "Rule 403 does not provide a shield for defendants who engage in outrageous acts, permitting only the crimes of Caspar Milquetoasts to be described fully to a jury. It does not generally require the government to sanitize its case, to deflate its witnesses' testimony, or to tell its story in a monotone." *Id.*; *accord U.S. v. Rivera*, 83 F.3d 542, 547 (1st Cir. 1996) (where charged crime was carjacking, evidence that victim was also raped) " 'Unless trials are to be conducted on scenarios, on unreal facts tailored and sanitized for the occasion, the application of Rule 403 must be cautious and sparing.' " *Id.* (quoting *U.S. v. McRae*, 593 F.2d 700, 707 (5th Cir. 1979)).

Additional References

Graham, Handbook of Federal Evidence § 403.1 (7th ed., 2012)

Treatises and Practice Aids

Goode and Wellborn, Courtroom Handbook On Federal Evidence Chapter 5, Rule 403 and Obj. 70 (annual ed.)

Mueller & Kirkpatrick, Federal Evidence, § 6:89 (3d ed. 2007)

Wright & Graham, Federal Practice and Procedure: Evidence § 5215

McCormick, Evidence § 185 (6th ed. 2006)

Park, Trial Objections Handbook § 2:5 (2nd ed. 2001)

VAGUE AND AMBIGUOUS QUESTION

See:

Fed.R.Evid. 611(a)
Mil.R.Evid. 611(a)

Objection

- Objection. The question is vague and ambiguous because [*specify*].

Response

- [*Unless the question is clear and the objection merely a stalling tactic, it is better to rephrase the question*].

Commentary

Fed.R.Evid. 611(a) provides that the court shall exercise reasonable control over the mode of interrogating witnesses so as to make the interrogation effective for the ascertainment of truth. A question should be posed in a reasonably clear and specific manner so that the witness can understand what is being asked. A vague and ambiguous question is one which is indefinite and uncertain as to its meaning or susceptible to several different interpretations. *U.S. v. Wall*, 371 F.2d 398 (6th Cir. 1967) (reversing perjury conviction which had been based on response to ambiguous question). A witness is not required to answer questions which are uncertain in meaning. *See U.S. v. Clark*, 613 F.2d 391, 407 (2d Cir. 1979) ("The question excluded was confusing to court, counsel and the witness alike.").

Additional References

Graham, Handbook of Federal Evidence § 611.19 (7th ed. 2012)

Treatises and Practice Aids

Goode and Wellborn, Courtroom Handbook on Federal Evidence Chapter 5 Rule 611 and Obj. 1 (annual ed.)

Mueller & Kirkpatrick, Federal Evidence, §§ 6:60 *et seq.* (3d ed. 2007)

Wright & Gold, Federal Practice and Procedure: Evidence § 6164

Park, Trial Objections Handbook § 6:13 (2nd ed. 2001)

VOIR DIRE OF WITNESS (AS TO ADMISSIBILITY OF TESTIMONY OR DEMONSTRATIVE EVIDENCE)

See:

Fed.R.Evid. 104(a), 611(a)
Mil.R.Evid. 104(a), 611(a)

Form

- Objection, this witness is incompetent to give testimony because [*specify*]. I respectfully ask the court's permission to conduct voir dire of the witness. I believe I will be able to show that her testimony is not admissible.
- I object to the testimony of plaintiff's expert and request the right to conduct voir dire. I will be able to show that he lacks the knowledge, skill, training or experience to render an opinion in this case.
- I object to the admissibility of Exhibit 5 and request permission to conduct voir dire. I will be able to show that the witness cannot properly authenticate the document.

Commentary

As a preliminary question under Rule 104(a), the trial court has discretion to allow opposing counsel to challenge the competency of an expert or other person by voir dire of the witness. This is done by interrupting direct examination and allowing opposing counsel to examine the witness by leading questions for the purpose of establishing grounds for an objection.

Courts also will permit voir dire questioning if the attorney appears able to establish the inadmissibility of the evidence. Usually, the opposing attorney can ask a reasonable number of questions to establish lack of admissibility. The interrogation may not develop into questions that should be asked on cross-examination. Questioning that extends beyond proper voir dire and into cross-examination should be objected to as improper. *See* Fed.R.Evid. 611(a).

The request for voir dire is often preceded by an objection that there is no foundation for the evidence sought to be admitted. "Lack of foundation" is a shorthand way of asserting that the party offering the testimony has not met certain requirements of the rules of evidence. This objection may be employed with respect to at least each of the following:

1. Competency of a lay witness, Fed.R.Evid. 601.
2. Qualifications of an expert witness, Fed.R.Evid. 702.
3. Introduction of opinion testimony including a determination of scientific reliability and validity, Fed.R.Evid. 701 to 705.
4. Personal knowledge, Fed.R.Evid. 602.
5. Unavailability in connection with a hearsay exception, Fed.R.Evid. 804(a).
6. Satisfaction of the requirements of a hearsay exemption or exception, Fed.R.Evid. 801(d), 803, 804(b).
7. Authentication or identification, Fed.R.Evid. 901.
8. Admissibility of evidence other than the original writing, Fed.R.Evid. 1004.
9. The existence or waiver of a privilege, Fed.R.Evid. 501.
10. Relevancy, Fed.R.Evid. 401.

Graham, Handbook of Federal Evidence § 611.9 (4th ed. 1996).

When expert testimony is challenged, voir dire must demonstrate that the witness lacks knowledge, skill, training or experience in the area upon which he is to give an opinion. *See, e.g., Sullivan v. Rowan Companies, Inc.*, 952 F.2d 141 (5th Cir. 1992) (after extensive voir dire, expert found not qualified to testify on whether hand tool was defective and on cause of its failure).

With the court's permission, voir dire also can be used to show that certain demonstrative evidence is inadmissible. For example, a witness may identify a document which the proponent offers. By interposing an objection and requesting voir dire, the opposing attorney may question the witness in an attempt to show that the witness cannot sufficiently authenticate the document.

These principles are also illustrated in the following cases: *U.S. v. Stoecker*, 215 F.3d 788 (7th

Cir. 2000) (after voir dire regarding circumstances under which witness surrendered real estate license, certain cross-examination questions were precluded); *U.S. v. Corey*, 207 F.3d 84 (1st Cir. 2000) (after making foundation and hearsay objections, defense counsel permitted to voir dire federal agent as to any testimony about where firearm had been manufactured).

Additional References

Graham, Handbook of Federal Evidence § 611.9 (7th ed. 2012)

Treatises and Practice Aids

Goode and Wellborn, Courtroom Handbook on Federal Evidence Chapter 5, Rule 611 and Obj. 2 (annual ed.)

McCormick, Evidence § 52 (6th ed. 2006)

APPENDIX

FEDERAL RULES OF EVIDENCE

Effective July 1, 1975

Latest Amendments Effective December 1, 2011

Table of Rules

ARTICLE V. PRIVILEGES

ARTICLE VI. WITNESSES

ARTICLE VII. OPINIONS AND EXPERT TESTIMONY

ARTICLE VIII. HEARSAY

ARTICLE IX. AUTHENTICATION AND IDENTIFICATION

ARTICLE X. CONTENTS OF WRITINGS, RECORDINGS, AND PHOTOGRAPHS

ARTICLE XI. MISCELLANEOUS RULES

ARTICLE I GENERAL PROVISIONS

Rule 101. Scope; Definitions

(a) Scope. These rules apply to proceedings in United States courts. The specific courts and proceedings to which the rules apply, along with exceptions, are set out in Rule 1101.

(b) Definitions. In these rules:

(1) "civil case" means a civil action or proceeding;

(2) "criminal case" includes a criminal proceeding;

(3) "public office" includes a public agency;

(4) "record" includes a memorandum, report, or data compilation;

(5) a "rule prescribed by the Supreme Court" means a rule adopted by the Supreme Court under statutory authority; and

(6) a reference to any kind of written material or any other medium includes electronically stored information.

Rule 102. Purpose

These rules should be construed so as to administer every proceeding fairly, eliminate unjustifiable expense and delay, and promote the development of evidence law, to the end of ascertaining the truth and securing a just determination.

Rule 103. Rulings on Evidence

(a) Preserving a Claim of Error. A party may claim error in a ruling to admit or exclude evidence only if the error affects a substantial right of the party and:

(1) if the ruling admits evidence, a party, on the record:

(A) timely objects or moves to strike; and

(B) states the specific ground, unless it was apparent from the context; or

(2) if the ruling excludes evidence, a party informs the court of its substance by an offer of proof, unless the substance was apparent from the context.

(b) Not Needing to Renew an Objection or Offer of Proof. Once the court rules definitively on the record — either before or at trial — a party need not renew an objection or offer of proof to preserve a claim of error for appeal.

(c) Court's Statement About the Ruling; Directing an Offer of Proof. The court may make any statement about the character or form of the evidence, the objection made, and the ruling. The court may direct that an offer of proof be made in question-and-answer form.

(d) Preventing the Jury from Hearing Inadmissible Evidence. To the extent practicable, the court must conduct a jury trial so that inadmissible evidence is not suggested to the jury by any means.

(e) Taking Notice of Plain Error. A court may take notice of a plain error affecting a substantial right, even if the claim of error was not properly preserved.

Rule 104. Preliminary Questions

(a) In General. The court must decide any preliminary question about whether a witness is qualified, a privilege exists, or evidence is admissible. In so deciding, the court is not bound by evidence rules, except those on privilege.

(b) Relevance That Depends on a Fact. When the relevance of evidence depends on whether a fact exists, proof must be introduced sufficient to support a finding that the fact does exist. The court may admit the proposed evidence on the condition that the proof be introduced later.

(c) Conducting a Hearing So That the Jury Cannot Hear It. The court must conduct any hearing on a preliminary question so that the jury cannot hear it if:

(1) the hearing involves the admissibility of a confession;

(2) a defendant in a criminal case is a witness and so requests; or

(3) justice so requires.

(d) Cross-Examining a Defendant in a Criminal Case. By testifying on a preliminary question, a defendant in a criminal case does not become subject to cross-examination on other issues in the case.

(e) Evidence Relevant to Weight and Credibility. This rule does not limit a party's right to introduce before the jury evidence that is relevant to the weight or credibility of other evidence.

Rule 105. Limiting Evidence That Is Not Admissible Against Other Parties or for Other Purposes

If the court admits evidence that is admissible against a party or for a purpose — but not against another party or for another purpose — the court, on timely request, must restrict the evidence to its proper scope and instruct the jury accordingly.

Rule 106. Remainder of or Related Writings or Recorded Statements

If a party introduces all or part of a writing or recorded statement, an adverse party may require the introduction, at that time, of any other part — or any other writing or recorded statement — that in fairness ought to be considered at the same time.

ARTICLE II JUDICIAL NOTICE

Rule 201. Judicial Notice of Adjudicative Facts

(a) **Scope.** This rule governs judicial notice of an adjudicative fact only, not a legislative fact.

(b) **Kinds of Facts That May Be Judicially Noticed.** The court may judicially notice a fact that is not subject to reasonable dispute because it:

(1) is generally known within the trial court's territorial jurisdiction; or

(2) can be accurately and readily determined from sources whose accuracy cannot reasonably be questioned.

(c) **Taking Notice.** The court:

(1) may take judicial notice on its own; or

(2) must take judicial notice if a party requests it and the court is supplied with the necessary information.

(d) **Timing.** The court may take judicial notice at any stage of the proceeding.

(e) **Opportunity to Be Heard.** On timely

request, a party is entitled to be heard on the propriety of taking judicial notice and the nature of the fact to be noticed. If the court takes judicial notice before notifying a party, the party, on request, is still entitled to be heard.

(f) Instructing the Jury. In a civil case, the court must instruct the jury to accept the noticed fact as conclusive. In a criminal case, the court must instruct the jury that it may or may not accept the noticed fact as conclusive.

ARTICLE III PRESUMPTIONS IN CIVIL CASES

Rule 301. Presumptions in Civil Cases Generally

In a civil case, unless a federal statute or these rules provide otherwise, the party against whom a presumption is directed has the burden of producing evidence to rebut the presumption. But this rule does not shift the burden of persuasion, which remains on the party who had it originally.

Rule 302. Applying State Law to Presumptions in Civil Cases

In a civil case, state law governs the effect of a presumption regarding a claim or defense for which state law supplies the rule of decision.

ARTICLE IV RELEVANCY AND ITS LIMITS

Rule 401. Test for Relevant Evidence

Evidence is relevant if:

(a) it has any tendency to make a fact more or less probable than it would be without the evidence; and

(b) the fact is of consequence in determining the action.

Rule 402. General Admissibility of Relevant Evidence

Relevant evidence is admissible unless any of the following provides otherwise:

- the United States Constitution;
- a federal statute;

- these rules; or
- other rules prescribed by the Supreme Court.

Irrelevant evidence is not admissible.

Rule 403. Excluding Relevant Evidence for Prejudice, Confusion, Waste of Time, or Other Reasons

The court may exclude relevant evidence if its probative value is substantially outweighed by a danger of one or more of the following: unfair prejudice, confusing the issues, misleading the jury, undue delay, wasting time, or needlessly presenting cumulative evidence.

Rule 404. Character Evidence; Crimes or Other Acts

(a) Character Evidence.

(1) ***Prohibited Uses.*** Evidence of a person's character or character trait is not admissible to prove that on a particular occasion the person acted in accordance with the character or trait.

(2) ***Exceptions for a Defendant or Victim in a Criminal Case.*** The following exceptions apply in a criminal case:

(A) a defendant may offer evidence of the defendant's pertinent trait, and if the evidence is admitted, the prosecutor may offer evidence to rebut it;

(B) subject to the limitations in Rule 412, a defendant may offer evidence of an alleged victim's pertinent trait, and if the evidence is admitted, the prosecutor may:

(i) offer evidence to rebut it; and

(ii) offer evidence of the defendant's same trait; and

(C) in a homicide case, the prosecutor may offer evidence of the alleged victim's trait of peacefulness to rebut evidence that the victim was the first aggressor.

(3) ***Exceptions for a Witness.*** Evidence of a witness's character may be admitted under Rules 607, 608, and 609.

(b) Crimes, Wrongs, or Other Acts.

(1) ***Prohibited Uses.*** Evidence of a crime, wrong, or other act is not admissible to prove a person's character in order to show that on a particular occasion the person acted in accordance with the character.

(2) ***Permitted Uses; Notice in a Criminal Case.*** This evidence may be admissible for another purpose, such as proving motive, opportunity, intent, preparation, plan, knowledge, identity, absence of mistake, or lack of accident. On request by a defendant in a criminal case, the prosecutor must:

(A) provide reasonable notice of the general nature of any such evidence that the prosecutor intends to offer at trial; and

(B) do so before trial — or during trial if the court, for good cause, excuses lack of pretrial notice.

Rule 405. Methods of Proving Character

(a) **By Reputation or Opinion.** When evidence of a person's character or character trait is admissible, it may be proved by testimony about the person's reputation or by testimony in the form of an opinion. On cross-examination of the character witness, the court may allow an inquiry into relevant specific instances of the person's conduct.

(b) **By Specific Instances of Conduct.** When a person's character or character trait is an essential element of a charge, claim, or defense, the character or trait may also be proved by relevant specific instances of the person's conduct.

Rule 406. Habit; Routine Practice

Evidence of a person's habit or an organization's routine practice may be admitted to prove that on a particular occasion the person or organization acted in accordance with the habit or routine practice. The court may admit this evidence regardless of whether it is corroborated or whether there was an eyewitness.

Rule 407. Subsequent Remedial Measures

When measures are taken that would have made an earlier injury or harm less likely to occur, evidence of the subsequent measures is not admissible to prove:

- negligence;
- culpable conduct;
- a defect in a product or its design; or
- a need for a warning or instruction.

But the court may admit this evidence for another purpose, such as impeachment or — if disputed — proving ownership, control, or the feasibility of precautionary measures.

Rule 408. Compromise Offers and Negotiations

(a) Prohibited Uses. Evidence of the following is not admissible — on behalf of any party — either to prove or disprove the validity or amount of a disputed claim or to impeach by a prior inconsistent statement or a contradiction:

(1) furnishing, promising, or offering — or accepting, promising to accept, or offering to accept — a valuable consideration in compromising or attempting to compromise the claim; and

(2) conduct or a statement made during compromise negotiations about the claim — except when offered in a criminal case and when the negotiations related to a claim by a public office in the exercise of its regulatory, investigative, or enforcement authority.

(b) Exceptions. The court may admit this evidence for another purpose, such as proving a witness's bias or prejudice, negating a contention of undue delay, or proving an effort to obstruct a criminal investigation or prosecution.

Rule 409. Offers to Pay Medical and Similar Expenses

Evidence of furnishing, promising to pay, or offering to pay medical, hospital, or similar expenses resulting from an injury is not admissible to prove liability for the injury.

Rule 410. Pleas, Plea Discussions, and Related Statements

(a) Prohibited Uses. In a civil or criminal case, evidence of the following is not admissible against the defendant who made the plea or participated in the plea discussions:

(1) a guilty plea that was later withdrawn;

(2) a nolo contendere plea;

(3) a statement made during a proceeding on either of those pleas under Federal Rule of Criminal Procedure 11 or a comparable state procedure; or

(4) a statement made during plea discussions with an attorney for the prosecuting authority if the discussions did not result in a guilty plea or they resulted in a later-withdrawn guilty plea.

(b) Exceptions. The court may admit a statement described in Rule 410(a)(3) or (4):

(1) in any proceeding in which another statement made during the same plea or plea discussions has been introduced, if in fairness the statements ought to be considered together; or

(2) in a criminal proceeding for perjury or false statement, if the defendant made the statement under oath, on the record, and with counsel present.

Rule 411. Liability Insurance

Evidence that a person was or was not insured against liability is not admissible to prove whether the person acted negligently or otherwise wrongfully. But the court may admit this evidence for another purpose, such as proving a witness's bias or prejudice or proving agency, ownership, or control.

Rule 412. Sex-Offense Cases: The Victim's Sexual Behavior or Predisposition

(a) Prohibited Uses. The following evidence is not admissible in a civil or criminal proceeding involving alleged sexual misconduct:

(1) evidence offered to prove that a victim engaged in other sexual behavior; or

(2) evidence offered to prove a victim's sexual predisposition.

(b) **Exceptions.**

(1) ***Criminal Cases.*** The court may admit the following evidence in a criminal case:

(A) evidence of specific instances of a victim's sexual behavior, if offered to prove that someone other than the defendant was the source of semen, injury, or other physical evidence;

(B) evidence of specific instances of a victim's sexual behavior with respect to the person accused of the sexual misconduct, if offered by the defendant to prove consent or if offered by the prosecutor; and

(C) evidence whose exclusion would violate the defendant's constitutional rights.

(2) ***Civil Cases.*** In a civil case, the court may admit evidence offered to prove a victim's sexual behavior or sexual predisposition if its probative value substantially outweighs the danger of harm to any victim and of unfair prejudice to any party. The court may admit evidence of a victim's reputation only if the victim has placed it in controversy.

(c) **Procedure to Determine Admissibility.**

(1) ***Motion.*** If a party intends to offer evidence under Rule 412(b), the party must:

(A) file a motion that specifically describes the evidence and states the purpose for which it is to be offered;

(B) do so at least 14 days before trial unless the court, for good cause, sets a different time;

(C) serve the motion on all parties; and

(D) notify the victim or, when appropriate, the victim's guardian or representative.

(2) ***Hearing.*** Before admitting evidence under this rule, the court must conduct an in camera hearing and give the victim and parties a right to attend and be

heard. Unless the court orders otherwise, the motion, related materials, and the record of the hearing must be and remain sealed.

(d) Definition of "Victim." In this rule, "victim" includes an alleged victim.

Rule 413. Similar Crimes in Sexual-Assault Cases

(a) Permitted Uses. In a criminal case in which a defendant is accused of a sexual assault, the court may admit evidence that the defendant committed any other sexual assault. The evidence may be considered on any matter to which it is relevant.

(b) Disclosure to the Defendant. If the prosecutor intends to offer this evidence, the prosecutor must disclose it to the defendant, including witnesses' statements or a summary of the expected testimony. The prosecutor must do so at least 15 days before trial or at a later time that the court allows for good cause.

(c) Effect on Other Rules. This rule does not limit the admission or consideration of evidence under any other rule.

(d) Definition of "Sexual Assault." In this rule and Rule 415, "sexual assault" means a crime under federal law or under state law (as "state" is defined in 18 U.S.C. § 513) involving:

(1) any conduct prohibited by 18 U.S.C. chapter 109A;

(2) contact, without consent, between any part of the defendant's body — or an object — and another person's genitals or anus;

(3) contact, without consent, between the defendant's genitals or anus and any part of another person's body;

(4) deriving sexual pleasure or gratification from inflicting death, bodily injury, or physical pain on another person; or

(5) an attempt or conspiracy to engage in conduct described in subparagraphs (1)-(4).

Rule 414. Similar Crimes in Child-Molestation Cases

(a) Permitted Uses. In a criminal case in which a defendant is accused of child molestation, the court may admit evidence that the defendant committed any other child molestation. The evidence may be considered on any matter to which it is relevant.

(b) Disclosure to the Defendant. If the prosecutor intends to offer this evidence, the prosecutor must disclose it to the defendant, including witnesses' statements or a summary of the expected testimony. The prosecutor must do so at least 15 days before trial or at a later time that the court allows for good cause.

(c) Effect on Other Rules. This rule does not limit the admission or consideration of evidence under any other rule.

(d) Definition of "Child" and "Child Molestation." In this rule and Rule 415:

(1) "child" means a person below the age of 14; and

(2) "child molestation" means a crime under federal law or under state law (as "state" is defined in 18 U.S.C. § 513) involving:

(A) any conduct prohibited by 18 U.S.C. chapter 109A and committed with a child;

(B) any conduct prohibited by 18 U.S.C. chapter 110;

(C) contact between any part of the defendant's body — or an object — and a child's genitals or anus;

(D) contact between the defendant's genitals or anus and any part of a child's body;

(E) deriving sexual pleasure or gratification from inflicting death, bodily injury, or physical pain on a child; or

(F) an attempt or conspiracy to engage in conduct described in subparagraphs (A)-(E).

Rule 415. Similar Acts in Civil Cases Involving Sexual Assault or Child Molestation

(a) **Permitted Uses.** In a civil case involving a claim for relief based on a party's alleged sexual assault or child molestation, the court may admit evidence that the party committed any other sexual assault or child molestation. The evidence may be considered as provided in Rules 413 and 414.

(b) **Disclosure to the Opponent.** If a party intends to offer this evidence, the party must disclose it to the party against whom it will be offered, including witnesses' statements or a summary of the expected testimony. The party must do so at least 15 days before trial or at a later time that the court allows for good cause.

(c) **Effect on Other Rules.** This rule does not limit the admission or consideration of evidence under any other rule.

ARTICLE V PRIVILEGES

Rule 501. Privilege in General

The common law — as interpreted by United States courts in the light of reason and experience — governs a claim of privilege unless any of the following provides otherwise:

- the United States Constitution;
- a federal statute; or
- rules prescribed by the Supreme Court.

But in a civil case, state law governs privilege regarding a claim or defense for which state law supplies the rule of decision.

Rule 502. Attorney-Client Privilege and Work Product; Limitations on Waiver

The following provisions apply, in the circumstances set out, to disclosure of a communication or information covered by the attorney-client privilege or work-product protection.

(a) **Disclosure Made in a Federal Proceeding or to a Federal Office or Agency; Scope of a Waiver.** When the disclosure is made in a federal proceeding or to a federal office or agency and waives the attorney-client privilege or work-product protection, the waiver extends to an undisclosed communication or information in a federal or state proceeding only if:

(1) the waiver is intentional;

(2) the disclosed and undisclosed communications or information concern the same subject matter; and

(3) they ought in fairness to be considered together.

(b) Inadvertent Disclosure. When made in a federal proceeding or to a federal office or agency, the disclosure does not operate as a waiver in a federal or state proceeding if:

(1) the disclosure is inadvertent;

(2) the holder of the privilege or protection took reasonable steps to prevent disclosure; and

(3) the holder promptly took reasonable steps to rectify the error, including (if applicable) following Federal Rule of Civil Procedure 26(b)(5)(B).

(c) Disclosure Made in a State Proceeding. When the disclosure is made in a state proceeding and is not the subject of a state-court order concerning waiver, the disclosure does not operate as a waiver in a federal proceeding if the disclosure:

(1) would not be a waiver under this rule if it had been made in a federal proceeding; or

(2) is not a waiver under the law of the state where the disclosure occurred.

(d) Controlling Effect of a Court Order. A federal court may order that the privilege or protection is not waived by disclosure connected with the litigation pending before the court — in which event the disclosure is also not a waiver in any other federal or state proceeding.

(e) Controlling Effect of a Party Agreement. An agreement on the effect of disclosure in a federal proceeding is binding only on the parties to the agreement, unless it is incorporated into a court order.

(f) Controlling Effect of this Rule. Notwithstanding Rules 101 and 1101, this rule applies to state proceedings and to federal court-annexed and federal court-mandated arbitration proceedings, in the circumstances set out in the rule. And notwithstanding Rule 501, this rule applies even if state law provides the rule of decision.

(g) Definitions. In this rule:

(1) "attorney-client privilege" means the protection that applicable law provides for confidential attorney-client communications; and

(2) "work-product protection" means the protection that applicable law provides for tangible material (or its intangible equivalent) prepared in anticipation of litigation or for trial.

ARTICLE VI WITNESSES

Rule 601. Competency to Testify in General

Every person is competent to be a witness unless these rules provide otherwise. But in a civil case, state law governs the witness's competency regarding a claim or defense for which state law supplies the rule of decision.

Rule 602. Need for Personal Knowledge

A witness may testify to a matter only if evidence is introduced sufficient to support a finding that the witness has personal knowledge of the matter. Evidence to prove personal knowledge may consist of the witness's own testimony. This rule does not apply to a witness's expert testimony under Rule 703.

Rule 603. Oath or Affirmation to Testify Truthfully

Before testifying, a witness must give an oath or affirmation to testify truthfully. It must be in a form designed to impress that duty on the witness's conscience.

Rule 604. Interpreter

An interpreter must be qualified and must give an oath or affirmation to make a true translation.

Rule 605. Judge's Competency as a Witness

The judge presiding at the trial may not testify in that trial as a witness. No objection need be made in order to preserve the point.

Rule 606. Juror's Competency as a Witness

(a) At the Trial. A juror may not testify as a witness before the other jurors at the trial. If a juror is called to testify, the court must give a party an opportunity to object outside the jury's presence.

(b) During an Inquiry into the Validity of a Verdict or Indictment.

(1) ***Prohibited Testimony or Other Evidence.*** During an inquiry into the validity of a verdict or indictment, a juror may not testify about any statement made or incident that occurred during the jury's deliberations; the effect of anything on that juror's or another juror's vote; or any juror's mental processes concerning the verdict or indictment. The court may not receive a juror's affidavit or evidence of a juror's statement on these matters.

(2) ***Exceptions.*** A juror may testify about whether:

(A) extraneous prejudicial information was improperly brought to the jury's attention;

(B) an outside influence was improperly brought to bear on any juror; or

(C) a mistake was made in entering the verdict on the verdict form.

Rule 607. Who May Impeach a Witness

Any party, including the party that called the witness, may attack the witness's credibility.

Rule 608. A Witness's Character for Truthfulness or Untruthfulness

(a) Reputation or Opinion Evidence. A witness's credibility may be attacked or supported by testimony about the witness's reputation for having a character for truthfulness or untruthfulness, or by testimony in the form of an opinion about that character. But evidence of truthful character is admissible only after the witness's character for truthfulness has been attacked.

(b) Specific Instances of Conduct. Except for a criminal conviction under Rule 609, extrinsic evidence is not admissible to prove specific instances of a witness's conduct in order to attack or support the witness's character for truthfulness. But the court may, on cross-examination, allow them to be inquired into if they are probative of the character for truthfulness or untruthfulness of:

(1) the witness; or

(2) another witness whose character the witness being cross-examined has testified about.

By testifying on another matter, a witness does not waive any privilege against self-incrimination for testimony that relates only to the witness's character for truthfulness.

Rule 609. Impeachment by Evidence of a Criminal Conviction

(a) In General. The following rules apply to attacking a witness's character for truthfulness by evidence of a criminal conviction:

(1) for a crime that, in the convicting jurisdiction, was punishable by death or by imprisonment for more than one year, the evidence:

(A) must be admitted, subject to Rule 403, in a civil case or in a criminal case in which the witness is not a defendant; and

(B) must be admitted in a criminal case in which the witness is a defendant, if the probative value of the evidence outweighs its prejudicial effect to that defendant; and

(2) for any crime regardless of the punishment, the evidence must be admitted if the court can readily determine that establishing the elements of the crime required proving — or the witness's admitting — a dishonest act or false statement.

(b) Limit on Using the Evidence After 10 Years. This subdivision (b) applies if more than 10 years have passed since the witness's conviction or release from confinement for it, whichever is later. Evidence of the conviction is admissible only if:

(1) its probative value, supported by specific facts and circumstances, substantially outweighs its prejudicial effect; and

(2) the proponent gives an adverse party reasonable written notice of the intent to use it so that the party has a fair opportunity to contest its use.

(c) Effect of a Pardon, Annulment, or Certificate of Rehabilitation. Evidence of a conviction is not admissible if:

(1) the conviction has been the subject of a pardon, annulment, certificate of rehabilitation, or other equivalent procedure based on a finding that the person has been rehabilitated, and the person has not been convicted of a later crime punishable by death or by imprisonment for more than one year; or

(2) the conviction has been the subject of a pardon, annulment, or other equivalent procedure based on a finding of innocence.

(d) Juvenile Adjudications. Evidence of a juvenile adjudication is admissible under this rule only if:

(1) it is offered in a criminal case;

(2) the adjudication was of a witness other than the defendant;

(3) an adult's conviction for that offense would be admissible to attack the adult's credibility; and

(4) admitting the evidence is necessary to fairly determine guilt or innocence.

(e) Pendency of an Appeal. A conviction that satisfies this rule is admissible even if an appeal is pending. Evidence of the pendency is also admissible.

Rule 610. Religious Beliefs or Opinions

Evidence of a witness's religious beliefs or opinions is not admissible to attack or support the witness's credibility.

Rule 611. Mode and Order of Examining Witnesses and Presenting Evidence

(a) Control by the Court; Purposes. The court should exercise reasonable control over the mode and order of examining witnesses and presenting evidence so as to:

(1) make those procedures effective for determining the truth;

(2) avoid wasting time; and

(3) protect witnesses from harassment or undue embarrassment.

(b) Scope of Cross-Examination. Cross-examination should not go beyond the subject matter of the direct examination and matters affecting the witness's credibility. The court may allow inquiry into additional matters as if on direct examination.

(c) Leading Questions. Leading questions should not be used on direct examination except as necessary to develop the witness's testimony. Ordinarily, the court should allow leading questions:

(1) on cross-examination; and

(2) when a party calls a hostile witness, an adverse party, or a witness identified with an adverse party.

Rule 612. Writing Used to Refresh a Witness's Memory

(a) Scope. This rule gives an adverse party certain options when a witness uses a writing to refresh memory:

(1) while testifying; or

(2) before testifying, if the court decides that justice requires the party to have those options.

(b) Adverse Party's Options; Deleting Unrelated Matter. Unless 18 U.S.C. § 3500 provides otherwise in a criminal case, an adverse party is entitled to have the writing produced at the hearing, to inspect it, to cross-examine the witness about it, and to introduce in evidence any portion that relates to the witness's testimony. If the producing party claims that the writing includes unrelated matter, the court must examine the writing in camera, delete any unrelated portion, and order that the rest be delivered to the adverse party. Any portion deleted over objection must be preserved for the record.

(c) **Failure to Produce or Deliver the Writing.** If a writing is not produced or is not delivered as ordered, the court may issue any appropriate order. But if the prosecution does not comply in a criminal case, the court must strike the witness's testimony or — if justice so requires — declare a mistrial.

Rule 613. Witness's Prior Statement

(a) **Showing or Disclosing the Statement During Examination.** When examining a witness about the witness's prior statement, a party need not show it or disclose its contents to the witness. But the party must, on request, show it or disclose its contents to an adverse party's attorney.

(b) **Extrinsic Evidence of a Prior Inconsistent Statement.** Extrinsic evidence of a witness's prior inconsistent statement is admissible only if the witness is given an opportunity to explain or deny the statement and an adverse party is given an opportunity to examine the witness about it, or if justice so requires. This subdivision (b) does not apply to an opposing party's statement under Rule 801(d)(2).

Rule 614. Court's Calling or Examining a Witness

(a) **Calling.** The court may call a witness on its own or at a party's request. Each party is entitled to cross-examine the witness.

(b) **Examining.** The court may examine a witness regardless of who calls the witness.

(c) **Objections.** A party may object to the court's calling or examining a witness either at that time or at the next opportunity when the jury is not present.

Rule 615. Excluding Witnesses

At a party's request, the court must order witnesses excluded so that they cannot hear other witnesses' testimony. Or the court may do so on its own. But this rule does not authorize excluding:

(a) a party who is a natural person;

(b) an officer or employee of a party that is not a natural person, after being designated as the party's representative by its attorney;

(c) a person whose presence a party shows to be essential to presenting the party's claim or defense; or

(d) a person authorized by statute to be present.

ARTICLE VII OPINIONS AND EXPERT TESTIMONY

Rule 701. Opinion Testimony by Lay Witnesses

If a witness is not testifying as an expert, testimony in the form of an opinion is limited to one that is:

(a) rationally based on the witness's perception;

(b) helpful to clearly understanding the witness's testimony or to determining a fact in issue; and

(c) not based on scientific, technical, or other specialized knowledge within the scope of Rule 702.

Rule 702. Testimony by Expert Witnesses

A witness who is qualified as an expert by knowledge, skill, experience, training, or education may testify in the form of an opinion or otherwise if:

(a) the expert's scientific, technical, or other specialized knowledge will help the trier of fact to understand the evidence or to determine a fact in issue;

(b) the testimony is based on sufficient facts or data;

(c) the testimony is the product of reliable principles and methods; and

(d) the expert has reliably applied the principles and methods to the facts of the case.

Rule 703. Bases of an Expert's Opinion Testimony

An expert may base an opinion on facts or data in the case that the expert has been made aware of or personally observed. If experts in the particular field would reasonably rely on those kinds of facts or data in forming an opinion on the subject, they need not be admissible for the opinion to be admitted. But if the facts or data would otherwise be inadmissible, the proponent of the opinion may disclose them to the jury only if their probative value in helping the jury evaluate the opinion substantially outweighs their prejudicial effect.

Rule 704. Opinion on an Ultimate Issue

(a) **In General — Not Automatically Objectionable.** An opinion is not objectionable just because it embraces an ultimate issue.

(b) **Exception.** In a criminal case, an expert witness must not state an opinion about whether the defendant did or did not have a mental state or condition that constitutes an element of the crime charged or of a defense. Those matters are for the trier of fact alone.

Rule 705. Disclosing the Facts or Data Underlying an Expert's Opinion

Unless the court orders otherwise, an expert may state an opinion — and give the reasons for it — without first testifying to the underlying facts or data. But the expert may be required to disclose those facts or data on cross-examination.

Rule 706. Court-Appointed Expert Witnesses

(a) **Appointment Process.** On a party's motion or on its own, the court may order the parties to show cause why expert witnesses should not be appointed and may ask the parties to submit nominations. The court may appoint any expert that the parties agree on and any of its own choosing. But the court may only appoint someone who consents to act.

(b) Expert's Role. The court must inform the expert of the expert's duties. The court may do so in writing and have a copy filed with the clerk or may do so orally at a conference in which the parties have an opportunity to participate. The expert:

(1) must advise the parties of any findings the expert makes;

(2) may be deposed by any party;

(3) may be called to testify by the court or any party; and

(4) may be cross-examined by any party, including the party that called the expert.

(c) Compensation. The expert is entitled to a reasonable compensation, as set by the court. The compensation is payable as follows:

(1) in a criminal case or in a civil case involving just compensation under the Fifth Amendment, from any funds that are provided by law; and

(2) in any other civil case, by the parties in the proportion and at the time that the court directs — and the compensation is then charged like other costs.

(d) Disclosing the Appointment to the Jury. The court may authorize disclosure to the jury that the court appointed the expert.

(e) Parties' Choice of Their Own Experts. This rule does not limit a party in calling its own experts.

ARTICLE VIII HEARSAY

Rule 801. Definitions That Apply to This Article; Exclusions from Hearsay

(a) Statement. "Statement" means a person's

oral assertion, written assertion, or nonverbal conduct, if the person intended it as an assertion.

(b) Declarant. "Declarant" means the person who made the statement.

(c) Hearsay. "Hearsay" means a statement that:

(1) the declarant does not make while testifying at the current trial or hearing; and

(2) a party offers in evidence to prove the truth of the matter asserted in the statement.

(d) Statements That Are Not Hearsay. A statement that meets the following conditions is not hearsay:

(1) ***A Declarant-Witness's Prior Statement.*** The declarant testifies and is subject to cross-examination about a prior statement, and the statement:

(A) is inconsistent with the declarant's testimony and was given under penalty of perjury at a trial, hearing, or other proceeding or in a deposition;

(B) is consistent with the declarant's testimony and is offered to rebut an express or implied charge that the declarant recently fabricated it or acted from a recent improper influence or motive in so testifying; or

(C) identifies a person as someone the declarant perceived earlier.

(2) ***An Opposing Party's Statement.*** The statement is offered against an opposing party and:

(A) was made by the party in an individual or representative capacity;

(B) is one the party manifested that it adopted or believed to be true;

(C) was made by a person whom the party authorized to make a statement on the subject;

(D) was made by the party's agent or employee on a matter within the scope of that relationship and while it existed; or

(E) was made by the party's coconspirator during and in furtherance of the conspiracy.

The statement must be considered but does not by itself establish the declarant's authority under (C); the existence or scope of the relationship under (D); or the existence of the conspiracy or participation in it under (E).

Rule 802. The Rule Against Hearsay

Hearsay is not admissible unless any of the following provides otherwise:

- a federal statute;
- these rules; or
- other rules prescribed by the Supreme Court.

Rule 803. Exceptions to the Rule Against Hearsay — Regardless of Whether the Declarant Is Available as a Witness

The following are not excluded by the rule against hearsay, regardless of whether the declarant is available as a witness:

(1) ***Present Sense Impression.*** A statement describing or explaining an event or condition, made while or immediately after the declarant perceived it.

(2) ***Excited Utterance.*** A statement relating to a startling event or condition, made while the declarant was under the stress of excitement that it caused.

(3) ***Then-Existing Mental, Emotional, or Physical Condition.*** A statement of the declarant's then-existing state of mind (such as motive, intent, or plan) or emotional, sensory, or physical condition (such as mental feeling, pain, or bodily health), but not including a statement of memory or belief to prove the fact remembered or believed unless it relates to the validity or terms of the declarant's will.

(4) ***Statement Made for Medical Diagnosis or Treatment.*** A statement that:

(A) is made for — and is reasonably pertinent to — medical diagnosis or treatment; and

(B) describes medical history; past or present symptoms or sensations; their inception; or their general cause.

(5) ***Recorded Recollection.*** A record that:

(A) is on a matter the witness once knew about but now cannot recall well enough to testify fully and accurately;

(B) was made or adopted by the witness when the matter was fresh in the witness's memory; and

(C) accurately reflects the witness's knowledge.

If admitted, the record may be read into evidence but may be received as an exhibit only if offered by an adverse party.

(6) ***Records of a Regularly Conducted Activity.*** A record of an act, event, condition, opinion, or diagnosis if:

(A) the record was made at or near the time by — or from information transmitted by — someone with knowledge;

(B) the record was kept in the course of a regularly conducted activity of a business, organization, occupation, or calling, whether or not for profit;

(C) making the record was a regular practice of that activity;

(D) all these conditions are shown by the testimony of the custodian or another qualified witness, or by a certification that complies with Rule 902(11) or (12) or with a statute permitting certification; and

(E) neither the source of information nor the method or circumstances of preparation indicate a lack of trustworthiness.

(7) ***Absence of a Record of a Regularly Conducted Activity.*** Evidence that a matter is not included in a record described in paragraph (6) if:

(A) the evidence is admitted to prove that the matter did not occur or exist;

(B) a record was regularly kept for a matter of that kind; and

(C) neither the possible source of the information nor other circumstances indicate a lack of trustworthiness.

(8) ***Public Records.*** A record or statement of a public office if:

(A) it sets out:

(i) the office's activities;

(ii) a matter observed while under a legal duty to report, but not including, in a criminal case, a matter observed by law-enforcement personnel; or

(iii) in a civil case or against the government in a criminal case, factual findings from a legally authorized investigation; and

(B) neither the source of information nor other circumstances indicate a lack of trustworthiness.

(9) ***Public Records of Vital Statistics.*** A record of a birth, death, or marriage, if reported to a public office in accordance with a legal duty.

(10) ***Absence of a Public Record.*** Testimony — or a certification under Rule 902 — that a diligent search failed to disclose a public record or statement if the testimony or certification is admitted to prove that:

(A) the record or statement does not exist; or

(B) a matter did not occur or exist, if a public office regularly kept a record or statement for a matter of that kind.

(11) ***Records of Religious Organizations Concerning Personal or Family History.*** A statement of birth, legitimacy, ancestry, marriage, divorce, death, relationship by blood or marriage, or similar facts of personal or family history, contained in a regularly kept record of a religious organization.

(12) ***Certificates of Marriage, Baptism, and Similar Ceremonies.*** A statement of fact contained in a certificate:

(A) made by a person who is authorized by a religious organization or by law to perform the act certified;

(B) attesting that the person performed a marriage or similar ceremony or administered a sacrament; and

(C) purporting to have been issued at the time of the act or within a reasonable time after it.

(13) ***Family Records.*** A statement of fact about personal or family history contained in a family record, such as a Bible, genealogy, chart, engraving on a ring, inscription on a portrait, or engraving on an urn or burial marker.

(14) ***Records of Documents That Affect an Interest in Property.*** The record of a document that purports to establish or affect an interest in property if:

(A) the record is admitted to prove the content of the original recorded document, along with its signing and its delivery by each person who purports to have signed it;

(B) the record is kept in a public office; and

(C) a statute authorizes recording documents of that kind in that office.

(15) ***Statements in Documents That Affect an Interest in Property.*** A statement contained in a document that purports to establish or affect an interest in property if the matter stated was relevant to the document's purpose — unless later dealings with the property are inconsistent with the truth of the statement or the purport of the document.

(16) ***Statements in Ancient Documents.*** A statement in a document that is at least 20 years old and whose authenticity is established.

(17) ***Market Reports and Similar Commercial Publications.*** Market quotations, lists, directories, or other compilations that are generally relied on by the

public or by persons in particular occupations.

(18) ***Statements in Learned Treatises, Periodicals, or Pamphlets.*** A statement contained in a treatise, periodical, or pamphlet if:

(A) the statement is called to the attention of an expert witness on cross-examination or relied on by the expert on direct examination; and

(B) the publication is established as a reliable authority by the expert's admission or testimony, by another expert's testimony, or by judicial notice.

If admitted, the statement may be read into evidence but not received as an exhibit.

(19) ***Reputation Concerning Personal or Family History.*** A reputation among a person's family by blood, adoption, or marriage — or among a person's associates or in the community — concerning the person's birth, adoption, legitimacy, ancestry, marriage, divorce, death, relationship by blood, adoption, or marriage, or similar facts of personal or family history.

(20) ***Reputation Concerning Boundaries or General History.*** A reputation in a community — arising before the controversy — concerning boundaries of land in the community or customs that affect the land, or concerning general historical events important to that community, state, or nation.

(21) ***Reputation Concerning Character.*** A reputation among a person's associates or in the community concerning the person's character.

(22) ***Judgment of a Previous Conviction.*** Evidence of a final judgment of conviction if:

(A) the judgment was entered after a trial or guilty plea, but not a nolo contendere plea;

(B) the conviction was for a crime punishable by death or by imprisonment for more than a year;

(C) the evidence is admitted to prove any fact essential to the judgment; and

(D) when offered by the prosecutor in a criminal case for a purpose other than impeachment, the judgment was against the defendant.

The pendency of an appeal may be shown but does not affect admissibility.

(23) ***Judgments Involving Personal, Family, or General History, or a Boundary.*** A judgment that is admitted to prove a matter of personal, family, or general history, or boundaries, if the matter:

(A) was essential to the judgment; and

(B) could be proved by evidence of reputation.

(24) [***Other Exceptions.***] [Transferred to Rule 807.]

Rule 804. Exceptions to the Rule Against Hearsay — When the Declarant Is Unavailable as a Witness

(a) **Criteria for Being Unavailable.** A declarant is considered to be unavailable as a witness if the declarant:

(1) is exempted from testifying about the subject matter of the declarant's statement because the court rules that a privilege applies;

(2) refuses to testify about the subject matter despite a court order to do so;

(3) testifies to not remembering the subject matter;

(4) cannot be present or testify at the trial or hearing because of death or a then-existing infirmity, physical illness, or mental illness; or

(5) is absent from the trial or hearing and the statement's proponent has not been able, by process or other reasonable means, to procure:

(A) the declarant's attendance, in the case of a hearsay exception under Rule 804(b)(1) or (6); or

(B) the declarant's attendance or testimony, in the case of a hearsay exception under Rule 804(b)(2), (3), or (4).

But this subdivision (a) does not apply if the statement's proponent procured or wrongfully caused the declarant's unavailability as a witness in order to prevent the declarant from attending or testifying.

(b) The Exceptions. The following are not excluded by the rule against hearsay if the declarant is unavailable as a witness:

(1) ***Former Testimony.*** Testimony that:

(A) was given as a witness at a trial, hearing, or lawful deposition, whether given during the current proceeding or a different one; and

(B) is now offered against a party who had — or, in a civil case, whose predecessor in interest had — an opportunity and similar motive to develop it by direct, cross-, or redirect examination.

(2) ***Statement Under the Belief of Imminent Death.*** In a prosecution for homicide or in a civil case, a statement that the declarant, while believing the declarant's death to be imminent, made about its cause or circumstances.

(3) ***Statement Against Interest.*** A statement that:

(A) a reasonable person in the declarant's position would have made only if the person believed it to be true because, when made, it was so contrary to the declarant's proprietary or pecuniary interest or had so great a tendency to invalidate the declarant's claim against someone else or to expose the declarant to civil or criminal liability; and

(B) is supported by corroborating circumstances that clearly indicate its trustworthiness, if it is offered in a criminal case as one that tends to expose the declarant to criminal liability.

(4) ***Statement of Personal or Family History.*** A statement about:

(A) the declarant's own birth, adoption, legitimacy, ancestry, marriage, divorce, relationship by blood, adoption, or marriage, or similar facts of personal or family history, even though the declarant had no way of acquiring personal knowledge about that fact; or

(B) another person concerning any of these facts, as well as death, if the declarant was related to the person by blood, adoption, or marriage or was so intimately associated with the person's family that the declarant's information is likely to be accurate.

(5) [***Other Exceptions.***] [Transferred to Rule 807.]

(6) ***Statement Offered Against a Party That Wrongfully Caused the Declarant's Unavailability.*** A statement offered against a party that wrongfully caused — or acquiesced in wrongfully causing — the declarant's unavailability as a witness, and did so intending that result.

Rule 805. Hearsay Within Hearsay

Hearsay within hearsay is not excluded by the rule against hearsay if each part of the combined statements conforms with an exception to the rule.

Rule 806. Attacking and Supporting the Declarant's Credibility

When a hearsay statement — or a statement described in Rule 801(d)(2)(C), (D), or (E) — has been admitted in evidence, the declarant's credibility may be attacked, and then supported, by any evidence that would be admissible for those purposes if the declarant had testified as a witness. The court may admit evidence of the declarant's inconsistent statement or conduct, regardless of when it occurred or whether the declarant had an opportunity to explain or deny it. If the party against whom the statement was admitted calls the declarant as a witness, the party may examine the declarant on the statement as if on cross-examination.

Rule 807. Residual Exception

(a) In General. Under the following circumstances, a hearsay statement is not excluded by the rule against hearsay even if the statement is not specifically covered by a hearsay exception in Rule 803 or 804:

(1) the statement has equivalent circumstantial guarantees of trustworthiness;

(2) it is offered as evidence of a material fact;

(3) it is more probative on the point for which it is offered than any other evidence that the proponent can obtain through reasonable efforts; and

(4) admitting it will best serve the purposes of these rules and the interests of justice.

(b) Notice. The statement is admissible only if, before the trial or hearing, the proponent gives an adverse party reasonable notice of the intent to offer the statement and its particulars, including the declarant's name and address, so that the party has a fair opportunity to meet it.

ARTICLE IX AUTHENTICATION AND IDENTIFICATION

Rule 901. Authenticating or Identifying Evidence

(a) In General. To satisfy the requirement of authenticating or identifying an item of evidence, the proponent must produce evidence sufficient to support a finding that the item is what the proponent claims it is.

(b) Examples. The following are examples only — not a complete list — of evidence that satisfies the requirement:

(1) ***Testimony of a Witness with Knowledge.*** Testimony that an item is what it is claimed to be.

(2) ***Nonexpert Opinion About Handwriting.*** A nonexpert's opinion that handwriting is genuine, based on a familiarity with it that was not acquired for the current litigation.

(3) ***Comparison by an Expert Witness or the Trier of Fact.*** A comparison with an authenticated specimen by an expert witness or the trier of fact.

(4) ***Distinctive Characteristics and the Like.*** The appearance, contents, substance, internal patterns, or other distinctive characteristics of the item, taken together with all the circumstances.

(5) ***Opinion About a Voice.*** An opinion identifying a person's voice — whether heard firsthand or through mechanical or electronic transmission or recording — based on hearing the voice at any time under circumstances that connect it with the alleged speaker.

(6) ***Evidence About a Telephone Conversation.*** For a telephone conversation, evidence that a call was made to the number assigned at the time to:

   (A) a particular person, if circumstances, including self-identification, show that the person answering was the one called; or

   (B) a particular business, if the call was made to a business and the call related to business reasonably transacted over the telephone.

(7) ***Evidence About Public Records.*** Evidence that:

   (A) a document was recorded or filed in a public office as authorized by law; or

   (B) a purported public record or statement is from the office where items of this kind are kept.

(8) ***Evidence About Ancient Documents or Data Compilations.*** For a document or data compilation, evidence that it:

   (A) is in a condition that creates no suspicion about its authenticity;

   (B) was in a place where, if authentic, it would likely be; and

   (C) is at least 20 years old when offered.

(9) ***Evidence About a Process or System.*** Evidence describing a process or system and showing that it produces an accurate result.

(10) ***Methods Provided by a Statute or Rule.*** Any method of authentication or

identification allowed by a federal statute or a rule prescribed by the Supreme Court.

Rule 902. Evidence That Is Self-Authenticating

The following items of evidence are self-authenticating; they require no extrinsic evidence of authenticity in order to be admitted:

(1) ***Domestic Public Documents That Are Sealed and Signed.*** A document that bears:

(A) a seal purporting to be that of the United States; any state, district, commonwealth, territory, or insular possession of the United States; the former Panama Canal Zone; the Trust Territory of the Pacific Islands; a political subdivision of any of these entities; or a department, agency, or officer of any entity named above; and

(B) a signature purporting to be an execution or attestation.

(2) ***Domestic Public Documents That Are Not Sealed but Are Signed and Certified.*** A document that bears no seal if:

(A) it bears the signature of an officer or employee of an entity named in Rule 902(1)(A); and

(B) another public officer who has a seal and official duties within that same entity certifies under seal — or its equivalent — that the signer has the official capacity and that the signature is genuine.

(3) ***Foreign Public Documents.*** A document that purports to be signed or attested by a person who is authorized by a foreign country's law to do so. The document must be accompanied by a final certification that certifies the genuineness of the signature and official position of the signer or attester — or of any foreign official whose certificate of genuineness relates to the signature or attestation or is in a chain of certificates of genuineness relating to the signature or attestation. The certification may be made by a secretary of a United States embassy or legation; by a consul general, vice consul, or consular agent of the United States; or by a diplomatic or consular official of the foreign country assigned or accredited to the United States. If all parties have been given a reasonable opportunity to investigate the document's authenticity and accuracy, the court may, for good cause, either:

(A) order that it be treated as presumptively authentic without final certification; or

(B) allow it to be evidenced by an attested summary with or without final certification.

(4) ***Certified Copies of Public Records.*** A copy of an official record — or a copy of a document that was recorded or filed in a public office as authorized by law — if the copy is certified as correct by:

(A) the custodian or another person authorized to make the certification; or

(B) a certificate that complies with Rule 902(1), (2), or (3), a federal statute, or a rule prescribed by the Supreme Court.

(5) ***Official Publications.*** A book, pamphlet, or other publication purporting to be issued by a public authority.

(6) ***Newspapers and Periodicals.*** Printed material purporting to be a newspaper or periodical.

(7) ***Trade Inscriptions and the Like.*** An inscription, sign, tag, or label purporting to have been affixed in the course of business and indicating origin, ownership, or control.

(8) ***Acknowledged Documents.*** A document accompanied by a certificate of acknowledgment that is lawfully executed by a notary public or another officer who is authorized to take acknowledgments.

(9) ***Commercial Paper and Related***

Documents. Commercial paper, a signature on it, and related documents, to the extent allowed by general commercial law.

(10) ***Presumptions Under a Federal Statute.*** A signature, document, or anything else that a federal statute declares to be presumptively or prima facie genuine or authentic.

(11) ***Certified Domestic Records of a Regularly Conducted Activity.*** The original or a copy of a domestic record that meets the requirements of Rule 803(6)(A)-(C), as shown by a certification of the custodian or another qualified person that complies with a federal statute or a rule prescribed by the Supreme Court. Before the trial or hearing, the proponent must give an adverse party reasonable written notice of the intent to offer the record — and must make the record and certification available for inspection — so that the party has a fair opportunity to challenge them.

(12) ***Certified Foreign Records of a Regularly Conducted Activity.*** In a civil case, the original or a copy of a foreign record that meets the requirements of Rule 902(11), modified as follows: the certification, rather than complying with a federal statute or Supreme Court rule, must be signed in a manner that, if falsely made, would subject the maker to a criminal penalty in the country where the certification is signed. The proponent must also meet the notice requirements of Rule 902(11).

Rule 903. Subscribing Witness's Testimony

A subscribing witness's testimony is necessary to authenticate a writing only if required by the law of the jurisdiction that governs its validity.

ARTICLE X CONTENTS OF WRITINGS, RECORDINGS AND PHOTOGRAPHS

Rule 1001. Definitions That Apply to This Article

In this article:

(a) A "writing" consists of letters, words, numbers, or their equivalent set down in any form.

(b) A "recording" consists of letters, words, numbers, or their equivalent recorded in any manner.

(c) A "photograph" means a photographic image or its equivalent stored in any form.

(d) An "original" of a writing or recording means the writing or recording itself or any counterpart intended to have the same effect by the person who executed or issued it. For electronically stored information, "original" means any printout — or other output readable by sight — if it accurately reflects the information. An "original" of a photograph includes the negative or a print from it.

(e) A "duplicate" means a counterpart produced by a mechanical, photographic, chemical, electronic, or other equivalent process or technique that accurately reproduces the original.

Rule 1002. Requirement of the Original

An original writing, recording, or photograph is required in order to prove its content unless these rules or a federal statute provides otherwise.

Rule 1003. Admissibility of Duplicates

A duplicate is admissible to the same extent as the original unless a genuine question is raised about the original's authenticity or the circumstances make it unfair to admit the duplicate.

Rule 1004. Admissibility of Other Evidence of Content

An original is not required and other evidence of the content of a writing, recording, or photograph is admissible if:

(a) all the originals are lost or destroyed, and not by the proponent acting in bad faith;

(b) an original cannot be obtained by any available judicial process;

(c) the party against whom the original would be offered had control of the original; was at that time put on notice, by pleadings or otherwise, that the original would be a subject of proof at the trial or hearing; and fails to produce it at the trial or hearing; or

(d) the writing, recording, or photograph is not closely related to a controlling issue.

Rule 1005. Copies of Public Records to Prove Content

The proponent may use a copy to prove the content of an official record — or of a document that was recorded or filed in a public office as authorized by law — if these conditions are met: the record or document is otherwise admissible; and the copy is certified as correct in accordance with Rule 902(4) or is testified to be correct by a witness who has compared it with the original. If no such copy can be obtained by reasonable diligence, then the proponent may use other evidence to prove the content.

Rule 1006. Summaries to Prove Content

The proponent may use a summary, chart, or calculation to prove the content of voluminous writings, recordings, or photographs that cannot be conveniently examined in court. The proponent must make the originals or duplicates available for examination or copying, or both, by other parties at a reasonable time and place. And the court may order the proponent to produce them in court.

Rule 1007. Testimony or Statement of a Party to Prove Content

The proponent may prove the content of a writing, recording, or photograph by the testimony, deposition, or written statement of the party against whom the evidence is offered. The proponent need not account for the original.

Rule 1008. Functions of the Court and Jury

Ordinarily, the court determines whether the proponent has fulfilled the factual conditions for admitting other evidence of the content of a writing, recording, or photograph under Rule 1004 or

1005. But in a jury trial, the jury determines — in accordance with Rule 104(b) — any issue about whether:

(a) an asserted writing, recording, or photograph ever existed;

(b) another one produced at the trial or hearing is the original; or

(c) other evidence of content accurately reflects the content.

ARTICLE XI MISCELLANEOUS RULES

Rule 1101. Applicability of Rules

(a) To Courts and Judges. These rules apply to proceedings before:

- United States district courts;
- United States bankruptcy and magistrate judges;
- United States courts of appeals;
- the United States Court of Federal Claims; and
- the district courts of Guam, the Virgin Islands, and the Northern Mariana Islands.

(b) To Cases and Proceedings. These rules apply in:

- civil cases and proceedings, including bankruptcy, admiralty, and maritime cases;
- criminal cases and proceedings; and
- contempt proceedings, except those in which the court may act summarily.

(c) Rules on Privilege. The rules on privilege apply to all stages of a case or proceeding.

(d) Exceptions. These rules — except for those on privilege — do not apply to the following:

(1) the court's determination, under Rule 104(a), on a preliminary question of fact governing admissibility;

(2) grand-jury proceedings; and

(3) miscellaneous proceedings such as:

- extradition or rendition;

- issuing an arrest warrant, criminal summons, or search warrant;
- a preliminary examination in a criminal case;
- sentencing;
- granting or revoking probation or supervised release; and
- considering whether to release on bail or otherwise.

(e) **Other Statutes and Rules.** A federal statute or a rule prescribed by the Supreme Court may provide for admitting or excluding evidence independently from these rules.

Rule 1102. Amendments

These rules may be amended as provided in 28 U.S.C. § 2072.

Rule 1103. Title

These rules may be cited as the Federal Rules of Evidence.